Brief Contents

Contents

Preface

We wrote *Consumer Behavior: A Framework* to provide a concise yet complete overview of the field of consumer behavior. Our goal was to strip away all of the excess baggage found in today's textbooks on consumer behavior. *Framework* contains the factual material that students and professionals need to understand the factors that influence consumer behavior and to develop managerial strategies to market products to consumers. With this concise primer in mind, we also include a comprehensive set of ads, diagrams, cases, exercises, and glossary terms that the student can access at www.consumerbehavior.net. Together, text and Web site provide the essence of consumer behavior.

Framework offers three key benefits. First, most noticeable to students is that the book is inexpensive and easy to carry around because of its slim size.

The second benefit of the book is that it retains the key strengths of our longer text, *Consumer Behavior*, Fifth Edition. That is, *Framework* provides high knowledge content, high managerial content, and high technology content. Despite its slimmed down size, *Framework* contains the key information that students need to know about the field. We take a balanced approach to the field by integrating throughout the text the three perspectives on consumer behavior: the decision making, the experiential, and the behavioral.

In order to emphasize the managerial applications of consumer behavior, each chapter concludes with a summary of how the consumer behavior concepts can be employed to develop managerial strategy. An entire chapter (chapter 2) is devoted to identifying the managerial applications areas to which the concepts can be applied. Each chapter then concludes with a summary of how the consumer-behavior concepts can be employed to develop managerial strategy. We use the acronym PERMS, to summarize the strategies: Product positioning and differentiation, Environmental analysis, marketing Research, Marketing mix development, and Segmentation.

The third benefit of *Framework* is that it is instructor friendly. We have created a Web site, www.consumerbehavior.net, that is accessible to instructors and students. The site contains cases to which the answers may be found in the instructor's manual. The site also contains the most complete and thoroughly developed PowerPoint presentations of any consumer behavior book. The PowerPoint presentations are accessible to students so that they can be downloaded for class. Instructors can modify the presentations as they wish. Also included on the Web site are lecture notes and links to sites on the World Wide Web. Of course, adopters are provided with a comprehensive instructor's manual, which includes lecture outlines and a lengthy test bank.

Furthermore, *Framework* can be packaged with a diverse set of additional materials offered either free or for a nominal price.

➤ Printed versions of the cases found on the Web

➤ *E-Biz for e-Marketing Guide 2001*

➤ *E-Marketing*, Second Edition, by Strauss and Frost

➤ *Marketing PlanPro* software

➤ *PhotoWars* simulation

➤ Custom exercises

In sum, we believe that instructors and students will find *Consumer Behavior: A Framework* to be informative, interesting to read, managerially relevant, and technologically sophisticated.

Of course, without the support of many people, *Framework* could not have been written. Both authors thank Bruce Kaplan and Whitney Blake of Prentice Hall for their support during the editorial process. Professor Minor thanks the members of his Ph.D. seminar in consumer behavior for reading and commenting on several chapters.

Finally, our fondest thanks go to our families (John's family: Maryanne, Katherine, and Cara; Michael's family: Karen and Amy) for their support, confidence, and good humor. They are truly special people.

An Introduction to Consumer Behavior

After studying this chapter, you should be able to discuss each of the following concepts:

1. Consumer behavior.
2. Consumer primacy.
3. Environmental analysis.
4. Positioning and product differentiation.
5. Segmentation.
6. The role of theory in consumer behavior.
7. Research perspectives on consumer behavior.
8. Exchange processes.
9. Role of ethics in consumer behavior.
10. The organizing framework of consumer behavior.

Here are just four examples of the types of questions that the study of consumer behavior can help answer. First, why do women and men risk pain and the possible physical deformity of cosmetic surgery to enhance their physical appearance? Second, how can a company use the World Wide Web to generate word of mouth communications about a new pop singer?[1] Third, why do people enjoy going to horror movies and being scared half to death? Fourth, how can an understanding of consumer decision making be used to design a product?*

---

*The answers to the questions posed in this paragraph are (1) they may have low self-esteem, (2) it monitors what teenagers are saying in Internet chat rooms, (3) they are bored and are attempting to increase their level of physiological activation, and (4) they identify the most important features desired by the target market and design the product appropriately.

Consumer behavior is an exciting field of study. Because all of us buy goods and services, we can draw on our everyday experiences in the marketplace to understand the field's concepts and theories. One of the goals of this book is to examine, through the use of copious examples, how corporations, public-policy makers, and nonprofit organizations use consumer-behavior concepts in order to investigate buying habits and make managerial marketing decisions on both a national and international level. This book also aims to sensitize readers to issues involving ethics and social responsibility.

Consider cosmetic surgery, which even teenagers are undergoing. The purchase of this service is a consumer behavior in the same manner as purchasing jewelry, cosmetics, cologne, or a nice suit. Although relatively few of us (as of yet) have had cosmetic surgery, any one of us may wear an earring or tattoo—each of which requires a form of surgery. One goal of the surgery is to make us feel more physically attractive. Certainly, all of us have purchased clothing, cosmetics, or jewelry for the same purpose. For example, in the summer of 1999, the fad among upscale, conservative women was to wear custom-made toe rings made of gold, platinum, or diamonds. One analyst described the fad as representing the "newest incarnation of the haute hippie look."[2]

Indeed, some consumer actions can be truly bizarre. In the United States, one recent cosmetic surgery trend is the metal scalp implant. After anesthetizing the patient, a one-inch incision is made on the top of the head and a metal bar containing four threaded posts is inserted between skin and bone. Spikes, which can be up to four inches long, are then screwed into the posts and stick out of the skin.[3]

In addition to investigating unusual buying activities, such as scalp implants, the study of consumer behavior is also critical for managerial decision making. Cosmetic surgery, for example, is an industry. In order to be successful, physicians must sell a product, and the marketing process requires an understanding of consumer needs and wants. By understanding their customers, clinics can develop alternative plastic surgery products—from face-lifts and liposuction to penile enlargement, breast augmentation, and hair implants. Providers must also develop promotional appeals that target the specific needs of their potential customers. Thus, when appealing to men, they may want to emphasize competing against younger rivals. The findings of consumer research can also be used to more effectively segment the market. For example, the market for plastic surgery is better on the coasts than in the midsection of the United States.[4]

Consumer behavior also has relevance to international marketing. The study of cross-cultural processes and of how people in different countries react to marketing efforts is central to the field. For example, plastic surgery's siren call is being heard internationally as well as in the United States. Spurred by President Carlos Menem's penchant for fixing his receding hairline and his ex-wife's many face-lifts, the entire country of Argentina appears to have gone under the knife. As one Argentinean psychiatrist has noted, "This surgery, this frivolity, is the consequence of our terrible history."[5]

Finally, the study of consumer behavior highlights concerns about ethics and social responsibility in the marketplace. For example, because of the high degree of trust that must be present in the patient–physician relationship, it is critical that both parties exercise high levels of ethical behavior. The results of plastic surgery can be horrible. For example, the penile enlargement business is unregulated. Numerous lawsuits have been filed because of infections, uneven surfaces, and impotence resulting from the procedure. Similarly, the turmoil over silicone breast implants has caused many women to avoid breast augmentation surgery. Another goal of our book is to sensitize readers to issues involving ethics and social responsibility in the consumer domain.

WHAT IS CONSUMER BEHAVIOR?

The study of consumer behavior is a young discipline: The first textbooks were written in the 1960s. Its intellectual origins, however, are much older. For example, Thorstein Veblen talked about conspicuous consumption in 1899. In the early 1900s, writers began to discuss how advertisers could use psychological principles.[6] In the 1950s ideas from Freudian psychology were popularized by motivation researchers and used by advertisers. It was not until the enunciation of the marketing concept in the 1950s, however, that the need to study consumer behavior was recognized.

The **marketing concept** embodies "the view that an industry is a customer-satisfying process, not a goods-producing process. An industry begins with customer and his needs, not with a patent, a raw material, or a selling skill."[7] The recognition that an organization can exist only as long as it fulfills consumer needs and wants by thoroughly understanding their exchange partners (i.e., customers) makes the study of the consumer essential.[8]

Consumer behavior is defined as the study of the buying units and the exchange processes involved in acquiring, consuming, and disposing of goods, services, experiences, and ideas. Within this simple definition, a number of important concepts are introduced. First, included in the definition is the word *exchange*. A consumer inevitably resides at one end of an **exchange process** in which resources are transferred between two parties. For example, an exchange takes place between a doctor and patient. The physician trades medical services for money. In addition, other resources, such as feelings, information, and status, may also be exchanged between the parties.

This book views the exchange process as a fundamental element of consumer behavior. Exchanges occur between consumers and companies. Exchanges also occur between companies, such as in industrial buying situations. Finally, exchanges occur between consumers themselves, such as when a neighbor borrows a cup of sugar or a lawn mower.

Consider again the definition of consumer behavior. Notice that the term *buying unit* is used rather than *consumer*. This is because purchases may be made by either individuals or groups. An important area of study for consumer researchers is that of organizational buying behavior. Particularly in business-to-business marketing, the purchase decision may be made by a group of individuals in a buying center rather than a single person. Fortunately, the same basic principles apply to organizational buying behavior as to consumer behavior.

As the definition of consumer behavior also reveals, the exchange process involves a series of steps, beginning with the acquisition phase, moving to consumption, and ending with the disposition of the product or service. When investigating the **acquisition phase,** researchers analyze the factors that influence the product and service choices of consumers. Much of the research in consumer behavior has focused on this phase. One factor associated with the search for and selection of goods and services is product symbolism. That is, people may acquire a product to express to others certain ideas and meanings about themselves. For example, some people undergo cosmetic surgery and wear body rings or tattoos to make a symbolic statement to others about who and what they are.

The consumption and disposition phases have received much less attention by consumer researchers than the acquisition phase. When investigating the **consumption**

phase, the researcher analyzes how consumers actually use a product or service and the experiences that the consumer obtains from such use. The investigation of the consumption process is particularly important for service industries. In some industries, such as restaurants, amusement parks, and rock-concert promotions, the consumption experience is the reason for the purchase.

The **disposition phase** refers to what consumers do with a product once they are done using it. In addition, it addresses the level of satisfaction that consumers experience after the purchase of a good or service. For example, one critical problem faced by physicians and patients concerns the level of satisfaction with the results of the medical procedure. If consumers have unrealistic expectations, the anticipated outcomes are not likely to occur and dissatisfaction will result. From the surgeon's perspective, such customer dissatisfaction is likely to increase the likelihood that lawsuits will be filed. For the patient, unfulfilled expectations may result in a loss of self-esteem and possibly increase the desire for even more cosmetic surgery. For example, after five face-lifts a woman found that her hairline had now moved to behind her ears. At this point she was completely distraught, began filing lawsuits, and sought another plastic surgeon to correct the problem.

The student of consumer behavior will also be struck by the diversity of the field. It incorporates theories and concepts from all the behavioral sciences. When studying the acquisition, consumption, and disposition of products, services, and ideas, one also explores the disciplines of marketing, psychology, social psychology, sociology, anthropology, geography, demography, and economics.

WHY STUDY CONSUMER BEHAVIOR?

Possessing an understanding of consumers and the consumption process provides a number of benefits. These benefits include assisting managers in their decision making, providing marketing researchers with a knowledge base from which to analyze consumers, helping legislators and regulators create laws and regulations concerning the purchase and sale of goods and services, and assisting the average consumer in making better purchase decisions. In addition, the study of consumers can help us understand the social science factors that influence human behavior.

Consumer Analysis as a Foundation of Marketing Management

The importance of understanding the consumer is found in the definition of **marketing** as a "human activity directed at satisfying needs and wants through human exchange processes."[9] From this definition emerge two key marketing activities. First, marketers attempt to satisfy the needs and wants of their target market. Second, marketing involves the study of the exchange process by which two parties transfer resources between each other. In the exchange process, companies receive monetary and other resources from consumers. In return, consumers receive products, services, and other resources of value. For marketers to create a successful exchange, they must have an understanding of the factors that influence the needs and wants of consumers.*

---

*The American Marketing Association developed the following definition of marketing: "Marketing is the process of planning and executing the conception, pricing, promotion, and distribution of ideas, goods, and services to create exchanges that satisfy individual and organizational objectives." Although this definition emphasizes the importance of the exchange concept, it neglects the concept that marketing functions to fulfill the needs and wants of consumers. In the authors' view, downplaying a consumer focus is a setback for marketing. The field of consumer behavior can assist the marketer in obtaining this information.

Indeed, the principle of **consumer primacy** is the central point on which the marketing field is based.[10] According to this concept, the consumer should be at the center of the marketing effort. As Peter Drucker, a well-known management scholar, has explained, "Marketing is the whole business seen from the point of view of its final result, that is, from the customer's point of view."[11] Similarly, in his critique of General Motors Corporation, Ross Perot proclaimed that, for the company to turn around, managers must perceive that "the consumer is king."[12]

As society increasingly relies on electronics to function, a focus on the consumer is growing in importance. A recent issue of *Business Week* magazine was devoted to "The Internet Age." The cover story, entitled, "Customers Move into the Driver's Seat," began as follows:

> A Copernican revolution of sorts is under way. Executives used to imagine their companies as the center of a solar system orbited by suppliers and customers. The Internet is changing that—dramatically. Now, the customer is becoming the center of the entire business universe.[13]

Public Policy and Consumer Behavior

A knowledge of consumer behavior can also assist in the development of public policy. As it pertains to consumer behavior, **public policy** involves the development of the laws and regulations that have an impact on consumers in the marketplace. In its legislative, regulatory, and judicial roles, the federal government often deals with issues involving consumers. For example, proposals have been made to limit, or even cut off entirely, the ability of cigarette manufacturers to advertise their product.

Also falling into the public-policy domain of consumer behavior is the study of consumer misbehavior. Sometimes called the dark side of consumer behavior, the field investigates how consumers can act unethically, misuse products, and engage in behaviors that risk their financial resources and even place their lives in danger. By understanding the causes of consumer misbehavior, such as the reasons people compulsively buy products and consume illegal substances, public-policy makers maximize the likelihood that they can implement laws and regulations that will benefit society.

Consumer Behavior and Altruistic Marketing

The ideas and concepts of marketing may also be applied to nontraditional business areas. For example, various nonprofit groups, such as political parties, religious organizations, and charitable groups (e.g., United Way of America) engage in consumer research; rather than marketing tangible products, however, these organizations market intangible ideas. For example, the United Way promotes the idea that if thousands of individuals volunteer to help others through nonprofit organizations, such as Big Brothers/Big Sisters and the Red Cross, the United States will be a better place to live.

Indeed, consumer researchers have recently argued that many of the most important problems faced by society today involve choices that consumers make, such as decisions to eat high-fat foods, smoke, drink and drive, take drugs, or use the services of prostitutes. Research by consumer-behavior scholars can benefit society by finding ways to influence people to act more responsibly in their consumption of such goods and services. Thus, consumer researchers have much to contribute to the new field of **altruistic marketing.** Altruistic marketing can be defined as a field of study that seeks to (1) perform studies to determine the causes of negligent consumer behavior and (2) apply the research findings to develop treatment and preventive methods to reduce the maladaptive actions of consumers.[14]

The Personal Value of Consumer Behavior

A general knowledge of consumer behavior also has personal value. It can help people become better consumers by identifying the factors that influence their own consumption activities. In addition, it can assist consumers in the buying process by informing them of some of the strategies companies use to market their products. Knowing the factors that influence consumption has intrinsic value for many people. On one level, it is simply fun to know why product rumors start, why subliminal advertising messages are unlikely to influence buying, and why some celebrities, such as ex-basketball player Michael Jordan, can be effective product endorsers even after their sports career have ended. Finally, being able to understand one's own personal consumption motivations, as well as those of others, is satisfying and is part of being a well-rounded, educated person.

The study of consumer behavior can provide three types of information: (1) orientation, (2) facts, and (3) theories. First, it helps to orient managers and public-policy makers so that they consider the impact of their actions on consumers. It also provides facts, such as what choice processes consumers use to make a product purchase or what values particular cultures emphasize. Finally, the study of consumer behavior provides theories. The description of a set of ideas as a theory is sometimes ridiculed with statements such as, "That's only theory; it has nothing to do with what really happens." In fact, nothing is more practical than a theory. We base our actions on theories of what causes what. Detectives develop theories for why a crime was committed, medical doctors develop theories for why a person gets sick, and managers develop theories for why a product fails to sell.

A **theory** is defined as a set of interrelated statements defining the causal relationships among different variables. Theories may be big or small, but all should have research support. A major practical reason for studying consumer behavior is that the field has a variety of theories that do have research support and that can be used to understand and solve managerial and public-policy problems. Table 1.1 summarizes the reasons for studying the field of consumer behavior.

Reasons for Studying Consumer Behavior

1. Consumer analysis should be the foundation of marketing management. It assists managers to:
   a. Design the marketing mix.
   b. Segment the marketplace.
   c. Position and differentiate products.
   d. Perform an environmental analysis.
   e. Develop market research studies.
2. Consumer behavior should play an important role in the development of public policy.
3. The study of consumer behavior will enable one to be a more effective consumer.
4. Consumer analysis provides knowledge of overall human behavior.
5. The study of consumer behavior provides three types of information:
   a. A consumer orientation.
   b. Facts about human behavior.
   c. Theories to guide the thinking process.

TABLE 1.1

THREE RESEARCH PERSPECTIVES ON CONSUMER BEHAVIOR

A key feature of the field of consumer behavior is its research base. As a social science field, it employs research methods and procedures from each of the behavioral sciences. This book organizes research in consumer behavior into three research perspectives that act as guides for how to think about and identify the factors that influence consumer acquisition behavior: (1) the decision-making perspective, (2) the experiential perspective, and (3) the behavioral influence perspective.[15]

The Decision-Making Perspective

During the 1970s and early 1980s, researchers focused on the view that consumers are rational decision makers. According to the **decision-making perspective,** buying results from consumers first perceiving that a problem exists and then moving through a series of steps in a rational problem-solving process. These steps include problem recognition, search, alternative evaluation, choice, and postacquisition evaluation. The roots of this approach are in cognitive psychology and in economics.

Thinking back to the question of why people purchase cosmetic surgery services, the decision-making perspective focuses attention on the steps through which consumers move when deciding which physician to hire to do cosmetic surgery. For example, in analyzing the choice process, researchers would attempt to identify the characteristics sought by consumers in their physician, such as his or her qualifications, bedside manner, explanation of risks, and price charged. Next, the researcher would identify the nature of the search process used to obtain information on the procedure. The alternative evaluation process would be investigated along with how consumers chose between alternatives. Finally, the researcher would assess the factors influencing the postpurchase satisfaction of consumers.

The Experiential Perspective

The **experiential perspective** on consumer buying proposes that in some instances consumers do not make their purchases according to a strictly rational decision-making process. Instead, people sometimes buy products and services in order to have fun, create fantasies, and obtain emotions and feelings.[16] Classified within the experiential perspective are impulse and variety-seeking purchases. Variety seeking occurs when consumers switch brands to lower boredom levels and obtain stimulation.[17] The process may be described as one in which consumers base their purchase on a "how-do-I-feel-about-it" rule of thumb.[18] Many consumer services and products bought for leisure purposes have a strong experiential component to them, including such activities as going to rock concerts, symphonies, amusement parks, and movies. For example, in 1999 sales of personal computers (PCs) unexpectedly surged. The reason was that consumers realized that PCs could be used as stereos, recording studios, and entertainment centers. As a result, PC makers such as Dell and Gateway began marketing their brands for leisure pursuits, as well as for educational needs.[19]

The roots of the experiential perspective are in motivational psychology and in areas of sociology and anthropology. In particular, researchers who take an experiential perspective will frequently use **interpretive research methods.** Interpretivists believe that researchers inevitably influence the data collection effort, focus on understanding rather than prediction, and believe that reality is socially constructed. Interpretivists frequently employ naturalistic research methods in which the investigator directly observes and records the activities of interest or even actively participates in the activities.[20] They can even be found recording the folklore and traditions of society in order to obtain an understanding of their consumption process.[21]

The Behavioral Influence Perspective

Behavioral influence occurs when strong environmental forces propel consumers to make purchases without necessarily first developing strong feelings or beliefs about the product. In this instance the consumer does not necessarily go through a rational decision-making process or rely on feelings to purchase a product or service. Instead, the action results from the direct influence of behavior by environmental forces, such as sales promotion devices (e.g., contests), cultural norms, the physical environment, or economic pressures.[22]

The behavioral influence perspective provides another viewpoint for understanding the reasons people undergo cosmetic surgery. For example, strong group or social pressures might propel an individual to have her breasts enhanced or have his chin given that chiseled look. In such instances the person may actually have a distaste for the procedure but still engage in the act because of the force of social pressures.

Most purchases, of course, will have some elements of each of the three perspectives. For example, the purchase of the services of a plastic surgeon involves some level of decision making, such as when a consumer searches for information, evaluates alternatives, and makes an informed choice. It is likely, however, that an experiential process is also operating, in which strong emotional elements drive the consumer to engage in actions that have a high level of symbolic meaning, such as having a face-lift to create a youthful image. Finally, as previously noted, strong pressures found in a social situation may also impact the behavior. It is therefore useful to examine consumer behavior from each perspective to fully appreciate the impact of logical decision making, of feelings and emotions, and of environmental influences on consumer behavior.

EXCHANGE PROCESSES AND CONSUMER BEHAVIOR

Central to the study of consumer behavior is a focus on exchange processes. Whenever a good, service, idea, or experience is transferred from one entity to another, an exchange takes place. Formally, **exchange** may be defined as a process that involves the "transfer of something tangible or intangible, actual or symbolic, between two or more social actors."[23]

The idea that exchange is fundamental to marketing has been discussed for over 40 years. In 1957 Wroe Alderson, one of the early founders of the field, stated that "[m]arketing is the exchange which takes place between consuming groups and supplying groups."[24] In 1985 the American Marketing Association defined marketing as "the process of planning and executing the conception, pricing, promotion, and distribution of ideas, goods, and services to create exchanges that satisfy individual and organizational objectives."[25] In each of these definitions, the concept of exchange is central to defining the field of marketing.

When investigating exchange, it is important to examine what makes one person willing to give up one thing to receive something else in return. If one person has one collection or assortment of goods and another person has a second collection or assortment of goods, what will make them enter into an exchange? The basic reason for exchanging one good for another is that different people possess divergent tastes and preferences. Thus, if I have something that has lower value to me than to you, and if you have something that has lower value to you than to me, we have a basis for exchange.[26] In such instances both parties profit from the exchange because each receives something that they value more than what they gave up.

The Elements of Exchange

Researchers have worked hard to identify what is exchanged between two people or between two social units (e.g., a family and a firm).[27] One categorization system has

Examples of the Six Categories of Resources

1. *Feelings.* Expressions of affectionate regard, warmth, or comfort.
2. *Status.* Evaluative judgment conveying high or low prestige, regard, or esteem.
3. *Information.* Any advice, opinion, or instruction.
4. *Money.* Any coin or token that has some standard of exchange value.
5. *Goods.* Any product or object that has exchange value.
6. *Services.* Any performance of labor done for someone else.

Source: Based in part on Gregory Donnenworth and Uriel Foa, "Effects of Resource Class on Retaliation to Injustice in Interpersonal Exchange," *Journal of Personality and Social Psychology,* 29 (1974): 785–93.

TABLE 1.2

identified six types of resources that may be exchanged: goods, services, money, status, information, and feelings.[28] Table 1.2 provides examples of each of the six categories of resources.

Figure 1.1 presents a diagram of the exchange process, illustrating that each party to the exchange possesses certain resources. The resources input by one party represent his or her costs and become the outcomes received by the other party. Outcomes are derived not only from the resources exchanged but also from the experiences obtained from engaging in the exchange act. Thus, each party may derive rewards or costs from the exchange process itself, in addition to those obtained from the goods, services, or money transferred.

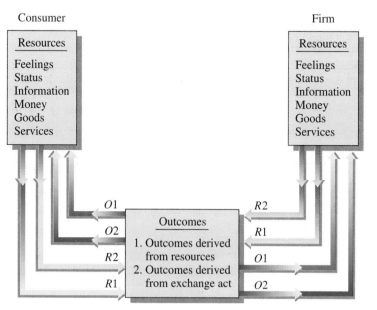

R1 and R2 = Resources input to exchange
O1 and O2 = Outcomes received from exchange

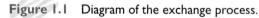

Figure 1.1   Diagram of the exchange process.

Dimensions of Exchange Relations

Four types of consumer exchange relations have been identified: (1) restricted versus complex, (2) internal versus external, (3) formal versus informal, and (4) relational versus discrete (see Table 1.3).

Restricted versus Complex Exchanges. The most simple type of exchange, called a **restricted exchange,** involves two parties interacting in a reciprocal relationship.[29] An example is a consumer and her stockbroker or a patient and his physician. At the most complicated level, one finds complex exchanges. **Complex exchanges** involve a set of three or more actors enmeshed in a set of mutual relations, for example, a channel of distribution in which an automobile goes from manufacturer (e.g., Ford) to a dealer, which then sells it to a customer. Each party depends on the other to supply resources. Even though car buyers and manufacturers are separated by a dealer, the consumer depends on the manufacturer to build a quality product. Similarly, the manufacturer needs consumers to purchase its automobiles.

Internal versus External Exchanges. A second dimension of exchange relations concerns whether they occur within a group (an internal exchange) or between parties that are in separate groups (an external exchange).[30] An example of an **internal exchange** is the complex sets of relations that occur within a family. Internal exchanges involve a situation in which the members of an organization or group avoid going into the market to obtain a good or service. Instead, the particular need is satisfied within the organization. An example of an **external exchange** is the transactions that occur between members of a family or company and retailers. Here, members of the group are importing goods or services from an outside source to fulfill a need.

Consumer researchers in general have focused on developing an understanding of external exchanges. Nonetheless, internal exchanges are also important. For example, should an automobile company produce its own car motors or should it purchase the engines from another supplier (e.g., Ford purchasing a motor from Yamaha for its Taurus SHO car)?

Formal versus Informal Exchanges. Exchanges can occur either formally or informally. A **formal exchange** involves an explicit written or verbal contract and will frequently occur in external exchanges. Exchanges can also occur informally. In an **infor-**

Types of Exchange Relations
1. Restricted vs. Complex
a. *Restricted exchange.* Concerns a two-party relation.
b. *Complex exchange.* Involves a set of three or more actors.
2. Internal vs. External
a. *Internal exchange.* Occurs within a group.
b. *External exchange.* Occurs between groups.
3. Formal vs. Informal
a. *Formal exchange.* Involves explicit written or verbal contracts.
b. *Informal exchange.* Involves unwritten, unspoken social contracts.
4. Relational vs. Discrete
a. *Relational exchange.* Creates long-term relations.
b. *Discrete exchange.* Constitutes one-time exchange in which no relations are formed.

TABLE 1.3

mal exchange, unwritten, social contracts are created between parties. This type of exchange occurs more frequently in internal exchanges, where one finds that social norms and peer pressure replace formal contracts.

One arena in which informal exchanges frequently occur is in dating. From an exchange perspective, people can be viewed as possessing a set of resources that are exchanged. As such, people have attributes, such as physical beauty, intelligence, money, a high-status occupation, and a good personality. These characteristics are the resources exchanged when individuals become involved in romantic exchanges. Thus, the dating process may be argued to consist of men and women exchanging various resources.

In one study the researcher investigated personal dating advertisements found in *The Washingtonian* and *New York* magazines.[31] In both magazines males and females publish short descriptions of themselves and of the type of person they would like to meet. Here is an example of a personal dating advertisement:

> Very attractive, college-educated, professional female (in science), 28, 5′ 8″, dark hair, exercise fanatic, active and outgoing, seeks male counterpart: Tall, handsome, (blond?), muscular, secure, professional man (Law, MD) under 36, for sports, fun dates, and possibly great relationship. Note and photo appreciated.

The researcher performed a content analysis of the personal advertisements in the two magazines. The resources offered and sought were placed into 10 categories: love, physical attractiveness/beauty, money, occupational status, educational status, intellectual status, entertainment services, information–personality, information–ethnic, and information–demographic. Table 1.4 depicts the set of resources that men and women were hypothesized to offer and seek. Women were hypothesized to offer (and men were proposed to seek) physical attractiveness, love, entertainment services, and information. In contrast, men were proposed to offer (and women were proposed to seek) money, educational status, intellectual status, and occupational status.

The results revealed that women more than men offered physical attractiveness resources and sought monetary resources. Conversely, men offered monetary resources and sought physical attractiveness resources. Somewhat sadly, both men and women sought love resources much more frequently than they offered them. Perhaps the lack of willingness to give love accounted for why these individuals were resorting to personal ads.

Resource Exchanges Between Men and Women in the Dating Setting

I. Resources hypothesized to be advertised by men and women:
  a. Women advertise physical attractiveness, love, entertainment services, and information.
  b. Men advertise money, educational status, intellectual status, and occupational status.
II. Actual resources found in study to be advertised and sought:
  a. Women offered physical attractiveness.
   Women sought monetary resources and love.
  b. Men offered monetary resources and occupational status.
   Men sought physical attractiveness and love.

Source: Elizabeth C. Hirschman, "People as Products: Analysis of a Complex Marketing Exchange," *Journal of Marketing*, Vol. 51 (January 1987), 98–108.

TABLE 1.4

Relational versus Discrete Exchange. Exchanges are also categorized as to whether they are discrete or relational in nature. A **discrete exchange** is a short, one-time interaction in which money is paid for an easily measured commodity. Discrete exchanges, therefore, do not involve the creation of a relationship. In contrast, a **relational exchange** involves a transaction involving a long-term commitment in which trust and the development of social relations play an important role.[32]

Relational exchanges have been equated to a marriage between buyer and seller. As one author has stated: "The sale merely consummates the courtship. Then the marriage begins. How good the marriage is depends on how well the relationship is managed by the seller."[33] Thus, when viewed from a relational exchange perspective, transactions should be analyzed in terms of their history and anticipated future. Such transactions are noted for the social relations that occur as well as for the benefits derived from the characteristics of the product or service obtained.

Consumers will make long-term commitments with marketers to reduce overall transaction costs (e.g., by minimizing search costs), to lower risk, and to gain the positive feelings that result from interacting with someone they like. Table 1.5 depicts some of the characteristics of relational exchanges.

Examples of relational exchanges are found in both the industrial and consumer sectors. For instance, a company producing a complex product—such as a jet aircraft, submarine, or large building—must contract with other corporations to supply specific components and services. One survey of banking, high-tech, and manufacturing customers found that respondents considered "the personal touch" to be the most important element of providing good service. Personal touch was defined as "how committed a company representative is to a client and whether he or she remembers a customer's name." The personal-touch factor was found to be more important than convenience, speed of delivery, and how well the product worked.[34] Personal touch is simply another way to describe what happens in relational exchanges.

Social relations are particularly important in facilitating exchanges at home buying parties. The term **market embeddedness** has been used to describe the situation in which the social ties between buyer and seller supplement product value to increase the perceived value of the exchange.[35] The importance of social relations has been recognized by companies such as Tupperware and Mary Kay Cosmetics. These companies frequently employ parties to sell their merchandise. In these parties one finds a

Some Characteristics of Relational Exchanges

1. *Timing.* Long term; reflects an ongoing process.
2. *Obligations.* Obligations are customized and detailed. Promises are made, and laws and regulations may apply.
3. *Relationship expectations.* Conflicts are anticipated, but they are countered by trust and efforts to create unity.
4. *Rewards.* Rewards are derived from economic and noneconomic means.
5. *Communications.* Communications are extensive through formal and informal means.
6. *Cooperation.* A great deal of cooperation is needed to maintain exchange.
7. *Power.* Increased interdependence increases the importance of judicious application of power in the exchange.
8. *Planning.* There is a significant focus on the process of exchange. Detailed planning is required for future exchanges.

TABLE 1.5

Summary of Some Key Findings Concerning Relationship Exchanges
1. Relational exchanges become more important when services and products are complex, customized, and delivered over time.
2. Relationships are more important when buyers are relatively unsophisticated.
3. Relationships are more important when the buying environment is dynamic.
4. Consumers make purchases partly for the product or service and partly for the feelings that result from the exchange.
5. Trust and satisfaction with the past performance of the exchange partner influence perceptions of relationship quality.

TABLE 1.6

hostess, a demonstrator, and the invitees. Usually, close relationships exist within the group of invitees and between the invitees and the hostess.

Table 1.6 summarizes the important findings concerning relationship exchanges.

ETHICAL ISSUES IN CONSUMER EXCHANGE RELATIONS

Within exchanges, the trust between the buyer and seller is an extremely important element. One factor that influences the bonds of trust is the ethical conduct of the buyer and seller. **Ethics** is the study of the normative judgments concerned with what is morally right and wrong, good and bad.[36] Judgments of what is morally right or wrong are based on standards that (1) deal with serious human injuries and benefits, (2) may or may not be laid down by authoritative bodies, (3) override self-interest, and (4) are based on impartial considerations.

Ethical judgments frequently involve a conflict between one's own self-interest and a standard of conduct. Thus, plastic surgeons, for example, are obligated to think first of their client's interests rather than their own. When making a decision that may have ethical implications, the person must use impartial considerations in reaching the decision. Such a decision should be based on moral guidelines and not on who is helped or hurt by the outcome of the action.[37]

The problems faced by cosmetic surgeons in their relationships with patients illustrate an ethical dilemma. An **ethical dilemma** is defined as "a decision that involves the trade-off between lowering one's personal values in exchange for increased organizational or personal profits."[38] Therefore, whenever consumers engage in exchange relationships, ethical principles are likely to come into play.

The following components generally occur in an **ethical exchange:**[39]

1. Both parties will know the full nature of the agreement that they are entering.
2. Neither party to the exchange will intentionally misrepresent or omit relevant information to the other.
3. Neither party to the exchange will unduly influence the other.

Most discussions of ethics deal with industrial or consumer marketing and typically focus on the company's actions in such areas as misleading advertising, selling products that fail to comply with the claims made about them, producing unsafe products, exerting undue influence (e.g., bribery), and failing to disclose important relevant information (e.g., not telling a customer that a product has been used previously). In addition, however, consumers also have a responsibility to act ethically in their exchanges with companies and with other consumers. Thus, if an acquaintance wishes to purchase your old car or lawn mower, you have an ethical duty to warn the person of safety problems, to avoid coercing the person to make the purchase, and to avoid misleading the person regarding how the item will perform.

Consumers should also act ethically in their dealings with businesses. For example, when consumers return products to a retailer, they have an ethical duty to return the product in satisfactory condition. They also have a duty not to mislead the store as to the reasons for the return. For example, is it ethical to purchase a dress, wear it on a single special occasion, and then return it, claiming that it simply did not fit properly? Similarly, consumers should avoid the unethical act of **free riding,** which occurs when a person obtains a resource, such as information, from a company and then fails to pay back resources in return. For instance, a person may go to a full-service camera store to obtain product information and to identify satisfactory alternatives. If the person obtains product information from sales personnel and then uses the information to make a purchase from a low-cost discount store (that does not offer personal service), the person is guilty of free riding. The consumer is acting unethically in such an instance because he or she had no intention of making a purchase. Harm is done to the retailer because the consumer received informational and service resources while having no intention of buying.

A reciprocity exists between consumers and businesses. When sufficient numbers of consumers act unethically, businesses will have to respond in some manner. If large numbers of consumers engage in free riding, real harm results because full-service retail stores will either close their doors or become discount stores. Consumers will then lose an important source of marketplace information. Similarly, if too many consumers abuse return privileges, companies will be forced to install no-return policies. Ethical behavior is a two-way street: Consumers have a right to expect businesses to act ethically, and companies have a right to expect consumers to act ethically.

It is critical to develop within a company a culture that emphasizes ethical core values.[40] Researchers have identified four rules that managers and consumers should follow to ensure that their decisions are ethical.[41] By keeping these rules in mind when making decisions, a business can develop an ethical culture. Although originally designed to apply to managers, these rules for ethical decision making pertain to consumers as well. As a result, the four rules have been slightly rewritten to link them to both consumer and managerial decision making, as follows:

1. *The golden rule.* Act in a way that you would expect others to act toward you.
2. *The professional ethic.* Take only actions that would be viewed as proper by an objective panel of colleagues.
3. *Kant's categorical imperative.* Act in a way such that the action taken under the circumstances could be a universal law of behavior for everyone facing those same circumstances.
4. *The TV test.* Always ask, "Would I feel comfortable explaining this action on TV to the general public?"

AN ORGANIZING FRAMEWORK OF CONSUMER BEHAVIOR

The organizing model shown in Figure 1.2 provides an overview of the broad field of consumer behavior. As the figure illustrates, the consumer-behavior model has five primary components that form the field's core areas of study: the buying unit, the exchange process, the marketer's strategy, the individual influencers, and the environmental influencers.

Buying units in this model represent the customers of products, services, experiences, and ideas offered by marketers. They are connected to the marketer via an

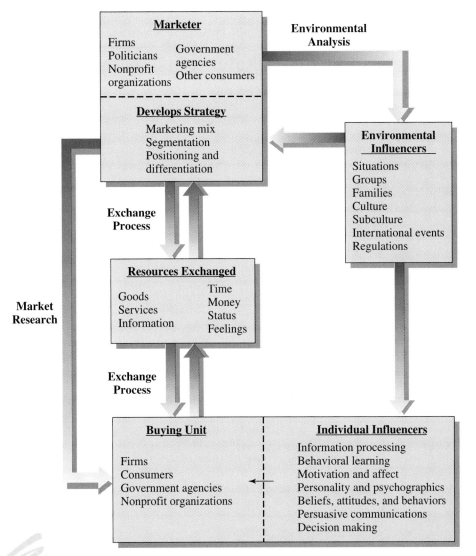

Figure 1.2   An organizing framework of consumer behavior.

exchange relationship. Buying units may consist of an individual, family, or organization that makes a purchase decision. In addition, buying units may be either consumers (individuals or households) or profit or nonprofit organizations making purchases. In other words, the principles of consumer behavior apply to business-to-business marketing as well as business-to-consumer marketing.

   The term *marketer* is used extremely broadly in the model; a marketer could be a company selling a good or service, a nonprofit organization, a governmental agency, a political candidate, or another consumer who wishes to sell or trade something. The marketer seeks to create an exchange with consumers by implementing a marketing strategy through which it attempts to reach its long-term customer and profit goals. A major focus of the text will involve identifying how an understanding of the exchange process, the individual influencers, and the environmental influencers can be used to develop marketing strategy.

A **marketing strategy** is implemented by developing segmentation, positioning, and marketing-mix objectives for a product. Segmentation refers to the division of the marketplace into relatively homogeneous subsets of consumers having similar needs and wants. Positioning involves influencing how consumers perceive a brand's characteristics relative to those of competitive offerings. In order to implement the segmentation and positioning objectives, the marketer develops a marketing-mix strategy. The **marketing mix** consists of the product itself, together with how it is priced, promoted, and distributed.

To develop strategy, the marketer conducts environmental-analysis studies in order to identify the likely effects of the environmental influencers. In addition, the marketer uses market research to obtain information on individual consumers. Based on environmental analysis and market research, managers develop positioning and segmentation strategies, which are implemented through the marketing mix. Consumer-behavior findings and ideas are critical to the development of marketing strategy. Chapter 2 discusses how managers can use these concepts to market their goods, services, ideas, and experiences.

The model of consumer behavior connects the buying unit to both the individual influence factors and the environmental influencers outlined in Figure 1.2. The **individual influence factors** represent the psychological processes that affect individuals engaged in acquiring, consuming, and disposing of goods, services, and experiences. The **environmental influencers** represent those factors outside of the individual that affect individual consumers, decision-making units, and marketers.

The individual influencers and the environmental influencers lie on a continuum that moves from a highly micro- to a broad macrofocus. The continuum begins at the microlevel by focusing on the individual and the basic psychological processes involving perception and learning. As one goes along the continuum, the analysis moves to the study of personality, attitudes, persuasion, and finally, consumer decision making. At this point the emphasis changes from the study of the individual to investigations of the impact of situations and groups of people on consumer behavior. At this end of the continuum, consumer researchers examine how people in different nations and cultures acquire, consume, and dispose of goods, services, experiences, and ideas.

ORGANIZATION OF THE TEXT

The three major sections of this book are organized around the consumer-behavior model shown in Figure 1.2. Part I, an overview of the field, consists of two chapters. In the present chapter, we have defined the field and presented the organizing framework of consumer. Chapter 2 identifies how a knowledge of consumer behavior can be used to develop marketing strategy and then discusses how consumer-behavior concepts can be employed by managers of organizations to develop the marketing mix, segment the marketplace, position and differentiate products, perform environmental analysis, and conduct market research.

Part II consists of a set of chapters concerning the factors that influence individual consumers. As shown in Figure 1.2, individual consumer processes include information processing, motivation, personality and psychographics, attitudes, persuasive communications, and decision making.

Finally, part III considers the environmental influencers that affect buyers and sellers, including consumer situations, group processes, culture, subcultures, and international and cross-cultural consumer behavior. The book concludes with a chapter that focuses on the dark side of consumer behavior and its public-policy implications.

If you develop an understanding of the key consumer-behavior concepts introduced at the beginning of each chapter of this book, we believe that you will have the information required to gain an advantage in the marketplace. This advantage results because you have the knowledge to create exchanges that are mutually profitable for both the consumer and your organization. We hope that the process is as enjoyable as it is lucrative.

Notes

1. Erin White, "Chatting a Singer up the Pop Charts," *Wall Street Journal,* October 5, 1999, pp. B1, B4.
2. Alisha Davis, "A Summer Foot Festish," *Newsweek,* August 16, 1999, p. 63.
3. Joe Aylward, "Don't Try This at Home," *Newsweek,* August 12, 1996, p. 5.
4. Charles Siebert, "The Cuts That Go Deeper," *New York Times Magazine,* July 7, 1996, pp. 20–35, 40–44.
5. Jonathan Friedland, "Argentina Is a Land of Many Faces, Fixed by Plastic Surgeons," *Wall Street Journal,* February 2, 1996, pp. A1, A5.
6. Scott Ward and Thomas Robertson, "Consumer Behavior Research: Promise and Prospects," in *Consumer Behavior: Theoretical Sources,* ed. Scott Ward and Thomas Robertson (Upper Saddle River, NJ: Prentice Hall, 1973), 3–42.
7. Theodore Levitt, "Marketing Myopia," in *Modern Marketing Strategy,* ed. Edward Bursk and John Chapman (Cambridge, MA: Harvard University Press, 1964).
8. Philip Kotler, *Marketing Management* (Upper Saddle River, NJ: Prentice Hall, 2000), 21.
9. Brent Stidsen, "Directions in the Study of Marketing," in *Conceptual and Theoretical Developments in Marketing,* ed. Neil Beckwith et al. (Chicago, IL: American Marketing Association, 1979), 383–98.
10. As cited in Kotler, *Marketing Management,* 3.
11. Frank Houston, "The Marketing Concept: What It Is and What It Is Not," *Journal of Marketing* (April 1986): 81–87.
12. Ross Perot, "How I Would Turn Around GM," *Fortune,* February 15, 1988, p. 45.
13. Otis Port, "Customers Move into the Driver's Seat," *Business Week,* October 4, 1999, pp. 103–6.
14. Richard E. Petty and John T. Cacioppo, "Addressing Disturbing and Disturbed Consumer Behavior: Is It Necessary to Change the Way We Conduct Behavioral Science?" *Journal of Marketing Research* 33 (February 1996): 1–8.
15. John C. Mowen, "Beyond Consumer Decision Making," *Journal of Consumer Marketing* 5 (winter 1988): 15–25.
16. Morris Holbrook and Elizabeth C. Hirschman, "The Experiential Aspects of Consumption: Consumer Fantasies, Feelings, and Fun," *Journal of Consumer Research,* September 9, 1982, pp. 132–40.
17. For a review of variety seeking, see Leigh McAlister and Edgar E. Pessemier, "Variety Seeking Behavior: An Interdisciplinary Review," *Journal of Consumer Research,* December 9, 1982, pp. 311–22. Also see Werner Kroeber-Riel, "Emotional Product Differentiation by Classical Conditioning," in *Advances in Consumer Research,* ed. Thomas Kinnear (Ann Arbor, MI: Association for Consumer Research, 1984), 11:538–43.
18. Michel Tuan Pham, "Representativeness, Relevance, and the Use of Feelings in Decision Making," *Journal of Consumer Research* 25 (September 1998): 144–59.
19. Gary McWilliams, "New PCs Say, 'Let Me Entertain You,' and Sales Get Unexpected Lift," *Wall Street Journal,* September 28, 1999, pp. B1, B6.
20. Russell Belk, John Sherry, and Melanie Wallendorf, "A Naturalistic Inquiry into Buyer and Seller Behavior at a Swap Meet," *Journal of Consumer Research,* March 14, 1988, pp. 449–69.
21. John Sherry, "Some Implications of Consumer Oral Tradition for Reactive Marketing," in *Advances in Consumer Research,* ed. Thomas Kinnear (Ann Arbor, MI: Association for Consumer Research, 1984), 11:741–47.
22. Michael L. Rothschild and William Gaidis, "Behavioral Learning Theory: Its Relevance to Marketing and Promotions," *Journal of Marketing* 45 (spring 1981): 70–78. Also see Peter H. Reingen and Jerome B. Kernan, "More Evidence on Interpersonal Yielding," *Journal of Marketing Research* 16 (November 1979): 588–93.

23. For additional work on exchange, see Richard Bagozzi, "Marketing as Exchange," *Journal of Marketing* 39 (October 1975): 431–47.

24. Wroe Alderson, *Marketing Behavior and Executive Actions* (Homewood, IL: Richard D. Irwin, 1957).

25. "AMA Board Approves New Marketing Definition," *Marketing News,* March 1, 1985, p. 1.

26. These ideas are based on the law of exchange articulated by Wroe Alderson, *Dynamic Marketing Behavior* (Homewood, IL: Richard D. Irwin, 1965).

27. Franklin Houston and Jule Gassenheimer, "Marketing and Exchange," *Journal of Marketing* 51 (October 1987): 3–18. This excellent article was the basis for a number of the ideas expressed in the section on exchange processes.

28. Uriel Foa and Edna Foa, *Societal Structures of the Mind* (Springfield, IL: Charles C. Thomas, 1974). Foa and Foa employ love, not feelings, as the sixth resource. The change was made in this text because *love* is an unsuitable term for the types of feelings engendered in a consumer exchange. In addition, in some contexts negative, rather than positive, feelings may be communicated.

29. Richard P. Bagozzi, "Toward a Formal Theory of Marketing Exchanges," in *Conceptual and Theoretical Developments in Marketing*, ed. O. C. Ferrell, Stephen W. Brown, and Charles W. Lamb Jr. (Chicago, IL: American Marketing Association, 1979), 32–39.

30. Robert F. Lusch, Stephen W. Brown, and Gary J. Brunswick, "A General Framework for Explaining Internal vs. External Exchange," *Journal of the Academy of Marketing Science* 20 (1992): 119–34.

31. Elizabeth C. Hirschman, "People as Products: Analysis of a Complex Marketing Exchange," *Journal of Marketing* 51 (January 1987): 98–108.

32. F. Robert Dwyer, Paul Schurr, and Sejo Oh, "Developing Buyer–Seller Relationships," *Journal of Marketing* 51 (April 1987): 11–27.

33. Theodore Leavitt, *The Marketing Imagination* (New York: Free Press, 1983), 111.

34. "What Customers Really Want," *Fortune,* June 4, 1990, pp. 58–68.

35. Jonathan K. Frenzen and Harry L. Davis, "Purchasing Behavior in Embedded Markets," *Journal of Consumer Research* 17 (June 1990): 1–12.

36. Morris B. Holbrook, "Ethics in Consumer Research: An Overview and Prospectus," in *Advances in Consumer Research*, ed. Chris T. Allen and Deborah Roedder John (Provo, UT: Association for Consumer Research, 1994), 21:566–71.

37. For a recent discussion of ethics and marketing, see Craig J. Thompson, "A Contextualist Proposal for the Conceptualization and Study of Marketing Ethics," *Journal of Public Policy and Marketing* 14 (fall 1995): 177–91.

38. Gene R. Laczniak and Patrick E. Murphy, "Fostering Ethical Marketing Decisions," *Journal of Business Ethics* 10 (1991): 259–71.

39. Manuel Velasquez, *Business Ethics: Concepts and Cases* (Upper Saddle River, NJ: Prentice Hall, 1982).

40. Anusorn Singhapakdi, Kenneth L. Kraft, Scott J. Vitell, and Kumar C. Rallapelli, "The Perceived Importance of Ethics and Social Responsibility on Organizational Effectiveness: A Survey of Marketers," *Journal of the Academy of Marketing Science* 23 (winter 1995): 49–56.

41. Laczniak and Murphy, "Fostering Ethical Marketing Decisions."

Consumer Behavior and the Marketing Manager

After studying this chapter, you should be able to describe each of the following concepts, together with their managerial relevance:

1. The five managerial application areas (PERMS).
2. Product positioning.
3. Product differentiation.
4. The elements of the consumer environment.
5. Behavioral economics.
6. The role of consumer behavior in performing marketing research.
7. The role of consumer behavior in the development of the marketing mix.
8. Bases for the segmentation of the marketplace.
9. Behavioral segmentation.
10. Managerial applications analysis.

As described in chapter 1, an understanding of consumer-behavior theories and concepts is critical for marketing managers and public-policy makers. Specifically, in order to develop marketing strategy, managers must know the factors that influence the acquisition, consumption, and disposition of goods, services, and ideas. This chapter identifies and discusses five managerial applications areas to which consumer behavior concepts apply and from which marketing strategy is derived: (1) product positioning and differentiation, (2) environmental analysis, (3) marketing research, (4) marketing-mix development, and (5) segmentation.

Five Managerial Application Areas of Consumer-Behavior Concepts

Managerial Application Area	Definition
1. Product positioning	The attempt to influence product demand by developing and promoting a product with specific characteristics that differentiate it from competitors.
2. Environmental analysis	The assessment of the external forces that act upon the firm and its customers and that create threats and opportunities.
3. Market research	Applied consumer research designed to provide management with information on factors that impact consumers' acquisition, consumption, and disposition of goods, services, and ideas.
4. Marketing-mix strategy	The coordination of marketing activities involving product development and the promotion, pricing, and distribution of the product.
5. Segmentation	The division of the marketplace into distinct subsets of customers with similar needs and wants, each subset to be reached with a different marketing mix.

TABLE 2.1

The acronym PERMS—positioning, environmental analysis, research, marketing mix, and segmentation—can be used to recall the five managerial application areas of consumer behavior concepts. Table 2.1 briefly defines each managerial application area. First, the positioning and differentiation of a product must be based on an understanding of the product benefits sought by the target market. Second, environmental analysis is facilitated by understanding the culture of a target markets. Third, research into consumer markets cannot be conducted without a thorough understanding of the factors that impact consumer buying. Similarly, marketing-mix strategy must be based on a solid understanding of the target market's characteristics. Finally, the segmentation of the marketplace is based on identifying differences in how groups of consumers think, feel, and behave. In sum, whenever the question, "What is the managerial implication of such-and-such consumer behavior concept?" is asked, you should immediately consider each of the five PERMS concepts.

By developing a basic understanding of the five areas of managerial strategy that apply to consumer-behavior principles, you will have a basis for using the consumer-behavior concepts discussed throughout the rest of the book for marketing and public-policy decision making.

PRODUCT POSITIONING AND PRODUCT DIFFERENTIATION

Through **product positioning** an organization influences how consumers perceive a brand's characteristics relative to those of competitive offerings. The goal of product positioning is to influence demand by creating a product with specific characteristics (i.e., brand attributes) and a clear image that differentiate it from competitors. **Product differentiation** is the process of manipulating the marketing mix so as to position a product in a manner that allows consumers to perceive meaningful differences between a brand and its competitors.

Positioning a product and segmenting customers go hand in hand: A segment of customers is identified, and a product is then developed and positioned to fulfill the needs of that segment. For example, in 1996 Starbucks announced that it would open coffee shops in Japan, and the news sent shivers down the spines of Japanese coffee-bar owners. Starbucks had recognized that the Japanese are the world's number-three coffee consumers and as such, the country represented an untouched market. Starbucks is positioned as an upscale, hip place to drink espresso, caffe latte, caffe mocha, and Seattle coffee. Because its image is highly differentiated from the mom-and-pop coffee bars in Japan, its earnings potential is extremely high. One Japanese advertising executive described the current coffee merchants as "like a dry lake bed—void of new ideas. . . . That's why the whole industry is stirred up about Starbucks."[1]

Two types of positioning strategies may be followed. In **specific positioning** the company seeks to create strong linkages in consumers' minds among the product, certain key attributes, and benefits. Market leaders in particular will attempt to establish attribute–need linkages in order to create a strong product image. In this approach, even though other brands are not specifically mentioned, the goal is still to differentiate the brand's qualities from the competition's. Procter & Gamble did this effectively with Crest toothpaste by creating the image of a strong tooth-decay fighter.

A second approach to product positioning is frequently employed by brands that are not market leaders. In this approach the secondary brand attempts to position itself in relation to a market leader. Called **competitive positioning,** its goal is to emphasize the attributes possessed by the brand in relation to a leading brand. In this approach the company will often use comparative advertising.[2]

An example of competitive positioning strategy is Pepsi-Cola's positioning of its brand to Coca-Cola. Pepsi-Cola has positioned its beverage as a "hip" product targeted to the more unconventional person. Interestingly, Coca-Cola does not appear to have a clear positioning strategy. As the sales leader, it attempts to stand above the competition and let other companies react to its moves.

One key problem for marketers is assessing a brand's position. Perhaps the most frequently used approach to this involves the creation of **perceptual maps.** Perceptual maps seek to show how consumers position various brands relative to each other on graphs whose axes are formed by product attributes.

Figure 2.1 displays a perceptual map that was created to assess consumer perceptions of various types of meat products.[3] It was developed by asking consumers to rate the meat products on a series of attributes, including taste, cost, calories, quality, and preparation time. A computer program called multidimensional preference scaling was used to create the map. The program graphs how consumers perceive various products in relation to each other as well as to various attributes that describe them. For example, in the upper-right-hand quadrant of the figure are a number of attributes clustered together—healthy, low fat, light, low calorie, and tender. The products positioned closest to these attributes are fish, chicken, and tuna. On the other side, the meat products beef roast, pork roast, pork chop, and ham are clustered together. The attributes closest to them are great taste and good aroma.

The perceptual map shown in Figure 2.1 helps to identify some of the reasons consumption of beef has fallen over the past 15 years: Consumers have become highly concerned about the value of their time and the importance of eating in a healthy manner. Beef roast and pork are both positioned far away from these attributes on the perceptual map. In contrast, food products that are becoming more prevalent, such as fish, chicken, and turkey, are positioned much closer to the clusters of adjectives relating to health and ease of cooking.

One of the benefits of creating perceptual maps is the ability to identify whether consumers differentiate one product from another. As the perceptual map in Figure

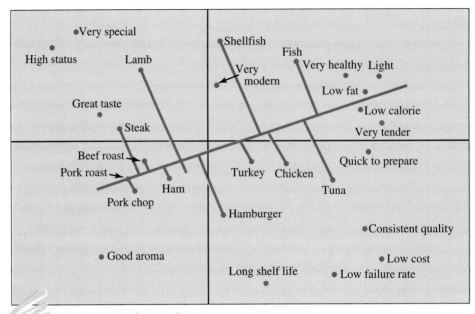

Figure 2.1   A perceptual map of meats.

Source: Adapted form a discussion in John Kinski, "Consumer Perceptions of Meat Products," Master's Thesis, Oklahoma State University, 1985.

2.1 shows, consumers perceived beef roast, pork roast, pork chops, and ham to be very close together. In other words, these products are *not* differentiated well by consumers.

Companies gain a number of benefits when consumers are able to differentiate one brand from others. In particular, product differentiation adds perceived value to the product. The increase in perceived value helps to increase the leverage of the various components of the marketing mix.[4] Thus, for example, in the pricing area, brand differentiation can allow the company to command premium prices for a product. In the promotion area, product differentiation helps creative personnel to develop messages that promote only the brand advertised and not competitors as well. An example of a clearly differentiated brand using a claim effectively was Mercedes with its unique selling proposition, "Engineered like no other car in the world." Mercedes stands out in its engineering, and the claim is highly believable. Because of its ability to differentiate itself from other brands in the United States, Mercedes can price its cars significantly higher in the United States than in Germany.

ENVIRONMENTAL ANALYSIS

Environmental analysis consists of the assessment of the external forces that act upon a company and its customers and that create both threats and opportunities. In large organizations the task of performing environmental analysis may take place in the market research department or in the strategic planning group. In smaller organizations the chief executive office (CEO) and key staff members perform the analysis. A company should monitor on an ongoing basis a number of different components of the external consumer environment.[5] These components include the demographic, economic, natural, technological, political, and cultural environments. Table 2.2 lists

Market Environments and Their Applications to Consumer-Behavior Areas	
Environment	**Consumer-Behavior Area**
Demographic	Population changes and cultural values of various demographic groups based on such factors as age, sex, income, eduction, ethnicity, and geography.
Economic	Factors influencing consumer economic sentiment and patterns of savings and spending.
Natural	Consumers' reactions to changing weather patterns and to natural disasters such as earthquakes.
Technological	The diffusion of technological innovations and consumers' reactions to the innovations; the user-friendly characteristics of machines and computers.
Political	The impact of laws, rules, and regulations on consumers.
Cultural	Rituals, values, mores, customs, and norms of a culture and how they influence consumption behavior within that culture.

TABLE 2.2

the environments and the areas of consumer behavior that are applicable to their understanding.

One goal of the consumer analyst is to predict future changes in these environments and how these changes will influence consumers. For example, the publisher of this book, Prentice Hall, must be able to predict changes in the number of consumers who are likely to read its textbooks. An analysis of population trends suggests that, beginning at the turn of the century, an area of emphasis should be on textbooks used in colleges and universities. That is because between 2000 and 2005 the number of college students will increase dramatically. In contrast, during this same time period, the number of students entering grade school will sharply decrease. These demographic trends have major implications for developing segmentation strategy: Environmental analysis suggests that textbook publishers target the college-market segment of consumers.

The field of consumer behavior includes critical information on how the cultural, cross-cultural, subcultural, demographic, and situational environments lead to marketing opportunities or liabilities. These disciplines are discussed in detail in part III. Although the focus of this text is not on the ways in which economic, natural, and technological environments impact consumer behavior and marketing strategy, these areas are discussed briefly in the following sections.

The Economic Environment and Consumer Behavior

The economic environment consists of the monetary resources, natural resources, and human resources that influence the behavior of individuals and groups. At the local, national, and international levels, the economic environment influences the consumption patterns of millions of people. In the long term, it dramatically influences the lifestyle and well-being of entire nations. For example, in the nineteenth century, Britain was the wealthiest country in the world. A century later the standard of living of its consumers lags far behind the United States, Germany, Japan, and Scandinavia.

One area of economics, called **behavioral economics,** has particular relevance to consumer behavior. Behavioral economics is the study of the economic decisions made by individual consumers and the behavioral determinants of those economic decisions. Although economic theories, such as the law of demand, can be applied at the individual level, traditional economists are most comfortable talking about aggregates of people. (The law of demand states that an inverse relationship exists between the price of a product and the quantity demanded of the product.) Behavioral economists take another approach and analyze consumers individually. This idea, developed by George Katona, proposes that the attitudes, motives, and expectations of individual consumers can be built up to make predictions concerning the economy as a whole. This "bottom-up" approach was a radical departure from traditional economic thinking.

Behavioral economists have made three major contributions to the understanding of consumer-spending patterns. First, they originated and documented the idea that the consumer sector strongly influences the course of the aggregate economy. Part of the impetus for the development of behavioral economics was the recognition that the U.S. economy is consumer driven. Fully two-thirds of the U.S. gross national product results from consumer spending. Second, they investigated the factors that influence the decisions of families to buy or save. By understanding the intentions of families to buy and save, one can develop a picture of the future of the overall economy. Traditional economists focused on the aggregate economy that emerged from the study of secondary data, such as measures of the gross national product and inflation.

The third contribution of behavioral economists was the development of a methodology for making predictions of aggregate economic activities based on consumer surveys. The use of the survey research methodology was a major break from the traditional econometric studies of the economy. In the survey approach, representative samples of consumers are interviewed to obtain information on consumer attitudes and expectations about their forthcoming buying behavior. Begun in 1946 the surveys of consumer sentiment continue today at the University of Michigan Survey Research Center. In addition, other groups, such as the Conference Board, have developed their own indices of consumer sentiment. Such indices now play an important role in helping private and governmental forecasters estimate the future course of the economy.

The Natural Environment and Consumer Behavior

Features of the natural environment important to the marketer include the types of raw materials available, pollution, consumer fear of contracting deadly diseases, the expansion of desert regions around the globe, and various weather phenomena such as hurricanes or drought. Each factor can influence consumption behavior.

Shortages of raw materials, such as oil, can dramatically influence prices of product and cause consumers to change their buying patterns. Pollution can wipe out or degrade important waterways and ruin industries. For example, the oyster industry in Virginia's Chesapeake Bay has been severely harmed by pollution. The effects of disease on consumer behavior are illustrated by the AIDS virus; fear of the deadly disease has changed the behavior patterns of sexually active people. Even shifts in weather patterns are linked to short-term changes in consumer behavior. Obviously, short-term cold snaps or rainy spells influence the purchase of clothing. Natural disasters can change buying patterns of affected regions. For example, after Hurricane George devastated the Mississippi Gulf coast in 1998, car dealerships in the region had record sales. Indeed, the purchase of goods and services explodes after a disaster in the United States as the region is rebuilt. A phenomenon results that is called the "Jacuzzi effect"—not only do people rebuild after a disaster, but they also add extras, such as whirlpool bathtubs.[6]

The Technological Environment and Consumer Behavior

Technological changes can dramatically influence the lifestyle of consumers and can also be an important source of new product ideas. The birth-control pill, television, radio, computer, automobile, and airplane have all dramatically influenced consumer lifestyles. (Consumer lifestyle, or the way people live, is discussed in chapter 6.) An overlooked area of research relating technology to consumer behavior is that of investigating the people–machine interface. At issue is how to produce machines and products that are easy to use. As applied to consumers, the problem is how to make machines user friendly. For the consumer researcher, the goal should be to anticipate what changes in the technological environment will occur and how these will influence the lifestyle and consumption patterns of consumers.

The Reciprocity of Consumers and the Environment

It is important to realize that consumers can influence the environment, just as the environment can influence consumers. Thus, changes in consumer spending and saving patterns can influence the economy. Similarly, the behavior of millions of consumers acting together can influence the natural environment. For example, many researchers believe that one of the primary causes of the widening of the deserts in Africa is the actions of people who allow cattle to overgraze and who cut down trees for firewood.

MARKET RESEARCH

Market research may be defined as applied consumer research designed to provide management with information on factors that impact consumers' acquisition, consumption, and disposition of goods, services, and ideas. Unless the market researcher has a firm grasp of the factors that impact consumer behavior, he or she has no way of determining what to measure or what pitfalls may occur doing the research.

Consumer researchers provide many of the scales and instruments used by market researchers. These instruments are employed to measure a myriad of issues—from attention to advertisements and memory for promotions to attitudes, decision processes, customer satisfaction, and personality and psychographic characteristics.

In some cases consumer research can determine whether regulators allow a product to be marketed. For example, in 1996 Procter & Gamble began marketing its new synthetic fat substitute, named Olestra. The product has a huge market potential as a medium for cooking potato chips, french fries, and so on. Because the product cannot be absorbed into the human body, extra calories and fat are not added. The downside, however, is that it may cause abdominal problems. Prior to allowing Procter & Gamble to market the product, the Federal Drug Administration (FDA) required the company to do consumer research to assess the product's effects on the gastrointestinal system. Although some minor problems were found, the FDA gave its approval.

Even after the FDA's approval, the company continued its research. When a potato chip product made by Frito-Lay, which was fried in the oil, was initially test-marketed in several midsized cities, Procter & Gamble researchers carefully monitored consumer response. The company discovered that only one alleged adverse health effect happened for every 3,000 bags of chips sold—a rate lower than that found in the tests done for the FDA. The results of the consumer analysis helped to combat charges made by one consumer group that the product is unsafe and should be banned.[7]

MARKETING-MIX DEVELOPMENT

Marketing-mix development involves the development and coordination of activities involving the product and its promotion, pricing, and distribution. The facts, theories, and concepts of consumer behavior directly impact the development of the marketing mix. These applications are discussed in the following subsections.

Product Development

This book uses the term *product* broadly to include goods, services, places, organizations, ideas, and even people.[8] For example, the product of an organization such as the Sierra Club is a set of ideas. Similarly, the product of a political campaign is the candidate and his or her ideas. Principles of consumer behavior can be applied to four separate areas of the process of new-product development—(1) idea generation, (2) concept testing, (3) product development, and (4) market testing.

Within the area of new-product development, consumer-behavior concepts perhaps have the greatest impact on **idea generation.** No less than five major areas of consumer behavior can be used to help managers develop ideas for new products. These include the analysis of consumer attitudes, lifestyle changes, situational factors, other cultures, and subcultures. For example, a company can use the study of consumer attitudes regarding existing products to identify consumer desires for particular product attributes. If consumers believe that existing products fail to possess attributes that are desired, a new-product opportunity may exist. Colgate-Palmolive, for example, recognized that consumers wanted to have toothpaste that was easier to dispense. The company developed a pump that was economical and easy to use. The result was that Colgate toothpaste rapidly increased its market share and threatened to replace Crest as the number-one-selling toothpaste.

Concept testing involves the pretesting of the product idea. A product concept is defined as the particular "consumer meaning that the company tries to build into a product idea."[9] For example, the product concept for a new personal computer may be to build a computer that consumers perceive to be user friendly, portable, IBM-compatible, powerful, and low priced. In order to determine whether a market exists for such a product concept, the firm can do product-positioning analysis and surveys to determine the attitudes consumers may possess toward such a concept.

After determining whether consumers perceive the product concept as management intends, the company can begin the process of **product development.** Here, prototypes are developed, tested, named, and packaged. A variety of consumer-behavior concepts are important in this phase. For example, researchers should be concerned with how consumers process information about the product. Is the product user friendly (easy to use, not too complex, etc.)? Does the product's packaging gain attention? Can consumers remember the name of the product?

The researchers must also be concerned about the attitude-formation process when testing the product and packaging. Do consumers like the prototype product? Do they believe the claims made about it? Do they like the packaging?

After the product-development phase is concluded satisfactorily, a product is often moved into **market testing.** Market testing, when done, involves placing the product into limited distribution to consumers in order to identify any potential problems and to test the entire marketing mix. In this phase additional attitudinal measures are taken to determine if consumers are forming the expected beliefs, affective reactions, and buying intentions. In addition, postpurchase satisfaction is examined. Are consumers happy with the product after purchase? Are they rebuying it? Are they showing signs of developing brand loyalty? The manager will also want to know if consumers are using the product in the expected situations. In general, the goal of the market test is to determine if the marketing strategy seems to be working. Therefore, all the areas of consumer behavior previously mentioned will apply.

Throughout the new-product-development process, managers must be concerned with the products and actions of competitors. Consumers will not perceive a brand in isolation of competitors. Thus, assessment of how the product compares with competitive offerings is crucial. A decision to move into full-scale production would be a gross mistake if it were based on the finding that consumers rate your product as "good" on various attributes but rate competitors as "excellent" on the same attributes. Furthermore, managers cannot assume that the competitive environment will remain constant while product development occurs. When engaging in product development, managers are constantly trying to hit a moving target. Changes occurring in the cultural, economic, and natural environments make the process exceptionally risky.

Promotional Strategy Implications

For the marketing manager, consumer behavior has broad application to promotional strategy. Consumer-behavior concepts apply to each component of the promotional mix—from advertising and personal selling to sales promotion to public relations. The strategic and practical implications of consumer behavior on each element of the promotional mix are discussed in the following subsections.

Advertising and Personal Selling Implications. When developing advertising materials, it is useful to think in terms of the ideas, images, and feelings the creative minds in an advertising agency should attempt to evoke in consumers. One approach to developing concepts for the advertising theme is to analyze the motivations and psychographic characteristics of the target market. Particularly for experiential products such as beer, perfume, and cigarettes, developing a theme and image for the product is crucial.

The frog and lizard ads for Budweiser beer illustrate the development of an advertising campaign based on knowledge of the demographic and psychographic characteristics of a target market. Targeted to consumers born after 1964 (the so-called Generation X), the ads show ugly but amusing frogs and lizards going to great lengths to "get a Bud." In one ad a frog shoots out its tongue to latch onto a speeding Budweiser truck. In another ad a gang of frogs hijack an alligator to invade a party and steal a case of Bud. Although these descriptions sound ridiculous when described verbally, the ads are irreverent and absurd in a cute way—qualities that appeal to Generation Xers.

The investigation of consumer attitudes is another particularly important area for advertisers. The goal of many advertisements is to create beliefs about the attributes of a product. In order to know the beliefs on which to focus, market researchers must identify the attributes that the target market views as most important. In addition, the advertiser must have information on the type of message to use to influence the beliefs. Should fear appeals be used? Would a celebrity endorser be the most effective source of information? Should comparative advertising be used? The knowledge of attitude formation and change can assist the manager in answering these types of questions.

Many of the areas important to advertisers are also relevant to those engaged in personal selling. Knowledge of attitude formation and change processes can assist marketers in developing specific messages for their sales force. Similarly, the analysis of cultural and subcultural differences between the sales force and clients can help the company avoid various problems that can arise through inappropriate statements or actions. For example, when dealing with Japanese business personnel, a manager does not want his or her sales force to be too forceful or act too informally with the more reserved and polite Japanese. Another area of consumer behavior that is of particular importance to personal selling is personal influence, which is discussed in chapter 8.

Sales Promotion Applications. Sales promotion has been defined as all of the supplementary promotional activities done in addition to advertising and personal selling.[10] It includes such items as supplying product literature via direct mail, providing dealer incentives, using point-of-purchase (POP) materials, and providing consumer incentives.

Consumer-behavior principles can influence planning in each of these areas, but the applications are particularly strong in the domains of direct mail, POPs, and consumer incentives. Direct-mail marketers attempt to identify highly specific segments of consumers to whom they can direct advertising materials or catalogs. The goal of these attempts is to pinpoint precisely a segment of consumers that is likely to be influenced by the materials received and then reach the group directly through the mail. Accordingly, sophisticated direct-mail marketers develop precise demographic and psychographic profiles of the segment that they plan to reach. By combining the demographic information that can be obtained from zip codes and census information with information obtained from lists of magazine readers and catalog readers, marketers can pinpoint segments quite precisely.

Consumer-behavior principles also apply in the creation of effective sales incentives. Sales incentives include such devices as price-off deals, sampling, contests, and the use of premiums, coupons, and trading stamps. A number of these sales incentives concern techniques to change the price of the product. Such devices as rebates, coupons, trading stamps, and price-off deals effectively change the price the consumer pays for the product. (The perceptual processes described in chapter 3 have particular relevance to the development of such sales incentives.)

Public Relations. Public relations is a broad area that focuses on the interface between the corporation and consumers. Areas of concern include managing the publicity that emerges from the company and handling consumer questions and complaints. The areas of consumer behavior that apply most directly to public relations are those of attitude formation and change. In particular, the manager of public relations must be concerned with the effects of negative publicity on the company and its products. Negative information has a relatively greater influence on consumers than does positive information. As a result, those in public relations must monitor news media and consumers constantly in order to identify quickly any negative information about the company that is seeping into the marketplace. Types of negative information a manager may have to deal with include rumors, product recalls (e.g., the recall of Coke in Europe in 1999), product disasters (e.g., an airplane crash), corporate financial problems, illegal activities of senior corporate officials, and complaints made by consumer groups concerning advertising.

When planning public-relations activities, the manager must be concerned with how the public will perceive that source of information and the message that is given. In many instances corporate officials will act as spokespersons for the company. Providing training to these individuals on how to present themselves is an important task for companies with a high public profile.

Pricing and Distribution Applications

One major area for applying consumer-behavior principles to pricing is predicting the likely impact of price changes on consumers. That is, how will consumers react when companies raise or lower the price of a product? Principles of perception apply to this question. As will be discussed in chapter 3, unless the price change is greater than some threshold level, consumers may not notice a difference. If the price is being lowered, it should be lowered enough so that consumers will perceive that a change has occurred. In contrast, if the price is being raised, in most instances the company would prefer that the price increase not be enough for consumers to perceive a difference. Pricing issues will also be discussed in chapters on consumer decision making and in sections on the relationship between price and quality (see chapters 3 and 7).

Consumer-behavior principles can also apply to the distribution component of the marketing mix. In particular, understanding how consumers make their purchase decisions will have an impact on product distribution. That is, the extent to which consumers engage in search behavior should influence the intensity of a company's distribution efforts. If a product is bought under low-involvement conditions, it is unlikely that consumers will engage in much search behavior prior to buying it. Therefore, companies selling low-involvement products should seek to place the product in as many retail outlets as possible in order to have the product available whenever a need arises that it could fulfill. A classic example is the distribution strategy of soft-drink companies—in particular, Coca-Cola. In most urban areas, a consumer can find a vending machine or retailer selling Coca-Cola within several hundred feet of wherever he or she stands.

Geodemographics is yet another consumer behavior that has application to physical distribution (see chapter 14). Through geodemographic analysis market researchers assess the demographic characteristics of consumers in divergent geographical areas. Companies must be concerned about where to place new retail outlets and where to place distribution centers. Analyzing population shifts among regions of the country can pay dividends in the form of lowering costs and in matching the distribution of the product to growth areas. Similarly, companies must be concerned with the placement of retail stores in cities and towns.

THE SEGMENTATION OF THE MARKETPLACE

Market segmentation is defined as the dividing of a market into distinct subsets of customers with similar needs and wants, each of which can be reached with a different marketing mix.[11] For segments to be useful, they should possess the characteristics of *measurability, accessibility,* and *substantiality*. For the measurement criterion, a manager must be able to assess the segment's characteristics, needs, and wants via various demographic, psychographic, attitude, and personality measures. In order for a market segment to meet the accessibility criterion, customers must be reachable via the marketing mix. That is, if a market segment cannot be reached so that they receive promotional messages and the product itself, the market segment is not a viable target. Finally, the segment must be substantial enough in size and income to generate sufficient sales for it to be managerially useful.

The advantage of segmentation to a company is that the marketing mix can be tailored to meet the needs and wants of homogeneous subsets of customers. Because these subsets of consumers may have unique needs and wants not shared by larger groupings of consumers, the total market potential for a general class of product may be expanded. For example, the overall market potential for watches was increased when companies identified specialized needs and wants of consumers for fashion watches, diving watches, running watches, pocket watches, dress watches, and so forth. If only one type of all-purpose watch were offered, total sales would be much lower than they currently are. By developing watches for particular segments, the overall number of watches sold increased.

Bases for Segmenting Consumer Markets

Segments are identified by finding groupings of consumers with similar needs and wants. For consumer goods a market segment may be composed of millions of people. For industrial goods a segment may be composed of tens, hundreds, or thousands of companies. The goal for the manager is to identify the **bases for segmentation.** In other words, on what variables can distinct grouping of people or companies be identified? A number of factors have been identified by which people and companies can be grouped. Because the bases for segmenting consumer and industrial markets are somewhat different, they are discussed separately.

For consumer markets, four classifications of segmentation variables exist: (1) the characteristics of the person, (2) the nature of the situation in which the product or service may be purchased, (3) geography, and (4) the culture and subculture adopted by the consumer. These are summarized in Table 2.3.

Characteristics of the Person. Each individual within a population has a unique set of needs, wants, and aspirations. Fortunately for marketers, particular needs and wants are often shared by large enough numbers of people that the manager can develop a particular product or service to fulfill these needs and wants. It is the sum of large numbers of individual consumers who share certain needs and wants that creates a market segment. The characteristic of people on which markets can be formed may be classified into four categories—demographic, behavioral, psychographic, and personality characteristics.

Demographic Characteristics. Chapter 14 discusses a number of demographic measures used to describe the characteristics of various groups of people. These **demographic characteristics** include age, sex, income, religion, marital status, nationality, education, family size, occupation, and ethnicity. Such demographic measures of consumers have two important uses in the segmentation process. First, they can be used either singly or in combination to describe various subcultures whose members share certain values, needs, rituals, and behaviors. For example, by using a combination of education, occupation, and income, a measure of social class can be developed. Similarly, by using a combination of age, marital status, and number of children, a measure of the stage of the family life cycle can be obtained. Thus, demographic variables help to identify cultures and subcultures that the marketing manager can target with the marketing mix.

The second use of demographic variables is to describe consumers who are classified into segments via other means. For example, suppose that the product manager of Coke wants to segment Coke drinkers into heavy, medium, and light users so that different promotions can be targeted to each group. A large consumer survey is developed, and 3,000 people are contacted via the telephone. Questions are asked about how frequently they consume soft drinks, and Coke in particular. Suppose that, of the 3,000 people contacted, 1,000 fall into the medium-usage category. The marketing manager would like to target them for promotional messages and sales promotions (e.g., contests, coupons, etc.) to increase their consumption. The question is how to describe and reach this segment. The solution is to include in the consumer survey a series of questions that obtain demographic information. By knowing the age, ethnicity, geographic location, sex, education, and income of this group, it can be reached in a cost-effective way.

Demographic data are perhaps the single most important type of information a marketing manager can gather for the purpose of segmentation. The reason for this strong statement is that demographic information is the most readily available type of

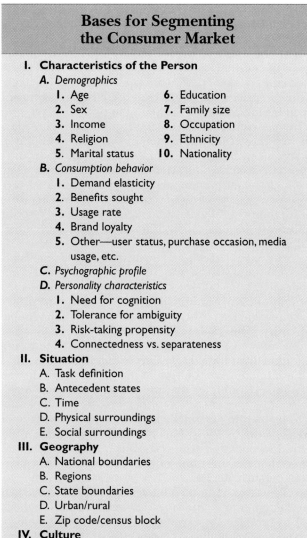

Bases for Segmenting the Consumer Market

I. Characteristics of the Person
  A. *Demographics*
   1. Age   6. Education
   2. Sex   7. Family size
   3. Income   8. Occupation
   4. Religion   9. Ethnicity
   5. Marital status   10. Nationality
  B. *Consumption behavior*
   1. Demand elasticity
   2. Benefits sought
   3. Usage rate
   4. Brand loyalty
   5. Other—user status, purchase occasion, media usage, etc.
  C. *Psychographic profile*
  D. *Personality characteristics*
   1. Need for cognition
   2. Tolerance for ambiguity
   3. Risk-taking propensity
   4. Connectedness vs. separateness
II. Situation
  A. Task definition
  B. Antecedent states
  C. Time
  D. Physical surroundings
  E. Social surroundings
III. Geography
  A. National boundaries
  B. Regions
  C. State boundaries
  D. Urban/rural
  E. Zip code/census block
IV. Culture
  A. Cultural mores, customers, values, and norms
  B. Subcultural mores, customs, values, and norms

TABLE 2.3

information on individual consumers. The federal government collects a wealth of demographic data through the census. Magazines, newspapers, and television and radio stations collect demographic information on their audiences. Private research companies collect and provide demographic information on various groups of people. With such information the manager can then make rational choices concerning the type of media to use to reach the target market as well as to make pricing and distribution decisions.

Behavior as a Basis for Segmentation. A complementary approach to using demographic variables to segment the market involves dividing consumers into homogeneous groups based on various aspects of their buying behavior. A number of different types of **behavioral segmentation** can be identified. These include price elasticity, benefits sought, and usage rate.

The concept of segmenting on **price elasticity** is based on the economic concept that different groups of consumers may react divergently to changes in the price of a product or service. Thus, customers who are price elastic will change their buying a great deal in response to price changes. In contrast, customers who are price inelastic show little change in buying patterns in response to price changes.

Airlines use the price elasticity of consumers to price their product. They create business-class and first-class seating arrangements for those willing to pay more for increased seating space and higher levels of service. In addition, the airlines charge more to those who have to make reservations closer in time to when their desired flight leaves. Price-inelastic customers include those with higher incomes, business travelers, and those who are traveling because of an emergency. In contrast, price-elastic consumers are most typically vacationers, who can make reservations early, and others who can substitute another mode of travel (e.g., the automobile) for flying if the price of an airline seat is too high.

The development of strategies to take advantage of segments possessing different price elasticities has a number of advantages for managers. Foremost, such practices allow companies to increase their total sales and possibly increase the overall efficiency of their operation. For example, by creating different prices for divergent segments, airlines can maximize profits by filling the maximum number of seats at the maximum possible price. Thus, because the marginal cost of filling empty seats in a plane is minimal, the fares for price-elastic vacationing passengers can be much lower while going almost directly to the bottom line. When done correctly, segmenting via price elasticity will not influence the image of the product. In other words, less likelihood exists that customers will infer that the product has lower quality because it is lower priced.

In addition to segmenting by price elasticity, companies may divide the market by the benefits sought by consumers. Called **benefit segmentation,** the concept is to develop products and services that possess specific qualities desired by homogeneous groups of consumers. For example, one of the benefits sought by many consumers is foods that are low in fat and calories.

Another type of behavior employed for segmentation is **usage behavior,** or usage rate. A company will attempt to identify through market research the light, moderate, and heavy users of its products or services. The company will then try to distinguish the demographic and psychographic characteristics of these groupings of users. This will allow the marketing manager to develop strategies to target one or more of the groups by manipulating the marketing mix. In general, companies target heavy users of products.

In addition to segmenting via usage rate, the manager can also segment by user status. Thus, the manager may be able to obtain from marketing research profiles of consumers who are nonusers, ex-users, potential users, first-time users, or regular users. In a similar manner, the manager may decide to segment based on the amount of brand loyalty shown by various user groups. Consumers who are brand loyal to the product or service may be separated from other user groups for special promotional messages. Managers may want to attempt to reach and influence users who show a tendency to switch between brands through sales promotion devices such as coupons or contests.

Psychographic and Personality Characteristics. As will be discussed in chapter 6, markets can be segmented by the psychographic and personality characteristics of consumers. Psychographics refers to the analysis of the lifestyles, interests, activities, and opinions of consumers. Personality refers to the distinctive patterns of behavior, including thoughts and emotions, that describe how a person responds to the situations of his or her life.

In most instances psychographic or personality segmentation is combined with behavioral segmentation. That is, the marketer will first divide consumers into heavy, moderate, and light users of a brand. One or more of these segments is then further analyzed via psychographic or personality inventories. Based on the segment's personality or psychographic characteristics, the marketer will then design promotional messages and distribution and pricing strategies that will be most effective.

For example, Merrill Lynch wanted to identify the psychographic characteristics of heavy users of brokerage services. The company employed a psychographic inventory called VALS (values and lifestyles). It found that an upwardly mobile, independent-thinking segment, labeled "achievers," described the heavy users of brokerage services quite well. Based on a knowledge of the characteristics of the achiever, the company changed its advertising from a theme of herds of bulls thundering across the plains to a single bull making intelligent choices about what directions in which to move.[12] The VALS inventory had shown that achievers are not followers but leaders, who make their decisions independently.

The Situation as a Segmentation Basis. Chapter 11 discusses how the situation in which a product or service is purchased is an important factor influencing consumption behavior. Consumer situations consist of the temporary environmental factors that form the context within which a consumer activity occurs at a particular time and place. For many types of products, segmentation by situation is the rule. For example, clothing and footwear have to be designed specifically for the physical surroundings (warm or cold weather, sun or rain) as well as for the task definition (party, sleep, casual, etc.). Research has shown that the situation also strongly impacts the choice of snack food, meat products, and fast-food chains.[13] Consumers will purchase vastly different snack foods if the task definition is a cocktail party as compared with a picnic.

Geographic Segmentation. For many products and services, an important basis for segmentation is geography. Managers can employ geography to segment the market by region, by the size of cities, counties, or even census blocks. Other means of geographic segmentation include density of population and climate.

Over the past decade, researchers have combined the fields of geography and demography (the study of demographics) to create the new discipline of geodemographics.[14] Geodemographic analyses allow the marketer to analyze the demographic characteristics of groups of people who live in particular census blocks or zip codes. The information is particularly useful for deciding where to locate a new business, such as a grocery store, fast-food restaurant, or golf course. Much more will be said about geodemographics in chapter 14.

Culture and Subcultures as a Basis for Segmentation. Culture may be defined as the way of life of the people of a society. In contrast, a subculture is a subdivision of a national culture. A subculture is based on some unifying characteristic, such as social status or nationality, and its members share a similarity of behavior somehow distinct from the national culture in which they live. For example, the United States, Japan, and Germany have distinctive national cultures. Yet within each of these cultures, a myriad of subcultures coexist. Culture is most clearly used as a segmentation variable when engaging in international marketing.

Marketers frequently target subcultures within a national culture. Usually, the subcultures are described by demographic variables. Thus, particular religious groups, such as Mormons, fundamentalist Christians, and Jews, may be identified as targets for a marketing offering. Similarly, a company may develop and promote a product to carefully selected ethnic groups. For example, an insurance company may identify Asians or Hispanics for a particular type of insurance product.

Segmenting Business Markets

Like consumer markets, business markets are also divided into segments. A significant system for categorizing all businesses into homogeneous groups has been developed, called the **North American Industry Classification System** (NAICS). This database classifies and identifies groups of business firms that produce the same type of product. Developed by the partners in the North American Free Trade Agreement (NAFTA), the NAICS assists industrial marketers in identifying potential new customers, estimating market potential, and delineating groups of companies that are likely to have similar product or service needs.

Another approach for segmenting industrial markets is identifying the macrobases and microbases for segmentation.[15] **Macrosegmentation** identifies groups of companies that have similar buying organizations and face similar buying situations. Table 2.4 identifies a number of these macrobases for segmentation. Examples of segmentation categories based on the characteristics of the organization include size of the company, its geographical location, its usage rate, and whether the company is centralized or decentralized. An example of a segmentation category based on a characteristic of the buying situation is whether the purchase is a new task, a modified rebuy, or a straight rebuy. Finally, the use of the NAICS classification system is an example of a product application macrobasis of industrial segmentation.

Microsegmentation in industrial marketing focuses on identifying the characteristics of the decision-making units within each of the various macrosegments. As such, microsegmentation requires an in-depth knowledge of buying organizations. One example of a basis for microsegmentation is the key decision criteria used by the buying organization. Analogous to benefit segmentation in consumer marketing, the

Some Macrobases for Segmentation	
Segmentation Basis	**Example**
1. Characteristics of buying organization	
a. Size	Small, medium, large; can be based on overall sales
b. Geographic location	New England vs. Southwest
c. Usage rate	Light, moderate, heavy user
d. Buying structure	Centralized vs. decentralized
2. Product application	
a. NAICS code	Varies by product
b. End market served	Varies by product
3. Characteristics of buying situations	
a. Type of buying situations	New task, modified rebuy, straight rebuy
b. Stage in decision process	Early vs. late stage

Source: Based on Michael D. Hutt and Thomas Speh, *Industrial Marketing Management* (New York: Dryden Press, 1981), 112.

TABLE 2.4

approach involves identifying the product and producer attributes sought by buyers. These could include quality of product, delivery reliability and speed, and supplier reputation.

CONSUMER BEHAVIOR AND SOLVING MANAGERIAL PROBLEMS

To develop managerial solutions to marketing problems, the analyst needs to have an understanding of consumer-behavior concepts, of the managerial-strategy elements, and of how to combine the two types of information to develop managerial plans. We advocate a three-step managerial-applications analysis:

Step 1. Gather information and identify the problem or opportunity.

Step 2. Identify the relevant consumer-behavior concepts and determine how they apply to the problem.

Step 3. Develop a managerial strategy by identifying the managerial implications of each applicable consumer-behavior concept.

In step 1 the analyst gathers as much information as possible about the case and carefully sifts through the information to identify the fundamental question(s) that needs to be answered. This step is important because the remainder of the analysis will flounder if inadequate information is gathered or if the problem is not correctly identified.

In step 2 the analyst systematically examines the problem(s) by identifying the consumer concepts relevant to it. The analyst then evaluates each of the topic areas from the individual level of analysis (discussed in part II) and from the environmental level of analysis (discussed in part III) for potential application to the problem. The key consumer-behavior concepts that may be used in this analysis are found in bold type in each chapter.

Finally, in step 3 the analyst identifies the managerial implications of the consumer-behavior concepts. The managerial implications will involve one or more of the five PERMS strategy elements discussed previously: positioning and differentiation, environmental analysis, market research, marketing-mix development, and segmentation. The analyst examines the extent to which the various consumer concepts affect each of the five managerial areas and develops managerial strategies from the concepts. Based on this analysis, a solution to the problem is identified.

Throughout the remainder of the book, we will discuss how the consumer-behavior concepts can be employed to develop managerial strategy. Indeed, whenever the issue of how managers can use consumer-behavior concepts for decision making comes up, you should immediately think "PERMS." Then, systematically consider how the consumer concept applies to position and differentiation, environmental analysis, market research, marketing-mix development, and segmentation.

Notes

1. Norihiko Shirouzu, "Japan's Staid Coffee Bars Wake Up and Smell Starbucks," *Wall Street Journal,* July 25, 1996, p. B1.
2. Philip Kotler, *Marketing Management* (Upper Saddle River, NJ: Prentice Hall, 2000).
3. John Kinski, "Consumer Perceptions of Meat Products," Master's thesis, Oklahoma State University, 1985.
4. Thomas Robertson, Joan Zielinski, and Scott Ward, *Consumer Behavior* (Glenview, IL: Scott, Foresman 1984).
5. Kotler, *Marketing Management.*
6. Robert Tomsho, "How Natural Disasters Can Change the Course of a Region's Growth," *Wall Street Journal,* October 5, 1999, pp. A1, A12.

7. Raju Narisetti, "P&G Says Fake-Fat Olestra Gets Fewer Complaints Than Expected," *Wall Street Journal*, July 25, 1996, p. B3.
8. Kotler, *Marketing Management*.
9. Ibid., 231.
10. Edmund Faison, *Advertising: A Behavioral Approach for Managers* (New York: Wiley, 1980).
11. Kotler, *Marketing Management*.
12. Joseph Plummer, "Emotions Important for Successful Advertising," *Marketing News*, April 12, 1985, p. 18.
13. Russell Belk, "Situational Variables and Consumer Behavior," *Journal of Consumer Research* 2 (December 1975): 157–64.
14. Eugene Sivades, George Mathew, and David J. Curry, "A Preliminary Examination of the Continuing Significance of Social Class to Marketing: A Geodemographic Replication," *Journal of Consumer Marketing* 14, no. 6 (1997): 463–79.
15. Michael D. Hutt and Thomas Speh, *Industrial Marketing Management* (New York: Dryden Press, 1981).

Information Processing I: Involvement and Perception

After studying this chapter, you should be able to describe each of the following concepts, together with their managerial relevance:

1. Consumer information processing.
2. The concepts of exposure, attention, and comprehension.
3. Consumer involvement.
4. The field of sensation.
5. Subliminal perception and absolute and difference thresholds.
6. Selective exposure and selective attention.
7. Weber's Law.
8. Adaptation level and the butterfly curve.
9. Expectations and the price–quality relationship.
10. Semiotics.

Consumer **information processing** is defined as the process through which consumers are exposed to information, attend to it, comprehend it, place it in memory, and retrieve it for later use. One of the most frequently reported problems encountered by marketers is getting consumers to receive, comprehend, and remember information about a product or service. The problem is particularly acute for advertisers. Millions of dollars can be spent developing and delivering a national campaign. If consumers fail to be exposed to the message, fail to attend to it, fail to comprehend it, or fail to remember it, the investment will be wasted.

Information is defined as the content of what is exchanged with the outer world as we adjust to it and make our adjustment felt upon it.[1] By reacting appropriately to information, or by generating information ourselves, we can adapt to and even influence the world around us. For example, the purchase of socially visible products, such as clothing or watches, provides information about a buyer's self-concept to others. Similarly, companies communicate meaning to consumers through the information transmitted in advertisements. Thus, the symbols employed in print advertisements are information units employed to influence consumers.

Consumer information is obtained through the senses of vision, hearing, taste, smell, and touch. It is important to note that the raw stimuli and the perception of the stimuli are quite different. The raw stimuli are composed of sound waves, light waves, bits of chemicals, textures, and levels of temperature. The interpretation of and meanings derived from the stimuli result from information processing. Different people may assign divergent meanings to exactly the same stimulus because its perception is influenced by their expectations and their general background. One cannot assume that, because two people receive exactly the same stimulus, for instance, in an advertisement, they will perceive it and react to it in a similar manner. For example, ask two avid fans of opposing basketball teams how well a game was refereed. Quite likely the two will have very different views of the officiating because of the differences in the way they perceived the game.

WHAT IS INFORMATION PROCESSING?

Figure 3.1 presents a simplified diagram of consumer information processing. The diagram shows that three factors influence information processing: perception, the level of consumer involvement, and memory. **Perception** is the process through which individuals are exposed to information, attend to the information, and comprehend

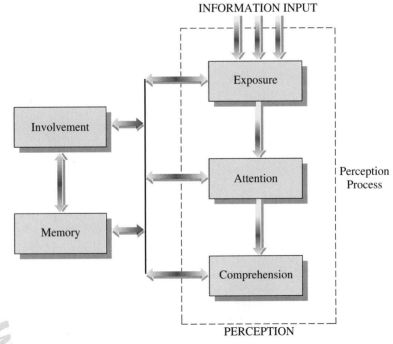

Figure 3.1   Consumer information-processing model.

the information. In the initial **exposure stage,** consumers receive information through their senses. In the **attention stage,** consumers focus on and allocate processing capacity to a stimulus. In the **comprehension stage,** they organize and interpret the information in order to obtain meaning from it.

The second factor that influences information processing is the degree of involvement of the consumer in the task. A consumer's involvement level influences whether he or she moves from the exposure through the attention to the comprehension stage of perception. In addition, involvement influences memory functions as well. Because an understanding of involvement is central to the understanding of information processing and perception, the next section discusses this important construct.

The final component of the information-processing model is the memory function. As can be seen in Figure 3.1, memory plays a role in each of the stages. Memory helps guide the exposure and attention processes by allowing consumers to anticipate the stimuli with which they may come into contact. It assists in the comprehension process by housing the consumer's knowledge about the environment. This knowledge base may be accessed in order to assist the person in comprehending the meaning of a stimulus. Because of the large role memory plays in information processing, chapter 4 deals with this component exclusively.

CONSUMER INVOLVEMENT

Consumer involvement is defined as the perceived personal importance or interest attached to the acquisition, consumption, and disposition of a good, service, or idea.[2] As involvement increases, consumers have greater motivation to attend, comprehend, and elaborate on information salient to the purchase.

Several factors influence the level a consumer's involvement level. They include (1) the type of product under consideration, (2) the characteristics of the communication received by the consumer, (3) the characteristics of the situation within which the consumer is operating, and (4) the personality of the consumer. For example, as the product or service under consideration becomes more expensive, socially visible, and risky to purchase, a consumer's involvement in the purchase will likely increase. Communications such as fear appeals can also raise a consumer's involvement by arousing emotions. The situation can influence involvement as well, by defining the context within which a purchase is made. Thus, if the consumer's goal is to buy a gift for an important person, such as a fiancée, involvement is likely to increase. In addition, different consumers may react with divergent levels of involvement to various products, situations, and communications.

Types of Consumer Involvement

Researchers have identified two different types of involvement.[3] **Situational involvement** occurs over a short time period and is associated with a specific situation, such as a need to replace a product that has broken (e.g., an automobile). In contrast, **enduring involvement** represents a longer commitment and concern with a product class; enduring involvement is indicated when a consumer consistently spends time thinking about the product on a day-to-day basis. Based on the combination of situational and enduring involvement, involvement responses result. **Involvement responses** refer to the level of complexity of information processing and the extent of decision making by a consumer.[4]

What happens when someone having high enduring involvement with a product suddenly needs to purchase the product? Research indicates that in such circumstances the effects of enduring and situational involvement add together. As a result, a high number of involvement responses occur because the total level of involvement is equal to the enduring plus situational involvement levels.[5]

The Effects of High Involvement

As their involvement level increases, consumers begin to process information in more depth.[6] Along with the increased information processing, one finds a general increase in arousal levels. Consumers give more diligent consideration to information relevant to the particular decision, which causes increased thinking about the decisions. In addition, higher levels of involvement are likely to lead consumers to engage in a more extended decision-making process and move through each of the decision stages in a more thorough manner. As will be discussed in chapter 9, the type of decision process diverges sufficiently in high- and low-involvement circumstances to warrant discussion of two categories of decision making—limited decision making in low-involvement circumstances and extended decision making in high-involvement circumstances.[7]

In sum, the involvement concept is critical to understanding not only information processing but also a variety of other consumer topics. For example, a consumer's involvement level has important implications for understanding memory processes, the decision-making process, attitude formation and change, and word-of-mouth communication.[8] Consumer involvement will be discussed throughout this text.[9]

THE EXPOSURE STAGE

As illustrated in Figure 3.1, exposure to a stimulus is the first step in the processing of information. With information exposure, a consumer's sensory organs are activated and the entire mechanism of information processing can begin. In order to influence consumers, marketers must expose them to information via marketing communications. If they do not, the result may be lower sales. For example, between 1991 and 1994, Nabisco slashed advertising spending on Planter's Peanuts by 70 percent. As one sales representative for the product line noted, "Mr. Peanut disappeared." Because of the drastic cut in ad spending, consumers were not exposed to Mr. Peanut. The result was a reduction in sales from $60 million in 1993 to about $15 million in 1996.[10] Corporations must spend money on advertising in order to expose consumers to their product.

One characteristic of the exposure stage is its selectivity. Through a process of **selective exposure,** consumers actively choose whether to expose themselves to information. Significantly, as involvement with particular type of product increases, consumers are more likely to selectively expose themselves to information about that product.

The concept of selective exposure is of great interest to advertisers. The tendency of consumers to selectively screen information to which they are exposed and to which they attend can dramatically lower the effectiveness of advertising dollars. The effects of selective exposure are illustrated by events that take place when a wildly popular event, such as the Super Bowl, is televised. Sanitation supervisors at water departments have found that during these events water consumption fluctuate dramatically. Over a two- or three-minute period, water-holding tanks would be drained and the system would be strained to capacity. Called the "flush factor," the sudden increase in water usage occurred during commercial breaks when consumers left their televisions to rush to their bathrooms. The flush factor illustrates the point that consumers watching television will selectively avoid exposing themselves to commercials and attend to other matters.[11]

The extent to which consumers engage in selective exposure to advertising has also been influenced by cable television. Remote-control devices on television have proliferated with the influx of cable television systems. With such devices consumers can rapidly and easily change from one channel to another. Called *zapping* or channel surfing in the industry, about 6 to 19 percent of consumers at any one time are zapping commercials by remotely switching channels. One study found that 64 percent of homes with cable zap advertisements.[12] How can advertisers respond to the problem of zapping? One executive commented that, to prevent people from selectively avoiding messages, advertisements must be made so well that people want to view them.[13]

The Study of Sensation

The analysis of the exposure stage begins with the study of sensation. **Sensation** refers to how people respond to the raw information received through the sense organs prior to attending to, comprehending, or giving meaning to the stimulus. Thus, a person studying sensation might ask the question, "How loud does a sound have to be before it is detected?" or "How much difference in the level of the hem of a skirt must there be before a consumer can detect the difference?" Four important concepts derived from the study of sensation are (1) the absolute threshold, (2) subliminal perception, (3) the difference threshold, and (4) consumer adaptation. These concepts are discussed in the next four sections.

The Absolute Threshold. Once someone is exposed to information, what factors determine whether that person goes beyond mere exposure to actively attend to and focus on the stimulus? One determinant is the intensity of the stimulus. The lowest level at which a stimulus can be detected 50 percent of the time is called the **absolute threshold.** As the intensity of a stimulus (such as the loudness of an advertisement) increases, the likelihood that it will be perceived also increases. Advertisers, therefore, have an incentive to make commercials as loud as possible without offending the consumer. Indeed, a common complaint by consumers is that television advertisements are louder than the programs they accompany. Although the maximum intensity of sound coming from a commercial is no greater than that coming from a program, advertisers do take steps to create the sensation that the loudness is greater, such as by recording the entire commercial near peak allowable levels.

Subliminal Perception. Closely related to the absolute threshold is the concept of subliminal perception. In 1957 audiences at a movie theater in New Jersey were exposed to briefly presented messages that said, "Drink Coca-Cola" and "Eat popcorn." The messages were superimposed on the movie and presented so quickly that the audience did not consciously realize that the messages had appeared. Although no evidence was presented, the marketing firm that created the messages claimed that sales of the items increased dramatically.

The media and consumers were shocked. *The New Yorker* stated that people's minds had been "broken and entered." However, others saw potential in subliminal messages, and a radio station began broadcasting subaudible messages that "TV's a bore."[14]

The term *subliminal* means below threshold. That is, a subliminally perceived stimulus cannot be reported because it is below the absolute threshold. **Subliminal perception** refers to the idea that stimuli presented below the level of conscious awareness may influence behavior and feelings. Three different types of subliminal stimulation have been identified—briefly presented visual stimuli, accelerated speech in low-volume auditory messages, and embedding or hiding sexual imagery or words in print advertisements.[15]

Does subliminal advertising work? According to one psychologist, the answer is, "No, what you see is what you get."[16] He argues that subliminal stimuli are extremely weak and most certainly overridden by a host of other, more powerful messages. In addition, because people are generally in control of their overt responses to stimuli, they will screen out attempts to affect undesired behavior.

More recently, however, evidence suggests that subliminal messages may impact consumers. In one study the authors investigated the effects of "subliminal embeds" on the ratings of ads by college students. Two print ads were used—one for a popular cigarette and the other for a well-known Scotch whiskey. After the embedded stimuli were pointed out by the experimenters, students reported that they could identify the nude body of a woman in the liquor ad and the representation of male genitals in the cigarette ad. A second version of each ad was created by having a professional photographer airbrush out the embedded material. Four other groups of students then evaluated the four ads. The results revealed that the ratings differed between the control (airbrushed ads) and the experimental ads (the ads with the sexually explicit stimuli) for the liquor advertisement with the nude body, but not for the cigarette ad. A second study was run in which measures of autonomic arousal were taken. In this study the students showed evidence of differences in arousal for both advertisements containing the embedded material.[17]

How does one explain the effects of subliminal advertisements? Two theories have been proposed.[18] **Incremental effects theory** states that, over many presentations of a stimulus, a stimulus representation is gradually built in the person's nervous system. At some point the representation reaches a behavioral threshold and causes changes in the actions of the consumer. However, the cause of the changes in actions is never recognized by the consumer.

The second theoretical approach is the **psychodynamic theory of arousal.** This theory assumes that unconscious wishes to engage in some behavior may be activated by unconsciously presented stimuli. Thus, in the liquor advertisement, one must assume that the students harbored an unconscious wish for sexual activity that was activated by the nude body embedded in the advertisement. The activation of this unconscious wish influences the perception of the ad.

Research on subliminal perception indicates that the phenomenon should not be dismissed. Clearly, additional work is needed on the topic—in part because of the public's intense interest in the area. Consumers are estimated to spend over $50 million a year on audiotapes that contain subliminal messages to help them quit smoking, lose weight, enhance self-esteem, and even improve sexual functioning. As noted by one author, however, great care must be taken in performing the research to ensure that alternative explanations of the effects are eliminated.[19]

The Just-Noticeable-Difference Threshold. In addition to the absolute threshold, a difference threshold exists. The **just-noticeable difference** (JND) is the minimum amount of difference in the intensity of a stimulus that can be detected 50 percent of the time. The study of difference thresholds has important implications for marketing research. For example, companies in the food industry are interested in producing products that give the optimum taste at the lowest cost.[20] In formulating the recipe for the product, they frequently have a choice between two ingredients that may differ in price. The question is, "Will a change in ingredient create a just-noticeable difference in the taste of the product?"[21]

One important finding is that the size of the JND varies with the level of the stimulus. Discovered by a German scientist, E. H. Weber, the relationship between the size of the JND and stimulus intensity has become known as Weber's Law. **Weber's Law** states that, as the intensity of the stimulus increases, the ability to detect a difference between the two levels of the stimulus decreases. Weber identified a formula that expresses these relationships, where I is the intensity level of the stimulus and K is a constant that gives the proportionate amount of change in stimulus level required for its detection:

$$JND = I \times K$$

One controversial application of Weber's Law is to pricing. A rule of thumb used by retailers is that markdowns must be at least 20 percent before consumers recognize them.[22] This 20 percent figure is equivalent to K, the constant in Weber's Law. For example, if a diamond ring is priced at $1,000, it must be marked down by $200 for the sale to be meaningful ($1,000 $\times$ .20 = $200). In contrast, if the diamond were priced at $8,000, the markdown must be $1,600 for the sale to be effective. Thus, the JND increases in size proportionate to K as the dollar value of a purchase increases. This application to pricing, however, is debatable. Strictly speaking, a small difference between any two prices (e.g., $1,000 and $1,001) is clearly noticeable; it just has little meaning to the consumer. When applied to pricing, it is better to label the process a "just-meaningful difference" rather than a "just-noticeable difference."

Information on absolute and difference thresholds can also be used to develop packaging strategy of companies. Why does Campbell's Soup package its pork and beans in a 20 3/4-ounce can while its major competitor uses a 21-ounce can? Probably because consumers do not notice the difference. Over millions of soup cans sold, this quarter-ounce difference can increase profits. Similarly, Bohemia Beer lowered the quantity of beer in each bottle from 12 to 11 ounces. The cost savings was used to increase the ad budget and develop a fancier container. As a result, sales nearly doubled.[23] The JND principle has been used to increase the size of portions as well as decrease them. After a 12-month test, the candy company M&M/Mars found that substantially increasing the size of its candy bars increased sales by 20 to 30 percent. As a result, the company changed nearly its entire product line.

Table 3.1 identifies a number of marketing uses of the concept of the JND.

Consumer Adaptation. Closely related to the concepts of the absolute threshold and the JND is that of adaptation. Everyone has experienced the process of adaptation. When first sitting in a hot bath, the steaming water may seem nearly unbearable. After a few minutes, however, the water feels quite pleasant. The change in sensation does not occur because the water gets colder; it occurs because nerve cells adapt to the water's temperature and no longer fire signals to the brain telling it that the water is

Some Marketing Examples of the JND	
Area of Application	**Example of Use**
Pricing	When raising the price, try to move less than a JND.
	When lowering the price for a sale, move more than a JND.
Sales promotion	Make coupons larger than the JND.
Product	Make decreases in size of food product less than JND (e.g., in shrinking candy bars).
	When the word *new* is used, make sure the product change is greater than the JND.
Packaging	To update package styling and logo, keep within the JND.
	To change image, make styling changes greater than the JND.

TABLE 3.1

too hot. Adaptation occurs, therefore, when an individual has repeated experience with a stimulus. The **adaptation level** is the amount or level of the stimulus to which the consumer has become accustomed. It is a reference point to which changes in the level of the stimulus are compared.

Consumer adaptation to stimuli has implications for both product and advertising strategies. Consumers become adapted to a certain look, style, or message over some period of time. In order to keep product or service communications fresh, marketers should attempt to vary them periodically. Eveready, for example, has used its Energizer Bunny ads, with the same theme of the drum-banging rabbit "going and going and going," for many years. Nonetheless, the message did not become boring because the dozens of different advertisements used various highly creative and humorous means to portray the idea that the batteries last a long time. The net result is a long-running advertising campaign that propelled the brand to become a leader in the marketplace.

The idea that people may perceive more positively something that is slightly different is supported by an effect called the butterfly curve. The degree of liking for a stimulus is illustrated on the vertical axis of the graph shown in Figure 3.2. The horizontal axis portrays the level of the stimulus and the position of the adaptation level. (This type of graph is called a butterfly curve because the shape of the curve is similar to the shape of the wings of a butterfly.) The **butterfly curve** shows that the preference for a stimulus is at its greatest level at points just higher or lower than the adaptation level. At the adaptation level, preference declines slightly because the person has become habituated to the stimulus. As the level of the stimulus moves too far from the adaptation level, however, the preference steadily decreases.[24]

The simple idea of the butterfly curve explains why fashion trends are constantly changing. Consumers quickly become adapted to a certain look, and its ability to give pleasure falls. Designers then modify the current look in some relatively small way, and it will appear fresh and interesting because the stimulus has diverged from the adaptation level. The up-and-down movement of the hems of skirts over the years illustrates the principle well. Similarly, the width of men's ties and lapels shows the same tendency of fashions to change.

The butterfly curve also suggests that unusual fashion looks are adopted slowly because they are at first too far away from the adaptation level. For example, when the singer Madonna first wore a bustier, the public was horrified. After a while, however, consumers adapted, and bustiers became familiar sights on dance floors and even in that fashion kingdom—the mall.

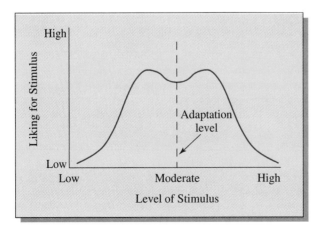

Figure 3.2
Butterfly curve.

Another phenomenon of consumer behavior that the butterfly curve can potentially explain is **spontaneous brand switching.** Consumers frequently switch brands, even when nothing indicates that they are unhappy with the brand previously used. The phenomenon seems to occur most frequently with low-involvement products for which little difference exists between brands. Applying the concept of the adaptation level, consumers may switch brands because they have adapted to the one most frequently used. Changing to a new brand moves the consumer off the adaptation level, thereby providing some increment in the pleasure received from the product class. Companies seem to implicitly recognize the problem and frequently come out with "new and improved" versions of their products.

Similarly, many companies periodically change their logos and other corporate symbols to maintain a fresh look. For example, Procter & Gamble made no less than 19 changes in the wrapper of Ivory Soap between 1898 and 1998.[25] The difference between any two of the changes was extremely subtle. When the 1898 and 1998 wrappers are compared, however, the differences are astounding. Similarly, General Mills has on a number of occasions changed the look of its famous, but fictitious, endorser of its cake mixes—Betty Crocker. The most recent change occurred in 1996. How was the new image of Betty Crocker chosen? A national contest was held in which women were asked to send photos of themselves and write a statement explaining how they "embody the ideas of Betty." From the thousands of entries, 75 photos were selected. All 75 photos were then computer digitized and combined to form a multiethnic image. The resulting image reveals a somewhat familiar, but exotic, face. Looking at Figure 3.2, consider where on the butterfly curve this stimulus resides.[26]

THE ATTENTION STAGE

Marketers must do more than expose consumers to information; they must also get them to attend to it. When **attention** occurs, cognitive capacity is allocated to a stimulus so that information is consciously processed. Thus, when a consumer attends to an advertisement, public-relations piece of information, or personal-selling communication, he or she is allocating cognitive capacity to the task. The more demanding the task, or the more involved the person is in the task, the greater the amount of attention focused on it.[27]

Preattention

Preattention is distinguished from attention. When a person attends to a stimulus, such as an advertisement, the individual is consciously aware of information being received. In contrast, during preattention a person is unconsciously and automatically scanning the environment. Thus, **preattention** can be defined as an unconscious process in which consumers automatically scan the features of the environment. Preattention occurs between the time the exposure stage occurs and when the consumer consciously attends to a stimulus. In the preattention stage, the information obtained is initially evaluated to determine whether it is of sufficient importance to be further processed. If it does have sufficient importance, additional cognitive resources will be allocated to the stimulus, and the person will move into the attention stage of information processing.[28]

One important finding is that preattention processes can influence consumer feelings. In one research study, a pictorial ad was placed either to the left or the right of an accompanying editorial.[29] The researcher found that, when the pleasing photograph was placed to the left of the editorial, the respondents liked the ad more than if it was placed to the right of the editorial. The researcher proposed that this occurred because when the ad was placed to the left of editorial, the information contained in the ad was transferred to the right hemisphere of the brain, that part of the brain responsible for forming holistic perceptions that directly impact feelings and emotions. As a result, the preconscious processing of the ad influenced the evaluations of the ad when it was placed to the left of the editorial. The respondents in the study had no conscious idea that the placement of the ad relative to the editorial impacted their evaluations.

Voluntary and Involuntary Attention

Attention can also be activated either voluntarily or involuntarily. With voluntary attention consumers actively search out information that has personal relevance. As involvement with a particular product increases, through a process called **selective attention,** people selectively focus attention on relevant information. For instance, consumers who are interested in buying a car, furniture, or an expensive camera will actively seek information about the product. When reading newspapers, they will be on the lookout for advertisements and articles that deal with the product sought. Conversely, if the marketing communication is not perceived as matching a particular goal, consumers will not focus attention on it. This is a major problem for advertisers on television and radio: Consumers may be exposed to the message but simply decide not to attend to the information contained in the communication because of their low-involvement level.

In addition to voluntary attention, attention can be placed on a stimulus involuntarily. Involuntary attention occurs when consumers are exposed to something so surprising, novel, threatening, or unexpected that they reflexively attend to the stimulus. Such stimuli result in an autonomic response in which the person turns toward and allocates attention to it. This response, which the consumer cannot consciously control, is called an **orientation reflex.**[30] Because most advertisements to which consumers are exposed are unrelated to the immediate goals of the audience, marketers go to some trouble to elicit the orientation reflex by using surprising and unexpected messages, sounds, and images in advertisements.

A critical issue for marketing researchers is how to measure the level of attention placed on a stimulus. When consumers attend to information, their physiological arousal increases. The arousal may result in an increase in blood pressure, a change in brain-wave patterns, a quickening of breathing, a slight sweating of the hands, and dilation of the pupils, among other things. One way of assessing the impact of advertisements is to measure the arousal elicited when consumers view the ad. In order to assess attention levels, market researchers have employed devices that measure arousal levels by assessing blood pressure, pupil dilation, brain-wave patterns, and even the temperature of the eardrum.

Capturing Consumers' Attention

Marketers attempt to capture attention by varying the nature of the stimulus that consumers receive. The goal is to activate the orientation reflex by adroitly creating stimuli that surprise, threaten, or violate the expectations of consumers. A number of stimulus factors can be used to achieve such a goal. For example, the Budweiser frog and lizard commercials discussed previously are effective in part because they surprise us by violating our expectations of how animals should behave.

In addition to using surprise, a variety of strategies can be employed to activate the orientation reflex. For example, movement attracts attention. Thus, on highways and in cities, one finds retailers using neon signs that simulate motion as lights in the series flash on and off. Unusual sounds can also be effective. Television advertisers have recently taken to using distinctive, nonverbal sounds to activate the orientation response. For example, ads for the financial corporation Shearson Lehman Brothers used a buzzing sound that grew louder as the commercial progressed. Executives claimed that ad awareness increased by 50 percent with the use of the peculiar sound in the commercials. The ad agency created the noise to mimic the sound of thinking in the ad campaign, which was called "Minds over Money." General Electric reported similar positive effects from its "beep ads," in which a symphony of peculiar beeps comes from digital kitchen appliances.[31]

Another factor that may influence attention is the size or magnitude of the stimulus. For example, all else being equal, consumers are more apt to attend to large-print advertisements than small ones. A loud television commercial is more likely to be processed than a soft one.

Color can also attract attention, particularly when it contrasts against a sea of black-and-white print materials and consumers are in a low-involvement state.[32] Thus, graphic artists employ the principle of contrast to increase the likelihood that consumers will attend to an advertisement. Contrast occurs when a stimulus diverges substantially from surrounding background stimuli. A loud noise in a quiet room or a print ad with very little copy in a sea of verbose ads illustrates the concept of contrast.

Finally, marketers can gain consumers' attention by placing ads in circumstances in which consumers have little choice but to attend to the information presented. An example is movie theaters playing commercials prior to the beginning of a show. Theater operators, however, are extremely cautious about what kinds of ads to show for fear of aggravating customers. Corporations that own large numbers of theaters will screen the ads to make sure that they are appropriate and that they avoid a hard sell. Thus, these commercials tend to be highly lavish productions. Although the cost per thousand viewers is higher than that of television advertising, theater advertising is claimed to be recalled three times better. There are problems with this type of advertising, however. Many national advertisers are reluctant to use movie advertising for fear of associating their products with violent or sex-laden movies. In addition, Walt Disney Productions forbids theater owners from showing advertisements with any of its movies.[33]

THE COMPREHENSION STAGE

In the comprehension stage, which follows the attention stage, consumers perceptually organize and interpret information in order to derive meaning from it. **Perceptual organization** is the process through which people perceive the shapes, forms, figures, and lines in their visual world. **Interpretation** is the process through which people draw upon their experience, memory, and expectations to attach meaning to a stimulus. The study of comprehension is particularly important for advertisers; researchers have found that, when people fail to correctly comprehend an advertisement, they are generally less persuaded by it.[34]

Perceptual Organization

Much of the work on perceptual organization comes from **Gestalt psychologists** active early in the twentieth century. (Gestalt theory is discussed further in chapter 4.) These individuals identified the rules that govern how people take disjointed stimuli and make sense out of the shapes and forms to which they are exposed. *Gestalt* is the German word for "pattern" or "configuration," which suggests these psychologists' goals of understanding how people perceive patterns in the world. One of the key ideas of the group was the familiar phrase, "the whole is greater than the sum of its parts." Thus, for example, a product is greater than the sum of its separate components. Porsche recognized this in the development of a new, lightweight car. The company's engineers recognized that light cars are less safe. In order to solve the problem,

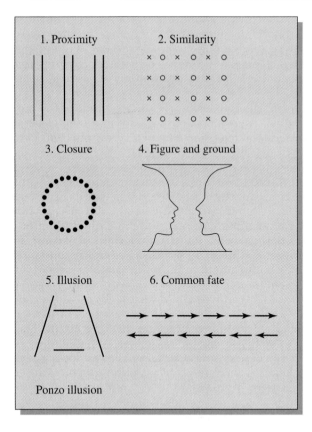

Figure 3.3

Some principles of perceptual organization.

they developed sophisticated computer programs that optimized the "whole vehicle rather than its separate parts."[35]

Figure 3.3 illustrates a number of the Gestalt rules of perceptual organization. For example, the so-called rule of common fate (example 6 in the figure) states that elements that move in the same direction are assumed to belong to each other. Other rules applicable to the problem of deciding "what goes with what" are similarity, proximity, illusion, and closure. Another area of Gestalt theory involves determining how people distinguish figure from ground in the visual world. Example 4 in Figure 3.3 illustrates figure–ground principles. At one moment the reversible figure resembles two faces looking at each other. The next moment it looks like a vase. The image switches back and forth because our brains cannot decipher whether the space inside or outside the drawing is the figure. In an advertising context, managers want their product to be the figure moving against the background of an ad because the figure attracts more attention than does the background.

From a marketer's point of view, the concepts of perceptual organization apply to visual communications, such as print ads, television ads, and package design. For example, when drawing an ad, the artist may consciously or unconsciously use Gestalt principles in order to create the desired effect on the consumer. In particular, the artist should be attentive to the figure–ground concept. For the product to be noticed, it must stand out from the background of the print ad. Similarly, if the goal is to associate the product with something else desirable—such as a popular celebrity endorser—the principles of proximity, closure, and common fate could be used.

Interpretation

In the interpretation stage, the consumer attempts to derive meaning from a stimulus in order to determine how to react. In this phase people retrieve from long-term memory their expectancies regarding what the stimulus "should be like" in order to interpret it. The personal inclinations and biases of the consumer also influence the interpretation of the stimulus. For example, if an individual believes a product to possess high quality, this expectation systematically biases the interpretation to increase quality ratings. (See chapter 10 for more on quality perceptions.)

One problem for marketers is that consumers may interpret the same stimulus differently. Classic illustrations of differences in interpretation can be found in cross-cultural marketing. Differences in the meaning of colors can be found throughout the world. For example, yellow flowers are a sign of death in Mexico, whereas in France they denote infidelity.[36]

The Role of Expectations. Expectations affect how consumers comprehend and interpret marketing stimuli. **Expectations** are a person's prior beliefs about what should happen in a given situation. The importance of taking into account how expectations influence interpretation is illustrated by the problems Adolph Coors had a few years ago. The company decided to change the label on its flagship brand from "Banquet Beer" to "Original Draft." The change was made in response to Miller Brewing's successful new entry of "Genuine Draft" into the market. The problem was that many Coors drinkers in the Southwest believed that the taste of the beer had been changed as well. As one Coors executive explained, "We tried to convince them it was the same product, and they'd say, 'Oh, no it isn't.' " With a change in the label, the Coors drinkers expected a change in the beverage. As a result of the expectation, they perceived a change in taste. When Coors changed the label back to the old one, a Coors distributor described customers as being elated and saying, "You brought it back just for me?" His response to each was, "You bet I did, old buddy."[37]

One function of market research is assessing the impact of consumer expectations on evaluations of marketing stimuli. One research study vividly indicates how the perception of taste can be influenced by visual cues that influence taste expectations. In this study the color of vanilla pudding was made either dark brown, medium brown, or light brown by adding a tasteless and odorless food coloring. Respondents then rated the puddings on a variety of scales. About 62 percent of the respondents rated the dark-colored pudding to have the best chocolate flavor and to be the thickest. The lighter-colored puddings were rated as more creamy than the dark pudding. As the authors of the article concluded, "It's the consumer's subjective perception of the product that counts, not the product's objective reality.[38] Other researchers have found that coloring food in unexpected colors (e.g., dyeing potatoes blue) can make people physically ill.[39]

The Price–Quality Relationship. An understanding of consumer expectations can have an important impact on pricing strategies. In general, the higher the price charged, the less likely a consumer is to buy a particular product item. Nonetheless, in some circumstances consumers develop expectations as to a **price–quality relationship.** Within certain price ranges of a product, consumers may expect that higher prices indicate greater product quality.[40] The price–quality relationship is probably learned over time through such aphorisms as "You get what you pay for." One summary of the evidence on the price–quality relationship gives the following occasions when price indicates the quality of a product:[41]

1. The consumer has some confidence that in the situation price predicts quality.

2. Real or perceived quality variations occur among brands.

3. Actual quality is difficult to judge through objective means or through brand name or store image.

4. Larger differences in price have a greater impact on perceived quality differences than do smaller price differences.

5. Consumers use price as an indicator of quality more frequently for familiar brands than for unfamiliar brands.

Significantly, the more information consumers receive about a product's characteristics, the less price is used as a quality indicator. In addition, researchers have found that perceived quality and perceived price combine together to influence the perceived value of the brand. In this case, however, the higher the price of the product, the lower the perceived value. Thus, **perceived value** can be defined as the trade-off that consumers make between perceived quality and perceived price when evaluating a brand.[42]

Managers must recognize, therefore, that a price–quality relationship exists. In certain circumstances consumers will infer quality from the price of the product. However, a higher price will also lower the perceived value of a brand.[43] The implication for managers is that extreme care should be taken prior to raising prices as a means of increasing sales.

SEMIOTICS

Consider the problem faced by distributors of motion picture videocassettes. How do you get buyers to notice and then rent a video of a movie that they have never heard of and that is lost in a sea of hundreds of other video boxes? The answer is to make a dynamite video box. As one executive explained, "A box has to look mainstream, sell the cast, tell the story, and jump off the shelf."[44] How, then, does one make a dynamite video box that "jumps off the shelf"? The answer—make great use of symbolism.

For example, as described in the *New York Times,* when the NC-17 video for *Showgirls* was released in 1996, the video box showed a "curve of flesh running from a woman's head to her toes. On the box of an R-rated alternative, . . . the skin extends only through the cleavage."[45] The length of "curve" symbolized the extent of nudity shown in the two versions of the film. Although the film flopped in theaters, it sold extremely well in video stores, in part because of the meanings captured by the symbols used on the video box.

The field of study that analyzes symbols and their meanings is called **semiotics.** The field was developed to analyze how people obtain meaning from signs. **Signs** are the words, gestures, pictures, products, and logos one person uses to communicate information to another.

Even nonverbal sounds can communicate meaning. For example, Harley-Davidson has attempted to trademark the distinctive sound made by its motorcycles. The low, guttural growl of Harley bikes has been described as sounding like a growling animal uttering, "potato-potato-potato." As a spokesperson for the company noted, "A lot of owners tell us they buy a Harley just for the sound." Of course, the sound symbolizes much more than just the motorcycle. It also stands for the Harley-Davidson image of macho, nonconformist, independent men and women. Of course, competitors are fighting the petition in court because the possibility of trademarking sounds could open up a Pandora's box of problems. As argued by one critic, "How about Rice Krispies? Do you think you can trademark the snap, crackle, pop?"[46]

The discipline of semiotics has been studied in one form or another since before the time of Socrates.[47] Indeed, some have argued that what sets the human species apart from others is its ability to adroitly use and manipulate symbols.[48] The field of semiotics is highly relevant to the entire area of promotional strategy in marketing: It is through the use of various symbols or signs that a company communicates information about a product or service to consumers.

The study of semiotics is an important aspect of the experiential perspective on consumer behavior. Thus, in order to understand how people emotionally react to symbols in the environment, one must gain an understanding of the shared meanings of various signs. Semiotics has relevance to a number of consumer-behavior areas, including the use of Freudian symbolism in advertising, the use of symbols to express one's self-concept, and cross-cultural communications. Researchers doing work on semiotics emphasize that meaning is in part determined by the cultural context within which the sign is embedded. Thus, a sign in one culture may have an entirely different meaning from a sign in another culture. For example, associating animals with products is done frequently and effectively in the United States. However, in some Asian cultures, the practice is viewed negatively. Thus, advertisements by an optical company showing cute little animals wearing eyeglasses failed miserably in Thailand because animals symbolize a lower form of life among many people in the Thai culture.

The field of semiotics has particular importance in marketing communications. Marketing and advertising managers must be alert to the use of symbols and how their target market will interpret them. Indeed, advertising has been described as "the modern substitute for myth and ritual and, directly or indirectly, it uses semiotics (the science of signs) to invest products with meaning for a culture whose dominant focus is consumption."[49]

The meaning of signs is learned early in life as a result of the general acculturation of a person. Whereas the ability to recognize the social implications of consumption choices is minimal among preschoolers, by the second grade children can make inferences about what it means to purchase a Cadillac versus a Mercedes or purchase a new, modern house versus an older, traditional house. By the sixth grade these skills are almost fully developed. Interestingly, college students show the greatest extent of consumption stereotyping and that the stereotyping then weakens with age.[50]

Semiotics has particular application to the positioning of brands. For example, colleges and universities are currently working hard to refine, and in some cases change, their logos and mascots. As described in the university trade publication *The Chronicle of Higher Education,* universities are attempting to create a "catchy symbol that paints a thousand words about the college and entices people to buy shirts and notebooks bearing the emblem." As one college official asserted, a distinctive logo "sets an institution apart in the eyes of alumni, donors, and students." In addition to helping to position a university, logos can bring in millions of dollars to a university through the sale of t-shirts, hats, and other memorabilia. The use of the logos can also be licensed to vendors typically for about a dollar per use. (Thus, one dollar of the cost of a T-shirt goes to the university for the use of its logo.) When Villanova University updated its logo to a more aggressive looking wildcat, profits from license fees jumped nearly 600 percent.[51]

MANAGERIAL IMPLICATIONS

The consumer-behavior concepts that emerge from investigations of involvement and perception have application to each of the managerial application areas. Applications to the five PERMS categories are summarized in the following sections.

Positioning and Differentiation

The areas of semiotics and consumer involvement have implications for product positioning and differentiation. Within the domain of semiotics, the symbols and signs that are linked to a brand or organization provide meanings that are interpreted and comprehended by consumers. For example, the names given to brands frequently make use of symbols. Consider the following automobile brand names—Mustang, New Yorker, Riviera, and Sebring. What are the meanings and images that are associated with these symbols?

Products can also be positioned and differentiated based on the level of consumer involvement with the product category. For example, kitchen appliances are targeted to consumers with different levels of involvement with cooking. Thus, KitchenAid mixers costing in excess of $400 are promoted to people for whom cooking is extremely important. Compare this brand to Black & Decker mixers costing less than $40.

Environmental Analysis

One function of environmental analysis is to identify the effects of cultural differences on the marketing effort. As noted in the discussion of semiotics, different cultures may impute very different meanings for the same symbol.

Research

In order to assess the level of consumer involvement with a brand, as well as determine the degree of exposure, attention, and comprehension of communications, a company must engage in marketing research. For example, when changing the size or composition of a food product, investigations into the JND are required. Similarly, research is required to determine the meanings that consumers derive from the symbols that are attached to products and organizations. Another research arena involves identifying the expectations that consumers have for the characteristics of a product.

Marketing Mix

Within the marketing mix, the concepts identified in this chapter have particular application to promotional strategy. Issues include how to cause consumers to be exposed to communications, attend to the messages, and comprehend the meanings in the desired manner. Messages, such as fear appeals, can be designed to influence the level of involvement of the target market. Concepts from Weber's Law have application to the pricing of products. The involvement level of consumers can influence strategies used to distribute brands. Concepts related to Weber's Law and the JND are also applicable to product development—particularly when changes in the size or composition of the product are considered.

Segmentation

The level of involvement consumers have with a product category is an important segmentation variable for marketers to consider. Markets can be divided into groups of consumers who are homogeneous with respect to their level of enduring involvement with a product. Based on their level of involvement, the degree of complexity of marketing communications, the distribution of the brand, and even the attributes and pricing of the brand may be influenced.

In sum, developing a good understanding of perception and consumer product involvement is critical for the successful marketing of goods, services, and ideas.

Notes

1. Norbert Wiener, "Cybernetics in History," in *Modern Systems Research for the Behavioral Scientist*, ed. Walter Buckley (Chicago, IL: Aldine Publishing, 1968), 31–36.
2. Richard L. Celsi and Jerry C. Olson, "The Role of Involvement in Attention and Comprehension Processes," *Journal of Consumer Research* 15 (September 1988): 210–24.

Also see Anthony Greenwald and Clark Leavitt, "Audience Involvement in Advertising: Four Levels," *Journal of Consumer Research* 11 (June 1984): 581–92. For a general review of the strength of involvement effects, see Carolyn Costley, "Meta Analysis of Involvement Research," in *Advances in Consumer Research,* ed. Michael Houston (Provo, UT: Association for Consumer Research, 1988), 15:554–62.

3. Marsha Richins and Peter H. Bloch, "After the New Wears Off: The Temporal Context of Product Involvement," *Journal of Consumer Research* 13 (September 1986): 280–85.

4. Marsha Richins, Peter H. Bloch, and Edward F. McQuarrie, "How Enduring and Situational Involvement Combine to Create Involvement Responses," *Journal of Consumer Psychology* 1, no. 2 (1992): 143–53.

5. Ibid.

6. Richard E. Petty, John T. Cacioppo, and David Schumann, "Central and Peripheral Routes to Advertising Effectiveness: The Moderating Role of Involvement," *Journal of Consumer Research* 10 (September 1983): 135–46.

7. Herbert Krugman, "The Impact of Television in Advertising: Learning without Involvement," *Public Opinion Quarterly* 30, 583–96.

8. Jong Won Park and Manoj Hastak, "Memory-Based Product Judgments: Effects of Involvement at Encoding and Retrieval," *Journal of Consumer Research* 21 (December 1994): 534–47.

9. For a discussion of how increased involvement and physiological arousal impacts the processing of information, see David M. Sanbonmatsu and Frank R. Kardes, "The Effects of Physiological Arousal on Information Processing and Persuasion," *Journal of Consumer Research* 15 (December 1988): 379–85.

10. Alex Markels and Matt Murray, "Call It Dumbsizing: Why Some Companies Regret Cost-Cutting," *Wall Street Journal,* May 14, 1996, pp. A1, A6.

11. Bernie Whalen, "$6 Billion down the Drain!" *Marketing News,* September 14, 1984, pp. 1, 37.

12. "Background on Zapping," *Marketing News,* September 14, 1984, p. 36.

13. Whalen, "$6 Billion down the Drain!"

14. Timothy E. Moore, "Subliminal Advertising: What You See Is What You Get," *Journal of Marketing* 46 (spring 1982): 38–47.

15. Ibid.

16. Ibid.

17. William Kilbourne, Scott Painton, and D. Ridley, "The Effect of Sexual Embedding on Responses to Magazine Advertisements," *Journal of Advertising* 14, no. 2 (1985): 48–56.

18. Joel Saegert, "Why Marketing Should Quit Giving Subliminal Advertising the Benefit of the Doubt," *Psychology and Marketing* (summer 1987): 107–20.

19. Philip M. Merikle and Jim Cheesman, "Current Status of Research on Subliminal Perception," in *Advances in Consumer Research,* ed. Melanie Wallendorf and Paul Anderson (Provo, UT: Association for Consumer Research, 1987), 14:298–302.

20. David Stipp, "A Flavor Analyst Should Never Ask, 'What's for Lunch?' " *Wall Street Journal,* August 3, 1988, pp. 1, 10.

21. Bruce Buchanan, Moshe Givon, and Arieh Goldman, "Measurement of Discrimination Ability in Taste Tests: An Empirical Investigation," *Journal of Marketing Research* 24 (May 1987): 154–63.

22. Richard Lee Miller, "Dr. Weber and the Consumer," *Journal of Marketing* (January 1962): 57–61.

23. John Koten, "Why Do Hot Dogs Come in Packs of 10 and Buns in 8s or 12s?" *Wall Street Journal,* September 21, 1984, pp. 1, 26.

24. Flemming Hansen, *Consumer Choice Behavior* (New York: Collier Macmillan, 1972).

25. Leon G. Schiffman and Leslie L. Kanuk, "Sequential Changes in Packaging that Fall below the J.N.D.," *Consumer Behavior* (Upper Saddle River, NJ: Prentice Hall, 1983), 140, fig. 6.1.

26. Stephen E. Stewart, "My Years with Betty," *Wall Street Journal,* July 5, 1996, p. A6.

27. Daniel Kahneman, *Attention and Effort* (Upper Saddle River, NJ: Prentice Hall, 1973). This section relies heavily on ideas from this classic book.

28. Chris Janiszewski, "Preattentive Mere Exposure Effects," *Journal of Consumer Research* 20 (December 1993): 376–92.

29. Ibid.

30. Ibid.

31. Sana Siwolop, "You Can't (Hum) Ignore (Hum) That Ad," *Business Week,* September 21, 1987, p. 56.

32. Pamela S. Schindler, "Color and Contrast in Magazine Advertising," *Psychology and Marketing* 3, no. 2 (1986): 69–78. Also see Joan Meyers-Levy and Laura A. Peracchio, "Understanding the Effects of Color: How the Correspondence between Available and Required Resources Affects Attitudes," *Journal of Consumer Research* 22 (September 1995): 121–38.

33. Ronald Alsop, "Coming Attractions: TV Ads at Movie Houses Everywhere," *Wall Street Journal,* July 3, 1986, p. 17.

34. David W. Stewart, "The Moderating Role of Recall, Comprehension, and Brand Differentiation on the Persuasiveness of Television Advertising," *Journal of Advertising Research* 25 (March–April 1986): 43–47.

35. "Make Mine a Porsche Lite," *Business Week,* October 4, 1999, p. 6.

36. E. T. Hall, *The Hidden Dimension* (New York: Doubleday, 1966).

37. Marj Charlier, "Beer Drinkers in Texas, California Don't Swallow Change in Coors Label," *Wall Street Journal,* December 29, 1988, p. B4.

38. Gail Tom, Teresa Barnett, William Lew, and Jodean Selmants, "Cueing the Consumer: The Role of Salient Cues in Consumer Perception," *Journal of Consumer Marketing* 4 (spring 1987): 23–27.

39. M. Tysoe, "What's Wrong with Blue Potatoes?" *Psychology Today* 19 (December 1985): 6, 8.

40. Kent B. Monroe, "The Influence of Price Differences and Brand Familiarity on Brand Preferences," *Journal of Consumer Research* 3 (June 1976): 42–49. Also see Valarie Zeithaml and Merrie Brucks, "Price as an Indicator of Quality Dimensions" (paper presented at the Association for Consumer Research Annual Conference, Cambridge, MA, October 9–11, 1987); and Chr. Hjorth-Anderson, "The Concept of Quality and the Efficiency of Markets for Consumer Products," *Journal of Consumer Research* 11 (September 1984): 708–18.

41. Kent B. Monroe and Akshay R. Rao, "Testing the Relationship between Price, Perceived Quality, and Perceived Value" (paper presented at the Association for Consumer Research Annual Conference, Cambridge, MA, October 9–11, 1987).

42. Tung-Zong Chang and Albert R. Wildt, "Price, Product Information, and Purchase Intention: An Empirical Study," *Journal of the Academy of Marketing Science* 22 (winter 1994): 16–27.

43. It should also be noted that different consumers form divergent beliefs about the relationship between price and quality. For example, see Karen H. Smith and N. Chinna Natesan, "Consumer Price–Quality Beliefs: Schema Variables Predicting Individual Differences," in *Advances in Consumer Research,* ed. Eric Arnould and Linda M. Scott (Provo, UT: Association for Consumer Research, 1999), 26:562–68.

44. Peter M. Nichols, "Dressed Up and Vying to Catch Your Eye," *New York Times,* January 26, 1996, pp. H9, H20.

45. Ibid.

46. Anna D. Wilde, "Harley Hopes to Add Hog's Roar to Its Menagerie of Trademarks," *Wall Street Journal,* June 23, 1995, p. B1.

47. David Mick, "Consumer Research and Semiotics: Exploring the Morphology of Signs, Symbols, and Significance," *Journal of Consumer Research* 13 (September 1986): 196–213.

48. Kenneth Boulding, *The Image* (Ann Arbor: University of Michigan Press, 1956), 44.

49. Richard Zakia and Mihai Nadin, "Semiotics, Advertising, and Marketing," *Journal of Consumer Marketing* 4 (spring 1987): 6.

50. Russell Belk, Kenneth Bahn, and Robert Mayer, "Developmental Recognition of Consumption Symbolism," *Journal of Consumer Research* 9 (June 1982): 4–17.

51. Julie L. Nicklin, "Marketing by Design," *Chronicle of Higher Education,* March 22, 1996, pp. A33–A34.

Information Processing II: Memory and Cognitive Learning

After studying this chapter, you should be able to describe each of the following concepts, together with their managerial implications:

1. The three types of memory and how they differ.
2. Miller's Law and its relationship to information overload.
3. Recognition and recall tasks.
4. Memory networks and schemas.
5. Retrieval cues.
6. Forgetting.
7. The serial-position effect.
8. The law of contiguity.
9. The Zeigarnik and von Restorff effects.
10. Affective processes and how they impact memory.

Developing an understanding of the factors that influence consumers' memory of information is critical to marketers. For example, Procter & Gamble and Philip Morris each spend over 2 billion dollars annually in the United States.[1] If consumers fail to recall the messages delivered, the money spent will be wasted.[2] In the marketplace of the twenty-first century, many consumer products have become so complicated that even engineers with Ph.D.'s cannot figure them out. An analyst for *Business Week* magazine described the effect of overly complex designs in this way: "Manufacturers of consumer products are not only losing the interest of their customers but they're also alienating them." Indeed, the ability to make personal computing simpler was the key contributing factor to the success of Apple's Macintosh computer and the recent success of its iMac brand. As one Apple executive explained, "On the desktop today, 80% of computing power is going toward ease of use, such as menus, windows, and pop-ups. Only 20% is actually going toward doing the job, such as calculating your spreadsheet."[3]

The problems of presenting information so that consumers can remember and understand it illustrates key issues involving the role of memory and knowledge in consumer information processing. This chapter begins by presenting a simplified model of memory. It then discusses the role of consumer knowledge in the purchase process. The chapter concludes with an explanation of how forgetting occurs and how feelings can influence what we remember.

A SIMPLIFIED MEMORY MODEL

The last chapter focused on perceptual processes in consumer information processing. Memory impacts the exposure, attention, and comprehension stages of perception. It allows consumers to anticipate and selectively expose themselves to the stimuli they might encounter. Similarly, memory influences attention processes by guiding a person's sensory system in order to focus selectively on particular stimuli. Finally, comprehension is affected by the expectations and associations elicited in memory by the stimuli encountered.

Figure 4.1 presents the **multiple-store model of memory,** which is composed of three different types of memory storage systems—sensory memory, short-term memory, and long-term memory.[4] As can be seen in the figure, information is first registered in sensory memory, where the preattention stage occurs. Here the stimulus is briefly and unconsciously analyzed to determine if additional processing capacity should be allocated to it. If the stimulus is perceived to be related to the person's goals, cognitive capacity will be allocated to it, and the information shifts to short-term mem-

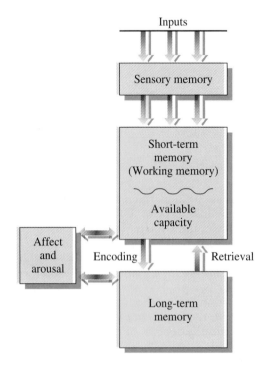

Figure 4.1

A simplified memory model.

ory. In short-term memory, people actively process information. Long-term memory is where the information is permanently stored. It is connected to short-term memory through encoding and retrieval processes. Finally, affective and arousal states are conceptualized as influencing short- and long-term memory.

Sensory Memory

The perception of a sight, sound, touch, smell, or taste occurs because a stimulus activates nerve fibers in a person's sensory organs. The electrical impulses that result from the firing of nerve cells form sensory memory. Lasting only a fraction of a second, the **sensory memory** of a stimulus consists of the immediate impression caused by the firing of the nerve cells. Because the nerve fibers fire for only very short lengths of time, the stimulus information will be quickly lost unless it is processed further.[5]

The firing of the nerve cells is monitored in the preattention stage. If the information is relevant to the person's goals or activates an orienting response, it will be actively monitored in short-term memory.

Short-Term Memory

Short-term memory is the site where information is temporarily stored while being processed. For example, when a consumer thinks about a television commercial or actively attempts to solve a problem, the cognitive processing is occurring in short-term memory. **Working memory,** another term for short-term memory, connotes the idea that individuals actively process information in this memory stage. Using a computer analogy, short-term memory is like random access memory (RAM).

Just as the images contained in sensory memory are lost if not attended to, so too the information contained in short-term memory. Evidence indicates that if information in short-term memory is not rehearsed, it will be lost within about 30 seconds.[6] **Rehearsal** occurs when a person silently repeats information to encode it into long-term memory. One way information is lost is through its replacement by other information in the limited storage capacity of short-term memory.[7]

The Limited Capacity of Short-Term Memory. Short-term memory has a number of important characteristics. First, it has a limited capacity. Psychologist George Miller proposed that the average person has the ability to process only about seven (plus or minus two) chunks of information at a time.[8] A chunk may be conceptualized as a single meaningful piece of information. It could be a single letter, a syllable, or an entire word. The recognition that people can handle seven (plus or minus two) bits of information at a time has been labeled **Miller's Law.** Some researchers have noted that Miller may have been too optimistic about the capacity of short-term memory. Indeed, in consumer contexts five (plus or minus two) bits may be a better estimate.

The limited capacity characteristic of short-term memory means that it acts as a bottleneck. If more information is received than the consumer can handle, some of it will be lost. This limited capacity is one reason why consumers suffer information overload when they must deal with overly complex products. **Information overload** describes a situation in which more information is received than can be processed in short-term memory. In addition to being unable to process all the information, consumers react to overload by becoming aroused and by more narrowly focusing attention on only certain aspects of the incoming stimuli.[9] The consumer may simply make a random choice, not buy anything, or focus on the wrong product qualities when making a product-choice decision.

The Internet is increasing the managerial relevance of information overload, whereby search engines routinely generate hundreds of Web sites that contain material possibly relevant to a purchase.[10] All of this information can quickly frustrate consumers. Information overload can also occur when a salesperson is explaining the characteristics of a complex product such as a computer. The uninformed buyer can soon become overwhelmed with facts and is likely to become aroused and nervous and to focus only on a limited number of product attributes (e.g., price and speed), which may result in a poor decision. Another occasion in which information overload can occur is when consumers make purchases in a culture in which they must speak a foreign language.[11] Under such circumstances information overload, high arousal levels, and discomfort can result in poor decision making.

Involvement and Short-Term Memory Capacity. The level of involvement experienced will influence the capacity of short-term memory.[12] In high-involvement situations consumers are likely to be more aroused and more attentive, thereby expanding the capacity of short-term memory to its maximal extent. In contrast, under low-involvement conditions the consumer's arousal level is apt to be low, so the consumer focuses relatively little cognitive capacity on the stimulus. Advertisers generally maintain that the number of copy points that can be transmitted in an ad are limited to about three or four. Because copy points are analogous to chunks of information, these findings indicate that consumers view television advertising from a low-involvement state. The managerial implications of these ideas are clear—when doing television or radio advertising, keep your messages simple.

Transferring Information from Short-Term to Long-Term Memory. One of the functions of short-term memory is to assist in the transfer of information to **long-term memory,** where information is permanently stored. As a person allocates more capacity to a stimulus, the likelihood of it being transferred to long-term memory increases. One way to allocate capacity to a stimulus is through the process of rehearsal. Rehearsal may involve the silent verbal repetition of information or the application of more energy to the task. An example of rehearsal is the repetition of a telephone number between the time you look it up and the time you dial the number.

One research study investigated the impact of rehearsal on the recall by young children of advertised products.[13] Children in the study either rehearsed or did not rehearse the names of the products by saying them aloud. The results revealed that the children (ages 4 to 9) who rehearsed the names of the products were better able to recall information about the brands. The implication of the study for advertisers is that commercials that induce repetition of material (e.g., using jingles and slogans) may possibly improve the transfer of information from short-term to long-term memory.

How long does it take to transfer a chunk of information into long-term memory? Researchers have found that it depends on just how the information is to be recalled from long-term memory. If the goal simply involves recognizing that a stimulus has been seen, it may take only two to five seconds for transfer if the information is processed. In contrast, if the information must be recalled without assistance at a later time, the transfer time is longer—from five to ten seconds for a single chunk.

These differences in transfer times have important implications for marketers. When developing messages for consumers, the marketer should consider whether the consumer will be in a recognition task or a recall task. In a **recognition task,** information is placed in front of a person, and the goal is to judge whether the information has been seen previously. In a **recall task,** the consumer must retrieve the information from long-term memory. Thus, in recognition tasks memory recall is said to be aided; in recall tasks the retrieval of memories is unaided.

Grocery shopping frequently involves consumers in a recognition task. For example, with a low-involvement product, such as laundry detergent, the shopper may merely scan the shelves for ideas on what to buy. Because the shopper is engaging in a

Summary of Short-Term Memory (STM) Processes

1. STM has a limited capacity of seven, plus or minus two, chunks of information.
2. STM is the site where information is processed and temporarily stored.
3. Information overload can occur if more information is received than can be processed in STM.
4. As involvement levels increase, consumers may allocate more capacity to a stimulus.
5. Information is transferred from STM to long-term memory by allocating more capacity to it. One method for allocating more capacity is rehearsal of the material to be learned.

TABLE 4.1

recognition task, the transmission time from short-term to long-term memory will be shorter than for recall tasks. As a consequence, the commercials used to advertise the brand may not have to be as long, be repeated as frequently, or attract as much attention as when the consumer must recall the information without aid.

In other instances the direct recall of a product name from memory may be required. For example, suppose that a group of friends decide to go out to lunch on the spur of the moment. Each person will name a restaurant choice, and the group will make a decision from this list of options. If the name of a particular restaurant is not recalled from memory, it simply will not be selected. This set of acceptable restaurants recalled from memory is called the **consideration set.** It is crucial that a company's product be included in the consideration set for it to have a chance to be chosen in such circumstances. Because the time required to transfer information from short- to long-term memory is longer when unaided recall is required, companies must go to greater lengths to promote their brands.

Short-term memory has a limited capacity, and temporarily stored information will be replaced with new information if it is not rehearsed. As a result, the earlier material may not be transferred to long-term memory. When consumers watch television or read a magazine, they are bombarded by dozens of advertisements competing for attention. If there are too many ads, **advertising clutter** results. Advertising clutter impedes the ability of consumers to move information from temporary storage in short-term memory to permanent storage in long-term memory, particularly when unaided recall is required.[14] For example, consider the Super Bowl football extravaganza, which typically lasts over three hours. During that time viewers see over 65 commercials. After one Super Bowl game a few years ago, a market research firm analyzed consumer recall for ads placed by the game's leading sponsor—PepsiCo. The researchers found that less than half of the respondents could remember any ads for PepsiCo's products. The cost of the ads was $6.8 million. There was so much clutter that it was hard for any company to break through.[15]

Table 4.1 summarizes some important points concerning short-term memory.

Long-Term Memory

In contrast to short-term memory, long-term memory has an essentially unlimited capacity to store information permanently.[16] Memory systems operate for each of the senses. Advertisers are particularly interested in information stored either semantically or visually. Semantic concepts are the verbal meanings attached to words, events, objects, and symbols. Thus, long-term memory stores the meanings of words, symbols, and such along with the associations among various semantic concepts. Long-term memory can also store information in terms of its sequence of occurrence (episodic memory), in terms of its modality (e.g., visual, smell, touch senses), and in terms of its affective, or emotional, content.[17]

The permanent nature of long-term memory is illustrated by the enduring quality of brand names. For example, in the 1980s General Motors discontinued the Nova brand of automobile because of poor sales. Another reason for discontinuing the brand was that the word *nova* means "no go" in Spanish. A number of years later, however, General Motors brought back the name *Nova* for a new car model despite its translation problems. The reason is that consumers in the United States retained an image of the brand as reliable and low cost, so it seemed appropriate for a new car built jointly with Toyota. One analyst noted: "Bringing back well-known brand names could be a clever idea because so much of the marketing work is done. People's memory of old advertising campaigns and packaging is remarkably persistent."[18]

Relative Superiority of Picture versus Word Memory. An important finding concerning long-term memory is that pictures tend to be more memorable than their verbal counterparts, particularly under low-involvement circumstances.[19] In one study consumers received one set of information about a brand from the written copy of the print ad and a different set of information from the pictorial content of the ad. Thus, the visual material pertained to one characteristic of the brand (e.g., its durability) and the verbal material talked about another characteristic (e.g., its value for the money). The results of the study revealed that significantly more pictorial information was recalled and recognized than verbally presented information.[20] The aphorism "a picture is worth a thousand words" thus has some scientific support.[21]

Another study found that, if the words in a message have high-imagery content, then the addition of pictures is not as important. (A high-imagery word would be *table*, a low-imagery word would be *future*.) In the study, high- and low-imagery versions of advertisements were created. The messages were either accompanied or not accompanied by a photograph. The results revealed that the photograph did not significantly enhance the recall of the message when high-imagery words were used. When low-imagery words were used, however, the picture did significantly enhance recall. Two managerial implications can be drawn from the research. First, advertisers should use high-imagery words whenever possible. Second, the use of photographs can significantly increase recall if the words in the message have relatively low-imagery content.[22]

Researchers have also found that visual material is particularly easily recognized if the objects to be remembered are perceived as interacting in some way. Thus, to associate a product with a famous endorser, the advertiser should show the endorser actually using the product in everyday scenes.[23]

One can make the following generalizations about the effects of the verbal and pictorial content of ads on memory:

1. In general, pictorial content is recognized and recalled more readily than verbal content, particularly if the verbal material has low-imagery content.
2. Verbal material is best recalled when it is processed under high-involvement circumstances.
3. If consumers are engaged in high-involvement information processing, greater overall recall may result by giving different information about a product via verbal and pictorial means.
4. Words and pictures should be used to complement each other in ads.[24]

Memory-Control Processes

How do people get information into and out of memory? Called **memory-control processes,** these methods of handling information may operate consciously or unconsciously to influence the encoding and retrieval of information.[25]

Encoding. **Encoding** refers to the process of transferring information from short-term to long-term memory. How the information is encoded impacts the speed of transfer and the placement of the information in memory. During rehearsal a consumer can simply repeat the stimulus over and over or attempt to link the stimulus to other information already placed into long-term memory. Significantly, if the consumer encodes the information by drawing associations between it and information already in memory, the storage process is enhanced.[26]

Researchers have found that, when given new information on a topic, experts recall more information than do novices. This occurs because experts have already developed elaborate memory networks and knowledge structures into which the information can be placed. This allows the information to be encoded more efficiently. In addition, it also makes the retrieval process easier. Finally, it allows the expert to better discriminate between important and unimportant information.[27] The ability to distinguish important from unimportant information helps the expert to make better decisions. (See chapter 9 for a discussion of decision making.)

The development of brand names by marketers should be governed by an understanding of encoding processes. If a product name is more closely associated with images and ideas evoked by the product class, there is proportional improvement in recall of the name.[28] For example, highly concrete names, which can be easily visualized, are remembered better because they can be coded both visually and verbally. In addition, such names can be better related to existing knowledge structures. In one study respondents were given either high-imagery or low-imagery brand names. Examples of high-imagery names were *ocean, orchestra, frog,* and *blossom.* Examples of low-imagery brand names were *history, capacity, truth,* and *moment.* The results revealed that subjects recalled more of the high-imagery names. An example of a product with a high-imagery name is Head & Shoulders shampoo.

Retrieval and Response Generation. The act of remembering something consists of the control processes of retrieval and response generation. In the **retrieval process,** the individual searches through long-term memory in order to bring the information back into short-term memory. It is through the process of **response generation** that the person develops a response by actively reconstructing the stimulus.[29] Consumers do not access stored replicas of the encoded stimulus information. Instead, traces of stimuli are activated and reconstructed into a recollection of the stimulus. People use logic, intuition, expectations, and whatever else is available to help reconstruct a memory.

A critical issue for advertisers is how to help consumers retrieve from memory information about their brand. One means is to provide consumers with retrieval cues on the packaging of a product. Such **retrieval cues** may be created by placing the verbal or visual information, originally contained in an ad, on the product or the packaging to assist consumers' memories during decision making.[30] This technique is frequently used by marketers of children's' cereals that feature animals in the ads and on the boxes of cereal.

Another approach for assisting retrieval and response generation is to employ music in advertisements. Research has shown that people recall messages better if they are sung. Music acts as a highly powerful retrieval cue that can substantially improve recall.[31] Indeed, jingles can stay in consumers' heads for years. For example, the maker of Mounds and Almond Joy candy bars brought back the "sometimes you feel like a nut" jingle. Even though the jingle had not played for years, customers still remembered it. By bringing it back, the company could capture an entire new generation of consumers with its message.

Advertising impacts the reconstruction of memories. That is, advertising can influence memories to make them consistent with how the ads depict past product

Summary of Long-Term Memory (LTM) Processes

1. LTM has unlimited capacity.
2. Information is stored semantically and visually, by its sequence of occurrence, by its modality, and in terms of its emotional content.
3. LTM is essentially permanent.
4. Generally, picture memory is superior to word memory.
5. The memory-control processes of encoding and response generation influence what is stored in and retrieved from memory.

TABLE 4.2

experience. For example, after seeing ads for a product, consumers may report more favorable product experiences than if they had not see the advertising. These results strongly suggest that advertisers should show scenes of satisfied consumers using a brand.[32] Not only will such ads influence expectations of future product performance, but they will also positively change consumers' recall of their own previous experience with the brand.

Table 4.2 summarizes key points on the impact of long-term memory on consumer information processing.

CONSUMER KNOWLEDGE

Stored in long-term memory is a person's knowledge about the consumption environment. **Consumer knowledge** is defined as the amount of experience with and information that a person has about particular products or services.[33] As consumer knowledge increases, a person can think about a product across a greater number of dimensions and make finer distinctions among brands. For example, a consumer with large amounts of knowledge about wine can think in terms of multiple dimensions, such as a wine's color, bouquet, nose, acidity, and so on. A novice might think in terms of one dimension (e.g., how much he or she likes its taste).[34]

Three types of consumer knowledge can be identified. First, there is objective knowledge, or the correct information about a product class that a consumer has stored in long-term memory. Second, there is subjective knowledge, or a consumer's perception of what or how much he or she knows about a product class. Interestingly, objective and subjective knowledge are not highly correlated.[35] Wide differences exist in how much people think they know and how much they really know. Third, there is information about the knowledge of others. For example, product engineers sometimes fail to recognize that consumers do not have sufficient knowledge to readily understand and use a particular product.

What are the implications for marketing managers of the study of consumer knowledge? As consumer knowledge increases, consumers become better organized, they are more efficient and accurate in their information processing, and they have better recall of information. Managers should consider the extent of consumer knowledge when developing and promoting the product. For example, much more complex communications can be sent to people who are knowledgeable because these consumers are less prone to information overload.

How Consumers Gain Knowledge

Consumers obtain their knowledge through the process of cognitive learning. **Cognitive learning** is defined as the processes responsible for how people form associations among concepts, learn sequences of concepts (e.g., learn a list), solve problems, and have insights. Such learning involves an intuitive hypothesis-generating process in which people adapt their beliefs to make sense of new data.[36] Thus, cognitive learning is an active process in which people seek to control the information obtained.[37]

People learn about the consumer environment through education and through experience.[38] **Learning through education** involves obtaining information from companies in the form of advertising, sales personnel, and the consumer's own directed efforts to seek data. In contrast, **learning through experience** involves the process of gaining knowledge through actual contact with products. Overall, learning from experience is more effective because the consumer is involved in the learning experience and because the information obtained is more vivid, concrete, and salient.

The Gestalt Approach to Knowledge. A group of researchers active in the early twentieth century made an important contribution to our understanding of cognitive learning and knowledge. The **Gestalt psychologists** argued that people perceive the inputs from the environment as part of a total context. Furthermore, they argued that a person is not a static organism who responds automatically to inputs from the environment. Rather, the Gestalt psychologists focused on the active, creative nature of learning and action.[39] As one noted consumer researcher stated:

> When we look at an automobile, we do not see glass and steel and plastic and bolts and paint. We see instead an organized whole, an automobile. And perhaps not even just an automobile but also comfortable transportation, prestige, status, and a symbolic sense of achievement. This is the familiar Gestalt dictum; the whole is different from, if not greater than, the sum of the isolated parts.[40]

The work of the Gestalt psychologists has important implications for marketers. Market researchers tend to perceive products in terms of their individual characteristics, such as price, color, features, reliability, and so forth. In contrast, consumers perceive the product as an integrated whole. In isolation a particular color or style may be judged as unacceptable. When seen in the overall context of a product, however, the characteristic could be quite satisfactory. Thus, when considered in isolation, using plaid seats in a car might seem silly; however, when placed in a sports car, the multicolor seats might fit quite well.

Another contribution of the Gestalt school is the idea that consumers engage in problem-solving activities and have sudden bursts of insight. Many products or situations can activate the consumer so that he or she begins problem-solving activities. For example, consumers can become highly involved in purchasing of an automobile, in selecting which mutual funds to place their retirement savings, or in identifying which college to attend.

Forming Associations. Another approach to cognitive learning is analyzing the associations that consumers form between marketing stimuli. Two discoveries have important implications for consumer researchers—the serial-position effect and paired-associate learning.

The study of **serial learning** concerns how people put into memory and recall information that is received in a sequential manner. For example, consider what happens at a commercial break during a television show. Viewers can be exposed to six or more advertisements in a two-minute time period. One important question is whether the position of an ad in the series influences how well it is remembered. A **serial-position effect** occurs when the order of presentation of information

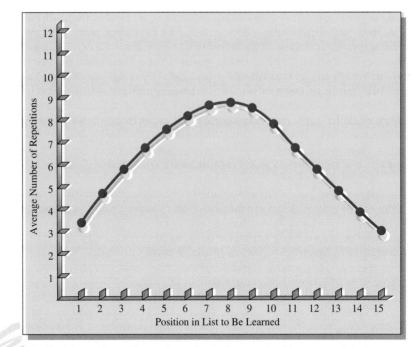

Figure 4.2   Serial position effect: a hypothetical example. More repetitions are required to learn the material in the middle of the list.

Source: The hypothetical curve shown here is based in part on serial-position curves found in Charles E. Osgood, *Method and Theory in Experimental Psychology* (New York: Oxford University Press, 1964).

influences recall of the information in the list. As illustrated in Figure 4.2, researchers have found that items in the beginning of the list and items at the end of the list are the most readily learned. In contrast, items in the middle of the list are learned much less rapidly.[41]

One explanation for the serial-learning effect is that the beginning and end of a list become anchors for learning. Due to limitations of short-term memory, people identify reference points for when to attempt to start or end the learning process. With the ability to store only limited amounts of information in short-term memory at a time, people recall most readily only the items right around the beginning and end of the list. Items in the middle take many more repetitions of the material to be recalled.

The serial-learning effect has some important implications for marketers. First, key information in an advertisement should be placed at the beginning or end of the message. If important information is embedded in the middle of the communication, it may take a larger number of repetitions of the advertisement for consumers to learn the information.[42] Second, it makes a difference where a commercial is placed. Networks know this, so the advertisements placed in the first and last position of a series of commercials, called **bookend ads,** command higher prices. The most recent research on the serial-position effect indicates that, given a choice of placing an ad at the beginning or end of a series, one should actually place it at the beginning. Over time, say a week or so, the first ad in a series is recalled better than the last ad. This finding provides evidence for a primacy effect for ads.[43]

In addition to studying how consumers learn lists of information, the researchers studying the role of association also investigated how consumers remember words that are paired with each other, called **paired-association learning.** One principle relating to this is the **law of contiguity,** which states that things that are experienced together become associated.[44] This law explains how people connect words with each other. For example, three pairs of stimulus and response words might be Maytag–quality, Nike–Tiger Woods, and Volvo–crash protection. *Maytag, Nike,* and *Volvo* are the stimulus words, and the response words are *quality, Tiger Woods,* and *crash protection,* respectively. An important finding in paired-associate learning is that learning is enhanced if the stimulus and response items can be readily associated with each other and are familiar.[45] In particular, if mental images can be developed between stimulus and response words, learning is more rapid.

The findings of studies in paired-associate learning suggest that, for these associations to be learned most rapidly, the following conditions should be met:

1. The stimulus and response words should be easily pronounceable.

2. The person should be familiar with the stimulus and response words.

3. The stimulus and response words should be meaningful.

4. The stimulus and response words should be easily associated.

5. Visual images should be created to link the stimulus and response words together.

Marketers instinctively use ideas from the law of contiguity when creating cooperative advertising campaigns. In such campaigns two distinct products are promoted together. For example, Alka-Seltzer and H&R Block developed a joint campaign in which the product and the service were touted as helping "tax-time upsets." As one Alka-Seltzer manager explained, "Alka-Seltzer has a heritage of being caring, empathetic, like Mother Theresa. This touches an underlying emotion at tax time."[46] In this case the stimulus words (*tax-time upsets*) and the response word (*Alka-Seltzer*) were easily associated.

Another way that marketers use the law of contiguity is to create brand names that suggest the product's use. For example, the names *Head & Shoulders* and *Lean Cuisine* identify the task that the brand is designed to perform. Because the products' use and the brand names are associated, the consumer's ability to recall the names increases. The brand name can even be suggestive of specific attributes of the brand. For example, the name of Sears' DieHard battery connotes that the product resists losing its charge. Recent research indicates that such suggestive names increase the recall of the benefits claimed by the brand name. Interestingly, however, the research also shows that recall is inhibited for benefits unrelated to the attribute suggested by the brand name. Thus, one would expect that an attribute of "low price" would be inhibiting for recalling the DieHard battery.[47]

The law of contiguity can also cause problems for marketers. When ads are positioned beside an unflattering ad or news story, the impact of the promotion may be reduced or may even become negative. For example, most companies check carefully to ensure that their television advertisements are not shown in conjunction with programs that could be offensive to their target market. Recent research has investigated whether corporate sponsorships of philanthropic organizations can mitigate the effects of negative publicity. For example, suppose that the organization is an oil company. Can an association with a positive stimulus (e.g., support of a children's hospital or an environmental group) reduce the effects of negative publicity (e.g., reports of an oil spill)? Preliminary results indicate that supporting an unrelated cause (the children's hospital) may minimize the negative publicity to a greater extent than supporting a related cause (the environmental group).[48]

Semantic Memory Networks

Semantic memory refers to how people store the meanings of verbal material in long-term memory. Researchers have found that semantic memory is organized into networks.[49] Figure 4.3 presents an example of what a memory network for automobiles might look like. The network is a series of memory nodes that represent the stored semantic concepts; the lines connecting the nodes indicate the associations that exist.

According to one popular theory of semantic memory, information is recalled from the semantic network via spreading activation.[50] Thus, if a stimulus activates a node, activation will spread through the network and activate other nodes. Each node that is activated represents a memory that is recalled.

Researchers have argued that five types of consumer information can be stored at the memory nodes:[51]

1. The brand name.
2. The brand's characteristics advertisement.
3. Advertisements about the brand.
4. The product category.
5. Evaluative reactions to the brand and the ad.

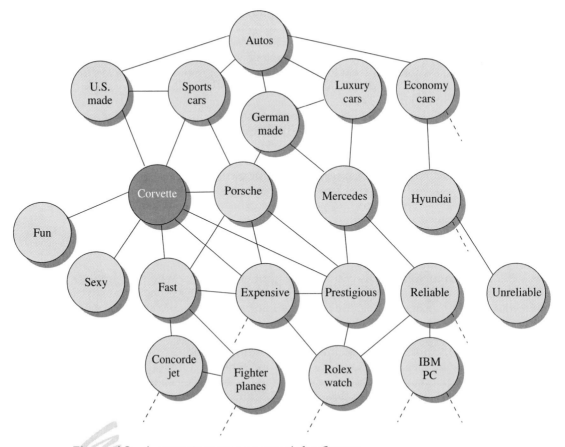

Figure 4.3 A semantic memory network for *Corvette*.

Suppose, for example, that the Corvette node shown in Figure 4.3 was activated by someone mentioning his or her plans to buy one. The activation of the node would result in a spreading of activation into the semantic network. As a result a number of additional nodes will be activated. These nodes become the associations that a person will have with the semantic concept of *Corvette*. Thus, various attributes of the car could be elicited as associations (e.g., sports car, fast, expensive, and prestigious). In addition, similar other brands of cars could be activated in memory (e.g., Porsche), as could various evaluative reactions stored in memory. Of course, consumers possess divergent memory structures, and the activation of a semantic concept may result in quite different sets of associations for different people.

As illustrated in Figure 4.3, consumers form a set of semantic associations with a brand name. A consumer's **brand knowledge** can be defined as consisting of a "brand node in memory to which a variety of associations have been linked."[52] Thus, in Figure 4.3 the brand name *Corvette* forms a node to which a variety of concepts are associated, such as its characteristics (e.g., goes fast, is expensive), brand connections (sports cars, Porsche), and evaluative reactions (e.g., fun, sexy).

Schemas

The total package of associations brought to mind when a node is activated is called a schema. Specifically, **schemas** "stored frameworks of knowledge about some object or topic and are represented by nodes in semantic memory.[53] Thus, the Corvette schema in Figure 4.3 consists of those associations and expectations that a particular person has about the car.

Researchers have found that, when provided with new information that is inconsistent with a schema, consumers engage in more diligent processing and consequently have improved memory about the stimulus. Thus, when a consumer receives information that deviates from expectation, he or she places more cognitive capacity on the information (i.e., processes it in greater depth). In such circumstances it is more likely that the information will be transferred from short-term to long-term memory.[54]

Indeed, creativity in advertising results in part from the violation of a schema. For example, in the late 1990s, the "milk mustache" campaign by the Milk Marketing Board was identified as the number-one advertising campaign in the United States. The highly memorable ads portrayed physically attractive celebrities wearing a circle of milk above their lip. The ads attract attention and are memorable because they violate the schema of how such people should look.

One study tested the effectiveness of violating schema in a personal-selling situation.[55] Suppose a customer in a clothing store encounters a salesperson who interacts with the person in a different style. If the customer is surprised by the sales approach, he or she might pay more attention to the information and recall it better in the future. The research results supported this hypothesis. When the seller met expectations of the typical salesperson, product evaluations were not affected by the quality of the arguments of the sales speech. However, when the salesperson violated the schema, subjects recalled more about what the salesperson said about the product and generally had more positive attitudes about the product.

Table 4.3 summarizes the major implications of memory processes for promotional strategy.

FORGETTING

If long-term memory is permanent, why do people forget? The answer is that, even though information has been placed in long-term memory, it may be impossible to

Summary of Major Implications of Memory Processes for Promotional Strategy

Memory Area	Implications
Short-term memory	Develop messages that match the capacity level of consumers' STM.
Long-term memory	Enhance message presentation by using vivid visual information as well as verbal information.
Consumer knowledge	1. Construct messages that match target's knowledge. 2. Construct messages inconsistent with consumer schemas. 3. Attempt to understand target market's schemas and semantic memory networks that include your product/service, and create messages that fit into these schemas.
Forgetting	1. Create promotional material with distinctive characteristics in order to minimize interference in target market's memory caused by competing material. 2. Create interruptions in advertisements that enhance their recall. 3. To maintain memory for ads, use a pulsing strategy of showing ads periodically, rather than spending an entire budget in a short time period.
Cognitive learning	1. Recognize that consumers are insightful information processors who perceive products as integrated wholes. 2. Make use of the law of contiguity by pairing product/service with positive association. 3. Do not bury key product information in the middle of a commercial. 4. Avoid allowing your advertisements to be buried in the middle of a series of commercials.
Affect and memory	In general, attempt to cause people to be in positive mood states when evaluating your product/service.

TABLE 4.3

retrieve. In one study over 10,000 people were polled on the advertisements that they could remember. Of these, 53 percent were unable to remember any specific ad that they had seen, heard, or read in the last 30 days.[56] These results are devastating to advertising managers because the recall of ads is an important measure of advertising effectiveness. In order to improve on the recall of advertisements, one must first understand the process of how people forget.

Interference Processes

Two factors that can cause problems in encoding, retrieval, and response generation are proactive interference and retroactive interference. When **retroactive interference** occurs, new material presented after old material has been learned interferes with the recall of the old material. That is, the learning of new material interferes with the retrieval or the response generation from memory of the old material. With **proactive interference** material learned prior to the new material interferes with the learning of the new material.[57] Such interference is an enormous problem for advertisers because consumers are exposed to between 300 and 600 commercials per day.[58]

A number of techniques can help advertisers minimize the effects of proactive and retroactive interference. A classic finding is that interference between material to be learned increases as the similarity of their content increases.[59] Thus, if consumers receive a series of commercials in which similar claims are made, confusion will result and learning will be impeded. Indeed, the confusion will grow proportionally to the degree that the competing commercials involve similar types of products or that different products use similar adjectives to describe their performance (such as high quality, low cost, low maintenance, etc.). These effects have been found to be particularly strong for unfamiliar brands.[60] Of course, this means that there are important advantages in the marketplace for brands that are familiar to consumers. A second finding is that interference lessens if information is provided bimodally, via both spoken and written information. This occurs because spoken and written information is processed via different neural pathways.[61]

The von Restorff Effect. A finding of particular importance to advertisers is called the **von Restorff effect.**[62] Experiments have shown that people tend to recall a unique item in a series of relatively similar items much more easily. This occurs because the effects of proactive and retroactive interference are minimized.

The von Restorff effect illustrates the importance of information salience. **Information salience** refers to the level of activation of a stimulus (e.g., a brand name) in memory.[63] The level of salience is increased if the person has just purchased a product. It also be increased by making something unique, by using continuously high levels of advertising, and by using cues (e.g., point-of-purchase displays) to remind consumers of a product.[64] In addition, stimulus factors such as novelty, contrast, color, surprise, movement, and size can all act to make a stimulus salient. Generally, the more salient something is, the more likely it will be encoded into memory and later recalled. One of an advertiser's primary goals should be to make an advertisement highly salient to the consumer.

Researchers have also found that if one brand is highly salient to consumers, the recall of competing brands is lowered.[65] Thus, if a manager can develop the marketing mix so that a brand is highly salient to consumers, recall of competing brands as a part of the consideration set may be decreased. The reason for this is that through retroactive interference the presence of the salient brand in memory inhibits the recall of competitors.

The Zeigarnik Effect. Another factor that influences whether something will be forgotten is called the Zeigarnik effect. Named after the German Gestalt scientist who discovered it, the **Zeigarnik effect** occurs when an individual is involved in a task that is interrupted or not completed.[66] Comparisons between the recall of information of a task that has been interrupted and one that has been completed consistently show that material in the interrupted task is recalled better.[67]

The Zeigarnik effect may explain in part the effectiveness of "soap-opera" ads, such as those developed for Taster's Choice coffee. These ads featured an on-going romance between a man and a woman. Of course, the trials and tribulations of the couple revolve around the drinking coffee. Each ad acts as a mini-episode of the drama. As the ad ends, the couple is caught in a conflict that has not been resolved. The lack of resolution piques the interest of consumers, and they "hold in mind" the ad until this particular conflict is resolved in the next act.

Time and Forgetting

Because of proactive and retroactive interference, the recall of verbal information decreases over time.[68] Figure 4.4 shows the results of a classic experiment by

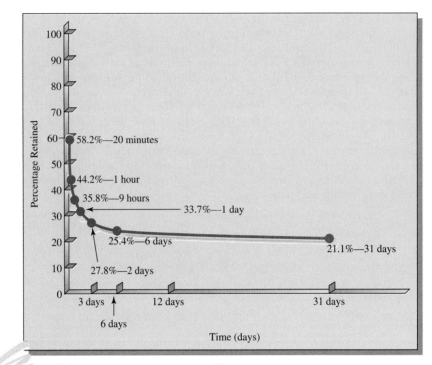

Figure 4.4   Relationship between time and forgetting.

Source: Data from H. Ebbinghaus, *Memory*, H. A. Ruger and C. E. Bussenius, trans. (New York: New York Teachers College, 1913).

H. Ebbinghaus concerning such effects. After learning a list of nonsense words (e.g., xlp, mqv, etc.), the percentage of words the participants remembered decreased dramatically at first and then leveled off over time.

The rapid forgetting that occurs immediately after learning has been shown to occur in advertising as well. In another classic experiment by Hubert Zielske, advertisements for a product ran once a week for 13 weeks.[69] At the end of the 13-week period, 63 percent of the housewives in the experiment could recall having seen the ad. After 13 weeks no more ads were shown, and forgetting showed the same pattern as that found 70 years earlier by Ebbinghaus—very rapidly at first and then leveling off. After 20 weeks the recall of the ads had dropped to below 30 percent; by the time nine months had passed, less than 10 percent of those surveyed could remember the ads.

In addition to giving one group of housewives one ad a week for 13 weeks, Zielske showed another group 13 ads that were spaced four weeks apart. In this case the ability to recall the ads increased slowly, but at the end of the year some 48 percent could remember the ads. The difference between the group shown the ads bunched together and the group who received the ads spaced over time has important implications for advertisers. If an advertiser wants to obtain rapid awareness of a product, a high frequency of ads over a short period of time will be most effective. However, rapid forgetting occurs after the burst of advertisements. If the goal is to build long-term awareness of the product, the commercials should be pulsed such that they are seen by consumers regularly over a long period of time. Often companies will combine the approaches and use a high-intensity campaign to bring out a product and then pulse regularly after the introduction to maintain awareness.

AFFECT AND MEMORY

One of the major themes of this book is that, when investigating consumer behavior, the researcher must be concerned with experiential, or affective processes. The term **affect** refers to the feelings, emotions, and moods that consumers may experience. A **mood** is a transient feeling state that occurs in a specific situation or time. It is not a personality variable because moods are temporary in nature, whereas personality is longer lasting. Similarly, it is not an emotion, which is more intense and attention getting.[70] Despite a mood's short duration and mild intensity, research suggests that people are better able to recall information that has the same affective quality as their mood state. Thus, when people are sad, they are more likely to recall information that is sad. Conversely, when people are happy, they are more likely to remember happy information.[71] Recent research indicates that positive mood states enhance the learning of brand names compared with neutral moods.[72]

In one study researchers asked consumers to think about happy, sad, or neutral past experiences in order to induce positive, negative, or neutral moods. They were then shown a single print advertisement for a Mazda RX7 sports car. When the respondents were asked to form an impression of the car while reading the ad, the mood affected their rating of the car 48 hours later. The researchers hypothesized that, when the evaluation was made at the time the ad was read, the participants' mood state influenced how the information was encoded. A sad mood caused the evaluation to be lower than did a neutral mood state. Similarly, the highest ratings occurred when the subjects encoded the information when in a positive mood state.[73]

The research on the relationship between affect and memory has managerial implications. In general, one can argue that marketers should attempt to place consumers in a positive mood state when they are receiving information on a product or service. A number of devices can be used to create these moods, such as the use of humor in an advertisement or purchasing a nice meal for a client in a personal-selling situation. To the extent that using a product causes negative moods, however, it may inhibit the learning of information and actually slow the learning process.

THE MANAGERIAL IMPLICATIONS
OF MEMORY AND COGNITIVE LEARNING

The principles and concepts of memory and cognitive learning have application to each of the five PERMS concepts, as discussed in the following sections.

Positioning and Differentiation

A critical issue for organizations is identifying and evaluating how consumers in their target market encode into memory the brand names of products, as well as the name of the organization. How information is encoded into memory can be determined by measuring the connections in the semantic memory network of individuals in the target market. This analysis results in the identification of the schema associated with a brand or with an organization. The schema will provide information on the positioning of the brand relative to other brands and to important attributes (or characteristics) on which the brand is evaluated. For example, if the schema for the brand Oldsmobile includes such associations as old-fashioned, Buick, grandfather, boxy, and long, it says much about the positioning of the brand. It also tells managers that consumers may not be differentiating the brand from Buick.

Environmental Analysis

When promoting a brand, managers must carefully examine the actions of competitors in the marketplace. To the extent that the communications environment is cluttered with competing advertisements, managers must consider the effects of information overload and the use of the Zeigarnik and von Restorff effects in order to improve the encoding and retrieval of information.

Research

Market research is required in order to identify the semantic memory network and schema of the target market for the organization and the brand. Studies to evaluate the consumers' recall and recognition of key advertising points is also necessary. In addition, companies should conduct research to assess the knowledge and involvement level of consumers in the target market. Such studies are critical for determining how much information to transmit in messages and the complexity of the design of the product. Market research should also be conducted to determine the affect associated with a brand or organization. Negative affective associations will tend to elicit other semantic memories that have a similar affective charge.

Marketing Mix

The concepts in this chapter are particularly relevant to the product development and promotional strategy elements of the marketing mix. By identifying the knowledge and involvement level of the target market, managers possess information relevant to the design of the product and the creation of promotional messages. Similarly, by understanding the Zeigarnik and von Restorff effects, managers receive guidance for the development of marketing communications. Having knowledge of the serial-position effect gives a manager direction as to the usefulness of purchasing the more expensive bookend ads. The law of contiguity is particularly important for the public-relations component of the promotional mix. That is, publicists must be on constant lookout for situations in which the brand or organization is paired with unfavorable information. Finally, if marketing research indicates that the brand or organization is associated with stimuli having a negative affective charge, marketing communications must be developed that seek to change the feelings associated with the brand or organization.

Segmentation

The knowledge level of consumers can be used as an important segmentation variable. That is, different messages and potentially even different products can be targeted to consumers with divergent knowledge levels.

Notes

1. R. C. Endicott, "Top Global Marketers," *Advertising Age*, November 1997, p. 9.
2. For a recent article on memory effects in advertising, see H. Shanker Krishnan and Dipankar Chakravarti, "Memory Measures for Pretesting Advertisements: An Integrative Conceptual Framework and a Diagnostic Template," *Journal of Consumer Psychology* 8, no. 1 (1999): 1–37.
3. Bruce Nussbaum and Robert Neff, "I Can't Work This Thing!" *Business Week*, April 29, 1991, pp. 58–66.
4. James R. Bettman, "Memory Factors in Consumer Choice: A Review," *Journal of Marketing* 43 (spring 1979): 37–53. The evidence is mixed as to whether three types of memory exist and, if so, whether memories are stored in three separate locations in the brain. Other approaches to memory have been proposed, such as one suggesting that short- and long-term memories are distinguished only by the depth of processing. Researchers have also identified another type of memory, called *implicit memory*. For a discussion of this concept, see Abhijit Sanyal, "Priming and Implicit Memory: A Review and Synthesis Relevant for Consumer Behavior," in *Diversity in Consumer Behavior: Advances in Consumer Research*, ed. John F. Sherry Jr. and Brian Sternthal (Provo, UT: Association for Consumer Research, 1992), 19:795–805. For even newer views of memory processes, see Alan J. Malter, "An

Introduction to Embodied Cognition: Implications for Consumer Research," in *Advances in Consumer Research,* ed. Kim Corfman and John Lynch (Provo, UT: Association for Consumer Research, 1996), 23:272–76. However, because the multiple-store theory has a strong intuitive appeal, and its predictions are generally consistent with other approaches to memory, it is the approach used in this discussion.

5. George Sperling, "The Information Available in Brief Visual Presentations," *Psychological Monographs* 74 (1960): 498.

6. Herbert Simon, *The Sciences of the Artificial* (Cambridge, MA: MIT Press, 1969).

7. Richard M. Shiffrin and R. C. Atkinson, "Storage and Retrieval Processes in Long-Term Memory," *Psychological Review* 76 (1969): 179–93.

8. George A. Miller, "The Magical Number Seven, plus or minus Two: Some Limits on Our Capacity to Process Information," *Psychological Review* 63 (1956): 81–97. Other researchers have argued about the capacity of short-term memory. Some have argued that it is limited to as few as three chunks of information. Others have argued that it can be as high as 20.

9. Daniel Kahneman, *Attention and Effort* (Upper Saddle River, NJ: Prentice Hall, 1973).

10. Jacob Jacoby, "Perspectives on Information Overload," *Journal of Consumer Research* 10 (March 1984): 432–35.

11. Claudia Dolinsky and Richard Feinberg, "Linguistic Barriers to Consumer Information Processing: Information Overload in the Hispanic Population," *Psychology and Marketing* 3, no. 4 (1986): 261–71.

12. Kahneman, *Attention and Effort.*

13. M. Carole Macklin, "Rehearsal Processes in Children's Recall of Advertised Products," in *Proceedings of the Division of Consumer Psychology,* ed. Wayne Hoyer (Washington, DC: American Psychological Association, 1986), 21–25.

14. Tom J. Brown and Michael L. Rothschild, "Reassessing the Impact of Television Advertising Clutter," *Journal of Consumer Research* 20 (June 1993): 138–46. This important article found little evidence of the negative effects of clutter on the recognition of advertisements embedded in television programming. Additional research, however, is required before we can conclude that clutter presents few, if any, problems for advertisers.

15. Kevin Goldman, "Barrage of Ads in Super Bowl Blurs Messages," *Wall Street Journal,* February 3, 1993, p. B6.

16. For a more detailed description of memory and memory-control processes, see Bettman, "Memory Factors."

17. Benton Underwood, "Attributes of Memory," *Psychological Review* 76 (November 1969): 559–73.

18. Ronald Alsop, "Old Chewing-Gum Favorites Find There's Life after Death," *Wall Street Journal,* September 11, 1986, p. 37.

19. Terry Childers and Michael Houston, "Conditions for a Picture-Superiority Effect on Consumer Memory," *Journal of Consumer Research* 11 (September 1984): 643–54.

20. Terry Childers, Susan Heckler, and Michael Houston, "Memory for the Visual and Verbal Components of Print Advertisements," *Psychology and Marketing* 3 (fall 1986): 147–50.

21. Recent research has found, however, that the superiority of visual over verbal recall may not occur for preschool children. See M. Carole Macklin, "The Impact of Audio-Visual Information on Children's Product-Related Recall," *Journal of Consumer Research* 21 (June 1994): 154–64. For additional information on the persuasive effects of visual and verbal information, see Charles S. Areni and K. Chris Cox, "The Persuasive Effects of Evaluation, Expectancy, and Relevancy Dimensions of Incongruent Visual and Verbal Information," in *Advances in Consumer Research,* 21, ed. Chris Allen and Ceborah Roedder John (Provo, UT: Association for Consumer Research, 1994), 21:337–42.

22. H. Rao Unnava and Robert E. Burnkrant, "An Imagery-Processing View of the Role of Pictures in Print Advertising," *Journal of Marketing Research* 28 (May 1991): 226–31.

23. For a review of this literature, see Kathy Lutz and Richard Lutz, "Effects of Interactive Imagery on Learning: Applications to Advertising," *Journal of Applied Psychology* 62 (August 1977): 493–98.

24. Michael Houston, Terry Childers, and Susan Heckler, "Picture–Word Consistency and the Elaborative Processing of Attributes," *Journal of Marketing Research* 24 (November 1987): 359–69. Closely related is the field of mental imagery. For a review of this area, see Laurie A. Babin, Alvin Burns, and Abhijit Biswas, "A Framework Providing Direction for Research on Communications Effects of Mental Imagery-Evoking Advertising Strategies," in *Diversity*

in Consumer Behavior: Advances in Consumer Research, ed. John F. Sherry Jr. and Brian Sternthal (Provo, UT: Association for Consumer Research, 1992), 19:621–28.

25. Bettman, "Memory Factors."
26. R. N. Kanungo, "Effects of Fittingness, Meaningfulness, and Product Utility," *Journal of Applied Psychology* 52 (August 1968): 290–95.
27. Elizabeth J. Cowley, "Recovering Forgotten Information: A Study of Consumer Expertise," in *Advances in Consumer Research,* ed. Chris Allen and Ceborah Roedder John (Provo, UT: Association for Consumer Research, 1994), 21:58–63.
28. Kim Robertson, "Recall and Recognition Effects of Brand Name Imagery," *Psychology and Marketing* 4 (spring 1987): 3–15.
29. Bettman, "Memory Factors."
30. Kevin L. Keller, "Memory Factors in Advertising: The Effect of Advertising Retrieval Cues on Brand Evaluations," *Journal of Consumer Research* 14 (December 1987): 316–33.
31. Wanda T. Wallace, "Jingles in Advertising: Can They Improve Recall?" in *Advances in Consumer Research,* ed. Marvin Goldberg and Gerald Gorn (Provo, UT: Association for Consumer Research, 1990), 17:239–42.
32. Kathryn A. Braun, "Postexperience Advertising Effects on Consumer Memory," *Journal of Consumer Research* 25 (March 1999): 319–34.
33. Joseph Alba and J. Wesley Hutchinson, "Dimensions of Consumer Expertise," *Journal of Consumer Research* 13 (March 1987): 411–54.
34. For a different perspective on knowledge structures, see Robert Lawson, "Consumer Knowledge Structures: Networks and Frames," in *Advances in Consumer Research,* ed. Joseph W. Alba and J. Wesley Hutchinson (Provo, UT: Association for Consumer Research, 1998), 25:334–40.
35. Concerning objective and subjective knowledge, see C. Whan Park, David L. Mothersbaugh, and Lawrence Feick, "Consumer Knowledge Assessment," *Journal of Consumer Research* 21 (June 1994): 71–82.
36. Stephen J. Hoch and John Deighton, "Managing What Consumers Learn from Experience," *Journal of Marketing* 53 (April 1989): 1–20.
37. For additional information on the transfer of consumer knowledge, see Jennifer Gregan-Paxton and Deborah Roedder John, "Consumer Learning by Analogy: A Model of Internal Knowledge Transfer," *Journal of Consumer Research* 24 (December 1997): 266–84.
38. Hoch and Deighton, "Managing What Consumers."
39. David Horton and Thomas Turnage, *Human Learning* (Upper Saddle River, NJ: Prentice Hall, 1976).
40. Harold H. Kassarjian, "Field Theory in Consumer Behavior," in *Consumer Behavior: Theoretical Sources,* ed. Scott Ward and Thomas Robertson (Upper Saddle River, NJ: Prentice Hall, 1973), 120.
41. Marvin Goldberg and Gerald Gorn, "Happy and Sad TV Programs: How They Affect Reactions to Commercials," *Journal of Consumer Research* 14 (December 1987): 387–403.
42. Frank R. Kardes and Paul M. Herr, "Order Effects in Consumer Judgment, Choice, and Memory: The Role of Initial Processing Goals," in *Advances in Consumer Research,* ed. Marvin Goldberg and Gerald Gorn (Provo, UT: Association for Consumer Research, 1990), 17:541–46.
43. Rik G. M. Pieters and Tammo H. A. Bijmolt, "Consumer Memory for Television Advertising: A Field Study of Duration, Serial Position, and Competition Effects," *Journal of Consumer Research* 23 (March 1997): 362–72.
44. Horton and Turnage, *Human Learning.*
45. Ibid.
46. Sandra Atchison, "Block, Block, Fizz, Fizz," *Business Week,* March 30, 1987, p. 36.
47. Kevin L. Keller, Susan E. Heckler, and Michael J. Houston, "The Effects of Brand Name Suggestiveness on Advertising Recall," *Journal of Marketing* 62 (January 1998): 48–57.
48. Erica Mina Okada and David J. Reibstein, "When !@#? Happens...Effects of Related and Unrelated Positive Associations on the Influence of Negative Secondary Associations," in *Advances in Consumer Research,* 25, ed. Joseph W. Alba and J. Wesley Hutchinson (Provo, UT: Association for Consumer Research, 1998), 25:349–356.
49. John Lynch and Thomas Srull, "Memory and Attentional Factors in Consumer Choice: Concepts and Research Methods," *Journal of Consumer Research* 9 (June 1982): 18–37.
50. Alan Collins and Elizabeth Loftus, "A Spreading Activation Theory of Semantic Processing," *Psychological Review* 56 (1975): 54–59.

51. J. Wesley Hutchinson and Daniel Moore, "Issues Surrounding the Examination of Delay Effects of Advertising," in *Advances in Consumer Research*, ed. Thomas Kinnear (Provo, UT: Association for Consumer Research, 1984), 11:650–55.

52. Kevin L. Keller, "Conceptualizing, Measuring, and Managing Customer-Based Brand Equity," *Journal of Marketing* 57 (January 1993): 1–22.

53. Tom J. Brown, "Schemata in Consumer Research: A Connectionist Approach," in *Diversity in Consumer Behavior: Advances in Consumer Research*, ed. John F. Sherry Jr. and Brian Sternthal (Provo, UT: Association for Consumer Research, 1992), 19:787–94.

54. Houston, Childers, and Heckler, "Picture–Word Consistency."

55. Mita Sujan, James Bettman, and Harish Sujan, "Effects of Consumer Expectations on Information Processing in Selling Encounters," *Journal of Marketing Research* 23 (November 1986): 346–53.

56. Julie Franz, "$95 Billion for What: Ads Remembered as Forgettable in 1985," *Advertising Age* 57 (March 3, 1986): 4.

57. Ernest Hilgard, Richard Atkinson, and Rita Atkinson, *Introduction to Psychology* (New York: Harcourt Brace Jovanovich, 1975).

58. Raymond Burke and Thomas Srull, "Competitive Interference and Consumer Memory for Advertising," *Journal of Consumer Research* 15 (June 1988): 55–68.

59. Charles E. Osgood, *Method and Theory in Experimental Psychology* (New York: Oxford University Press, 1964).

60. Robert Kent and Chris T. Allen, "Competitive Interference Effects in Consumer Memory for Advertising: The Role of Brand Familiarity," *Journal of Marketing* 58 (July 1994): 97–105.

61. Nader T. Tavassoli, "Language in Multimedia: Interaction of Spoken and Written Information," *Journal of Consumer Research* 25 (June 1998): 26–37.

62. Ibid.

63. Joseph Alba and Amitava Chattopadhyay, "Salience Effects in Brand Recall," *Journal of Marketing Research* 23 (November 1986): 363–69.

64. Lynch and Srull, "Memory and Attentional Factors."

65. Ibid.

66. Osgood, *Method and Theory.*

67. An interesting question is whether the interrupted story or the inserted material causing the interruption is recalled better. Research indicates that the inserted material may actually be more salient. See Richard Harris et al. "Language in Advertising: A Psycholinguistic Approach," *Current Issues and Research in Advertising* 9 (1986): 1–26.

68. H. Ebbinghaus, *Memory*, trans. H. A. Ruger and C. E. Bussenius (New York: Teachers College, 1913).

69. Hubert A. Zielske, "The Remembering and Forgetting of Advertising," *Journal of Marketing* 23 (January 1959): 231–43.

70. Meryl Gardner, "Mood States and Consumer Behavior: A Critical Review," *Journal of Consumer Research* 12 (December 1985): 281–300.

71. Patricia A. Knowles, Stephen J. Grove, and W. Jeffrey Burroughs, "An Experimental Examination of Mood Effects on Retrieval and Evaluation of Advertisement and Brand Information," *Journal of Academy of Marketing Science* 21 (spring 1993): 135–42. Also see Meryl Gardner, "Effects of Mood States on Consumer Information Processing," *Research in Consumer Behavior* 2 (1987): 113–35.

72. Angela Y. Lee and Brian Sternthal, "The Effects of Positive Mood on Memory," *Journal of Consumer Research* 26 (September 1999): 115–27.

73. Thomas Srull, "Memory, Mood, and Consumer Judgment," in *Advances in Consumer Research*, ed. Melanie Wallendorf and Paul Anderson (Provo, UT: Association for Consumer Research, 1986), 14:404–7.

Consumer Motivation

After studying this chapter, you should be able to describe each of the following concepts, together with their managerial relevance:

1. The concept of motivation.
2. Consumer needs.
3. Operant conditioning.
4. Classical conditioning.
5. Vicarious learning.
6. Opponent-process theory.
7. Optimum stimulation level.
8. Reactance theory.
9. Perceived risk.
10. Consumer attributions.

The investigation of motivation is central to understanding the acquisition, consumption, and disposition of goods, services, and ideas. Because of the practical importance of understanding consumer needs and desires, corporations spend billions of dollars on research to understand how they can motivate people to purchase the full range of consumer products—from automobiles to clothing to medical services. Investigating the dark side of consumer behavior, public-policy makers seek to determine what motivates people to consume cocaine, heroin, and other addictive drugs. Finally, the study of motivation helps to explain why some people enjoy such high-risk sports such as hang gliding, in which 1 in 250 participants dies each year.[1]

In this chapter we first define the concept of motivation. Next, we discuss four broad theories of motivation: (1) McClelland's theory of learned needs, (2) classical conditioning, (3) operant conditioning, and (4) vicarious learning. We then identify a number of midrange approaches to motivation, such as perceived risk. The chapter concludes with a discussion of the managerial implications of the consumer concepts.

WHAT IS MOTIVATION?

Motivation refers to an activated state within a person that leads to goal-directed behavior.[2] It consists of the varios needs, feelings, and desires that propel people to goal-directed behavior. Motivation begins with the presence of a stimulus that spurs the recognition of a need. The stimulus may come from inside the consumer; feeling hungry or the pursuit of a goal (e.g., a desire to travel) are types of internal stimuli that can result in need recognition. The stimulus can also come from outside the consumer, for example, an advertising message or a friend's comment about a product. If the stimulus causes an actual state of being to diverge from a desired state of being, a need results. **Need recognition** occurs when a perceived discrepancy exists between an actual and a desired state of being.

Researchers have differentiated between expressive and utilitarian needs.[3] **Expressive needs** involve desires by consumers to fulfill social, ego, or aesthetic requirements. Expressive needs are closely related to the maintenance of the self-concept of consumers. For example, expressive needs may be felt when outdated clothing fails to match a person's self-concept of being at the forefront of fashion. **Utilitarian needs** involve desires by consumers to solve basic problems, such as filling a car's gas tank or having enough money to pay bills.

Various generalizations have been made concerning the operation of needs. First, needs can be either innate or learned. People are genetically programmed to have various physiological needs, such as the need for food, air, water, and perhaps human contact. In addition, needs can be learned through conditioning processes and consumer socialization. A second generalization about needs is that they are never fully satisfied. That is, if one need is fulfilled, another will spring up to take its place. Of course, marketers attempt to fulfill these needs by creating products and services. Finally, a need state is accompanied by feelings and emotions.

The general term **affect** is used to describe the feelings, emotions, and moods experienced by consumers. As noted in chapter 4, emotions are differentiated from moods by their greater intensity and psychological urgency.[4] Researchers have identified 10 different emotional states that people can experience: interest, joy, surprise, anger, distress, disgust, contempt, fear, shame, and guilt.[5] Not surprisingly, researchers have also found that, when consumers' goals are satisfied, they experience a positive affective state. In contrast, when goals are thwarted, negative affect results.[6] In addition, emotions vary in terms of the amount of arousal associated with them. When the positive or negative affective state is combined with the level of arousal, four quadrants of emotions result. Thus, emotions can be positive–high arousal (e.g., joy, delight, ecstasy, elation), positive–low arousal (e.g., contented, serene, tranquil), negative–high arousal (e.g., anger, disgust, contempt), and negative–low arousal (e.g., fear, shame, guilt, depressed).[7]

SOME GENERAL THEORIES OF MOTIVATION

Most textbook discussions of motivation focus on describing certain well-known theories, such as Maslow's hierarchy of needs and Murray's social needs. (Figure 5.1 presents a brief review of the needs identified by Maslow and by Murray.) Indeed, by the

A.   Maslow's Hierarchy of Needs

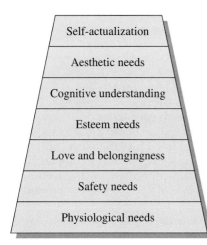

B.   Murray's List of Human Needs

Abasement	Harm avoidance
Achievement	Infavoidance
Affiliation	Nurturance
Aggression	Order
Autonomy	Play
Counteraction	Rejection
Defendance	Sentience
Deference	Sex
Dominance	Succorance
Exhibition	Understanding

Figure 5.1

Needs identified by Maslow and Murray.

Source: A. H. Maslow, *Motivation and Personality,* 2nd ed. (New York: Harper & Row, 1970); and H.A. Murray, Exploration in Personality (New York: Oxford, 1938).

time students take a consumer-behavior course, they have usually been exposed to the Maslow hierarchy in several other classes. The findings of the research performed on these theories, however, has been quite inconsistent. In particular, Maslow's hierarchy has been criticized for proposing a hierarchy of needs. For example, young adults have been found to focus more on self-actualization needs than older adults.[8] This finding is inconsistent with Maslow's concept that self-actualization is the last of the needs to be realized.

Although the ideas from the Maslow hierarchy have received mixed reviews, other broad theories of motivation have received research support. This section first describes McClelland's theory of learned needs and then presents three additional broad-based motivational theories that are derived from alternative views of behavioral learning—classical conditioning, operant conditioning, and vicarious learning.

McClelland's Theory of Learned Needs

David McClelland developed an important stream of research around the idea that four basic learned needs motivate people—the needs for achievement, affiliation, power, and uniqueness or novelty.[9] Those with a high **achievement motivation** seek to get ahead, strive for success, and take responsibility for solving problems. The **need for affiliation** reflects people's motivation to make friends, become members of groups, and associate with others. Those with a high need for affiliation tend to place the desire to be with others ahead of the need to succeed. The **need for power** refers to the desire to obtain and exercise control over others. The goal is to influence, direct, and possibly dominate other people. The need for power can take two directions, according to McClelland. It can be positive, resulting in persuasive and inspirational power, or it can be negative, resulting in the desire to dominate and obtain submission from others. Finally, the **need for uniqueness** refers to desires to perceive ourselves as different and original.

Some research has investigated the relationship between McClelland's ideas and consumer behavior. For example, a recent study investigated the motives for creating personal Web pages. The results were consistent with McClelland's learned needs: Among the possible motive statements, 74 percent matched one of the learned needs. The two motives most frequently identified were the need for affiliation (through personal portrayal and social interaction) and the need for power (by conquering technology). Surprisingly, the need for uniqueness was identified as the predominant motive in less than 25 percent of the respondents, and the need for achievement in less than 20 percent of the respondents.[10]

A clear prediction from McClelland's work is that products can be advertised with motivational themes derived from the four motives. Using the four needs identified by McClelland, managers can assess the predominant motives of the target market via market research. They can then develop advertising themes to activate the motive, which in turn influence attitudes, beliefs, and behaviors.

Classical Conditioning

Through the process of classical conditioning, a motivational state can be created that leads consumers to engage in a variety of behaviors that include responding more positively to advertisements, developing positive attitudes toward brands, purchasing more in restaurants and grocery stores, and purchasing more with their credit cards. In classical conditioning a neutral stimulus, such as a brand name, is paired with a stimulus that elicits a response. Through a repetition of the pairing, the neutral stimulus takes on the ability to elicit the response.

The Russian physiologist Ivan Pavlov discovered classical conditioning when he was working with dogs. The dogs had the propensity to begin salivating profusely (the response) each time meat powder (the stimulus) was presented to them. The stimulus of the meat powder reflexively elicited the response of salivation. When a bell was rung just prior to the dogs receiving the meat powder, the dogs began salivating to the sound of the bell. Thus, the neutral stimulus (the bell) began to activate a response (salivating).

When classical conditioning occurs, a previously neutral stimulus (called the **conditioned stimulus,** or CS) is repeatedly paired with the eliciting stimulus (called the **unconditioned stimulus,** or UCS). In such a pairing, the CS needs to occur prior to the UCS so that it predicts the UCS. After a number of such pairings, the ability to elicit an **unconditioned response** is transferred to the CS. The response elicited by the CS is called the **conditioned response** (CR).

Research on classical conditioning emphasizes that mere contiguity (or closeness in time) of the pairing of the CS with the UCS is not enough to achieve classical conditioning.[11] Conditioning results from the informational relationship of the CS and the UCS. For the CS to provide information about the UCS, it must predict the occurrence of the UCS. Figure 5.2 depicts these relationships. For optimal conditioning to occur, the CS should slightly precede the UCS in time.[12] In the experiments by Pavlov, the presence of the meat powder (the UCS) was preceded in time by the ringing of a bell (the CS). After a number of such pairings, the mere ringing of the bell would elicit the conditioned response of salivation (the CR).

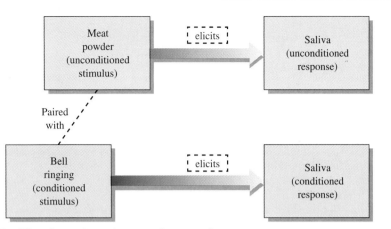

Figure 5.2 The classical-conditioning framework.

Researchers have found that a variety of stimuli may classically condition consumers. For example, music may influence consumers via a classical-conditioning process. In one experiment the tempo of music played in a grocery was varied over a nine-week period. At various times customers heard either no music, slow-tempo music, or fast-tempo music. When the pace at which customers moved between two points was measured, it was found that those in fast-tempo conditions moved significantly faster than did those in the slow-tempo conditions. Interestingly, daily gross sales volume was found to be 38 percent higher in the slow-tempo conditions.[13]

These results suggest that shoppers may be classically conditioned to respond to music. Thus fast-paced music elicits a response in which customers move faster. The fast pace, then, impedes buying. Similar findings have been obtained in a restaurant setting. When slow-tempo music was played, customers stayed longer at tables and purchased more from the bar. The estimated gross margin of the restaurant was significantly higher because of the increased bar sales.[14,]

In other studies researchers have found that credit-card insignias elicit spending responses.[15] In a carefully controlled series of studies, one group of subjects was placed in a spending situation in which the MasterCard logo was in view. Another group of subjects was placed in the same situation, but with the logo not present. The studies showed that the presence of the logo caused respondents to do the following: make buying decisions to spend more quickly, indicate that more would be spent on a clothing purchase and other consumer goods, estimate that they would give more to a charity, and actually give more to a charity.

In explaining the results, the author of the study proposed that credit cards become paired with the buying act. For many people the buying act takes on the properties of an unconditioned stimulus that elicits the unconditioned response of positive feelings. Through many pairings of the credit card with the buying act, the credit card becomes a conditioned stimulus that elicits a conditioned response of positive feelings. The positive feelings elicited by the credit card in turn make it more likely that a person will spend money when it is present.

In sum, evidence is accumulating that consumers respond to a variety of stimuli in a manner consistent with a classical-conditioning interpretation.[16] Through the conditioning process, unconditioned stimuli (such as brand names, credit-card logos, and so forth) take on motivational properties by influencing the desired state of

Some Key Concepts from Classical Conditioning That Apply to Consumer Behavior

1. *Unconditional stimulus.* The stimulus that elicits a response. For example, soothing music may elicit the responses of relaxation and positive feelings. Other examples of unconditioned stimuli in a consumer context are physically attractive people, beautiful visual scenes, the American flag (for U.S. citizens), and religious symbols.
2. *Unconditioned response.* The responses elicited by unconditioned stimulus.
3. *Conditioned stimulus.* A previously neutral stimulus that takes on some of the properties of the unconditioned stimulus when appropriately paired with it.
4. *Conditioned response.* The response elicited by the conditioned stimulus. It is generally a reduced version of the unconditioned response.
5. *Sign tracking.* The attention-drawing ability of unconditioned and conditioned stimuli.
6. *Higher-order conditioning.* The ability of a conditioned stimulus to classically condition another previously neutral stimulus.

TABLE 5.1

being. Table 5.1 summarizes the key concepts found in classical conditioning that apply to consumer behavior.

Operant Conditioning

Operant conditioning is a process by which the frequency of occurrence of a particular behavior is modified by the consequences of the behavior.[17] Thus, when a consumer emits a behavior, such as buying a product, the consequences of that behavior will change the probability of that behavior occurring again. If the behavior is positively reinforced—for example, the product performs well or friends compliment the fine purchase—the likelihood that the consumer will make the purchase again increases. If the behavior is punished—for example, the product fails or friends ridicule the purchase—the likelihood that the consumer will make the purchase again decreases. Reinforcers and punishers are strong motivators that dramatically impact consumer behavior.

The concepts of operant conditioning have wide application to consumer behavior and marketing management. Of particular importance is the analysis of the **contingencies of reinforcement** that impact consumers when purchasing and using goods or services. The study of the contingencies of reinforcement refers to the analysis of all the reinforcers and punishers that accompany the purchase of a product. The relationship, or contingency, between the time the reinforcers or punishers occur and the consumer's behavior influences the likelihood of that behavior occurring again. For instance, consider a consumer who goes into a fast-food restaurant to make a purchase. A variety of stimuli will act to reinforce or punish the consumer. Such factors as the cleanliness of the restaurant, speed of the lines, courtesy of the employees, and quality and price of the food can act as either reinforcers or punishers. Managers must carefully analyze these contingencies of reinforcement to determine their motivational impact on customers.

Table 5.2 identifies and defines nine key concepts of operant conditioning. These are discussed more fully in the sections that follow.

Reinforcement and Influencing Behavior. As noted previously, a **reinforcer** is anything that occurs after a behavior and that changes the likelihood that the behavior will occur again.[18] As such, reinforcers have strong motivational properties. There are

Some Basic Operant-Conditioning Principles

1. *Reinforcer.* A stimulus that increases the probability of repetition of the behavior that it follows.
2. *Positive reinforcer.* A stimulus whose *presence* as a consequence of a behavior increases the probability of the behavior recurring.
3. *Negative reinforcer.* A stimulus whose *disappearance* as a consequence of a behavior increases the probability that the behavior will recur.
4. *Secondary reinforcer.* A previously neutral stimulus that acquires reinforcing properties through its association with a primary reinforcer.
5. *Punisher.* A stimulus whose presence after a response decreases the likelihood of the behavior recurring.
6. *Shaping.* A process through which a new operant behavior is created by reinforcing successive approximations of the desired behavior.
7. *Extinction.* A gradual reduction in the frequency of occurrence of an operant behavior resulting from a lack of reinforcement of the response.
8. *Schedule of reinforcement.* The frequency and timing of reinforcers form a schedule of reinforcement that can dramatically influence the pattern of operant responses.
9. *Discriminative stimuli.* Stimuli that occur in the presence of a reinforcer and do not occur in its absence.

TABLE 5.2

three different types of reinforcers that influence the probability that these various behaviors will recur. A **positive reinforcer** involves placing an appropriate reward immediately after a behavior occurs. The reinforcer acts to increase the likelihood that a person will repeat the behavior. Giving consumers a $2,500 rebate if they purchase a particular brand of car is an example of a positive reinforcer.

A second type of reinforcer is a negative reinforcer. **Negative reinforcers** involve the removal of an aversive stimulus. That is, if a behavior results in the elimination of something negative, it is more likely to occur again in the future. Purchasing car insurance exemplifies a behavior performed to eliminate the effects of a negative stimulus (i.e., the cost of repairing a car or paying the medical bills of another). One humorous example of the use of a negative reinforcer happened in a fund drive sponsored by a nonprofit organization that operated a shelter for teenagers. The fund drive was called "The Great Gerbil Giveaway." People received a letter indicating that their name had been placed in a drawing to receive two gerbils. However, they could buy insurance against the possibility of winning the gerbils for a $5 or $10 contribution to the shelter. The letter noted that, without the insurance, "you just might WIN Gus and Gwendolyn who, we have it on an unimpeachable authority, 'Go for the Gusto,' and have multiplying personalities."[19] In other words, recipients had to engage in the behavior of making a cash contribution to avoid receiving a negative reinforcer in the form of two gerbils. Of course, the premise was that most people would rather pay $5 than receive the gerbils as a gift.

The third type of reinforcer is a **secondary reinforcer,** a previously neutral stimulus that acquires reinforcing properties through its association with a primary reinforcer. Early in one's life, all reinforcers are of a primary nature. Examples are the necessities required for life, such as food, water, salt, and soft touching. Over a period of time, previously neutral stimuli can become secondary reinforcers through their association with the primary reinforcer. The process occurs by pairing the neutral stimulus over and over with the primary stimuli. As a result of the pairing, the neutral stimulus will take on reinforcing properties similar to those of the primary stimuli. For example, if a mother coos softly just prior to softly touching her baby, over a period of time the soft cooing will itself become reinforcing to the baby. The result may be, however, that a mother might unconsciously condition a baby to cry so as to be picked up. If the mother cooed each time she picked up the child, the cooing would become a secondary reinforcer, leading the baby to emit behaviors simply to obtain the cooing.

In the marketing environment, most reinforcers are of a secondary nature. A product performing well, a reduction in price, and a friendly "hello" by a salesperson are all examples of secondary reinforcers. Even though they are secondary reinforcers, they still have a major impact on behavior.

Another operant-conditioning concept of importance to marketers is that of a punisher. A **punisher** is any stimulus whose presence after a behavior decreases the likelihood of the behavior recurring. For a marketer a key goal is to avoid punishing consumers for using the company's product or service. A great number of punishers exist in the environment to discourage product purchases. Some examples include poor product performance, ridicule of the product by friends, irritating actions or remarks by a salesperson, or stock outages of a product.

Extinction and Eliminating Behaviors. Once an operant response is conditioned, it will persist as long as it is periodically reinforced. However, if the operant response goes without reinforcement for an extended number of occasions, it will tend to disappear. This disappearance of a response due to lack of reinforcement is called **extinction.** Interestingly, immediately after the reinforcement ceases, the vigor of the response may actually increase. In humans the reaction is often anger. Suppose, for example, that a salesman over the years has reinforced his customers for buying his product by taking them out to lunch each time the product was purchased. Suddenly the salesman decides that this is too expensive and quits providing the reinforcer. The initial reaction of the customer may be anger, and the eventual outcome could be the extinction of the buying response.

Schedules of Reinforcement. The way in which reinforcers are applied can have an enormous impact on the behavior of consumers. A reinforcer does not have to be applied each time a particular behavior is emitted to reinforce it. In these intermittent **schedules of reinforcement,** the behavior is reinforced after a certain number of repetitions or after a certain length of time has passed. One outcome of using schedules of reinforcement is that the operant responses become more resistant to extinction. Thus, the reinforcer can be omitted for quite a number of cases and the behavior will still persist.

Automobile rebates provide an example of consumers being placed on an intermittent schedule of reinforcement. Automobile companies employ what is called a variable interval schedule—that is, the timing of when the rebates go into effect varies. Sometimes a rebate is put in place relatively quickly after the last one is discontinued. In other cases a considerable length of time passes before a new rebate program is initiated. This schedule conditions consumers to wait for rebates; such behavior is resistant to extinction. In a similar manner, casinos employ schedules of reinforcement to provide rewards to gamblers. For example, slot machines employ a variable ratio schedule in which people win only after the one-armed bandits are fed coins an indeterminate number of times.

Discriminative Stimuli. **Discriminative stimuli** are those stimuli that occur in the presence of a reinforcer and do not occur in its absence. They are like signals that indicate whether a reinforcer will be present if a behavior is emitted. Because the discriminative stimulus is paired with the reinforcer, the likelihood of the operant response occurring increases. The organism learns to emit the operant response when the discriminative stimulus is present and not to emit the response when it is absent. There is nothing special about a discriminative stimulus. For example, the word "sit" has no particular impact on a dog until it is followed by a dog biscuit (if the animal does sit on the floor). If the word is consistently followed by a reward after the behavior has appeared, it will come to gradually elicit the instrumental response of sitting.

From an operant-conditioning perspective, the messages and information that consumers receive about products and services act as discriminative stimuli.[20] Such information can signal the reinforcements that may result from a purchase. Discriminative stimuli are found in advertisements, on product packaging, and in the brand names, product logos, and other symbols used by marketers. The strategy of using branded products illustrates the managerial use of discriminative stimuli. Companies with broad product lines may identify each product as being a part of the same brand. Thus, for example, Campbell's clearly displays its name on every one of its soup products to cue consumers that each is produced by the same company. The distinctive cans have become discriminative stimuli that indicate to consumers that their contents will be reinforcing. The use of corporate logos has a similar function. Figure 5.3 diagrams the relationship among the discriminative stimulus, the behavior, and the reinforcer.

Shaping Consumer Responses. Have you ever wondered how animal trainers are able to teach assorted animals, such as dogs, killer whales, and elephants, to do bizarre tricks? Certainly, jumping through a hoop filled with fire is not an instinctive behavior for the average killer whale. Trainers use a process called shaping to teach animals such amazing tricks. Through **shaping,** totally new operant behaviors can be created by selectively reinforcing behaviors that successively approximate the desired instrumental response.

Companies strive to arrange contingencies so as to shape consumers. For instance, a car dealership might use the shaping process to encourage consumers to buy cars. First, they might provide free coffee and doughnuts to anyone who comes into the dealership. Next, the dealership would give $5 to a licensed driver who test drives a car. Third, they would give a $500 rebate to the person for buying the car. Finally, the dealership would provide outstanding service to the customer when the car is brought in for maintenance. The ultimate behavior desired is repeat buying from the dealership. To obtain the behavior, the actions of the consumer that lead to a desired terminal behavior are selectively reinforced.[21]

Vicarious Learning

Vicarious learning, which is also called **observational learning,** is a phenomenon whereby people observe the actions of others to develop "patterns of behavior."[22] For example, the observation of the effects of reinforcers and punishers on other people acts to influence the behavior of the observer. Vicarious learning creates a motivational state that may impact a variety of consumer behaviors from purchasing a product to learning a skill (e.g., riding a bicycle) to avoiding the buying of drugs.

Figure 5.3   The relationship among the discriminative stimulus, the behavior, and the reinforcer.

Three important ideas have emerged from observational-learning theory.[23] First, observational-learning theorists view people as symbolic beings who foresee the probable consequences of their behavior. People anticipate the future and vary their behavior accordingly. Second, people have the ability to regulate their own behavior. Through this self-regulatory process, people supply their own rewards and punishments internally by feeling either self-critical or self-satisfied. Third, people learn by watching the actions of others and the consequences of these actions (i.e., by vicarious learning). In particular, social-learning theorists emphasize the importance of models in transmitting information through observational learning.

A **model** is someone whose behavior a person attempts to emulate. The effectiveness of a model has been shown to increase in the following instances: [24]

1. The model is physically attractive.
2. The model is credible.
3. The model is successful.
4. The model is similar to the observer.
5. The model is shown overcoming difficulties and then succeeding.

The ability of models to cause consumers to engage in new behaviors is particularly important for companies introducing innovative products. For example, in order to broaden the appeal of its personal computers, IBM used principles of observational learning in its ads. One series of ads showed regular people, such as a "good-old-boy" farmer, going into a computer store, purchasing an IBM, and then using it effectively. The farmer was shown being reinforced by the positive consequences of using the computer when his neighbors were amazed that he could use such a device. Modeling processes can also be used to inhibit undesirable behaviors, such as using drugs. Finally, models can be employed to increase the likelihood that a previously learned behavior will occur. Examples of this type of vicarious learning may be found in attempts of companies to reposition a product or service. The Florida Citrus Growers Association, for instance, has for years attempted to persuade consumers to drink orange juice at times other than breakfast by showing attractive people drinking juice at lunch and dinner.

A Word of Warning

Although classical-conditioning, operant-conditioning, and observational-learning principles have major implications for managers and public-policy makers, a word of warning is in order. Some critics have questioned the consumer research that supports the applicability of classical conditioning. Similarly, in many of the consumer-behavior examples of operant conditioning, it is debatable whether people can be conditioned with so few pairings of behavior with reinforcer. It is possible that other theories, such as associative learning, may also explain the findings in classical and operant conditioning. For the manager, however, the key issue concerns whether one can influence consumer behavior by implementing classical-conditioning, operant-conditioning, and observational-learning procedures. The answer is a definite "yes." For the manager interested only in obtaining results, knowing exactly what processes account for the behavioral change is of little importance.

MIDRANGE THEORIES OF MOTIVATION

The trend over the past 20 years has been to move away from using broad theories of motivation, such as McClelland's social needs or operant conditioning, to using more

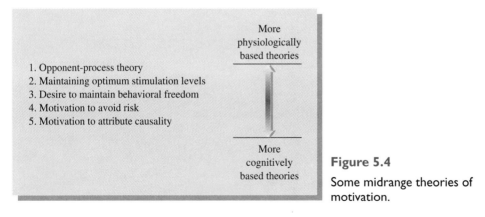

1. Opponent-process theory
2. Maintaining optimum stimulation levels
3. Desire to maintain behavioral freedom
4. Motivation to avoid risk
5. Motivation to attribute causality

More
physiologically
based theories

More
cognitively
based theories

Figure 5.4

Some midrange theories of
motivation.

restricted midrange theories to explain consumer motivation. The goal of each of the
midrange theories is to explain a narrower facet of human behavior.

Figure 5.4 lists the midrange theories of motivation that this chapter will discuss.
Their order of description moves from the more physiologically based theories (e.g.,
opponent-process theory) to the more cognitively oriented (e.g., attribution theory).

Opponent-Process Theory

A researcher once made an interesting observation about the emotional reactions of
parachutists. During their first free fall, before the parachute opens, beginners show
every sign of experiencing terror. They yell, their eyes bulge, their bodies go stiff, and
they breathe irregularly. Upon landing safely, they at first walk around stunned, with
stony-faced expressions. Then they begin smiling, talking, gesticulating, and showing
every indication of being elated. Why would someone who was in terror suddenly
become elated? The answer is found in a theory of motivation called the opponent-
process theory of acquired motivation.[25]

According to **opponent-process theory,** when a person receives a stimulus that
elicits an immediate positive or negative emotional reaction, two things happen. First,
the immediate positive or negative emotional reaction is felt. Next, a second emotional reaction occurs that has a feeling opposite to that initially experienced. The
combination of the two emotional reactions results in the overall feeling experienced
by the consumer. Because the second emotional reaction is delayed, the consumer
first experiences the initial positive or negative feeling. After some time period, however, this feeling gradually declines and the opposite feeling begins to be felt. Thus,
the parachutists first felt extreme fear, but after landing the fear turned to its opposite
emotion—elation. Figure 5.5 diagrams these relationships.

Although opponent-process theory is quite simple, it has broad explanatory
power. It accounts for a variety of consumer behaviors, such as drug addiction, cigarette smoking, jogging and marathoning, sauna bathing, and playing video games. For
example, why would seemingly sane individuals go through the pain of running a
marathon? The answer is that, through the operation of opponent processes, the pain
that accompanies the endurance run is followed by physiological pleasure. When such
a feeling is combined with the positive reinforcement from friends and acquaintances,
marathoning for some people is extremely positive.

Opponent-process theory can also explain why some consumers sink into debt
from overusing their credit cards. According to this theory, in order to make themselves

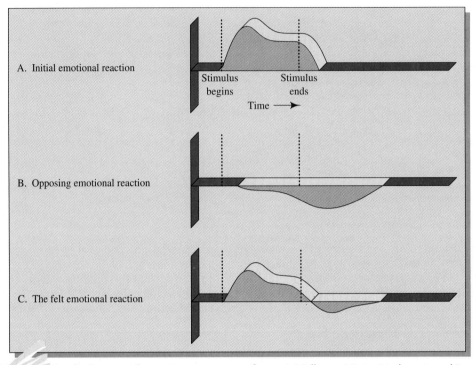

A. Initial emotional reaction

Stimulus begins   Stimulus ends

Time ⟶

B. Opposing emotional reaction

C. The felt emotional reaction

Figure 5.5   A diagram of opponent processes for an initially positive stimulus, e.g., taking an addictive drug.

feel better, consumers use a credit card to make a purchase. After the purchase, however, the good feelings begin to turn bad because of the negative rebound. The bills that inevitably arrive further exacerbate the negative feelings. To combat the negative feelings, the consumer again visits the local mall or calls a favorite mail-order company to make another purchase. The vicious circle can result in major financial problems.

Another concept that has emerged from opponent-process theory is priming. **Priming** occurs when a small amount of exposure to a stimulus (e.g., food, playing a video game, or navigating the Internet) leads to an increased drive to be in the presence of the stimulus. An example is taste cravings. After eating one potato chip, it is extremely hard for most people to stop and not have more. The taste of the first potato chip activates the person such that the drive to consume additional chips is greater than the drive was prior to eating the first one.

Marketers intuitively use principles of priming on a regular basis. Providing samples in a supermarket is a classic example of priming. In one study it was found that providing free samples of donuts to grocery-store shoppers resulted in consumers spending more than they had intended.[26]

Maintaining Optimum Stimulation Levels

Consumers have a strong motivation to maintain an **optimum stimulation level,** which is defined as a person's preferred amount of physiological activation or arousal. Activation may vary from very low levels (e.g., sleep) to very high levels (e.g., severe panic). Individuals are motivated to maintain an optimum level of stimulation and will take action to correct the level when it becomes too high or too low.

Internal and external factors may influence a person's level of stimulation at any given point in time. Internal factors include the individual's age, learning history, and personality characteristics. For example, people who prefer higher levels of stimulation score high on a scale that measures sensation seeking.[27] To maintain the high levels of stimulation required, sensation seekers are more apt to engage in such activities as parachute jumping, mountain climbing, gambling, and such. External factors influencing the stimulation level are those that affect the uncertainty and risk of the environment. Thus, if a person seeks a goal and some doubt exists as to whether the goal can be reached, his or her level of activation tends to rise. If the arousal level is too high, the individual takes steps to lower it. Conversely, if activation is too low, the individual takes action to raise the amount of stimulation in order to maintain an optimum level.

The desire to maintain an optimum stimulation level explains why consumers seek variety in their purchases, such as for restaurants, music, and leisure activities. **Variety seeking** occurs when a consumer selects a new brand or activity while still having a high degree of satisfaction with the current brand. Indeed, researchers have found that consumers will even switch temporarily to less-preferred options just to create variety in their lives.[28]

The desire of people to maintain an optimum stimulation level has wide implications for marketers because a host of products and services act to arouse or depress a person's activation level. For example, various types of drugs lower arousal levels (e.g., sleep aids) or raise arousal levels (e.g., stimulants such as caffeine and amphetamines). Many leisure activities strongly influence levels of arousal, such as parachute jumping, white-water rafting, and hunting. Indeed, the desire of consumers to attend sporting events is likely to be influenced in part by the need for excitement. Similarly, some rides at amusement parks are built to scare their customers, thus raising the stimulation level.

The desire for hedonic experiences is closely related to the need to maintain an optimum stimulation level. For consumer researchers, **hedonic consumption** refers to the needs of consumers to use products and services to create fantasies, to gain feelings through the senses, and to obtain emotional arousal.[29] The feelings that consumers seek to gain, however, may not be uniformly pleasurable. Particularly in their leisure activities, consumers may seek to experience a variety of emotions, such as love, joy, and fear. It may seem odd that someone would seek out negative experiences, such as fear. However, remember that roller coasters are built to create fear. Even their names are designed to instill fright, such as "Screamer" and "The Beast." Horror movies are created to frighten and disgust people. Similarly, the writer Steven King has made millions of dollars selling fear in his novels. People go to movies and read books to experience a variety of secondhand emotions, such as love, excitement, and fear. In each case the underlying goal involves maintaining optimum stimulation levels.

The Desire to Maintain Behavioral Freedom

Psychological reactance is the negative motivational state that results when a person's behavioral freedom has been threatened.[30] The motive to maintain behavioral freedom has broad implications for marketers. If the freedom to select a product or service is impeded, consumers respond by reacting against the threat.

An example of reactance was found among loyal users of Crayola crayons in response to actions by the product's producer, Binney & Smith. A few years ago, corporate managers of Binney & Smith retired eight colors from the popular 64-crayon flip-top box and replaced them with more contemporary colors. "Boring" colors such as raw umber, maize, and lemon yellow were eliminated and replaced by sexy new hues, including wild strawberry, fuchsia, teal blue, and cerulean. Consumers reacted to the change with a boycott. In one march protestors carried a coffin. One marcher declared, "They call it a retirement. I call it a burial." A first grader named Ebony Faison said, "Whenever I draw me, I use raw umber. What color should I color now?"[31] For a year following the change, the company received over 300 calls and letters each month protesting the change. One spokesperson admitted, "We were aware of the loyalty and nostalgia surrounding Crayola crayons, but we didn't know we hit such a nerve."[32]

In some cases marketers intentionally use reactance principles to influence consumers. Thus, sharp restrictions of the supply of products can increase demand because their perceived value increases as a result of reactance. For example, one-day-only sales increase consumer desires to make purchases more than do three-day-only sales.

Two types of threats can lead to reactance. **Social threats** involve external pressure from other people to induce a consumer to do something. Examples include pressing the consumer to buy a certain product, go to a certain play, or vote for a particular political candidate. If the pressure is too great, the consumer may react against it—resulting in a "boomerang effect." In such instances the consumer moves in the opposite direction intended by the person engaging in the social-influence attempt. In the personal-selling area of marketing, the problem of boomerang effects is great. Salespeople must take definite steps to persuade customers to buy their products. However, they cannot push too hard or they risk alienating the prospect. A time-tested strategy is to give customers information so that they can persuade themselves that the product is the right one to buy.

A second threat to behavioral freedom comes from impersonal sources. Generally, **impersonal threats** are barriers that restrict the ability to buy a particular product or service. The barriers may result from a shortage of the product, from the possibility that someone else will buy the product, or even from a rise in its price. In each case something comes between the consumer and the purchase of the product. The consumer's likely reaction is to reevaluate the product and want it even more. Even the decision to buy one product over another can result in the person's reevaluating the unchosen alternatives more positively.[33]

For consumers to experience reactance, three requirements must be met. First, the consumer must believe that he or she has the freedom to make a free choice in a given situation. If the general ability to make a choice is unavailable—perhaps because there are no alternative products—reactance will not occur. Second, a threat to the freedom must be experienced. Third, the decision must be one that is of some importance to the consumer.[34]

Perceived Risk and Consumer Motivation

Perceived risk is defined as a consumer's perception of the overall negativity of a course of action based on an assessment of the possible negative outcomes and of the likelihood that those outcomes will occur.[35] As such, perceived risk consists of two major concepts—the negative outcomes of a decision and the probability that these outcomes will occur.

Consumers are constantly faced with decisions that involve uncertainty and the possibility of negative outcomes. Indeed, almost any high-involvement decision a consumer makes involves uncertainty. In general, consumers are risk averse in their actions, although exceptions to the rule do exist. As previously noted, some consumers appear to seek risk in part to raise their activation levels to optimum levels.[36]

Types of Consumer Risks. The first discussion of the concept of perceived risk appeared in marketing literature in 1960.[37] Since that time much of the effort of con-

Types of Perceived Risk

1. *Financial.* Risk that the outcome will harm the consumer financially (e.g., will buying a car cause financial hardship?).
2. *Performance.* Risk that the product will not perform as expected (e.g., will the car really accelerate faster than a Porsche 928?).
3. *Physical.* Risk that the product will physically harm the buyer (e.g., will the car collapse in a crash?).
4. *Psychological.* Risk that the product will lower the consumer's self-image (e.g., a swinging single wonders, will I look like a typical housewife if I buy this car?).
5. *Social.* Risk that friends or acquaintances will deride the purchase (e.g., will my best friend think that I am trying to show him up by buying a Porsche?).
6. *Time.* Risk that a decision will cost too much time (e.g., will buying a sports car cost me time because I have to tune it so frequently?).
7. *Opportunity cost.* Risk that by taking one action the consumer will miss out on doing something else he or she would really prefer to do (e.g., by buying a Porsche 928, will I miss out on buying several expensive oil paintings?).

TABLE 5.3

sumer researchers has been to identify the various types of risk that impact consumers. Table 5.3 lists seven different types of risk to which consumers may respond: financial, performance, physical, psychological, social, time, and opportunity cost.[38]

The promotional work of marketers is often geared toward lowering the perceived risk of consumers. Advertisements may be used to point out how a particular product or service may lower risk. For example, insurance advertising stresses the reduction of financial risk. Automobile manufacturers, such as Volvo, mention the reduction of physical risk when touting the safety of their brands. Many advertisements for personal-use products use a theme of reducing social risk. For example, products are available to help consumers ward off "ring around the collar," bad breath, and dandruff, all of which can cause social embarrassment. Deodorant ads frequently use a social-risk theme. For example, by using the right deodorant, you can "raise your hand, if you're sure."

Factors Influencing the Perception of Risk. Researchers have found that a number of factors influence the amount of risk consumers perceive in a given situation. First, the characteristics of the individual consumer influence his or her perception of risk. Researchers have found that the following personal characteristics are associated with a greater willingness to accept risk: higher self-confidence, higher self-esteem, lower anxiety, and lower familiarity with the problem.

Second, the nature of the task influences risk perception. For example, researchers have found that voluntary risks are more acceptable to people than involuntary risks.[39] Voluntary risks include such things as choosing to drive a car on a trip or to go on a ski vacation. Involuntary risks include living in a home near where a nuclear power plant is being built or undergoing surgery for a life-threatening condition. For voluntary activities consumers perceive systematically less risk than there really is. In contrast, for involuntary activities consumers perceive more risk than is actually present.

Third, the characteristics of the product or service can also influence perceived risk. In general, products or services whose use may result in highly negative outcomes are quite logically perceived as riskier. Factors associated with such negative outcomes include its cost, its social visibility, and the potential physical danger in its use. For example, most people consider owning a gun as posing risk.

Finally, risk perception may also be influenced by the saliency of the negative outcomes that could result from a purchase or activity. When negative outcomes resulting from product or service failures are highly salient, they may be more available in memory, and consumers may erroneously perceive the product or service as riskier than it really is.[40] For example, in 1996 a ValuJet passenger plane crashed into the Everglades swamp in Florida. A new, start-up airline, ValuJet was grounded for many months until questions concerning its safety and maintenance practices were answered. The publicity over the crash and over the safety of new airlines scared consumers. Their perception of the risk of flying all new airlines increased. As a result, passengers avoided carriers such as Kiwi International Air Lines and Frontier Airlines. As one airline president noted, media coverage left the impression that "if you're not a major airline, you're not safe.[41]

How Consumers Reduce Perceived Risk. Because some degree of perceived risk is inherent in nearly all consumer decisions, individuals must have methods that help them to make decisions with some confidence. One important theory is that consumers compare their perception of the amount of risk present to some criterion of how much risk is acceptable. In this view consumers may be seen as comparing the perceived risk to the acceptable risk.[42] If the perceived risk is greater than the acceptable risk, the consumer is motivated to either reduce the risk in some way or forgo making the decision. What actions do consumers take to reduce the amount of risk perceived in a decision? In general, all the risk-reduction strategies involve taking steps to lower the perceived likelihood that negative outcomes will occur. The following are six such risk-reduction strategies:

1. Be brand loyal and consistently purchase the same brand.
2. Buy through brand image and purchase a quality national brand.
3. Buy through store image from a retailer that you trust.
4. Seek out information in order to make a well-informed decision.
5. Buy the most expensive brand, which is likely to have high quality.
6. Buy the least expensive brand in order to reduce financial risk.

The Motivation to Attribute Causality

As consumers move through their everyday life, events happen for which they seek explanations. The performance of a good or service may fall below expectations, a product endorser may strongly tout a brand of soft drink, a salesperson may flatter a customer's ego, or a company-related disaster may occur (e.g., the crash of an airliner). In each case consumers will seek to understand the cause for the action. They will want to identify why the product brought dissatisfaction, why the endorser advocated buying the soft drink, why the salesperson was so ingratiating, or why the airliner crashed.[43]

The explanation of the processes by which people make such determinations of the causality of action has been labeled attribution theory.[44] According to **attribution theory,** people attempt to determine whether the cause of an action was something internal or external to the person or object in question. Thus, if the referent is another person (e.g., a product endorser), a consumer may ask whether the endorser recommended the product because he or she actually liked the product (an **internal attribution**) or because he or she was paid for endorsing it (an **external attribution**). Similarly, if someone asks the person why he or she bought a particular brand, the consumer then seeks to determine if the cause of action was something internal to the product (e.g., the product's good qualities) or something external to the product (e.g., pressure from a salesperson or a temporary reduction in price). By identifying the reason for an action, people gain control over their environment, which is important. Indeed, researchers have recently found that one reason that people are attracted to the World Wide Web is that it gives them a sense of control.[45]

People are motivated to make attributions as to the cause of an action in order to determine how to act in the future. Thus, if a consumer decides that an endorser advocates a product merely because he or she is paid a great deal of money, the consumer will attribute the cause of the message to an external factor (the money) rather than to an internal factor (the endorser's liking for the product). Such an attribution will result in the message having little or no impact on the consumer's attitude toward the product. Because consumers frequently make external attributions to the endorsements of highly paid celebrities, companies seek endorsers who have not previously endorsed products. In 1999 examples of such endorsers were Michelle Pfeiffer, Bruce Willis, and Harrison Ford.

Consumers also make attributions as to the cause of the purchase of a brand. For example, if a brand is purchased when a large price discount is given, consumers may reveal less brand loyalty because they attribute the purchase to the sale rather than to the quality of the product. Interestingly, however, if the consumer believes that he or she was responsible for receiving the price discount, the attitude toward the brand increases, which results in repurchases and positive word-of-mouth communications.[46] One means for retailers to influence self-responsibility attributions is to give out cards that are punched each time the consumer makes a purchase. After 10 or so purchases, the person gets a free video rental, submarine sandwich, or whatever.

In addition, circumstances can cause attributions that will benefit a brand. For example, suppose that a consumer has purchased a high-priced brand. If asked why he or she bought such a high-priced product, the consumer may attribute the purchase to the high quality of the product. It is as though the consumer said to him- or herself, "The product must be good, or why would I have bought it at such a high price?" The consumer made an internal attribution because the product was bought despite its high price.

Attribution theory is actually composed of a family of theories, each of which explains how people determine causality in various situations. Insufficient space exists to discuss each of the attribution theories; only two will be examined here—the augmenting–discounting model of Harold Kelley and the theory of the fundamental attribution error.

The Augmenting–Discounting Model. The augmenting–discounting model is based on the idea that people examine the environmental pressures that impede or propel a particular action in order to determine the underlying cause for the behavior.[47] The **discounting principle** states that the role of a particular cause in producing a given outcome is discounted if other plausible causes are also present. Thus, discounting occurs if external pressures could provoke someone to act in a particular way. That is, the actions would be expected given the circumstances. In this case people believe that the actions were caused by the environment rather than by the person's actual beliefs, feelings, and desires. In such circumstances the person discounts the action as representing the other's real beliefs. An example would be making the judgment that the money paid to a celebrity caused him or her to endorse a particular product.

What happens if a person moves against environmental pressures to do something? In this instance the action would be unexpected given the circumstances. As a consequence, the observer infers that the person must have been highly internally motivated. The **augmenting principle** states that, when a person moves against the forces of the environment to do something unexpected, the belief that the action represents the person's actual opinions, feelings, and desires is increased. An example of the augmenting principle is a computer salesperson who tells a prospective customer that a competitor's computer is superior to one this company sells. In such an instance, the salesperson would be moving against his or her own best interests. Such an unexpected event would augment the consumer's feeling that the salesperson really believed the statement. It would also increase the customer's trust in the salesperson.

One of the major difficulties faced by marketers is how to avoid having consumers discount their messages. Consumers recognize that pressures exist to sell products and to make profits. Thus, when they watch advertisements on television or receive promotional messages, they tend to discount the message and make external attributions. In general, consumers are not particularly confident that promotional messages accurately describe the characteristics of products. For example, over 59 percent of the respondents in one study found "statistical" claims in advertisements to be unbelievable.[48]

The Fundamental Attribution Error. The fundamental attribution error states that people have a systematic bias to make internal attributions for the cause of the action of others. According to this view, when an individual or organization engages in an action that results in a particular outcome, observers tend to believe that the cause of the action was the person's or organization's true beliefs or policies. This occurs even when in reality the person or organization had no choice in the matter or the outcome was caused by purely external forces.[49]

The fundamental attribution error can have both positive and negative effects for corporations. On the positive side, it can benefit both salespeople[50] and celebrity endorsers because the bias causes consumers to believe that the salesperson or celebrity endorser strongly advocates the brand because of their true feelings (i.e., an internal attribution) rather than because of the money they receive (i.e., an external attribution).[51] On the negative side, if a problem occurs in the provision of a service (e.g., a product is received late or a bad experience occurs in a restaurant), the fundamental attribution error increases the likelihood that blame will be placed on the company rather than to external causes.[52]

Table 5.4 summarizes the managerial applications of attribution theory.

Managerial Applications of Attribution Theory

1. *Develop believable advertisements.* Use strategies that enhance message augmentation by influencing consumers to perceive that the endorsement was made for internally caused, rather than externally caused, reasons.
2. *Develop messages that give both sides of arguments.* Particularly include messages that would be unexpected from the organization.
3. *Resolve product problems.* Respond quickly and proactively to product problems to enhance consumer beliefs that the cause of the problem should be attributed to bad luck rather than to the intentions or negligence of the firm.
4. *Assess sales promotions.* Use sales promotions cautiously to avoid having consumers attribute the cause of their purchase to the incentive rather than to the product's qualities.

TABLE 5.4

THE MANAGERIAL IMPLICATIONS OF MOTIVATION

The principles and concepts of motivation have application to each of the five PERMS concepts. These are discussed in the following sections.

Positioning and Differentiation

The principles underlying discriminative stimuli in operant conditioning have direct application to positioning and differentiation. Brand names, product logos, and various symbols can be employed that denote the brand and distinguish it from others. Such symbols can act to uniquely position the brand and differentiate it from competitors. In addition, brands can be positioned by associating them with specific motivational needs that they fulfill. For example, Volvo has associated its cars with fulfilling needs for safety. In contrast, Pontiac has associated its vehicles with arousal needs (e.g., the "We Build Excitement" ad campaign).

Environmental Analysis

As used in operant-conditioning theory, the study of the contingencies of reinforcement involves an examination of the punishers and reinforcers that consumers receive when purchasing a good or service. In this examination managers must carefully analyze the nature of the environment in which the purchase is made. The analysis should include attention to the temperature, lighting, and smells in the retail store, the smiles and frowns of sales personnel, and the time taken to serve consumers. All of these factors and more represent aspects of environmental stimuli that have either reinforcing or punishing qualities.

The nature of the environment also influences the perception of risk by consumers. For example, the tourism industry is strongly impacted by the threat of terrorism. Similarly, tourism can be impacted by the natural environment, which can lead to perceptions of risks, such as when a hurricane threatens or when an earthquake rocks a country (e.g., Turkey in 1999).

Research

Marketing research is required to measure the dominant motivational tendencies of the target market. In particular, managers should perform analyses to assess a target market's dominant needs. For example, from the perspective of McClelland's social needs, is the target market focused more on the need for affiliation, power, achievement, or uniqueness? Similarly, what is the need for arousal of the target market? Does the target market perceive a high degree of risk associated with the category of the product a company offers?

Marketing Mix

The study of motivation has particular relevance to the product and promotion components of the marketing mix. Products can be designed to fulfill the motivational needs of consumers, for example, offering extremely safe products (e.g., a safe car or an insurance policy) to a segment of consumers that places a high premium on risk avoidance. Other consumers may place a high value on affiliation needs. Products can then be developed that meet such desires, such as resorts that cater to college students at spring break.

The motivational needs of consumers can also be identified and promotional messages designed to link a product to fulfilling these needs. Thus, a resort that targets college students at spring break will employ themes and images that emphasize affiliation and the fulfillment of the need for arousal. Conversely, a resort that targets young couples with children would employ themes involving a focus on safety, security, and entertainment.

Segmentation

The motivational needs of consumers can also be employed as segmentation variables. For example, marketers have recently recognized that a segment of consumers possesses a high need for arousal and seeks high-risk vacations. In response, companies are promoting adventures, such as climbing Mount Everest, riding in a jet fighter, and rafting down white-water rapids. Similarly, cereal brands target consumers with divergent motivational needs. Thus, Total cereal targets those motivated to protect their bodies (the physical needs of Maslow), whereas Wheaties targets those motivated to achieve in sports.

Notes

1. Richard L. Celsi, Randall L. Rose, and Thomas W. Leigh, "An Exploration of High-Risk Leisure Consumption through Skydiving," *Journal of Consumer Research* 20 (June 1993): 1–23.
2. Ernest Hilgard, Richard Atkinson, and Rita Atkinson, *Introduction to Psychology*, 6th ed. (New York: Harcourt Brace Jovanovich, 1975).
3. Robert A. Westbrook, "Product/Consumption-Based Affective Responses and Post-purchase Processes," *Journal of Marketing Research* 24 (August 1987): 258–70.
4. Deborah J. MacInnis and Bernard J. Jaworski, "Information Processing from Advertisements: Toward an Integrative Framework," *Journal of Marketing* 53 (October 1989): 1–23.
5. Carroll E. Izard, *Human Emotion* (New York: Plenum Press, 1977).
6. John P. Murray Jr. and Peter A. Dacin, "Cognitive Moderators of Negative-Emotion Effects: Implications for Understanding Media Context," *Journal of Consumer Research* 22 (March 1996): 439–47.
7. Elizabeth C. Hirschman and Barbara B. Stern, "The Roles of Emotion in Consumer Research," in *Advances in Consumer Research*, ed. Eric J. Arnould and Linda M. Scott (Provo, UT: Association for Consumer Research, 1999), 26:4–11.
8. Lynn Kahle, David Bousch, and Pamela Homer, "Broken Rungs in Abraham's Ladder: Is Maslow's Hierarchy Hierarchical?" *Proceedings of the Society for Consumer Psychology* (1988).
9. David C. McClelland, *Human Motivation* (New York: Cambridge University Press, 1987).
10. George M. Zinkhan et al., "Motivation Underlying the Creation of Personal Web Pages: An Exploratory Study," *Advances in Consumer Research*, ed. Eric J. Arnould and Linda M. Scott (Provo, UT: Association for Consumer Research, 1999), 26:69–74.
11. Robert Rescorla, "Pavlovian Conditioning: It's Not What You Think It Is," *American Psychologist* 43 (March 1988): 151–60. A "cognitive revolution" has taken place in the understanding of classical conditioning. The idea that actions follow stimuli in a reflexive manner is no longer held by theorists. See Terence A. Shimp, "The Role of Subject Awareness in Classical Conditioning: A Case of Opposing Ontologies and Conflicting Evidence," in *Advances in Consumer Research*, ed. Rebecca Holman and Michael Solomon (Provo, UT: Association for Consumer Research, 1991), 18:158–63.
12. An excellent review of applications of classical conditioning and operant conditioning to marketing may be found in Walter R. Nord and J. Paul Peter, "A Behavior Modification Perspective on Marketing," *Journal of Marketing* 40 (spring 1980): 36–47.
13. Ronald E. Milliman, "Using Background Music to Affect the Behavior of Supermarket Shoppers," *Journal of Marketing* 42 (summer 1982): 86–91.
14. Ronald E. Milliman, "The Influence of Background Music on the Behavior of Restaurant Patrons," *Journal of Consumer Research* 13 (September 1986): 286–89; Elnora W. Stuart, Terence A. Shimp, and Randall W. Engle, "Classical Conditioning of Consumer Attitudes: Four Experiments in an Advertising Context," *Journal of Consumer Research* 14 (December 1987): 334–49.
15. Richard A. Feinberg, "Credit Cards as Spending Facilitating Stimuli: A Conditioning Perspective," *Journal of Consumer Research* 13 (December 1986): 348–56.
16. Terence A. Shimp, Elnora W. Stuart, and Randall W. Engle, "A Program of Classical Conditioning Experiments Testing Variations in the Conditioned Stimulus and the Context," *Journal of Consumer Research* 18 (June 1991): 1–12.
17. This section on operant conditioning relies heavily on G. S. Reynolds, *A Primer of Operant Conditioning* (Glenview, IL: Scott Foresman, 1968).

18. William Gaidis and James Cross, "Behavior Modification as a Framework for Sales Promotion Management," *Journal of Consumer Marketing* 4 (spring 1987): 65–74. Gordon Foxall has developed another view on the types of reinforcers in which he distinguishes hedonic from informational reinforcers; see Gordon R. Foxall, "The Behavioral Perspective Model of Purchase and Consumption: From Consumer Theory to Marketing Practice," *Journal of the Academy of Marketing Sciences* 20 (spring 1992): 189–98.

19. Dolores Curran, "Putting the 'Fun' Back in Fundraisers," *Eastern Oklahoma Catholic,* April 21, 1991, p. 21.

20. Foxall, "Behavioral Perspective Model."

21. This example may be found in Nord and Peter, "Behavior Modification Perspective."

22. Albert Bandura, *Social Learning Theory* (Upper Saddle River, NJ: Prentice Hall, 1977).

23. Hilgard, Atkinson, and Atkinson, *Introduction to Psychology.*

24. Charles C. Manz and Henry P. Sims, "Vicarious Learning: The Influence of Modeling on Organizational Behavior," *Academy of Management Journal* 6 (January 1981): 105–13.

25. Richard L. Solomon, "The Opponent-Process Theory of Acquired Motivation," *American Psychologist* 35 (August 1980): 691–712.

26. Sandon A. Steinberg and Richard F. Yalch, "When Eating Begets Buying: The Effects of Food Samples on Obese and Nonobese Shoppers," *Journal of Consumer Research* 4 (March 1978): 243–46.

27. Marvin Zuckerman, *Sensation Seeking: Beyond the Optimum Level of Arousal* (Hillsdale, NJ: Lawrence Erlbaum, 1979).

28. Rebecca K. Ratner, Barbara E. Kahn, and Daniel Kahneman, "Choosing Less-Preferred Experiences for the Sake of Variety," *Journal of Consumer Research* 26 (June 1999): 1–15; Satya Menon and Barbara E. Kahn, "The Impact of Context on Variety Seeking in Product Choice," *Journal of Consumer Research* 22 (December 1995): 285–95.

29. Morris Holbrook and Elizabeth Hirschman, "The Experiential Aspects of Consumption: Consumer Fantasies, Feelings, and Fun," *Journal of Consumer Research* 9 (September 1982): 132–40.

30. Jack W. Brehm, *A Theory of Psychological Reactance* (New York: Academic Press, 1966). For a review of consumers research on reactance, see Greg Lessne and M. Venkatesan, "Reactance Theory in Consumer Research: The Past, Present, and Future," in *Advances in Consumer Research,* ed. Thomas K. Srull (Provo, UT: Association for Consumer Research, 1989), 16:76–78.

31. Virginia Daut, "Roses Were Reds, Violets Blues, till They Redid Crayola's Hues," *Wall Street Journal,* September 11, 1990, p. B1.

32. Suein L. Hwang, "Hue and Cry over Crayola May Revive Old Colors," *Wall Street Journal,* June 14, 1991, p. B1.

33. Darwyn Linder and Katherine Crane, "Reactance Theory Analysis of Predecisional Cognitive Processes," *Journal of Personality and Social Psychology* 15 (July 1970): 258–64.

34. Mona Clee and Robert Wicklund, "Consumer Behavior and Psychological Reactance," *Journal of Consumer Research* 6 (March 1980): 389–405.

35. G. R. Dowling, "Perceived Risk: The Concept and Its Measurement," *Psychology and Marketing* 3 (fall 1986): 193–210. For another discussion of problems in defining the concept, see James Bettman, "Information Integration in Consumer Risk Perception: A Comparison of Two Models of Component Conceptualization," *Journal of Applied Psychology* 60 (1975): 381–85.

36. For a recent discussion and model of perceived risk, see Grahame R. Dowling and Richard Staelin, "A Model of Perceived Risk and Intended Risk-Handling Activity," *Journal of Consumer Research* 21 (June 1994): 119–34.

37. Raymond A. Bauer, "Consumer Behavior as Risk Taking," in *Dynamic Marketing for a Changing World,* ed. Robert S. Hancock (Chicago, IL: American Marketing Association, 1960), 87.

38. The first five risks in Table 5.3 were identified by Jacob Jacoby and Leon Kaplan, "The Components of Perceived Risk," in *Advances in Consumer Research,* ed. M. Venkatesan (Chicago, IL: Association for Consumer Research, 1972), 3:382–83. Social risk was identified by J. Paul Peter and Michael Ryan, "An Investigation of Perceived Risk at the Brand Level," *Journal of Marketing Research* 13 (May 1976): 184–88. Opportunity cost was identified by William Zikmund and Jerome Scott, "A Factor Analysis of the Multi-Dimensional Nature of Perceived Risk," *Proceedings of the Southern Marketing Association* (Houston, TX: 1973), 1036.

39. Baruch Fischhoff, Paul Slovic, and Sarah Lichtenstein, "Which Risks Are Acceptable?" *Environment* 21 (January 1979): 17–38.

40. Valerie S. Folkes, "The Availability Heuristic and Perceived Risk," *Journal of Consumer Research* 15 (June 1988): 13–23.

41. Susan Carey and Martha Brannigan, "Fearful Fliers Avoid Discount Carriers," *Wall Street Journal*, August 30, 1996, p. B1.

42. Donald Popielarz, "An Exploration of Perceived Risk and Willingness to Try New Products," *Journal of Marketing Research* 4 (November 1967): 368–72.

43. Brian K. Jorgensen, "Consumer Reaction to Company-Related Disasters: The Effect of Multiple versus Single Explanations," in *Advances in Consumer Research*, ed. Chris Allen and Deborah Roedder John (Provo, UT: Association for Consumer Research, 1994), 21:348–53.

44. For a general review of the attribution process in consumer behavior, see Valerie Folkes, "Recent Attribution Research in Consumer Behavior: A Review and New Directions," *Journal of Consumer Research* 14 (March 1988): 548–65.

45. Michelle L. Peterman, Harper A. Roehm Jr., and Curtis P. Haugtvedt, "An Exploratory Attribution Analysis of Attitudes toward the World Wide Web as a Product Information Source," in *Advances in Consumer Research*, ed. Eric J. Arnould and Linda M. Scott (Provo, UT: Association for Consumer Research, 1999), 26:75–79.

46. Robert M. Schindler, "Consequences of Perceiving Oneself as Responsible for Obtaining a Discount: Evidence for Smart-Shopper Feelings," *Journal of Consumer Psychology* 7 (1998): 371–92.

47. Harold H. Kelley, "The Process of Causal Attribution," *American Psychologist* 28 (February 1973): 107–28.

48. Nancy Millman, "Product Claims Not Believable," *Advertising Age,* March 15, 1984, pp. 1, 32.

49. Lee Ross, "The Intuitive Psychologist and His Shortcomings: Distortion in the Attribution Process," in *Advances in Experimental Social Psychology*, vol. 10 (New York: Academic Press, 1977).

50. Robert Baer, "Overestimating Salesperson Truthfulness: The Fundamental Attribution Error," in *Advances in Consumer Research*, ed. Marvin Goldberg et al. (Provo, UT: Association for Consumer Research, 1990): 17:501–7.

51. Maria L. Cronley et al., "Endorsing Products for the Money: The Role of the Correspondence Bias in Celebrity Advertising," in *Advances in Consumer Research*, ed. Eric Arnould and Linda M. Scott (Provo, UT: Association for Consumer Research, 1999): 26:627–31.

52. John R. O'Malley Jr., "Consumer Attributions of Product Failures to Channel Members," *Advances in Consumer Research*, ed. Kim Corfman and John Lynch (Provo: UT: Association for Consumer Research, 1996): 23:342–45.

Personality and Psychographics

After studying this chapter, you should be able to describe each of the following concepts, together with their managerial relevance:

1. Personality.
2. Psychographics.
3. Psychoanalytic approach to personality.
4. Trait theory.
5. Self-concept.
6. Product images and self-images.
7. Symbolic interactionism.
8. Consumer lifestyle.
9. VALS II.
10. LOV scale.

This chapter introduces the concepts of personality, self-concept, and psychographics. Each describes a different approach to identifying individual differences in consumer behavior. **Individual difference variables** describe how one person varies from another in his or her distinctive patterns of behavior. Individual difference variables have three important managerial uses. First, a sufficient number of people who share similar personality, self-concept, or psychographic characteristics may be a large enough segment that can then be targeted by a company. Second, by developing an understanding of a target market's personality, self-concept, or psychographic characteristics, a company can develop promotional messages that will optimally tap into the group's needs and wants. Third, it may be possible to position a brand based on a dominant individual difference characteristic of a target market.

This chapter will first discuss the use of personality measures in consumer research. The word *personality* comes from the Latin term *persona*, which means "actor's face mask." Like a mask, a personality is worn as a person moves from situation to situation during a lifetime. **Personality** can be defined as "the distinctive patterns of behavior, including thoughts and emotions, that characterize each individual's adaptation to the situations of his or her life."[1] The goal for consumer researchers is to identify personality variables that distinguish large groups of people from each other.

Next, this chapter analyzes the **self-concept,** which is defined as the "totality of the individual's thoughts and feelings having reference to himself as an object."[2] People have a strong need to act consistently with who and what they think they are.[3] In addition, they purchase products and services to build their self-image and to express themselves to others.

Finally, this chapter investigates psychographic analysis. Through **psychographic analysis,** market researchers attempt to measure the lifestyles of consumers. The chapter concludes by outlining the managerial implications of the concepts from the study of personality, self-concept, and psychographics.

PERSONALITY AND CONSUMER BEHAVIOR

The concept of personality has four essential characteristics. First, to be called a personality characteristic, a person's behavior should show consistency across time. Second, the particular behaviors should distinguish the person from others. A personality characteristic cannot be shared by all consumers. Third, researchers cannot accurately predict an individual's behavior on one specific occasion from a single measure of personality.[4] For example, one cannot predict how many cans of peas a person will buy or the brand of furniture a person will own by measuring personality characteristics. What can be predicted by personality variables are enduring tendencies to engage in general classes of behaviors. For example, by knowing a person's personality characteristics, researchers can do a good job of predicting such behavioral tendencies as compulsive buying, sports participation, healthy lifestyles, and bargaining proneness.[5] Although personality variables cannot predict what sport an individual will participate in, they can predict the degree to which a person participates in all sports.

A fourth characteristic of personality is that it moderates the effects of messages and situations on consumer behavior. Within the domain of personality, a **moderating variable** is an individual difference variable that interacts with the situation or the type of message communicated. As will be discussed further in chapter 11, consumer situations refer to those temporary environmental factors that form the context in which a consumer activity occurs. One type of situation is the social context in which purchases occur. Researchers have found that consumers act differently depending on whether other people are observing their purchase behavior. This situational variable may interact with a personality characteristic that distinguishes people on their tendency to conform to social pressures when making purchases. A scale called the ATSCI (attention to social comparison interaction) has been developed to measure this disposition to conform to others.[6]

Figure 6.1 shows how the situational context may interact with a person's tendency to conform to others to influence purchase behavior. In most circumstances people go shopping with plans to make certain purchases. The findings illustrated in the figure show that the social situation interacts with the tendency to conform to others so as to impact the extent that the consumer *fails* to make the intended purchases. People who have a *low tendency to conform* will tend to make their desired purchases

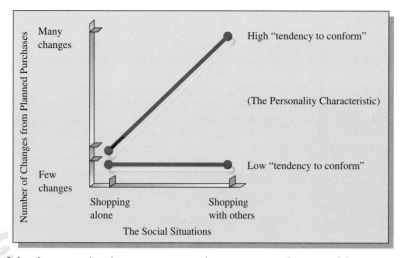

Figure 6.1 A personality (attention to social comparison information) by situation (whether or not shopping with others) interaction.

Note: The "tendency to conform" is a personality characteristic based on the ATSCI scale. See William O. Bearden and Randall L. Rose, "Attention to Social Comparison Information: An Individual Difference Factor Affecting Conformity," *Journal of Consumer Research* 16 (March 1990): 461–71.

whether they shop alone or with a group. In contrast, people with a *high tendency to conform* will make many more changes in purchase plans when shopping with a group than when shopping alone. Thus, the personality variable ATSCI moderates the impact of the situation on consumer behavior.

There are two distinct approaches to personality that are of particular use to consumer researchers: the psychoanalytic theory approach and the trait approach. These are discussed in the following sections.

Psychoanalytic Theory

Sigmund Freud's **psychoanalytic theory of personality** has had a major impact on our understanding of human makeup. Freud argued that the human personality results from a dynamic struggle between inner physiological drives (such as hunger, sex, and aggression) and social pressures to follow laws, rules, and moral codes. Furthermore, he proposed that individuals are aware of only a small portion of the forces that drive their behavior. From his perspective, humans have a conscious, preconscious, and an unconscious mind. This idea—that much of what propels humans to action is a part of the unconscious mind and is not available for scrutiny—revolutionized the understanding of the human personality.[7]

The Structure of the Personality. According to Freud, personality results from the clash of three forces—the id, ego, and superego. Present at birth, the **id** represents the physiological drives that propel a person to action. These drives are completely unconscious and form a chaotic cauldron of seething excitations.[8] The id requires instant gratification of its instincts. As such, it operates on the **pleasure principle.** That is, the id functions to move a person to obtain positive feelings and emotions.

The ego begins to develop as the child grows. The function of the **ego** is to curb the appetites of the id and help the person to function effectively in the world.

According to Freud, the ego stands for "reason and good sense while the id stands for untamed passions."[9] Freud viewed the ego as operating on the reality principle, which helps the person to be practical and to move efficiently through the world.

The **superego** can be understood as the conscience, or voice within a person that echoes the morals and values of parents and society. Only a small portion of it is available to the conscious mind. According to Freud, the superego is formed during middle childhood through the process of identification. The superego actively opposes and clashes with the id; one role of the ego is to resolve these conflicts. The focus on the conflict between the id and superego is what classifies the psychoanalytic view of personality as a conflict theory.

Psychoanalytic Theory and Promotional Strategy. Embraced by motivation researchers in the 1950s, psychoanalytic thought has had a major impact on marketing. Advertising firms hired psychoanalysts to help develop promotional themes and packaging to appeal to the unconscious minds of consumers. Psychoanalytic theory emphasizes the use of dreams, fantasy, and symbols to identify the unconscious motives behind a person's actions. Still used by some marketing researchers today, it is employed to identify the symbols and fantasies that unconsciously propel people to buy. Indeed, advertising that employs an experiential orientation, as compared with a rational decision approach, seeks to provide consumers with pleasant fantasies involving the use of products.

According to psychoanalytic theory, the unconscious wishes of people are expressed through **symbols,** which can be used by marketers. For example, phallic (male) and ovarian (female) symbols were thought to activate the release of sexual energy, or **libido.** Indeed, some writers have sold large numbers of books by sensationalizing the charge that advertising agencies place ovarian and phallic symbols in advertisements to arouse sexual energy and thereby generate sales.[10] Phallic symbols are represented by figures that are long and cylindrical, whereas ovarian symbols are represented by figures that are round and receptive. In some instances it is quite clear that companies make use of such symbols. For example, the concave shape of Jovan perfume and the convex shape of Jovan aftershave are highly symbolic.

According to psychoanalytic theory, people also have a death wish, which is symbolized in advertising by death masks. Death masks are facial covers that portray the contorted faces of people in unbearable pain. One author has argued that liquor advertisers place death masks in the ice cubes shown in liquor advertisements to activate the death wish of heavy drinkers.[11]

Do advertising agencies really engage in such activities? The answer is a qualified no. A college professor conducted a survey that asked advertising people if they ever deliberately embedded a subliminal message—such as a word, symbol, or sexual organ—in advertising artwork for a client. Of those surveyed, 96 percent said they did not. When asked if they knew of anyone doing it, 91 percent said they did not.[12] Although the percentage admitting to awareness of the use of embedded symbols in ads was low, it is somewhat surprising that anyone admitted to the practice at all.

Psychoanalytic Theory and Consumer Research. The psychoanalytic approach to personality has had the greatest impact on consumer behavior through its research methods. In particular, psychoanalytic theorists developed projective techniques to identify the unconscious motives that spur people to action. Examples of the projective techniques include word-association tasks, sentence-completion tasks, and thematic apperception tests (TATs). (TATs are ambiguous drawings about which people are asked to write stories.)

Freud's major therapeutic tool was to have people lie on a couch and relax both physically and psychologically, thus allowing patients to lower their defenses and understand better their unconscious motivations. Later, psychologists began to bring people together for group therapy. Marketers have adapted these two approaches by employing depth interviews and focus groups. **Depth interviews** are long, probing, one-on-one interviews undertaken to identify hidden reasons people purchase products and services. **Focus groups** employ long sessions in which 5 to 10 consumers are encouraged to talk freely about their feelings and thoughts concerning a product or service.

An example of depth interviews is found in work at the McCann-Erickson ad agency. Researchers there asked the question, "Why weren't low-income women from the South responding positively to a new roach killer in a tray, which they believed was more effective and less messy than traditional products?" Psychologists performed depth interviews and asked the women to draw roaches. The women portrayed the roaches as male scavengers. One woman wrote, "A man likes a free meal you cook for him; as long as there is food he will stay." Paula Drillman, the director of strategic planning at the ad agency, explained, "Killing the roaches with a bug spray and watching them squirm and die allowed the women to express their hostility toward men and have greater control over the roaches."[13]

Trait Theory

In the trait-theory approach, people are classified according to their dominant characteristics or traits. A **trait** is "any characteristic in which one person differs from another in a relatively permanent and consistent way."[14] Trait theories describe people in terms of their predispositions as measured by a series of adjectives or short phrases. As such, a person's personality is depicted in terms of a particular combination of traits.

For the trait approach to be useful to marketers, the measured personality characteristics must have direct relevance to the specific buying behavior being investigated. In addition, a trait scale must show strong evidence of being reliable and valid. **Reliability** is revealed when the scale is shown to be internally consistent (i.e., each question measures the same general construct) and gives similar results when an individual is retested after a period of time. One way of increasing reliability is to take multiple measures of behavior. Single measures of behavior are highly unreliable.[15] **Validity** occurs when the scale can be shown to measure the trait that it is designed to assess.

The 3M Model of Personality and Motivation. Studies by consumer researchers that employ a trait approach have been criticized as weak and inconclusive.[16] In addition, a large number of traits have been identified by consumer researchers and by psychologists that have no organizing principle. Recently, John Mowen developed a new approach to understanding the impact of traits on consumer behavior.[17] Called the "3M model of motivation and personality," the approach shows promise in providing an organizational structure for understanding how traits impact behavior. (3M stands for "meta-theoretic model of motivation.")

The 3M model identifies four levels of traits based on their level of abstraction: surface, situational, compound, and elemental traits. At the most concrete level are **surface traits,** which are defined as enduring dispositions to act in context-specific domains. Examples of surface traits are bargaining proneness, compulsive buying, healthy-diet behaviors, sports participation, and coupon proneness. Closely related to enduring product involvement (see chapter 3), hundreds of these behavior-specific traits exist. At the second level of abstraction are **situational traits,** which are defined as dispositions to act within general situational contexts. Dozens of situational traits exist; examples include value consciousness, general sports interest, product innovativeness, and health motivation. Situational traits are predictive of the more concrete surface traits. For example, the situational trait of value consciousness has been found to be predictive of both coupon proneness[18] and bargaining proneness.[19]

In the 3M model, situational traits result from the interaction of the situational context with more basic personality characteristics. For example, value consciousness represents the enduring tendency to seek quality at a good price in buying situations. In contrast, health motivation represents the tendency to behave within various health situations. In addition to the general context impacting situational traits, more basic personality characteristics also account for these tendencies.

There are two types of basic psychological traits: elemental traits and compound traits. **Elemental traits** are defined as the most basic underlying predispositions of individuals that arise from genetics and early learning history. The 3M model proposes eight elemental traits (see Table 6.1). Combinations of elemental traits create **compound traits,** which are defined as predispositions that result from the effects of multiple elemental traits, a person's learning history, and the cultural environment. A couple of dozen compound traits are proposed to exist; examples include self-efficacy, competitiveness, and the need for activity.

Figure 6.2 presents the results of a study that employed the 3M model to investigate healthy-diet lifestyles.[20] As can be seen in the figure, four elemental traits are predictive of the compound trait of self-efficacy: the need for arousal, introversion, emotional stability, and conscientiousness. In turn, the situational trait of health motivation is predicted by self-efficacy and the need for body resources. Finally, the measure of healthy-diet lifestyles is predicted by health motivation and by the need for body resources. The model accounted for over 40 percent of the variance in healthy-diet lifestyles in this study, which was measured as the enduring tendency to avoid foods with sugar and fat and to consume three meals per day.

The 3M model provides a means of understanding the nature of trait scales previously identified by consumer researchers and psychologists. For example, the scale measuring ATSCI, discussed earlier in this chapter, represents a compound level trait that is predicted by three of the eight elemental traits. In the study consumers high in

---

Definitions of the Eight Elemental Traits of the 3M Model

1. *Openness to experience.* The need to find novel solutions, express original ideas, and use the imagination in performing tasks.
2. *Conscientiousness.* The need to be organized, orderly, and efficient in carrying out tasks.
3. *Extroversion.* Operationalized as introversion; the tendency to reveal feelings of bashfulness and shyness.
4. *Agreeability.* The need to express kindness and sympathy to others.
5. *Neuroticism (emotional instability).* The tendency to emotionality as expressed by moodiness and by being temperamental.
6. *Material needs.* The need to collect and possess material goods.
7. *The need for arousal.* The desire for stimulation and excitement.
8. *Physical/body needs.* The need to maintain and enhance the body.

Note: The acronym OCEAN MAP provides a mnemonic device for remembering the traits.

TABLE 6.1

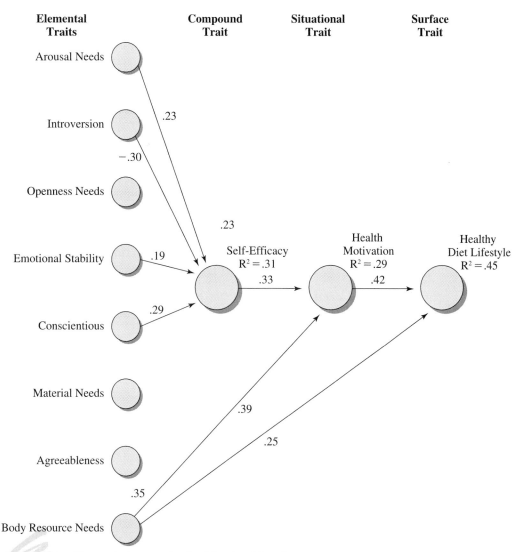

Figure 6.2 The path diagram for healthy-diet lifestyle.

Source: John C. Mowen, *The 3M Model of Motivation and Personality: Theory and Empirical Applications to Consumer Behavior,* (Boston, MA: Kluwer Academic Press, 2000).

Note: R^2 is the amount of variance accounted for in the variable.

attention to social comparison information were higher in agreeability, higher in need for material resources, and lower in openness to experience.[21] Similarly, the scale measuring the **tolerance-for-ambiguity** trait operates at the compound level. This trait predicts how a person will react to situations that have varying degrees of ambiguity or inconsistency.[22] Those individuals who are tolerant of ambiguity react to situational inconsistency in a positive way. In contrast, those identified as intolerant of ambiguity tend to view situational inconsistency as threatening and undesirable.

Tolerance for ambiguity influences consumers in a number of situations. For example, consumers high in tolerance for ambiguity have been shown to have increased tendencies to search for information.[23] Another study found that those categorized as tolerant of ambiguity reacted more positively to new products than those intolerant of ambiguity. Thus, tolerance for ambiguity predicts the situational trait of product innovativeness. When introducing a new product, managers should attempt to identify the level of their target market's tolerance for ambiguity. If the target market has a very low tolerance for ambiguity, it will likely be very difficult to launch the new product successfully.

In his work on the 3M model, Mowen suggested that the trait of **need for cognition** operates at the elemental level because it is closely related to the elemental trait of openness to experience. The need for cognition measures the extent to which consumers have an intrinsic motivation to engage in problem solving activities.[24] Consumers who consistently exert high amounts of effortful cognitive activities are said to have a high need for cognition. Those with a high need for cognition act as though they are in a high-involvement state. As a result, such people tend to think more prior to making a purchase.[25] When they receive a communication, they are influenced most by the quality of the arguments in the message because they examine it more carefully. In addition, they have greater recall of the information in the ad than people with a low need for cognition. Researchers have also found that consumers with a low need for cognition are influenced more by the characteristics of the source, such as his or her physical attractiveness and likability, than by the quality of the arguments in the ad.[26]

Information on a target market's need for cognition has relevance for advertisers.[27] More complex messages may be developed for consumers with a high need for cognition than for consumers with a low need. Thus, when targeting consumers with a high need for cognition, the marketer should consider using print advertising. In addition, messages should be quite detailed and focus on providing strong arguments for why the person should purchase the brand. In contrast, when targeting consumers with a low need for cognition, the advertiser should consider using television. The messages should be simple and delivered by attractive and likeable people. (The need for cognition personality variable is discussed further in chapter 9.)

In the 3M model, personality characteristics form aspects of a consumer's self-concept. As a result, traits act as reference values for evaluating the outcomes that result from our actions. Two of the elemental traits identified in the 3M model are the need for material resources and the need for body resources. Taking an evolutionary perspective, the 3M model proposes that, as a result of the human species adapting to the environment, needs arose to use and make tools, clothing, and shelter (i.e., obtain material resources) and to protect and enhance the body (i.e., protect physical or body resources).

The Needs for Material and Body Resources. When the need for material resources reaches extreme levels, it leads to materialism. Formally, **materialism** is defined as the importance a consumer attaches to worldly possessions. At the highest levels of materialism, possessions assume a central place in a person's life and provide the greatest sources of satisfaction and dissatisfaction.[28]

In his work on the 3M model, Mowen found that the need for material resources is associated with achievement orientation, competitiveness, impulsiveness, bargaining proneness, value consciousness (negative relation), tightwadism[29] (negative relation), compulsive buying, and product innovativeness. These findings are consistent with the idea that the need for material resources has both positive and negative implications for consumers.[30] That is, higher levels of materialism have the positive effect of leading to greater amounts of achievement motivation. On the other hand, it can also lead to impulsiveness and compulsive buying. These ideas are also consistent with the proposal that material needs form a component of self-concept. That is, "What we possess is, in a very real way, part of ourselves."[31] Indeed, William James in 1890 stated that we are the sum total of all our possessions.[32]

Just as people vary in their need for material possessions, they also differ in their need to protect and enhance the body. The need for body resources can be defined as the enduring disposition to seek to protect and enhance the body. Mowen found that the need for body resources was predictive of a number of compound and situational traits, including health motivation, competitiveness, value consciousness (i.e., people who seek to protect their body also seek to protect their finances), and sports interest. Like the need for material resources, the need for body resources has both positive and negative effects. On the positive side, it leads to higher levels of health motivation and healthy-diet lifestyles. On the negative side, too great a focus on the body may lead to vanity and possibly eating disorders such as anorexia nervosa.

Interestingly, other researchers have found that the different body parts vary in importance to people. Eyes, hair, heart, legs, and genitals have been identified as most essential to the sense of self. In contrast, throat, liver, kidneys, chin, knees, and nose are perceived as less central to the self. The implication is that if one loses a body part central to one's identity, the person will feel a loss to part of his or her identity. Evidence also suggests that women perceive their bodies as more central to their identities than men.

The concept that different body parts have different levels of importance to a consumer's self-concept has an important practical element. One major medical problem today is finding sufficient body parts for organ transplants. From a psychological perspective, transplanting important body organs can be extremely traumatic for both the donor and recipient. Furthermore, decisions by next of kin to donate organs of a deceased person are based in part on how sacrosanct the organs are perceived to be. Thus, organs important to the self-concept, such as the eyes and heart, are most frequently vetoed for donation.[33]

Compulsive Buying as a Personality Trait. Consumers falling into debt and going bankrupt is currently a major societal problem in the United States. Although overspending can result from factors beyond a person's control (such as unexpectedly losing a job), poor money management may also result from compulsive buying. Compulsive buying can be described as "chronic, repetitive purchasing that becomes a primary response to negative events or feelings."[34] As such, compulsive buying is part of the dark side of consumer behavior. Compulsive buyers have been found to have lower self-esteem, to fantasize more frequently than typical, and to reveal higher-than-average levels of depression and anxiety.

Consumer researchers have developed an instrument to measure the tendency to engage in compulsive buying.[35] The instrument can be used to screen consumers in order to identify those at risk of becoming compulsive buyers and thus encountering severe financial difficulties. The following are some of the statements on the instrument that successfully identified compulsive buyers:

➤ Bought things even though I couldn't afford them.

➤ Felt others would be horrified if they knew of my spending habits.

➤ Felt anxious or nervous on days I didn't go shopping.

➤ Bought something in order to make myself feel better.

Answering "yes" to one or two of the statements on the scale does not necessarily indicate potential problems. A consistent pattern in which a individual answers "yes" to most of the statements, however, suggests that the person should seek assistance from a professional. Research into compulsive buying may provide guidance for counseling programs to reduce this addiction and exemplifies how consumer research can be used to enhance society and the individuals who comprise it.

In the 3M model, compulsive buying is viewed as a surface trait. The following variables are associated with compulsive buying in a motivational network of traits: impulsiveness, emotional instability, the need for material resources, low conscientiousness, and introversion. These findings suggest that counseling programs that assist people in becoming more conscientious, more emotionally stable, and less impulsive will help them to overcome the buying addiction.

Separateness-Connectedness. A trait that resides at the compound level is **separateness-connectedness,** which is defined as the extent to which people perceive their self-concept as autonomous and separate from other people (i.e., separated) or as interdependent and united with other people.[36] Connected people consider significant others as part of the self or as an extension of the self. In contrast, separated people distinguish themselves from others and set a clear boundary between "me" and "not me." Researchers have found that separateness-connectedness (SC) differs across a number of demographic variables. For example, females have been found to have a more connected self-concept than males. Similarly, people from Asian cultures have a more connected self-concept than people from the United States, Canada, and Europe.

A recent study has shown that the SC trait moderates consumer responses to advertisements.[37] Respondents in the study respondents first completed the SC scale and two weeks later evaluated advertisements for the Discover credit card that employed either a separated or a connected theme. The following is a portion of each ad, illustrating how the themes of connectedness and separateness were communicated:

> *Separated Theme.* "Our marriage brings me and Chris together, but it doesn't make me lose my self-identify. I have a world of my own and I am keeping my individuality and unique life style. . . . Be what you want, but always be you. Your credit card shouldn't be like someone else's."

> *Connected Theme.* "Our marriage brings us together and it makes each "me" become part of the "us." Our family becomes our life. . . . We contribute to our relationship by our communal activities and joint decisions."

The results of the study revealed that respondents scoring high on separateness rated the individualistic ad very positively and the communal ad relatively lower. In contrast, respondents scoring high on connectedness rated the communal ad highly and the individualistic ad relatively lower. Other research has found that individuals in a collectivist culture preferred ads focusing on empathy and peacefulness. In contrast, people in individualistic cultures preferred ego-focused ads that emphasized pride and personal happiness.[38] Described another way, SC moderates the effects of the ads on consumer responses.

The results have clear managerial implications. Managers should match the theme of their ad to the self-concept of the target market. In addition, the market may be segmented and the brand positioned based on the SC construct. Thus, a brand could be positioned as made for "individualists" and targeted to men. In contrast, a brand could be positioned as made for "those who are connected" and targeted to women.[39]

Additional Personality Trait Scales. Consumer researchers have identified numerous other traits that have managerial relevance. For example, researchers have assessed vanity,[40] deal proneness,[41] consumer cognitive complexity,[42] verbal versus visual information processing,[43] gender schema theory,[44] consumer anxiety,[45] consumer ethno-centrism,[46] extroversion and neuroticism,[47] need for emotion,[48] and compliance, aggression, and detachment.[49] One objective of future research is to identify where in the hierarchical model of the 3M each of these traits fits.

On the Managerial Use of Scales Measuring Personality Traits

A key issue for marketing managers and market researchers concerns how to make practical use of personality scales. For example, suppose that managers sought to increase the purchase frequency of moderate users of a brand such as Pepsi-Cola. They would first obtain a large random sample of consumers and pay these individuals to complete an instrument that assesses the consumers' demographic characteristics, frequency of and feelings about drinking Pepsi and other soft drinks (the surface trait), and a set of personality traits, such as those found in the 3M model. The managers then perform analyses to determine how the low, moderate, and high consumers of Pepsi differ on the demographic and personality characteristics. Based on these relationships, the managers then develop strategies to position and differentiate the brand from competitors. Advertisements and other promotional messages are then created that implement the positioning strategy by employing themes consistent with the traits that differentiate the moderate users from the low users.

SELF-CONCEPT AND CONSUMER RESEARCH

Self-concept represents the "totality of the individual's thoughts and feelings having reference to himself as an object."[50] It is as though an individual turns around and evaluates in an objective fashion just who and what he or she is.[51] Because people have a need to behave consistently with their self-concept, this perception of themselves forms part of the basis for the personality. By acting in a manner consistent with their self-concept, consumers can maintain their self-esteem and gain predictability in interactions with others.

An important finding is that people have more than one self-concept. Table 6.2 identifies nine dimensions of self-concept. The "actual self" relates to how a person actually perceives him- or herself. The "ideal self" denotes how a person would like to perceive him- or herself.[52] The "social self" concerns how a person believes that others

Various Types of Self-Concept

1. *Actual self.* How a person *actually* perceives him- or herself.
2. *Ideal self.* How a person *would like* to perceive himself or herself.
3. *Social self.* How a person thinks *others* perceive him or her.
4. *Ideal social self.* How a person *would like others* to perceive him or her.
5. *Expected self.* An image of self somewhere in between the actual and ideal selves.
6. *Situational self.* A person's self-image in a specific situation.
7. *Extended self.* A person's self-concept that includes the impact of personal possessions on self-image.
8. *Possible selves.* What a person would like to become, could become, or is afraid of becoming.
9. *Connected self.* The extent that a person defines him- or herself in terms of his or her connection with other groups or individuals.

TABLE 6.2

perceive him or her. In contrast, the "ideal social self" relates to how a person would like others to view him or her. The "expected self" describes how a person would like to act. The "situational self" portrays how a person would like to act in various contexts. For example, at a sporting event a person might want to be carefree. In contrast, when conducting a business deal, the person would want to be serious. The "extended self" denotes the impact of possessions on self-image. Researchers have also identified a self-perception called "possible selves." This perspective on the self refers to what a person would like to become, could become, or is afraid of becoming. Thus, the possible-selves idea has a more future orientation than the other self-concept types.[53] Finally, the "connected self" depicts the extent to which people define themselves in terms of other people or groups with whom they are affiliated.

Symbolic Interactionism and the Self

Proponents of the **symbolic-interactionism** school view consumers as living in a symbolic environment; how people interpret these symbols determines the meanings derived.[54] Within a society people develop shared meanings as to what symbols represent. By linking themselves to these symbols, consumers can depict to others their own self-concept. Indeed, managers seek to give brands strong personalities so that consumers can appropriate the brand characteristics for themselves through the purchase of the product. Because the brand meanings are shared, marketers are helping to construct the self-concept of consumers.[55]

The idea of the "looking-glass self" plays an important role within the symbolic interactionist perspective.[56] A looking glass is a mirror, and the metaphor of the looking-glass self relates to the idea that people obtain signals about who they are by looking at how other people react to them. It is as though we see reflections of ourselves in the faces of others as we interact with them. We define ourselves in part by how we perceive other people's reactions to us. Thus, a woman may be shy and retiring as an office worker because that is how she believes that her bosses and coworkers view her. In contrast, on the weekends she may be a party animal as she moves from one bar to another. In part, she is using the reactions of others to determine her self-concept, which diverges markedly from that emerging in an office situation.

Self-Concept and Product Symbolism. As noted by the symbolic interactionists, products may act as symbols for consumers. Some writers have argued that people buy many products not for their functional benefits but for their symbolic value.[57] In such a view, consumers' personalities can be defined through the products they use. Indeed, our possessions represent extensions of ourselves. Thus, a relationship may be found between the self-image of a person and of certain products that he or she buys. Products for which such self-image–product-image congruence have been found include automobiles, health products, cleaning products, grooming products, leisure products, clothing, retail-store patronage, food products, cigarettes, home appliances, magazines, and home furnishings.[58]

Products most likely to be viewed as symbols that communicate one's self-concept to others have three characteristics.[59] First, they must have visibility in use: Their purchase, consumption, and disposition are readily apparent to others. Second, the product must show variability—that is, some consumers must have the resources to own the product, whereas others do not have the time or financial resources to possess it. If everyone owned the product or could use the service and if it were identical for everyone, it could not be a symbol. Third, the product should have personalizability. Personalizability refers to the extent to which a product denotes a stereotypical image of the average user. One can easily see how such symbolic products as automobiles or jewelry possess the characteristics of visibility, variability, and personalizability.

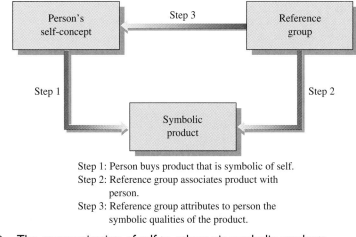

Step 1: Person buys product that is symbolic of self.
Step 2: Reference group associates product with person.
Step 3: Reference group attributes to person the symbolic qualities of the product.

Figure 6.3 The communication of self to others via symbolic products.

The importance of recognizing the symbolic nature of products is depicted in Figure 6.3. The three boxes in the figure represent (1) a person's self-concept, (2) an audience or reference group, and (3) a product that acts as a symbol. In step 1 the consumer buys a product that may communicate his or her self-concept to the audience. In step 2 the consumer hopes that the reference group will have the desired perception of the symbolic nature of the product. In step 3 the consumer hopes that the reference group views him or her as having some of the same symbolic qualities as the product.[60] Thus, consumers are conceptualized as purchasing products to communicate symbolically their self-concept to others. The theory that consumers select products and stores that correspond to their self-concept has been called the **image-congruence hypothesis.**[61]

An Approach to Measuring Self-and-Product Image Congruity. One of the problems for the market researcher is knowing how to assess the self-concept of consumers in a market segment and the image that these consumers have of a brand. In one recently developed approach, respondents are first asked to think about the type of person who uses product X. The instructions continue:

> Imagine this person in your mind and then describe this person using one or more personal adjectives such as, stylish, classy, masculine, sexy, old, athletic or whatever. . . . Once you've done this, indicate your agreement or disagreement to the following statement: This (product X) is consistent with how I see myself (in situation X).[62]

This approach has been shown to be effective in predicting brand preference, brand attitude, and consumer satisfaction.

When engaging in advertising and or personal selling, companies should seek to enhance the self-image of consumers. American Express successfully used such a strategy. In 1980 slightly over 100 million credit cards were owned by consumers in the United States. By 1995 almost 350 million credit cards were in the hands of consumers. How can such an increase be explained?[63] One psychologist argued that

:redit card enhances a person's self-esteem. He stated, "The great modern
is discovering that you're unrecognized, a nobody. With that card you can
ded by strangers, but you walk up and say, 'Look what I've got in my
n its "Do You Know Me" campaign, American Express used this need to
ompany into a leadership position in the credit-card industry.

E AND PSYCHOGRAPHIC ANALYSIS

nt of lifestyles through psychographic analysis represents a third
approach for identifying individual differences among consumers. Through psychographic analysis consumer researchers describe segments of consumers in terms of
how they live, work, and play. This section discusses these concepts.

Consumer Lifestyles

Lifestyle has been defined simply as "how one lives."[65] It has been used to describe
three different levels of aggregation of people—an individual, a small group of interacting people, and larger groups of people (e.g., a market segment).[66] The concept of
lifestyle denotes a set of ideas quite distinct from that of personality. Lifestyle relates to
how people live, how they spend their money, and how they allocate their time. It concerns the overt actions and behaviors of consumers. In contrast, standard models of
personality describe the consumer from a more internal perspective.[67] From this perspective, personality delineates the consumer's "characteristic pattern of thinking,
feeling, and perceiving."[68]

Of course, lifestyle and personality are closely related. A consumer who has a
personality categorized as low in need for arousal is unlikely to possess a lifestyle that
includes an occupation as a speculator in the futures market or activities such as
mountain climbing, hang gliding, and jungle exploration. From the perspective of the
newly developed 3M model, a lifestyle represents a surface trait, or an enduring disposition to engage in a particular set of behaviors. This surface trait, or lifestyle, can then
be predicted by combinations of situational, compound, and elemental traits.

Marketers measure lifestyles by psychographic analysis, which is discussed in the
following section.

Psychographic Analysis

The term *psychographics* refers to the idea of describing (*graph*) the psychological (*psy-
cho*) makeup of consumers. In practice, researchers employ psychographics to assess
consumers' lifestyles and factors associated with these lifestyles. Lifestyles are assessed
by measuring consumer's activities, interests, and opinions (AIOs). The goals of psychographic research are usually of an applied nature. That is, psychographic research is
used by market researchers to describe a consumer segment so as to help an organization better reach and understand its customers. Psychographic studies usually include
questions to assess a target market's lifestyle, its personality characteristics, and its
demographic characteristics. In sum, **psychographics** may be defined as the quantita-
tive investigation of consumers' lifestyles, personality, and demographic characteristics.

Psychographics and AIO Statements. In order to understand the lifestyles of consumers, psychographic researchers use questions called AIO statements. **AIO statements** describe the lifestyles of consumers by identifying their activities, interests, and
opinions. Activity questions ask consumers to indicate what they do, what they buy,
and how they spend their time. Interest questions focus on the consumers' preferences and priorities. Opinion questions ask for consumers' views and feelings on such

Some Typical Questions Found in AIO Inventories

I. *Activity Questions*
- **a.** What outdoor sports do you participate in at least twice a month?
- **b.** How many books do you read a year?
- **c.** How often do you visit shopping malls?
- **d.** Have you gone outside of the United States for a vacation?
- **e.** To how many clubs do you belong?

2. *Interest Questions*
- **a.** In which of the following are you most interested—sports, church, or work?
- **b.** How important to you is it to try new foods?
- **c.** How important is it to you to get ahead in life?
- **d.** Would you rather spend two hours on a Saturday afternoon with your wife or in a boat fishing alone?

3. *Opinion Questions (Ask the respondent to agree or disagree.)*
- **a.** The Russian people are just like us.
- **b.** Women should have free choice regarding abortion.
- **c.** Educators are paid too much money.
- **d.** CBS, Inc.™ is run by East Coast liberals.
- **e.** We must be prepared for nuclear war.

TABLE 6.3

things as world, local, moral, economic, and social affairs. Table 6.3 lists questions representative of AIO items.

No hard-and-fast rules exist for developing AIO items. One dimension on which they frequently differ is their level of specificity. AIO questions may be highly specific and ask the respondent to provide information on his or her attitudes and preferences regarding a specific product or service. For example, a researcher for General Mills might be interested in consumer perceptions of Post Grape-Nuts. The researcher might ask respondents to agree or disagree with the following highly specific questions:

I find Grape-Nuts to be too hard to chew.

Grape-Nuts remind me of the outdoors.

When I eat Grape-Nuts, it makes me feel healthful.

On the other hand, AIO questions can be much more general. Some highly general questions researchers might ask consumers to agree or disagree with include the following:

I consider myself an outdoor person.

I believe in world peace.

I think cities are where the action is.

Of course, researchers will have different purposes for asking the two types of questions. The highly specific questions give researchers information on what consumers think about the product and how that product relates to themselves. From such information products may be developed or changed and specific messages created. Indeed, unique selling propositions may be formulated. A unique selling proposition is a quick, hard-hitting phrase that captures a major feature of a product or service. For example, the makers of Wheaties have used for many years the unique selling proposition "The Breakfast of Champions." By asking people to describe the specific product through AIO statements, companies may create such unique selling propositions.

Consumer profiles can be developed from the responses to AIO questions and then used to develop an understanding of the general lifestyle of the targeted consumer segment. Based on the profile, advertisers can develop ideas for the themes of ads and for the setting within which to place an ad. For example, in a project called "Project Virile Female," RJR Nabisco found that an important aspiration of its target market of young, blue-collar women was to have an ongoing relationship with a man. Such knowledge suggests employing an advertising theme in which an attractive male is highly visible.

The psychographic inventory receiving the most attention among corporations is VALS (values and lifestyles). More recently, consumer researchers have begun to address a second approach, called LOV (list of values). These two inventories are discussed next.

The VALS Psychographic Inventory

Perhaps the most frequently used psychographic inventory of consumers is the **VALS lifestyle classification scheme.** Developed by the Stanford Research Institute (SRI), VALS has been widely used by U.S. corporations to segment the market and to provide guidance for developing advertising and product strategy.[69] SRI has in fact developed two psychographic inventories. The first, VALS, is based on motivational and developmental psychological theories—in particular, Maslow's theory of the hierarchy of needs (discussed further in chapter 5). The second approach, called VALS 2, was developed specifically to measure consumer buying patterns. Both inventories are currently being used by companies. However, this section discusses only the VALS 2 inventory.

The goal of VALS 2 is to identify specific relationships between consumer attitudes and purchase behavior. It divides the American population into eight segments based on their self-identity and their resources (see Table 6.4). The VALS 2 researchers identified three different categories of self-identity orientations: principle, status, and action. Those oriented toward principle make consumer choices based on their beliefs rather than on feelings, events, or a desire for approval. Consumers oriented toward status make choices based on their perception of whether others will approve of their purchases. Finally, consumers oriented toward action make decisions based on desires for activity, variety, and risk taking.

The second major dimension in the VALS 2 classification scheme is the resources of the consumer. Resources are defined broadly to include not only financial–material resources but also psychological and physical resources. People with abundant resources are at one end of the spectrum, whereas those with minimal resources occupy the other end. Figure 6.4 shows the VALS 2 network, using the eight categories of consumers listed in Table 6.4.

Transport Canada (the equivalent of the U.S. Department of Transportation) used VALS 2 to survey travelers at Canadian airports. The results revealed that most of the travelers were actualizers (37 percent). Actualizers have high incomes, and they buy products as an expression of their good taste, independence, and character. These characteristics suggested to the researchers that stores like The Sharper Image or Nature Company could do well in airports. As the researcher explained, "Actualizers are a good market for quality arts and crafts."[70] Table 6.5 identifies activity patterns and product ownership of the eight VALS 2 categories.

A problem with assessing the utility of the VALS psychographic inventories is that they are proprietary instruments (i.e., not in the public domain). SRI allows little

Descriptions of the VALS 2 Consumer Segments

1. *Actualizers*. High resources with focus on principle and action. Active, take-charge expression of taste, independence, and character. College educated, they compose 8% of the population. Median age is 43. Income is $58,000.

2. *Fulfilleds*. High resources with focus on principle. Mature, satisfied, well-informed people for whom image has little importance. Generally married with older children. Composing 11% of population, their median age is 48, they are college educated, and their median income is $38,000.

3. *Believers*. Low resources with focus on principle. Traditional and moralistic, they live predictable lifestyle tied to family and church. Loyal to American products—noninnovative. High school educated, they represent 16% of the population. Median age is 58, with income of $21,000.

4. *Achievers*. High resources with focus on status. Successful, career-oriented individuals. Low risk takers, they respect authority and status quo. Highly image conscious, they buy expensive, expressive autos. College educated, they represent 13% of the population. Median age is 36 and median income is $50,000.

5. *Strivers*. Low resources with focus on status. Impulsive and trend conscious, these individuals seek social approval for actions. Money defines success for them. They frequently have some college education and represent 13% of the population. Median income is $25,000, and median age is 34.

6. *Experiencers*. High resources with focus on action. Young, enthusiastic individuals who like sports and risk taking. Single and impulsive purchasers, they have not yet completed their education. Representing 12% of the population, their median age is 26 and their income is $19,000.

7. *Makers*. Low resources with focus on practical action. Conservative and practical, they focus on family, working with their hands. High school educated, they represent 13% of the population. Median age is 30 and income is $30,000.

8. *Strugglers*. Poor, with little education, they have few resources and must focus on living for the moment. Cautious but loyal shoppers, they represent 14% of the population. High school educated. Median age is 61 and income is $9,000.

Source: SRI International.

TABLE 6.4

access to the instruments by outside consumer researchers. Therefore, their reliability and validity are difficult to assess.[71] However, the survey itself is available on the World Wide Web. Interestingly, the majority of Web users are classified as "strivers" in the VALS 2 typology.[72]

The List-of-Values Approach

A scale that shows promise of correcting some of the problems of VALS is called the list-of-values (LOV) scale. The goal of the LOV scale is to assesses the dominant values of a person.[73] Although not strictly a psychographic inventory (because it does not use AIO statements), it has been applied to the same types of problems as VALS. Furthermore, because it is available for public scrutiny, its validity and reliability can be evaluated. The LOV scale assesses nine values:

1. Self-fulfillment.
2. Excitement.

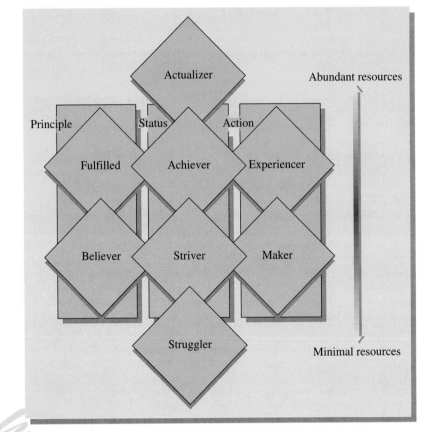

Figure 6.4   The VALS 2 network.

Source: SRI International.

3. Sense of accomplishment.

4. Self-respect.

5. Sense of belonging.

6. Being well respected.

7. Security.

8. Fun and enjoyment.

9. Warm relationships with others.

When LOV is used for market research, questions to assess the respondent's demographic profile are added to the questions used to identify the nine values. The LOV scale has three dimensions. Questions regarding the first four items (self-fulfillment, excitement, sense of accomplishment, and self-respect) concern individual values that are of an internal nature. The next three questions (sense of belonging, being well respected, and security) concern a focus on the external world. For example, a person who worries a lot about crime and unemployment would tend to have a need for security. The third dimension consists of the last two questions (fun and enjoyment and warm relationships with others) and reflects an interpersonal orientation.[74]

Buying and Activity Patterns of VALS 2 Segments

Activity Patterns

Segment

Item	Actualizer	Fulfilled	Believer	Achiever	Striver	Experiencer	Maker	Struggler
Buy hand tools	148	65	105	63	59	137	170	57
Barbecue outdoors	125	93	82	118	111	109	123	50
Do gardening	155	129	118	109	68	54	104	80
Do gourmet cooking	217	117	96	103	53	133	86	47
Drink coffee daily	120	119	126	88	87	55	91	116
Drink domestic beer	141	88	73	101	87	157	123	50
Drink herbal tea	171	125	89	117	71	115	81	68
Drink imported beer	258	93	41	130	58	216	88	12
Do activities with kids	155	129	57	141	112	89	116	32
Play team sports	114	73	69	104	110	172	135	34
Do cultural activities	293	63	67	96	45	154	63	14
Exercise	145	114	69	123	94	143	102	39
Do home repairs	161	113	85	82	53	88	171	58
Camp or hike	131	88	68	95	84	156	158	33
Do risky sports	190	48	36	52	59	283	171	7
Socialize weekly	109	64	73	90	96	231	94	62

Buying Patterns

Segment

Item	Actualizer	Fulfilled	Believer	Achiever	Striver	Experiencer	Maker	Struggler
Own SLR camera	163	124	80	138	83	88	115	29
Own bicycle > $150	154	116	90	33	83	120	88	43
Own compact disc player	133	108	119	97	96	94	94	69
Own fishing equipment	87	91	114	87	84	113	142	67
Own backpacking equipment	196	112	64	100	56	129	148	29
Own home computer	229	150	59	136	63	82	109	20
Own < $13K import car	172	128	80	143	68	109	89	44
Own > $13K import car	268	105	70	164	79	119	43	32
Own medium/small car	133	117	89	101	112	92	112	54
Own pickup truck	72	96	115	104	103	91	147	52
Own sports car	330	116	43	88	102	112	90	5

Note: Figures under each segment are the index for each segment (100 = base rate usage).

Source: SRI International.

TABLE 6.5

117

The LOV scale has been extensively tested and can differentiate consumers along the three dimensions of internal focus, interpersonal focus, and external focus. One study revealed that consumers with an emphasis on internal values seek to control their lives. This desire for control extended to such decisions as where to eat and where to shop and was expressed by a need to obtain good nutrition and to avoid food additives by purchasing "natural" foods. In contrast, those with an external orientation tended to avoid natural foods, perhaps out of a desire to conform with society at large.[75]

A Warning

Psychographic research has become extremely popular over the past 15 years. Consumer researchers and corporations have invested large amounts of time and financial resources in these studies. Classifying consumers into neat pigeonholes can be risky, however, by grossly oversimplifying the understanding of the buying process. The danger of oversimplification arises in part because of the neat and tidy descriptions that can be developed from psychographic analysis. For example, RJR Nabisco profiled the virile female market in the following way: She is a "white 18–24-year old female. She has only a high school degree and work is a job, not a career. Her free time is spent with her boyfriend, doing whatever he is doing. That includes going to tough-man competitions, tractor pulls, hot rod shows, and cruising. She watches lots of television."[76] This type of description can potentially cause managers and researchers to disparage the segment and view it as more homogeneous than it really is—if it ever really existed.

THE MANAGERIAL IMPLICATIONS OF PERSONALITY AND PSYCHOGRAPHICS

The principles and concepts derived from the study of personality and psychographics have application to each of the five PERMS concepts. These are discussed in the following sections.

Positioning and Differentiation

By identifying the dominant personality and psychographic characteristics of the target market, marketing managers have a means to develop strategies that position and differentiate a product from the competitors'. For example, if the target market has a dominant tendency to reveal a high need for arousal, the brand can be positioned being used or consumed while doing exciting, thrilling, and risky activities. The advertising of Mountain Dew employs this approach to position and associate the brand with youth, enthusiasm, and daring.

Environmental Analysis

Managers must recognize that the values of the dominant culture or subculture in which the target market resides will have an impact on their personality. In particular, culture and subculture can impact the compound and situational traits found in the 3M model. For example, because the U.S. culture communicates the importance of individualism and achievement motivation, U.S. citizens tend to score higher on measures of these characteristics than do individuals in Asian cultures. The identification of the values of the dominant culture or subculture of the target managers can provide managers with indications of what compound and situational traits to measure.

Research

Marketing research is required to measure the personality, self-concept, and psychographic characteristics chosen for investigation. Managers should also employ research to test whether the messages designed to communicate positioning strategies are being interpreted by the target market in the desired way.

Marketing Mix

The study of personality, self-concept, and psychographics has clear implications for promotional and product strategy. As previously indicated, one can use an understanding of the dominant personality, self-concept, and psychographic characteristics of the target market to design a promotion strategy. For example, advertising and public-relations themes and messages can be derived from the analysis. In addition, identifying the dominant traits of the target market will have implications for product design. For example, suppose that the target market is high in conscientiousness, low in the need for arousal, low in material needs, and low in openness to experience. For a automobile manufacturer, this combination of traits suggest developing a very safe, inexpensive, reliable, and visually plain vehicle, such as the Toyota Camry.

Segmentation

Segmentation represents the most important managerial use of the concepts described in this chapter. That is, the fundamental purpose for investigating personality, self-concept, and psychographics is to provide an empirical means of identifying variables that break a heterogeneous population into homogeneous subgroups with similar needs, wants, wishes, and desires.

Notes

1. Walter Mischel, "On the Future of Personality Measurement," *American Psychologist* 32 (April 1977): 2. For a general review of personality in consumer behavior, see Harold H. Kassarjian and Mary Jane Sheffet, "Personality and Consumer Behavior: An Update," in *Perspectives in Consumer Behavior,* 4th ed., ed. Harold H. Kassarjian and Thomas S. Robertson (Upper Saddle River, NJ: Prentice Hall, 1991), 281–303.
2. Morris Rosenberg, *Conceiving the Self* (New York: Basic Books, 1979).
3. Darrell Bem, "Self-Perception Theory," in *Advances in Experiential Social Psychology,* vol. 6, ed. L. Berkowitz (New York: Springer Press, 1965).
4. Harold H. Kassarjian and Mary Jane Sheffet, "Personality and Consumer Behavior: One More Time," *American Marketing Association 1975 Combined Proceedings* 37 (1975): 197–201.
5. John C. Mowen, The 3M Model of Motivation and Personality: Theory and Empirical Applications to Consumer Behavior (Boston, MA: Kluwer Academic Press, 2000).
6. William O. Bearden and Randall L. Rose, "Attention to Social Comparison Information: An Individual Difference Factor Affecting Consumer Conformity," *Journal of Consumer Research* 16 (March 1990): 461–71.
7. For an interesting overview of psychoanalytic theory, see Spencer Rathus, *Psychology* (New York: Holt, Rinehart and Winston, 1981).
8. Sigmund Freud, "New Introductory Lectures," in *The Standard Edition of the Complete Works of Freud,* vol. 22, James Strachey, ed. (London: Hogarth Press, 1964).
9. Ibid.
10. Wilson Bryan Key, *Subliminal Seduction: Ad Media's Manipulation of a Not So Innocent America* (Upper Saddle River, NJ: Prentice Hall, 1973).
11. Ibid.
12. Jack Haberstroh, "Can't Ignore Subliminal Ad Charges," *Advertising Age,* September 17, 1984, pp. 42, 44. Also see John Caccavale, Thomas Wanty, and Julie Edell, "Subliminal Implants in Advertisements: An Experiment," in *Advances in Consumer Research,* ed. Andrew Mitchell (Ann Arbor, MI: Association for Consumer Research, 1981), 9:418–23.
13. Ronald Alsop, "Advertisers Put Consumers on the Couch," *Wall Street Journal,* May 13, 1988, p. 17.
14. Ernest Hilgard, Richard Atkinson, and Rita Atkinson, *Introduction to Psychology,* 6th ed. (New York: Harcourt Brace Jovanovich), 1975.
15. John Lastovicka and Erich Joachimsthaler, "Improving the Detection of Personality-Behavior Relationships in Consumer Research," *Journal of Consumer Research* 14 (March 1988): 583–87.

16. Harold Kassarjian, "Personality and Consumer Behavior: A Review," *Journal of Marketing Research* 8 (1971): 409–18.

17. Mowen, *3M Model.*

18. Donald R. Lichtenstein, Richard G. Netemeyer, and Scot Burton, "Distinguishing Coupon Proneness from Value Consciousness: An Acquisition-Transaction Utility Theory Perspective," *Journal of Marketing* 54 (July 1990): 54–67.

19. Mowen, *3M Model.*

20. Ibid.

21. Ibid.

22. Stanley Budner, "Intolerance for Ambiguity as a Personality Variable," *Journal of Personality* 30 (1962): 29–50.

23. Charles Schaninger and Donald Sciglimpaglia, "The Influence of Cognitive Personality Traits and Demographics on Consumer Information Acquisition," *Journal of Consumer Research* 8 (September 1981): 208–15.

24. James W. Peltier and John A. Schibrowsky, "Need for Cognition, Advertisement Viewing Time, and Memory for Advertising Stimuli," in *Advances in Consumer Research,* ed. Chris T. Allen and Deborah Roedder John (Provo, UT: Association for Consumer Research, 1994), 21:244–50.

25. Curtis P. Haugtvedt, Richard E. Petty, and John T. Cacioppo, "Need for Cognition and Advertising: Understanding the Role of Personality Variables in Consumer Behavior," *Journal of Consumer Psychology* 1, no. 3: 239–60.

26. Curt Haugtvedt et al., "Personality and Ad Effectiveness: Exploring the Utility of Need for Cognition," in *Advances in Consumer Research,* ed. Michael Houston (Provo, UT: Association for Consumer Research, 1988), 15:209–12.

27. Haugtvedt, Petty, and Cacioppo, "Need for Cognition."

28. Russell Belk, "Materialism: Trait Aspects of Living in the Material World," *Journal of Consumer Research* 12 (December 1985): 265–80.

29. For a recent research study on frugality and tightwadism, see John L. Lastovicka et al., *Journal of Consumer Research* 26 (June 1999): 85–98.

30. Kathleen S. Micken and Scott D. Roberts, "Desperately Seeking Certainty: Narrowing the Materialism Construct," in *Advances in Consumer Research,* ed. Eric Arnould and Linda M. Scott (Provo, UT: Association for Consumer Research, 1999), 26:513–18.

31. Russell Belk, "My Possessions Myself," *Psychology Today,* July–August 1988, pp. 50–52.

32. William James, *The Principles of Psychology,* vol. 1 (New York: Henry Holt, 1890).

33. Belk, "Materialism."

34. Ronald J. Faber and Thomas C. O'Guinn, "A Clinical Screener for Compulsive Buying," *Journal of Consumer Research* 19 (December 1992): 459–69.

35. Ibid.

36. Cheng Lu Wang and John C. Mowen, "The Separateness–Connectedness Self Schema: Scale Development and Application to Message Construction," *Psychology and Marketing* 8, no. 4 (1999): 23–34.

37. Ibid.

38. Jennifer L. Aaker and Patti Williams, "Empathy versus Pride: The Influence of Emotional Appeals across Cultures," *Journal of Consumer Research* 25 (December 1998): 241–61.

39. For additional work on "affiliation versus autonomy seeking," see Susan Schultz Kleine, Robert E. Kleine III, and Chris T. Allen, "How Is a Possession 'Me' or 'Not Me'? Characterizing Types and an Antecedent of Material Possession Attachment," *Journal of Consumer Research* 22 (December 1995): 327–43.

40. Richard G. Netemeyer, Scot Burton, and Donald R. Lichtenstein,, "Trait Aspects of Vanity: Measurement and Relevance to Consumer Behavior," *Journal of Consumer Research* 21 (March 1995): 612–26.

41. Donald R. Lichtenstein, Richard G. Netemeyer, and Scot Burton, "Assessing the Domain Specificity of Deal Proneness: A Field Study," *Journal of Consumer Research* 22 (December 1995): 314–26.

42. George Zinkhan and Abhijit Biswas, "Using the Repertory Grid to Assess the Complexity of Consumers' Cognitive Structures," in *Advances in Consumer Research,* ed. Michael Houston (Provo, UT: Association for Consumer Research, 1988), 15:493–97.

43. Evelyn Gutman, "The Role of Individual Differences and Multiple Senses in Consumer Imagery Processing: Theoretical Perspectives," in *Advances in Consumer Research,* ed. Michael Houston (Provo, UT: Association for Consumer Research, 1988), 15:191–96. Also

see Deborah MacInnis, "Constructs and Measures of Individual Differences in Imagery Processing: A Review," in *Advances in Consumer Research*, ed. Melanie Wallendorf and Paul Anderson (Provo, UT: Association for Consumer Research, 1987): 14:88–92.

44. See Bernd H. Schmitt, France Leclerc, and Laurette Dube-Rious, "Sex Typing and Consumer Behavior: A Test of Gender Schema Theory," *Journal of Consumer Research* 15 (June 1988): 122–28.

45. See Ronald Hill, "The Impact of Interpersonal Anxiety on Consumer Information Processing," *Psychology and Marketing* 4 (summer 1987): 93–105.

46. Terence Shimp and Subhash Sharma, "Consumer Ethnocentrism: Construction and Validation of CETSCALE," *Journal of Marketing Research* 24 (August 1987): 280–89.

47. Todd A. Mooradian, "Personality and Ad-Evoked Feelings: The Case for Extroversion and Neuroticism," *Journal of the Academy of Marketing Science* 24 (spring 1996): 99–109.

48. Niranjan V. Raman, Prithviraj Chattopadhyay, and Wayne D. Hoyer, "Do Consumers Seek Emotional Situations: The Need for Emotion Scale," in *Advances in Consumer Research*, ed. Frank R. Dardes and Mita Sujan (Provo, UT: Association for Consumer Research, 1995), 22:537–42.

49. Shimp and Sharma, "Consumer Ethnocentrism." For information on the CAD scale, see J. Noerager, "An Assessment of CAD," *Journal of Marketing Research* 16 (February 1979): 53–59.

50. Rosenberg, *Conceiving the Self.*

51. Raj Mehta and Russell Belk, in "Artifacts, Identity, and Transition: Favorite Possessions of Indians and Indian Immigrants to the United States," *Journal of Consumer Research* 17 (March 1991): 398–411, note, however, that concepts of self differ cross-culturally. Hindus, for example, are less susceptible to the Western view of self as both subject and object.

52. For an excellent review of the self-concept in consumer behavior, see M. Joseph Sirgy, "Self-Concept in Consumer Behavior: A Critical Review," *Journal of Consumer Research* 9 (December 1982): 287–300. Also see Newell D. Wright, C. B. Claiborne, and M. Joseph Sirgy, "The Effects of Product Symbolism on Consumer Self-Concept," in *Advances in Consumer Research*, ed. John F. Sherry Jr. and Brian Sternthal (Provo, UT: Association for Consumer Research, 1992), 19:311–18.

53. Amy J. Morgan, "The Evolving Self in Consumer Behavior: Exploring Possible Selves," in *Advances in Consumer Research*, ed. Leigh McAlister and Michael L. Rothschild (Provo, UT: Association for Consumer Research, 1993), 20:429–32.

54. George H Mead, *Mind, Self, and Society* (Chicago, IL: University of Chicago Press, 1934).

55. Mark Ligas and June Cotte, "The Process of Negotiating Brand Meaning: A Symbolic Interactionist Perspective," in *Advances in Consumer Research*, ed. Eric Arnould and Linda M. Scott (Provo, UT: Association for Consumer Research, 1999), 26:609–14.

56. Charles H. Cooley, *Human Nature and the Social Order* (New York: Scribners, 1902).

57. Sidney J. Levy, "Symbols for Sale," *Harvard Business Review* 37 (1959): 117–24.

58. Russell Belk, Kenneth D. Bahn, and Robert N. Mayer, "Developmental Recognition of Consumption Symbolism," *Journal of Consumer Research* 9 (June 1982): 4–17.

59. Rebecca H. Holman, "Product as Communication: A Fresh Appraisal of a Venerable Topic," in *Review of Marketing*, ed. Ben M. Enis and Kenneth J. Roering (Chicago, IL: American Marketing Association, 1981), 106–19.

60. Edward L. Grubb and Harrison Grathwohl, "Consumer Self-Concept, Symbolism, and Market Behavior: A Theoretical Approach," *Journal of Marketing* 31 (October 1967): 22–27. The author conceived of these relations from the work of Fritz Heider on balance theory. See Fritz Heider, *The Psychology of Interpersonal Relations* (New York: Wiley, 1958).

61. Sak Onkvisit and John Shaw, "Self-Concept and Image Congruence: Some Research and Managerial Issues," *Journal of Consumer Marketing* 4 (winter 1987): 13–23.

62. M. Joseph Sirgy et al., "Assessing the Predictive Validity of Two Methods of Measuring Self-Image Congruence," *Journal of the Academy of Marketing Science* 25 (summer 1997): 229–41.

63. Charles McCoy and Steve Swartz, "Big Credit-Card War May Be Breaking Out, to Detriment of Banks," *Wall Street Journal*, March 19, 1987, pp. 1, 24.

64. Ibid., p. 24.

65. Del Hawkins, Roger Best, and Kenneth Coney, *Consumer Behavior: Implications for Marketing Strategy* (Plano, TX: Business Publications, 1983).

66. W. Thomas Anderson and Linda Golden, "Lifestyle and Psychographics: A Critical Review and Recommendation," in *Advances in Consumer Research*, ed. Thomas Kinnear (Ann Arbor, MI: Association for Consumer Research, 1984), 11:405–11.

67. Lifestyle has been distinguished from "cognitive style" by Anderson and Golden, "Lifestyle and Psychographics."

68. Ron J. Markin, *Consumer Behavior: A Cognitive Orientation* (New York: Macmillan, 1974).

69. For an in-depth discussion of VALS, see Arnold Mitchell, *The Nine American Lifestyles* (New York: Macmillan, 1983), 57.

70. Rebecca Piirto, "VALS the Second Time," *American Demographics,* July 1991, p. 6.

71. A number of researchers have noted that there are problems with the original VALS inventory. See John L. Lastovicka, John P. Murry Jr., and Eric Joachimsthaler, "Evaluating the Measurement Validity of ATSCI Typologies with Qualitative Measures and Multiplicative Factoring," *Journal of Marketing Research* (February 1991): 11–23. Also see Lynn R. Kahle, Sharon Beatty, and Pamela Homer, "Alternative Measurement Approaches to Consumer Values: The List Values (LOV) and Values and Life Style (VALS)," *Journal of Consumer Research* 13 (December 1986): 405–9; Sharon E. Beatty, Pamela Homer, and Lynn Kahle, "Problems with VALS in International Marketing Research: An Example from an Application of the Empirical Mirror Technique," in *Advances in Consumer Research,* ed. Michael Houston (Provo, UT: Association for Consumer Research, 1988), 15:375–80.

72. SRI International, June 7, 1995 <vals@sri.com>. Go to the Web site www.consumerbehavior.net for a hyperlink to VALS 2 and other Web sites relevant to consumer behavior.

73. Kahle, Beatty, and Homer, "Alternative Measurement Approaches."

74. Pamela Homer and Lynn Kahle, "A Structural Equation Test of the Value–Attitude–Behavior Hierarchy," *Journal of Personality and Social Psychology* 54 (April 1988): 638–46.

75. Kahle, Beatty, and Homer, "Alternative Measurement Approaches." Also see Thomas P. Novak and Bruce MacEvoy, "On Comparing Alternative Segmentation Schemes: The List of Values (LOV) and Values and Life Styles (VALS)," *Journal of Consumer Research* (June 1990): 105–9. For an article that further explores the LOV scale, see Wagner A. Kamakura and Thomas P. Novak, "Value-System Segmentation: Exploring the Meaning of LOV," *Journal of Consumer Research* 19 (June 1992): 119–32.

76. Alix Freedman and Michael McCarthy, "New Smoke from RJR under Fire," *Wall Street Journal,* February 20, 1990, pp. B1, B4.

Belief, Attitude, and Behavior Formation and Change

After studying this chapter, you should be able to describe each of the following concepts, together with their managerial relevance:

1. Beliefs, attitudes, and behavioral intentions.
2. Attributes.
3. Direct formation of beliefs, attitudes, and behaviors.
4. Hierarchies of effects.
5. The attitude-toward-the-object model.
6. The behavioral intentions model.
7. The elaboration likelihood model.
8. Balance theory.
9. Attitude toward the advertisement.
10. Behavioral influence techniques of persuasion.

The concepts of beliefs, attitudes, and behavior are closely linked together. The generic phrase *consumer-attitude formation* is often used to describe the field. In fact, more has been written on consumer attitudes than any other single topic in the field of consumer behavior.[1] This chapter describes how beliefs, attitudes, and behaviors are formed and changed. In addition, it discusses how such knowledge can assist marketing managers and public-policy makers.

CONSUMER BELIEFS

Consumer beliefs result from cognitive learning. They represent the knowledge and inferences that a consumer has about objects, their attributes, and their benefits provided. **Objects** are the products, people, companies, and things about which people hold beliefs and attitudes. **Attributes** are the features or characteristics of an object. Finally, **benefits** are the positive outcomes that objects provide to the consumer.

The beliefs held by consumers about a product's attributes may not match reality, however. For example, halo effects can cause misperceptions about product attributes in the marketplace. A **halo effect** occurs when consumers assume that, because a product is good or bad on one product characteristic, it is also good or bad on another product characteristic. Thus, for example, a consumer who believes that the Explorer sport utility vehicle (SUV) has good traction may also believe that it has good handling as well. Halo effects can even extend from a company's specific product to the company as a whole. For example, if consumers believe that Gucci makes high-quality handbags, they will extrapolate the belief that all Gucci products are high in quality.[2]

Attributes differ widely in their importance to consumers. **Attribute importance** is defined as a person's assessment of the significance of an attribute for a specific good or service.[3] Researchers have found that attribute importance is strongly influenced by the amount of attention directed to the specific feature of a product. That is, the greater the attention directed to an attribute, the more important it becomes. Several factors have been found to influence attribute importance. One factor is the self-concept of the consumer. For example, if a consumer has a self-concept that includes "ruggedness," the attribute of toughness in a truck could attract this person's attention. Second, advertising can influence the importance of attributes by directing attention to specific features of a product. For example, if the copy in an advertisement that pertains to an attribute is highly concrete and vivid, it may direct attention to that attribute and increase its perceived importance.

CONSUMER ATTITUDES

Over the past 30 years, the term *attitude* has been defined in numerous ways. This book employs the definition proposed by L. L. Thurstone, one of the originators of modern-attitude-measurement theory. According to Thurstone, an **attitude** is "the amount of affect or feeling for or against a stimulus."[4] The idea that attitudes refer to affect or a general evaluative reaction has been expressed by many researchers.[5] Whereas beliefs are the cognitive knowledge about an object, attitudes are the affective feelings that people have about objects.

Attitudes are stored in long-term memory and serve four important functions for consumers.[6] First, the utilitarian function specifies that people express feelings to maximize rewards and minimize punishments received from others. In this sense, the expression of an attitude is like an operantly conditioned response. For example, a salesperson might learn that making positive comments to a client (i.e., expressing favorable attitudes) is more likely to result in a sale (i.e., a positive reinforcer). Second, attitudes can serve an ego-defense function. In their ego-defensive role, attitudes act to protect people from basic truths about themselves or from the harsh realities of the external world. An example would be smokers who hold positive attitudes toward smoking to defend themselves against the reality of what they are doing to their bodies.

Attitudes also provide knowledge and value-expressive functions, their third and fourth roles. In their knowledge function, attitudes serve as guidelines in order to simplify decision making. For example, consumers may develop attitudes toward salespeople in "loud" jackets or toward retail stores with soft music and plush interiors. The knowledge function also helps to explain the effects of brand loyalty. By remaining brand loyal and maintaining a positive attitude toward a product, consumers can simplify decision making by avoiding a long, drawn-out search process for information on alternative brands. Finally, through the value-expressive function, consumers can express their central values and self-concept to others. The value-expressive function can be seen in cases in which people wear clothing adorned with the logos of brand to make a statement about themselves.[7]

BEHAVIORS AND INTENTIONS TO BEHAVE

Consumer behaviors consist of all the actions taken by consumers related to acquiring, disposing, and using products and services. Examples of consumer behaviors include buying a product or service, providing word-of-mouth information about a product or service to another person, disposing of a product, and collecting information for a purchase.

Prior to engaging in an action, people may develop behavioral intentions regarding their likelihood of engaging in the behavior. **Behavioral intentions** are defined as expectations to behave in a particular way with regard to the acquisition, disposition, and use of products and services. Thus, a consumer may form the intention to search for information, tell someone else about an experience with a product, buy a product or service, or dispose of a product in a certain way. Because they are highly predictive of actual behavior (especially in high-involvement circumstances), measuring behavioral intentions is important to market researchers.

HOW BELIEFS, ATTITUDES, AND BEHAVIORS ARE FORMED

Beliefs, attitudes, and behaviors may be formed in two distinct ways. The first is through direct formation in which a belief, attitude, or behavior is created without either of the other states occurring first. After a belief, attitude, or behavior is formed directly, the states build on each other to create hierarchies of effects. **Hierarchies of effects** identify the order in which beliefs, attitudes, and behaviors occur. The next two sections discuss these processes.

The Direct Formation of Beliefs, Attitudes, and Behaviors

Disparate processes cause the direct formation of beliefs, attitudes, and behaviors, and these processes are directly linked to the three research perspectives on consumer behavior. Recall from chapter 1 that these are the decision-making, experiential, and behavioral influence perspectives.

Forming Beliefs Directly. The decision-making perspective explains how beliefs are directly formed. Thus, beliefs directly emerge from the information-processing and cognitive-learning activities of the consumer. As described in chapter 4, information about the attributes of a product are received, encoded into memory, and later retrieved from memory for use.

Forming Attitudes Directly. Three mechanisms from the experiential perspective explain how attitudes are formed directly: classical conditioning, the mere-exposure phenomenon, and the influence of mood states. From a classical-conditioning perspective, an attitude is a conditioned emotional response that can be elicited by a conditioned stimulus.[8] The "hot," "sexy" ads for Calvin Klein's products illustrate the attempt to classically condition consumers so that feelings and emotions are elicited by a brand.

Another method by which positive feelings may be formed is through repeated exposures with a stimulus. All else being equal, through the **mere-exposure phenomenon,** people's liking for something may increase simply because they see it over and over again.[9] The all-else-equal caveat is important: If the consumer perceives the stimulus negatively, the repeated exposures could lead to an increase in the dislike for the stimulus.[10] An interesting aspect of the mere-exposure phenomenon is that it is not cognitively based. The positive feelings created from repeated exposures can occur without the person consciously knowing or perceiving that the object is familiar.[11] The omnipresence of the Coca-Cola brand name is an example. One sees it repeatedly flashed on the television, at baseball parks, in theaters, in restaurants, on buses, and elsewhere. The effects of mere exposure may be one of the factors that makes Coke the largest-selling soft drink.

The mood of the consumer also has direct impact on attitude formation. Researchers have found that, when consumers are initially exposed to an object, their mood state at the time will impact the attitude formed. Therefore, when consumers first learn about a new product, such as a digital audio recorder, their mood at that time will impact their evaluation. A positive mood increases the attitude; a negative mood decreases the evaluation. When introducing consumers to new products, retailers should do everything possible to place consumers in a positive affective state.[12]

Creating Behavior Directly. Traditionally, consumer researchers have viewed the behavior of buying a product or service as occurring after the formation of beliefs and attitudes. However, consistent with the behavioral influence perspective, behavior may be influenced directly without consumers first having developed strong beliefs or attitudes about the product. Behavior can be directly influenced when strong situational or environmental forces propel the consumer to action. The design of the physical environment is an excellent example of how behaviors can be directly induced.[13] For example, the appropriate arrangement of aisles in a supermarket can move customers in desired directions past high-margin food and nonfood items.

Operant conditioning can also be used to influence behavior directly. Shaping is an example of the direct influence of behavior through operant conditioning. Auto dealerships are skillful shapers of behavior. For example, a few years ago Buick attempted to improve sales of its slow-selling Regal by coordinating its sales promotion efforts with the Buick Open golf tournament. The division ran a large contest, called the "Longest Drive Sweepstakes," that gave any person who entered a showroom a chance of winning $126,000. If the person test drove a Regal, he or she was given a sleeve of golf balls. Finally, the customer was given large discounts on the purchase of a Regal.

Hierarchies of Beliefs, Attitudes, and Behaviors

Beliefs, attitudes, and behaviors can be formed indirectly through hierarchies of effects, and the type of purchase process controls which hierarchy is implemented. Table 7.1 identifies four different purchase processes and the four hierarchies that result: the high-involvement hierarchy, the low-involvement hierarchy, the experiential hierarchy, and the behavioral influence hierarchy.

Decision-Making Hierarchies. The high- and low-involvement hierarchies represent two forms of decision-making hierarchies. In the **high-involvement hierarchy,** beliefs occur first, followed by affect, which is in turn followed by behavior.[14] As its name suggests, this hierarchy of effects occurs when consumers are in a high-involvement state. In this situation consumers increase their problem-solving activities and search extensively for information about alternative products. As a result, large number of beliefs

The Four Hierarchies of Effects	
Purchase Process	**Hierarchy of Effects**
High involvement	High-involvement hierarchy: Beliefs—attitude—behavior
Low involvement	Low-involvement hierarchy: Beliefs—behavior—affect
Experiential/impulse	Experiential hierarchy: Affect—behavior—beliefs
Behavioral influence	Behavioral influence hierarchy: Behavior—beliefs—affect

TABLE 7.1

are formed about the alternatives. An affective charge is attached to each belief, and the sum of these charges creates the attitude. After the formation of beliefs and attitudes, behavior occurs.

In **low-involvement hierarchy** consumers first form beliefs about a product.[15] These beliefs are then followed directly by the product's purchase. Only after the purchase does the consumer develop an attitude regarding the product.[16] Thus, the flow of events is quite different when consumers are involved in a low-involvement decision. In these cases consumers are not motivated to engage in extensive problem solving. Instead, they move through a limited decision process in which only a few alternatives are considered in a superficial manner. As a result, the consumers form only a limited number of beliefs about the product alternatives. Furthermore, because they do not evaluate alternatives closely, the consumers may not form any attitudes. In sum, when consumers have low involvement in a purchase, they tend to engage in limited problem solving and move through a process of belief formation, then behavior, and finally attitude formation.[17]

Experiential Hierarchy. The **experiential hierarchy** begins with a strong affective response. Behavior then results from the strong feelings. Finally, beliefs are developed in order to justify and explain the behavior. Impulse purchases exemplify the experiential hierarchy. In an **impulse purchase,** a strong positive feeling is followed by the buying act.[18] If questioned about the purchase, the consumers would be able to voice a series of beliefs. However, the belief statements they make may be done to justify the decision.[19]

Behavioral Influence Hierarchy. In the **behavioral influence hierarchy,** strong situational or environmental forces propel a consumer to engage in an action without first having formed either feelings or affect about the object of the purchase. Behavior is therefore directly influenced without beliefs or attitudes intervening. When behavior is induced directly through the operation of environmental or situational factors, the hierarchy of effects begins with the behavior. Whether feelings or beliefs follow the behavior in the hierarchy has not been definitely answered. One researcher has argued that the hierarchy moves from behavior to feelings to beliefs.[20] This has been called the "do–feel–learn" hierarchy.

The study of beliefs and attitudes and their relationship to purchase behavior has major implications for promotional strategy. How companies promote a brand depends on the type of buying process that the brand's target market uses in buying

Some Promotional Strategies Based on the Type of Consumer Purchase Process	
Buying Process	**Possible Promotional Strategies**
High involvement	Emphasize developing product-attribute and product-benefit beliefs through cognitive-learning procedures. Can stress print advertising and personal selling. Help create affect through product demonstrations and advertising using classical-conditioning procedures.
Low involvement	Emphasize developing product-attribute beliefs through repetition of simple messages. Tie point-of-purchase displays to advertising. Place product and displays in high-traffic area.
Experiential/impulse	Emphasize the fun and feelings that can be obtained by experiencing the product or service. Emphasize creating affect through the classical conditioning of positive feelings toward the product.
Behavioral influence	Use sales-promotion techniques, such as sweepstakes, rebates, samples, or coupons.

TABLE 7.2

products from its particular category. Table 7.2 summarizes some promotional strategies that companies may use depending on the buying process involved.

PREDICTING CONSUMER ATTITUDES THROUGH MULTIATTRIBUTE MODELS

Multiattribute models describe how consumers combine their beliefs about product attributes to form attitudes about brand alternatives, corporations, or other objects in high-involvement circumstances. Numerous multiattribute models have been developed.[21] This chapter presents two of these models. The first focuses on predicting the attitude that a consumer forms toward a specific object, such as a product, service, person, or idea. The second model focuses on predicting the behavioral intentions of consumers to perform an action, such as buying a product or service.

Attitude-Toward-the-Object Model

The **attitude-toward-the-object model** identifies three major factors that are predictive of attitudes.[22] First, a person's salient beliefs influence attitude formation about an object. **Salient beliefs** represent knowledge about the attributes of the object that are activated in memory when attention is focused on an object. The second factor is the strength of the person's belief that an object has a particular attribute in question. The strength of the object–attribute linkage is assessed by asking a person, "How likely is it that object *x* possesses attribute *y*?" To measure strength of the belief, a 10-point scale is used. For example, if researchers are measuring consumer beliefs about the Land Rover SUV, they may ask, "What number represents how likely it is that the Land Rover is extremely rugged?"

Extremely Unlikely   1   2   3   4   5   6   7   8   9   10   Extremely Likely

The third component of this model is the evaluation of the goodness or badness of each of the salient attributes. For example, in the Land Rover example, some consumers may evaluate "ruggedness" positively and some may evaluate it negatively.

(That is, while "ruggedness" allows the vehicle to go off the road, it also makes the vehicle look awkward and slow.) Researchers obtain evaluation ratings of the attribute by asking consumers how good or bad the attributes are. In the Land Rover example, the researcher would ask consumers to rate the following two questions:

1. How bad or good is it for a vehicle to be extremely rugged?

    Very bad   −3   −2   −1   0   +1   +2   +3   Very good

2. How bad or good is it for a vehicle to have great handling?

    Very bad   −3   −2   −1   0   +1   +2   +3   Very good

In this example different segments of consumers will give divergent evaluations of the goodness or badness of the attribute of ruggedness. Some consumers may evaluate more favorably the attribute of off-road capability, whereas others will rate more favorably the attribute of good handling. On this attribute ratings may range widely from minus 3 to plus 3.

When attempting to predict a consumer's attitude, information on the evaluation and strength of the salient beliefs is combined via an algebraic formula. The formula is:

$$A_o = \sum_{i=1}^{N} b_i \, e_i$$

where: A_o = the overall attitude toward object o
b_i = the strength of the belief of whether object o has some particular attribute I
e_i = the evaluation of the goodness or badness of attribute I
n = the number of beliefs

Table 7.3 presents a hypothetical example of the attitudes held by two market segments—Macho Mikes and Racy Ritas—regarding three vehicles: a Toyota Celica, a Land Rover, and a Toyota RAV 4. Macho Mikes are young males who are risk takers, like to participate in sports, and love to drink beer. Racy Ritas are young, professional women who live in urban areas and work out at health clubs. Assume that for this example members of each market segment evaluated the vehicles on five salient attributes—sporty styling, outstanding handling, high cost, ruggedness, and off-road capability.

The predicted attitude is calculated by first multiplying the belief ratings for each attribute by the evaluation of the attribute. For example, Macho Mikes gave an evaluation of "+3" for off-road ability. This number is then multiplied by the belief rating of "7" for the Land Rover to give "21." In contrast, for Racy Ritas, the evaluation of off-road ability is "−3." This number is multiplied by the belief rating of "9" to give "−27." The "belief × evaluation" scores for each attribute are then added for each object to provide an estimate of the attitude. Note that the overall attitude score (e.g., 18 for Land Rover by Macho Mikes) is virtually meaningless in and of itself. Only when compared to the scores for Racy Ritas does it take on meaning.

An inspection of Table 7.3 shows that the Macho Mikes prefer the RAV 4 (an attitude of 47), followed by the Land Rover (attitude of 18) and the Celica (attitude of −5). In contrast, Racy Ritas like the Celica the best (attitude of 35) followed by the RAV 4 (attitude of −1) and the Land Rover (attitude of −5). The belief ratings of the two market segments were similar for the three autos. Each group viewed the Land Rover as costly, rugged, and as possessing off-road capability. The RAV 4 was viewed as costing less than the Land Rover and the Celica. The Celica was viewed as possessing

Predicting the Attitudes of Two Consumer Segments

Segment A: Macho Mikes

Attribute	e_i	Land Rover b_i	$b_i \times e_i$	RAV 4 b_i	$b_i \times e_i$	Celica b_i	$b_i \times e_i$
Sporty styling	−1	5	−5	7	−7	7	−7
Great handling	+1	5	5	6	6	8	8
High cost	−3	8	−24	2	−6	7	−21
Ruggedness	+3	7	21	9	27	4	12
Off-road ability	+3	7	21	9	27	1	3
Attitude score =			18		47		−5

Segment B: Racy Ritas

Attribute	e_i	Land Rover b_i	$b_i \times e_i$	RAV 4 b_i	$b_i \times e_i$	Celica b_i	$b_i \times e_i$
Sporty styling	+2	4	8	6	12	8	16
Great handling	+3	5	15	3	9	9	27
High cost	−1	8	−8	2	−2	7	−7
Ruggedness	+1	7	7	7	7	5	5
Off-road ability	−3	9	−27	9	−27	2	−6
Attitude score =			−5		−1		35

Note: b_i = strength of belief (1 = extremely unlikely, 10 = extremely likely).
  e_i = evaluation of goodness/badness (−3 = very bad, +3 = very good).
  A_o = Attitude toward object O.

TABLE 7.3

sporty styling and good handling, but as lacking in ruggedness and off-road capability. The extreme differences in the preferences of the two market segments was caused by the wide variations in their evaluations of the attributes. Macho Mikes strongly desired ruggedness and off-road capability. In contrast, Racy Ritas strongly desired sporty styling and great handling.

In sum, the attitude-toward-the-object model suggests that three factors influence attitude formation: (1) the salient attributes, (2) the extent to which consumers believe that the object possesses the attributes, (3) the degree of positivity or negativity of each of the attributes. Marketing managers must obtain this information from their key target markets. This knowledge will influence how the product is developed and how it is promoted. In addition, the information will influence the selection of the promotional messages designed to influence beliefs concerning the extent to which an object possesses an attribute.

How does the attitude-toward-the-object model deal with differences in the importance of the attributes? Interestingly, the model makes no direct attempt to measure the importance of attributes. The omission of ratings of importance, however, has little impact on the ability of the model to predict attitudes. This is because the importance of an attribute is in part assessed by the evaluation ratings. That is, as the importance of an attribute increases, the evaluation ratings become more extreme.[23]

Global Attitudes versus Attitudes-Toward-the-Object. The measure of attitude obtained from a multiattribute model is an indirect measure of attitude. In other words, the researcher can estimate the level of consumers' attitudes toward an object by measuring the strengths of their beliefs about the attributes possessed and their evaluations of the attributes of the object. In contrast, direct measures of consumers' global attitudes can be taken. A **global-attitude measure** is the direct measurement of the overall affect and feelings held by a consumer regarding an object.

To measure global attitudes, researchers ask several questions on semantic differential scales. (Semantic differentials scales ask respondents to rate an object on various scales anchored by meaning adjectives.) For example, global attitudes regarding a Land Rover might be phrased in the following manner: "Please describe your feelings about Land Rovers by circling the appropriate number on the scales."

Good   1 2 3 4 5   Bad
Positive 1 2 3 4 5   Negative

Whenever possible, market researchers collect data on global attitudes together with sufficient information to predict the attitudes through an attitude-toward-the-object model. The results of the two estimates can then be compared. If global attitudes and predicted attitudes are highly correlated, researchers can be confident that they have a good understanding of the factors influencing consumer-attitude formation. In contrast, if predicted and global attitudes fail to correlate, additional research is required to identify what is happening.

When Do Attitudes Predict Behavior? An important issue for consumer researchers involves explaining why knowledge of consumer attitudes does not necessarily predict actual behavior. In fact, many consumer researchers are pessimistic about the ability of attitudes to predict overt behavior.[24] Recently, researchers have recognized that the issue is one of knowing when attitudes predict behavior. A variety of factors have been found to influence the extent to which attitudes predict behaviors.[25] The ability of attitudes to predict behavior increases in the following circumstances: Consumer involvement is high, the attitude measure are reliable and valid, the attitudes are strongly held,[26] and situational factors do not intervene (e.g., interventions by other people, sickness, or promotional efforts of other brands).

The Behavioral Intentions Model

The behavioral intentions model, also called the **theory of reasoned action,** was developed for the purpose of improving on the ability of the attitude-toward-the-object model to predict consumer behavior. It extends the basic attitude-toward-the-object model in several ways.[27] First, it proposes that behavior results from the formation of specific intentions to behave. Thus, the model does not attempt to predict behavior per se, but rather intentions to act. Researchers have found that this model is superior to the attitude-toward-the-object model for predicting behavior.[28]

Second, the behavioral intentions model contains a new construct called the subjective norm. The **subjective norm** (SN) assesses what consumers believe other people think that they should do. In other words, SN introduces into the formulation the powerful effects of opinion leaders and reference groups on behavior. For example, one study investigated the use of condoms by adults. The results revealed that perceived pressure from others was by far the best predictor of condom usage. Pressure from socially important people was more important than other variables, such as AIDS knowledge, perceived susceptibility, and condom-use outcome expectancies.[29] Other studies have shown that the opinions of others influence a consumer's evaluations of a brand, particularly when the opinions are offered before the consumer tries the brand.[30]

The third change in the model involves the object to which attitudes are directed. Instead of assessing the consumer's attitude toward the brand itself, the model assesses the consumer's attitude toward the overt behavior of purchasing the product. The key difference in assessing attitude toward behavior rather than attitude toward the object is that the focus is on the consumer's perception of what the consequences of the purchase will be. When the consequences of the purchase are assessed—not whether the product possesses certain attributes—the researcher can better take into consideration factors that may act to impede intentions to behave. For example, consider the purchase of a sport utility vehicle. The following are some of the possible consequences: (1) buying the car would mean the person could not take a vacation; (2) buying the car would mean the person would have to deal with obnoxious salespeople; (3) buying the car would mean a loan at very high interest rates. Models that assess only the attitude toward the object have difficulty accounting for these types of effects.

The Mere-Measurement Effect. Consumer researchers have found that merely asking consumers about their purchase intentions influences their subsequent purchases. In one study of the mere-measurement effect, also called the self-prophecy effect, researchers asked nearly 5,000 consumers whether they intended to purchase a new car.[31] Next, they determined whether the consumers actually made a purchase during the next six months. These results were compared to a control group of 5,000 similar consumers who were not asked the purchase-intent question. The researchers found that those who received the purchase-intent question were significantly more likely to actually make the purchase, regardless of whether they said "yes" or "no." Significantly, this research has been replicated in a variety of other settings.[32] The results provide a new reason for doing marketing research.[33] The very act of asking behavioral intentions questions could increase the likelihood that consumers will purchase a product.[34]

PERSUASION: BELIEF, ATTITUDE, AND BEHAVIOR CHANGE

So far, this chapter has discussed how beliefs, attitudes, and behaviors are formed and how they may be predicted. In many instances, however, the goal is to persuade by changing preexisting attitudes and beliefs. **Persuasion** is defined as the explicit attempt to influence beliefs, attitudes, or behaviors. One could argue that consumers rarely enter a situation with absolutely no preexisting attitudes and beliefs about an object. Because of previous experience, consumers may already have an initial positive or negative feeling toward a new product or service. Thus, even when introducing new products, communicators are seeking to persuade consumers.

Persuasion can be understood from the three perspectives on consumer behavior: decision making, experiential, and behavioral influence. Look first at the decision-making approach.

The Decision-Making Approach to Attitude Change

An approach to understanding the persuasion process, called the **elaboration likelihood model** (ELM), illustrates the decision-making path to belief, attitude, and behavior change.[35] In the ELM (depicted in Figure 7.1) the persuasion process begins when the consumer receives a message. Upon receiving the message, the consumer begins

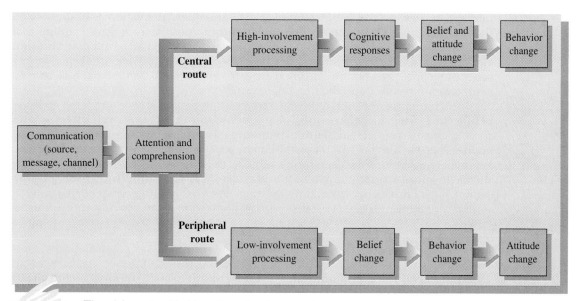

Figure 7.1   The elaboration likelihood mode of persuasion.

to process it. Depending on such factors as the message content, the nature of the consumer, and the consumer's situation, the person processes a communication with higher or lower amounts of involvement.

As described in chapter 3, involvement refers to the perceived personal relevance of the information. Depending on the amount of involvement, belief and attitude change may take one of two routes. When high-involvement information processing occurs, the person is said to take the **central route to persuasion.** In contrast, when in low-involvement circumstances, the consumer is said to be engaging in the **peripheral route to persuasion.**

When attitude and belief change occur via the central route, the high-involvement hierarchy of effects operates. As a result, the consumer attends more carefully to the message being received and diligently considers the communication, comparing it to his or her own attitudinal position. If the consumer has the ability to process the information, he or she is likely to generate a number of cognitive responses to the communication.[36] (**Cognitive responses** are the favorable or unfavorable thoughts generated by consumers as a result of a communication.) Based in part on the extent to which the cognitive responses are supportive or nonsupportive of the message, belief change occurs. Following the changes in beliefs, the consumer then experiences attitude change, which in turn leads to behavior change.

When belief and attitude change occur through the central route, the effects are relatively enduring and predictive of behavior.[37] In these involvement circumstances, consumers employ central cues when evaluating the message. **Central cues** refer to ideas and supporting data that bear directly on the quality of the arguments developed in the message.[38]

In the peripheral route to persuasion, the low-involvement hierarchy of effects occurs. There are minimal numbers of cognitive responses because the consumer is not carefully considering the pros and cons of the issue. Instead, consumers use peripheral cues to determine whether to accept or reject the message. **Peripheral**

persuasion cues include such factors as the attractiveness and expertise of the source, the mere number of arguments presented, and the positive or negative stimuli that form the context within which the message was presented (e.g., pleasant music). Under low-involvement circumstances, beliefs may change, but it is unlikely that attitudes or feelings are also influenced. If attitudes are formed, they are likely to be relatively temporary and unpredictive of behavior.[39]

You have probably heard the old aphorism, "If you say something often enough, people will come to believe you." A phenomenon called the truth effect relates directly to this saying. The **truth effect** states that, if something is repeated often enough, people who are in a low-involvement processing mode will begin to believe it. It occurs regardless of the actual truth value of the statement. In addition, it has been shown to more strongly impact elderly consumers compared with younger consumers.[40] The truth effect therefore illustrates one type of peripheral cue that may act to persuade consumers in low-involvement conditions—the repetition of information.[41]

Individual Differences in the Route to Persuasion. The ELM proposes that consumers may chronically use either a central or peripheral route. One can measure a trait called the **need for cognition,** which is the extent to which consumers chronically exhibit high- versus low-involvement processing of information.[42] Consumers who have a high need for cognition engage in high amounts of effortful cognitive activities. Such people habitually evaluate argument quality and employ the central route to persuasion. Consumers with a low need for cognition employ the peripheral route to persuasion. Information on a target market's need for cognition has importance for advertisers. In particular, more complex messages may be developed for consumers with a high need for cognition than for consumers with a low need for cognition.[43] In contrast, the use of celebrity endorsers (i.e., a peripheral cue) will be more effective for consumers with a low need for cognition.

Multiattribute Models and the Decision-Making Path to Persuasion

The concepts underlying multiattribute models of attitude formation can be applied to help change the beliefs, attitudes, and behaviors of a target. First, consider the attitude-toward-the-object model. Recall that in the model an attitude results from three factors: (1) the salient attributes on which a person evaluates an object, (2) a rating of the evaluation of the goodness or badness of the various attributes of an object, and (3) a rating of the person's belief of the extent to which the object possesses each of the attributes. Each of these factors can be employed to change an existing attitude.

First, communicators can attempt to change the perceived evaluation of an attribute. For example, an automobile company may use a fear appeal to place high emphasis on safety. The goal is to increase consumers' evaluations of the attribute of safety. A second strategy involves introducing a new attribute, rather than attempting to change the evaluation of an existing attribute. One such example of this strategy is an ad for Rembrandt Mouth Rinse that informed people that the brand is alcohol free. Because the most popular mouthwash (Listerine) is 52 proof, Rembrandt effectively added a new reason for buying its product.

A third way of influencing attitudes through the attitude-toward-the-object model is to change the belief that an object has a particular attribute. This is probably the easiest of the three approaches because a company can use a variety of methods to show that the particular characteristic of the product has changed. For example, a company could use demonstrations or trustworthy endorsers to show and explain the change.

The behavioral intentions model suggests additional approaches to attitude change. For example, marketers can influence perceptions of the consequences of a behavior. Thus, in the "Drug-Free America" campaign, advertisers identified at least one new consequence of taking drugs. That is, the children of nursing mothers can become addicts. By making salient this additional negative outcome of using cocaine, the campaign may have persuaded consumers not to engage in such behavior.

A second implication of the behavioral intentions model for attitude change involves the SN component. The model explicitly considers the impact of other people on a consumer's intentions to behave. In the "Drug-Free America" campaign researchers recognized the importance of teenagers' peer groups in developing questions for the market-research study. The results of the study confirmed the importance of reference groups, and advertisements were developed that showed one peer helping another.

Table 7.4 summarizes the implications of multiattribute models for attitude change and behavior.

Five Methods of Changing Attitudes: A Multiattribute Perspective

Method 1
Change the perceived evaluation of the attributes.
Advantage: Can increase the attitude rating of a product or service without changing the product or service in any way.
Disadvantage: Very difficult to do because evaluation ratings are often tied to the consumer's self-concept.

Method 2
Change the product-attribute beliefs.
Advantage: Easier to do because the company can use demonstrations or trustworthy sources to present the message. Beliefs about the extent to which products contain attributes are not usually connected to the consumer's self-concept.
Disadvantage: May involve changing the product.

Method 3
Add a new attribute for consideration.
Advantage: Beliefs and attitudes are easier to change when they are weakly held.
Disadvantage: May involve changing the product or service. Requires extensive promotional efforts to get new information to target market.

Method 4
Influence perceptions of consequences of behavior.
Advantage: Can identify consequences not previously recognized.
Disadvantage: Target may not evaluate consequences as desired or may not perceive them to be likely.

Method 5
Influence perceptions of reference group's reactions to behavior.
Advantage: Reference groups have a large impact on intentions to behave.
Disadvantage: Motivation to comply may be very low.

TABLE 7.4

The Experiential Path to Attitude Change

The persuasion process can also occur along an experiential path. When consumers follow the experiential path, attitudes are influenced directly, and beliefs about the object do not necessarily change beforehand. Two approaches have particular relevance to the experiential path to persuasion: balance theory and attitudes toward the advertisement.

Balance Theory

Researchers have found that attitudes may be changed by creating cognitive imbalance within the target of persuasion. The objective is to make use of people's tendency to maintain cognitive consistency among the various ideas and concepts about which they think. **Cognitive consistency** is the term applied to the human desire to maintain a logical and consistent set of interconnected attitudes. Thus, by deliberately creating cognitive inconsistency, the skillful communicator can induce consumers to change their attitudes because of this unconscious desire to bring their cognitive system back into balance. To explain the mechanisms behind the operation of cognitive consistency, it is first necessary to explain balance theory.

Balance theory specifies the relationships that an observer (*o*) perceives between him- or herself and another person (*p*) and an impersonal object (*x*). In a consumer-behavior setting, the observer represents the consumer, the other person might be a product endorser, and the impersonal object could be a brand. The observer, person, and object are called cognitive elements. Balance theory states that cognitive elements form a system in which each is linked to the other. They are similar to the nodes found in a semantic memory network, as discussed in chapter 4.

Figure 7.2 shows an example of a triad of cognitive elements. Two types of connections join the elements—sentiment connections and unit relations. Sentiment connections are identical in definition to the term *attitude* as used in this text. They are the positive or negative feelings that the observer may have toward the other person and the object. **Sentiment connections** are given a positive (+), negative (−), or neutral (0) algebraic sign depending on whether the feeling toward *p* or *x* is positive, negative, or neutral.

The second type of connection is called a **unit relation,** which occurs when the observer perceives that the person and object are connected to each other. The fac-

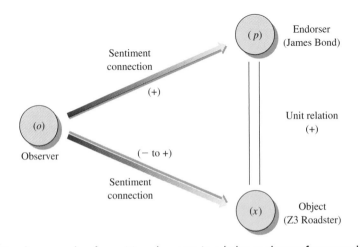

Figure 7.2   An example of cognitive elements in a balance-theory framework.

tors that govern whether a person perceives a connection are the same principles of perceptual organization discussed in chapter 3. Thus, p and x would be perceived as having a unit relation through such principles as proximity, similarity, continuation, and common fate. As in the case of sentiment connections, the relationship between p and x may be either positive, negative, or neutral. A positive unit relation indicates that p and x are perceived as related and as forming a unit. A negative sign indicates that the two elements are in opposition to each other. A neutral sign indicates that no relation exists between p and x. In such a case, the observer would not view the three elements as forming a unit, and no cognitive consistency forces would operate.

The basic premise of **balance theory** is that people have a preference to maintain a balanced state among the cognitive elements of p, o, and x. A balanced state was defined by Fritz Heider (the originator of balance theory) as a situation in which the cognitive elements fit together harmoniously with no stress for change. Such "harmony" occurs when the multiplication of the signs of the connections between the elements result in a positive value. As shown in Figure 7.3, a balanced state results from three positive signs or from two negative signs and one positive sign. An imbalanced state occurs if two signs are positive and one sign is negative or if all three signs are negative.

Balanced states are preferred to unbalanced states. Further, if a person experiences an imbalanced state, he or she is motivated to change the signs of one or more of the cognitive relations. Through a type of unconscious, mental rationalization, the person changes the weakest sign in order to bring the system into balance.

Although companies may not realize that they are using cognitive consistency procedures to change attitudes, one can identify numerous cases in which their strategies employ principles of balance theory. Indeed, the use of celebrity endorsers to sponsor products fits balance-theory principles quite well. Companies strive to select endorsers who are viewed as positively as possible by consumers. From the perspective of balance theory, these companies are attempting to maximize the strength of the sentiment connection between the observer (o) and the endorser (p). In addition, suc-

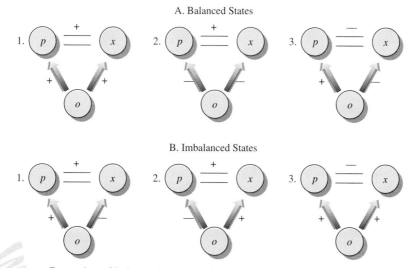

Figure 7.3 Examples of balanced and imbalanced states.

cessful companies attempt to create a unit relation between the endorser and the brand (x). Various ways of establishing this unit relation include the following: hiring endorsers who are known experts in using the product; signing the endorser to long-term, exclusive contracts so that the celebrity is associated only with the company's brand and no others; and having the endorser consistently wear or use the product when in public view so that he or she is strongly associated with the product. When a highly positive endorser is used and he or she is strongly connected to the product, then the sentiment relation between the consumer and the brand should become more positive.

Consumers, however, do not always change attitudes as marketing managers plan. In general, one finds that consumers change the sign of the weakest connection in an imbalanced cognitive system.[44] Thus, if consumers perceive that a celebrity endorses a brand only for the money, a unit connection may not develop between the celebrity and the product. As a result, no attitude change would occur. It is possible that celebrities, such as Michael Jordan, who endorse many products may gradually lose their effectiveness over time because no unit connection is formed between them and the products that they extol.

Attitude Toward the Advertisement

A second approach to directly influencing brand attitudes without necessarily changing beliefs is to influence consumer attitudes toward the advertisement. Researchers have found that consumers develop attitudes toward advertisements, just as they do brands.[45] In turn, these attitudes toward ads may influence attitudes toward the brand. An **attitude toward the ad** is a consumer's general liking or disliking for a particular advertising stimulus during a particular advertising exposure.[46] Attitudes toward advertisements can result from a number of factors, including the content and imagery vividness of the ad, the mood of the consumer, the consumer's emotions elicited by the advertisement, and by consumers' liking for the television program in which the ad is embedded.[47] Evidence indicates that these factors can influence attitude toward the ad under both high- and low-involvement conditions and regardless of whether the consumer is familiar with the brand.[48]

Researchers have also found that ads containing high levels of imagery strongly impact attitudes toward the ad.[49] The term *imagery* refers to the extent that an ad causes consumers to imagine their use of the product and to connect the ad to their own feelings and beliefs. Ads that employ concrete words, vivid verbal or pictorial images, instructions to imagine the use of the brand, and high levels of plausibility have been found to strongly impact consumers' attitudes toward the ad.

Another beneficial impact of creating strong positive attitudes toward ads is that it increases the time spent watching the commercial. Consumers have two direct means of controlling the time spent watching an ad. First, they can "zap" the ad by switching to a new channel. Second, they can "zip" the ad by fast-forwarding through programs already recorded. Researchers have found that both zipping and zapping are reduced as the pleasure and arousal caused by an ad increases.[50] These findings reveal that a firm should attempt to create ads that have positive emotional and informational qualities in order to reduce zipping and zapping.

The Behavioral Influence Route to Behavior Change

So far, this chapter has discussed the processes through which beliefs and attitudes are changed. As noted earlier, our actions can be affected through behavioral influence without necessarily first influencing either beliefs or attitudes about the behavior. For example, the ecological design of buildings and spaces can strongly affect the behavior of people without their being aware of the influence. Similarly, strong reinforcers or punishers in the environment can induce people to take actions that they would prefer to avoid.

Behavioral influence techniques have been developed that cause people to comply to requests by making use of strong norms of behavior. The techniques have been implemented by charities, by honest salespersons, and by everyday people. Unfortunately, the techniques also can be employed by unscrupulous individuals to gain their own illicit ends. The following sections discuss four behavioral influence techniques: ingratiation, the foot-in-the-door technique, the door-in-the-face technique, and the even-a-penny-will-help technique.

Ingratiation Tactics. The term **ingratiation** refers to self-serving tactics engaged in by one person to make him- or herself more attractive to another.[51] In this case attractiveness refers to the overall positivity or negativity with which one person views another. An ingratiator builds on the knowledge that, as the attractiveness of one person increases, the likelihood of another complying with his or her wishes increases. It is a subtle way of obtaining increased power over another person. Of course, everyone attempts to make him- or herself more attractive to favored others. With ingratiation, however, the efforts are manipulative and calculating. A number of different ingratiation techniques are available for use, but the common denominator among all the tactics is that the ingratiator subtly rewards the target. The techniques include appearing to be similar to the target, conforming to the target's wishes, offering compliments and gifts, expressing liking,[52] asking advice, and remembering someone's name.[53]

Ingratiation tactics are effective methods of achieving increased power in a short-term relationship, such as a personal-selling situation. Indeed, one of the primary tactics of the skilled salesperson is to create a "close relationship" with the client. Recent work on ingratiation indicates that it may be the most frequently used influence tactic.[54] A major problem can occur, however, if the ingratiator is caught in the attempt to manipulate the target. If the target recognizes that he or she is being deliberately manipulated, the influence attempt is likely to boomerang, resulting in a loss rather than a gain of power. An ingratiator's dilemma, therefore, exists. The ingratiator cannot be too obvious in his or her attempts to reward the target.[55]

The Foot-in-the-Door Technique. An old saying states that if a good salesman can merely get his foot in the door, he can make the sale. The foot-in-the-door technique shows that the adage has scientific support. A requester can increase the likelihood that a prospect will say "yes" to a moderate request if the person can be persuaded first to say "yes" to a smaller request. Thus, by getting a prospect to let him or her in the door, the skilled salesperson has persuaded that person to capitulate to a small request. The task of selling the person the product then becomes that much easier.

The **foot-in-the-door technique** operates through a self-perception mechanism—by complying to the first, small request, the prospect forms an impression that he or she is the type of person who does such a thing. Later, when the second request is made, the person is more likely to agree to the request because of a need to be consistent with that self-perception.[56] The foot-in-the-door technique has been shown to influence people in a wide variety of settings. For example, in comparison with control groups, those who were first asked to do something very small more frequently agreed to a larger request when asked. Examples include giving blood, counting traffic for a fictitious safety committee, and completing market-research surveys. Similarly, one study found that people who were first contacted over the phone and asked a few short questions were later more likely to complete a long written questionnaire than were people who had not been contacted first on the phone.[57]

The Door-in-the-Face Technique. The **door-in-the-face technique** also involves making two requests. However, instead of being very small, the initial request is extremely large. In fact, it is so large that no one would be expected to comply to it. After the respondent says "No!" to the first request, a smaller second request is made. In comparison with control groups that do not receive an initial request, groups met with the two-step approach display a greater degree of compliance to the second request. Areas in which the door-in-the-face technique have been found to increase the rate of compliance include asking people to complete marketing surveys, take juvenile delinquents to the zoo, and count automobiles for a traffic-safety committee.

The success of the door-in-the-face strategy operates through the norm of reciprocity.[58] The **norm of reciprocity** states that, if a person does something for you, you should do something in return for that person. The norm helps to grease the wheels of society by ensuring that efforts to help someone else will not go unrewarded. When the door-in-the-face strategy is implemented, the norm is illicitly invoked—that is, the requester makes the large request and never expects the person to comply with it. He or she then makes the smaller, more moderate request. The key to success is that the requester must make it appear that he or she has given up something when the smaller request is made. The target then feels as though he or she must return the favor. The only possible way of reciprocating the imaginary gift is to say "yes" to the second request.

Even-a-Penny-Will-Help Technique. The foot-in-the-door and the door-in-the-face techniques are based on the norms of looking good to others, being self-consistent, and reciprocating the concessions of others. The **even-a-penny-will-help technique** is based on the universal tendency for people to want to make themselves look good. Most often used in charity contexts, the approach operates by asking the target to give money and by tacking on the phrase "even a penny will help" at the end of the request. Because everyone has a penny, the person would look foolish in saying "no" to the request. Thus the person must say "yes." The problem is that the target cannot simply give a penny because he or she would look completely foolish. Thus, the person tends to give whatever is normatively appropriate for the situation and the charity.

Research investigating the technique has found that the total amount given to charities increases when the technique is used. Although individuals give slightly less money, on average, in comparison with those who did not receive the request and still contributed, the larger number of people giving something more than compensates for the slightly smaller individual contributions.[59] It is important to recognize that the compliance tactic can be implemented in many ways in addition to merely saying, "even a penny will help." A market researcher could ask the respondent to complete a survey and add the phrase "even answering a question or two would help." A salesperson making a cold call could state "even two minutes of your time would be appreciated." The adaptations of the technique are limitless.[60]

Ethical Implications of the Techniques of Personal Influence

An important note should be added concerning the ethics of using the techniques of personal influence. Each of the four techniques has a Machiavellian element. In each case the influencer attempts to manipulate another individual by engaging in a subtle subterfuge. In the case of the door-in-the-face technique, for example, the influencer lies to the respondent; the first request is a sham. This tactic is then in conflict with the critical principle that marketers and researchers should never lie to consumers. Fortunately, the ability to abuse the compliance techniques is self-limiting—that is, if overused, consumers will readily identify them and turn against those who employ the tactics.

THE MANAGERIAL IMPLICATIONS OF ATTITUDE FORMATION AND CHANGE

The principles and concepts derived from the study of attitudes, beliefs, and behavior formation and change have applications to each of the five PERMS concepts. These are discussed in the following sections.

Positioning and Differentiation

By identifying the salient attributes that have high importance ratings and are given extremely positive evaluation ratings in the attitude-toward-the-object model, managers have a means of positioning and differentiating a brand. For example, Burger King differentiates its burgers from McDonald's with its "Have it your way" slogan: Having the ability to order a burger with the trimmings that you want is an important attribute, and Burger King uses the slogan and backs it up with service to position and differentiate its brand.

Environmental Analysis

In order to implement the behavioral influence approach to behavior change, the analyst must carefully evaluate the environment in which the influence technique is to take place. For example, if the goal is to influence the movement of consumers through a retail store, the analyst must carefully evaluate the direct effects of the arrangement of aisles and the atmospheric variables, such as the sounds, smells, and textures of the store. On the other hand, if an influence technique such as ingratiation is to be employed, it is important to identify the norms of the culture and subculture that impact the target of influence. For example, offering a gift may be appropriate in many Asian cultures but inappropriate in the United States.

Research

Market research is required to identify the salient attributes that are of high importance to consumers in a product category. It is also critical to perform research studies to compare your brand to competitors' in terms of overall attitudes and of the belief ratings of the extent that it possesses key attributes. Other areas of research include identifying the involvement level of the target market and evaluating consumers' attitudes toward the advertisements that are being developed. Finally, it is important to conduct research in order to identify the key benefits that consumers are seeking in a product category.

Marketing Mix

The investigation of consumer beliefs, attitudes, and behaviors has particular relevance to product development and promotional strategy. First, after identifying the important product benefits, companies can develop brands that have attributes that provide these benefits. Indeed, new-product development should begin with an evaluation of the product benefits consumers seek and the attributes that provide them. Second, promotional strategy should be based on communicating to consumers the messages that evolve from the positioning strategy that emerges from the identification of key attributes. Other promotional issues that emerge include how to employ balance-theory principles and behavioral influence techniques to persuade and influence consumers. Finally, it is important to work with the creatives on the advertising staff to fashion communications toward which consumers will have positive attitudes.

Segmentation

The identification of important product attributes is the foundation of benefit segmentation. **Benefit segmentation** is the division of the market into homogeneous groups of consumers based on a similarity of benefits sought in a product category. Procter & Gamble has built huge market shares for many of its brands by establishing a strategy of focusing on how a product provides a benefit that fulfills one particular consumer need. For example, Crest toothpaste's dominant market share was built around providing one primary benefit—decay prevention. Similarly, Charmin toilet tissue has built its market share around providing the benefit of softness.

Notes

1. James Helgeson, Alan Kluge, John Mager, and Cheri Taylor, "Trends in Consumer Behavior Literature: A Content Analysis," *Journal of Consumer Research* 10 (March 1984): 449–54.
2. Christopher Joiner and Barbara Loken, "The Inclusion Effect and Category-Based Induction: Theory and Application to Brand Categories," *Journal of Consumer Psychology* 7, no. 2 (1998): 101–29.
3. Scott Mackenzie, "The Role of Attention in Mediating the Effect of Advertising on Attribute Importance," *Journal of Consumer Research* 13 (September 1986): 174–95.
4. The definition is found in John Cacioppo, Stephen Harkins, and Richard Petty, "The Nature of Attitudes and Cognitive Responses and Their Relations to Behavior," in *Cognitive Responses in Persuasion,* ed. Richard Petty, Thomas Ostrom, and Timothy C. Brock, eds. (Hillsdale, NJ: Lawrence Erlbaum, 1981), 31.
5. Chris T. Allen, Karen A. Machleit, and Susan Schultz Kleine, "A Comparison of Attitudes and Emotions as Predictors of Behavior at Diverse Levels of Behavioral Experience," *Journal of Consumer Research* 18 (March 1992): 493–504. For a similar definition, see Darrel J. Bem, *Beliefs, Attitudes, and Human Affairs* (Belmont, CA: Brooks/Cole, 1970). Also see Martin Fishbein and Icek Ajzen, *Belief, Attitude, Intention, and Behavior: An Introduction to Theory and Research* (Reading, MA: Addison-Wesley, 1975); and Phillip Zimbardo, E. Ebbesen, and C. Maslach, *Influencing Attitudes and Changing Behavior* (Reading, MA: Addison-Wesley, 1977).
6. Daniel Katz, "The Functional Approach to Attitudes," *Public Opinion Quarterly* 24 (1960): 163–204. Also see Sharon Shavitt, "Products, Personalities, and Situations in Attitude Functions: Implications for Consumer Behavior," in *Advances in Consumer Research,* ed. Thomas Srull (Provo, UT: Association for Consumer Research, 1989), 16:300–305.
7. For an excellent discussion on the functions and role of attitudes in consumer behavior, see Richard J. Lutz, "The Role of Attitude Theory in Marketing," in *Perspectives in Consumer Behavior,* ed. Harold Kassarjian and Thomas Robertson (Upper Saddle River, NJ: Prentice Hall, 1991), 317–39.
8. Elnora Stuart, Terence Shimp, and Randall Engle, "Classical Conditioning of Consumer Attitudes: Four Experiments in an Advertising Context," *Journal of Consumer Research* 14 (December 1987): 334–49.
9. Robert Zajonc, "The Attitudinal Effects of Mere Exposure," *Journal of Personality and Social Psychology* monograph, vol. 9 (1968), 2, pt 2, 1–27.
10. Mackenzie, "Role of Attention."
11. William Wilson, "Feeling More Than We Know: Exposure Effects without Learning," *Journal of Personality and Social Psychology* 37 (June 1979): 811–21.
12. John Hadjimzrcou, John W. Barnes, and Richard S. Jacobs, "The Effects of Context-Induced Mood States on Initial and Repeat Product Evaluations: A Preliminary Investigation," in *Advances in Consumer Research,* ed. Kim P. Corfman and John G. Lynch Jr. (Provo, UT: Association for Consumer Research, 1996), 23:337–41.
13. Walter Nord and J. Paul Peter, "A Behavior Modification Perspective on Marketing," *Journal of Marketing* 44 (spring 1980): 36–47.
14. Michael Ray, "Marketing Communications and the Hierarchy-of-Effects," in *New Models for Mass Communications,* ed. P. Clarke (Beverly Hills, CA: Sage Publications, 1973), 147–76.
15. Herbert Krugman, "The Impact of Television Advertising: Learning without Involvement," *Public Opinion Quarterly* 29 (October 1961): 59–62. A variety of definitions of involvement have been proposed. For a good review, see John H. Antil, "Conceptualization and

Operationalization of Involvement," in *Advances in Consumer Research*, ed. Thomas C. Kinnear (Provo, UT: Association for Consumer Research, 1984), 11:203–9.

16. Richard W. Olshavsky and Donald H. Granbois, "Consumer Decision Making: Fact or Fiction?" *Journal of Consumer Research* 6 (September 1979): 93–100.

17. For an excellent discussion of low-involvement decision making, see F. Stewart De Bruicker, "An Appraisal of Low-Involvement Consumer Information Processing," in *Attitude Research Plays for High Stakes*, ed. John Maloney and Bernard Silverman (Chicago, IL: American Marketing Association, 1979), 112–30.

18. Dennis W. Rook and Stephen J. Hoch, "Consuming Impulses," in *Advances in Consumer Behavior* (Provo, UT: Association for Consumer Research, 1985), 12:23–27.

19. Such justifications would work through a self-perception process. See Bem, *Beliefs, Attitudes, and Human Affairs.*

20. These ideas were expressed to me by Professor Russell Belk.

21. Numerous approaches to the study of attitudes exist. For a discussion of several of these, see Lutz, "Role of Attitude Theory."

22. For a full discussion of the attitude-toward-the-object model, see Fishbein and Ajzen, *Belief, Attitude, Intention, and Behavior.*

23. For a recent discussion of this issue, see Mackenzie, "Role of Attention."

24. Allan Wicker, "Attitudes versus Actions: The Relationship of Verbal and Overt Behavioral Responses to Attitude Objects," *Journal of Social Issues* 25 (autumn 1969): 65.

25. Robert Cialdini, Richard Petty, and John Cacioppo, "Attitude and Attitude Change," *Annual Review of Psychology* 32 (1981): 366.

26. Linda F. Alwitt and Ida E. Berger, "Understanding the Link between Environmental Attitudes and Consumer Product Usage: Measuring the Moderating Role of Attitude Strength," in *Advances in Consumer Research*, ed. Leigh McAlister and Michael Rothschild (Provo, UT: Association for Consumer Research, 1992), 20:189–94.

27. Icek Ajzen and Martin Fishbein, "Attitude–Behavior Relations: A Theoretical Analysis and Review of Empirical Research," *Psychological Bulletin*, September 1977, pp. 888–918. Readers should note that the behavioral intentions model is now called the theory of reasoned action. We retain the older name to emphasize its focus on predicting behavioral intentions.

28. For an example of an article that finds the behavioral intentions model to be superior to attitude-toward-the-object model, see Michael J. Ryan and E. H. Bonfield, "Fishbein's Intentions Model: A Test of External and Pragmatic Validity," *Journal of Marketing* 44 (spring 1980): 82–95.

    Readers should note that work continues on behavioral intentions models. For a recent comparison of three models of behavioral intentions, see Richard Netemeyer, J. Craig Andrews, and Scrinvas Durvasula, "A Comparison of Three Behavioral Intentions Models: The Case of Valentine's Day Gift-Giving," in *Advances in Consumer Research*, ed. Leigh McAlister and Michael Rothschild (Provo, UT: Association for Consumer Research, 1992), 20:135–41.

29. Martin Fishbein, Susan E. Middlestadt, and David Trafimow, "Social Norms for Condom Use: Implications for HIV Prevention Interventions of a KABP Survey with Heterosexuals in the Eastern Caribbean," in *Advances in Consumer Research*, ed. Leigh McAlister and Michael Rothschild (Provo, UT: Association for Consumer Research, 1992), 20:292–96.

30. David B. Wooten and Americus Reed II, "Informational Influence and the Ambiguity of Product Experience: Order Effects on the Weighting of Evidence," *Journal of Consumer Psychology* 7, no. 1 (1998): 79–99.

31. Vicki G. Morwitz, Eric Johnson, and David Schmittlein, "Does Measuring Intent Change Behavior?" *Journal of Consumer Research* 20 (June 1993): 46–61.

32. For a review of this research, see David E. Sprott, Eric R. Spangenberg, and Andrew W. Perkins, "Two More Self-Prophecy Experiments," in *Advances in Consumer Research*, ed. Eric Arnould and Linda M. Scott (Provo, UT: Association for Consumer Research, 1999), 26:621–26.

33. The mere-measurement effect was recently supported in research by Eric R. Spangenberg and Anthony G. Greenwald, "Social Influence by Requesting Self-Prophecy," *Journal of Consumer Psychology* 8, no. 1 (1999): 61–89.

34. Gavan J. Fitzsimons and Vicki G. Morwitz, "The Effect of Measuring Intent on Brand-Level Purchase Behavior," *Journal of Consumer Research* 23 (June 1996): 1–11.

35. Richard Petty, John Cacioppo, and D. Schumann, "Central and Peripheral Routes to Advertising Effectiveness: The Moderating Role of Involvement," *Journal of Consumer Research* 10 (September 1983): 135–46.

36. Richard Petty and John Cacioppo, "The Elaboration Likelihood Model of Persuasion," in *Advances in Experiential Social Psychology,* ed. Leonard Berkowitz (New York: Academic Press, 1986), 19:123–205.

37. Cialdini, Petty, and Cacioppo, "Attitude and Attitude Change."

38. Recent research has been supportive of key elements of the ELM model. See Jong-Won Park and Manoj Hastak, "Effects of Involvement on On-Line Brand Evaluations: A Stronger Test of the ELM," in *Advances in Consumer Research* ed. Frank R. Kardes and Mita Sujan (Provo, UT: Association for Consumer Research, 1995), 22:435–39.

39. Cacioppo, Harkins, and Petty, "Nature of Attitudes," 31–54. Also see Petty, Cacioppo, and Schumann, "Central and Peripheral Routes." A number of studies have found evidence supportive of predictions made by the elaboration likelihood model. The work on the ELM is still relatively new, however, and several authors have noted that it has weaknesses. See Charles Areni and Richard Lutz, "The Role of Argument Quality in the Elaboration Likelihood Model," in *Advances in Consumer Research,* ed. Michael Houston, ed. (Provo, UT: Association for Consumer Research, 1988), 15:197–203. Also see Paul Miniard, Peter Dickson, and Kenneth Lord, "Some Central and Peripheral Thoughts on the Routes to Persuasion," in *Advances in Consumer Research,* ed. Michael Houston, ed. (Provo, UT: Association for Consumer Research, 1988), 15:204–8. Another recent article is Paul W. Miniard, Deepak Sirdeshmukh, and Daniel E. Innis, "Peripheral Persuasion and Brand Choice," *Journal of Consumer Research* 19 (September 1992): 226–39.

40. Sharmistha Law, Scott A. Hawkins, and Fergus I. M. Craik, "Repetition-Induced Belief in the Elderly: Rehabilitating Age-Related Memory Deficits," *Journal of Consumer Research* 25 (September 1998): 91–107.

41. Scott A. Hawkins and Stephen J. Hoch, "Low-Involvement Learning: Memory without Evaluation," *Journal of Consumer Research* 19 (September 1992): 212–24.

42. Curtis P. Haugtvedt, Richard E. Petty, and John T. Cacioppo, "Need for Cognition and Advertising: Understanding the Role of Personality Variables in Consumer Research," *Journal of Consumer Psychology* 1, no. 3 (1992): 239–60.

43. Curt Haugtvedt, Richard Petty, John Cacioppo, and Theresa Steidley, "Personality and Ad Effectiveness: Exploring the Utility of Need for Cognition," in *Advances in Consumer Research,* ed. Michael Houston (Provo, UT: Association for Consumer Research, 1988), 15:209–12.

44. M. J. Rosenberg, "An Analysis of Affective-Cognitive Consistency," in *Attitude Organization and Change,* ed. M. J. Rosenberg, C. I. Hovland, W. J. McGuire, R. P. Abelson, and J. W. Brehm (New Haven, CT: Yale University Press, 1960), 15–64.

45. Andrew A. Mitchell and Jerry Olson, "Are Product Attribute Beliefs the Only Mediator of Advertising Effects of Brand Attitude?" *Journal of Marketing Research* 18 (1981): 318–32.

46. Richard Lutz, "Affective and Cognitive Antecedents of Attitude toward the Ad: A Conceptual Framework," in *Psychological Processes and Advertising Effects: Theory, Research, and Application,* ed. L. F. Alwitt and A. A. Mitchell (Hillsdale, NJ: Lawrence Erlbaum, 1985), 45–63.

47. Kenneth R. Lord, Myung-Soo Lee, and Paul L. Sauer, "Program Context Antecedents of Attitude toward Radio Commercials," *Journal of the Academy of Marketing Science* 22 (winter 1994): 3–15.

48. Joseph Phelps and Esther Thorson, "Brand Familiarity and Product Involvement Effects on the Attitude toward an Ad–Brand Attitude Relationship," in *Advances in Consumer Research,* ed. Rebecca H. Holman and Michael R. Solomon (Provo, UT: Association for Consumer Research, 1991), 18:202–9.

49. Paula Fitzgerald Bone and Pam Scholder Ellen, "The Generation and Consequences of Communication-Evoked Imagery," *Journal of Consumer Research* 19 (June 1992): 93–104. For more information on the effects of pictures on information processing and brand preferences, see Carolyn L. Costley and Merrie Brucks, "Selective Recall and Information Use in Consumer Preferences," *Journal of Consumer Research* 18 (March 1992): 464–84.

50. James Boles and Scot Burton, "An Examination of Free Elicitation and Response Scale Measures of Feelings and Judgments Evoked by Television Advertisements," *Journal of the Academy of Marketing Science* 20 (summer 1992): 225–33.

51. Edward E. Jones, *Ingratiation: A Social Psychological Analysis* (New York: Appleton-Century-Crofts, 1964).

52. Michael J. Dorsch and Scott W. Kelley, "An Investigation into the Intentions of Purchasing Executives to Reciprocate Vendor Gifts," *Journal of the Academy of Marketing Science* 22 (fall 1994): 315–27.

DELIVERY ADDRESS
CPI Liverpool
Blackwells University Bookshop
Unit 2/3 Block 1 Crown Place,
Peach Street,
LIVERPOOL
Merseyside,
L3 5UH,
UNITED KINGDOM

Bookbarn International Ltd
Unit 1 Hallatrow Business Park, Wells
Road, Hallatrow,
Bristol
Somerset, BS39 6EX,
UNITED KINGDOM

Packing Slip / Invoice
Price: £3.31

Standard

Order Date: 07/02/2019

Customer Contact: Liverpool CPI

BBI Order Number: 902364

NOS1

Website Order ID: 203-7573867-8820317

NOS2

SKU InvID	Locators	Item Information
2605520 9875152	C32-09-01 279025 Green PAP ExLib - N U:G	**Consumer Behavior: A Framework** Mowen, John C. & Minor, Michael S. Previous owners Annotations/Highlighting.

If you wish to contact us regarding this order, please email us via Amazon quoting your order number.

amzuk

Thanks for shopping with us

www.bookbarninternational.com

*9 0 2 3 6 4 *

Greetings from Bookbarn International,

Thank you so much for placing an order with us, in doing so you've helped us grow as an independent bookseller.

We hope you're happy with your purchase, however if you have any issues or queries please do not hesitate to contact us.
Log into the website you bought from, locate your order in your order or purchase history and **Contact Seller.**
Our small and committed team provides a fast response to ensure you are fully satisfied.

Kind regards & happy reading!
The BBI Team

Bookbarn Internationalからのご挨拶、

この度はご注文していただきありがとうございます。
おかげさまで私たちはインディペンデント系書店として成長することができております。

ご注文いただいた商品に問題がある場合や質問がある場合は、どうかお気軽にお問い合わせください。

連絡方法は、お客様がご注文されたウェブサイトにログインしていただき、注文履歴のリストから出品者に連絡するボタンより直接ご連絡ください。

当社の小規模で献身的なチームは、お客様が完全に満足していただけることを確実にするために迅速な対応をいたします。

どうぞよろしくお願いいたします。

読書をお楽しみいただけますよう願っております！
BBI チーム

Salutations de Bookbarn International,

Merci beaucoup d'avoir passé une commande chez nous. Vous nous avez aidé à grandir en tant que libraire indépendant.

Nous espérons que vous êtes satisfait de votre achat. Si vous avez des questions ou des questions, n'hésitez pas à nous contacter.

Connectez-vous au site Web où vous avez commandé votre livre, trouvez votre commande dans votre historique d'achat et contactez le vendeur.

Notre équipe petite et engagée fournit une réponse rapide pour s'assurer que vous êtes pleinement satisfait.

Bonne lecture!

Cordialement,
L'équipe BBI

Saludos desde Bookbarn International,

Muchas gracias por hacer un pedido con nosotros. Nos ha ayudado a crecer como librería independiente.

Esperamos que esté satisfecho con su compra. Si tiene algún problema o consulta, no dude en contactarnos: Inicie sesión en el sitio web que utilizó para efectuar su compra, busque su pedido en su historial de compras y comuníquese con el vendedor.

Somos un equipo pequeño, comprometido con brindar una respuesta rápida para garantizar su completa satisfacción.

Saludos cordiales y feliz lectura!

El equipo de BBI

Grüße von Bookbarn International,

Vielen Dank für Ihre Bestellung. Sie haben uns dabei geholfen, ein unabhängiger Buchhändler zu werden.

Wir hoffen, dass Sie mit Ihrem Kauf zufrieden sind. Wenn Sie jedoch Probleme oder Fragen haben, zögern Sie bitte nicht, uns zu kontaktieren.

Gehen Sie auf Meine Bestellungen, suchen Sie Ihre Bestellung in der Liste und klicken Sie auf Verkäufer kontaktieren.

Unser kleines und engagiertes Team bietet eine schnelle Antwort, um sicherzustellen, dass Sie voll zufrieden sind.

Mit freundlichen Grüßen und viel Spaß beim Lesen!
Das BBI-Team

UK +44 (0)1761 451 777 | bookbarn@bookbarninternational.com

53. Daniel J. Howard, Charles Gengler, and Ambuj Jain, "What's in a Name? Complimentary Means of Persuasion," *Journal of Consumer Research* 22 (September 1995): 200–211.

54. Lynnea Mallalieu and Corinne Faure, "Toward an Understanding of the Choice of Influence Tactics: The Impact of Power," in *Advances in Consumer Research,* ed. Joseph W. Alba and J. Wesley Hutchinson (Provo, UT: Association for Consumer Research, 1998), 25:407–14.

55. Edward E. Jones and Harold B. Gerard, *Foundations of Social Psychology* (New York: Wiley, 1967).

56. Peter H. Reingen and J. B. Kernan, "Compliance with an Interview Request: A Foot-in-the-Door, Self-Perception Interpretation," *Journal of Marketing Research* 14 (August 1977): 365–69.

57. Robert A. Hansen and Larry M. Robinson, "Testing the Effectiveness of Alternative Foot-in-the-Door Manipulations," *Journal of Marketing Research* 17 (August 1980): 359–64.

58. John C. Mowen and Robert Cialdini, "On Implementing the Door-in-the-Face Compliance Strategy in a Marketing Context," *Journal of Marketing Research* 17 (May 1980): 253–58.

59. Robert Cialdini and David Schroeder, "Increasing Compliance by Legitimizing Paltry Contributions: When Even a Penny Helps," *Journal of Personality and Social Psychology* 34 (October 1976): 599–604.

60. For a single theoretical explanation of the four compliance techniques based on the availability–valence hypothesis, see Alice Tybout, Brian Sternthal, and Bobby Calder, "Information Availability as a Determinant of Multiple Request Effectiveness," *Journal of Marketing Research* 20 (August 1983): 279–90. Also see Edward Fern, Kent Monroe, and Ramon Avila, "Effectiveness of Multiple Request Strategies: A Synthesis of Research Results," *Journal of Marketing Research* 23 (May 1986): 144–52.

Persuasive Communications

After studying this chapter, you should be able to describe each of the following concepts, together with their managerial implications.

1. The communications model.
2. Source credibility.
3. Source attractiveness.
4. Source likability.
5. Comparative advertisements.
6. Fear appeals versus humor appeals.
7. Rhetorical figures of speech.
8. Lectures and dramas.
9. Message repetition and wear-out.
10. Primacy and recency effects.

Communications are omnipresent in our lives. Radio and television commercials, print advertisements, billboards, packaging, and sales personnel all seek to communicate with us and ultimately to influence us. Researchers have estimated that on average American consumers receive from 200 to 500 commercial messages a day. Yet they are aware of only 15 percent and actively process only 4 to 5 percent of the messages.[1] In addition, in our encounters with friends and acquaintances, persuasive communications are commonplace. A friend who says, "Hey, there's a great new movie. Do you want to go?" is engaging in a persuasion attempt.

As exemplified by the exploding interest in the Internet and e-mail, a telecommunications revolution is also occurring. For example, Lexus kicked off a $60 million ad campaign for its ES300 model with e-mails to drivers of rival automakers.[2] The U.S. Post Office estimates that 25 percent of future mail volume is "at risk" because of advances in telecommunications.[3] (And this may be a very low estimate!) On the other hand, the amount of unwanted e-mail, called spam, has exploded as well. Busy executives frequently receive over a hundred e-mails each day, and answering each is a huge time drain.

A **communication** involves the use of a sign to convey meaning. A **sign** may be a verbalization, utterance, body movement, written word, picture, odor, touch, or even stones on the ground to denote a property boundary. When one speaks of a communication, the referent may be the specific words spoken, a subtle change in voice quality, the written word, a pictorial representation, or a gesture. Communications are received through all the senses. Extremely unambiguous messages can be communicated through smell and touch. Perfumes are worn to communicate sensual thoughts and feelings. A touch can communicate feelings of tenderness, sadness, and anger. Even silence can have meaning and increase listener retention of ad information.[4]

An important point is that the meanings conveyed by signs are strongly influenced by culture. For example, the gesture for indicating "okay" in the United States consists of joining the thumb and index finger to form a circle. However, in many Latin American countries, such a sign is an insult having scatological (i.e., obscene references to excrement) connotations.

Researchers have developed a **communications model** that depicts the relationships among the various factors that influence the effectiveness and impact of persuasive communications.[5] Figure 8.1 presents one version of this model. The model identifies five factors that control the effectiveness of communications: source characteristics, message content, medium characteristics, contextual factors, and receiver or audience characteristics.

As shown in Figure 8.1, persuasive communications begin with a source of information who encodes and delivers a message. Messages can be coded in many ways. For example, a communicator must think through such issues as whether to use a fear appeal, humor, a lecture, or a drama in a television advertisement.

The message is delivered through some medium or channel of transmission. The medium could be face to face, print, radio, telephone, billboards, television, or the World Wide Web. The characteristics of the channel influence the interpretation of the message, as well as how its information is processed. The message is then received by members of an audience who decode and interpret the communication.

Various characteristics of the audience can moderate the effects of persuasive communications. Such factors as personality, sex, intelligence, and involvement in the issue mediate how receivers decode the information and react to the communication. Finally, the entire communications process takes place within a general environmental

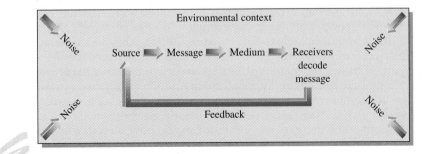

Figure 8.1   A communications model.

context. Various environmental stimuli may inhibit the communications process by distracting consumers, influencing their mood, or acting to create "noise" in the transmission of the message.

This chapter analyzes in detail two key factors that influence the effectiveness of the communication process: the characteristics of the source of information and the characteristics of the message that is communicated. Three other factors important to the communications process are not discussed in the chapter. They are (1) the context within which the message is delivered, (2) the nature of the channel or vehicle through which the message is communicated, and (3) the receiver. The receiver of the communication is an individual. (Individual differences in consumer behavior are discussed in chapter 6.)

The channel through which a message is transmitted may also influence the effectiveness of the communication. **Channels** are the media through which messages flow. Examples of channels are face-to-face interactions (e.g., a sales call), television, radio, billboards, newspapers, and magazines. The Internet is the newest channel through which information flows. Its impact extends from consumer buying to industrial buying. For example, it is changing the behavior of steel purchasers. Previously, companies using small amounts of steel in their products could not negotiate prices. Now these companies can click to a Web site, www.MetalSite.com, and get quotes from a half-dozen steelmakers.[6] The net effect is lower prices and better service.

Because communication begins with an information source, this element is discussed first.

SOURCE CHARACTERISTICS

Understanding the factors that influence the effectiveness of sources of information is extremely important to marketing managers and public-policy makers. For example, advertisers frequently hire endorsers to advocate a product or service. In one study that investigated 243 commercials, over 38 percent used some type of endorser.[7] The importance that advertisers attribute to finding the "right" source is illustrated by the huge sums they are willing to pay celebrity endorsers. For example, when the young golfer Tiger Woods turned professional, Nike and Titleist paid the 20 year old a combined $40 million to endorse their products over a three-year period.[8]

A **source** is defined as an individual or character who delivers a message. **Source characteristics** are the features that impact the effectiveness of the source. They include the source's credibility, physical attractiveness, likability, and meaningfulness.

Source Credibility

The term **source credibility** refers to the perception of the degree of a source's credence, based on the perception of the expertise and trustworthiness of the source. Thus, the greater the expertise and trustworthiness of a source of information, the more likely an observer will perceive the source as credible. The credibility of the source has a large impact on consumer behavior. For example, critics from the *New York Times* have been found to have twice the impact on the success of Broadway shows of critics from the *Daily News* or the *New York Post*.[9] One reason for the differential impact is the higher credibility of the critics who write for the *New York Times*.

Source expertise refers to the extent of knowledge the source is perceived to have about the subject on which he or she is communicating. **Source trustworthiness** refers to the extent that the source is perceived to provide information in an unbiased, honest manner.[10] Among the various types of source variables, source expertise has been found to have the greatest impact on respondent's reactions to communications.[11]

Source expertise and trustworthiness make an independent contribution to source effectiveness. Thus, if someone is perceived to be trustworthy, he or she can influence an audience, even if perceived to have relatively little expertise. Similarly, even though someone may be perceived to be untrustworthy, if perceived to be an expert, he or she will have persuasive ability.[12]

In advertisements, one factor that influences trust is the attributions made for the cause of the endorsement. If an endorser is perceived as presenting a message because of his or her own self-interest, trust will be substantially lower. These effects are magnified if multiple endorsers are used in an advertising campaign. If multiple trustworthy endorsers are employed to convey a message, the formation of positive attitudes is enhanced. Conversely, if multiple "untrustworthy" endorsers are employed, attitudes dramatically decrease. Thus, risks are run if the endorsers appear to be motivated primarily because they are paid rather than because they really believe in the product.[13] Advertising campaigns such as for basketball shoes, beer, and milk have used multiple endorsers. For example, in the award-winning "Milk Mustache" campaign, endorsers in this humorous campaign included Spike Lee, Florence Griffith Joyner, and Steve Young.

Another important positive effect of using credible endorsers is that they reduce counterargumentation. Advertisers realize that consumers often develop their own thoughts in response to a message. These thoughts, called **cognitive responses,** may be positive regarding the message (i.e., support arguments), may be negative toward the message (i.e., counterarguments), or may concern the characteristics of the source (source derogations).[14] When a highly trustworthy and expert endorser is used, however, people lower their defenses and produce fewer cognitive responses. In particular, because highly credible sources inhibit counterargumentation, they may be more persuasive than less credible sources.

In sum, highly credible sources are more effective than are less credible sources.[15] Highly credible sources have been found to do the following:

1. Produce more positive attitude change toward the position advocated.
2. Induce more behavioral change than less credible sources.
3. Enhance the ability to use fear appeals, which involve physical or social threats.
4. Inhibit the creation of counterarguments to the message.

The Physical Attractiveness of the Source

To recognize the importance of **physical attractiveness,** one has only to watch television or examine print advertisements. Most television and print ads use physically attractive people. Indeed, researchers have found that physically attractive communicators are more successful than unattractive ones in changing beliefs.[16] In addition, people tend to form positive stereotypes about physically attractive people. For example, one study found that college men and women expected physically attractive people to be more sensitive, warm, modest, happy, and so forth. Indeed, the results of the study were summarized as "What is beautiful is good."[17]

In the advertising arena, researchers have found that attractive individuals are perceived more positively and reflect more favorably on the brand endorsed. For example, in one study respondents were shown slides of either an attractive or an average-looking person who worked at the Cincinnati Zoo.[18] Respondents were asked to give their impressions of the presentation and of the person. In addition, they were asked if they would be willing to volunteer to assist the zoo. The results revealed that impressions of the slide show were significantly more favorable when an attractive model was used. The effect was particularly strong for males who saw an attractive female. Males exposed to the attractive female were significantly more interested in attending a meeting and in passing a levy to finance the zoo.

Physical attractiveness also interacts with other variables.[19] In one study highly attractive and less attractive people endorsed either a coffee product or a perfume. The results showed that the more attractive model produced greater intentions to buy the product when the product had a sexual appeal (i.e., when the product was the perfume). In contrast, if the product had nothing to do with attracting the opposite sex (i.e., the product was coffee), the unattractive source had more impact. Respondents in the study may have inferred that physically attractive endorsers would know something about perfume but have little knowledge of coffee. These results indicate that using physically attractive and sexy models may not be appropriate for some types of products, such as coffee.

These results illustrate the importance of matching the nature of the product with the characteristics of the endorser. This **match-up effect** states that endorsers are more effective in changing attitudes, beliefs, and intentions when the dominant characteristics of the product match the dominant features of a source. This explains the results of the study just described: Because perfume is used to entice members of the opposite sex, a physically attractive source "fits" the product. In contrast, a characteristic of coffee is the difficulty of brewing a good cup, which is not associated with physical attractiveness. Researchers have also found that matching source and brand is particularly important when consumers are in a high-involvement state.[20] Finally, another benefit of matching endorser to product is that it leads to increased persistence in the attitudes that are formed as a result of the association.[21]

A potentially negative effect of using extremely attractive models is that it can harm the self-image of women. Researchers have found that even preadolescent girls compare their own physical attractiveness to that of models.[22] As a result of the comparison process, standards for physical attractiveness increased. Such comparisons have been shown to lower the self-esteem of young girls.[23]

Advertisers have moved from simply using physically attractive models to employing highly sexually suggestive ads. One such example are the ads for Victoria's Secret run in 1999, in which prime-time television ads revealed sensuous models clad in skimpy underwear. A writer in *Advertising Age* stated: "If you want to catch people's attention—which after all is the point of advertising—sex is one way to break the message out of the clutter. Associating product with pleasure propels purchases."[24]

In the United States, television ads showing models in their undergarments was taboo until 1987. That situation has now changed. As one ad researcher noted, "Sex is everywhere. Advertisers are going to see what they can get away with on network TV."[25] Similarly, billboards for one brand of bras were placed in Britain, Germany, France, and Italy. They displayed a model clad in her underwear stretched sexily on a bed of grass. The billboard read, "Who Said a Woman Can't Get Pleasure from Something Soft?" Such steamy ads have begun to draw protests. For example, in Mexico a woman's group forced Playtex to put a dress on the model shown on billboards for Wonderbra.[26]

Academic research has shown that sexy advertisements attract attention, enhance ad recall, and improve attitude toward the ad. However, responses to highly explicit ads can be negative. For example, one study found that the presence of physically attractive, partially clad models positively influenced an automobile's image.[27] The same study also found that, if the erotic content of the ad was too high, it actually harmed recall of the ad when memory was measured a week after exposure to the ad.

Because of the increasing prevalence of male nudity in advertising, such as used by Calvin Klein, researchers have begun to analyze its effects on consumer reactions.[28] In one study male and female respondents saw males in various states of dress (from fully dressed to suggestive to nude) as models for body oil or a ratchet wrench set. The results paralleled the findings for female nudity. Male consumers preferred ads in which the male models had on their clothes. In contrast, females preferred suggestive ads and nude ads of males for the body oil product. However, when the wrench set was the product, full nudity "turned off" the women because the nudity had no relationship to the product.

The following generalizations can be made about nudity in advertising. First, the nudity should be appropriate to the product. Second, increasing nudity draws attention to the ads and increases the arousal levels of observers. Third, the nude images decrease the cognitive processing of the brand and ad message because of distraction effects. Fourth, suggestive or nude models appeal more to the opposite sex.[29]

Likability of the Source

Source likability refers to the positive or negative feelings that consumers have toward a source of information. Likability is increased when the source behaves in a way that matches the desires of those who observe him or her. In addition, likability increases when a source says pleasant things.[30] Finally, a source may be likable because he or she acts in ways or espouses beliefs that are similar to those of the audience. The phenomenal success of Michael Jordan and Bill Cosby as endorsers is due in part to their extreme likability. In contrast, infamous personalities such as O. J. Simpson and Mike Tyson cannot be used as endorsers because of their disagreeableness.

Source Meaningfulness

Sources of information also provide meanings to consumers. As a result of the connection between the source and a brand, such meanings can then be transferred. For example, by hiring Michael Jordan and connecting him with its salty-sweet beverage in advertisements, Gatorade hopes to transfer to its product the message that consuming the drink can enhance athletic potential. In this case Jordan acts as a symbol representing a number of qualities (e.g., athleticism and being a winner), which may be transferred to the beverage.

The transfer of meaning from celebrity to product to consumer is diagrammed in Figure 8.2. The figure presents a flowchart in which a celebrity plays a number of roles over his or her career.[31] (Note that, although celebrities frequently come from show business, they may also gain their fame from politics, sports, business, or other area that places them in the public eye.) Based on these roles, meanings become attached to the celebrity that are shared within a culture.

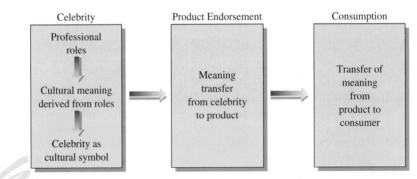

Figure 8.2 The transfer of meaning from celebrity to product to consumer.

In sum, celebrities are cultural symbols. When the celebrity endorses a product in an advertisement, associations are formed so that the culturally derived meanings may be transferred to the product. In the consumption phase, the meaning may then be transferred from the product to the consumer. Thus, when consumers drink Gatorade, some of the qualities of Michael Jordan may become symbolically attached to them.

A study was conducted to identify the meanings that are transferred from the celebrity Cher to Scandinavian Health Spas—a company that she has endorsed in the past.[32] Respondents were asked to describe the associations that they made between Cher and the spas based on her advertisements for the company. Table 8.1 presents the results. Among the eight categories of responses, the most frequently mentioned association was becoming attractive and having a "great body" like Cher's. Most of the associations were quite positive, except for one category—"lacks credibility." For this category respondents would occasionally mention that Cher obtained her body as much through plastic surgery as hard work. In addition, males and females diverged on some categories. For example, males more frequently viewed a spa as a place to meet the opposite sex, more frequently felt that Cher lacked credibility, and more often associated the word "sexy" with Cher and Scandinavian Health Spas. In contrast, females more frequently associated the words "hard work" with the advertisements.

Managerial Implications of Source Effects

A crucial decision for managers concerns what kind of source to use when developing advertising communications. The source of information is a vital component in delivering a message to an audience. The specific source used can help a company to position a product. For example, consumers would perceive a brand promoted by Bill Cosby quite differently from a brand promoted by Sylvester Stallone. Careful market-research studies should be performed to investigate audience reactions to the source and to track changes in reactions over time.

Finding a celebrity who is willing to make the endorsement and who is not already overexposed is difficult. In fact, one major advertising firm (Ogilvy & Mather)

Associations Between Cher and Scandinavian Health Spas

Association	Number of Responses Made	
	Males	Females
Attractive/great body like Cher's	15	17
Health/fitness	12	6
Hard work	5	11
Sexy	11	5
Lacks credibility	10	4
Place to meet opposite sex	6	0

Source: Based on Lynn Langmeyer and Mary Walker, "A First Step to Identify Meaning in Celebrity Endorsers," in *Advances in Consumer Research,* ed. Rebecca Holman and Michael Solomon (Provo, UT: Association of Consumer Research, 1991), 18:364–71.

TABLE 8.1

Summary of Key Findings on Impact of Source Effects
1. Important source-effect variables include credibility, expertise, trust, physical attractiveness, likability, meaning, and matchup with the product.
2. Source expertise has been found to have a greater impact on consumer responses than other source-effect variables.
3. Sources with high credibility are more effective, enhance the advertiser's ability to use fear appeals, and inhibit the formation of counterarguments.
4. In general, physically attractive people are more effective than less physically attractive people as sources.
5. To maximize source effectiveness, the source and the product should be a good matchup.
6. Meanings derived from the characteristics of the source can be transferred to the product through their close association.
7. The perceived characteristics and personality of the source interact with the nature of the product. Thus, in some circumstances highly physically attractive or highly likable people may not be the most effective sources of information.

TABLE 8.2

stopped using celebrities because of research showing that the audience assumes that the celebrity has been bought off.[33] Because of the problem of overexposure and the likelihood that consumers discount the endorsement of celebrities, a premium is paid for the services of "virgin" endorsers.

One final managerial issue concerns whether hiring celebrity endorsers is worth it. One study investigated the impact of hiring a celebrity endorser on the stock price of companies. Interestingly, the research revealed that, although investors in the stock market sometimes reacted negatively to the hiring of a celebrity, the action overall more frequently increased the stock price of companies. On the whole, the market acts as though hiring celebrities will increase the profits of firms.[34]

Table 8.2 summarizes the major findings on source effects.

MESSAGE CHARACTERISTICS

The effects of message content and construction on receivers has been intensively studied by researchers. **Message content** refers to the strategies that may be used to communicate an idea to an audience. Examples of such strategies include decisions of whether to use fear or humor in ads and whether to develop complex or simple messages. In contrast, **message construction** refers to the problem of how to physically construct a message. Examples of this include deciding where information should be placed in a message to get maximum impact and how often information should be repeated in a message. Issues in message content and construction are discussed in the sections that follow.

Developing Message Content

The logical first step in creating a message is to decide on its content. That is, the sender must decide what signs to use to communicate meaning. Creating an effective message is an art. This section discusses 10 different approaches to developing message content (see Table 8.3 for a summary of these approaches).

Using Rhetorical Figures of Speech. The goal of rhetoric is to "discover the most effective way to express a thought in a given situation."[35] Examples of rhetorical figures of

Types of Message Content
1. *Rhetorical figures of speech.* The use of rhyme, puns, hyperbole, metaphor, irony, and paradox to increase interest and provide additional meaning to messages.
2. *Message complexity.* The decision of how much information to place in a message.
3. *Drawing conclusions.* The issue of whether to directly state the inference that consumers are expected to obtain from the message—i.e., "buy this product."
4. *Comparative messages.* The question of whether to directly, indirectly, or not compare your brand to another brand.
5. *One- versus two-sided messages.* The issue of whether to present an audience with both sides of an issue.
6. *Fear appeals.* The decision of whether to develop a message that activates a fear response in consumers.
7. *Humor.* The decision of whether to employ humor in a message.
8. *Vivid versus abstract information.* The importance of using vivid and salient information in messages.
9. *Lectures versus dramas.* The decision of whether to persuade by having a source directly address the audience or employing characters to indirectly address the audience by speaking to each other.
10. *Life themes.* The goal of developing messages around the critical values and goals that influence consumers at different stages of their lives.

TABLE 8.3

speech include rhyme, puns, hyperbole (e.g., exaggerated claims), metaphors, and irony. Issues of rhetoric are found in the development of all marketing messages, from advertisements to packaging to personal selling to public relations.

One reason to use rhetorical devices is to make otherwise dull prose more interesting. For example, consider the use of paradox. A paradox is a rhetorical figure of speech that refers to a statements that are self-contradictory, false, or impossible.[36] Suppose that a copywriter wants to advertise a baseball batting glove made by Franklin, Inc. He or she might say something boring, such as, "While using our batting glove, Mark McGuire hit 70 home runs last year." On the other hand, the copywriter could use the principle of paradox and say: "Mark McGuire hit 70 home runs last year. But we held the bat." The use of paradox here adds punch to otherwise dull copy.

Another rhetorical figure of speech is the metaphor. A metaphor substitutes one object for another for the purpose of giving it meaning. For example, in 1999 Panasonic advertised a new cordless phone—the GigaRange Extreme. The headline read, "It's the SUV of Cordless Phones." The copy continued, "Our toughest and longest distance cordless phone ever . . . shock resistant/splash resistant." The ad featured the phone leaning against the wheel of a dirt-covered SUV. The SUV metaphor attached the meanings of toughness and dependability to the cordless phone.

It is important to recognize that rhetorical devices can be created visually, as well as in verbal or written form. For example, a visual metaphor was used in an ad for Pramnol motion-sickness medicine. The ad showed a seat belt with a package of Pramnol as the buckle. Through a visual effect, the ad presents the metaphor that Pramnol is a seat belt that keeps you in the car. In tests of the ad's effectiveness, researchers found that it increased consumer's attitude toward the ad.[37]

Message Complexity. From an information-processing perspective, for a message to have impact, the receiver must go through the exposure, attention, and comprehension stages. A factor that strongly influences comprehension is **message complexity.** If the information is too complex or worse yet, presented in a garbled, confusing manner, receivers are less likely to comprehend and be persuaded by the information.[38]

Excessively high message complexity frequently results from attempts to place too much information in a communication. As noted in chapter 4, consumers have a limited ability to process information. If too much information is given, they become overloaded and react negatively. In the context of television commercials, the general rule is that no more than four major copy points can be communicated. If celebrity endorsers are used, even fewer bits of information can be processed by consumers because part of their cognitive capacity is allocated to the endorser rather than to the message.[39]

The problem of creating excessively complex messages can directly impact corporate profits. With the deregulation of long-distance telephone service, consumers have been bombarded with extremely complex pricing schemes, as well as constant appeals to change carriers. Within this confusing situation, Sprint came out with the "Dime Lady" campaign, in which Candice Bergen is forced into seclusion because everyone she encounters wants to talk about the "dime-a-minute" price for Sprint calls. Sprint's long-distance volume increased four times faster than AT&T's. The phenomenal growth was fueled in part by the extremely simple and appealing message. As one Sprint executive explained, "We recognize that in such a complex category as telecommunications today, that simplicity of product and message is extremely important. . . . That's exactly what Sprint Sense offers."[40]

Drawing Conclusions. Another question involving the development of message content is whether the communicator should draw a conclusion for the audience. In a message the communicator may generate a number of arguments that support a particular position. These arguments may logically build on one another and lead to an inference that the audience should buy the product. Thus an advertiser might state, "Our brand is built better, will last longer, and is priced lower than other brands." The conclusion that could be drawn is that the consumer should go out and buy it. However, the question is, "Should the communication expressly draw the conclusion and tell the audience to go out and buy the product or let the audience draw the conclusion itself?"

Research on the effects of drawing conclusions indicates that whether to leave advertisements open-ended depends on the complexity of the message and the involvement of the audience.[41] If the message is relatively complex or if the audience is not involved in the topic, a conclusion should be drawn in the message. In contrast, if the audience is highly involved and the message is strong, without being too complex, it is better to let the audience make the inference.[42]

Comparative Messages. A **comparative message** is one in which the communicator compares the positive and negative aspects of his or her position to the positive and negative aspects of a competitor's position. The approach is used by advertisers in order to explicitly identify one or more competitors for the purpose of claiming superiority over them.[43]

Since the early 1970s, the Federal Trade Commission has encouraged the use of comparative advertising out of the belief that naming a competitor would assist consumers in evaluating a claim of superiority.[44] Comparative advertising is useful for small companies who are trying to enter a market, particularly if their claims are based on research done by independent third parties.[45] The opinion of many marketing managers was expressed by a Coca-Cola executive, who stated, "Comparative ads are good when you're new, but when you're the standard, it just gives a lot of free publicity to your competitors."[46] In European countries, however, comparative ads are viewed quite negatively. They are banned in Germany, Italy, and Belgium.[47]

Comparative ads can be used to position and differentiate a brand. By directly comparing a low-market-share product to the dominant brand, managers can anchor it close to the position of the dominant brand in the consumer's mind.[48] Using the product category of toothpaste, researchers found that comparative advertisements were superior to noncomparative ads in anchoring a new brand closer to a dominant brand and in creating a clearer brand image. Thus, direct comparisons between an unfamiliar brand and a market leader act to reposition the unfamiliar brand so that consumers perceive it to be more similar to the market leader.[49]

Two different types of comparative advertisements have been identified. In **direct comparative advertisements,** one brand is compared specifically with another brand. In **indirect comparative advertisements,** the comparison brand is not specifically mentioned. Rather, the ad compares the brand indirectly to "competitors." Deciding which type of comparative ad to use depends on the market share of the brand. One study found that low-market-share brands should directly compare themselves to the market leader. In contrast, moderate-market-share brands should use indirect comparative ads to avoid mentioning the name of the competitor and confusing consumers. Finally, the results revealed that market-share leaders should generally avoid comparative ads entirely.[50]

Several conclusions can be drawn from the research on comparative advertising:

1. Comparative ads can be effective for low-market-share or new brands in reducing perceived differences with the leading brands.[51]

2. Moderate-market-share brands should use only indirect comparative advertising when comparisons are made to other moderate-share brands.

3. To differentiate its brand from another, a company should compare it to the competitor on important attributes.

4. In general, market leaders should avoid comparative advertising.[52]

One-Sided versus Two-Sided Messages. Another communications issue concerns whether to present an audience with one or both sides of an issue. Research on the effectiveness of two-sided messages has shown that it can be an effective persuasion technique. Presenting both sides of an argument gives the appearance of fairness and may lower the tendency of consumers to argue against the message and the source. Particularly in cases when the audience is unfriendly, when it knows that opposition arguments exist, or when it is likely to hear arguments from the opposition, two-sided communications may be effective.[53] Because comparative ads frequently give information on both favorable and unfavorable aspects of a brand, they also represent two-sided messages.

Two-sided messages, however, are not always the most effective. In some instances giving only one side of an issue may result in the greatest attitude change. When the audience is friendly, when it is not likely to hear the other side's arguments, when it is not involved in the issue, or when it is not highly educated, one-sided messages may be more effective. In such instances presenting the other side to a message may simply confuse the audience and weaken the effects of the arguments for the issue.[54] Because many of the purchases that consumers make occur in low-involvement circumstances, marketers should probably have good evidence from market-research studies that a two-sided message is effective before using it.[55]

Fear Appeals. In a **fear appeal,** the communicator seeks to activate consumer anxiety by identifying one or more risks than can occur in the consumer environment. Each of the sources of risk identified in chapter 5 can be employed to create fear appeals. For example, the risk of bodily harm has been used to generate fear by companies who sell the safety of burglar alarms and by automakers who advertise the crash protection of their cars. Fear of financial risk is used by insurance companies. Social risk is also used effectively to generate fears by a variety of companies. Various companies selling deodorants, dandruff shampoo, and laundry detergents have successfully used social-risk fear appeals. By buying their products, consumers can avoid such "awful" maladies as "ring around the collar," they can "raise their hand if they're Sure," and they can scratch their heads without people snickering over their dandruff.

For fear appeals to be effective, researchers have found that the message should provide one or more of the following types of information:

1. Give specific instructions on how to cope with and solve the problem.
2. Provide an indication that following the instructions will solve the problem.
3. Avoid giving high-fear messages to audiences that feel highly threatened and vulnerable to the threat.
4. Avoid giving high-fear messages to audiences that are low in self-esteem.

As noted by one set of authors, if these precautions are satisfied, "very frightening messages are almost always more persuasive than more factual appeals to reason."[56] One reason fear appeals can be successful is that they create emotional responses. These emotions then focus a person's attention on how to cope with the problem. The increased attention on coping responses makes it more likely that the person will learn how to respond to the threat.[57] As long as the emotional response does not interfere with the processing of information about how to solve the problem, the fear appeal is likely to be effective.[58]

Humor in Messages. Like the use of fear appeals, the effectiveness of inserting **humor in messages** has been debated among marketing researchers. Nonetheless, humor is used frequently in advertisements. One study found that as much as 24.4 percent of prime-time television commercials played in the United States used humor.[59]

What makes something funny? One theory states that humor results from incongruity or deviations from expectations.[60] For example, in 1999 an investment company used humor to focus its target market's attention on financial planning. In one print ad, the headline read, "How do you plan on funding your retirement?" The picture showed a diver wearing a snorkel and wet suit in the wishing well of a water fountain. An arm was shown reaching over the edge of the pool dropping pennies into a steel bucket. Apparently, the person was saving for retirement by harvesting money from wishing wells. The ad makes you smile because of the incongruity of saving for retirement through such bizarre means.

Humor can result in unanticipated negative effects, however. First, humor can reduce the comprehension of the message. For example, one study compared the recall of ad content in humorous ads to that in serious ads. The results showed that recall was significantly better in the serious version of the ad.[61] Second, using humor may shorten the life span of the ads. Particularly if the humor is of a "gag" type, it may quickly fade and lose its positive effects. Third, humorous ads can also have unanticipated negative effects on various audiences. For example, ads for Budweiser beer were shown in Britain. In one ad a truck driver for Chieftain Cement walks into a bar crowded with American Indians. The driver has a ghostly pale face and is quite out of place in the bar. Just as the scene is about to turn ugly, the driver dunks his head into a bucket of water. It turns out that he is also an Indian and was only covered with cement dust. The scene ends with the man gulping down a bottle of beer. Although the English loved the ad, Native Americans hated it because it encouraged the stereo-type of alcoholism among their group.[62] The ad executives were quite oblivious to the problem and astonished at the furor it caused.

Humor's negative effects are in part explained by findings that different audiences may react in diverse ways to the same humorous message. One study found that females react more negatively to the injection of humor in ads than males.[63] Another study found that a variety of audience characteristics impact reactions to the effects of humor, including sex, race, national origin, personality, and social attitudes.[64] In addition, humor may have a negative impact because it distracts the audience from the message and lower comprehension.[65]

Despite these potential negative effects, humor can influence attitudes and behaviors.[66] Three factors account for these positive effects. One is that humor places people in a good mood, which in turn lowers counterarguments to the message.[67] Second, humor can attract attention to an ad and increase its recall and comprehension. Third, the strongest effect of humor is that it enhances the liking for the advertisement.[68] As described in the previous chapter, attitude toward the ad directly impacts attitude toward the product.

Two additional points are important for understanding the effects of humor on consumers. First, the humor should be related to the product or situation in some way. Second, the effects of humor interact with the prior brand evaluation of consumers to influence attitudes.[69] One particular study created either humorous or nonhumorous ads for a pen. In addition, prior evaluations of the pen were varied by giving fictitious *Consumer Reports* ratings. Thus, some respondents rated the pen very positively and others rated it negatively. The results revealed that, when the ad was humorous and their prior evaluations were positive, their attitudes and purchase intentions increased substantially. However, when the ad was humorous and their prior evaluations were negative, their attitudes and purchase intentions plummeted. In contrast, the opposite pattern emerged for the serious ads. When prior evaluations were negative, attitudes and purchase intentions increased when a serious ad was used; when prior evaluations were positive, attitudes and purchase intentions decreased when a serious ad was used. Figure 8.3 diagrams the effect for the measure of purchase intention. From a managerial perspective, then, humorous ads are best employed in order to reinforce positive attitudes.

Vivid versus Abstract Information. A well-established finding in psychology is that messages using vivid, concrete words tend to have greater impact on receivers than messages containing more abstract information.[70] **Vivid messages** attract and hold attention, as well as promote the receiver to use his or her imagination. As such, vivid messages are more likely to be placed into long-term memory and later recalled than more pallid information.

What makes information vivid? Three factors have been found to increase the vividness of messages. First, to the extent that the message has personal relevance, it will tend to have a greater impact. As the involvement level of the message increases, so too should its impact. A second factor is concreteness. A concrete message gives a high degree of detailed, specific information about people, actions, and situations. Finally, the information should be as close as possible to the receiver in terms of time, spatial proximity, and sensory proximity. Time proximity simply refers to using information that is as fresh and new as possible. For example, when a new-product breakthrough occurs, managers should announce it as quickly as possible. Spatial proximity refers to the idea of placing information in a context that is linked as closely as possible to that experienced by the audience. Thus, if a product is targeted to one region of the country, television ads should be filmed in recognizable parts of the region.

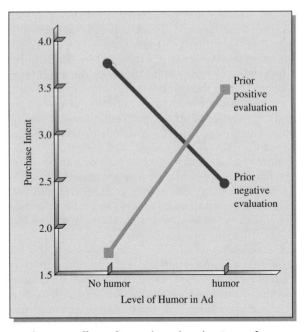

Figure 8.3   The moderating effect of prior brand evaluations of consumer responses to humorous ads.

Source: Based on Amitava Chattopadhyay and Kunal Basu, "Humor in Advertising: The Moderating Role of Prior Brand Evaluation," *Journal of Marketing Research* 27 [November 1990]: 466–76.

Sensory proximity refers to the concept of having the ideas in the message experienced firsthand by the audience or by someone else, such as an endorser, who can tell the audience what he or she experienced. One reason why automobile salespeople are so anxious to get you to drive a car is to have you obtain firsthand sensory experiences of the car.

Lectures versus Dramas. A **lecture** occurs when a source speaks directly to the audience in an attempt to inform and persuade.[71] It is like an oration in which evidence is presented and arguments made. We frequently see lectures in television ads. Here, a source talks to the audience and gives them information about the product. In contrast to a lecture, in a **drama** the characters speak to each other and not to the audience. The viewer is an eavesdropper who observes an imaginary setting that concerns a product or service.

When a person receives a lecture, facts are given, and the consumer recognizes that a persuasion attempt is unfolding. In such cases characteristics of the source become extremely important, and the advertiser must be concerned with the types of cognitive responses developed by the audience. Dramas work through a different mechanism. Because dramas are stories about the world, observational learning occurs. Viewers learn from the lessons revealed by the models in the communication. When a commercial drama rings true, the consumer is drawn into it and develops conclusions that may be applied to everyday life. As a result, fewer counterarguments emerge.

Lectures have the advantage of presenting information in a highly condensed form. However, they can frequently be dry and boring and spur counterargumentation. In contrast, dramas have the potential to increase audience interest by creating emotional responses and by transforming the meaning of using a product. **Transformational advertising** is defined as the attempt to cause a consumer to associate the experience of using a product with a set of psychological characteristics not typically associated with the use of a product.[72] For example, an advertisement in which a woman is swept off her feet by an impassioned lover after getting the dishes "squeaky clean" is attempting to transform the experience of washing dishes. Normally, one does not associate sex with dishwashing. Such a commercial attempts to transform the experience by giving it a new psychological meaning.

When successful, transformational ads involve the audience emotionally in the advertisement. They change how the audience thinks and feels about the product or service advertised. The marketing of perfume and colognes is based largely on attempts to transform the dabbing of something on one's skin into a romantic, sensual experience. In fact, one goal of such ads seems to be to transform a woman (or man) into a gorgeous (handsome) creature having tremendous allure to the opposite sex.[73]

Researchers have begun the process of investigating the effects of dramas and lectures on consumer responses. In one study respondents were shown ads for an automobile employing either a lecture or drama format. The results revealed that the lecture-format ad resulted in more counterarguments. In addition, respondents seeing the lecture ad revealed much less empathy and self-participation with the events in the ad.[74]

Researchers have found that dramas are associated with the expression of greater amounts of feelings and less counterargumentation. In addition, drama increases the respondents' perception of the authenticity of the commercial as well as their empathy toward the ad. In sum, lectures are processed evaluatively whereas dramas are processed empathically. Thus, effective lectures depend on the quality of the arguments overcoming the counterargumentation that results. In contrast, effective dramas work to the extent that they involve consumers emotionally and to the extent that they seem authentic and create empathy.[75]

Life Themes. **Life themes** represent critical values and goals that influence consumers at different stages of their lives. When skillfully employed, they influence beliefs, attitudes, and behaviors because consumers interpret communications from within the perspective of their own lives.[76] Consider the copy in an advertisement for Georgia-Pacific that appeared in *Newsweek* magazine:

> You've remade yourself a hundred times, searching for what would fit, and last. College kid, philosopher, James Dean wannabe. Now you're looking at an ad for vinyl siding and it is stirring you to imagine new ways of remaking your living space. Would you say your interests have evolved?

The ad then continues by identifying one of vinyl siding's key attributes—it is low hassle because it does not need to be repainted. Targeted to long-time homeowners (middle-class people 60-plus years old), the ad connects vinyl siding to their current life theme (that is, wanting to minimize hassle and future costs when they live on a fixed retirement income). Whereas the life theme of avoiding hassle and minimizing future costs appeals to older consumers, it is completely inappropriate for younger people.

From a managerial perspective, it is important to identify the life themes that influence the thinking of important market segments. By linking an advertisement to life themes (e.g., freedom, achievement, or the avoidance of hassle), the consumers' level of attention and involvement increases. In addition, more positive attitudes toward the ad will be created.

A final comment must be made about message content. There are many more types of messages than those identified here. For example, advertisers can employ guilt appeals.[77] Even the intentional use of silence in a television ad represents a type of message.[78]

Message Structure

Although communicators must worry about message content, they should also be concerned with how the messages are structured. **Message structure** refers to how the content of the message is organized. For example, where in the message should important information be placed? Another structural problem concerns how many times key pieces of information should be repeated in a message.

Primacy and Recency Effects. Primacy and recency effects refer to the relative impact of information placed either at the beginning or the end of a message. **A primacy effect** occurs when material early in the message has the most influence; a **recency effect** occurs when material at the end of the message has the most influence. The question is not trivial. Whether in a television commercial or in a formal presentation by a salesperson, the communicator wants to ensure that each piece of information has the maximum impact on the receiver. In addition, primacy and recency effects can occur when a series of messages is received. For example, when a number of commercials appear in succession on television, do those at the beginning, middle, or end of the sequence have the most impact?

Some consistent findings are beginning to emerge on primacy–recency effects. First, over time, primacy effects have more impact than recency effects. Particularly when recall is measured after a delay of several days, the material heard early in the message tends to be persuasive for the simple reason that it is heard first.[79] Second, the primacy effect particularly occurs to a larger extent for verbal material, such as that in a radio advertisement, than for visual material found in a print ad.[80]

One finding can be stated unequivocally, however. Material presented in the middle of a message is relatively poorly remembered and has the least impact. Research on serial learning presented in chapter 4 demonstrates the greater difficulty in retaining information placed in the middle of lists of material to be learned. Therefore, communicators should try to avoid placing the important parts of a message in the middle of a communication.

Repetition Effects. In chapter 5 we noted that the repetition of information is required for learning to take place. With this knowledge in mind, one must ask how many times the information should be repeated. Herbert Krugman has suggested that as few as three exposures to an advertisement may be sufficient.[81] Indeed, too much repetition will result in increasingly negative responses—a phenomenon called **advertising wear-out.**

Advertising wear-out was found in one study where members of church groups received either one, three, or five exposures to an advertisement for a fictitious toothpaste during a one-hour television show. The results showed that the number of counterarguments to the commercials increased as the number of repetitions increased.[82] Other researchers have found that too much repetition can cause attitudes toward the ad to become more negative.[83]

Sophisticated advertisers, however, rarely present the same commercial over and over again. Instead, they create a series of different ads that carry the same basic message. In one study researchers tested such an approach by varying the content of each ad slightly. In this study the number of positive cognitive responses increased and the number of negative cognitive responses decreased as the message was repeated.[84] The variations in ad execution substantially improved the recall of the ads that were repeated without causing wear-out to occur.[85] In addition, consumers were more resistant to attack ads by competitors.[86] Finally, researchers have found that if exposures to repetitive ads are voluntary, distributed over time, made in the presence of ads by competitors, and made in the cluttered environment found in the "real world," repetitive ads improve "top-of-the-mind awareness" and brand choice.[87]

Two-factor theory explains the effects of message repetition. The theory proposes that two different psychological processes are operating as people receive repetitive messages. In one process the repetition of a message causes a reduction in uncertainty and increased learning about the stimulus, resulting in a positive response.[88] However, in the other process, tedium or boredom begins to occur with each repetition. At some point the tedium overtakes the positive effects, and the receiver begins to react negatively to the ad. Two-factor theory suggests that, to avoid the negative effects of boredom, the communicator should vary the ad with each repetition. Figure 8.4 diagrams the relationships proposed by the two-factor theory.[89]

Lists versus Narratives. Another structural issue concerns whether the information in a print advertisement should use a list format (i.e., key points are bulleted) or a narrative format, in which a story is told in paragraph form. Research on the topic indicates that attitude toward the messages was improved when the narrative form was used. For example, if a travel agency describes the experiences that you will have on a vacation,

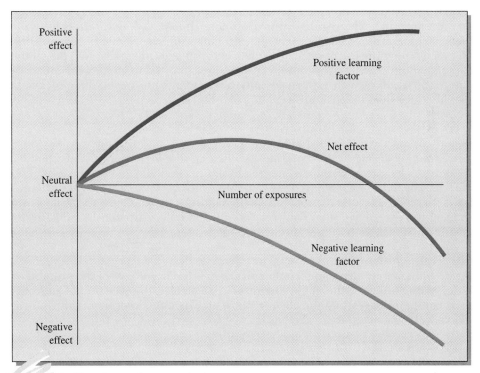

Figure 8.4   Two-factor theory and advertising wear-out.

Source: Arno Rethans, John Swasy, and Lawrence Marks, "Effects of Television Commercial Repetition, Receiver Knowledge, and Commercial Length: A Test of the Two-Factor Model," *Journal of Marketing Research* 23 [February 1986]: 59–61, published by the American Marketing Association.

it is better to use the narrative than list the points in a bulleted format. The effect is particularly strong when negative information about the trip is included.[90]

THE MANAGERIAL IMPLICATIONS OF PERSUASIVE COMMUNICATIONS

The principles and concepts derived from the study of persuasive communications have applications to each of the five PERMS managerial applications areas. These are discussed in the following sections.

Positioning and Differentiation

The development of persuasive communications must be based on the positioning and differentiation strategy of the company. For example, if the strategy is to position a brand as fun, exciting, and off-beat, advertisers should use a drama format in which attractive models are shown engaged in fun, off-beat, exciting activities. Conversely, if the strategy is to position the brand as decreasing the risk of an important problem, a fear-appeal message communicated by a credible source in a lecture format may be most appropriate.

Environmental Analysis

In order to decide which type of comparative advertisement to employ, managers need to analyze the competitive environment. If one's product is the brand leader, research suggests that comparative ads should be avoided. In contrast, if your brand lags far behind the market leaders, the relationships suggest that direct comparative ads are warranted. The regulatory environment should also be carefully examined when deciding on message content. In particular, different nations have different rules concerning the use of sexually explicit and comparative ads. Finally, the cultural and subcultural environments should be examined in order to identify potential reactions to the use of sexually explicit ads and the meanings attached to different celebrities who may be employed as message sources.

Research

In general, market research should be employed to test pilot audience reactions to sources and to messages. More specifically, research should be employed to identify in advance how a target market perceives the likability, credibility, and meaningfulness of sources. Research is also required prior to using strong fear appeals. In particular, the degree to which the audience feels threatened must be ascertained because if its members feel too threatened, they will react poorly to strong fear appeals. Similarly, low-self-esteem audiences react negatively to strong fear appeals.

Marketing Mix

The development of marketing communications is the major role of the promotional strategy component of the marketing mix. In particular, the selection of sources of information, messages, and the channel through which the information flows is critical to advertising and public relations.

Segmentation

Divergent segments of consumers may require different sources of information and message content. For example, when targeting heterosexual men with sexually explicit advertising, female models should be employed. In contrast, females respond better when male models are employed. In addition, consumers with higher levels of expertise on a topic can be given more complex messages than those with lower levels of expertise. Another example involves creating stronger fear appeals for high-self-esteem consumers than low-self-esteem consumers. In general, it is critical for marketers to develop a full understanding of the characteristics of divergent segments in order to select the best source, message, and channels in order to communicate most persuasively.

Notes

1. Scott A. Hawkins and Stephen J. Hoch, "Low Involvement Learning: Memory without Evaluation," *Journal of Consumer Research* 19 (September 1992): 212–26.
2. Bradley Johnson, "Lexus Tries E-Mail for Auto Intro," *Advertising Age,* October 7, 1996, p. 4.
3. Wendy Bounds and Matt Murray, "Card Makers Try New Ways to Greet a Paperless World," *Wall Street Journal,*" March 19, 1996, p. B1.
4. G. Douglas Olsen, "Creating the Contrast: The Influence of Silence and Background Music on Recall and Attribute Importance," *Journal of Advertising* 24 (winter 1995): 29–44.
5. C. I. Hovland and I. L. Janis, *Personality and Persuasibility* (New Haven, CT: Yale University Press, 1959).
6. Robert Guy Matthews, "Web Sites Made of Steel," *Wall Street Journal,* September 16, 1999, pp. B1, B4.
7. Terrence Shimp, "Methods of Commercial Presentation Employed by National Television Advertisers," *Journal of Advertising* 5 (fall 1976): 30–36.
8. Jeff Jensen, "Woods Hits Golf Jackpot," *Advertising Age,* September 2, 1996, p. 6.
9. Srinivas K. Reddy, Vanitha Swaminathan, and Carol M. Motley, "Exploring the Determinants of Broadway Show Success," *Journal of Marketing Research* 35 (August 1998): 370–83.
10. Note that not all researchers define trust in the manner described here. In some cases trust has been defined as including expertise within its bounds. That is, trust is defined in the same manner as we have defined credibility in the chapter. See, for example, Christine Moorman, Rohit Deshpande, and Gerald Zaltman, "Factors Affecting Trust in Market Research Relationships," *Journal of Marketing* 57 (January 1993): 81–101.
11. Elizabeth J. Wilson and Daniel L. Sherrell, "Source Effects in Communication and Persuasion Research: A Meta-Analysis of Effect Size," *Journal of the Academy of Marketing Science* 21 (spring 1993): 101–12.
12. Josh Wiener and John C. Mowen, "The Impact of Product Recalls on Consumer Perceptions," *Mobius: The Journal of the Society of Consumer Affairs Professionals in Business,* spring 1985, pp. 18–21.
13. David J. Moore, John C. Mowen, and Richard Reardon, "Multiple Sources in Advertising Appeals: When Product Endorsers Are Paid by the Advertising Sponsor," *Journal of the Academy of Marketing Science* 22 (1994): 234–43.
14. Peter Wright, "Cognitive Processes Mediating Acceptance of Advertising," *Journal of Marketing Research* 10 (February 1973): 53–62.
15. For an excellent review of the material on source credibility, see Brian Sternthal, Lynn Phillips, and Ruby Dholakia, "The Persuasive Effect of Source Credibility: A Situational Analysis," *Public Opinion Quarterly* 42 (fall 1978): 285–314.
16. Shelley Chaiken, "Communicator Physical Attractiveness and Persuasion," *Journal of Personality and Social Psychology* 37 (August 1979): 1387–97.
17. Karen Dion, E. Berscheid, and E. Walster, "What Is Beautiful Is Good," *Journal of Personality and Social Psychology* 24 (December 1972): 285–90.
18. Kathleen Debevec and Jerome Kernan, "More Evidence on the Effects of Presenter's Physical Attractiveness: Some Cognitive, Affective, and Behavioral Consequences," in *Advances in Consumer Research,* ed. Thomas Kinnear (Provo, UT: Association for Consumer Research, 1984), 11:127–32. For additional information on the impact of attractiveness, see also Paul Speck, David Schumann, and Craig Thompson, "Celebrity Endorsements—Scripts, Schema and Roles: Theoretical Framework and Preliminary Tests," in *Advances in Consumer Research,* ed. Michael Houston (Provo, UT: Association for Consumer Research, 1988), 15:69–76.
19. Michael Baker and Gilbert Churchill, "The Impact of Physically Attractive Models on Advertising Evaluations," *Journal of Marketing Research* 14 (November 1977): 538–55.
20. Amma Kirmani and Baba Shiv, "Effects of Source Congruity on Brand Attitudes and Beliefs: The Moderating Role of Issue-Relevant Elaboration," *Journal of Consumer Psychology* 7, no. 1 (1998): 25–47.

21. Jaideep Sengupta, Ronald C. Goodstein, and David S. Boninger, "All Cues Are Not Created Equal: Obtaining Attitude Persistence under Low-Involvement Conditions," *Journal of Consumer Research* 23 (March 1997): 351–61.

22. Mary C. Martin and Patricia F. Kennedy, "Advertising and Social Comparison: Consequences for Female Preadolescents and Adolescents," *Psychology and Marketing* 10 (November/December 1993): 513–30.

23. Marshal Richins, "Social Comparison and the Idealized Images of Advertising," *Journal of Consumer Research* 18 (June 1991): 71–83.

24. Judy Kuriansky, "Sex Simmers, Still Sells," *Advertising Age,* spring 1995, p. 49.

25. Pat Sloan, "Underwear Ads Caught in Bind over Sex Appeal," *Advertising Age,* July 8, 1996, p. 27.

26. Juliana Koranteng and Richard Bruner, "Sexy Bras Drawing Protests," *Advertising Age International,* July 1996, p. 16.

27. M. Steadman, "How Sexy Illustrations Affect Brand Recall," *Journal of Advertising Research* 9 (March 1969): 15–19. Also see Robert Chestnut, Charles LaChance, and Amy Lubitz, "The Decorative Female Model: Sexual Stimuli and the Recognition of Advertisements," *Journal of Advertising* 6 (fall 1977): 11–14.

28. Penny M. Simpson, Steve Horton, and Gene Brown, "Male Nudity in Advertisements: A Modified Replication and Extension of Gender and Product Effects," *Journal of the Academy of Marketing Science* 24 (summer 1996): 257–62.

29. Stephen M. Smith, Curtis P. Haugtvedt, John M. Jadrich, and Mark R. Anton, "Understanding Responses to Sex Appeals in Advertising: An Individual Difference Approach," in *Advances in Consumer Research,* ed. Frank R. Kardes and Mita Sugan (Provo, UT: Association for Consumer Research, 1995), 22:735–39.

30. Jean-Charles Chebat, Michael Laroche, Daisy Baddoura, and Pierre Filiatrault, "Effects of Source Likeability on Attitude Change through Message Repetition," in *Advances in Consumer Research,* ed. Leigh McAlister and Michael L. Rothschild (Provo, UT: Association for Consumer Research, 1993), 20:353–58.

31. Grant McCracken, "Who Is the Celebrity Endorser? Cultural Foundations of the Endorsement Process," *Journal of Consumer Research* 16 (December 1989): 310–21.

32. Lynn Langmeyer and Mary Walker, "A First Step to Identify the Meaning in Celebrity Endorsers," in *Advances in Consumer Research,* ed. Rebecca Holman and Michael Solomon (Provo, UT: Association for Consumer Research, 1991), 18:364–71.

33. David Ogilvy, *Ogilvy on Advertising* (New York: Vintage Books, 1983).

34. Jagdish Agrawal and Wagner A. Kamakura, "The Economic Worth of Celebrity Endorsers: An Event Study Analysis," *Journal of Marketing* 59 (July 1995): 56–62.

35. Edward F. McQuarrie and David Glen Mick, "Figures of Rhetoric in Advertising Language," *Journal of Consumer Research* 22 (March 1996): 424–38.

36. Ibid.

37. Edward F. McQuarrie and David Glen Mick, "Visual Rhetoric in Advertising: Text—Interpretive, Experimental, and Reader-Response Analyses," *Journal of Consumer Research* 26 (June 1999): 37–54.

38. Alice Eagly, "The Comprehensibility of Persuasive Arguments as a Determinant of Opinion Change," *Journal of Personality and Social Psychology* 29 (1974): 758–73.

39. For more information on the impact of message complexity, see Tina M. Lowrey, "The Effects of Syntactic Complexity on Advertising Persuasiveness," *Journal of Consumer Psychology* 7, no. 2 (1998): 187–206.

40. Kim Cleland, "Spring Sense Wins Credit for Carrier's Growth Spurt," *Advertising Age,* September 9, 1996, pp. 3, 64.

41. Bertram Raven and Jeffrey Rubin, *Social Psychology* (New York: Wiley, 1983).

42. Alan G. Sawyer and Daniel J. Howard, "Effects of Omitting Conclusions in Advertisements to Involved and Uninvolved Audiences," *Journal of Marketing Research* 28 (November 1991): 467–74.

43. Kanti V. Prasad, "Communications Effectiveness of Comparative Advertising: A Laboratory Analysis," *Journal of Marketing Research* 13 (May 1976): 128–37.

44. Gerald Gorn and Charles Weinberg, "The Impact of Comparative Advertising on Perception and Attitude: Some Positive Findings," *Journal of Consumer Research* 11 (September 1984): 719–27.

45. William Wilkie and Paul Farris, "Comparison Advertising: Problems and Potential," *Journal of Marketing* 39 (November 1975): 7–15.

46. "Creating a Mass Market for Wine," *Business Week,* March 15, 1982, pp. 108–18.

47. Martin Du Bois and Tara Parker-Pope, "Philip Morris Campaign Stirs Uproar in Europe," *Wall Street Journal*, July 1, 1996, pp. B1, B6.

48. Cornelia Droge and Rene Darmon, "Associative Positioning Strategies through Comparative Advertising: Attribute versus Overall Similarity Approaches," *Journal of Marketing Research* 24 (November 1987): 377–88.

49. For a more detailed look at comparative ads, see Cornelia Pechmann and S. Ratneshwar, "The Use of Comparative Advertising for Brand Positioning: Association versus Differentiation," *Journal of Consumer Research* 18 (September 1991): 145–60.

50. Cornelia Pechmann and David W. Stewart, "The Effects of Comparative Advertising on Attention, Memory, and Purchase Intentions," *Journal of Consumer Research* 17 (September 1990): 180–91.

51. Gorn and Weinberg, "Impact of Comparative Advertising."

52. This conclusion has been challenged in the following research: Paul W. Miniard, Michael J. Barone, Randall L. Rose, and Kenneth C. Manning, "A Re-Examination of the Relative Persuasiveness of Comparative and Noncomparative Advertising," in *Advances in Consumer Research*, ed. Chris T. Allen and Deborah Roedder John (Provo, UT: Association for Consumer Research, 1994), 21:299–303.

53. See, for example, studies by Russell Jones and Jack Brehm, "Persuasiveness of One- and Two-Sided Communications as a Function of Awareness: There Are Two Sides," *Journal of Experimental Social Psychology* 6 (1970): 47–56; Alan G. Sawyer, "The Effects of Repetition of Refutational and Supportive Advertising Appeals," *Journal of Marketing Research* 10 (February 1973): 23–33; and Michael Kamins and Henry Assael, "Two-Sided versus One-Sided Appeals: A Cognitive Perspective on Argumentation, Source Derogation on Argumentation, Source Derogation, and the Effect of Disconfirming Trial on Belief Change," *Journal of Marketing Research* 24 (February 1987): 29–39.

54. G. C. Chu, "Prior Familiarity, Perceived Bias, and One-Sided versus Two-Sided Communications," *Journal of Experimental Social Psychology* 3 (1967): 243–54. Also see Cornelia Pechmann, "How Do Consumer Inferences Moderate the Effectiveness of Two-Sided Messages?" in *Advances in Consumer Research*, ed. Marvin E. Goldberg, Gerald Gorn, and Richard Pollay (Provo, UT: Association for Consumer Research, 1990), 17:337–41.

55. Raven and Rubin, *Social Psychology*.

56. John F. Tanner Jr., James B. Hunt, and David R. Eppright, "The Protection Motivation Model: A Normative Model of Fear Appeals," *Journal of Marketing*, July 1991, pp. 329–36.

57. Ibid.

58. Punam Anand Keller and Lauren Goldberg Block, "Increasing the Persuasiveness of Fear Appeals: The Effect of Arousal and Elaboration," *Journal of Consumer Research* 22 (March 1996): 448–59.

59. Different studies have obtained divergent estimates of the percentage of commercials using humor. The 24.9 percent estimate came from Marc G. Weinberger and Harlan E. Spotts, "Humor in U.S. versus U.K. TV Advertising," *Journal of Advertising* 18 (1989): 39–44. Slightly lower estimates (16 percent) were obtained by Dana L. Alden, Wayne D. Hoyer, and Chol Lee, "Identifying Global and Culture-Specific Dimensions of Humor in Advertising: A Multinational Analysis," *Journal of Marketing* 57 (April 1993): 64–75. Also see Brian Sternthal and C. Samuel Craig, "Humor in Advertising," *Journal of Marketing* 37 (October 1973): 12–18.

    One critical issue concerns the question, "What makes something humorous?" This topic is beyond the scope of this book. However, for a related discussion, see Alden, Hoyer, and Lee, "Identifying Global and Culture-Specific Dimensions." Also see Edward F. McQuarrie and David Glen Mick, "On Resonance: A Critical Pluralistic Inquiry into Advertising Rhetoric," *Journal of Consumer Research* 19 (September 1992): 180–97.

60. Alden, Hoyer, and Lee, "Identifying Global and Culture-Specific Dimensions of Humor in Advertising: A Multinational Analysis."

61. Joan Cantor and Pat Venus, "The Effects of Humor on the Recall of a Radio Advertisement," *Journal of Broadcasting*, winter 1980, p. 14.

62. Tara Parker-Pope, "British Budweiser Ads Rankle American Indians," *Wall Street Journal*, July 16, 1996, pp. B1, B5.

63. H. Bruce Lammers, "Humor and Cognitive Responses to Advertising Stimuli: A Trade Consolidation Approach," *Journal of Business Research* 11 (June 1983): 182.

64. Sternthal and Craig, "Humor in Advertising." Also see Thomas J. Madden and Marc Weinberger, "The Effects of Humor on Attention in Magazine Advertising," *Journal of Advertising* 11 (March 1982): 1.

65. John H. Murphy, Isabella Cunningham, and Gary Wilcox, "The Impact of Program Environment on Recall of Humorous Television Commercials," *Journal of Advertising* 8 (spring 1979): 17–21.

66. Cliff Scott, David M. Klein, and Jennings Bryant, "Consumer Responses to Humor in Advertising: A Series of Field Studies Using Behavioral Observation," *Journal of Consumer Research* 16 (March 1990): 498–501. Also see Young Zhang and George M. Zinkhan, "Humor in Advertising: The Effects of Repetition and Social Setting," in *Advances in Consumer Research*, ed. Rebecca Holman and Michael Solomon (Provo, UT: Association for Consumer Research, 1991), 18:813–18.

67. P. Kelly and Paul J. Solomon, "Humor in Television Advertising," *Journal of Advertising* 4 (summer 1975): 33–35.

68. Marc G. Weinberger and Charles S. Gulas, "The Impact of Humor in Advertising: A Review," *Journal of Advertising* 21 (December 1992): 35–59.

69. Amitava Chattopadhyay and Kunal Basu, "Humor in Advertising: The Moderating Role of Prior Brand Evaluation," *Journal of Marketing Research* 27 (November 1990): 466–76. For another recent study on humor in advertising, see Stephen M. Smith, "Does Humor in Advertising Enhance Systematic Processing?" in *Advances in Consumer Research*, ed. Leigh McAlister and Michael L. Rothschild (Provo, UT: Association for Consumer Research, 1993), 20:155–58. Smith found evidence that humor in an ad tends to lead to more peripheral processing so that the strength of ad claims are not evaluated as closely as when more serious ads are employed. Thus, a more humorous ad positively impacted ratings only when weak claims were employed.

70. This section relies heavily on material found in Richard Nisbett and Lee Ross, *Human Inference: Strategies and Shortcomings of Social Judgment* (Upper Saddle River, NJ: Prentice Hall, 1980).

71. William Wells, "Lectures and Dramas" (paper presented at the Association of Consumer Research, fall 1987).

72. Christopher Puto and William Wells, "Informational and Transformational Advertising: The Differential Effects of Time," in *Advances in Consumer Research*, ed. Thomas Kinnear (Provo, UT: Association for Consumer Research, 1984), 11:638–43.

73. For a model of transformational advertising, see Vanitha Swaminathan, George M. Zinkhan, and Srinivas K. Reddy, "The Evolution and Antecedents of Transformational Advertising: A Conceptual Model," in *Advances in Consumer Research*, ed. Kim P. Corfman and John G. Lunch Jr. (Provo, UT: Association for Consumer Research, 1996), 23:49–55.

74. Gregory W. Boller, "The Vicissitudes of Product Experience: 'Songs of Our Consuming Selves' in Drama Ads," in *Advances in Consumer Research*, ed. Marvin E. Goldberg, Gerald Gorn, and Richard Pollay (Provo, UT: Association for Consumer Research, 1990), 17:321–26. For additional analysis of transformational ads, see John Deighton, Daniel Romer, and Josh McQueen, "Using Drama to Persuade," *Journal of Consumer Research* 16 (December 1989): 335–43.

75. Deighton, Romer, and McQueen, "Using Drama to Persuade."

76. David Glen Mick and Claus Buhl, "A Meaning-Based Model of Advertising Experiences," *Journal of Consumer Research* 19 (December 1992): 317–38.

77. Robin Higie, June Cotte, and Melissa Lunt Moore, "Believe It or Not: Persuasion, Manipulations, and Credibility of Guilt Appeals," in *Advances in Consumer Research*, ed. Eric J. Arnould and Linda M. Scott (Provo, UT: Association for Consumer Research, 1999), 26:288–94.

78. Swee Hoon Ang, Siew Meng Leong, and Wendy Yeo, "When Silence Is Golden: Effects of Silence on Consumer Ad Response," in *Advances in Consumer Research*, ed. Eric J. Arnould and Linda M. Scott (Provo, UT: Association for Consumer Research, 1999), 26:295–99.

79. Curtis P. Haugtvedt and Duane T. Wegener, "Message Order Effects in Persuasion: An Attitude Strength Perspective," *Journal of Consumer Research* 21 (June 1994): 205–18.

80. H. Rao Unnava, Robert E. Burnkrant, and Sunil Erevelles, "Effects of Presentation Order and Communication Modality on Recall and Attitude," *Journal of Consumer Research* 21 (December 1994): 481–90.

81. Herbert Krugman, "Why Three Exposures May Be Enough," *Journal of Advertising Research* 12 (December 1972): 11–14.

82. George E. Belch, "The Effects of Television Commercial Repetition on Cognitive Response and Message Acceptance," *Journal of Consumer Research* 9 (June 1982): 56–65.

83. Marian Burke and Julie Edell, "Ad Reactions over Time: Capturing Changes in the Real World," *Journal of Consumer Research* 13 (June 1986): 114–18.

84. The following study supports this conclusion: Dena Cox and Anthony Cox, "What Does Familiarity Breed? Complexity as a Moderator of Repetition Effects in Advertising Evaluation," *Journal of Consumer Research* 15 (June 1988): 111–16. Also see Arno Rethans, John Swasy, and Lawrence Marks, "Effects of Television Commercial Repetition, Receiver Knowledge, and Commercial Length: A Test of the Two-Factor Model," *Journal of Marketing Research* 23 (February 1986): 50–61.

85. The encoding variability hypothesis also applies to the effects of repetition. See H. Rao Unnava and Robert E. Burnkrant, "Effects of Repeating Varied Ad Executions on Brand Name Memory," *Journal of Marketing Research* 28 (November 1991): 406–16. Also see Robert Burnkrant and Hanumantha Unnava, "Effect of Variation in Message Execution on the Learning of Repeated Brand Information," in *Advances in Consumer Research,* ed. Mellanie Wallendorf and Paul Anderson (Provo, UT: Association for Consumer Research, 1987), 14:173–76.

86. Curtis P. Haugtvedt, David W. Schumann, Wendy L. Schneier and Wendy L. Warren, "Advertising Repetition and Variation Strategies: Implications for Understanding Attitude Strength," *Journal of Consumer Research* 21 (June 1994): 176–89.

87. Giles D'Souza and Ram C. Rao, "Can Repeating an Advertisement More Frequently Affect Brand Preference in a Mature Market?" *Journal of Marketing* 59 (April 1995): 32–42.

88. L. McCullough and Thomas Ostrom, "Repetition of Highly Similar Messages and Attitude Change," *Journal of Applied Psychology* 59 (June 1974): 395–97.

89. D. E. Berlyne, "Novelty, Complexity, and Hedonic Value," *Perception and Psychophysics* 8 (November 1970): 279–86.

90. Rashmi Adaval and Robert S. Wyer Jr., "The Role of Narratives in Consumer Information Processing," *Journal of Consumer Psychology* 7, no. 3 (1998): 207–45.

CHAPTER 9

Consumer Decision Processes

After studying this chapter, you should be able to describe each of the following concepts, together with their managerial relevance:

1. Generic decision-making model.
2. Three perspectives on consumer decision making.
3. Impulse and variety-seeking purchases.
4. Problem recognition.
5. Search processes.
6. Consideration set.
7. Alternative evaluation.
8. Choice processes.
9. High-involvement choice models.
10. Low-involvement choice models.

P rior to making an acquisition, consumers move through a decision process. **Consumer decision making** is defined as the processes involved in recognizing problems, searching for solutions, evaluating alternatives, choosing among options, and evaluating the outcomes of the choice. Not only do consumers make decisions regarding which brand options to choose but they also decide what quantity of the good to purchase.[1] Consumers make decisions in order to reach goals, which include making the best choice among alternative actions, reducing the effort in making the decision, minimizing negative emotions, and maximizing the ability to justify the decision. Decision making is a constructive process. That is, consumers make decisions "on the fly," and the process employed is influenced by the problem's difficulty, the knowledge and charac-

171

teristics of the consumer, and the characteristics of the situation.[2] It is critical for managers to identify the type of decision process employed by a target market because it will influence each of the managerial applications areas.

The **generic decision-making model** identifies the stages through which consumers move when making decisions. There are five stages: (1) problem recognition, (2) search, (3) alternative evaluation, (4) choice, and (5) postacquisition evaluation. (The stages are diagrammed in Figure 9.1.) In the problem recognition stage, consumers discern that a need exists. If sufficiently strong, the need may motivate the person to enter the second stage, the search for information. The search for information may be either extensive or limited depending on the involvement level of the consumer. In the third stage, consumers evaluate the alternatives that are identified for solving the problem. Alternative evaluation is synonymous with the formation of beliefs and attitudes regarding the alternatives. Material presented in chapter 7 concerning attitudes is particularly applicable to the evaluation stage.

Choice is the fourth stage. It involves deciding which alternative action to select (e.g., which brand to choose, whether to spend or save, from which store to purchase the product). Finally, in the postacquisition stage, buyers consume and use the acquisition. In addition, they evaluate the outcomes of the consequences of the behavior and engage in the disposal of the waste resulting from the purchase.[3] (Chapter 10 focuses specifically on such postacquisition processes.)

The generic decision-making process describes the steps in making choices employed by businesses and organizations, as well as by consumers. For example, one researcher sent questionnaires to over 2,000 purchasing managers of companies of

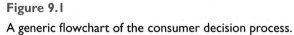

Figure 9.1

A generic flowchart of the consumer decision process.

varying sizes.[4] The dimensions that she identified closely correspond to the stages of the generic decision-making process.

This chapter has three goals. First, it discusses decision making from the three research perspectives on consumer behavior—the decision making, experiential, and behavioral influence—presenting both traditional and more recent views of decision making. The second goal is to discuss in detail the first four components of the decision-making process—problem recognition, search for information, alternative evaluation, and choice. Finally, this chapter identifies the managerial applications of the study of consumer decision making.

ALTERNATIVE PERSPECTIVES ON CONSUMER DECISION MAKING

From the late eighteenth century through much of the 1970s, researchers viewed people as moving linearly through the generic decision-making process outlined in Figure 9.1. In the late 1970s, however, authors began to question the concept that all consumer purchases result from a careful, analytical process. Some authors suggested that in many instances consumers may not engage in any decision making at all prior to making a purchase. As stated in one article, "We conclude that for many purchases a decision process never occurs, not even on the first purchase."[5] In addition, researchers recognized that many consumer behaviors do not involve the purchase of goods, such as automobiles and toothpaste. People also purchase experiences in the form of services, such as vacation excursions, rock concerts, theater, parachuting, movies, art, opera, and gambling.[6]

Due to the limitations of the traditional consumer decision process, researchers proposed alternative decision-making models that place different levels of emphasis on each of the stages identified in the generic flowchart. For these reasons, we have identified the three perspectives on consumer behavior—the traditional decision-making perspective, the experiential perspective, and the behavioral influence perspective. Each perspective defines a divergent type of decision process. Table 9.1 summarizes the acquisition process from the viewpoint of each of the three perspectives. Table 9.2 summarizes how the marketing mix of a company changes depending on which of the three decision-making perspectives the target market is using. The following sections discuss in more detail the implications of the three perspectives for understanding consumer decision making.

The Decision-Making Perspective

The traditional **decision-making perspective** emphasizes the rational, information-processing approach to consumer purchase behavior. It is closely related to the high-involvement hierarchy of effects approach to attitude formation discussed in chapter 7. According to this approach, consumers move through each of the stages of the decision process in a linear fashion, with high levels of information processing occurring.

Researchers in the 1970s, however, recognized that consumers do not always go through an extended decision process. Rather, under low-involvement conditions, limited decision making takes place and less search behavior occurs.[7] Furthermore, because the low-involvement hierarchy of effects is operative when limited decision making occurs, the alternative evaluation stage is largely absent from the decision process. Thus, in limited decision making, the choice among alternative brands is made in a relatively simple manner, and simplified decision rules are used.[8] In sum, the decision-making perspective includes both the high-involvement and low-involvement routes to making decisions.

Three Perspectives on Decision Making

I. Traditional Decision-Making Perspective

A. *High-Involvement Decisions*

Problem recognition	→Extensive search	→Extended alternative evaluation	→Complex choice	→Acquisition evaluation

B. *Low-Involvement Decisions*

Problem recognition	→Limited search	→Minimal alternative evaluation	→Simple choice processes	→Acquisition evaluation

II. Experiential Perspective

Problem recognition (affect driven)	→Search for affect-based solutions	→Alternative evaluation (comparison of affect)	→Choice (affect-based)	→Acquisition evaluation

III. Behavioral Influence Perspective

Problem recognition (results from discriminative stimulus)	→Search (learned response)	→Choice (behavior results from reinforcers)	→Acquisition evaluation (self-perception process)

TABLE 9.1

Some Marketing-Mix Strategies for Products Bought via High- and Low-Involvement Decision Processes

I. High-Involvement Decision Processes

A. *Promotional Strategy*
  1. Sell product via skilled sales force.
  2. Utilize strong persuasive arguments in messages.

B. *Distribution Strategy*
  1. Utilize a more limited distribution system.
  2. Ensure that distributors are trained to provide outstanding service.

C. *Pricing Strategy*
  1. Consider charging premium prices.
  2. Avoid use of frequent sales.
  3. Consider policy of price bargaining with customers.

II. Low-Involvement Decision Processes

A. *Promotional Strategy*
  1. Place greater weight on mass advertising to create sales awareness.
  2. Use heavy amounts of message repetition.
  3. Utilize likable/attractive endorsers.
  4. Keep arguments in advertisements simple.

B. *Distribution Strategy*
  1. Utilize an extensive distribution strategy.

C. *Pricing Strategy*
  1. Attempt to be a low-cost producer.
  2. Consider use of coupons and other price incentives to reach more price-conscious groups.

TABLE 9.2

The Experiential Perspective

In contrast to the decision-making perspective, the experiential perspective recognizes consumers as "feelers" as well as thinkers—that is, they consume many types of products for the sensations, feelings, images, and emotions that the products generate.[9] When problems are examined from the experiential perspective, managers focus on entertainment, arts, and leisure products rather than on more functional consumer goods. The experiential perspective recognizes that products carry subjective symbolic meanings for consumers.[10] In particular, products such as flowers, jewelry, perfume, after-shave lotion, and so forth are bought largely for the meanings they provide.

From an experiential perspective, problem recognition results from the realization that a difference exists between actual and desired affective states. Similarly, the search process involves seeking information concerning the affective impact of choice options. In the alternative evaluation stage, the options are evaluated based on their affective quality. Choice is based on affective criteria (such as "Which product will make me feel better?") Finally, postacquisition evaluation is based on whether the outcome meets the emotional expectations of the consumer.

Behavioral Influence Perspective

When approaching problems from the **behavioral influence perspective,** researchers focus on the behaviors of consumers and the contingencies of the environment that influence the behaviors. For example, the physical environment can be used to induce behaviors from consumers. The use of textures, smells, and lighting can also create an atmosphere that elicits desired responses from consumers. Arranging aisles in a retail store to funnel consumers by desired products illustrates how the physical environment can impact behavior without changing either beliefs or feelings about the action. Similarly, the mere arrangement of the containers of food products on shelves in a grocery store can impact consumer buying decisions independently of their beliefs and attitudes about the product alternatives.[11] Other researchers have found that, as the level of lighting is lowered, people sit closer to each other and talk in lower voices. If the goal is to create an intimate, quiet atmosphere, low lighting levels should be used.[12]

It should be noted that the discussion of the experiential and behavioral influence perspectives is controversial to some researchers. Indeed, arguments can be made that decision making occurs whenever consumers engage in a behavior. The experiential and behavioral influence perspectives are discussed here, however, to emphasize the role of feelings and environmental factors in causing consumer actions. A single-minded focus on belief formation and rational information processing fails to capture adequately the richness of consumer behavior.

The following sections discuss the first four states of decision making—problem recognition, search, alternative evaluation, and choice. Chapter 10 describes the final stage of the decision-making process—postacquisition evaluation.

PROBLEM RECOGNITION

Problem recognition occurs when a discrepancy develops between an actual and a desired state of being. (Note that the definition of problem recognition is identical to that of need state discussed in chapter 5.) If the satisfaction with the **actual state** decreases, or if the level of the **desired state** increases beyond a critical level, a problem is recognized that propels a consumer to action.[13]

A variety of factors may cause the actual state to decrease below acceptable levels. A person could run out of a product (such as gasoline or toothpaste), a product could wear out, or a product may simply go out of style. Similarly, the person could use the product and find that it simply fails to meet expectations. Internal states of consumers, such as perceptions of hunger, thirst, or boredom, can decrease the perception of the actual state. Negative mood states can also lower the actual state. For example, the person could receive bad news, or a general situation could make the person uncomfortable (e.g., a consumer could be placed in a new social situation).

The desired state is influenced by factors that affect consumers' aspirations and circumstances. Influences such as culture, subculture, reference groups, and lifestyle trends can cause a person to change his or her desired state. For example, if a person joins an organization, such as a fraternity, sorority, or corporation, the pressures of the social group may change the person's perception of the appropriateness of wearing certain types of clothing. When a student graduates from college, a whole new set of dress requirements may be imposed. The desired state therefore changes, and needs develop for nice suits, briefcases, and shoes that would be considered inappropriate in a college environment.

Because consumers have a capacity to think, plan, and dream, they can create new consumption visions. Consumption visions are defined as "self-constructed mental simulations of future consumption situations."[14] By being able to imagine themselves in new situations or owning new possessions, consumers may influence their own desired state. Of course, advertisers seek to encourage such thinking by showing off products and services in highly inviting ways.

Because consumers can plan and anticipate future needs, products and services may be purchased on a preneed basis. In fact, an entire range of products have been identified as **preneed goods.** Growth areas in preneed marketing include liability insurance, self-diagnostic health kits, prepaid legal services, and prepaid tuition plans for colleges. In some respects the ultimate in preneed problem recognition is the purchase of funeral services and burial plots long before the consumer's demise.[15]

CONSUMER SEARCH BEHAVIOR

After consumers identify a problem, they begin a search process to acquire information about products that may eliminate the problem. **Consumer search behavior** is defined as the actions taken to identify and obtain information as the means of solving a consumer problem.

Researchers have identified two types of consumer **search processes**—internal search and external search.[16] In **internal search** consumers retrieve from long-term memory information on products or services that may help to solve a problem. In contrast, in **external search** consumers acquire information from outside sources, such as friends, advertisements, packaging, *Consumer Reports,* sales personnel, and so forth.

In addition to distinguishing internal and external search, researchers have also made the distinction between prepurchase search and ongoing search. **Prepurchase search** involves the information-seeking activities that consumers engage in to facilitate decision making concerning a specific purchase in the marketplace that occurs because problem recognition has taken place. **Ongoing search,** on the other hand, involves the search activities that are independent of specific purchase needs or decisions.[17] Ongoing search is found particularly among individuals who have built a hobby around a particular consumer product or activity. For example, car, gardening, computer, and photography enthusiasts are constantly reading and studying because of their intrinsic interest in the topic.

Internal Search

After a problem is recognized, consumers engage in an internal search for information. When consumers engage in an internal search for information, they attempt to retrieve from long-term memory the brands that may or may not solve the problem. Figure 9.2 identifies five different categories into which a brand must fall.[18] As the figure illustrates, internal search is viewed as proceeding via a two-stage process. First, the consumer retrieves from long-term memory those products and brands of which he or she is aware. This **awareness set** is a subset of the total universe of potential brand and products available. At a minimum a company wants its brand to be a part of the awareness set. If consumers are unaware of a brand, they are unlikely to ever consider it, unless they discover it in the external search process.

The importance of getting your brand into the awareness set is illustrated by a company called Avia International. What does Avia make? Market research indicated that only 4 percent of consumers knew that it made sneakers and sports apparel. As the marketing vice president for the company noted, "There's a whole segment of people who are not buying our shoes because they don't know who we are." As a result, the company undertook a major advertising campaign to create brand awareness. The importance of this strategy is supported by the finding that over 90 percent of new products are pulled within three years of their introduction. One expert explained the major reason: "In most cases, failures were the result of a lack of product recognition."[19]

After identifying the awareness set, the consumer separates the awareness group into three additional categories—the consideration set, the inert set, and the inept set. The **consideration set** consists of those brands and products that are acceptable for further consideration.[20] The **inert set** consists of the brands and products to which the consumer is essentially indifferent. The **inept set** consists of the brands and products

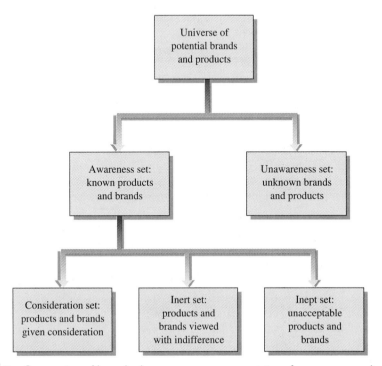

Figure 9.2 Categories of brands that consumers may retrieve from memory during internal search.

that are considered unacceptable. The goal of a company, of course, is to have its brand placed in the evoked set and not in the inept set.

Researchers have made a number of findings about the size of the consideration set. First, the size of the consideration set is dynamic and may change as more information is added through external search.[21] Indeed, even incidental exposure to a commercial can cause a person to add the brand to the consideration set.[22] The size of the consideration set has been found to decrease as the satisfaction and brand loyalty of consumers increases. In addition, as the consideration set increases, retailer search behavior increases, which results in a higher tendency to switch from one brand to another.[23] Factors associated with an increase in the size of the consideration set include the education level of consumers, the size of consumers' families, the size of the awareness set, and the extent to which consumers recognize that different brands can be used in different situations.[24]

How large are the awareness and consideration sets of consumers? Researchers have found that awareness set sizes ranged from a low of 3.5 brands for mouthwash to a high of 19.3 brands for laundry detergent. In general, consideration-set size paralleled the size of the awareness set. Thus for mouthwash 1.3 brands were in the consideration set, whereas for laundry detergent 5.0 brands were in the consideration set.[25] In general, the larger the awareness set, the larger the consideration set.[26]

External Search

During external search consumers solicit information from outside sources.[27] Table 9.3 identifies the basic types of information sought in external search. These include information on the alternative brands available, the evaluative criteria on which to compare brands, the importance of the criteria, and the performance of the brands on the attributes.[28] Note that the amount and types of information sought in external search can be derived directly from the concepts involved in attitude formation and change (discussed in chapter 7).

Measuring External Search. It is important for managers to measure the extent to which consumers in the target market search because it directly impacts distribution strategies. If they find that consumers engage in little external search, extensive distribution is necessary, such as that found for soft drinks. Several approaches have been employed to measure the extent of external search. Some of these indicators include (1) the number of stores visited, (2) the number of friends with whom the person discusses the product, (3) the number of buying guides consulted, (4) the number of store employees with whom the consumer talks, and (5) the number of advertisements that the consumer sees, hears, or reads.

The Types of Information Sought via External Search

1. Alternative brands available.
2. Evaluative criteria on which to compare brands.
3. Importance of various evaluative criteria.
4. Information on which to form beliefs:
   Attributes that brands possess.
   Benefits that various attributes provide.

TABLE 9.3

Another approach to assessing the degree of external search is to measure the extent to which a person relies on any particular source.[29] Also called the **instrumentality of search,** the approach involves assessing the extent to which the person relies on or finds useful the various sources of information.

Factors Influencing the Degree of External Search. Economists argue that consumers search as long as the marginal gains from search exceed the marginal costs of such a search.[30] From this viewpoint, consumers will continue searching only as long as the incremental gains that result from search are greater than the costs incurred to make the additional search.[31] The more costly it is for consumers to engage in external search, the less they will engage in the activity.

Working from an information-processing perspective, researchers have found that consumers engage in heavy amounts of external search when in a high-involvement state and doing extensive problem solving.[32] Researchers investigating the search process reported the following findings:

1. As time availability increases, search effort increases.
2. As perceived risk increases, total search effort increases.[33]
3. As attitudes toward shopping increase, total search effort increases.[34]
4. As education, income, and socioeconomic status increase, external search increases.[35]

The characteristics of the market situation may also influence the amount of external search. Researchers have found that, as the number of product alternatives available increases, greater amounts of search result.[36] Similarly, the number of stores available and their proximity also influence the amount of external search. When stores are numerous and in close physical proximity, consumers tend to engage in larger amounts of external search.[37] As one would expect, consumers engage in large amounts of external search when shopping in large malls where a number of stores are in close proximity to each other. Thus, as search costs are reduced, search increases. It can be anticipated that, because the use of the Internet decreases search costs, overall search will increase as increasing numbers of people buy products through the World Wide Web.

A recent summary of the literature discusses how product experience influences the amount of search. The authors of this study concluded that an inverted-U relationship exists. At low levels of experience, little search occurs. As experience increases, search increases, but only up to a certain point. At high levels of experience, sufficient knowledge exists to make search unnecessary. Thus, at very high levels of product experience, relatively little search occurs.[38]

The Amount of Search by Consumers

Research has shown that consumers engage in surprisingly little external search, even when in extended problem-solving situations. For example, one study investigated the external search behavior for refrigerators.[39] The author found that 42 percent of the respondents visited only one store. Furthermore, 41 percent considered only one brand. Another study found that, in 77 percent of the cases, consumers visited only one store when purchasing a small appliance.[40] Other researchers investigated the external search behavior for major appliances and automobiles. They concluded that "the amount of information sought by many buyers is small, even though information is accessible."[41]

Although consumers may visit few stores prior to purchasing appliances, one would expect them to engage in greater external search when options are easily compared, such as when shopping in a grocery store. In one study, however, shoppers were found to spend only 12 seconds in their selection process for each good purchased.[42] Immediately after they made a selection, they were asked to give the price of the brand selected. The researchers found that only 59 percent of the shoppers claimed to have checked the price. Less than half were actually able to state the correct price, and 32 percent gave a price that was off by an average of 15 percent. In fact, when a product was selling for a reduced price, less than half were even aware of the sale. The authors reported that executives of leading packaged goods firms were surprised and concerned with these results. Consumers search very little, even in a grocery store. As a result, it is difficult to communicate with them via promotional strategy.

Why do consumers engage in so little information search? One reason is that they may have engaged in extensive amounts of prepurchase search. Research indicates that a majority of consumers exhibit high levels of presearch decision activities.[43] Such presearch activities may result from the passive, low-involvement reception of information from marketing communications. They may also result from consumers who have an enduring involvement with a product class and who consistently engage in high-involvement prepurchase search activities.[44] Finally, consumers may perceive that they obtain few benefits in relation to the costs of additional search.

It should also be added, however, that consumer self-report surveys used to gather information may understate the actual amount of search by consumers. That is, when asked to describe their search process, many consumers forget all the steps they took in the search process.[45] Thus, consumers may actually be searching more than the data indicate.

ALTERNATIVE EVALUATION

In the alternative evaluation stage of the acquisition process, the consumer compares the options identified as potentially capable of solving the problem that initiated the decision process. When the options are compared, consumers form beliefs, attitudes, and intentions about the alternatives under consideration. (Chapter 7 identifies the concepts applicable to understanding the alternative evaluation stage of the decision process, including hierarchy of effects.)

Alternative evaluation is influenced by the type of hierarchy of effects occurring. From a high-involvement decision-making perspective, alternative evaluation follows the standard learning model, in which beliefs lead to affect formation resulting in behavioral intentions and behavior. In such instances the multiattribute models of attitude formation may be used to describe the evaluation process. In low-involvement situations alternative evaluation consists of the formation of a few rudimentary beliefs about the options under consideration. Indeed, relatively little alternative evaluation tends to occur under low-involvement conditions. Strong affective reactions (i.e., attitudes) are viewed as developing only after behavior occurs.

From the experiential perspective, the evaluation process is viewed as affect driven. The focus is not on belief formation but rather on affect creation. Thus, the researcher investigates what feelings and emotions are elicited by the acquisition that is about to be made. Finally, from the behavioral influence perspective, consumers are conceptualized as never consciously comparing alternatives. Table 9.4 summarizes the alternative evaluation process from the decision-making, experiential, and behavioral influence perspectives.

In the alternative evaluation stage, consumers consider the extent to which options possess various attributes. In addition, they begin to consider the importance and the goodness or badness of these attributes. Interestingly, when circumstances cause a person to have to exert greater effort to evaluate one alternative in comparison with another, negative affect occurs. For example, suppose that it is difficult to find

Alternative Evaluation and the Hierarchies of Effects

Hierarchy of Effect	How Alternatives Compared
High-involvement hierarchy	Beliefs about attributes are compared. Affective reactions are compared.
Low-involvement hierarchy	Limited number of beliefs about attributes are compared.
Experiential hierarchy	Affective reactions are compared.
Behavioral influence hierarchy	No internal comparison processes are recognized as occurring prior to behavior.

TABLE 9.4

information about the attributes of a particular brand. The result is that people avoid choosing the option that requires greater cognitive effort.[46]

In sum, it is through alternative evaluation that consumers gain the information needed to make a final choice, which is the next step in the decision-making process.

THE CONSUMER CHOICE PROCESS

After engaging in an evaluation of the alternatives, the consumer's next step in the decision process is to make a choice among alternatives, such as between different brands, services, or stores. In addition to choosing between two brands of a particular product, consumers may also choose between noncomparable alternatives. For example, people may choose between going on an expensive vacation, purchasing a car, or building a swimming pool. This section discusses each of these types of choices—choices between brands, stores, and noncomparable alternatives.

How consumers go about making choices is strongly influenced by the type of decision process in which they are engaged. The choice process differs if consumers use a high-involvement approach as compared to a low-involvement approach. Similarly, if the consumer is using an experiential orientation, the choice process is altered. (When behavioral influence is taking place, the consumer is considered not to be making any type of conscious, mentalistic choice.) The next two sections discuss the choice process from the high-involvement, low-involvement, and experiential perspectives. These are followed by a discussion of consumer choices among noncomparables and choices among stores. Table 9.5 summarizes these approaches to the choice process.

Choice Under High- and Low-Involvement Conditions

The study of choice under high- and low-involvement conditions has focused on identifying how consumers structure and select the rules in order to decide which alternative to purchase.[47] These investigations have identified two broad categories of choice models—compensatory and noncompensatory. Compensatory models are employed in high-involvement conditions. In these models high-belief ratings on one attribute can compensate for low ratings on another attribute. The attitude-toward-the-object model is an example of a compensatory model. In contrast, noncompensatory models are used in low-involvement conditions. In these models high ratings on one attribute may not compensate for low ratings on another attribute.[48]

Table 9.6 illustrates an example involving a decision faced by one of the authors concerning which brand of power lawn mower to purchase. His consideration set

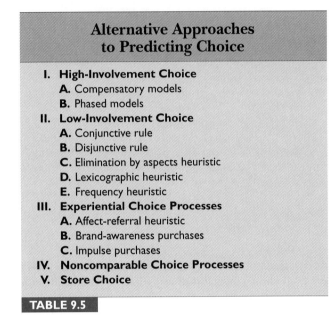

Alternative Approaches to Predicting Choice

I. High-Involvement Choice
  A. Compensatory models
  B. Phased models
II. Low-Involvement Choice
  A. Conjunctive rule
  B. Disjunctive rule
  C. Elimination by aspects heuristic
  D. Lexicographic heuristic
  E. Frequency heuristic
III. Experiential Choice Processes
  A. Affect-referral heuristic
  B. Brand-awareness purchases
  C. Impulse purchases
IV. Noncomparable Choice Processes
V. Store Choice

TABLE 9.5

consisted of four brands of self-propelled, gasoline-powered, 21-inch lawn mowers: a Toro recycler, a Toro rear bagger, a Lawnboy, and a John Deere. The Toro recycler was especially designed so that it would grind up the clippings into a fine mulch and deposit them back on the lawn so that they would be undetectable. The other models were standard rear-bagging lawn mowers with mulching attachments. The table identifies the attributes on which the lawn mowers were evaluated, the evaluations of the goodness or badness of the ratings, the estimates of the likelihood that the models possessed the

Which Lawn Mower to Choose?
An Example of the Use of AlternativeChoice Models

			Belief Rating and Consideration Set*†			
Attribute	**Evaluation Rating**	**Importance Rating**	**Toro Recycler**	**Toro Bagger**	**Lawnboy Bagger**	**John Deere Bagger**
Low cost	+1	4	7(7)	2(2)	2(2)	6(6)
Blade brake clutch‡	+2	8	1(2)	9(18)	10(20)	8(16)
Ease of operation	+2	7	9(18)	5(10)	4(8)	5(10)
Mulching§	+3	9	9(27)	5(15)	6(18)	5(15)
Consumer Reports rating	+2	5	8(16)	7(14)	6(12)	5(10)
			$\Sigma b_i e_i = 70$	$\Sigma b_i e_i = 59$	$\Sigma b_i e_i = 60$	$\Sigma b_i e_i = 57$

*Assume that a 5 or better on the belief ratings is required to surpass cutoff points on conjunctive and elimination by aspects models. Assume that 10 is required as a cutoff for the disjunctive model.
†$\Sigma b_i e_i$ is the formula for the attitude-toward-the-object model discussed in chapter 7. Numbers in parentheses represent the multiplication of the evaluation times the belief ratings.
‡The blade brake clutch allows the engine to run without the blade turning. This is important when bagging grass.
§The mower cuts grass into fine bits, which then are deposited back on the lawn. If this works well, no grass clippings are detectable after mowing.

TABLE 9.6

attributes (i.e., both concepts derived from the attitude-toward-the-object model), and the importance ratings of each of the attributes. The choice of lawn mower depends on whether the author is using a compensatory or a noncompensatory model.

The following subsections discuss how a choice would be predicted in high-involvement circumstances and then under low-involvement conditions, using the lawn mower example to illustrate the different outcomes.

High-Involvement Choice. Under conditions of high involvement, consumers act as though they are using a compensatory model. In **compensatory models of choice,** consumers analyze each alternative in a broad evaluative fashion so that high ratings on one attribute may compensate for low ratings on other attributes.[49] In such a process, all the information on the attributes of a brand are combined into an overall judgment of the preference for the brand. Such an evaluation is made for each of the brand alternatives. According to the compensatory model, the brand that has the highest overall preference is then chosen. If consumers employ a compensatory model, they do not necessarily reject an option because it has low ratings on any particular attribute. For example, a consumer may rate a particular brand of automobile as poor in acceleration. However, because the car is rated highly on other attributes and because judgment is based on a global evaluation, the brand could still be chosen. The attitude-toward-the-object model discussed in chapter 7 illustrates a compensatory model.

In the lawn mower selection problem shown in Table 9.6, if one assumes that the author employed a high-involvement decision process, the attitude-toward-the-object model should predict the purchase selection. As seen in the table, the predicted attitude is computed in exactly the same manner as described in chapter 7. The lawn mower with the highest rating is the Toro recycler, with an overall attitude score of 70. The closest competitor is the Lawnboy, with a rating of 60. The major reasons for the selection of the Toro recycler were its mulching and ease of operation features, each of which had high goodness evaluations along with belief ratings of 9. Note that the belief ratings on these attributes compensated for the low ratings on the blade brake clutch attribute, which this model lacked entirely.

Phased Strategies. In a **phased strategy,** consumers sequentially use two noncompensatory models or use a noncompensatory model and then a compensatory approach. For example, a consumer first may use a conjunctive model to reduce the alternatives considered to three or four. The consumer could then use a lexicographic approach or the attitude-toward-the object model to make the final choice. Such phased models are most likely used under high-involvement conditions.

Low-Involvement Choice. In low-involvement circumstances consumers act as though they use **noncompensatory models of choice.** In these models, high ratings on some attributes may not compensate for low ratings on other attributes. These noncompensatory models are also called **hierarchical models of choice.** They are hierarchical because the consumer is viewed as comparing alternatives on attributes one at a time: One attribute is chosen and all alternatives are compared on it. The person then moves to the next attribute and compares alternatives on it. The process then continues in a hierarchical manner. For the decision maker, one advantage of noncompensatory choice models is that they are relatively simple to implement. When consumers are in a low-involvement situation, they are unwilling to engage in the large amounts of information-processing effort required by a compensatory model.

The noncompensatory models are used as shortcuts to reach satisfactory decisions rather than optimal ones. Such a process has been called **satisficing** and depicts a goal of reaching a decision that is "good enough" rather than optimal.[50] The non-compensatory models have also been called heuristic models of choice. Heuristics are simple rules of thumb that people use to make satisfactory decisions rather than perfect ones. The use of heuristic choice models in low-involvement circumstances makes sense. In such cases consumers are unconcerned with reaching optimal decisions; they merely want to make a decision that is "good enough."

Several noncompensatory choice models have been identified, including the conjunctive rule, the disjunctive rule, the elimination-by-aspects heuristic, the lexicographic heuristic, and the frequency heuristic.[51]

The Conjunctive Rule. In many instances, such as purchasing a car, consumers are faced with a decision for which a large number of brand alternatives are available. Clearly, it would be impossible to investigate each brand in detail, so a shortcut is needed to simplify the process. One such shortcut involves the use of the **conjunctive rule,** in which the consumer sets minimum cutoffs on each attribute that he or she wishes to investigate. If the product fails to surpass the minimum cutoff level on each attribute, the alternative is rejected. If the cutoff levels are set very stringently, it is possible that only one alternative is left after all others are eliminated. More frequently, cutoff points are set lower so that a number of alternatives remain. As such, the conjunctive rule is often used as an initial screening device to eliminate enough brands so that a more complex decision approach, such as a compensatory model, can be applied to select from the remaining alternatives.

In the lawn mower example shown in Table 9.6, suppose that the belief ratings had to equal or surpass a cutoff of 5 or more to be considered. Using this rule, only the John Deere bagger has belief ratings that reach the cutoff on each attribute. Each of the remaining alternatives has at least one belief rating below the cutoff point. Therefore, based on the conjunctive model, the John Deere would be selected.

Disjunctive Rule. The **disjunctive rule** is similar to the conjunctive rule in that minimum standards are set for each attribute under consideration. Alternatives are then evaluated on the attributes. The disjunctive rule differs in that any alternative that surpasses the minimum cutoff on any attribute is accepted. Usually the cutoff point is set very stringently. The alternative chosen by the disjunctive rule is the one that is rated extremely high on some attribute. It is as though the person is saying that he or she wants an alternative that is "great" on some attribute.

Suppose that belief ratings in the lawn mower example have to reach the extremely high cutoff score of 10 for the alternative to be considered under a disjunctive model. The only brand to have a 10 on any attribute is the Lawnboy bagger, which has a 10 on the blade brake clutch feature. Thus, if a disjunctive model were employed, the analysis would predict that the consumer would select the Lawnboy.

Note the key difference in the conjunctive and disjunctive models. Both set minimum standards for each attribute. However, in the conjunctive model, if a rating falls below the standard on any attribute, it is rejected. In the disjunctive model, if a rating is above the cutoff level on any attribute, the alternative is accepted. Therefore, as one might expect, cutoffs for the disjunctive model are typically set higher than for the conjunctive model.

Elimination by Aspects. According to the **elimination-by-aspects heuristic,** each alternative is thought of as a collection of aspects or attributes. Choice occurs via a hierarchical process in which the alternatives are compared on the most important attribute. Alternatives not surpassing a cutoff on the attribute are eliminated. The decision maker then moves on to the next most important attribute and eliminates alternatives not surpassing the cutoff point. The process continues until only one alternative remains. The likelihood of choosing any one attribute with which to compare alternatives is based on its importance to the decision maker.

Suppose that a cutoff point on the belief rating is set at 6. When the elimination-by-aspects heuristic is applied to the lawn mower example in Table 9.6, one predicts that the Lawnboy would be selected. On the most important attribute of mulching, only the Toro recycler and the Lawnboy both equaled or surpassed the cutoff value of 6. On the second most important attribute, blade brake clutch, the Toro recycler was eliminated. This left only the Lawnboy, which is the predicted choice.

The Lexicographic Heuristic. The **lexicographic heuristic** has strong similarities to the elimination-by-aspects approach. Both start with the consumer ranking the attributes in their order of importance. The consumer then rates all alternatives on the most important attribute. At this point, however, the two approaches diverge. If a lexicographic model is used, the consumer then selects the alternative that is best on the most important attribute. If a tie occurs, the consumer moves to the next attribute and selects the alternative rated best on that attribute, and so forth. Thus, the lexicographic model uses a harsher standard of choice than the elimination-by-aspects model. The elimination-by-aspects model eliminates alternatives only if they fail to possess an attribute that surpasses a cutoff point. In contrast, in the lexicographic model, an alternative is eliminated if it does not have the highest rating on the most important attribute. Only in cases of ties does one move on to the next most important attribute.

Looking again at the lawn mower example, consider which lawn mower the consumer is predicted to select. If the lexicographic heuristic is used, the analysis would predict the choice of the Toro recycler. On the most important attribute of mulching, it received the highest rating and all other options would be eliminated. One can readily see why the lexicographic model is noncompensatory. That is, an alternative could be eliminated merely because it did not at least achieve a tie in the rating of the most important attribute.

The Frequency Heuristic. The **frequency heuristic** states that, when consumers are in a low-involvement state, choice may be influenced by the "mere number of positive and negative attributes associated with a brand or by the mere number of dimensions on which one brand outperforms another."[52] When a frequency heuristic is used, consumers act as though they simply count the number of features on which one brand surpasses another. Little or no attention is allocated to the relative importance of the features.[53]

Commercials that use a **piecemeal report strategy** are employing the frequency heuristic. For example, automakers have used comparative advertising in which their brand is selectively compared to a series of competitors on a number of different attributes. The ad might state that the vehicle has a trunk larger than a Mercedes, goes from 0 to 60 miles per hour faster than an Audi, and has more leg room than a BMW. In fact, the car might be a very poor brand and be exceeded by its competitors on every other dimension. However, because the attributes on which it surpasses the competition are systematically selected, the illusion is created that it has a high frequency of positive attributes.

Which Choice Models Do Consumers Use? One study asked respondents to make choices among various automobile alternatives after being given seven attributes on which to rate the cars.[54] Table 9.7 presents the results. The study found that almost 61 percent of the respondents used a lexicographic model. Next most frequently used was a compensatory model (32.1 percent). A phased strategy of using a conjunctive

Frequency of Use of Choice Models in Brand Choice

Model/Choice	Verbal Description	Percentage Using Approach
Conjunctive (noncompensatory)	I chose the car that had a really good rating on at least one characteristic.	0.6
Lexicographic (noncompensatory)	I looked at the characteristic that was most important to me and chose the car that was best in that feature. If two or more cars were equal on that feature, I then looked at my second most important feature to break the tie.	60.7
Multiattribute (compensatory)	I chose the car that had a really good rating when you balance the good ratings with the bad ratings.	32.1
Phased (conjunctive-compensatory)	I first eliminated the cars with a really bad rating on any feature and then chose from the rest the one that seemed the best overall when you balance the good ratings with the bad ratings.	5.4
Other	(Category composed of several other types of heuristic models.)	1.8

Source: Adapted from M. Reilly and R. Holman, "Does Task Complexity or Cue Intercorrelation Affect Choice of an Information Processing Strategy? An Empirical Investigation," in *Advances in Consumer Research,* ed. W. D. Perreault Jr. (Atlanta, GA: Association for Consumer Research, 1977), 4:189.

TABLE 9.7

model to screen alternatives followed by a compensatory approach was used 5.4 percent of the time. These three strategies accounted for 98.2 percent of the choices. Although the researchers did use a simulated buying situation and used students as respondents, it does indicate that consumers are likely to use noncompensatory models frequently in their decision making. It should be added, however, that the study did not analyze the extent to which respondents used all the types of choice models. For example, it did not analyze whether respondents used an elimination-by-aspects model or the frequency heuristic. More research is needed on this important issue.

Experiential Choice Processes

From the experiential perspective, choice is viewed as resulting from consumers considering their feelings about alternatives. Thus, little emphasis is placed on the development of beliefs about attributes.[55] As a result, the purchase is made with little cognitive control and seems to happen in a largely automatic manner.[56] Several types of consumer choice can be categorized as experiential processes. These are discussed in the following sections.

The Affect–Referral Heuristic. When consumers employ the **affect–referral heuristic,** they base their choice on their overall emotional response to an alternative. Rather than examining attributes or beliefs about attributes, consumers use a holistic approach in which they choose the alternative toward which they have the most positive feelings. Affect–referral explains how consumers make brand-loyal purchases. As will be discussed in chapter 10, consumers who express strong brand loyalty also reveal highly positive affect toward the brand. Thus, when making a purchase, they do not go through an extended or even a limited decision process. Rather, they simply refer to their feelings when making a choice. In a similar manner, impulse purchases represent cases in which consumers base their decision on a strong affective response. Finally, affect–referral can cause consumers to postpone needed purchases. Some choices create trade-offs between attributes that produce a negative affective state. For example, people know that they should buy life insurance, but the process makes them think about death and dying. This conflict produces a negative emotional state that causes the person to put off buying the insurance.[57]

The Effects of Brand Awareness. Brand awareness may also influence consumer choice through an affect–referral process. In particular, new brands face an extremely difficult problem in capturing market share because national brands are purchased in part because of the positive affect associated with them. One explanation for these effects is the mere-exposure phenomenon (discussed in chapter 7). That is, because national advertising of a brand results in frequent exposure to it, consumers become familiar with it. The familiarity results in positive feelings when consumers are exposed to the brand. As a result, the more familiar brand is chosen.[58]

The effects of brand awareness were demonstrated in a study in which respondents chose among three alternative brands of peanut butter. In the awareness condition, one of the brands was a well-known national brand. In the unawareness condition, all three brands were unknown regional brands. As might be expected, when the national brand was known, 93.5 percent of the subjects chose it.[59] Indeed, the study demonstrated that brand awareness was more important than the actual taste of the peanut butter. That is, the researchers varied the quality of the peanut butter independently of the brand name. When the good-tasting peanut butter was placed in the unknown brand's jar, only 20 percent selected it—even after they had tasted the less good tasting alternatives. In contrast, when the good-tasting peanut butter was placed in the national brand's jar, 77 percent chose it.[60]

Impulse Purchases. An **impulse purchase** has been defined as a "buying action undertaken without a problem having been previously recognized or a buying intention formed prior to entering the store."[61] An impulse to buy is accompanied by a sudden, powerful, persistent, and unplanned urge to buy something immediately. In addition, impulse buying is prone to occur with diminished regard for the decision's consequences.[62] Impulse purchases represent mindless reactive behavior. They are the antithesis of the rational consumption processes that one finds in high-involvement purchases and to a certain extent in low-involvement purchases.[63] Impulse purchases occur frequently; various studies have found that as many as 39 percent of department store purchases and 67 percent of grocery store purchases may be unplanned.[64]

In one study of impulse purchases, researchers conducted depth interviews, asking respondents to report on their feelings when they made purchases.[65] One subject reported the following:

> I was in Beverly Hills just walking around, not intending to buy, when I saw some shoes on sale. So I went inside and tried them on and they fit fine. At that time I thought about buying one pair, then I got the feeling I had to try everything. They were just calling to me. You suddenly feel compelled to buy something. It feels like getting an idea. It's a fast feeling, and if I don't get it right away, I'll think of reasons why I don't need it.

In this case strong positive affective feelings created a buying impulse that dominated all rational thought. The affective state led directly to a behavior without the person forming beliefs or thinking very hard about the purchase.

Variety-Seeking Purchases. Variety seeking refers to the tendency of consumers to spontaneously buy a new brand of product even though they continue to express satisfaction with the previously purchased brand. One explanation of variety seeking is that consumers attempt to reduce boredom by purchasing a new brand.[66] The theory of optimum stimulation has been proposed to explain this tendency to avoid boredom. Discussed more fully in chapter 5, optimum stimulation theory posits if one's activation falls too low or moves too high, he or she takes steps to change it.[67] The switching of brands may be a method of increasing stimulation by bringing something new into a consumer's life.

Effects of Mood States on Choice. Mood states influence whether a person uses a decision-making or an experiential approach to choice. One research team found that people in a positive mood state responded more favorably to emotional appeals than to informational appeals. In contrast, people in negative mood states responded more favorably to informational appeals than emotional appeals. These findings were extended by the researchers to the choice process. They found that, when people were in negative moods, they tended to rely on an informational approach to product selection. When in positive moods, their choice was more closely related to a focus on their feelings and fantasies about using particular brands.[68]

Choices Among Noncomparable Alternatives

As already noted, choices are not always made among comparable alternatives. Rather than merely deciding which brand of 35mm camera to purchase, a consumer must sometimes decide between divergent alternatives. For example, should the consumer spend $600 to purchase a high-quality camera, new stereo speakers, or a new business suit? The traditional noncompensatory models are of little assistance here because they require the decision maker to form beliefs about alternatives on common attributes. What do consumers do when the alternatives have no attributes in common other than price?

In one study in which subjects had to choose among noncomparable alternatives, the researchers noticed two trends.[69] First, subjects focused on using more abstract attributes in their comparison of alternatives. When comparing cameras to business suits, for example, they would compare the alternatives on such attributes as necessity, stylishness, cost, and innovativeness. Second, the respondents shifted to a more holistic strategy in which overall attitudes toward the alternatives were compared. In addition to comparing each alternative on abstract attributes, the respondents evaluated each alternative separately to compare overall impressions of the products.[70]

The study of noncomparable alternatives is important because some of the most important decisions made by consumers involve very different product alternatives. For example, consumers may make a choice between purchasing a car or building a new kitchen. Similarly, an 18 year old must make the choice between going to college or taking a job. A woman may be forced to choose between starting a family, concentrating on a career, or trying to do both.

Choices Among Stores

Another area of research on choice concerns the store selection process. A critical issue for retailers involves developing an understanding of the factors that consumers use when selecting from which store to purchase a product. The approaches to choice identified in the preceding sections are directly relevant to the issue. Using a decision-making perspective, retailers can identify the attributes that people use to evaluate alternative stores, determine whether consumers are in high- or low-involvement states, and identify the appropriate choice model. Researchers have found that consumers consider such attributes as the store's distance from their home, the overall prices of brands carried, and service.[71]

Another factor that influences store choice is the **decision context.** Context refers to those situational or extrinsic factors that dictate the options available to the decision maker.[72] Thus, the types of stores available, how many stores are available, and the presence of mail-order alternatives influence the nature of the choice process.

Other research on store choice has focused on the type of choice set used by consumers.[73] The research found that consumers evaluate retailers based on the same types of sets discussed earlier in this chapter concerning products (i.e., awareness, inert, inept, and consideration sets). In addition, several new types of sets were found. For example, the **interaction set** consists of those stores in which a consumer allows him- or herself to be exposed to personal selling. Such stores have an opportunity to sell that is not shared by those in the **quiet set.** Consumers may enter stores belonging to the quiet set, but they tend not to interact with any sales personnel.

THE MANAGERIAL IMPLICATIONS OF CONSUMER DECISION MAKING

The principles and concepts derived from the study of consumer decision making have applications to each of the five PERMS concepts. These are discussed in the following sections.

Positioning and Differentiation

The analysis of problem recognition has direct relevance to positioning and differentiation strategies. Problem recognition and need recognition processes both result from a perceived discrepancy between an actual and a desired state. These desired states represent benefits that consumers seek. Thus, products can be positioned as fulfilling these benefits. For example, a consumer may have a desired state of protecting and enhancing the body. A product such as a sunscreen can then be positioned as performing this function by preventing sunburn and potentially skin cancer. Alternative evaluation processes also have relevance to positioning: Products can be positioned by identifying the attributes that consumers perceive as extremely important. For example, in the lawn mower example, the Toro recycler could be positioned based on its mulching capability.

Environmental Analysis

The nature of the consumer environment may have large effects on consumer search behavior. As a result, managers should evaluate the number of competing stores in a region. Interestingly, placing one's store in close proximity to competitors lowers consumer search costs, resulting in higher traffic. Also, the number of competitors will impact the size of consumer consideration sets, which will in turn impact internal search. Managers should also evaluate the impact of the consumer environment from a behavioral influence perspective. In particular, it is important to carefully assess the effects of the physical environment (e.g., the layout and atmospherics of stores) on consumers.

Research

It is important to conduct appropriate research studies to identify the extent of external search in which consumers engage in the purchase of brands in a product class. This will have important implications for distribution strategies. In addition, it is even more important to determine the type of choice processes employed by the target market. Whether consumers engage in high-involvement, low-involvement, or experiential choice can impact both promotional product strategy. For example, if a company finds through market research that the target market employs a lexicographic choice model, it is critical to design and promote a product so that it is perceived as the best on the most important attribute. Similarly, if consumers use a conjunctive choice process, it is critical to ensure that the product exceeds a minimum cutoff level on each of the attributes.

Marketing Mix

As already noted, the identification of the attributes that consumers rate as extremely important has implications for product and promotional strategy. Similarly, an understanding of the type of choice process employed by the target market will influence product and promotional strategy. For example, if the target market is found to employ a high-involvement choice model, it suggests that managers do not have to be concerned about optimizing each of the features of the brand. Rather, the focus should be on identifying the attributes rated as most important by the target market and working to create strong beliefs that the brand possesses these attributes. In addition, do not forget that price can be an attribute as well. For some product categories, price is the most important attribute. In cases in which price is extremely important, managers must ensure that their brands are priced competitively. Distribution and promotional strategies should be based in part on an understanding of the extent of consumer search. For example, if limited search occurs, the product must be promoted heavily and distributed widely.

Segmentation

The extent of external search and the type of choice model employed by consumers can act as segmentation variables. For example, a strategy may be to target a high-involvement target market consisting of the early adopters in the product category. These individuals can be expected to engage in extended search processes, including preneed search. In addition, they will likely employ a phased decision process that culminates in using a compensatory choice model. The approach to reach and influence these individuals will be very different from that employed to market a brand to consumers using either a low-involvement or experiential decision process.

Notes

1. Brian Wansink, Robert J. Kent, and Stephen J. Hoch, "An Anchoring and Adjustment Model of Purchase Quantity Decisions," *Journal of Marketing* 35 (February 1998): 71–81.
2. James R. Bettman, Mary Frances Luce, and John W. Payne, "Constructive Consumer Choice Processes," *Journal of Consumer Research* 25 (December 1998): 187–237.
3. For a discussion of cross-cultural issues in consumer decision making, see Kathleen Brewer Doran, "Exploring Cultural Differences in Consumer Decision Making: Chinese Consumers in Montreal," in *Advances in Consumer Research,* ed. Chris T. Allen and Deborah Roedder John (Provo, UT: Association for Consumer Research, 1994), 21:318–22.
4. Michele D. Bunn, "Taxonomy of Buying Decision Approaches," *Journal of Marketing* 57 (January 1993): 38–56.
5. Richard Olshavsky and Donald Granbois, "Consumer Decision Making: Fact or Fiction," *Journal of Consumer Research* 6 (September 1979): 98.
6. Morris Holbrook and Elizabeth Hirschman, "The Experiential Aspects of Consumption: Consumer Fantasies, Feelings, and Fun," *Journal of Consumer Research* 9 (September 1982): 132–40.
7. Herbert Krugman, "The Impact of Television in Advertising: Learning without Involvement," *Public Opinion Quarterly* 30 (fall 1965): 349–56.
8. For an excellent discussion of low-involvement decision making, see Stewart De Bruicker, "An Appraisal of Low-Involvement Consumer Information Processing," in *Attitude Research*

Plays for High Stakes, ed. John Maloney and Bernard Silverman (Chicago, IL: American Marketing Association, 1979), 112–30.

9. Meera P. Venkatraman and Deborah J. MacInnis, "The Epistemic and Sensory Exploratory Behaviors of Hedonic and Cognitive Consumers," in *Advances in Consumer Research,* ed. Elizabeth Hirschman and Morris Holbrook (Provo, UT: Association for Consumer Research, 1985), 12:102–7.

10. Sidney J. Levy, "Symbols for Sales," *Harvard Business Review* 37 (July–August 1959): 117–24.

11. Itamar Simonson and Russell S. Winer, "The Influence of Purchase Quantity and Display Format on Consumer Preference for Variety," *Journal of Consumer Research* 19 (June 1992): 133–38.

12. Jeff Meer, "The Light Touch," *Psychology Today,* September 1985, pp. 60–67.

13. Gordon C. Bruner and Richard J. Pomazal, "Problem Recognition: The Crucial First Stage of the Consumer Decision Process," *Journal of Consumer Marketing* 5 (winter 1988): 53–63.

14. Diane M. Phillips, "Anticipating the Future: The Role of Consumption Visions in Consumer Behavior," in *Advances in Consumer Research* ed. Kim P. Corfman and John G. Lynch Jr. (Provo, UT: Association for Consumer Research, 1996), 23:70–75.

15. C. Jayachandran and Nyroslaw Kyj, "Pre-Need Purchasing Behavior: An Overlooked Dimension in Consumer Marketing," *Journal of Consumer Marketing* 4 (summer 1987): 59–66.

16. James R. Bettman, *An Information Processing Theory of Consumer Choice* (Reading, MA: Addison-Wesley, 1979).

17. Peter Bloch, Daniel Sherrell, and Nancy Ridgway, "Consumer Search: An Extended Framework," *Journal of Consumer Research* 13 (June 1986): 119–26.

18. For information on the categories of brands that consumers may retrieve from long-term memory, see F. May and R. Homans, "Evoked Set Size and the Level of Information Processing in Product Comprehension and Choice Criteria," in *Advances in Consumer Research,* ed. W. D. Perreault (Chicago, IL: Association for Consumer Research, 1977), 4:172–75. Also see Naeim Abougomaah, John Schlacter, and William Gaidis, "Elimination and Choice Phases in Evoked Set Formation," *Journal of Consumer Marketing* 4 (fall 1987): 67–73.

19. Joseph Pereira, "Name of the Game: Brand Awareness," *Wall Street Journal,* February 14, 1991, p. B1.

20. For an excellent discussion of the consideration set, see Allan D. Shocker, Moshe Ben-Akiva, Bruno Boccara, and Prakash Nedungadi, "Consideration Set Influences on Customer Decision Making and Choice: Issues, Models, and Suggestions," *Marketing Letters,* August 1991, pp. 181–98.

21. John Howard and Jagdish Sheth, *The Theory of Buyer Behavior* (New York: Wiley, 1969).

22. Stewart Shapiro, Deborah J. MacInnis, and Susan E. Heckler, "The Effects of Incidental Ad Exposure on the Formation of Consideration Sets," *Journal of Consumer Research* 24 (June 1997): 94–104.

23. Rajan Sambandam and Kenneth R. Lord, "Switching Behavior in Automobile Markets: A Consideration-Set Model," *Journal of the Academy of Marketing Science* 23 (winter 1995): 57–65.

24. Ibid.

25. Ayn E. Crowley and John H. Williams, "An Information Theoretic Approach to Understanding the Consideration Set/Awareness Set Proportion," in *Advances in Consumer Research,* ed. Rebecca Holman and Michael Solomon (Provo, UT: Association for Consumer Research, 1991), 18:780–87.

26. For more technical discussions of the factors that influence whether a brand enters the consideration set, see J. Wesley Hutchinson, Kalyan Raman, and Murali K. Mantrala, *Journal of Marketing Research* 31 (November 1994): 441–61. Also see Andreas G. Lazari and Donald A. Anderson, "Designs of Discrete Choice Set Experiments for Estimating Both Attribute and Availability Cross Effects," *Journal of Marketing Research* 31 (August 1994): 375–83.

27. Sharon Beatty and Scott Smith, "External Search Effort: An Investigation across Several Product Categories," *Journal of Consumer Research* 14 (June 1987): 84.

28. For an excellent current review of the factors associated with the extent of external search, see Beatty and Smith, "External Search Effort."

29. Jeff Blodgett and Donna Hill, "An Exploratory Study Comparing Amount-of-Search Measures to Consumers' Reliance on Each Source of Information," in *Advances in*

Consumer Research, ed. Rebecca Holman and Michael Solomon (Provo, UT: Association for Consumer Research, 1991), 18:773–79.

30. Arieh Goldman and J. K. Johansson, "Determinants of Search for Lower Prices: An Empirical Assessment of the Economics of Information Theory," *Journal of Consumer Research* 5 (December 1978): 176–86.

31. For a discussion of how children respond to the costs and benefits of search, see Jennifer Gregan-Paxton and Deborah Roedder John, "Are Young Children Adaptive Decision Makers? A Study of Age Differences in Information Search Behavior," *Journal of Consumer Research* 21 (March 1995): 567–80.

32. For a conceptual discussion of the factors that influence retail search processes, see Philip A. Titus and Peter B. Everett, "The Consumer Retail Search Process: A Conceptual Model and Research Agenda," *Journal of the Academy of Marketing Science* 23 (spring 1995): 106–19.

33. D. S. Sundaram and Ronald D. Taylor, "An Investigation of External Information Search Effort: Replication in In-Home Shopping Situations," in *Advances in Consumer Research,* ed. Joseph W. Alba and J. Wesley Hutchinson (Provo, UT: Association for Consumer Research, 1998), 25:440–45.

34. Beatty and Smith, "External Search Effort."

35. N. Capon and M. Burke, "Individual, Product Class, and Task Related Factors in Consumer Information Processing," *Journal of Consumer Research* 7 (August 1972): 249–57.

36. D. R. Lehmann and W. L. Moore, "Validity of Information Display Boards: An Assessment Using Longitudinal Data," *Journal of Marketing Research* 17 (November 1980): 450–59.

37. G. S. Cort and L. V. Dominquez, "Cross Shopping and Retail Growth," *Journal of Marketing* 14 (May 1977): 187–92.

38. Sridhar Moorthy, Brian T. Ratchford, and Debabrata Talukdar, "Consumer Information Search Revisited: Theory and Empirical Analysis," *Journal of Consumer Research* 23 (March 1997): 263–77.

39. W. Dommermuth, "The Shopping Matrix and Marketing Strategy," *Journal of Marketing Research* 2 (May 1965): 128–32.

40. J. Udell, "Prepurchase Behavior of Buyers of Small Appliances," *Journal of Marketing* 30 (October 1966): 50–52.

41. J. Newman and R. Staelin, "Prepurchase Information Seeking for New Cars and Major Household Appliances," *Journal of Marketing Research* 9 (August 1972): 249–57.

42. Peter R. Dickson and Alan G. Sawyer, "The Price Knowledge and Search of Supermarket Shoppers," *Journal of Marketing* 54 (July 1990): 42–53.

43. Girish Punj, "Presearch Decision Making in Consumer Durable Purchases," *Journal of Consumer Marketing* 4 (winter 1987): 71–82.

44. Peter Bloch and Marsha Richins, "Shopping without Purchase: An Investigation of Consumer Browsing Behavior," in *Advances in Consumer Research,* ed. Richard Bagozzi and Alice Tybout (Ann Arbor, MI: Association for Consumer Research, 1983), 10:389–93.

45. J. Newman and B. Lockeman, "Measuring Prepurchase Information Seeking," *Journal of Consumer Research* 2 (December 1975): 216–22.

46. Ellen C. Garbarino and Julie A. Edell, "Cognitive Effort, Affect, and Choice," *Journal of Consumer Research* 24 (September 1997): 147–58.

47. Eloise Coupey, "Restructuring: Constructive Processing of Information Displays in Consumer Choice," *Journal of Consumer Research* 21 (June 1994): 83–99.

48. For recent discussions of choice models, see Pratibha A. Dabholkar, "Incorporating Choice into an Attitudinal Framework: Analyzing Models of Mental Comparison Processes," *Journal of Consumer Research* 21 (June 1994): 100–118. Also see Maryon F. King and Siva K. Balasubramanian, "The Effects of Expertise, End Goal, and Product Type on Adoption of Preference Formation Strategy," *Journal of the Academy of Marketing Science* 22 (spring 1994): 146–59.

49. This section on noncompensatory models relies heavily on work by Peter Wright, "Consumer Choice Strategies: Simplifying versus Optimizing," *Journal of Marketing Research* 11 (February 1976): 60–67. Also see Dennis Gensch and Rajshekhar Javalgi, "The Influence of Involvement on Disaggregate Attribute Choice Models," *Journal of Consumer Research* 14 (June 1987): 71–82.

50. Alan Newell and Herbert Simon, *Human Problem Solving* (Upper Saddle River, NJ: Prentice Hall, 1972).

51. Wright, "Consumer Choice Strategies."

52. Joseph W. Alba and Howard Marmorstein, "The Effects of Frequency Knowledge on Consumer Decision Making," *Journal of Consumer Research* 14 (June 1987): 14–25.
53. Ibid.
54. M. Reilly and R. Holman, "Does Task Complexity or Cue Intercorrelation Affect Choice of an Information-Processing Strategy? An Empirical Investigation," in *Advances in Consumer Research,* ed. W. D. Perrault Jr. (Atlanta, GA: Association for Consumer Research, 1977), 4:185–90.
55. Banwari Mittal, "A Study of Affective Choice for Consumer Decisions," in *Advances in Consumer Research,* ed. Chris T. Allen and Deborah Roedder John (Provo, UT: Association for Consumer Research, 1994), 21:256–63.
56. P. Weinberg and W. Gottwald, "Impulsive Consumer Buying as a Result of Emotions," *Journal of Business Research* 10 (March 1982): 43–87.
57. Mary Frances Luce, "Choosing to Avoid: Coping with Negatively Emotion-Laden Consumer Decisions," *Journal of Consumer Research* 24 (March 1998): 409–33. Also see Mary Frances Luce, John W. Payne, and James R. Bettman, "Emotional Trade-Off Difficulty and Choice," *Journal of Marketing Research* 36 (May 1999): 143–59.
58. Marc Vanhuele, "Why Familiar Stimuli Are Liked: A Study on the Cognitive Dynamics Linking Recognition and the Mere Exposure Effect," in *Advances in Consumer Research,* ed. Frank R. Kardes and Mita Sujan (Provo, UT: Association for Consumer Research, 1995), 22:171–175.
59. Wayne D. Hoyer and Steven P. Brown, "Effects of Brand Awareness on Choice for a Common, Repeat-Purchase Product," *Journal of Consumer Research* 17 (September 1990): 141–48.
60. Not all research is supportive of mere-exposure effects. For example, see John W. Pracejus, "Is More Exposure Always Better? Effects of Incidental Exposure to a Brand Name on Subsequent Processing of Advertising," in *Advances in Consumer Research,* ed. Frank R. Kardes and Mita Sujan (Provo, UT: Association for Consumer Research, 1995), 22:319–27.
61. Dennis Rook and Stephen Hoch, "Consuming Impulses," in *Advances in Consumer Research,* ed. E. Hirschman and M. Holbrook (Ann Arbor, MI: Association for Consumer Research, 1985), 12:23–27.
62. For a recent review and analysis of impulse purchasing, see James E. Burroughs, "Product Symbolism, Self-Meaning, and Holistic Matching: The Role of Information Processing in Impulsive Buying," in *Advances in Consumer Research,* ed. Kim P. Corfman and John G. Lynch Jr. (Provo, UT: Association for Consumer Research, 1994), 23:463–69.
63. Rook and Hoch, "Consuming Impulses."
64. "Industrial Retail Selling Strategies Designed to Induce Impulse Sales," *Beverage Industry,* June 3, 1977, pp. 6 ff.
65. Rook and Hoch, "Consuming Impulses."
66. M. Venkatesan, "Cognitive Consistency and Novelty Seeking," in *Consumer Behavior: Theoretical Sources,* ed. Scott Ward and Thomas Robertson (Upper Saddle River, NJ: Prentice Hall, 1973), 354–84.
67. P. S. Raju, "Optimum Stimulation Level: Its Relationship to Personality, Demographics, and Exploratory Behavior," *Journal of Consumer Research* 7 (December 1980): 272–82. For a review of variety seeking, see Leigh McAlister and Edgar Pessemier, "Variety Seeking Behavior: An Interdisciplinary Review," *Journal of Consumer Research* 9 (December 1982): 311–22.
68. Meryl Gardner and Ronald Hill, "Consumers' Mood States: Antecedents and Consequences of Experiential vs. Information Strategies for Brand Choice," *Psychology and Marketing* (in press).
69. Michael Johnson, "Consumer Choice Strategies for Comparing Noncomparable Alternatives," *Journal of Consumer Research* 11 (December 1984): 741–53. Also see Barbara Kahn, William Moore, and Rashi Glazer, "Experiments in Constrained Choice," *Journal of Consumer Research* 14 (June 1987): 96–113.
70. A topic related to choice comparability is decision difficulty. For a discussion, see Eloise Coupey and Carol W. DeMoranville, "Information Processability and Restructuring: Consumer Strategies for Managing Difficult Decisions," in *Advances in Consumer Research,* ed. Kim Corfman and John G. Lynch Jr. (Provo, UT: Association for Consumer Research, 1996), 23:225–30.

71. James Bruner and John Mason, "The Influence of Driving Time upon Shopping Center Preference," *Journal of Marketing* 32 (April 1968): 57–61.
72. Susan Spiggle and Murphy Sewall, "A Choice Sets Model of Retail Selection," *Journal of Marketing* 51 (April 1987): 97–111.
73. Ibid.

CHAPTER 10

After We Buy: Satisfaction and Loyalty

After studying this chapter, you should be able to discuss each of the following concepts, together with their managerial relevance:

1. The consumption experience.
2. The formation of brand expectations.
3. The equity approach to understanding postacquisition satisfaction.
4. The expectation confirmation approach to understanding postacquisition satisfaction.
5. The two major reasons consumers complain.
6. The extent to which consumers take overt action to complain when they are dissatisfied.
7. The eight factors that influence consumer complaining.
8. The various ways in which consumers may dispose of a product.
9. Four actions companies can take to help ensure postacquisition satisfaction.
10. Brand loyalty.

Chapter 9 discussed the first four stages of the consumer decision process: problem recognition, information search, alternative evaluation, and choice. This chapter focuses on the last stage of consumer decision making, postacquisition processes. **Postacquisition processes** refer to the consumption, postchoice evaluation, and disposition of goods, services, experiences, and ideas. During the postchoice evaluation stage, purchase satisfaction or dissatisfaction may occur. Indeed, providing high levels of satisfaction is a major goal of most corporations, from local restaurants to Delta Airlines to General Motors.

Figure 10.1 presents a model of the consumer postacquisition process, which encompasses five major topics: (1) product usage or consumption, (2) consumer

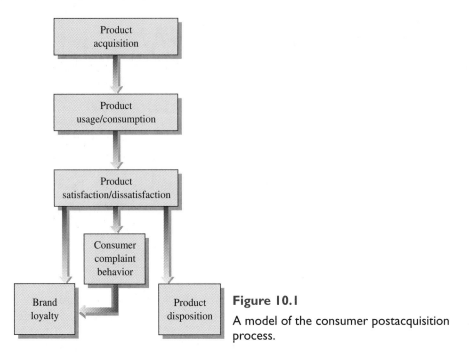

Figure 10.1

A model of the consumer postacquisition process.

satisfaction and dissatisfaction, (3) consumer complaint behavior, (4) the disposition of goods, and (5) the formation of brand loyalty. During the consumption stage, consumers use and experience the product. This stage is followed by the development of consumer satisfaction or dissatisfaction. If consumers are dissatisfied with the product's performance, complaint behavior may occur. The final two stages of the postacquisition process involve how consumers dispose of the goods that they purchase and how brand loyalty and future buying intentions are formed.

THE CONSUMPTION EXPERIENCE

A consumer's **consumption experience** may be defined as the cognitions and feelings experienced by a person during the use of a product or service. In the following subsections, the three elements of the consumption experience will be discussed: product use, the consumption of performance, and the impact of moods and feelings on the overall consumption experience.

Product Use

Product use involves the actions and experiences that take place during the time period in which a consumer is directly experiencing a good or service. The observation of how consumers use goods can lead to the development of new market offerings. For example, a general manager at Kodak observed a tourist in Japan attempting to pry open a Kodak film container while holding his camera. The feat was impossible with one hand, and the man had to use his teeth to tear off the lid. The manager returned to headquarters, reported the problem, and now the lids can be pulled off with one hand.[1]

Another area in which information on product usage can be important is in avoiding product liability problems. Companies must design a product so that it is safe in the use for which it was designed. In addition, companies should take steps to anticipate unintended uses of their products and either design them for safe use or provide warnings that they should not be used in certain applications. For example, aluminum stepladders warn consumers not to stand on the top of the ladder and to avoid use near electrical lines.

Marketers have identified three factors that are particularly important when assessing product usage.[2] First, the **consumption frequency** should be analyzed. Some products are used continuously (e.g., refrigerators and hot water heaters); most products, however, are used discontinuously (e.g., dishwashers, medical services, toothpaste, autos, etc.). In general, companies want consumers to use their products or service as frequently as possible (exceptions include efforts to reduce or eliminate the abuse of drugs.)[3]

Second, **consumption amount** is important for marketers to evaluate. In many cases companies may develop strategies to increase the average amount of a product consumed. General Mills realized that it could influence the consumption amount of its cereals via shelf placement. Because most people are right-handed, they naturally reach for cereals that are on the right side of a display. By putting larger packages toward the right, larger packages are more often bought.[4]

The **consumption purpose** is the third category that researchers consider. A classic example of a company that has attempted to increase the number of purposes for which a product may be used is Arm & Hammer. A few of the alternative uses suggested for its baking soda include baking, brushing teeth, freshening a carpet, and serving as an antacid. Consumption purpose is closely related to what is called *usage occasion*. More will be said about usage occasions in chapter 11.

The Consumption of Performance

Marketing researchers suggest that in Western society people frame the consumption experience as though they were participating in a performance. Using naturalistic research methods borrowed from the fields of anthropology and sociology, researchers have investigated dramatic consumer performances such as sky diving[5] and white-water river rafting.[6]

What does it mean to say that consumers are participating in a performance? From a dramaturgical perspective, consumers and marketers act as though they are in a theatrical performance.[7] For example, when rafting down the Colorado River, the participants and their guide are actors. The boat, life vests, food, mosquito repellants, and so on are the props for the play. The Colorado River and the canyon form the stage. Within this backdrop a story is told. In the first stage of the story, conflicting forces are introduced. For example, the participants ask themselves if they really want to participate in a white-water experience. During the second stage, tensions and emotions build as they experience fear, hunger, and cold. In the conclusion, the conflict is resolved and emotions are released.

Marketers seek to script the exchange performance that occurs with customers. Indeed, consumers and marketers can be viewed as being in an "exchange play" in which each performs to a greater or lesser degree. For our purposes a **consumer performance** can be defined as an event in which a consumer and marketer act as performers or audience in a situation in which obligations and standards exist.[8] It is important to distinguish a performance from an occurrence. An occurrence happens as the result of an accident or "act of nature." It is unplanned and does not arise from any obligation.

Table 10.1 distinguishes occurrences from three different types of performances. In a **contracted performance,** the consumer and marketer play only minimal roles. Contracted performances most frequently involve the purchase and use of low-involvement products, such as detergent, toothpaste, motor oil, and checking accounts.

Types of Consumer Performances

1. *Contracted performance.* Both the consumer and the marketer have minimal interactions. Occurs with low-involvement goods.
2. *Enacted performance.* Both the consumer and the marketer have sufficient latitude to place blame for the outcome of the transaction. Occurs most frequently with high-involvement products.
3. *Dramatistic performance.* Both the consumer and the marketer know that a show is occurring. Each party becomes concerned with the motives of the other. Occurs most frequently in the highest-involvement situations, such as skydiving or buying an automobile.

TABLE 10.1

When the audience recognizes that a satisfactory exchange depends on the performance of a person, an **enacted performance** takes place. Here the exchange occurs in a manner in which the consumer or marketer can blame or give credit to the other for the outcome of the transaction. Enacted performance occurs most frequently in service exchanges or with high-involvement goods. For example, the performance involved in being a passenger on an airline or a patient in the dentist's chair is enacted. Similarly, the purchase of a car involves both the consumer and the salesperson in a complex exchange in which blame or credit can be assessed by either party.

The third type of performance, **dramatistic performance,** occurs when both the consumer and marketer know that a show is occurring, and each monitors the other's role. The producer is putting on a show, and the consumer knows it. In dramatistic performance the stakes are large and the consumer's and marketer's involvement levels are quite high. In such instances each actor is an audience to the other and each becomes alert to the motives of the other in the performance, recognizing that the actions of the other could be contrived. An example is a situation in which a consumer believes that he or she has been wronged by a company and begins to complain. Another example is the performances that occur on a white-water rafting expedition or during skydiving, which also have a dramatistic flare. In other words, in both enacted and dramatistic performances, there is an element of theater, but in dramatistic performances the marketer is deliberately trying to contrive an effect.

Particularly when purchasing services, the metaphor of a drama is appropriate. The dramaturgy metaphor may also hold for the purchase and use of goods as well as services. Indeed, a good can be described as merely the "frozen potential for performance."[9] Thus, consumers not only choose goods but also consume performances when they use the good. We even speak of a detergent or a car as "performing well." At the extreme, building a house in which tens or hundreds of thousands of dollars are invested can take on the characteristics of Greek tragedy.

Mood States and the Consumption Experience

Moods are temporary positive or negative affective states. An important issue concerns the impact of the consumption experience on mood states. As discussed in chapters 4 and 9, consumer mood states may have a strong impact on what is remembered and on which brand is chosen. Moods may be influenced by what happens during the consumption of a product. The mood state that is created during the consumption process may, in turn, influence the overall evaluation of the product.

One study investigated the impact of music on consumer mood states and on subsequent product evaluations.[10] Respondents in the study either heard music that they had rated very positively or that they rated very negatively. While listening to the music, they rated the taste of peanut butter. Premeasures indicated that the positively rated music influenced the respondents to be in a more positive mood than those exposed to the negatively rated music. Different groups of subjects rated one of three different types of peanut butter, which in pretests were determined to taste very good, neutral, or very bad. The results revealed that the type of music did *not* impact brand evaluations for the good- or the bad-tasting peanut butter. However, for the neutral-tasting peanut butter, brand evaluations were significantly higher when the music was liked as compared to when it was disliked.

In sum, consumer feelings about the consumption experience will impact their evaluations of the product independent of the actual quality of the product. Postpurchase evaluation of products is closely related to the development of feelings of satisfaction or dissatisfaction with the exchange process, which is the topic of the next section.

THE DEVELOPMENT OF POSTACQUISITION SATISFACTION AND DISSATISFACTION

During and after the consumption and use of a product or service, consumers develop feelings of satisfaction or dissatisfaction. **Consumer satisfaction** is defined as the overall attitude regarding a good or service after its acquisition and use. It is a postchoice evaluative judgment resulting from a specific purchase selection and the experience of using or consuming it.[11]

From a managerial perspective, maintaining or enhancing customer satisfaction is critical. One recent study examined the satisfaction level of customers with Swedish companies. The results revealed that, over a five-year period, an annual 1 percent increase in customer satisfaction resulted in an 11.4 percent increase in the companies' return on investment. The researchers found that satisfied customers positively influence future cash flows. Thus, programs to increase customer satisfaction should be treated as investments.[12]

What are the factors that contribute to feelings of consumer satisfaction or dissatisfaction (CS/D)? Figure 10.2 presents a model of CS/D. In the model consumers are shown as consuming or using the good or service. Based on this experience, they evaluate its overall performance. This assessment of performance has been found to be closely related to the ratings of the quality of the product.[13] These perceptions of product quality are compared to the consumer's expectations of the product's performance. An evaluation process then takes place in which consumers act as though they compare actual performance to expected performance. Based on the comparison of expected quality to performance quality, consumers will experience positive, negative, or neutral emotions depending on whether expectations were confirmed. These emotional responses then act as inputs into the overall satisfaction–dissatisfaction perception.

In addition, the level of satisfaction or dissatisfaction will also be impacted by the consumer's evaluation of the equity of the exchange. Finally, attributions of the cause of the product's performance will also impact the attitude of satisfaction or dissatisfaction. The following sections discuss each of these ideas.

The Evaluation of Product Performance and Quality

Over the past 15 years, companies throughout the world have embraced the ideas that successful companies should continuously improve the quality of their products and that quality is defined by the customer. **Product quality** is defined as the customers' overall evaluation of the excellence of the performance of a good or service.[14] A key issue in assessing perceived product performance concerns what dimensions consumers use to make this assessment. Researchers in the services area have identified

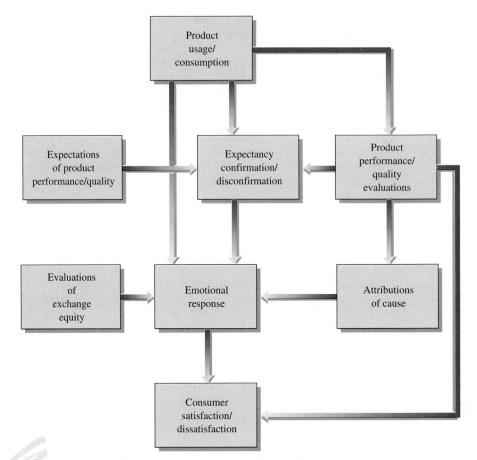

Figure 10.2   A model of consumer satisfaction/dissatisfaction.

five dimensions on which consumers evaluate service quality. These dimensions are found in part A of Table 10.2.[15]

The five dimensions of service quality identified in part A of Table 10.2 can be viewed as attributes on which consumers evaluate the overall performance of *services*. As applied to goods, however, they present a problem because, with the exception of the "tangibles" category, they focus exclusively on the interaction between employees and customers. What is needed is a set of dimensions that includes the concrete attributes consumers associate with goods.

Such a set of eight dimensions has been proposed to assess product quality. These eight categories are listed in part B of Table 10.2. A careful analysis of Table 10.2 shows that there is an overlap among the concepts identified in the service-quality and product-quality dimensions. We believe that it is possible to combine these approaches to identify the following seven basic dimensions of quality:

1. *Performance.* The absolute level of performance of the good or service on the key attributes identified by customers. The extent to which the product or service is "done right." The number of attributes offered. The ability of employees to handle problems well. The quality of the information provided to the customer.

The Dimensions of Quality

A. Dimensions of Service Quality

1. *Tangibles.* Include physical facilities, equipment, and appearance of personnel.
2. *Reliability.* The ability of personnel to perform dependably and accurately.
3. *Responsiveness.* Providing customers with prompt service.
4. *Assurance.* The knowledge and courtesy of employees, as well as their ability to inspire trust and confidence.
5. *Empathy.* The ability of employees to care and to provide individualized attention.

Source: A. Parasuraman, Valarie A. Zeithaml, and Leonard L. Berry, "SERVQUAL: A Multiple-Item Scale for Measuring Consumer Perceptions of Service Quality," *Journal of Retailing* 64 (spring 1988): 12–36.

B. Dimensions of Product Quality

1. *Performance.* Performance on primary operating characteristics.
2. *Features.* The number of bells and whistles that supplement primary characteristics.
3. *Reliability.* Probability of failing or malfunctioning.
4. *Durability.* The life of the product.
5. *Serviceability.* Ease of repair, and the speed, courtesy, and timeliness of personnel.
6. *Aesthetics.* How the product looks, feels, and sounds.
7. *Conformance to specifications.* Degree to which the product meets production benchmarks.
8. *Perceived quality.* A catchall category that includes the effects of brand image and other intangible factors that influence customers' perceptions of quality.

Source: David A. Garvin, *Managing Quality: The Strategic and Competitive Edge* (New York: The Free Press, 1988)

TABLE 10.2

2. *Employee interactions.* The courtesy, friendliness, and empathy shown by people delivering the service or good. The overall credibility of the employees, including consumer trust in the employees and their perceptions of employee expertise.

3. *Reliability.* The consistency of the performance of the good, service, or store.

4. *Durability.* The product's life span and general sturdiness.

5. *Timeliness and convenience.* How quickly the product is received or repaired. How quickly information is provided or service is received. The convenience of the purchase and service process, including accepting credit cards, operating hours, and parking.

6. *Aesthetics.* The physical appearance of the good or store. The attractiveness of the presentation of the service. The pleasantness of the atmosphere in which the service or product is received. The extent to which the design of the product is appealing.

7. *Brand equity.* The additional positive or negative impact on perceived quality that knowing the brand or store name has on the evaluation.[16]

Research is necessary to establish whether these seven categories fully represent the dimensions on which consumers evaluate quality. In particular, the category of product aesthetics requires additional research. One exploratory study on product design did find that consumers evaluated design in a gestalt (i.e., holistic) manner and did so largely unconsciously. Two factors seemed to be related to aesthetic preferences: proportion (the ratio of length and height of an object) and unity (the extent to which design elements appear to go together).[17]

Table 10.3 provides examples of how each of the seven categories can be applied to a good (e.g., an automobile) or a service (e.g., an elegant restaurant).

A key question concerns how the dimensions of product quality are combined to form an overall impression of quality. We view the formation of overall product quality as a type of overall consumer belief. That is, we think that consumers form beliefs about each of the product's quality dimensions and then sum up these beliefs to create an overall belief regarding the quality of the product. In effect, people act as though their perception of the overall performance quality of a product is formed via a type of multiattribute model.

A Revised Set of Categories of Product Quality Applied to a Good and a Service

Product Quality Dimension	Automobile Quality
1. Performance	Level of horsepower, handling, fit and finish, resale value, the number of features, such as air bags, ABS breaking system, premium sound system, cup holders.
2. Employee interactions	Friendliness, helpfulness, empathy, and credibility of service personnel.
3. Reliability	Freedom from breakdown of vehicle, consistency of personnel in providing expected levels of service.
4. Durability	How long the car lasts before it wears out from use or before it becomes technologically out-of-date.
5. Timeliness/convenience	The ability of the company to provide the vehicle and its service in a timely way. The convenience of providing service.
6. Aesthetics	The attractiveness and functionality of the layout and style of the car.
7. Brand equity	The extent that the vehicle's brand name results in customers believing that it has high or low quality.

Product Quality Dimension	Restaurant Meal Quality
1. Performance	The degree to which the food is prepared according to standards of taste and temperature. The degree to which staff know their jobs. The number of extra features provided with the meal, such as fresh flowers on the table, special breads provided as appetizers, free desserts.
2. Employee interactions	The friendliness and helpfulness of the staff.
3. Reliability	The consistency with which the restaurant provides a high-quality dining experience.
4. Durability	The number of years that the restaurant successfully pleases its customers.
5. Timeliness	The ability of the staff to provide service in a timely way.
6. Aesthetics	The atmosphere of the restaurant, the degree to which the food is pleasing to the eye, the physical attractiveness of the staff.
7. Brand equity	The extent that the restaurant's brand name results in customers believing that it has high or low quality.

TABLE 10.3

The Development of Satisfaction and Dissatisfaction

A model critical for understanding and influencing CS/D is the expectancy disconfirmation model. The expectancy disconfirmation model defines CS/D as the "evaluation rendered that the experience was at least as good as it was supposed to be."[18] Three additional approaches have been used to explain the formation of CS/D: equity theory, attribution theory, and experientially based affective feelings. In addition, the actual performance of a product has been found to impact CS/D.[19] This section discusses each of these approaches.

The Expectancy Disconfirmation Model. The process through which CS/D is formed begins with the use of a product, as well as the use of other brands in the product class. Because of this usage behavior, as well as communications from companies and other people, consumers develop expectations of how the brand *should* perform.

These performance expectations are compared to **actual product performance** (i.e., the perception of the product's quality). If quality falls below consumers' expectations, **emotional dissatisfaction** results. If it is above their expectations, they feel **emotional satisfaction.**[20] If performance is perceived as equal to expectations, consumers experience **expectancy confirmation.**[21] In fact, when expectations and actual performance coincide, evidence indicates that consumers may simply not consciously consider their level of satisfaction with the product. Thus, although expectancy confirmation is a positive state, it often does not result in strong feelings of satisfaction. Strong satisfaction is apparently experienced only when actual performance is markedly superior to expected performance.

Product expectations are the standard against which the actual performance of the product is assessed.[22] The level of performance expected of a product is influenced by the nature of the product itself, by promotional factors, by the effects of other products, and by the characteristics of the consumer. Consumers' prior experiences with the product, its price, and its physical characteristics all influence how they expect it to perform. Thus, if the product has a high price or if it has performed extremely well in the past, consumers will expect it to meet high performance standards.

How the company promotes the product through its advertising and through the communications of sales personnel also influences performance expectations. A consultant with a market-research firm noted that advertising hype can create expectations that are impossible to satisfy.[23]

Consumers' expectations of performance are also influenced by their experience with other similar products. For example, a key factor influencing consumer perceptions of the quality of medical services is the timeliness with which medical care is delivered. Physicians and hospitals have been slow to recognize that consumers form their expectations of timeliness as much from their experiences with banks and restaurants as from their experience with other medical facilities.

Finally, performance expectations are influenced by the individual characteristics of the consumer. Some consumers simply expect more of products than others do. Likewise, some consumers have wider latitudes of acceptance than others. Consumers with very narrow regions of acceptance are, of course, more easily dissatisfied than those with broad regions of acceptance.

Equity Theory and Consumer Satisfaction. Another approach to understanding consumer satisfaction is through equity theory. Researchers have found that people analyze the exchange between themselves and other parties to determine the extent to which those exchanges are equitable or fair.[24] **Equity theory** holds that people will analyze the ratio of their **outcomes** and **inputs** to the ratio of the outcomes and inputs of their partner in an exchange, and if they perceive that their ratio is higher, they will experience feelings of inequity. The following equation shows these ratios:[25]

$$\frac{\text{Outcomes A}}{\text{Inputs A}} = \frac{\text{Outcomes B}}{\text{Inputs B}}$$

The outcomes that person A receives from an exchange divided by the inputs of person A to the exchange should equal the outcomes of person B from the exchange divided by the inputs of person B to the exchange.

According to equity theory, the norm is that each party to an exchange should be treated fairly or equitably. Satisfaction therefore occurs when the ratios of outcomes and inputs for each party to the exchange are approximately equal. When the buyer believes that his or her ratio of inputs to outcomes is worse than the seller's, the buyer experiences inequity, and this feeling of inequity leads to dissatisfaction.

Just what are the inputs and outcomes to a consumer exchange? From the consumer's perspective, inputs are the information, effort, money, or time exerted to make an exchange possible. Outcomes for the consumer are the benefits and liabilities received from the exchange. Outcomes could consist of the good or service received from the marketer, the performance of the product, and the feelings obtained from the exchange.

A number of authors have investigated how equity theory can be applied to consumer behavior. One study looked at the exchange process between consumers and an airline.[26] For consumers, the inputs to the exchange consisted primarily of the money they paid for the ticket, and the outcomes consisted of the quality of the service they received and the speed with which the airline got them to their destination. The study revealed that if consumers perceived their inputs to be large because they paid higher-than-average fares, they tended to be dissatisfied with the service. Also, if they perceived that outcomes were poor because flights had been delayed for two hours, they revealed more dissatisfaction as well.[27]

Another study found that people consider the outcomes of other consumers in determining their own satisfaction with a transaction.[28] Respondents in the study pretended to be automobile buyers. After the purchase they found that another person had obtained either a better or worse deal on the same car. When the other consumer had received a better deal on the same car, the respondents were less satisfied with their own transaction and with the auto dealer than when the other consumer got a worse deal. This study shows that factors other than the performance of the product may strongly influence feelings of satisfaction—specifically, the evaluation of the overall equity of the purchase transaction.

Note that the process equity theory proposes to explain CS/D is different from the process proposed by the expectancy disconfirmation model. In the expectancy disconfirmation model, CS/D results from the comparison of actual performance to expected performance. Equity theory, on the other hand, holds that satisfaction *also* results from comparing one's inputs and outcomes with others.[29] What is the relative impact of equity versus expectancy disconfirmation on consumer satisfaction? In a study of over 400 new-car buyers, researchers obtained measures of satisfaction with the salesperson, the degree of equity or fairness in the transaction, and the inputs and outcomes of the salesperson and of the buyer.[30] Buyers were self-centered—that is, they perceived that a deal was fair when the buyer's outcome was high and the seller's inputs were high. Furthermore, perceptions of fairness or equity had a greater impact on overall satisfaction than did perceptions of expectation disconfirmation.

The managerial implications of equity theory are as follows. First, marketers should ensure that customers recognize all of the inputs the company has added to the transaction. Second, as the authors of the new-car buyer study stated, "equitable exchange from the point of view of the buyer may be seen as inequitable exchange by the salesperson."[31] Third, consumers do form judgments of equity, and these judgments may have a greater impact on satisfaction than expectancy disconfirmation. This combination of findings makes the salesperson's job extremely difficult because it forces the salesperson to manage impressions so that buyers believe they are getting a great buy while the salesperson is giving up a great deal to make the sale. Unfortunately, the need to create such an impression encourages salespeople to use hype and false statements to make sales.

Relating Attribution Theory, Product Failure, and Consumer Satisfaction. The attributions that people make can strongly influence their postpurchase satisfaction with a product or service. If a product fails (i.e., performance is below expectations), consumers will attempt to determine the cause of the failure. If they attribute the cause for failure to the product or service itself, they are likely to feel dissatisfied, but if they attribute the cause for failure to chance factors or to their own actions, they are not as likely to be dissatisfied.[32]

One study investigating consumer satisfaction with airlines that were experiencing many delayed flights found that satisfaction depended on the types of attributions consumers made.[33] When they attributed delays to uncontrollable factors such as fog or ice, they did *not* tend to get angry. However, when they attributed delays to factors such as the actions of airline personnel over whom the airline had control, they were likely to feel angry and dissatisfied. In general, attributional processes are most likely to impact CS/D when consumer involvement in and experience with (i.e., knowledge of) the good or service is high.[34]

Actual Product Performance. Researchers have found strong evidence that actual product performance influences satisfaction independently of expectations, equity, and attributions. Even when consumers expect a product to perform poorly, they still feel dissatisfied when it does. A study investigating the effects of performance together with the impact of attribution, expectations, and equity on satisfaction with a stock market selection found that performance influenced satisfaction independently of expectations.[35] It has also been found that perceived product performance and quality directly influences CS/D, particularly when the product is unambiguous and easy to evaluate.[36]

Affect and CS/D. CS/D may also be analyzed from an experiential perspective. The term **affect and CS/D** refers to the concept that the level of consumer satisfaction is influenced by the positive and negative feelings that consumers associate with the product or service after purchase and during use. One researcher investigating the level of satisfaction with automobiles and cable television services after their purchase found that there were two dimensions of affective responses: a set of positive feelings and a set of negative feelings.[37] These feelings were independent of each other. That is, consumers could simultaneously feel both positive and negative about a purchase. One can of course experience joy, interest, and excitement while also feeling anger, disgust, and contempt. For example, after purchasing a car, a consumer may feel excited and proud about the car while simultaneously being irritated and unhappy with the salesperson.[38]

The study also found that measures of CS/D were directly influenced by consumers' affective feelings. Researchers discovered a relationship in which a purchase led to affective reactions, which in turn led to feelings of CS/D.[39] Thus, in addition to the cognitive knowledge that expectancies were confirmed or disconfirmed, the feelings that surrounded the postacquisition process also appeared to affect satisfaction with a product. A similar pattern of results has been found in CS/D with restaurants and with automobiles. Affective responses predicted responses independently of customers' cognitive thoughts (i.e., beliefs about the server's attentiveness, friendliness, etc.). Particularly in high-involvement situations, such as the purchase of an automobile, customer satisfaction tends to have a strong emotional component.[40]

As can be seen in Figure 10.2, which diagrams the factors that influence CS/D, after a purchase and the use or consumption of the product, a series of cognitive and emotional reactions take place in the consumer, including expectancy confirmation or disconfirmation evaluations, evaluations of the equity of the exchange, evaluations of actual product performance, and attributions of the cause of the outcomes.

Also note that Figure 10.2 depicts emotions and attributions as interacting together to influence consumer satisfaction or dissatisfaction. For example, if a product important to the consumer fails, the consumer is likely to have the immediate emotional response of anger. However, the anger is influenced by the attribution of cause made by the customer. If the person attributes the cause of the failure to factors beyond the control of the company, the dissatisfaction and anger felt is likely to be very mild. The extent of satisfaction or dissatisfaction, then, results from the manner in which the attribution of cause interacts with the emotional response to the product performance evaluations.[41]

Another recent finding is that, as the involvement level in the purchase situation increases, the level of satisfaction or dissatisfaction with a purchase tends to be magnified.[42] Therefore, if outcomes exceed expectations, consumers will have higher levels of satisfaction if they are highly involved in the purchase. Likewise, if outcomes fall below expectations, consumers will have higher levels of dissatisfaction if they are highly involved in the purchase.

Measuring Consumer Satisfaction

Traditional measures of satisfaction have assessed consumers' overall evaluation of the product, as well as their evaluations of specific attributes. Likert scales are frequently used: A statement is made and consumers are asked to indicate their level of agreement with it. For example, to assess overall satisfaction with an airline, a questionnaire might give the following item: "Overall, I was highly satisfied with the service provided by Delta Airlines." A five-point scale could be used: "Agree 1 2 3 4 5 Disagree."

A newer approach to satisfaction measurement is to use rating scales with which respondents evaluate the performance of a service or good on various dimensions. Thus, one question might be, "Rate the timeliness of how the airline service was provided," followed by a five-point scale: "Very Bad 1 2 3 4 5 Very Good." Other questions would probe opinions about other characteristics of the service, such as customer–employee interactions, the aesthetics of the airplane (e.g., was it clean?), and the reliability of the service. Frequently, regression equations are developed to evaluate the ability of the attribute questions to predict overall satisfaction. This general approach can be used to evaluate satisfaction with virtually any good or service.

Researchers who use Likert and other rating scales to assess satisfaction treat satisfaction as though it were a type of attitude, a view that is validated by studies of airline services.[43] That being so, it seems likely that customers will place different importance weights on the various attributes of a good or service. That is, some dimensions of the service will have a greater impact on overall satisfaction than others. For example, the study on airlines found that punctuality and the quality of the meals served were extremely important in consumers' eyes. If the flight was delayed, not only did the importance of punctuality in predicting satisfaction increase but ratings were lower on other dimensions of the flight than they were if there was no delay in the flight. This finding illustrates a halo effect, which states that extreme ratings on one dimension of performance will influence ratings on other dimensions of performance.

Recently, researchers have identified a problem with traditional approaches to measuring satisfaction.[44] In self-reports of customer satisfaction, most respondents said they were satisfied. For example, the authors reported that, across hundreds of different studies, on average, 65 percent of customers reported "high levels of satisfaction." These findings are important for managers. A report stating that "the majority of customers revealed high levels of satisfaction" is virtually meaningless because this result is almost always obtained regardless of the quality of the service.

One way to correct this problem is to ask about dissatisfaction rather than satisfaction. Asking respondents to agree or disagree with the statement, "I was highly dissatisfied with the product" counteracts the positivity bias and allows the manager to focus on areas of dissatisfaction.

Another recent line of thought has observed that satisfaction does not necessarily translate into loyalty. Indeed, Frederick Reicheld may have coined the term *satisfaction trap*. Using data from the consultants Bain & Company, he notes that between 65 and 85 percent of consumers who claim to be satisfied or very satisfied will defect.[45] The idea of consumer loyalty is discussed more fully later in this chapter.

CONSUMER COMPLAINT BEHAVIOR

When consumers are dissatisfied with a product or service, what do they do about it? **Consumer complaint behavior** is a term that covers all the different actions consumers take when they are dissatisfied with a purchase.[46] Researchers have identified five common complaint behaviors, which are listed in Table 10.4.[47]

The first three behaviors—dealing with the retailer, not patronizing the brand or store and asking friends to also shun it, and complaining through third parties—are straightforward responses to product or service problems in which consumers either withdraw their business or seek some type of refund. The refund could be in the form of money or through a replacement product. The last two behaviors are more far reaching. Instead of merely withdrawing their own business (and perhaps that of friends and family), consumers who launch public boycotts are out to change marketing practices or to promote social change. Perhaps the most drastic behavior is the last: creating an entirely new organization to provide the good or service. Examples of

Types of Complaint Actions

1. Do nothing or deal with the retailer.
   a. Forget about the incident and do nothing.
   b. Definitely complain to the store manager.
   c. Go back or call retailer immediately and ask manager to take care of the problem.
2. Avoid using the retailer again and persuade friends to do the same.
   a. Decide not to use the retailer again.
   b. Speak to friends and relatives about your bad experience.
   c. Convince friends and relatives not to use the retailer.
3. Take overt action with third parties.
   a. Complain to a consumer agency.
   b. Write a letter to a local newspaper.
   c. Take some legal action against the retailer.
4. Boycott the organization.
5. Create an alternative organization to provide the good or service.

TABLE 10.4

such organizations are Consumers Union, food-buying co-ops (e.g. IGA grocery stores), credit unions, and the American Association of Retired Persons.

Studies of consumer complaint behavior have shown that a minority of dissatisfied customers actually take overt action against the company. For example, one study found that in a sample of 2,400 households, about one in five purchases resulted in some degree of dissatisfaction, but the buyer took action in less than 50 percent of these instances. The type of action taken by consumers depended in part on the type of product or service. For low-cost, frequently purchased products, fewer than 15 percent of consumers took any action when they were dissatisfied. But for household durables and automobiles, over 50 percent of dissatisfied consumers took some sort of action. The product type that is most likely to produce action from dissatisfied customers is clothing. As many as 75 percent of those experiencing dissatisfaction with clothing took some form of complaint action.[48]

The models of consumer complaint behavior have identified two major purposes for complaining.[49] First, consumers complain in order to recover an economic loss. They may seek to exchange the problem product for another product or to get their money back, either directly from the company or store or indirectly through legal means. The second reason consumers engage in complaint behavior is to rebuild self-image. In many instances the consumer's self-image is tied to the purchase of a product, so that if the product performs poorly, the person's self-image is lowered. To restore self-image, the consumer may use negative word-of-mouth communications, stop buying the brand, complain to the company or Better Business Bureau, or take legal action. The self-image maintenance aspects of consumer complaint behavior have been insufficiently studied by researchers and companies alike.

Factors Influencing Complaint Behavior

A number of factors have been found to influence whether consumers complain. As noted previously, one of them is the type of product or service involved. Another is the cost and social importance of the product. Some authors have suggested that the likelihood of complaint behavior increases when the following occur:

1. The level of the dissatisfaction increases.
2. The attitude of the consumer toward complaining becomes more positive.
3. The amount of benefit to be gained from complaining increases.
4. The company is blamed for the problem.
5. The product is important to the consumer.
6. The resources available to the consumer for complaining increase.[50]

Previous experience with complaining is also associated with increased complaint behavior. People who have complained in the past know how to go about contacting appropriate authorities and therefore are less bothered by the task than neophytes are.[51]

Attributions made by consumers relate to complaint behavior. When consumers attribute product problems to the company rather than to themselves, complaint behavior increases. Furthermore, if the problem is viewed as under the control of the company, complaining increases.[52] For example, if consumers attribute a problem with airline service to decisions purposely made by the company, they are much more likely to complain than if they believe the problem is beyond the company's control.

Researchers have been only partially successful in relating demographic factors to consumer complaining behavior.[53] In actuality, experience with complaining is a far better predictor of complaint behavior than any demographic factor.[54] Still, a modest correlation has been found between age and income and complaining behavior.

Consumers who engage in complaining behavior tend to be younger and have higher incomes and more education.[55]

Investigations into the relationship between complaining and personality variables have found that people who are more dogmatic (close-minded) and self-confident are somewhat more likely to complain.[56] Consumers who value their individuality and a sense of independence also tend to complain more often than others. Perhaps these people make themselves feel important and different from others by complaining.[57]

Corporate Reactions to Consumer Complaining

Many consumer-oriented companies do make special efforts to track CS/D with their products and services. The use of consumer hotlines is often used for this purpose. Procter & Gamble, Whirlpool, and 3M, for example, all have used such toll-free numbers effectively. Many companies also advertise their e-mail addresses, which can be used to register complaints.

Public-policy makers take great interest in consumer complaint behavior. If they believe that consumer complaints are too frequent in an industry, they are likely to develop regulations to ameliorate the problem. Managers, of course, prefer to avoid the encroachment of government—the mere possibility of government intervention can be a strong impetus to establish industry standards. For instance, in Microsoft's battle with the government over its anticompetitive stance, the company's competitors attempted to have Microsoft punished without increasing government regulation of the industry.

Managers should have mechanisms in place to handle complaints when they occur. The presence of toll-free numbers is one highly effective means of handling complaints. In addition, companies should establish a means of redress for legitimate consumer complaints.

When not at fault, companies should try hard to break the connection between themselves and the negative event. Several approaches are possible in these situations. First, the company can deny its involvement ("we didn't do it"). Second, the company can deflect culpability by blaming someone else ("a maniac is poisoning Tylenol pills"). Third, the company can explain the event and identify extenuating circumstances. Note that, in this third case, the company does not deny all responsibility. Rather, it is encouraging consumers to make a stronger external attribution for the event instead of blaming it completely on the company.

One interesting research study analyzed company reactions to corporate complaints and in addition had consumers evaluate the types of excuses offered by the companies. Most companies attempted to avoid responsibility, an approach viewed negatively by consumers. Consumers gave the highest ratings to companies that sought to minimize the unpleasantness of an outcome for the consumer and gave a reason for the action.[58]

The authors of this study suggested that companies use excuses strategically so that they accurately describe the causes and outcomes of the negative events that precipitated the complaints. The excuses provided by companies are an important source of information for consumers when they are deciding what course of action to pursue to correct a perceived wrong. Of course, consumers are not always right, and companies are not always wrong, so sometimes a courteous explanation can clear up a misunderstanding.

Complaints and Exit Behavior

Exit behavior refers to the consumer choice to either leave a relationship or to lower consumption levels of the good or service. Researchers investigating complaint behavior in the cellular telephone industry have found that consumers who complain are

(1) more likely to leave a relationship and (2) more likely to likely to decrease their consumption levels of the good or service. In addition, they found that, as the level of dissatisfaction increased, the likelihood of complaining increased. The researchers recommended a "get-it-right-the-first-time" attitude on the part of companies because in many cases it is simply not possible to appease a complaining customer. This recommendation is particularly important where the costs of obtaining new customers are high. In the cellular telephone industry it costs $600 to obtain a new customer but only $20 to retain an existing one.[59]

PRODUCT DISPOSITION

Although disposing of acquisitions is a fundamental part of the consumer decision process, little research has been done in the area. Basically, a consumer has three alternative dispositional options after using a product for some period of time—keep it, get rid of it permanently, or get rid of it temporarily.[60] Each of these alternatives has suboptions. For example, if the decision is to keep the product, the consumer can continue to use the product, convert it to a new use (e.g., use an old toothbrush to apply shoe polish), or store it. Similarly, if the decision is to get rid of the product permanently, the consumer has a number of options: throw it away, give it away, trade it, or sell it.

A classic study investigated consumers' disposition decisions regarding six different products.[61] One clear pattern was that the higher the value of the product, the more likely consumers were to dispose of the product in ways that maximized returns. Thus, refrigerators and stereo amplifiers were frequently sold, while toothbrushes were usually thrown away.

Product disposition can be extremely profitable. For some types of products, there is a thriving aftermarket that seriously cuts into sales of new products. For example, sales of used textbooks can severely lower the sales of new textbooks. Although students benefit in the short term by having to pay less for their books, in the long run the cost of new textbooks is increased because fewer new books are sold, and that raises the per-unit costs of production. Another enterprise based on product disposition is the used-car market. Hundreds of thousands of people make their living buying and selling used cars. And with publications such as *Consumer Reports* rating used cars, new-car buyers are beginning to make the resale value of a car one of the attributes they consider in the initial purchase decision. There are also large aftermarkets in used guitars and other musical equipment, and sometimes vintage equipment is worth more than a newly produced equivalent.

Another product disposition issue is the handling of the garbage resulting from consumer purchases. Indeed, dealing with the environmental hazards posed by the mountains of waste we create each year in using products is a major public concern. Consumers have generally positive attitudes regarding programs to reduce waste, such as recycling, garbage reduction, and composting, but despite these positive attitudes, participation in programs to reduce waste varies widely.[62] Researchers investigating the factors spurring consumer intentions to reduce waste found that individual consumer attitudes predicted intentions to a greater extent than the opinions of other people. Moreover, the greater the individual's perception that a recycling action would have societal benefits, the stronger was that individual's intention to take the action.[63]

BRAND LOYALTY

Closely related to consumer satisfaction and consumer complaining behavior is the area of brand loyalty. **Brand loyalty** can be defined as the degree to which a customer holds a positive attitude toward a brand, has a commitment to it, and intends to continue purchasing it in the future. Brand loyalty is directly influenced by the satisfaction or dissatisfaction with the brand that has accumulated over time, as well as by perceptions of the product's quality.[64] Because it is from four to six times less costly to retain old customers than to develop new ones, managers should give top priority to creating strategies that build and maintain brand loyalty.[65]

Air France has a program to nurture brand loyalty among the "jet-setters" who ride the supersonic Concorde on a once-a-month basis. These frequent fliers are given interesting and unusual gifts, such as a videocassette of Jean Cocteau's *Beauty and the Beast,* rather than a coupon for $50 off their next $6,000 round trip. As one well-known marketing consultant said, the point is to "bond a customer to a marketer."[66]

The definition we have given of brand loyalty is based on two general approaches to understanding the concept: behavioral measures and attitudinal measures of brand loyalty.

Behavioral Approaches to Brand Loyalty

Behavioral approaches to brand loyalty measure consumers' actual purchase behavior regarding the product. The **proportion-of-purchases method** is the most frequently used measure of brand loyalty. In this approach all of the brands purchased within a particular product category are determined for each consumer, and the proportion of purchases going to each brand is identified. Brand loyalty is then measured in terms of some arbitrary proportion of purchases going to a particular brand. For example, if more than 50 percent of the purchases went to a particular brand during some time period, that consumer would be said to be loyal to the brand.

The behavioral approaches make it clear that brand loyalty is not an all-or-nothing phenomenon. Instead, loyalty should be viewed as a continuum from complete loyalty to complete brand indifference. There are several types of loyalty besides undivided loyalty. In some cases consumers have a divided loyalty between two brands. In other cases they are largely loyal to one brand but occasionally switch to other brands, perhaps to break the monotony and raise their levels of arousal. In still other instances customers are completely indifferent to distinctions between brands.[67] These different buying patterns, in which A, B, C, and D are different brands, may be portrayed as follows:

1. *Undivided loyalty.* A A A A A A A A
2. *Occasional switch.* A A B A A A C A A D A
3. *Switch loyalty.* A A A A B B B B
4. *Divided loyalty.* A A A B B A A B B B
5. *Brand indifference.* A B D C B A C D

From the marketer's perspective, the problem with these behavioral measures of brand loyalty is that they do not identify the reasons consumers purchase a brand. A particular brand could be purchased because of convenience, availability, or price. If any of these factors change, consumers might rapidly switch to another brand. In such instances consumers cannot be said to exhibit brand loyalty because implicit in the idea of loyalty is that the consumer has more than a passing infatuation with the brand.

Attitudinal Measures of Brand Loyalty

The problems encountered in the behavioral measures of brand loyalty illustrate why it is important to distinguish between brand loyalty and repeat purchase behavior. **Repeat purchase behavior** means that the consumer is merely buying a product repeatedly without any particular feeling for it. The concept of brand loyalty, in contrast, implies that a consumer has some real preference for the brand. In light of this distinction, another approach to assessing brand loyalty was developed, one based on the consumers' attitude toward the product, as well as their purchase behavior. According to this approach, consumers exhibit brand loyalty only when they actively prefer the product.[68]

With brand loyalty comes a commitment. **Brand commitment** has been defined as an emotional or psychological attachment to a brand within a product class.[69] Whereas brand loyalty has both a behavioral and an attitudinal component, brand commitment tends to focus more on the emotional or feeling component. In one study of the brand commitment of consumers to soft drinks, researchers found that commitment results from purchase involvement, which, in turn, results from ego involvement with the brand category.[70] According to the authors of the study, such ego involvement happens when a product is closely related to the consumer's important values, needs, and self-concept.

In sum, brand commitment occurs most frequently with high-involvement products that symbolize consumers' self-concepts, values, and needs. These products tend to be higher-priced consumer durables that possess greater perceived risk,[71] although they may be such everyday emotion-laden products as soft drinks. Some evidence indicates that brand preferences are formed during childhood and adolescence,[72] which would suggest that managers should begin targeting their customers early in their life.

Identifying Brand-Loyal Consumers

One intriguing question for market researchers is whether there is a type of consumer who is brand loyal across various types of products. Research evidence so far indicates that brand loyalty is a product-specific phenomenon. Consumers who are loyal in one product category may or may not be loyal in any other product category. Efforts to identify demographic, socioeconomic, or psychological characteristics related to brand-loyal behavior have generally been unsuccessful.[73] There is, however, one variable that does predict brand loyalty, and that is store loyalty. Consumers who are loyal to particular stores also tend to be loyal to certain brands.[74] The connection here may be that consumers who repeatedly shop at the same stores may be forced to buy certain brands because they are the only ones available in these stores.

It is important to remember that marketing strategies involving sales promotion devices may actually work to inhibit brand loyalty. If consumers purchase brands because of the sales promotion rather than because of the product's intrinsic positive qualities, they may get into the habit of buying only when there are sales promotions. One study found that sales promotion devices may cause even brand-loyal customers to switch brands. However, these researchers also found that the likelihood that the consumers would repurchase the new brand was low.[75] All of the evidence points to the conclusion that the quality of the product and the advertising of the brand are the key factors in creating long-term brand loyalty.

Comparing Satisfaction and Loyalty

In coming years there may be an increasing emphasis on loyalty as opposed to satisfaction. As noted earlier, defection rates among even satisfied customers can be quite high. Thus, although satisfaction and loyalty are linked, the relation is asymmetric. Satisfaction is an unreliable determinant of loyalty. Richard Oliver suggests that there are several obstacles to loyalty, such as consumer idiosyncrasies (variety seeking and loyalty to multiple brands) and switching incentives (competitors may lure consumers away with enticing messages and incentives). He suggests, in fact, that loyal customers are beyond satisfaction and even enduring preference—they are "determined defenders" in the face of enticing counteroffers from competitors.[76] From this perspective satisfaction is a temporary, relatively passive state, and the burning question is how to convert this temporary state into enduring loyalty.

MANAGERIAL IMPLICATIONS

The consumer-behavior concepts that emerge from investigations of postacquisition processes have application to each of the PERMS managerial applications areas. These are discussed in the following sections.

Positioning and Differentiation

The loyalty programs mentioned in this chapter (such as frequent flier programs) can be viewed as an attempt to position one service provider from another. Many brands provide a celebrity or humanlike character (e.g., the Pillsbury Doughboy), which not only helps differentiate the brand but also provides an opportunity for adoration- or devotion-based commitment. This type of approach to positioning is perhaps most easily seen in promotions to children, who form strong attachments to dolls, stuffed animals, and animal-like objects (e.g., Barney).

Environmental Analysis

Scanning of the environment for threats from public-policy makers resulting from consumer complaints makes good business sense. When Coca-Cola found itself providing potentially dangerous products in Europe in 1999, failure to take dramatic action as quickly as possible resulted in a public relations fiasco. (This is discussed further in chapter 16.) A potentially even more damaging result might have occurred, however, had public-policy makers stepped in to increase regulation of the industry.

The kind of information that can be gained by employing a toll-free hotline or Web site can not only provide ideas for new products, as well as improvements to existing products, but also provide forewarning of significant problems emerging which may result in either a drop in sales, or actions from policy makers.

Research

One of the clearest applications emerging from this chapter is that companies need to understand how they should deal with consumer complaints. Market research provides them with tools for doing so.

As an exercise, perhaps evaluate your own behavior vis-à-vis satisfaction. Consider an occasion on which you have been most angry with a company as a result of a purchase of a good or service. What did they do to cause your emotions? What was the role of your own attributions in increasing or decreasing your anger? What specific actions could the company have taken that would have helped to resolve your complaint?

Another area in which research would be helpful follows from the discussion of equity theory. Feelings of inequity may occur when consumers perceive that the ratio of their outcomes to inputs is inferior to the retailer's, salesperson's, or manufacturer's outcomes to inputs.

Marketing Mix

Oliver's discussion of loyalty and satisfaction suggests that competitors can (and do) provide persuasive messages and incentives to lure loyal—or potentially loyal—customers away. The elements of the marketing mix need to be employed in such a way as to blunt the impact of such enticing messages and offers from competitors.

Segmentation

Clearly, it would be good if one could identify more-loyal customers from those less loyal and make offers based on the differences between the groups. As this chapter points out, little can be determined in terms of a demographic profile of loyal customers. Nonetheless, research can identify them based on store loyalty or the proportion of purchases method for determining brand loyalty.

Notes

1. Leslie Helm, "Why Kodak Is Starting to Click Again," *Business Week,* February 23, 1987, pp. 134–38.
2. Philip Hendrix, "Product/Service Consumption: Key Dimensions and Implications for Marketing" (Working Paper, Emory University, Atlanta, GA, August 1984).
3. Hendrix also identified consumption interval as a fourth factor; Hendrix, "Product/Service Consumption." However, interval and frequency of usage are essentially identical. As a result, only frequency is identified here as one of the factors.
4. This anecdote was related to one of the authors by Jeanne Verkinnes, a General Mills employee, September 23, 1999.
5. Richard L. Celsi, Randall L. Rose, and Thomas W. Leigh, "An Exploration of High-Risk Leisure Consumption through Skydiving," *Journal of Consumer Research* 20 (June 1993): 8.
6. Eric J. Arnould and Linda L. Price, "River Magic: Extraordinary Experience and the Extended Service Encounter," *Journal of Consumer Research* 20 (June 1993): 24–45.
7. Erving Goffman, *The Presentation of Self in Everyday Life* (New York: Basic, 1959).
8. This definition of performance was developed for the textbook and specifically designed to incorporate the notion that an exchange process is taking place. It borrows ideas from the work of John Deighton, "The Consumption of Performance," *Journal of Consumer Research* 19 (December 1992): 362–72.
9. Deighton, "Consumption of Performance," 362.
10. Paul W. Miniard, Sunil Bhatla, and Deepak Sirdeshmukh, "Mood as a Determinant of Postconsumption Product Evaluations: Mood Effects and Their Dependency on the Affective Intensity of the Consumption Experience," *Journal of Consumer Psychology* 1, no. 2 (1992): 173–95.
11. Richard Oliver has distinguished satisfaction from attitude toward the object in his work. He argues that attitude toward the product or brand represents a more generalized evaluation of a class of purchase objects. The approach taken in this text is that attitudes occur at different levels of specificity. They can be highly abstract, such as one's attitude to his or her country, or highly specific, such as one's satisfaction with specific purchase. All are affective reactions that range on a hedonic continuum from unfavorable to favorable. For an article using Oliver's approach, see Robert A. Westbrook and Richard L. Oliver, "The Dimensionality of Consumption Emotion Patterns and Consumer Satisfaction," *Journal of Consumer Research* 18 (June 1991): 84–91.
12. Eugene W. Anderson, Claes Fornell, and Donald R. Lehmann, "Customer Satisfaction, Market Share, and Profitability: Findings from Sweden," *Journal of Marketing* 58 (July 1994): 53–66.
13. J. Joseph Cronin and Steven A. Taylor, "Measuring Service Quality: A Reexamination and Extension," *Journal of Marketing* 56 (July 1992): 55–68. Also see R. Kenneth Teas, "Expectations, Performance Evaluation, and Consumers' Perceptions of Quality," *Journal of Marketing* 57 (October 1993): 18–34.
14. This definition extends the definition of service quality to goods as well. See Valerie A. Zeithaml, "Consumer Perceptions of Price, Quality, and Value: A Means-End Model and Synthesis of Evidence," *Journal of Marketing* 52 (July 1988): 2–22.
15. More-recent work on SERVQUAL is summarized in Valerie A. Zeithaml, Leonard L. Berry, and A. Parasuraman, "The Behavioral Consequences of Service Quality," *Journal of Marketing* 60 (April 1996): 31–46.
16. Kevin Lane Keller, "Conceptualizing, Measuring, and Managing Customer-Based Brand Equity," *Journal of Marketing* 57 (January 1993): 1–22.
17. Robert W. Veryzer, "Aesthetic Response and the Influence of Design Principles on Product Preferences," in *Advances in Consumer Research,* ed. Leigh McAlister and Michael L. Rothschild (Provo, UT: Association for Consumer Research, 1992), 22:224–28.

18. H. Keith Hunt, "CS/D: Overview and Future Research Directions," in *Conceptualization and Measurement of Consumer Satisfaction and Dissatisfaction,* ed. H. Keith Hunt (Cambridge, MA: Marketing Science Institute, 1977), 455–88.

19. Richard Oliver and Wayne DeSarbo, "Response Determinants in Satisfaction Judgments," *Journal of Consumer Research* 15 (March 1988): 495–507.

20. R. B. Woodruff, E. R. Cadotte, and R. L. Jenkins, "Modeling Consumer Satisfaction Processes Using Experience-Based Norms," *Journal of Marketing Research* 20 (August 1983): 296–304.

21. R. L. Oliver, "A Cognitive Model of the Antecedents and Consequences of Satisfaction Decisions," *Journal of Marketing Research* 17 (November 1980): 460–69.

22. Woodruff, Cadotte, and Jenkins, "Modeling Consumer Satisfaction."

23. Patricia Sellers, "How to Handle Customers' Gripes," *Fortune,* October 24, 1988, pp. 87–100.

24. J. S. Adams, "Toward an Understanding of Inequity," *Journal of Abnormal and Social Psychology* 67 (1963): 422–36.

25. The equity ratio shown has been criticized and is given primarily for pedagogical purposes. See John C. Alessio, "Another Folly for Equity Theory," *Social Psychological Quarterly* 43 (September 1980): 336–40.

26. R. P. Fisk and C. E. Young, "Disconfirmation of Equity Expectation: Effects on Consumer Satisfaction with Services," in *Advances in Consumer Research,* ed. E. C. Hirschman and M. B. Holbrook (Ann Arbor, MI: Association for Consumer Research, 1985), 12:340–45.

27. For other studies of equity in consumer behavior, see J. W. Huppertz, S. J. Arenson, and R. H. Evans, "An Application of Equity Theory to Buyer-Seller Exchange Situations," *Journal of Marketing Research* 15 (May 1978): 250–60.

28. John C. Mowen and Stephen L. Grove, "Search Behavior, Price Paid, and the Comparison Other: An Equity Theory Analysis of Post-Purchase Satisfaction," in *International Fare in Consumer Satisfaction and Complaint Behavior,* ed. Ralph Day and H. Keith Hunt (Bloomington: Indiana University School of Business, 1983), 57–63.

29. J. E. Swan and Alice Mercer, "Consumer Satisfaction as a Function of Equity and Disconfirmation," in *Conceptual and Empirical Contributions to Consumer Satisfaction and Complaining Behavior,* Sixth Annual Conference, ed. H. Hunt and R. Day (Bloomington: Indiana University Press, 1982), 2–8.

30. Richard L. Oliver and John E. Swan, "Consumer Perceptions of Interpersonal Equity and Satisfaction in Transactions: A Field Survey Approach," *Journal of Marketing* 53 (April 1989): 21–35.

31. Ibid., 33.

32. Valerie Folkes, "Consumer Reactions to Product Failure: An Attributional Approach," *Journal of Consumer Research* 10 (March 1984): 398–409.

33. Valerie Folkes, Susan Koletsky, and John Graham, "A Field Study of Causal Inferences and Consumer Reaction: The View from the Airport," *Journal of Consumer Research* 13 (March 1987): 534–39.

34. T. N. Somasundaram, "Consumers' Reaction to Product Failure: Impact of Product Involvement and Knowledge," in *Advances in Consumer Research,* ed. Leigh McAlister and Michael L. Rothschild (Provo, UT: Association for Consumer Research, 1992), 20:215–18.

35. Oliver and DeSarbo, "Response Determinants." Also see David Tse and Peter Wilton, "Models of Consumer Satisfaction Formation: An Extension," *Journal of Marketing Research* 25 (May 1988): 204–12.

36. Youjae Yi, "The Determinants of Consumer Satisfaction: The Moderating Role of Ambiguity," in *Advances in Consumer Research,* ed. Leigh McAlister and Michael L. Rothschild (Provo, UT: Association for Consumer Research, 1992), 20:502–6.

37. Robert Westbrook, "Product/Consumption-Based Affective Responses and Postpurchase Processes," *Journal of Marketing Research* 24 (August 1987): 258–70.

38. The finding that positive and negative dimensions of affect exist was also found by Haim Mano and Richard L. Oliver, "Assessing the Dimensionality and Structure of the Consumption Experience: Evaluation, Feeling, and Satisfaction," *Journal of Consumer Research* 20 (December 1993): 451–66.

39. Laurette Dube-Rioux, "The Power of Affective Reports in Predicting Satisfaction Judgments," in *Advances in Consumer Research,* ed. Marvin E. Goldberg, Gerald Gorn, and Richard W. Pollay (Provo, UT: Association for Consumer Research, 1990), 17:571–76.

40. Westbrook and Oliver, "Dimensionality of Consumption Emotion Patterns."

41. This model is based in part on Lalita A. Manrai and Meryl P. Gardner, "The Influence of Affect on Attributions for Product Failure," in *Advances in Consumer Research,* ed. Rebecca Holman and Michael Solomon (Provo, UT: Association for Consumer Research, 1991), 18:249–54.

42. Barry J. Babin, Mitch Griffin, and Laurie Babin, "The Effect of Motivation to Process on Consumers' Satisfaction Reactions," in *Advances in Consumer Research,* ed. Chris Allen and Deborah Roedder John (Provo, Utah: Association for Consumer Research, 1994), 21:406–11.

43. Shirley Taylor and John D. Claxton, "Delays and the Dynamics of Service Evaluations," *Journal of the Academy of Marketing Science* 22 (summer 1994): 254–64.

44. Robert A. Peterson and William R. Wilson, "Measuring Customer Satisfaction: Fact and Artifact," *Journal of the Academy of Marketing Science* 20 (winter 1992): 61–72.

45. This line of thought is captured in Richard L. Oliver, "Whence Consumer Loyalty?" *Journal of Marketing* (Special Issue 1999): 33–44.

46. This definition is highly similar to one developed by Jagdip Singh, "Consumer Complaint Intentions and Behavior: Definitional and Taxonomical Issues," *Journal of Marketing* 52 (January 1988): 93–107.

47. The first three types of complaint actions were identified by William Bearden and Jesse Teel, "Selected Determinants of Consumer Satisfaction and Complaint Reports," *Journal of Marketing Research* 20 (February 1983): 21–28. The last two were identified by Robert O. Herrmann, "The Tactics of Consumer Resistance: Group Action and Marketplace Exit," in *Advances in Consumer Research,* ed. Leigh McAlister and Michael L. Rothschild (Provo, UT: Association for Consumer Research, 1992), 20:130–34.

48. A. Andreason and A. Best, "Consumers Complain: Does Business Respond?" *Harvard Business Review* 55 (July–August 1977): 93–101.

49. R. E. Krapfel, "A Consumer Complaint Strategy Model: Antecedents and Outcomes," in *Advances in Consumer Research,* ed. E. Hirschman and M. Holbrook (Ann Arbor, MI: Association for Consumer Research, 1985), 12:346–50.

50. Diane Halstead and Cornelia Droge, "Consumer Attitudes toward Complaining and the Prediction of Multiple Complaint Responses," in *Advances in Consumer Research,* Rebecca Holman and Michael Solomon (Provo, UT: Association for Consumer Research, 1991), 18:210–16; and E. L. Landon, "A Model of Consumer Complaint Behavior," in *Consumer Satisfaction, Dissatisfaction, and Complaining Behavior,* Symposium Proceedings, ed. Ralph Day (Bloomington: Indiana University, School of Business, 1977), 20–22.

51. See K. Gronhaug and G. Zaltman, "Complainers and Noncomplainers Revisited: Another Look at the Data," in *Advances in Consumer Research,* ed. K. Monroe (Ann Arbor, MI: Association for Consumer Research, 1981), 8:83–87.

52. Folkes, Koletsky, and Graham, "A Field Study."

53. Gronhaug and Zaltman, "Complainers and Noncomplainers."

54. Ibid.

55. Michelle Morganosky and Hilda Buckley, "Complaint Behavior: Analysis by Demographics, Lifestyle, and Consumer Values," in *Advances in Consumer Research,* ed. Melanie Wallendorf and Paul Anderson (Provo, UT: Association for Consumer Research, 1987), 14:223–26.

56. See J. Faricy and M. Maxio, "Personality and Consumer Dissatisfaction: A Multi-Dimensional Approach," in *Marketing in Turbulent Times,* ed. E. M. Mazze (Chicago, IL: American Marketing Association, 1975), 202–8; and W. O. Bearden and J. E. Teel, "An Investigation of Personal Influences on Consumer Complaining," *Journal of Retailing* 57 (fall 1981): 3–20.

57. Morganosky and Buckley, "Complaint Behavior."

58. Donna J. Hill and Robert Baer, "Customers Complain—Businesses Make Excuses: The Effects of Linkage and Valence," in *Advances in Consumer Research,* ed. Chris T. Allen and Deborah Roedder John (Provo, UT: Association for Consumer Research, 1994), 21:399–405.

59. Ruth N. Bolton and Tim M. Bronkhorst, "The Relationship between Customer Complaints to the Firm and Subsequent Exit Behavior," in *Advances in Consumer Research,* ed. Frank Kardes and Mita Sujan (Provo, UT: Association for Consumer Research, 1995), 22:94–100.

60. J. Jacoby, C. K. Berning, and T. F. Dietvorst, "What About Disposition?" *Journal of Marketing* 41 (April 1977): 23.

61. Ibid.

62. J. A. McCarty and L. J. Shrum, "Recycling of Solid Wastes: Personal Values, Value Orientations, and Attitudes about Recycling as Antecedents of Recycling Behavior," *Journal of Business Research* 30 (May 1994): 53–62.

63. Shirley Taylor and Peter Todd, "Understanding Household Garbage Reduction Behaviors: A Test of an Integrated Model," *Journal of Public Policy and Marketing* 14 (fall 1995): 192–204.

64. William Boulding, Ajay Kalra, Richard Staelin, and Valarie A. Zeithaml, "A Dynamic Process Model of Service Quality: From Expectations to Behavioral Intentions," *Journal of Marketing Research* 30 (February 1993): 7–27.

65. Melanie Wells, "Brand Ads Should Target Existing Customers," *Advertising Age,* April 26, 1993, p. 47.

66. Cyndee Miller, "Rewards for the Best Customers," *27,* July 5, 1993, pp. 1, 6.

67. A similar point was made by J. Paul Peter and Jerry C. Olson, *Consumer Behavior and Marketing Strategy* (Homewood, IL: Richard D. Irwin, 1990), 435.

68. Jacob Jacoby and Robert Chestnut, *Brand Loyalty, Measurement, and Management* (New York: Wiley, 1978).

69. Sharon E. Beatty, Lynn R. Kahle, and Pamela Homer, "The Involvement–Commitment Model: Theory and Implications," *Journal of Business Research* 16, no. 2:149–67.

70. Ibid.

71. Charles L. Martin and Phillips W. Goodell, "Historical, Descriptive, and Strategic Perspectives on the Construct of Product Commitment," *European Journal of Marketing* 25, no. 1 (1991): 53–60.

72. Lester Guest, "Brand Loyalty Revisited: A Twenty Year Report," *Journal of Applied Psychology* 48 (April 1964): 93–97.

73. See, for instance, Ronald Frank, William Massy, and Thomas Lodahl, "Purchasing Behavior and Personal Attributes," *Journal of Advertising Research* 9 (December 1969): 15–24.

74. James Carmen, "Correlates of Brand Loyalty: Some Positive Results," *Journal of Marketing Research* 7 (February 1970): 67–76.

75. Michael Rothschild, "A Behavioral View of Promotions Effects on Brand Loyalty," in *Advances in Consumer Research,* ed. Melanie Wallendorf and Paul Anderson (Provo, UT: Association for Consumer Research, 1987), 119–20.

76. Oliver, "Whence Consumer Loyalty?"

CHAPTER 11

Situational Influences

After reading this chapter, you should be able to describe each of the following concepts, together with their managerial implications:

1. Consumer situations.

2. The five types of situational influences.

3. Five other means, besides music, through which physical surroundings can influence buying.

4. The effects of a store's location on consumer store choice.

5. Store atmosphere.

6. Task definition.

7. Five categories of gift-giving situations.

8. Three ways in which time may influence consumption activities.

9. The varying views of time held in different cultures.

10. Antecedent states and how both types might influence consumption.

This chapter discusses the impact of situational influences on consumer behavior. The **consumer environment** is composed of those factors existing independent of individual consumers and companies that influence the exchange process. Figure 11.1 diagrams the consumer environment and its effect on the exchange process.

The components of the consumer environment shown in the figure are found within the set of dotted lines. At the most macro level of analysis are the economic and cultural and cross-cultural environments. They influence both the subcultural and the regulatory environments, each of which influence group and family processes. In turn,

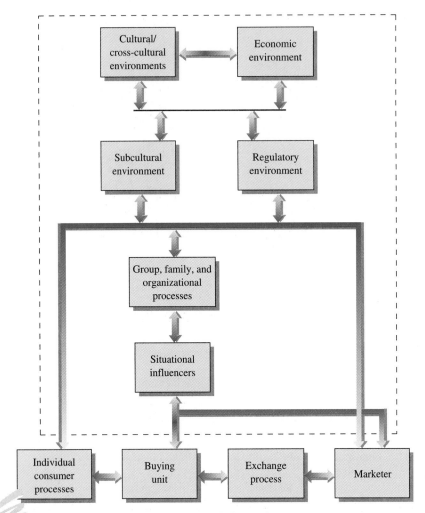

Figure 11.1   The consumer environment and the exchange process.

group and family processes affect the situational influences, as well as individual consumer processes and the marketer.

At the most micro level of analysis within the consumer environment are situational influences—the topic of this chapter. Situational influences affect the buying unit, the marketer, and the exchange process itself. Indeed, a marketing exchange can be conceptualized as resulting from the interaction of the buying unit, the marketer, and the situation at a particular time and place. This important interaction is called the **marketing triad.** All of the other factors identified in the text, from individual consumer processes to environmental influences, come together to influence the situation, the buying unit, and the marketer.

Part III of this book is generally organized from the micro to the macro level of the consumer environment. Part III begins with an analysis of situational influences—the environmental factors that operate at the most micro level.

INTRODUCTION TO SITUATIONAL INFLUENCES

Consumer situations consist of the temporary environmental factors that form the context within which a consumer activity occurs. Thus, a consumer situation is composed of those factors that (1) involve the time and place in which a consumer activity takes place, (2) explain why the action takes place, and (3) influence consumer behavior. Consumer situations are relatively short-term events and should be distinguished from more long-term environmental factors, such as the effects of culture, as well as personal factors that have a more long-lasting quality, such as an individual's personality. Examples of situations include the physical surroundings, social surroundings, time, the task definition, and antecedent states—all of which are described in Table 11.1.

Physical surroundings can have a major impact on the experiences obtained by consumers. In a gas station, for example, designers attempt to create an atmosphere making the experience as pleasant as possible, such as providing good lighting to enhance safety. If the physical surroundings are unpleasant, there is always another station down the road. Similarly, social surroundings are important. When filling up with gas, we step out of our cars and are relatively vulnerable. In this case we are concerned about avoiding unwanted social encounters.

Another situational element is time. For example, purchasing gasoline is not typically a preferred pastime. The extent to which the time needed to complete this transaction can be shortened may influence the willingness of customers to use a certain gas station.

A fourth situational element is **task definition,** which is defined as the reason or occasion for engaging in a consumer action. A gas gauge nearing "empty" defines a situation that sets the occasion for the set of activities required to find a gas station. A strategy of gasoline retailers is to increase the number of situational reasons for consumers to patronize them. Thus, many have added fast-food restaurants in order to satisfy the situational need of hunger.

The study of situations has important implications for managers. Products may be defined by the situations in which they are used. For example, wristwatches are positioned and consumers segmented in part based on usage situations. One can find formal watches, sports watches, everyday watches, and specialty watches (e.g., a diving watch). Thus, groups of people (i.e., segments) may be identified with an unfulfilled situational need, such as a desire to have a watch with a timing function for jogging. A product is then developed to fit the needs of that situation, in this case a durable timepiece with a

Five Types of Consumer Situations

1. *Physical surroundings.* The concrete physical and spatial aspects of the environment encompassing a consumer activity.
2. *Social surroundings.* The effects of other people on a consumer in a consumer activity.
3. *Time.* The effects of the presence or absence of time on consumer activities.
4. *Task definition.* The reasons that occasion the need for consumers to buy or consume a product or service.
5. *Antecedent states.* The temporary physiological states and moods that a consumer brings to a consumption activity.

Source: Russell Belk, "Situational Variables and Consumer Behavior," *Journal of Consumer Research* 2 (December 1975), 157–63.

TABLE 11.1

stopwatch capacity. Similarly, the company may create promotional materials that clearly position the product in reference to its situational use and to its competitors.

In addition to product design, segmentation, and positioning, the study of situations has a variety of other managerial uses. People may obtain information on products in specific situations (e.g., via the car radio while commuting). Thus, the promotional method may be influenced by situational variations in information reception. Similarly, certain products may be bought only in certain situations (e.g., as a gift). Such information has an impact on pricing, promoting, and distributing the product.

This chapter discusses each of the situational factors that may influence consumers. Special attention is paid to the effects of the physical environment on consumers. In addition, the effects of time and the task definition are given extensive treatment. Less attention is given to the impact of the social surroundings, which is discussed in chapter 12. Similarly, antecedent states are discussed only briefly because of their close relationship to mood, which has been addressed in a number of earlier chapters. After analyzing the various types of situations, this chapter presents the important topic of "situation" by "buying unit" by "market offering" interactions.

THE PHYSICAL SURROUNDINGS: A FOCUS ON THE STORE ENVIRONMENT

Physical surroundings are the concrete physical and spatial aspects of the environment encompassing a consumer activity. Such stimuli as color, noise, lighting, weather, and the spatial arrangement of people or objects can influence consumer behavior.

Physical surroundings influence consumer perceptions through the sensory mechanisms of vision, hearing, smell, and even touch. Surroundings have particular importance to retailers; perhaps their most important task is to manage the physical environment in order to influence behaviors, attitudes, and beliefs of consumers in a desired manner. For example, physical surroundings have important implications for building a store image. If a retailer wants to present an upscale image, it is crucial that the surroundings match this image.

The perception of safety is another factor controlled in part by the physical surroundings. Ample nearby parking, adequate outdoor lighting, and open spaces enhance the feeling of security for shoppers. The presence of such physical attributes could increase nighttime shopping, particularly among the elderly, who are highly conscious of their vulnerability to crime.

Researchers have investigated the impact of the physical environment on consumer perceptions and behavior in several retailing areas. These studies, discussed in the following sections, have analyzed how music, crowding, store layout, store location, and store atmosphere affect buyers.

The Effects of Music on Shoppers

One component of the physical environment in retail stores that has been shown to influence consumers is background music. Two studies examined the effect of music on consumers. In the first study, supermarket shoppers experienced either no music, slow-tempo music, or fast-tempo music over a nine-week period. The shoppers walked faster or slower depending on the tempo of the music and bought 38 percent more on a daily basis when slower music was played. No differences between the groups were found when customers were asked about their awareness of the music, suggesting that it operated below their consciousness.[1]

The second study obtained similar results. Fast- or slow-paced background music was randomly played on Friday and Saturday nights over eight consecutive weekends in a medium-sized restaurant in the Dallas/Fort Worth, Texas, area.[2] The pace of the music influenced consumers to spend more time in the restaurant. In slow-tempo conditions patrons took on average 56 minutes to complete their dinner. In contrast, it took 45 minutes to complete dinner in the fast-tempo conditions. The increased time in the restaurant had no statistically significant impact on food sales; however, liquor sales went up significantly. Overall, the average gross margin per group was $55.82 in the slow-tempo and $48.62 in the fast-tempo conditions.

The supermarket and restaurant studies demonstrate that the physical environment can influence buyer behavior. However, one should not immediately generalize and say that all retail businesses should play slow-paced music. There may be consumption situations in which fast music would be more appropriate. For example, restaurants that have low margins and depend on high volume must have a high occupant turnover rate. In this case playing fast-paced music may speed up customer use, thereby making seats available for other customers more quickly.

The presence of music in the consumer environment is pervasive. For example, when a customer is placed on hold on the phone, companies will frequently play music to fill the silence and help make the wait seem less negative. Surprisingly, however, research found that music rated as more pleasant does *not* make time seem to pass more quickly. Thus, "time does not necessarily fly" when people are having fun.[3] These results suggest that playing appealing, peppy music while people wait on "musical hold" or in waiting lines may prove counterproductive. A further study suggests that louder music increases the perception that "the pace of events" increases, but it also increases time duration estimates. So keep the volume down.[4]

Research also indicates that music is more effective if it matches the general situational context of the purchase. Just as the source should match the message (as discussed in the chapter on communications processes), the type of music should match the purchase context. For example, when classical music, as opposed to top-40 music, was played in a wine store, shoppers selected more expensive wines. As a result, they spent more money.[5] Clearly, the type of music should fit the situation.

The Effects of Crowding on Consumers

Crowding occurs when a person perceives that his or her movements are restricted because of limited space. The experience can result from an overabundance of people, from a limited physical area, or from a combination of the two. The concept has particular relevance to retailers who must decide how to arrange floor space. When consumers experience crowding, a number of different outcomes may occur.[6] They may react by reducing their shopping time, by altering their use of in-store information, or by decreasing their communication with store employees. Potentially, crowding may increase shopper anxiety, lower shopping satisfaction, and negatively affect store image.

Researchers have distinguished between the terms *density* and *crowding* (see Figure 11.2). **Density** refers to how closely packed people are. **Crowding** refers to the unpleasant feelings that may result when a person perceives that densities are too high and that perceived control of the situation has been reduced below acceptable levels.

Although one might assume that high density levels are always viewed negatively, they may actually sometimes be perceived as beneficial. When consumers are seeking an experience such as being in a bar or attending a sporting event, high levels of density may enhance the overall impact of the event. In any context there is probably some optimum level of density. For example, dining out is uncomfortable if the restaurant is nearly empty. Conversely, if the restaurant is so full that service is poor, the experience is equally negative. The optimum level of density is somewhere between the two extremes.

In a similar vein, people don't necessarily change their behavior just to limit crowding. Researchers in England found that only 6 percent of a large sample of

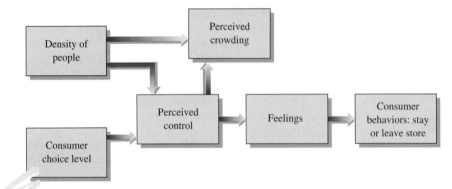

Figure 11.2   The effects of density and crowding on consumer behavior in a retail setting.

Source: Figure based on Michael K. Hui and John E. G. Bateson, "Perceived Control and the Effects of Crowding and Consumer Choice on the Service Experience," *Journal of Consumer Research* 18 (September 1991): 174–84.

supermarket shoppers shifted from busy to quiet periods to avoid congestion. Other elements, such as time of shopping in relation to work and weekends, are probably more important.[7]

Consumer Crowd Behavior. In some circumstances consumers show the same kinds of behavior as found in the actions of hysterical crowds. Consumers in such instances do things as part of a crowd that they would never do alone. In European and South American countries, for example, spectators at important soccer events have been known to turn into mobs. In October 1996 82 people were killed trying to squeeze into a World Cup soccer match in Guatemala City, Guatemala. Too many tickets had been sold, and fans who weren't allowed in tried to squeeze through a small causeway, where people inside were suffocated or trampled. Earlier in 1996 French farmers tried to give away fruit in Paris to protest low food prices but had to stop because unruly crowds overwhelmed them.

The factors that cause normal consumers to evolve into crowds are still not understood completely. In 1896 Gustav Le Bon suggested that people go into hypnotic trances when they are part of a mob, forming a collective mind. A more likely explanation is that very large groups cause a high degree of physiological arousal. The high arousal results in the tendency of each member of the crowd to act on his or her dominant idea. Because a similar idea brought the group together, the individuals within the crowd are likely to share a common tendency to action. In many instances the dominant tendency involves aggressiveness. Because each person in a crowd becomes inconspicuous, individual responsibility is lost. Thus, the usual norms that control behavior do not apply. The result is an unruly, highly aroused group of people who are not acting as individuals and are not subject to the standard norms that control behavior. The results can be riots, runs on banks, or panic buying of a product in short supply.

The Effects of Store Location

Real estate agents have a rule that states that the three primary factors influencing the value of a piece of property are *location, location,* and *location.* Those who study retailing echo this point, and location's contribution to store choice has been extensively researched.

Both actual distance and perceived distance may influence store selection. Research has shown that consumers have "cognitive maps" of the geography of a city.

Interestingly, consumer "maps" of the locations of retail stores may not match the actual relationships. Such factors as parking availability, merchandise quality, and the ease of driving to the shopping center can make the distance seem shorter or longer than it actually is.[8]

Also, it has been found that "image transference" exists: That is, the image of larger anchor stores in a shopping center affects the image of smaller stores in the center.[9] Small stores are better off located in a center with a department store as the anchor tenant rather than a discount store, unless the discount store is congruent with the smaller stores' image.

The Effects of Store Layout

Stores are designed to facilitate customer movement, assist in the presentation of merchandise, and help create a particular atmosphere. The overall goal is to maximize profits by increasing sales through a cost-effective store design. **Store layout** can influence consumer reactions and buying behavior. For example, the placement of aisles influences traffic flow. The location of items and departments relative to traffic flow can dramatically influence sales. One suggestion is that all convenience foods—salad bar, deli, bakery, frozen entrees, frozen pizza, rotisserie chicken, and prepared meals—should be brought together for the upscale, but harried, consumer.[10]

The design of seating arrangements can dramatically influence communication patterns. It has been argued that airport terminals are designed to discourage people from talking comfortably to each other. Chairs are bolted down and placed so that people cannot face each other and converse from a comfortable distance. The reason for the antisocial arrangement of furniture in airports is presumably to drive people into airport bars and food courts, where space is arranged more comfortably—and where customers spend money. This concept is being taken to great lengths, with casinos and department stores making an appearance in airports: one designer describes one such example, the Pittsburgh Airport, as "a mall with planes parked around it."[11]

The Effects of Atmospherics

A store's atmosphere delivers a message to consumers, for example, "This store has high-quality merchandise." **Atmospherics** is a more general term than store layout; it deals with how managers can manipulate the design of the building, the interior space, the layout of the aisles, the texture of the carpets and walls, and the scents, colors, shapes, and sounds experienced by customers. Even the arrangement of merchandise, types of displays, and poses of mannequins can influence consumers' perceptions of store atmosphere. These elements are pulled together well in the definition developed by Philip Kotler, which describes atmospherics as "the effort to design buying environments to produce specific emotional effects in the buyer that enhance his probability of purchase."[12]

Researchers have argued that store atmosphere influences the extent to which consumers spend beyond their planned levels in a store.[13] The store's atmosphere influences a shopper's emotional state, which then leads to increased or decreased shopping. Emotional state is made up of two dominant feelings—pleasure and arousal. The combination of these elements influences the consumer to spend either more or less time in the store.

Figure 11.3 presents a diagram of these relationships. When the atmosphere arouses the consumer and positive emotions already exist, the buyer tends to spend more time in the store and has an increased tendency to affiliate with people. This situation is likely to result in increased buying. In contrast, if the environment is not pleasurable, increased arousal could result in decreased buying. Research by psychologists has shown that dominant tendencies are more likely to be activated when

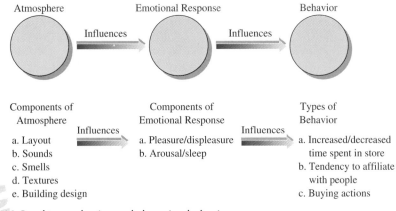

Figure 11.3 Atmospherics and shopping behavior.

Source: Adopted from a discussion in Robert Donovan and John Rossiter, "Store Atmosphere: An Environmental Psychology Approach," *Journal of Retailing* 58 (spring 1982): 34–57.

people become aroused. If the dominant tendency is to leave the store, increased arousal tends to increase the desire to leave.

The atmosphere of a retail store influences emotional responses. Indeed, the study of atmospherics is linked directly to the experiential perspective on consumer behavior. However, atmospherics can also be understood from the behavioral influence perspective on consumer behavior. In particular, the layout of buildings and the design of traffic corridors in cities, malls, and stores directly influence the movements of consumers in many cases without their behavior first being influenced by either beliefs or feelings. As Winston Churchill was quoted as saying, "First we shape our buildings and then they shape us."[14]

A variety of other studies have found that a building's atmosphere influences its inhabitants. Some researchers have suggested that increasing the number of windows and admitted sunlight can actually improve mood states. Wal-Mart opened a prototype store in Lawrence, Kansas, where half of the departments were illuminated by skylights, the other half by artificial light. It was found that sales were higher in the skylit area, and employees in the artificial-light areas of the store tried to have their departments moved to the skylit part of the store.[15]

One area that has recently attracted attention is olfactory cues and the store environment. A study found that shoppers return more often to scented stores and perceive goods sold there to be of better quality than in unscented stores. The intensity and nature of the actual scent seem to matter little, as long as it is inoffensive. However, the scent should be distinctive and congruent with product offerings, and managers need to pay attention to costs—diffusion methods can be expensive, as can the cost of the scents.[16]

The spatial arrangements found in a retail store have important consumer-behavior effects, which can be summarized in four statements:

1. Space modifies and shapes consumer behavior.

2. Retail store space affects consumers through the stimulation of the senses.

3. Retail stores, like other aesthetic surroundings, affect perceptions, attitudes, and images.

4. Stores can be programmed via space utilization to create desired customer reactions.[17]

Atmosphere becomes increasingly important as the number of competitors increases, as the differences in product and price decrease among the competitors, and as the market becomes segmented on lifestyle and social-class differences. A retail store's atmosphere can be used as a tool to differentiate one retailer from another and to attract specific groups of consumers who seek the feelings derived from the atmosphere.

In general, the nature of retail stores shapes the experience of acquiring a product or service. In a service setting, the physical and social surroundings may become a part of the service itself. For example, the nature of a concert or a play is shaped in large part by lighting, the characteristics of the set, the way sound is produced, and the characteristics of the other people who are sharing the experience. As a result, the investigation of the physical surroundings is a key element of market research.

SOCIAL SURROUNDINGS

The field of **social surroundings** deals with the effects of other people on a consumer in a consumption situation. For example, the presence of a group can result in conformity pressures on a consumer. If a college student belongs to a fraternity or sorority, pressures may exist to purchase particular brands of beverages, clothing, and even automobiles. Knowledge that a consumption situation involves the presence of other people can also dramatically influence a consumer's actions. The type of snack foods that someone buys may be affected by the knowledge that others will be present when the snacks are consumed. Light or salty snacks, for instance, tend to be bought in part as something to have around the house if friends should drop by.[18]

Similarly, other people can influence the impact of the communications situation on the consumer. For example, the presence of others in a room is likely to lessen the degree to which a television viewer pays attention to the advertisements that cross the screen. In a personal-selling situation, the presence of a friend could lower the impact of the sales presentation. Research on conformity found that subjects conformed to the views of a group even when they knew objectively that the group was wrong. However, if at least one other member of the group concurred with the subject in the experiments, the group conformity effect was lost.[19] Thus, in a sales encounter, it is likely that if a friend were brought along, he or she would lessen the impact of the sales presentation. That person might buttress the views of the buyer against the sales message of the seller.

Social motives sometimes explain why people go out and shop. Shopping can be an important social experience for consumers. One can meet new people and possibly make friends with them while shopping. In one study researchers recorded the social interactions of 100 randomly selected individuals who entered a large mall alone.[20] In 51 percent of the cases, the interactions between these subjects and others were informational, such as asking someone where to find an item. Twenty-three percent of the interactions were perfunctory, where the person acknowledged a person's presence. In 26 percent of the cases, however, social interactions occurred. In these instances a conversation took place between the person and someone else. The authors interpreted these results as indicative of the importance of social interaction in the shopping experience. They even suggest that the rebirth of central business districts and older malls lies in the rejuvenation of their social significance.

From a retailer's perspective, it is usually beneficial to encourage the social aspects of shopping. When a shopper is with others, he or she visits more stores and makes more unplanned purchases.[21] In fact, many products would not exist unless people gathered into social groupings. A small industry exists to supply party needs such as noisemakers, party napkins, specialized mixers, and so on. Even a basic beverage such as beer is consumed in contexts that are often social in nature. In an inventory of beer-drinking situations, half of the contexts dealt with social situations, such as entertaining close friends at home, attending a social event for which people bring their own beverages, going to a tavern after work, going to a restaurant or lounge on Friday or Saturday night, or taking a camping trip, beach trip, or extended picnic.[22]

THE TASK DEFINITION

The reasons people buy and consume a product or service are varied. These buying purposes form what is called the **task definition,** or the situational reasons for buying or consuming a product or service at a particular time and place. Examples of such buying purposes are plentiful. A purchase could be occasioned by some type of gift situation, such as Christmas, a birthday, graduation, or wedding. The reason for buying a beverage could be to satisfy thirst, to get a buzz, or to stay awake. In fact, the number of ways for consumers to define the task situation is probably infinite. It is up to the skilled marketing manager to identify those buying reasons that are not adequately met by existing products.

Closely related to the task definition is the usage situation. **Usage situations** form the context in which a product is used and influence the product characteristics sought by a consumer. For example, the usage situation of camping presents unique requirements for eating utensils, food packaging, bedding, and shelter. These requirements center around the need for light weight, portability, and durability. The task definition of "going camping," therefore, is a situational factor that may influence the design of products. Those who choose the situation of living outdoors for short periods of time can become a heavy-spending market segment, as Coleman has discovered.

Occasion-Based Marketing Opportunities

A problem for marketers is that a product can become locked into one usage situation, limiting its market potential. Consumers may come to use a product habitually in a particular situation and consider it inappropriate for other situations. Orange juice is a good example. By convention, orange juice has become associated with breakfast. Although nutritious and tasty, the beverage has not been adopted by consumers as a thirst-quenching beverage in a way that rivals soft drinks. The orange juice trade association has spent millions trying to redefine the task definition of the beverage. The campaign, based around the theme "Orange juice isn't just for breakfast anymore" has brought national attention to the thirst-quenching aspects of the beverage. A second attempt to redefine the task definition of orange juice concerns health. The trade association has teamed with the American Cancer Society, to explain the fruit's relationship to cancer prevention, and with the March of Dimes. The March of Dimes is concerned with birth defects, and one method of preventing birth defects is to increase the mother's folic acid intake, which can be done by drinking orange juice.

Examples of companies or trade associations attempting to change the usage situations of products are numerous. Turkey growers have attempted to persuade Americans to eat the big birds on occasions other than Thanksgiving and Christmas. The seasonal demand for turkey causes production problems for them. Another example is beef. Although beef held a three-to-one market-share advantage over poultry after World War II, by the 1990s the shares were about equal.[23] In an attempt to broaden the situational usage of the product, the beef trade association has sponsored commercials suggesting that beef makes a good breakfast meat.

The ability of companies to recognize new or overlooked usage situations can result in the discovery of profitable market segments. The forerunner of the Internet (the ARPANET) existed for many years as a tool for scientists and intellectuals, but using it was clumsy. In 1988 a Frenchman decided to write a "front end" to make it easier to get into, and maneuver around, the Internet. Thus, the prototype for the Web browser was born. Later, as the Internet rose in popularity, companies began writing more and more sophisticated browsers. Companies such as Netscape have vastly increased Internet usage and at the same time have made their shareholders wealthy.

Gift Giving

An important ritual in most societies is the giving and receiving of gifts. People build reciprocal relations by engaging in the ritual pattern of giving, receiving, and giving back. It has been suggested that gifts reflect status hierarchies, denote rights of passage, such as graduations, and influence the socialization of children through the formation of gender roles (e.g., little boys receive toy soldiers and little girls receive dolls). Gift giving has strong symbolic qualities. Similar to advertisers, gift givers manage meanings conveyed about who the giver is, who the receiver is, and the nature of their relationship. For example, the failure to remove a price tag from a gift violates the symbolic notion that gifts are nonmonetary expressions of affection.[24]

Gift giving has important economic consequences. In retail stores some 30 percent of sales occur during the Christmas season. More important, Christmas buying has been estimated to account for 50 percent of annual retail profits. So powerful is the effect of the Christmas season that consumers will even purchase gifts for those whom they consider to be "difficult." Difficult people include those who do not want or need gifts, are likely to be unappreciative of a gift, or are very different from the purchaser.[25] Retailers recognize how important gift giving is to their profits and take full advantage of the many gift occasions that have been prescribed by society.

The type of gift situation may influence a consumer's involvement in the purchase. For example, people usually engage in greater search efforts and buy more expensive, higher-quality presents for a rite of passage (a low-frequency, large-scale event such as the wedding of a close friend) than a rite of progression (high-frequency, small-scale events such as a birthday).[26] Researchers have found that people are more conservative (i.e., purchased "safe" traditional goods) when buying gifts for their spouses than for themselves.[27] One possible reason is that they perceived much greater risk in buying for their spouses than for themselves.

Why do people give gifts? Gift giving can be analyzed from the perspective of the matrix shown in Figure 11.4. On the vertical axis are two gift types—voluntary gifts and obligatory gifts.[28] Voluntary gifts are those made with a minimum of outside pressures forcing the action. In contrast, obligatory gifts are a result of strong social norms pressuring the person into action. On the horizontal axis is the degree to which self-interest influences the gift. In cases of low self-interest, the giver has few ulterior motives for the action. On occasions when high self-interest exists, ulterior motives play a predominant role in the gift giving.

Gift-giving motives are found in the four cells of the matrix found in Figure 11.4. When the gift is voluntary and low self-interest is present, an altruistic motive exists for the action. An example of an altruistic gift would be giving a friend a small present completely out of the blue to cheer him or her up. In contrast, when the gift is voluntary, but high self-interest exists, the motive is frequently one of creating an obligation. Giving a woman an expensive present in the hopes of creating an obligation that she may reciprocate is an example. On the other hand, low-involvement, ritual gifts occur when an obligation exists, but the giver has low self-interest in the exchange. Giving presents to acquaintances at Christmas, birthdays, and graduations fits this category. Finally, when an obligation exists, but the person has a high self-interest in the exchange, high-involvement reciprocity occurs. In such instances, there are strong pressures to give. The exchange relationship may be highly important to the person,

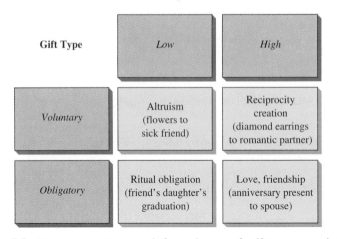

Figure 11.4   Gift-giving motivations result from degree of self-interest and gift type.

and love or friendship may be involved. (An example is purchasing an anniversary present for one's wife because forgetting the event would lead to dire consequences.)

The results of one study that investigated differences in the gift giving of 299 men and women at Christmas in a large Canadian city revealed that women were much more involved in the task than were men. Women started shopping earlier (October rather than November), spent more hours shopping per gift (2.4 versus 2.1 hours), and fewer of their gifts were exchanged (10 percent versus 16 percent). The only area in which men surpassed women was in the amount spent per gift: $91.25 versus $62.13 (Canadian dollars).[29]

Consumers not only give gifts to others; they also purchase gifts for themselves. Indeed, many of the same situational variables that influence purchasing gifts for others also motivate consumers to buy for themselves. **Self-gifts** are premeditated, indulgent, relevant to the self, and context bound. They may be given to reward an accomplishment (e.g., making a high grade on a consumer-behavior test), as therapy for a disappointment (e.g., failing to get a coveted job), or as part of a holiday or life transition (e.g., a birthday, graduation, or divorce).[30] Self-gifts may range from purchasing a donut to reward early-morning exercise to buying a new car to celebrate a promotion. Research has found that consumers higher in the personality trait of materialism tend to purchase self-gifts more frequently, particularly as a means to manage their moods. These individuals appear to associate buying with happiness.[31] A quote from one of the respondents in the study illustrates how a self-gift can be purchased in order to buy happiness:

> I bought a diamond ring for myself. It made me feel worthwhile, loved, secure. My husband doesn't believe in giving diamond rings, so I had to accept the fact that I had to buy one for myself if I wanted to get all those good feelings.

Readers should keep one finding in mind concerning gift giving. In a series of four studies, a researcher found strong evidence that those who give gifts should take great pains to wrap them nicely.[32] Wrapping a gift results in more positive attitudes toward owning the product. Nicely wrapped gifts appear to place the recipients in a better mood state, which causes them to enjoy the entire process more.

TIME AS AN ENVIRONMENTAL INFLUENCER

In his "Advice to a Young Tradesman," Ben Franklin wrote, "Remember that time is money." It was not until the mid-1970s, however, that time was recognized to be an important consumer-behavior variable. Since then, some authors have even suggested that time may be the most important variable in consumer behavior because it plays a role in so many areas.[33] As discussed earlier in the text, definitions of brand loyalty should specify the period of time over which the buying behavior is considered. Similarly, studies of the diffusion of innovations require the consideration of how rapidly in time a new product or service is adopted. Behavioral learning theory (see chapter 5) tells us that rewards must be given in close temporal proximity to a behavior to be effective. These examples represent only a few of the cases in which time is an important consumer-behavior variable.

Time can be analyzed from three different perspectives: (1) individual differences in the conception of time, (2) time as a product, and (3) time as a situational variable.

Individuals and Time

At the individual level, consumers use their time in four different ways—work, necessities, housework, and leisure.[34] These methods are arranged on a continuum of obligatory to discretionary uses of time. People have little control over when and how long they work. Somewhat more control exists concerning necessities, such as how long one sleeps and when one eats. The effort spent on housework is much more variable, with dual-earner families spending less time on "household production." Finally, people have the most discretion in how they use their leisure time.

Time can be viewed as a resource, and how people choose to spend their time says a great deal about them. The activities in which consumers engage can be categorized as to whether they are substitutable or complementary based on their relationship to time.[35] **Substitute activities** are separate activities that satisfy the same need for the consumer; furthermore, the two activities are mutually exclusive in the sense that they cannot occur together. For example, playing handball and racquetball are considered substitutes. **Complementary activities** are those that naturally take place together. Thus, a person may jointly engage in gardening and mowing the grass to fulfill the need of having a beautifully landscaped home. Complementary activities do not have to occur simultaneously, and may occur over a period of time, such as a week or a month. Consumer choices in the way they use their time says a great deal about their lifestyles.

Various constraining factors influence the substitutability and complementarity of activities. For example, the employment status of the wife and the presence or absence of children may strongly influence how time is spent by husbands and wives. (These issues are discussed in more detail in chapter 12). In fact, evidence exists that marital satisfaction is influenced by the extent to which couples share views on the complementarity and substitutability of activities. The evidence indicates that husbands and wives who jointly participate in activities have greater marital satisfaction.[36]

How individuals view time is even influenced by their culture.[37] North Americans and Western Europeans tend to run on *linear separable* time: the past, present, and future exist; time is divided up and allocated; and there is a future orientation. Time can be lost or wasted. It might be helpful to view businesspeople as running on linear time. For those on *circular traditional* time, time does not stretch into the future, and people tend to do today only what has to be done today. Those on linear separable time often find it frustrating to deal with those on circular time, because the latter may not see a relationship between time and money. Finally, those who keep *procedural traditional* time are governed by the task rather than the time. For them, meetings begin when the time is right, and as to how much time a meeting will take, well, it is "until it's over." The idea of wasting time is irrelevant, and completing the task is the key. This kind of time is reflected in Native American culture and is sometimes called "Indian time." Some evidence exists that Asians are also on procedural time.[38] Medical doctors also run on procedural time, creating conflicts with exasperated patients who are thinking in terms of linear time.

Time as a Product

Of course, time can also be a type of product. Many purchases are made to buy time. Appliances such as microwave ovens, garbage disposals, and trash compactors exist in part for the purpose of saving time. Fast-food restaurants have flourished because consumers have a need to obtain nourishment while on the go. A name has been given to the individual who engages in such behavior—the time-buying consumer.

Because time acts as a product attribute, advertisers use time-oriented appeals in their promotional materials. A study investigated the changing use of time-oriented appeals between 1890 and 1988 by analyzing ads in *The Ladies' Home Journal* over the period. The authors found that the proportion of ads that used time as the primary appeal increased dramatically. In 1890 less than 5 percent of the ads appealed predominantly to time. By the late 1980s, nearly 50 percent of the ads included a time-oriented appeal as a major component. An example can be found in an ad for Hunt's Manwich (from 1986) headlined, "When it's dinner time and time is tight."[39]

Time as a Situational Variable

In addition to recognizing time as a product, it is important to understand time as a **situational variable.** Generally, the situational characteristic of time that influences consumers is its availability. How much time a consumer has available to do a task, such as buying a product, will influence the strategy used to select and purchase it. Information search is particularly influenced by the availability of time. Researchers have found that, as time pressure increases, consumers spend less time searching for information. Similarly, the use of available information decreases, and negative or unfavorable information is given more weight in a decision when time pressures are severe.[40]

An experiment was conducted to directly assess the impact of time pressure on grocery shopping. Actual grocery shoppers were assigned either to a control group with no time pressure or to the experimental group, which was asked to complete their shopping in one-half the participants' expected shopping time. The time-pressured group more frequently failed to purchase intended products and made fewer unplanned purchases. Time pressure also caused a decrease in the total number of purchases. Finally, time pressures caused greater problems when the respondents were shopping in unfamiliar stores.[41] The managerial implication of the study is that to facilitate shopping by time-pressed consumers, retailers should create a shopping environment that makes it easy to locate desired products.

Time may also interact with other variables to influence purchase behavior. For example, the length of time elapsed since a shopper's last meal has been shown to influence how much they buy at a grocery store. As noted by the researchers, a person who shops while hungry may find that his or her "imagination readily places potatoes and onions around roasts and transforms pancake mix into a steaming, buttered snack."[42]

Interestingly, a situation–consumer interaction was found in the research on hunger and grocery shopping. The food buying of shoppers classified as overweight was not affected by how long they had gone since their last meal. The effect of buying more when hungry occurred mainly for people of average weight. The authors interpreted the results as indicating that overweight consumers fail to use internal cues to determine their hunger. Rather, they use the presence of food to determine how much to buy and consume.[43] Situation–consumer interactions is discussed in more detail later in this chapter.

Time of day is an important situational variable that can be used as means of segmenting products. For example, food products may be marketed for use in the morning (e.g., breakfast foods) or the evening. Michelob Lite beer created an entire advertising campaign whose theme was "The night belongs to Michelob Lite."

The situational element of time can influence distribution strategy as well. Consumers experiencing a shortage of time want to obtain products quickly and with minimal effort. The drive-through windows at fast-food restaurants exemplify a distribution system that allows customers to obtain burgers, fried chicken, and other foods rapidly. Mail-order, telephone-order, and computer-ordering systems (such as found on the Internet) for products have been developed so that consumers do not have to take the time to go to a retail store to make a purchase.

Finally, taking a long time is not necessarily negative. For example, luxury travel by rail is increasing in the United States. In this case time is substituted for luxury. In Europe the Orient Express between Paris and Istanbul has operated since 1919, despite faster airline service.[44]

ANTECEDENT STATES

Antecedent states are those temporary physiological and mood states that a consumer brings to a consumption situation. This situational factor relates closely to concepts of the individual consumer discussed in part II. Examples of antecedent states include such temporary conditions as hunger, thirst, lack of sleep, and mood. **Mood states** are temporary variations on how people feel, which range from happiness to very negative feelings. (The effect of mood on the information processing of consumers was discussed in some detail in chapter 4.)

An example of how temporary physiological states may influence buying behavior has already been given: Consumers who shop for groceries while hungry are in danger of making unnecessary impulse purchases. In the same vein, O'Doul's nonalcoholic brew pursued a strategy of capitalizing on the temporary state of thirst. In a commercial a man dripping with sweat was shown gulping down an O'Doul's while his equally thirsty dog panted unsuccessfully for a drink, then hit his master in the head with his water dish. The goal is to tie the beverage graphically to the physiological state it is designed to remedy.

These temporary physiological states may influence buying through two means. First, they may lead to problem recognition. For example, the gnawing hunger pangs in a person's stomach may cause the person to recognize a problem that needs to be solved.

The second way that physiological states may influence consumers is by changing the "feeling" component of the hierarchy of effects. (Hierarchy of effects models were discussed in chapter 7). For example, when a person is hungry, the presence of food is likely to create highly positive feelings concerning consumption. Thus, a hungry person who enjoys red meat will have very positive feelings when he or she sees a porterhouse steak. These positive feelings may then lead to an increased likelihood of purchasing the steak. Similarly, if a shopper is thirsty while in a store, the physiological state is likely to create positive feelings about thirst-quenching beverages.

The Effects of Temporary Mood States on Consumers

Mood states have also been found to influence consumer behavior. In one survey people were asked why they shopped. Two of the reasons given were that they wanted to alleviate either depression or loneliness.[45] In such instances consumers expressed the idea that they used the shopping and purchasing experience to influence their temporary mood state.

Psychologists have conducted studies that investigate the effects of mood on gifts to charities, to others, and to themselves. In these studies the researchers actually influenced the mood of subjects. After creating either positive or negative moods in the subjects, the researchers then took measures of how the changes in mood state affected behavior. In one study, a group of second- and third-grade children were asked to think of something that made them very happy. Another group was asked to think of something that made them feel very sad. A third group was asked not to think of anything in particular. After their mood was influenced, the children were given a chance to help themselves to candy from a treasure chest. The results revealed that in comparison to the control group, those with either a positive or a negative mood took more candy for themselves.

The mood study shows that people tend to reward themselves when they feel either good or bad. The mediator of the phenomenon appears to be the affective component of attitudes—the same concept suggested as the explanation for why hungry people buy more in a supermarket. As the authors of the mood study explained, "When one is feeling good, one tends to be more generous to oneself."[46] The phenomenon extends beyond self-generosity: People are also more generous to others when they are in a positive mood state.[47]

Why did the children in sad moods also indulge themselves more? The reason seems to be that they took more candy to make themselves feel better. Significantly, the impact of negative moods seems to extend to how much one person will help another. Research evidence suggests that people over the age of six will help others more when they are feeling bad, as well as when they are feeling good, than when they are in a neutral mood state. Again, the motivation seems to be that people derive good feelings from helping others. When a person feels bad, he or she may seek out ways to feel better and consequently help others more.

Recent evidence suggests that temporary mood states may influence consumer reactions to advertisements. In one experiment half of the subjects read an uplifting story that placed them in highly positive moods. All respondents then evaluated a print advertisement. The results revealed that those placed in a positive mood state had more favorable brand attitudes and fewer counterarguments to the ad. The author suggested that those in positive mood states engaged in less cognitive processing, which would cause fewer counterarguments to occur. In addition, a positive mood state tended to cause subjects to process information peripherally. Thus, those in good moods were less affected by central cues, such as argument quality, and more influenced by peripheral cues, such as source attractiveness.[48]

Research on the effects of mood on consumer behavior is still in its infancy. One cannot be sure that mood influences the buying of products in the same way that it affects the taking of candy or the distribution of coupons that can be used to obtain a prize.[49] But the evidence indicates that mood states may be particularly effective in influencing consumer buying behavior in retail settings—particularly at the point of purchase.

INTERACTIONS AMONG USAGE SITUATION, PERSON, AND PRODUCT

The buying act can be viewed as a two-way interaction in which consumer situations interact with personal factors (a situation–person interaction) or with the type of product or service being offered (a situation–product interaction). Alternatively, it can be a three-way interaction between person, product, and situation variables.[50]

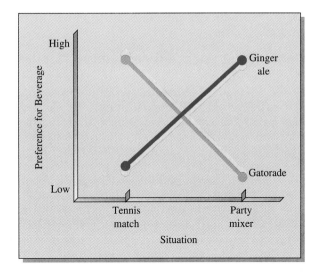

Figure 11.5
Situation–product interaction.

An **interaction** occurs when two or more factors combine to cause consumers to behave in a different manner than they would have behaved if the two factors were not combined. In a situation–product interaction, two products are viewed as useful in different situations. For example, Gatorade would be seen by most consumers as appropriate in situations where one has worked up a great thirst, such as after a competitive tennis match, whereas drinking Canada Dry ginger ale after a hard workout sounds perfectly awful. In contrast, Gatorade has little appeal as a mixer at a fashionable party, whereas Canada Dry ginger ale would be quite appropriate. Thus, the type of product and type of situation interact so that the type of product favored is determined by a situational context. Figure 11.5 diagrams these interactions.

Situation–product interactions form the basis for benefit segmentation. That is, different products are created to offer divergent benefits that may be used in different situations. For example, consider the various types of watches that are marketed. Diving watches were developed to allow someone to tell time while underwater. The benefit provided is the ability to know when one's air is about to run out. In contrast, formal watches were created as ornaments. Their benefit is that they look pretty.

An example of a situation–product interaction is illustrated by a study developed to probe how purchase agents react to lunches in fancy versus ordinary restaurants. In the study the fanciness of the restaurant represents the type of product, and the reason for the lunch represents the situational factor. (Specifically, the reason for the lunch is a task-definition factor). The researchers found that the buyers evaluated the suppliers' position more favorably in ordinary restaurant meetings than in fancy restaurant meetings. However, if the reason for the lunch had been a celebration for closing a contract, the fancy restaurant may have been more appropriate than the ordinary restaurant. The authors interpreted the results as indicating that sales representatives should be extremely careful in staging business lunches in fancy restaurants. They argued that the restaurant context should fit the business context.[51]

MANAGERIAL IMPLICATIONS

The consumer-behavior concepts that emerge from investigations of the consumer environment have application to four of the PERMS managerial applications areas.

(Because situational influences are a part of the environment, the "E" in PERMS is ignored.)

Positioning and Differentiation

The situational influences described—physical and social surroundings, time, task definition, and antecedent states—offer multiple opportunities for positioning products and differentiating them from others. A clear example is the use of time-saving features as a means of differentiating a product from competitive offerings. The Apple iMac was originally marketed without a floppy drive as standard equipment—it was clearly optimized as a computer for working in an Internet environment. Apple has also typically emphasized the use of their computers for tasks, such as publishing, where graphics are important, and for music recording and composing, where sound cards and digital-recording capabilities are critical.

In 1998 70 McDonald's restaurants in northern California experimented with the use of one line for serving, versus several lines.[52] The reason is that, although multiple lines actually move people faster, these multiple lines are more stressful. Jumping from line to line, or watching someone who arrived after us move toward the front faster, creates stress. McDonald's was investigating whether this point of differentiation—single versus multiple lines—would help to position McDonald's restaurants favorably versus those of competitors.

Research

Marketing research is required to determine which situational influences can be used to developed positioning strategies. Research may also indicate which consumer situations present opportunities for new products. For example, laptop computers arose as a means of allowing those "on the road" to do work comparable to that they could perform in their offices. Thus, laptops enable a person to perform the task definition of "working away from the office."

Marketing Mix

As an example of the degree to which situational influences may affect the marketing mix, one of the elements mentioned in this chapter—time as a product—may influence the marketing mix element of price. As consumers increasingly feel that they are rushed, the perception that it is acceptable to trade an increased product cost for the time-saving qualities that may exist in a more expensive product are likely to increase.

Situational influences may also be used as a guide to product development. The desire on the part of frequent fliers to take a substantial part of their belongings with them as carry-on baggage rather than checked luggage has created opportunities for the development of larger carry-on bags, which have become so big they've sprouted wheels.

Makers of dressier, professional clothing have had to adjust to the arrival of more casual wear during the week and even more to "casual Fridays." Thus, the product mix in upscale retail outlets such as Brooks Brothers is much more casual than was the case 10 years ago.

Segmentation

Markets can be divided into groups of consumers who are homogeneous in terms of a particular situational influence, and products can be developed that may present a solution to a problem or enhance that situation. For example, one result of increasing participation in work outside the home by females means that more males are needing to do their own gift purchasing. This creates potential opportunities to devise gift services that will appeal to these males.

Notes

1. Ronald E. Milliman, "Using Background Music to Affect the Behavior of Supermarket Shoppers," *Journal of Marketing* 46 (summer 1982): 86–91.
2. Ronald E. Milliman, "The Influence of Background Music on the Behavior of Restaurant Patrons," *Journal of Consumer Research* 13 (September 1986): 286–89.
3. James J. Kellaris and Robert J. Kent, "The Influence of Music on Consumers' Temporal Perceptions: Does Time Fly When You're Having Fun?" *Journal of Consumer Psychology* 1, no. 4 (1992): 365–76.
4. James J. Kellaris, Susan Powell Mantel, and Moses B. Altsech, "Decibels, Disposition, and Duration: The Impact of Musical Loudness and Internal States on Time Perceptions," in *Advances in Consumer Research*, ed. Kim P. Corfman and John J. Lynch Jr. (Provo, UT: Association for Consumer Research, 1996), 23:498–503.
5. Charles S. Areni and David Kim, "The Influence of Background Music on Shopping Behavior: Classical versus Top-Forty," in *Advances in Consumer Research*, ed. Leigh McAlister and Michael L. Rothschild (Provo, UT: Association for Consumer Research, 1993), 20:336–40.
6. G. Harrell, M. Hutt, and J. Anderson, "Path Analysis of Buyer Behavior under Conditions of Crowding," *Journal of Marketing Research* 17 (February 1980): 45–51.
7. Robert East, Wendy Lomax, Gill Willson, and Patricia Harris, "Decision Making and Habit in Shopping Times," *European Journal of Marketing* 28, no. 4 (1994): 56–71.
8. R. Mittelstaedt et al., "Psychophysical and Evaluative Dimensions of Cognized Distance in an Urban Shopping Environment," in *Combined Proceedings*, ed. R. C. Curhan (Chicago, IL: American Marketing Association, 1974), 190–93. Also see Priya Raghubir and Aradhna Krishna, "As the Crow Flies: Bias in Consumers' Map-Based Distance Judgments," *Journal of Consumer Research* 23 (June 1996): 26–39.
9. David J. Burns, "Image Transference and Retail Site Selection," *International Journal of Retail and Distribution Management* 20 (September–October 1992): 38–43.
10. Paul Kelly, "Reorganizing the Store," *Progressive Grocer*, March 1996, p. 21.
11. Paul Tarricone, "Real Estate: Airports Can Be a Launching Pad for Revenue," *Facilities Design and Management*, February 1996, p. 26.
12. Philip Kotler, "Atmospherics as a Marketing Tool," *Journal of Retailing* 49 (winter 1973–74): 48–64.
13. Robert Donovan and John Rossiter, "Store Atmosphere: An Environmental Psychology Approach," *Journal of Retailing* 58 (spring 1982): 34–57.
14. Cited by Mary Jo Bitner, "Consumer Responses to the Physical Environment in Service Settings," in *Creativity in Services Marketing: What's New, What Works, What's Developing*, ed. M. Venkatesan, Diane Schmalensee, and Claudia Marshall (Chicago, IL: American Marketing Association, 1986), 89–93.
15. John Pierson, "If the Sun Shines In, Workers Work Better, Buyers Buy More," *Wall Street Journal*, November 20, 1995, pp. B1, B7.
16. Eric R. Spangenberg, Ayn E. Crowley, and Pamela W. Henderson, "Improving the Store Environment: Do Olfactory Cues Affect Evaluations and Behaviors?" *Journal of Marketing* 60 (April 1996): 67–80: Also see Deborah J. Mitchell, Barbara E. Kahn, and Susan C. Knasko, "There's Something in the Air: Effects of Congruent or Incongruent Ambient Odor on Consumer Decision Making," *Journal of Consumer Research* 22 (September 1995): 229–38.
17. Ron Markin, Charles Lillis, and Chem Narayana, "Social-Psychological Significance of Store Space," *Journal of Retailing* 52 (spring 1976): 43–54.
18. Russell Belk, "An Exploratory Assessment of Situational Effects in Buyer Behavior," *Journal of Marketing Research* 11 (May 1974): 160.
19. Solomon E. Asch, *Social Psychology* (Upper Saddle River, NJ: Prentice-Hall, 1952).
20. Richard Feinberg, Brent Scheffler, and Jennifer Meoli, "Social Ecological Insights into Consumer Behavior in the Retail Mall," in *Proceedings of the Division of Consumer Psychology*, ed. Linda Alwitt (New York: American Psychological Association, 1987), 17–19.
21. Donald H. Granbois, "Improving the Study of Customer In-Store Behavior," *Journal of Marketing* 32 (October 1968): 28–33.
22. William Bearden and Arch Woodside, "Consumption Occasion Influence on Consumer Brand Choice," *Decision Sciences* 9 (April 1978): 275.
23. Eugene W. Anderson and Steven M. Shugan, "Repositioning for Changing Preferences: The Case of Beef versus Poultry," *Journal of Consumer Research* 18 (September 1991): 219–32.

24. Mary Finlay, "Motivations and Symbolism in Gift-Giving Behavior," in *Advances in Consumer Research,* ed. Marvin E. Goldberg, Gerald Gorn, and Richard W. Pollay (Provo, UT: Association for Consumer Research, 1990), 17:699–706.

25. Cele Otnes, Young Chan Kim, and Tina M. Lowrey, "Ho, Ho, Woe: Christmas Shopping for 'Difficult' People," in *Advances in Consumer Research,* ed. John Sherry Jr. and Brian Sternthal (Provo, UT: Association for Consumer Research, 1992), 19:482–88.

26. This distinction is noted in David Cheal, *The Gift Economy* (New York: Routledge, 1988), cited in Mary Finley Wolfinbarger and Mary C. Gilly, "An Experimental Investigation of Self-Symbolism in Gifts," in *Advances in Consumer Research,* ed. Kim P. Corfman and John G. Lynch Jr. (Provo, UT: Association for Consumer Research, 1996), 23:458–62.

27. E. W. Hart, "Consumer Risk Taking for Self and Spouse," Ph.D. dissertation, Purdue University, 1974.

28. The distinction between voluntary and obligatory gifts was pointed out by Cathy Goodwin, Kelly L. Smith, and Susan Spiggle, "Gift Giving: Consumer Motivation and the Gift Purchase Process," in *Advances in Consumer Research,* ed. Marvin E. Goldberg, Gerald Gorn, and Richard W. Pollay (Provo, UT: Association for Consumer Research, 1990), 17:690–98. For another perspective on why consumers give gifts, see Mary Finley Wolfinbarger and Laura J. Yale, "Three Motivations for Interpersonal Gift Giving: Experiential, Obligated, and Practical Motivations," in *Advances in Consumer Research,* ed. Leigh McAlister and Michael Rothschild (Provo, UT: Association for Consumer Research, 1993), 20:520–26.

29. Eileen Fischer and Stephen J. Arnold, "More Than a Labor of Love: Gender Roles and Christmas Gift Shopping," *Journal of Consumer Research* 17 (December 1990): 333–43.

30. David Glen Mick and Michele DeMoss, "Further Findings on Self-Gifts: Products, Qualities, and Socioeconomic Correlates," in *Advances in Consumer Research,* ed. John Sherry Jr. and Brian Sternthal (Provo, UT: Association for Consumer Research, 1992), 19:140–46.

31. Kim K. R. McKeage, Marsha L. Richins, and Kathleen Debevec, "Self-Gifts and the Manifestation of Material Values," in *Advances in Consumer Research,* ed. Leigh McAlister and Michael L. Rothschild (Provo, UT: Association for Consumer Research, 1993), 20:359–64.

32. Daniel J. Howard, "Gift-Wrapping Effects on Product Attitudes: A Mood-Biasing Explanation," *Journal of Consumer Psychology* 1, no. 3 (1992): 197–223.

33. F. M. Nicosia and R. Mayer, "Toward a Sociology of Consumption," *Journal of Consumer Research* 3 (September 1976): 65–76.

34. Laurence Feldman and Jacob Hornik, "The Use of Time: An Integrated Conceptual Model," *Journal of Consumer Research* 7 (March 1981): 407–19.

35. Morris Holbrook and Donald Lehmann, "Allocating Discretionary Time: Complementarity among Activities," *Journal of Consumer Research* 7 (March 1981): 395–406.

36. Ibid.

37. Robert Graham, "The Role of Perception of Time in Consumer Research," *Journal of Consumer Research* 7 (March 1981): 335–42.

38. Jay D. Lundquist, Sara Tacoma, and Paul M. Lane, "What Is Time? An Explanatory Extension toward the Far East," in *Developments in Marketing Science,* ed. Michael Levy and Dhruv Grewel (Coral Gables, FL: Academy of Marketing Science, 1993), 16:186–90.

39. Barbara L. Gross and Jagdish N. Sheth, "Time-Oriented Advertising: A Content Analysis of United States Magazine Advertising, 1890–1988," *Journal of Marketing* 53 (October 1989): 76–83.

40. Anthony D. Miyazaki, "How Many Shopping Days until Christmas? A Preliminary Investigation of Time Pressures, Deadlines, and Planning Levels on Holiday Gift Purchases," in *Advances in Consumer Research,* ed. Leigh McAlister and Michael L. Rothschild (Provo, UT: Association for Consumer Research, 1993), 20:331–35. Also see Peter Wright, "The Harassed Decision Maker: Time Pressures, Distractions, and the Use of Evidence," *Journal of Applied Psychology* 59 (October 1974): 555–61; and Frank Denton, "The Dynamism of Personal Lifestyle: How We Do More in Less Time," in *Advances in Consumer Research,* ed. Chris T. Allen and Deborah Roedder John (Provo, UT: Association for Consumer Research, 1994), 23:132–36.

41. C. Whan Park, Easwar S. Iyer, and Daniel C. Smith, "The Effects of Situational Factors on In-Store Grocery Shopping Behavior: The Role of Store Environment and Time Available for Shopping," *Journal of Consumer Research* 15 (March 1989): 422–33.

42. R. E. Nisbet and D. E. Kanouse, "Obesity, Food Deprivation, and Supermarket Shopping Behavior," *Journal of Personality and Social Psychology* 12 (August 1969): 289–94.

43. Ibid.
44. John Bigness, "Elegance Does an Encore on U.S. Rails," *Wall Street Journal,* January 26, 1996, p. B4.
45. E. M. Tauber, "Why Do People Shop?" *Journal of Marketing* 36 (October 1972): 47.
46. D. L. Rosenhan, B. Underwood, and B. Moore, "Affect Moderates Self-Gratification and Altruism," *Journal of Personality and Social Psychology* 30 (October 1974): 546–52.
47. B. Moore, B. Underwood, and D. L. Rosenhan, "Affect and Altruism," *Developmental Psychology* 8 (January 1973): 99–104.
48. Rajeev Batra, "The Role of Mood in Advertising Effectiveness," *Journal of Consumer Research* 17 (September 1990): 203–14.
49. D. Kenrick, D. Baumann, and R. Cialdini, "A Step in the Socialization of Altruism as Hedonism," *Journal of Personality and Social Psychology* 37 (May 1979): 747–55.
50. S. Ratneswar and Alan G. Sawyer, "The Use of Multiple Methods to Explore Three-Way Person, Brand, and Usage Context Interactions," in *Advances in Consumer Research,* ed. John Sherry Jr. and Brian Sternthal (Provo, UT: Association for Consumer Research, 1992), 19:116–22.
51. Paul Schurr and Bobby Calder, "Psychological Effects of Restaurant Meetings on Industrial Buyers," *Journal of Marketing* 50 (January 1986): 87–97.
52. Richard Gibson, "Merchants Mull the Long and the Short of Lines," *Wall Street Journal,* September 3, 1998, pp. B1, B4.

Group, Dyadic, and Diffusion Processes

After reading this chapter, you should be able to discuss each of the following concepts, together with their managerial implications:

1. The concept of the group and the various types of groups.
2. The concept of role.
3. Social comparison processes and their influence on consumers.
4. Group polarization.
5. Three major trends in household demographics over the past 20 years.
6. The influence of children on family decision making.
7. The dimensions on which organizational buying differs from consumer buying.
8. The service encounter as theater.
9. Market mavens.
10. Diffusion.

Group processes are important elements of the consumer environment. A major reason for studying groups is that, when people enter a group, they frequently act differently than when they are alone. As a result, groups are more than the sum of their parts. For example, why do restaurants usually add a 15 percent tip to the bill when more than four or five people eat together? The reason is that each member of a group gives a lower percentage tip than if they were eating alone. Being a part of a group causes each member to feel less responsible for providing a fair share of the tip.

This chapter is divided into five major sections, the first of which discusses how groups influence consumption. The two most important fundamental types of groups—families and organizational groups—are then discussed. The fourth section discusses dyadic exchanges. The information that passes from one individual to another within groups may have an important impact on such consumer decisions as which product to purchase or which store or service provider to use (e.g., which doctor, dentist, or hair stylist to patronize). The section focuses on word-of-mouth communications and the service encounter as examples of dyadic exchanges. The fifth section analyzes the processes through which information and innovations diffuse through the environment.

GROUP PROCESSES

A **group** is a set of individuals who interact with one another over some period of time and who share a common need or goal. The group itself typically serves as a means to achieving a goal. Consumers belong to numerous groups, each of which has some impact on buying behavior. For example, college students are likely to be members of families, sororities or fraternities, dorms, student organizations, or clubs. The family group is particularly important because it is an important buying unit within the economy.

Groups influence buying in two general ways. First, they may influence the purchases made by individual consumers: A fraternity member may buy a fraternity jacket. Second, group members must sometimes make decisions as a group. For example, a student club may have to decide where to hold a party and what refreshments to purchase.[1]

The study of group processes is also relevant to decision making within companies. The buying center within a company is usually composed of several individuals who jointly make purchase decisions. Also, employees often form groups to decide where to have parties, which restaurant to go to for a celebration, and which radio station to listen to as background music.

Types of Groups

Sociologists have developed a variety of terms to describe the different types of groups a person may belong to, aspire to join, or avoid.[2] Table 12.1 provides a brief definition of the various groups. These include reference groups, primary and secondary groups, and formal and informal groups. The most important of these groups is the reference group.

Types of Groups

Reference group. A group whose values, norms, attitudes, or beliefs are used as a guide for behavior by an individual.

Aspiration group. A group to which an individual would like to belong. If membership in it proves impossible, it becomes a symbolic group for the person.

Dissociative group. A group with which the person does not wish to be associated.

Primary group. A group of which a person is a member and with which that person interacts on a face-to-face basis. Primary groups are marked by intimacy among their members and by a lack of boundaries for the discussion of various topics.

Formal group. A group whose organization and structure are defined in writing. Examples are labor unions, universities, and classroom groups.

Informal group. A group that has no written organizational structure. Informal groups are often socially based, such as a group of friends who meet frequently to play golf, play bridge, or party together.

TABLE 12.1

Reference Groups. The term **reference group** is broad and encompasses a number of more specific types of groups. The common factor among the types of reference groups is that each is used by the consumer as a point of reference to evaluate the correctness of his or her actions, beliefs, and attitudes.

One type of reference group is the aspiration group. **Aspiration groups** are those sets of people with whom a consumer identifies. One can see the effects of aspiration groups on college students in the spring of their senior year. At this point in time, they are interviewing for jobs. Their aspiration group has suddenly changed, and along with it their clothing—from jeans and cutoffs to business suits.

A **dissociative group** is another type of reference group. The dissociative group is still a point of reference; however, it is a group with which the consumer wants to *avoid* being associated. For example, when individuals are striving to move into higher social classes, they may avoid buying the products and services used by the dissociative reference group.

How Groups Influence Consumers

Groups affect consumers through five basic means: (1) group influence processes, (2) the creation of roles within the group, (3) the development of conformity pressures, (4) social comparison processes, and (5) the development of group polarization. These are discussed in the following subsections.

Group Influence Processes. The type of group having the most impact on consumers is the reference group. Reference groups affect people through norms, via information, and through the value-expressive needs of consumers. A **norm** is a behavioral rule of conduct agreed upon by a majority of the group in order to establish behavioral consistency within the group. Norms are rarely written down but are nonetheless generally recognized as standards for behavior by group members. They represent shared value judgments about how things should be done by members of the group. **Normative influence** occurs when norms act to influence behavior. For example, the effects of unwritten corporate dress codes illustrate the impact of normative influence on the clothing purchased by employees. Similarly, norms can influence what and how much a person eats or drinks at a party and even the type of car a consumer purchases.

Groups can also influence consumers by providing them with information and encouraging the expression of certain types of values. **Informational influence** affects individuals because the group provides highly credible information that influences the consumer's purchase decisions. A reference group's values and attitudes toward consumption exert **value-expressive influence** on consumers. Because the person wishes to be a part of the group and to be liked by the members, he or she may act in ways that express these values and attitudes.

Finally, reference group influence may vary depending on the type of product purchased. It has been suggested that reference group influence is higher for "public" products, such as wristwatches and automobiles, than for "private" products, such as refrigerators and mattresses.[3]

Roles. A role consists of the specific behaviors expected of a person in a given position. When a person takes on a role, normative pressures exert influence on the person to act in a particular way. An important role in consumer behavior is that of the *decider*. This person makes the final decision concerning which brand to choose. In organizational buying settings, identifying the decider is crucial. Often, an individual outside of the purchasing department is actually responsible for the buying decision; reaching this individual with the promotional message can make the difference in whether a sale is made.

The term **role-related product cluster** has been given to the set of products necessary to play a particular role. For marketing managers, identifying those products that match the roles of consumers can be useful. For example, the role-related product cluster of a successful executive's office might include a personal computer, a window on an upper floor, and an exercise device in the corner. An advertising campaign for the exercise equipment could symbolically tie its product to the rest of the product cluster as necessities for the upward-moving business person.

Conformity Pressures. **Conformity** may be defined as a "change in behavior or belief toward a group as a result of real or imagined group pressure."[4] Two types of conformity can be identified. The first is simple **compliance,** in which the person merely conforms to the wishes of the group without really accepting the group's dictates. The second is **private acceptance,** in which the person actually changes his or her beliefs in the direction of the group. A number of factors may increase the conformity pressures of a group.

Factors Within the Group Leading to Conformity. Three aspects of groups may act to increase the conformity pressures felt by its members. One aspect is *cohesiveness,* which refers to how closely knit a group is. A group whose members have a high degree of loyalty and identification can exert greater influence on its members. The *expertise* of the group also affects conformity pressures. Because consumers are members of many groups, several different groups may have input into a particular purchase decision. The group whose members have more expertise relevant to the decision will have greater influence on the purchase.

The third group aspect that has been found to influence decisions is the *size* of the group, particularly when the group is of a transient nature. In a classic series of experiments, the psychologist Solomon Asch had people judge which of the series of lines on one card matched the length of a line on another card. The task was quite simple, and when done alone, the subjects made almost no errors. However, in the experiment Asch also used confederates who systematically made incorrect estimates and who succeeded in inducing wrong answers. The impact of the group was found to vary with the number of confederates. The likelihood of the subjects agreeing with the confederates increased until the size of the group reached about four people. After the group size got to four people, the impact of adding more individuals to the group was minimal.[5]

Factors Within the Person Leading to Conformity. The ability of a group to make a person conform depends on the nature and needs of the person as well as the properties of the group. One such personal factor is the amount of information that the person has available for a decision. When little information is available or when the information is ambiguous, the group has more impact on the person's decision.

The attractiveness of the group and the person's need to be liked by the group often work together to create conformity pressures. In most cases the more the person wants to be a part of the group, the more he or she also wishes to be liked by its members. In such circumstances the individual tends to conform to group norms and pressures in order to fit in as well as possible.

Type of Decision. The type of decision is a final factor that may influence the amount of conformity pressure felt by the person. When a product is highly salient and conspicuous to others, conformity pressures increase.

Perhaps the buying situation that best illustrates the impact of group conformity pressures involves home shopping parties. Nearly everyone who attends purchases something. In effect, strong friendship ties create a type of "moral economy" in which buying is expected.

Social Comparison Processes. Another way in which groups influence consumers involves people's need to assess their opinions and abilities by comparing themselves to others. The process through which people evaluate the "correctness" of their opinions, the extent of their abilities, and the appropriateness of their possessions has been called **social comparison.**[6] In addition to using groups to obtain factual information, consumers use groups to determine where they stand in terms of their opinions, abilities, and possessions.

It is important to note that people typically compare themselves to others who are at about the same level on the given attributes rather than to someone who shows great differences. Social comparison, however, is not limited to contrasting oneself with peers. The idealized images of how one should look that are obtained from advertising can also influence one's self-image. One study reported a series of experiments on the topic. In one of these experiments, college women viewed magazine ads that used either highly attractive models or no models.. After being exposed to the highly attractive models in the ads, the women were less satisfied with their own physical appearance. Thus, advertising does cause social comparison to occur, and these comparisons can affect our feelings about ourselves.[7]

Group Polarization. For several decades psychologists have studied a highly perplexing phenomenon—**group polarization.** Researchers in studies have provided groups and individuals with decision dilemmas and compared their choices. Although they first found that groups tended to select the riskier alternative, later research found that conservative as well as risky shifts could occur.[8]

The study of group polarization is particularly relevant to organizational sales. If a group decision to purchase an industrial product or service is made, the salesperson needs to recognize that risky or conservative shifts may occur. Because the dominant culture of most companies is toward financial conservatism, organizational sellers should probably tailor the marketing mix based on this dominant value.

FAMILIES AND HOUSEHOLDS

The term *family* is actually a subset of a more general classification—the household. **Households** are composed of all those people who occupy a living unit. Examples of households include roommates living in an apartment, unmarried couples living together, a husband and wife with children, a husband, wife, children, and grandparents living under one roof, or two couples sharing the same house. The key similarity among all of the examples is that the group must live in the same residence. Using the above definition, a husband, wife, and children who live together are a household as well as a family.

A number of different types of families exist. The **nuclear family** consists of a husband, a wife, and their offspring. The **extended family** consists of the nuclear family plus other relatives, such as the parents of the husband or wife. Although in many societies a husband and wife are expected to reside with one or the other of their parents, in the United States and Canada children from middle-class families tend to strike off on their own to form families away from their parents. Such a trend has been called the **detached nuclear family.**

Over the past two decades, major changes have occurred in the United States and Canada in the nature of households and families. New living arrangements have begun to be established that profoundly affect the number and size of households and families. Many of these changes are discussed in the next section.

The Demographics of Households

Two general types of households can be identified—families and nonfamilies. Data from the U.S. Bureau of the Census indicates that household growth has outpaced population growth. Since 1970 the average household size has fallen from 3.14 to 2.67 persons, and average family size has fallen from 3.58 to 3.20 persons. The trend toward smaller households lies in an increasing divorce rate, decisions of young people to leave home prior to marriage, and the tendency of older people to maintain their own homes after other family members are gone.[9]

Later marriage is another factor linked to the decreasing size of households. In 1966 the average male was 22.8 years old and the female 20.5 years old at the time of first marriage. By the late 1980s the ages had increased to 25.8 years for men and 23.6 years for women. In fact, by the mid-1990s 66 percent of women aged 20 to 24 had never married—more than double the number in 1980.[10]

The trend toward later marriage has a number of implications. First, it suggests that more people will remain single. Second, it implies that fertility rates will decrease because older couples simply have more trouble conceiving than younger couples. Later marriages also increase the chances for premarital pregnancies because women are sexually mature longer prior to marriage. Finally, by remaining single longer, young people have more time to invest in themselves by pursuing educational and work goals.

Divorce is a growing fact of life for couples in the 1990s. In the late 1970s, it was estimated that 35 percent of new marriages would end in divorce. That estimate is now about 50 percent. One result of the higher divorce rate is a large increase in the number of single men and women caring for children under 18 years of age. Between 1980 and 1994, this number increased by over 225 percent for men and 142 percent for women. A more positive sign, however, is that since the mid-1980s divorce rates have declined slightly, from about 5.3 per 1,000 population in 1981 to 4.7 in 1990 and 4.2 in 1999.[11]

Another major trend in family composition over the past 15 years is the increased frequency of two-career families. By 1993 64.7 percent of all married women in the United States were working, and this figure has continued to rise.[12]

Changes in family demographics can influence the design of the marketing mix in a variety of ways. For example, the rapid increase in the number of working women has dramatically changed the way marketers attempt to reach this group. The time demands on working women mean that the distribution system has had to be adjusted so that retail stores are open weekends and at night. Similarly, another result of the increasing tendency of women to work is that men are taking over more purchasing responsibility. Between 1987 and 1994, the number of men shopping from home via catalog increased 54 percent, compared with a smaller 39 percent increase in women catalog shoppers.[13] Companies in the clothing industry have introduced suits and skirts for working women that do not go out of style every year. Women are also buying more homes: Single women own 13.8 million homes, more than double the number of 30 years ago.[14]

Family Decision Making

During the course of everyday living, family members make thousands of decisions. The study of family decision making is quite difficult for three reasons. First, as in organizational buying units, the decision maker may not be the user or maintainer of the product. Second, families come in many different configurations. A family with a working mother, stay-at-home dad, and two small children will employ very different decision-making processes than a single mother living on welfare with two teenage sons. A third problem concerns the reliability and validity of the information obtained. For example, a general tendency exists among some couples for either the husband or wife to systematically overestimate his or her influence, participation, and authority in household decisions.

A number of issues in family decision making are discussed in this section. These include determining which family members have the most influence on various household decisions and identifying the role of children in family decision making.

Relative Influence of Decision Makers. A key question in studying family decision making concerns who in the family has the most influence on various types of decisions. An early effort to identify the relative influence of family members on household decisions was conducted in Belgium.[15] The classic study identified the following four role-specialization dimensions in the buying of products:

1. *Wife-dominated decisions.* The wife is largely independent in deciding what to buy.
2. *Husband-dominated decisions.* The husband is largely independent in deciding what to buy.
3. *Autonomic decisions.* Decisions of lesser importance that either the husband or wife may make independently of the other.
4. *Syncratic decisions.* Decisions in which the husband and wife participate jointly.

Research conducted in the United States has found similar patterns. One study investigated the decision patterns of financially secure, middle-aged couples.[16] In this study husband-dominated decisions tended to focus on the details of automobile purchases (e.g., where to purchase the car). Wife-dominated decisions tended to involve the detailed aspects of kitchen and laundry purchases, such as what brand the new washer and dryer should be. Syncratic decisions appeared to predominate in the study. Areas in which syncratic decisions were found included vacations, home electronic appliances, home selection, when to purchase the next car, and when to purchase new furniture.

Influence in the Family. Researchers have looked specifically at the ability of members of the family to influence decisions. They have identified three factors that strongly influence a member's family influence: financial resources of the family member, the importance of the decision to the family member, and the gender-role orientations of the family members.[17] Researchers have found that, as financial contribution to the family unit increases, influence also increases. Similarly, the importance of the decision to a family member also increases that person's influence on a particular decision.

The third factor affecting the amount of influence is the gender-role orientation of the spouses. Gender role relates to the extent to which a member of the family follows traditional normative conceptions of how males and females should behave. Research on the effects of gender role suggests that families that are less traditional in their gender-role orientation have a greater tendency to use a joint decision-making style. In general, gender-role orientation is instrumental in defining the decision-role responsibilities of husbands and wives.[18]

Finally, there is a change over the life of the family. Across a wide range of decisions (automobiles, vacations, electronic devices, furniture and appliances), the influence of the wife tends to increase over time, peaking in the retirement years. The startling exception is groceries, where the wife's influence decreases as the couple ages.[19]

The Role of Children in Family Decision Making. Children clearly make a difference in family decisions (this issue is also discussed in chapter 16). Even when children do not dominate the decision process, they have the potential to form alliances with either the husband or wife to produce a "majority" decision.

The influence of children on household decisions increases as they grow older. One study of adolescents and their parents found that, as the adolescent's age increased, his or her influence on the various decision stages also increased. Another major finding was that peer communication was related to mentioning and discussing purchases with parents. These results demonstrate the large impact that peer groups have on adolescents' product preferences. The study also found that, because adolescents increasingly earned money outside of the home, they had more input into purchase decisions.[20] A more recent study found that adolescents used bargaining, such as money deals (offers to pay for all or part of the cost), reasoning, and direct requests most effectively in dealing with their parents over family decisions. On the other hand, begging, whining, and declaring that "everyone else" was doing something were least effective.[21]

In other research adolescents' and mothers' perceptions of their influence on family purchase decisions were compared. As one would expect, the adolescents believed their influence was greater than the mothers rated it. Similarly, the mothers rated their own influence as greater than the adolescents believed. The study did show that adolescents are active participants in family purchase decisions, even for products not for their own use. For example, even in the purchase of the family car, both adolescents and mothers indicated that the young person had some impact on the decision.[22]

Childhood Consumer Socialization

One reason for the family's importance is its role as a socialization agent. Socialization may be defined as the process by which individuals acquire knowledge, skills, and dispositions that enable them to participate as members of society.[23] This general concept can be narrowed to that of **childhood consumer socialization,** which refers to the processes by which children acquire the skills and attitudes relevant to functioning as consumers.

Understanding how individuals are socialized into consumers is important for several reasons. First, knowledge of the factors influencing consumer socialization can provide information to marketers that may be useful in designing marketing communications. Children are potent consumers. It is estimated that children under 12 years old directly spend nearly $27.5 billion a year in the United States.[24] Second, public-policy decisions concerning the regulation of the marketing of products to children should in part be based on an understanding of the consumer socialization process.

A Model of Consumer Socialization. Figure 12.1 presents a simple model of consumer socialization. It suggests that consumer socialization is based on three components—

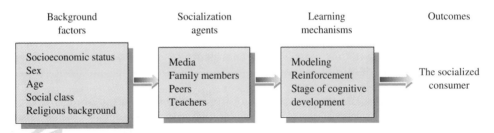

Figure 12.1 A model of consumer socialization.

background factors, socialization agents, and learning mechanisms such as cognitive learning, operant conditioning, and modeling.

Socialization background factors include such variables as socioeconomic status, sex, age, social class, and religious background. Socialization agents are those individuals directly involved with the consumer who have influence because of their frequency of contact, importance, or control over rewards and punishments given to the consumer. Examples of socialization agents include parents, brothers and sisters, peers, teachers, the media, and media personalities such as athletes, movie stars, and rock stars.

Researchers have investigated the impact of socialization agents and background factors on consumer socialization. In an important early study that analyzed the factors of family, mass media, newspaper readership, school, peers, age, social class, and gender, it was found that the family was crucial for teaching the "rational" aspects of consumption.[25] However, the influence of parents is situation specific. Their impact varies across the stage of the decision process, across various types of products, and across various personal characteristics, such as age, socioeconomic class, and sex of the child. Researchers have also suggested that children's perceptions of their parents' life satisfaction and financial skill contribute strongly to the willingness of the child to accept parents as consumption role models. Where parents were perceived as unsuccessful or unskilled, children turned elsewhere for role models.[26]

Peers were found to be an important socialization agent. They contributed particularly to the expressive element in which one buys for materialistic or social reasons (e.g., buying to "keep up with the neighbors"). For teenagers, buying to impress or be like others was clearly important. However, interaction among peers also was related to an increased awareness of goods and services in the marketplace.

ORGANIZATIONAL BUYING BEHAVIOR

Just as individual consumers and families make purchases, so do organizations. Businesses, government agencies, and nonprofit organizations all make purchases in order to produce goods or services. At the heart of the purchase process in organizations is the buying center. An **organizational buying center** is defined as those people in an organization who participate in the buying decision and who share the risks and goals of the decision.[27] Buying centers are not part of the company's organizational structure, and composition varies depending on purchase situations. For example, physicians are not involved in determining which floor cleaners to use in a hospital, but they are very likely to be active when expensive diagnostic equipment is being considered.

Because buying centers are composed of people, the same behavioral factors (psychological, sociological, and anthropological) that impact consumers also affect the individuals within a organization. Just as different members of a family may have greater influence over certain purchases, members of a buying center may use various strategies such as promises or threats to influence the final result.[28] However, because an organization differs from a family in terms of its mission and its situational environment, one can expect that divergent factors affect the two types of groups. For example, on the dimension of price, competitive bidding is used much more frequently in organizational buying than in consumer buying. If a family needs to purchase cooking oil, they will go to a local grocery store and buy a brand at list price. When McDonald's buys cooking oil, the company may take competitive bids, provide detailed specifications for the good, develop long-term relationships with suppliers, and involve management, R&D, and nutritionists in the decision.

Building Relationships in Organizational Buying

Perhaps the most-discussed concept in the field of marketing in the 1990s was relationship marketing. **Relationship marketing** can be defined as the overt attempt of exchange partners to build a long-term association in which purposeful cooperation and mutual dependence occurs and social, as well as structural, bonds are developed. When relationships are formed, the parties join together (either formally or informally) so that they share to some degree the gains or losses that occur in their business operations.[29] Marketing relationships exist along a continuum from simple, one-time transactions to fully integrated hierarchical companies.

The most recent form of relationship marketing that is beginning to be adopted by U.S. corporations is the network structure.[30] Somewhat similar to the Japanese *keiretsu,* networks may possess little or no formal organization but are characterized by mutual interdependence and long-term stability. Such networks of companies create a situation in which high levels of mutual trust can be formed.

Given this important trend in marketing to form relationships, the buying center of an organization must respond appropriately. In many respects the relationships that result may resemble marriages. As in marriages, managers must recognize that a give-and-take will exist with suppliers. Similarly, the sales force must be willing to adjust rapidly to the changing needs of its customers. Again as in marriages, the dissolution phase will be much more difficult than in traditional contractual exchanges.[31]

Two critical elements in building long-term relationships are trust and commitment. **Relationship trust** is "a willingness to rely on an exchange partner in whom one has confidence."[32] In order to develop trust in a relationship, the members must reveal vulnerability to each other. In such cases control of important resources is left with the other partner in the exchange. The exchange members must then rely on each other to fulfill their obligations. When high levels of trust exist, the exchange process becomes more flexible and bureaucratic and legal entanglements are minimized. Similarly, **commitment** is the belief of an exchange partner that the relationship with another "is so important as to warrant maximum efforts at maintaining it."[33]

Although the present discussion of relationships concentrates on organizational buying, it is also relevant to consumer behavior. For example, the establishment of a relationship with a supplier allows both the individual consumer and the organizational buyer to reduce the costs of search. Consumers often purchase the same goods repeatedly from the same store, and brand loyalty can be considered a form of relationship behavior. The idea that consumers prefer to reduce choices by engaging in an ongoing loyalty relationship with marketers has, in fact, been called the "fundamental axiom of relationship marketing."[34] It should be noted, however, that this view is a matter of controversy[35] because when consumers enter a relationship, for example, by signing up for an airline's frequent flier program, they often increase their choices: First, they develop relationships with a number of competing airlines; second, they increase their information flow from each airline so that they are aware of more, rather than fewer, choices.

DYADIC EXCHANGES

Dyadic exchange takes place when two individuals transfer resources between each other. We focus on two important types of dyadic exchange, word-of-mouth communications and the service encounter.

Word-of-Mouth Communications

Word-of-mouth communication refers to an exchange of comments, thoughts, or ideas between two or more consumers, none of whom represent a marketing source.[36]

Word-of-mouth communications have an extremely strong impact on consumer purchase behavior. One survey of consumers asked what factors influenced their purchases of 60 different products. The results revealed that referrals from others accounted for three times as many purchases as did advertising.[37] Another study found that word-of-mouth influence was twice as effective as radio advertising, four times more effective than personal selling, and seven times as effective as newspapers and magazines.[38] Research in the United Kingdom shows that, although six out of seven software users utilize pirated copies, these pirates are responsible for generating over 80 percent of new legal software buyers, due in part to word-of-mouth communications with other potential users.[39]

A **negativity bias** operates in word-of-mouth communications. One piece of negative information about a product or service influences a consumer more than one, two, or even three items of positive information. For example, a study of a new coffee product found that, after receiving positive information, 54 percent tried the product. However, after receiving negative information, only 18 percent tried it.[40]

A likely explanation for the disproportionate influence of negative information is that, because most products are pretty good, negative information is rather rare. When such information does occur, it takes on greater importance because of its high saliency. Also, because word-of-mouth information comes directly from another person, who describes his or her own experiences, information tends to be more vivid than in a medium such as printed communication. The net result is that word-of-mouth information is more accessible in memory and has a relatively greater effect on consumers.[41]

Why Word-of-Mouth Communication Occurs. The omnipresence of word-of-mouth communication results from the needs of both the sender and receiver of the information. The receiver may desire information because he or she fails to believe the advertisements and sales messages received in the marketplace. Also, the receiver may be seeking additional information in order to decrease anxiety about a risky purchase. When receivers are highly involved in a purchase decision, they tend to go through a longer search process for a product or service. In these high-involvement situations, personal influence is increasingly important.

Consumers may be motivated to seek the input of others in three additional purchase situations.[42] Consumers tend to seek the advice of others (1) when the products are highly visible to others, (2) when the product is highly complex, and (3) when the product cannot be easily tested against some objective criterion.

The process of influencing others also fulfills the needs of senders of information. The ability to provide information and to sway others in their decisions provides a person with feelings of power and prestige. Influencing others can also help influencers erase doubts about their own purchases. In addition, by providing information to others, a sender can increase his or her involvement with a group. Thus, providing information acts to increase social interaction and the general cohesion of the group.[43] Finally, people can engage in word-of-mouth communications in order to derive some benefit. That is, by giving someone else information, based on the norm of reciprocity, they should at some point return the favor.

Opinion Leadership. The study of word-of-mouth communication shows that some people provide information more frequently than others. Such individuals may become **opinion leaders,** defined as those consumers who influence the purchase decisions of others.

Opinion leadership does *not* appear to be a general trait held by specific individuals who influence others across a broad range of categories. Rather, opinion leadership is specific to the product category and situation. Within a single product category, such as appliances or household furnishings, an opinion leader may influence others across a number of different products. However, opinion leadership doesn't seem to occur across product categories.

Characteristics of Opinion Leaders. Attempts to find demographic and personality characteristics that pinpoint opinion leaders have not been very successful. The most clear-cut finding is that opinion leaders are involved with the product category. They are interested in the product category, tend to read special-interest magazines about it, and are knowledgeable about it. Some evidence exists that opinion leaders may be more self-confident and socially active than followers. Opinion leaders may also have a somewhat greater social status than followers; however, they do belong to the same peer group as followers. Finally, they tend to be more innovative in their purchases than followers, but they are not the consumers who are "product innovators."[44]

Comparing Opinion Leaders and Product Innovators. Opinion leaders and product innovators are similar in a variety of respects. Product innovators are the small set of people who are the first to buy new products. The innovator may be described as an adventurer who strikes off on his or her own to buy new products. In contrast, the opinion leader is like an editor who can influence others but who can never be too far away from the goals, values, and attitudes of those whose opinions are being influenced. Innovators are less integrated into social groups and feel freer to break group norms by adopting new products very early in their life cycle. In contrast, opinion leaders are more socially integrated and exert their influence in part because they do not espouse beliefs that are widely divergent from those of the group.[45]

A group of researchers has found that those most ready to use new technology demonstrate many of the characteristics of product innovators. They define *technology readiness* as composed of four dimensions—optimism (belief in the benefits of technology), innovativeness, comfort level (feeling of control over technology), and assurance.[46]

Mavens and Surrogates. In addition to opinion leaders and product innovators, researchers have identified two other sources of personal influence—the market maven and the surrogate consumer. **Market mavens** are "individuals who have information about many kinds of products, places to shop, and other facets of markets, and initiate discussions with consumers and respond to requests from consumers for market information."[47] As this definition suggests, these individuals play a broader personal influence role than do opinion leaders. The expertise of market mavens is not product specific; rather, it is based on more general market expertise. Market mavens may seek to obtain marketplace information in order to be useful to others in social exchanges and to provide a basis for conversations.[48]

The second new type of influencer that has been identified is the surrogate consumer. A **surrogate consumer** is a person who acts "as an agent retained by a consumer to guide, direct, and/or transact marketplace activities."[49] They can play a wide variety of roles, such as tax consultant, wine steward, interior decorator, stock broker, or car buyer. The surrogate consumer tends to be used in high-involvement purchases in which the consumer desires to surrender some control to a capable external agent. The consumer abdicates to the surrogate many of the information search, evaluation, and choice functions that take place in the consumer decision process. Table 12.2 summarizes the characteristics of the four types of influencers discussed here—opinion leaders, product innovators, market mavens, and surrogate consumers.

Characteristics of Four Types of Consumer Influencers

Influencer Type	Basis for Expertise	Characteristics
1. Opinion leader	Enduring involvement in product category.	Enduring involvement, higher status, integrated into social group.
2. Product innovator	Purchase of innovative product.	Less integrated into social groups than opinion leaders.
3. Market maven	General market knowledge.	Demographic characteristics unknown; enjoys having general knowledge about the marketplace.
4. Surrogate consumer	Knowledge specific to product category.	Frequently a paid professional.

TABLE 12.2

Service Encounters

The **service encounter** is a personal interaction that occurs between a consumer and a marketer. A service encounter can occur in "pure service contexts," such as a physician's examination, cashing a check, or ordering a meal at a restaurant. In addition, service encounters also occur in "mixed service contexts." For example, consider your involvement with your car. Certainly, automobiles are goods. However, a number of service encounters will have occurred during and after your purchase. That is, when you bought it, you interacted with the seller. When having it serviced or repaired, you encounter additional company representatives. In sum, during the service encounter, a consumption experience is occurring.

During the service encounter, the consumer and the marketer act as though they are on a stage reading from a common "service script." This script creates expectations on both actors' parts. To the extent that either violates the script in a negative manner, dissatisfaction may result. Thus, if the service provider violates expectations (perhaps by being too pushy), the consumer will be dissatisfied. Conversely, if the consumer violates expectations (perhaps by ridiculing the employee), the employee will be dissatisfied.

The use of theater as a metaphor to describe the service encounter provides a vocabulary for understanding the exchange process. Figure 12.2 presents a diagram that depicts the service encounter as theater.[50] Like any production, there is a stage where the play takes place. In addition, there are front and back regions for both consumer and firm. In the front region, both parties reveal impression management and protective practices. A backstage area also exists for both parties where rehearsal occurs, secondary support exists (e.g., other people help the production), and management functions reside.

As already noted, both the consumer and the employee follow scripted roles during the service encounter. Researchers have identified three themes that may occur for each party in the encounter.[51] The three themes for consumers are autonomy, mutuality, and dependence. They depict the nature of the relationship that the consumer desires to form with the service provider. Consumers desire autonomy when they believe they have the information that they need and seek to engage in

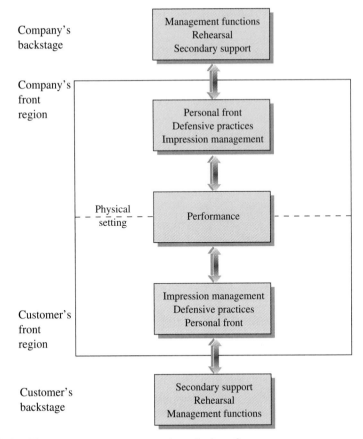

Company's
backstage

Company's
front
region

Physical
setting

Customer's
front
region

Customer's
backstage

Figure 12.2   The service encounter as theatrical performance.

Source: Adapted from Stephen Grove and Raymond Fisk, "The Service Encounter as Theater," in *Advances in Consumer Research,* ed. John F. Sherry Jr. and Brian Sternthal (Provo, UT: Association for Consumer Research, 1992), 19: 455–61.

self-service. Those who purchase relatively low-involvement goods from retail stores frequently desire autonomy. Consumers may also have a high degree of expertise and, as a result, seek autonomy. The sophisticated investor who purchases stocks from a discount brokerage exemplifies this case.

As product involvement increases and as consumer expertise decreases, consumers may seek either mutual cooperation or dependence in the relationship with the employee. Examples of mutual cooperation might include purchasing expensive clothing, original art, or stocks and bonds by a consumer with some knowledge of the risks and benefits involved. In contrast, if the consumer has limited knowledge or expertise, total dependence may be placed on the employee. In such instances the consumer wants the employee to take an active role and participate fully in the service encounter. At the extreme the employee becomes a surrogate consumer. The roles are not static, however. For example, in an extended service encounter (such as between a guide and a client in a rafting expedition), the customer is in a more dependent state at the beginning, with mutuality occurring as the encounter progresses. By the end of the trip the two are usually—at least temporarily—friends.[52]

Employee themes are symmetrical with the consumer themes. The three employee themes are indifference, cooperation, and dominance. If the customer wants mutual cooperation, the employee should provide it without attempting to become dominant. The indifference theme, however, is tricky. Generally, consumers who want autonomy do *not* want indifferent service providers. Rather, they desire providers who leave them alone until they need attention to complete the transaction.

DIFFUSION PROCESSES

The term *diffusion* refers to the idea that substances or even ideas can gradually spread through a medium and reach a state of equilibrium. In a consumer-behavior setting, **diffusion** refers to the process by which innovative ideas, products, and services spread through the consumer population.

Two different types of diffusion processes are of concern to marketers. The first is information diffusion and alternative models of information transmission. The second type of diffusion process involves the diffusion of innovations. This section identifies the factors that influence how innovative products become adopted by consumers.

Transmission Processes

A question of importance to marketers and sociologists concerns how communications flow within the consumer environment. Several models of how information is transmitted from the mass media to the general population have been proposed. The **trickle-down theory** holds that trends—particularly fashion trends—begin with the wealthy. The wealthy adopt styles of clothing and attitudes that distinguish themselves from the lower classes. The lower classes then attempt to emulate the wealthy by copying their actions. In this way the fashions and behaviors of the wealthy "trickle down." One problem with the trickle-down theory is that relatively little communication actually occurs between the classes. Most communications occur between people in the same social class. Second, in a mass-communication culture, information on fashion is transmitted almost instantaneously. Information transmission is much more like a flood than a trickle.

The approach that appears to represent the flow of personal influence much better is the **multistep flow model.** In this approach the mass media transmits information to three distinct sets of people—opinion leaders, gatekeepers, and followers.[53] Each type of person is viewed as having the capability of providing information to the other categories of people. The opinion leader is the person who influences others about the particular piece of information transmitted by the mass media. The gatekeeper is an individual who has the capability of deciding whether others in a group will receive information. That person's opinions may or may not influence the others, however. The followers are those who are influenced by the opinion leader or by the information provided by the gatekeeper.

The multistep flow model recognizes a number of important pieces of information:

1. Mass communications can directly reach nearly everyone in the population.
2. Opinion leaders are able to influence a group of followers. However, for different products the role of opinion leader and follower may be reversed.
3. Another group of individuals, the gatekeepers, can choose whether or not to provide information to opinion leaders and followers.
4. Communications can be transmitted back and forth between the three groups.

The Diffusion of Innovations

The study of the adoption of new products is important for marketers. In order to grow, a company must continually improve existing products and periodically develop new products for the changing marketplace. The study of product adoption is also important because of the relatively low success rate of new products. The overall cost of introducing a new consumer product has been estimated to be about $6 million. The chance of a new product being successful is about 53 percent for consumer goods.[54]

In the 1980s one study proposed a simple model of the diffusion process, identifying six key factors that influence the nature and extent of the diffusion of an innovation.[55] First, diffusion occurs within a social system or market. Second, diffusion depends on the individual adoption decisions of thousands or even millions of consumers. The individual adoption process is synonymous with individual consumer decision making, discussed earlier. The decisions of individuals are influenced by three factors—the characteristics of the innovation, the characteristics of innovators, and the personal-influence process. These three factors make up the third, fourth, and fifth elements of the diffusion process. The final element is the nature of the diffusion process, which results from the influence of the five preceding elements. The following subsections discuss in greater detail the elements of the diffusion process.

The Social System. The study of the social system in which products are diffused is closely related to the analysis of the impact of cultural and subcultural processes on consumers. Evidence indicates that the speed of diffusion is influenced by several aspects of the social system. First, the greater the compatibility between the innovation and the values of the members of the social system, the quicker the rate of diffusion. Second, the more homogeneous (i.e., nonsegmented) the social system, the faster the diffusion process. The diffusion of innovations across cultures is dependent upon the distance between the countries and the social similarity of the cultures.[56]

Characteristics of the Innovation. One approach to distinguishing the innovation characteristics of products and services concerns the technological versus symbolic aspects of the innovation.[57] A *symbolic innovation* communicates a different social meaning than it did previously because of the acquisition of new intangible attributes. A *technological innovation* results from a change in the characteristics of a product or service through the introduction of a technological change. An example of a technological innovation is a compact disc player. An example of a symbolic innovation is the diffusion of new hair styles or fashion styles.

Characteristics of Innovators. One of the important challenges faced by marketers of innovative products is identifying the characteristics of people who buy the product early in its life cycle.

People who are innovative tend to have higher incomes, higher levels of education, greater social mobility, higher opinion leadership in the product category, and more favorable attitudes toward risk.

Factors Influencing the Diffusion Pattern. Figure 12.3 identifies the normal pattern of innovative product diffusion through the population. Note that the curve describing the diffusion process in Figure 12.3 is S-shaped. During the introductory phase, the percentage of consumers adopting the product is small and slowly accelerating. As the product moves into the growth stage, the percentage accelerates, and the curve bends upward rapidly. During maturity, growth slows until it turns negative, marking the beginning of decline.

The exact shape of the curve depends on a number of factors. If the innovation is adopted very quickly, the fast pattern found in Figure 12.3 results. If the adoption

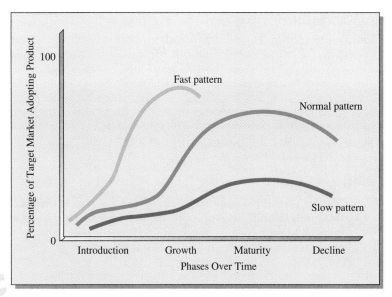

Figure 12.3   The shape of the diffusion process.

rate is slow, the pattern becomes much flatter and more drawn out. Three factors affect the rapidity with which an innovation is adopted and, as a consequence, the shape of the curve:

1. *Characteristics of the product.* The same factors that influence the likely success of an innovation also influence the rapidity with which it is adopted. To the extent that it fulfills a need, is compatible, has a relative advantage, has low complexity, has observable positive features, and is easily tried, the product will be adopted more quickly. For example, the Frisbee was widely adopted within six months of introduction.

2. *Characteristics of the target market.* Products targeted to different target groups will exhibit divergent adoption patterns. For example, products that appeal to younger, more highly educated, change-oriented individuals are often quickly adopted, but they also run the risk of rapidly moving into decline.

3. *Extent of the marketing effort.* Companies can influence the growth curve of a product by the quality and extent of their marketing effort.

The shape of the diffusion pattern, therefore, is not always S-shaped. In some instances it may show an exponential pattern—the curve starts out slowly and then increases at a rapid rate. Exponential patterns tend to result when the innovation is adopted via low-involvement decision making, when low switching costs exist, and when a relative lack of personal influence occurs. In contrast, the S-shaped curve tends to be found when personal influence is operating, when high switching costs exist, and when a high-involvement decision process is taking place.[58]

MANAGERIAL IMPLICATIONS

The preceding discussion of groups, dyadic exchanges, and diffusion adds a number of new concepts to our understanding of the consumer. Applications to the five PERMS concepts are summarized in the following sections.

Positioning and Differentiation

The discussion about opinion leaders suggests that opinion leaders are rather different than followers and that one should position an innovative product so that it is of interest to opinion leaders, and then possibly reposition the product as necessary to account for the differences between leaders and followers. For example, although new high-technology devices such as computers are often introduced to companies via opinion leaders (in this case, technology enthusiasts), these enthusiasts seldom have budgetary control, and a different appeal—probably one that relies more on the ability of innovations to improve the bottom line and less on the "whiz-bang" technology—may be necessary.

Environmental Analysis

Monitoring information transmission processes is also important for marketing managers. Marketing research should be employed to identify exactly what a company's customers are communicating to others about its products or services. It is crucial for companies to track customer satisfaction and then take quick steps to remedy problems that may occur.

Research

Through research into the diffusion process, the marketing manager can get a feel for the likely growth curve of the product. Will the product be a slow starter that must be nurtured for a substantial length of time, or will a strong marketing effort allow it to start fast?

As discussed in this chapter, research may help to identify whether a group polarization is more likely to be risky or conservative in the case of organizational purchases.

Marketing Mix

Knowledge of diffusion processes is important to managers, particularly those involved in marketing new products and services. Product managers need to investigate the extent to which an innovation has a relative advantage over competitors and is compatible with the values and lifestyle of their target market. Furthermore, the manager needs to assess the product's complexity, trialability, and observability.

It is worthwhile in consumer markets to consider the addition of promotional items that will attract children and thereby make use of their ability to influence family decisions. For example, in late 1999 the Burger King chain introduced 57 new Pokémon toys, each available with the purchase of a children's meal. It was reported at the time that parents were "bracing their stomachs for two months of hamburgers."[59] Although few parents may agree to eat hamburgers for 57 days, many families probably visited Burger King more than usual during this promotion.

Segmentation

Managers can segment the market based on group membership. Naturally existing groups of consumers make outstanding target markets for companies because they are readily identifiable and reachable. For example, numerous companies target military veterans, public teachers, government workers, church groups, the National Rifle Association, and so on.[60] Product and service offerings can be developed specifically for the members of the groups. Promotional strategy can be built around the concept that the product or service is positioned as being offered specifically to the members of the group. Environmental analysis should be performed to determine the extent to which new membership groups are establishing themselves. Finally, marketing research should be performed to assess the attitudes and psychographic characteristics of the individuals who make up these groups.

Notes

1. James C. Ward and Peter H. Reingen, "Sociocognitive Analysis of Group Decision Making among Consumers," *Journal of Consumer Research* 17 (December 1990): 245–62.
2. Michael S. Olmstead, *The Small Group* (New York: Holt, Rinehart & Winston, 1962). For a fascinating discussion of group influence on decision making, see Irving L. Janis, *Victims of Groupthink* (Boston, MA: Houghton Mifflin, 1972).
3. Francis Bourne, "Group Influence in Marketing and Public Relations," in *Some Applications of Behavioral Research,* ed. R. Likert and S. P. Hayes (Basil, Switzerland: UNESCO, 1957). For a study that tested these ideas, see William Bearden and Michael Etzel, "Reference Group Influence on Product and Brand Purchase Decisions," *Journal of Consumer Research* 9 (September 1982): 183–94.
4. Charles A. Kiesler and Sara B. Kiesler, *Conformity* (Reading, MA: Addison-Wesley, 1969), 7.
5. Solomon E. Asch, *Social Psychology* (Upper Saddle River, NJ: Prentice Hall, 1952).
6. Leon Festinger, "A Theory of Social Comparison Processes," *Human Relations* 7 (May 1954): 117–40.
7. Marsha L. Richins, "Social Comparison and the Idealized Images of Advertising," *Journal of Consumer Research* 18 (June 1991): 71–83.
8. R. E. Knox and R. K. Safford, "Group Caution at the Race Track," *Journal of Experimental Social Psychology* 12 (May 1976): 317–24.
9. U.S. Bureau of the Census, *Current Population Surveys* (Washington, D.C.: U.S. Bureau of the Census, 1991).
10. U.S. Department of Commerce, *Statistical Abstract of the United States, 1995* (Washington DC: U.S. Government Printing Office, 1995), 55.
11. U.S. Department of Commerce, *Statistical Abstract of the United States, 1995*, 61; U.S. Department of Commerce, *Statistical Abstract of the United States, 1998* (Washington DC: U.S. Government Printing Office, 1995), 76; and Centers for Disease Control and Prevention, *National Vital Statistics Reports* 48, no 2 (March 9, 2000).
12. U.S. Department of Commerce, *Statistical Abstract of the United States, 1995*, 477; U.S. Department of Commerce, *Statistical Abstract of the United States, 1998*, 410.
13. Callmetta Y. Coleman, "Mail Order is Turning into Male Order," *Wall Street Journal*, March 26, 1996, p. A6.
14. June Fletcher, "When Buying a House, Who Needs a Man?" *Wall Street Journal*, February 9, 1996, p. B10.
15. Harry L. Davis and Benny P. Rigaux, "Perception of Marital Roles in Decision Processes," *Journal of Consumer Research* 1 (June 1974): 51–62.
16. Alvin Burns, "Husband and Wife Purchase Decision-Making Roles: Agreed, Presumed, Conceded, and Disputed," in *Advances in Consumer Research*, ed. William Perreault (Atlanta, GA: Association for Consumer Research, 1977), 4:50–55.
17. William Qualls, "Household Decision Behavior: The Impact of Husbands' and Wives' Sex Role Orientation," *Journal of Consumer Research* 14 (September 1987): 264–79.
18. Ibid.
19. Cynthia Webster and Samantha Rice, "Equity Theory and the Power Structure in a Marital Relationship," in *Advances in Consumer Research*, ed. Kim P. Corfman and John G. Lynch Jr. (Provo, UT: Association for Consumer Research, 1996), 23:491–97.
20. George Moschis and Linda Mitchell, "Television Advertising and Interpersonal Participation in Family Consumer Decisions," in *Advances in Consumer Research*, ed. Richard Lutz (Provo, UT: Association for Consumer Research, 1986), 13:181–85.
21. Kay M. Palan and Robert E. Wilkes, "Adolescent–Parent Interaction in Family Decision Making," *Journal of Consumer Research* 24 (September 1997): 159–69.
22. Ellen Foxman and Patriya Tansuhaj, "Adolescents' and Mothers' Perceptions of Relative Influence in Family Purchase Decisions: Patterns of Agreement and Disagreement," in *Advances in Consumer Research*, ed. Michael Houston (Provo, UT: Association for Consumer Research, 1988), 15:449–53.
23. For a review of the literature on socialization, see Gregory M. Rose, "Consumer Socialization, Parental Style, and Developmental Timetables in the United States and Japan," *Journal of Marketing* 63 (July 1999): 105–19.

24. Richard Tomkins, "Selling to a Captivated Market," *Financial Times*, April 23, 1999, p. 10.

25. George Moschis and Roy Moore, "Decision Making among the Young: A Socialization Perspective," *Journal of Consumer Research* 6 (September 1979): 101–12.

26. Elizabeth S. Moore-Shay and Britto M. Berchmans, "The Role of the Family Environment in the Development of Shared Consumption Values: An Intergenerational Study," in *Advances in Consumer Research*, ed. Kim P. Corfman and John G. Lynch Jr. (Provo, UT: Association for Consumer Research, 1996), 23:484–90.

27. Michael D. Hutt and Thomas W. Speh, *Business Marketing Management* (Fort Worth, TX: Dryden Press, 1992), 66.

28. R. Venkatesh, Ajay K. Kohli, and Gerald Zaltman, "Influence Strategies in Buying Centers," *Journal of Marketing* 59 (October 1995): 71–82.

29. This definition of relationship marketing was developed by John C. Mowen. Ideas for the definition were developed in particular from Gregory T. Gundlach and Patrick E. Murphy, "Ethical and Legal Foundations of Relational Marketing Exchanges," *Journal of Marketing* 57 (October 1993): 35–46.

30. Ravi S. Achrol and Philip Kotler, "Marketing in the Network Economy," *Journal of Marketing* 63 (Special Issue 1999): 146–63.

31. Jeffrey J. Stoltman, James W. Gentry, and Fred Morgan, "Marketing Relationships: Further Consideration of the Marriage Metaphor with Implications for Maintenance and Recovery," *Enhancing Knowledge Development in Marketing*, American Marketing Association Educators' Proceedings, ed. David Cravens and Peter Dickson (Chicago, IL: American Marketing Association, 1993), 28–35.

32. Christine Moorman, Gerald Zaltman, and Rohit Deshpande, "Relationships between Providers and Users of Market Research: The Dynamics of Trust within and between Organizations," *Journal of Marketing Research* 29 (August 1992): 314–29.

33. Robert M. Morgan and Shelby D. Hunt, "The Commitment–Trust Theory of Relationship Marketing," *Journal of Marketing* 58 (July 1994): 2–38.

34. Jagdish N. Sheth and Atul Parvatiyar, "Relationship Marketing in Consumer Markets: Antecedents and Consequences," *Journal of the Academy of Marketing Science* 23 (fall 1995): 255–71.

35. Robert A. Peterson, "Relationship Marketing and the Consumer," *Journal of the Academy of Marketing Science* 23 (fall 1995): 278–81.

36. This definition is based in part on one developed by Paula Fitzgerald Bone, "Determinants of Word-of-Mouth Communications during Product Consumption," in *Advances in Consumer Research*, ed. John F. Sherry Jr. and Brian Sternthal (Provo, UT: Association for Consumer Research, 1992), 19:579–83.

37. Stephen P. Morin, "Influentials Advising Their Friends to Sell Lots of High-Tech Gadgetry," *Wall Street Journal*, February 28, 1983, p. 30.

38. Elihu Katz and Paul Lazarsfeld, *Personal Influence* (Glencoe, IL: Free Press), 1955.

39. Moshe Givon, Vijay Mahajan, and Eitan Muller, "Software Piracy: Estimation of Lost Sales and the Impact on Software Diffusion," *Journal of Marketing* 59 (January 1995): 29–37.

40. Johan Arndt, "Role of Product-Related Conversations in the Diffusion of a New Product," *Journal of Marketing Research* 4 (August 1967): 292. Similarly, Ford Motor Company found that satisfied customers told 8 people about their cars, but dissatisfied customers told 22 about their complaints. See Damon Darlin, "Although U.S. Cars Are Improved, Imports Still Win Quality Survey," *Wall Street Journal*, December 16, 1985, p. 27.

41. Paul M. Herr, Frank R. Kardes, and John Kim, "Effects of Word-of-Mouth and Product-Attribute Information on Persuasion: An Accessibility–Diagnosticity Perspective," *Journal of Consumer Research* 17 (March 1991): 454–62.

42. Thomas Robertson, Joan Zielinski, and Scott Ward, *Consumer Behavior* (Glenview, IL: Scott, Foresman, 1984).

43. Ernst Dichter, "How Word-of-Mouth Advertising Works," *Harvard Business Review* 44 (November–December 1966): 148.

44. Everett M. Rogers, *Diffusion of Innovations*, 4th ed. (New York: Free Press, 1995). Also see William H. Redmond, "Contemporary Social Theory and the Bass Diffusion Model," in *Enhancing Knowledge Development in Marketing*, ed. Cornelia Dröge and Roger Calantone (Chicago, IL: American Marketing Association, 1996), pp. 7:176–81.

45. Thomas Robertson and James Myers, "Personality Correlates of Opinion Leadership and Innovative Buying Behavior," *Journal of Marketing Research* 6 (May 1969): 168. For an extended application of similar notions to high-technology adoptions, see Geoffrey A.

Moore, *Inside the Tornado: Marketing Strategies from Silicon Valley's Cutting Edge* (New York: Harper Business, 1995).

46. A. Parasuraman and Charles Colby, "A Scale for Measuring Customer's Technology Readiness: Replication, Refinement, and Implications for Service Organizations" (paper presented at the Fourth Vanderbilt/AMA Frontiers in Services Conference, September 24–26, 1998).

47. Lawrence Feick and Linda Price, "The Market Maven: A Diffuser of Marketplace Information," *Journal of Marketing* 51 (January 1987): 83–87. Also see Linda Price, Lawrence F. Feick, and Audrey Guskey, "Everyday Market Helping Behavior," *Journal of Public Policy and Marketing* 12 (fall 1995): 255–66.

48. Todd A. Mooradian, "The Five Factor Model and Market Mavenism," in *Advances in Consumer Research*, ed. Kim P. Corfman and John G. Lynch Jr. (Provo, UT: Association for Consumer Research, 1996), 23:260–63. Also see Michael T. Elliott and Anne E. Warfield, "Do Market Mavens Categorize Brands Differently?" in *Advances in Consumer Research*, ed. Leigh McAlister and Michael Rothschild (Provo, UT: Association for Consumer Research, 1993), 20:202–8; and Terrell E. Williams and Mark E. Slama, "Market Mavens' Purchase Decision Evaluative Criteria: Implications for Brand and Store Promotion Efforts," *Journal of Consumer Marketing* 12, no. 3 (1995): 4–21.

49. Stanley C. Hollander and Kathleen M. Rassuli, "Shopping with Other People's Money: The Marketing Management Implications of Surrogate-Mediated Consumer Decision Making," *Journal of Marketing* 63 (April 1999): 102–18.

50. Stephen J. Grove and Raymond P. Fisk, "The Service Experience as Theater," in *Advances in Consumer Research*, ed. John F. Sherry Jr. and Brian Sternthal (Provo, UT: Association for Consumer Research, 1992), 19:455–61.

51. Michael Guiry, "Consumer and Employee Roles in Service Encounters," in *Advances in Consumer Research*, ed. John F. Sherry Jr. and Brian Sternthal (Provo, UT: Association for Consumer Research, 1992), 19:666–72.

52. Linda L. Price, Eric J. Arnould, and Patrick Tierney, "Going to Extremes: Managing Service Encounters and Assessing Provider Performance," *Journal of Marketing* 59 (April 1995): 83–97. Also see Linda Price and Eric J. Arnould, "Commercial Friendships: Service Provider–Client Relationships in Context," *Journal of Marketing* 63 (October 1999): 38–56.

53. Henry Assael, *Consumer Behavior and Marketing Action* (Boston, MA: Kent, 1983).

54. Derived from C. Merle Crawford, *New Products Management* (Burr Ridge, IL: Irwin, 1994).

55. Hubert Gatignon and Thomas Robertson, "A Propositional Inventory for New Diffusion Research," *Journal of Consumer Research* 11 (March 1985): 849–67.

56. Ibid. Also see Kristiaan Helsen, Kamel Jedidi, and Wayne S. DeSarbo, "A New Approach to Country Segmentation Utilizing Multinational Diffusion Patterns," *Journal of Marketing* 57 (October 1993): 60–71.

57. Elizabeth Hirschman, "Symbolism and Technology as Sources of the Generation of Innovations," in *Advances in Consumer Research*, ed. Andrew Mitchell (Provo, UT: Association for Consumer Research, 1981), 9:537–41.

58. Gatignon and Robertson, "A Propositional Inventory."

59. Stephen Lynch, "Pokémon Provides the Blueprint for the Perfect Pre-Teen Fad," *McAllen Monitor*, November 25, 1999, p. 1D.

60. For an interesting examination of an unusual group (Harley-Davidson motorcycle enthusiasts), see John W. Schouten and James H. McAlexander, "Subcultures of Consumption: An Ethnography of the New Bikers," *Journal of Consumer Research* 22 (June 1995): 43–61.

CHAPTER 13

Culture and Popular Culture

When you have finished this chapter, you should be able to discuss each of the following concepts, together with their managerial implications:

1. The concept of culture.
2. Components of culture.
3. The role of consumer goods in culture.
4. Seven core American values.
5. Cultural values and means-end-chain models.
6. Rituals.
7. Cultural symbols.
8. Popular culture.
9. Four examples of popular culture.
10. Fashion and the characteristics of fashion trends.

Culture has been defined in a variety of ways. One classic definition states that **culture** is a set of socially acquired behavior patterns transmitted symbolically through language and other means to the members of a particular society.[1] Cultures may be distinguished in terms of their regulation of behavior, the attitudes of the people, the values of the people, the lifestyle of the people, and the degree of tolerance of other cultures.[2] Another perspective comes from the symbolic interactionists, who view culture as composed of a set of competing images transmitted through media via important signs and symbols.[3]

Broadly speaking, culture is a way of life. It includes the material objects of a society, such as guns, footballs, autos, religious texts, forks, and chopsticks. It is also composed of ideas and values; for example, most Americans endorse the belief that people have a right to choose between different brands of products. Culture consists of a mix of institutions that include legal, political, religious, and even business organizations. Some may even symbolically represent a society—for example, McDonald's or French champagne. The ways we dress, think, eat, and spend our leisure time are all components of our culture.

A number of additional ideas are necessary to gain an overall understanding of culture. A culture is *learned*—it is *not* present in our genes. It is transmitted from generation to generation, influencing future members of the society. The process of learning one's own culture is called **enculturation.** The difficult task of learning a new culture is called **acculturation.** Researchers have distinguished the level of acculturation from the level of cultural identification. **Cultural identification** refers to the society in which a person prefers to live. As such, it is *attitudinal* in nature. In contrast, the level of acculturation is *behavioral,* referring to the extent to which the actions of the immigrant conform to the norms and mores of a new culture.[4]

A culture is also *adaptive*. It changes as a society faces new problems and opportunities. Just as organisms evolve, so do cultures. They take on new traits and discard old ones to form a new cultural base. The "sexual revolution" that occurred during the 1960s in the United States exemplifies such cultural adaptation. The development of the birth-control pill helped create an environment conducive to changes in the way society viewed women and sexual relations. More recently, the AIDS epidemic has influenced sexually active people, whether American, Ghanaian, or Bulgarian, to return to more conservative sexual values.

Finally, culture satisfies needs. By providing **norms,** or rules of behavior, a culture gives an orderliness to society. It provides **values,** delineating what is right, good, and important. People need to know what is expected of them, what is right and wrong, and what they should do in various situations. Culture fulfills such societal requirements.

Culture is so pervasive and automatically accepted that it is difficult to identify the elements of one's own culture In fact, it has been suggested that understanding one's own culture requires knowing something of another culture—which provides the perspective needed to realize that other people really do things differently.[5] For example, by international standards Americans are fanatics concerning personal hygiene and cleanliness. Refrigerators became more accepted in this country when wooden exteriors were replaced with "sanitary" white enamel.[6] In most other parts of the world, deodorants are rarely used, baths much less frequently taken, and teeth rarely brushed. Indeed, toilet paper is unheard of in some areas of the globe. However, cultural discomfort is bidirectional. Visitors from mainland China are somewhat revolted when they learn that Americans actually sell food for animals in the same place where food is sold for people.

Components of Culture

Scholars use a number of key concepts to describe cultures. As noted earlier, each culture has a set of values denoting the end states that people should strive to attain. When comparing and contrasting cultures, one sees that the relative importance of various values differs.

All societies have a distinctive set of norms. Norms are more specific than values and dictate acceptable and unacceptable behaviors. Two general types of norms exist. **Enacted norms** are those that are explicitly expressed, sometimes in the form of laws. An example is which side of the road you drive a car. In the United States, people drive on the right side, but in England and much of the former British Empire (Australia,

Hong Kong, Kenya, etc.), as well as Japan, people drive on the left. When one of the authors first traveled to Britain, he was almost run over by a car. He was crossing a busy traffic intersection, and a car was turning left in front of him. The person in the left-hand seat was smiling at him—an action he took to indicate that he should cross the street. As he stepped off the curb, the car nearly knocked him over. He had been looking at the passenger rather than the driver.

The second type of norm is embedded in the culture and only learned through extensive interaction with the people of the culture. Called **cresive norms,** they include three types:[7]

> *Customs*. Handed down from generation to generation, customs apply to basic actions such as what ceremonies are held and the roles played by the sexes.

> *Mores*. Mores are customs that emphasize the moral aspects of behavior. Frequently, mores apply to forbidden behaviors, such as the exhibition of skin by women in fundamentalist Muslim countries.

> *Conventions*. Conventions describe how to act in everyday life, and they frequently apply to consumer behavior. For example, yard landscaping varies widely from society to society. In the United States, yards are frequently very large and covered with grass. In Germany yards frequently feature neat flower gardens. In Japan yards are small, are elaborately planted with bushes, and frequently feature the sound of bubbling water.

Another element of culture is the myths held by its people. **Myths** are stories that express key values and ideals of a society. For example, in the United States, a popular mythological character is Superman. Superman displays important values within the American culture, such as great strength and a mild-mannered exterior. He fights crime and injustice. As one authority on the topic has noted, myths help to (1) explain the origins of existence, (2) reveal a set of values for the society, and (3) provide models for personal conduct.[8]

The creation of myths is extremely important to marketers. For example, the Superman myth was created via a comic book. Other consumer myths include fictional characters, such as Santa Claus, the Phantom, E.T., the Playboy Bunny, and the Easter Bunny. In addition, cultural myths may also be based on real people, such as George Washington cutting down the cherry tree and refusing to lie about it. A more recent cultural myth is based on Sam Walton, who built Wal-Mart and became the richest man in the United States while maintaining a frugal lifestyle.

Each culture also has its own set of symbols, rituals, and values to which marketers can tie their products and services. For example, in the United States, the eagle is a symbol representing strength, courage, and patriotism. Companies wanting to create such an image may use the eagle in their advertising or packaging: Commercials for Miller Beer, for example, feature an eagle. In Australia the koala is an important symbol that is used by companies to link themselves symbolically to the country. Various rituals are also important to culture. In late January of each year millions of people in the United States gather together in small groups, sit in front of a television set, and eat fattening food while watching the Super Bowl. To increase interest in similar rituals abroad, in the 1990s the U.S. National Basketball Association (NBA) targeted Asia. NBA games can now be seen in most countries in the area, and in countries like China where the sport is not well-known, the NBA and sporting goods suppliers are sponsoring competitions and clinics.[9] Similarly, National Football League (NFL) exhibition games are played in Japan, Europe, and Mexico. Cultural rituals may be borrowed from one country and spread to another. For example, the *quinceañera* is a coming-out ceremony for 15-year-old Hispanic girls that has been introduced into the United States from Mexico.

Values also vary widely across cultures. As an example, in the United States, the freedom to own guns is deeply ingrained. In the early 1990s, gun ownership by women increased by 20 percent (although only about 13 percent now own guns).[10] Other countries have less liberal laws for gun possession, and these laws reflect a different set of values about owning guns.

The Cultural Matrix

The cultural matrix shown in Figure 13.1 visually depicts three important sets of factors that compose a culture. It is the intertwining of sets of values, of the institutional–social environment, and of the material environment that creates the overall cultural fabric of a society. As shown in the figure, the material environment consists of such factors as the technical–scientific level of the society, the extent and type of natural resources present, the geographical features of the society, and its degree of economic prosperity. The institutional–social environment includes the legal, political, religious, business, and subcultural institutions and groups that compose the society. Discussed at length in chapter 14, subcultures are subdivisions of a national culture centered on some unifying characteristic, such as social class or ethnicity.

A culture is also influenced by the dominant values of the society. Values will be discussed in a separate section in the chapter. In the American culture, key values include individualism, freedom, and achievement.

It should also be noted that culture can be affected by additional factors, such as natural disasters and wars. For example, early European settlers decimated entire civilizations of native peoples in the Americas by bringing in diseases against which the natives had no defense. As another example, during the recent fighting in Bosnia and Herzegovina, warnings of the long-term effects of smoking were laughed away. When each day brings the possibility of being killed by snipers or bombs, you don't worry about developing cancer in 30 years. The extremes of war illustrate that the types of

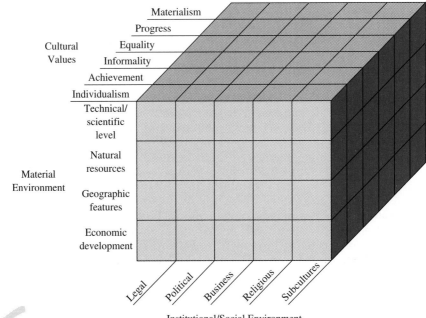

Figure 13.1   The cultural matrix.

consumer goods that are valued in a culture depend a great deal on the particular circumstances faced by the people.

As time passes, changes occur in the external environment, social institutions, and values found within the cultural matrix. In addition, a constant interplay of movements and countermovements takes place within the matrix. As a result, new ideas and trends are constantly bubbling to the surface. These ideas and trends form what is called *popular culture.*

Popular culture is constantly changing, bringing variations in fashion and lifestyles. These changes may lead to corporate catastrophes or marketing opportunities. For example, in the 1980s popular culture in the United States emphasized fitness and slimness. Marketers of running shoes, weight-lifting machines, and related athletic equipment experienced explosive growth. During this time period, the sales of a small Tulsa, Oklahoma–based company named Stair Master Corporation exploded as part-time athletes purchased these expensive devices to simulate the exercise of climbing stairs. However, popular culture changed. Between 1985 and 1990, participation in fitness declined by 10 percent.[11] The decline in physical activity occurred for all age groups—not just the aging baby boomers. Such changes created massive problems for companies selling fitness devices. Meanwhile, a shift from hard physical exercise to walking occurred, and manufacturers of walking shoes experienced rapid growth. Then, in the mid-1990s gyms reported a roughly threefold gain in participation in boxing, while parents began enrolling their children in private gym programs.[12] The challenge to marketers in the exercise industry is to anticipate these trends.

Chapter Overview

In this chapter we take up culture and its impact on consumer behavior. The chapter begins by analyzing the role of consumer goods within a culture. Next, we relate core American values to the cultural meanings that consumers hope to attach to themselves. The third and fourth sections present information on cultural rituals and symbols. Finally, we discuss popular culture, which represents the shorter trends that occur within the overall fabric of a society.

THE ROLE OF CONSUMER GOODS IN A CULTURE

Consumer-behavior researchers have long been interested in the role consumer goods play in a culture. Figure 13.2 diagrams the relationship among individual consumers, consumer goods, and the culturally constituted world. The significance of goods lies in their ability to carry and communicate cultural meaning.[13] **Cultural meanings** refer to these values, norms, and shared beliefs that are symbolically communicated. They are transferred from the culturally constituted world to consumer goods and from these goods to individuals.

The culturally constituted world is the lens through which individuals interpret the world around them. It is made up of the values, mores, and norms that define a particular society. It forms a kind of blueprint designating how people should act and behave. As shown in Figure 13.2, the transfer of meaning from culture to object may occur through advertising and fashion systems, while the transfer of meaning from consumer goods to individuals may take place through various rituals, including possession, exchange, grooming, and divestment.

Advertising is a conduit through which meaning pours from the culturally constituted world to consumer goods. By positioning a product, the advertiser imbues it with meaning. For example, Pontiac has used the theme "We build excitement" extensively. The company's goal is to position the brand as exciting and youthful. Through

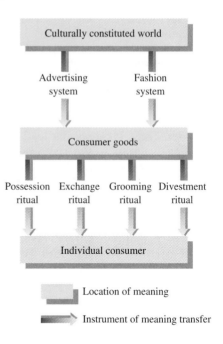

Figure 13.2

Communicating cultural meaning.

Source: Reproduced with permission from Grant McCracken, "Culture and Consumption: A Theoretical Account of the Structure and Movement of the Cultural Meaning of Consumer Goods," *Journal of Consumer Research* 13 (June 1986): 71–84.

this positioning process, meanings are drawn from the culturally constituted world and transferred to the automobile through the advertisements.

The fashion system is a broader, more diffuse set of agents of transfer. It includes magazines, newspapers, opinion leaders, and at the margins of society, hippies, punks, and gays. The characters in television shows often give meaning to various products and services. Television programs such as *Dynasty* and *Dallas* have acted to transfer meaning to clothing and accessories that represent the nouveau riche in American society.

Figure 13.2 depicts consumer goods and services as transferring cultural meanings to individuals. In essence, people use goods to link cultural meanings to themselves. If the meaning that we attach to our material objects is understood by others, we successfully portray who and what we are to others. As one authority has stated, "What can be said of clothing can be said of virtually all other high-involvement product categories and several low-involvement ones. Clothing, transportation, food, housing exteriors and interiors, and adornment all serve as media for the expression of the cultural meaning that constitutes the world.[14]

It has been argued that rituals are used to transfer meanings of objects to the individual. A ritual is a symbolic series of actions that link the person to the material good. The exchange of gifts at birthdays and Christmas illustrates such rituals. Gifts possess symbolic properties that act to transfer cultural meanings, such as love, from one person to another. We will discuss rituals in more detail later in the chapter.

CULTURAL VALUES IN THE UNITED STATES

Values are enduring beliefs about ideal end states and modes of conduct. In general, values tend to be few in number. They are more abstract than attitudes and serve as standards to guide actions, attitudes, and judgments. Specific attitudes about objects tend to reflect and support a person's values. Within a society **cultural values** represent the shared meanings of ideal end states and modes of conduct. Thus, cultural values depict a shared meaning of what is important and of what end states of existence people should seek.[15]

The values that make up the culturally constituted world in the United States have a variety of sources. One important source of our culture, of course, is the European heritage of the early settlers of the United States and Canada. The flight from religious persecution and authoritarian monarchies indelibly etched into the American culture the values of individualism and freedom. Some have argued that the frontier created the values of rugged individualism, informality, equality, and diligence.[16] Certainly, the Judeo-Christian heritage of early Americans also influenced what were to become core American values.[17]

A number of authors have developed lists of core American values. Frequently mentioned values include beliefs in the importance of the following:

1. Individualism	6. Achievement
2. Youthfulness	7. Efficiency
3. Progress	8. Informality
4. Materialism	9. Equality
5. Activity	10. Distrust of government

Other values sometimes mentioned include freedom, external conformity, humanitarianism, authority, respect for institutions, mastery of the environment, and religion. The so-called Protestant ethic also flows deeply through the social fabric of the United States. Thus, values relating to hard work and frugality are important to many Americans. Such themes are sometimes used by advertisers. It has also been proposed that one advantage of pioneer brands is that the notion of being a pioneer is a manifestation of the values of innovation and progress.[18]

In every society there are also countercurrents to the traditional cultural values. For example, in the United States, respect for institutions has been steadily falling since the mid-1970s. As noted earlier, culture is adaptive, and one should expect to occasionally see movements that are inconsistent with the traditional values of a culture.

Consumer Research on Cultural Values

One important research issue concerns how cultural values influence specific consumption decisions. Figure 13.3 shows the sequence of moving from global values to domain-specific values to evaluations of product attributes.[19] **Global values** consist of

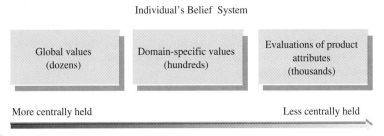

Figure 13.3 Organization of the value-attitude system.

Source: Adopted by permission from Donald E. Vinson, Jerome Scott, and Lawrence Lamont, "The Role of Personal Values in Marketing and Consumer Behavior," *Journal of Marketing* 41 (April 1977): 46, published by the American Marketing Association.

enduring beliefs about desired states of existence. **Domain-specific values** are beliefs pertaining to more concrete consumption activities. Examples include beliefs that manufacturers should give prompt service, guarantee their products, help eliminate environmental pollution, be truthful, and so forth. Evaluations of product attributes are highly specific beliefs about individual products. For example, how well does a Corvette handle? Is it easy to repair?

Researchers have found that people with different global values also exhibit divergent domain-specific values and product evaluations. Indeed, individual differences in global values translate to markedly different product preferences. For example, people whose global values emphasize logic, an exciting life, and self-respect tend to prefer compact cars and outdoor recreation, whereas those whose global values emphasize national security and salvation are more attracted to standard-sized cars and television.

Figure 13.3 exemplifies what are called **means-end-chain models.** Means–end chain models identify the linkages between consumer desires for specific product features with increasingly abstract concepts, such as benefits desired and values that are important to an individual. For example, consider a person who desires to purchase a car with a small fuel-efficient engine. Three major benefits result from this feature— good gas mileage, lower purchase and operating costs, and protection of the environment. In turn, these benefits lead to a frugal lifestyle. Finally, a frugal lifestyle leads to the terminal value of a clean environment. In sum, the purchase of a car with the attribute of a small engine acts as a means to reach the desired end state of a cleaner environment. The process of probing to identify the linkages between means (i.e., attributes) and terminal values (i.e., end states) is called **laddering.**[20]

As we will show later in the chapter, values are also closely connected to social change. As the culture of a society changes, so do the values of the individuals that make up the society. Changes in values can directly influence managerial strategy. For example, Stouffer's recognized that the values of many female grocery shoppers were shifting from emphasizing their roles as "providers for the family" and moving toward self-fulfillment. Acting upon this recognition, the company successfully introduced a line of frozen entrees that were positioned as fulfillment oriented. In fact, the positioning phrase used in advertisements was "Set yourself free."

Research on the List-of-Values Scale. An index developed specifically for consumer research on values is called the list-of-values (LOV) scale. One study using the scale investigated how values in the United States changed between 1976 and 1986.[21] The researchers conducted a national survey of consumers in 1976 and again in 1986. Overall values were quite stable over the time span. Between the 1976 and 1986 figures, the correlation ratio was .91 for males and .77 for females. These high correlations indicate only small changes in values. Note, however, that the correlation for females was lower than that of males, indicating a greater change in women's values. An analysis assessing the change in values by age showed that the most change occurred among people under 30.

Research on the LOV scale has shown that people's values influence their attitudes, which in turn influence behavior. One study investigated the characteristics of those who shop for natural foods. The results revealed that people who emphasize internal values (i.e., self-fulfillment, excitement, sense of accomplishment, and self-respect) like and purchase natural foods more than do people who emphasize external values (i.e., sense of belonging, being well respected, and having security).[22] A more recent study suggests that in the 1990s a "role-relaxed" person began to appear. The role-relaxed consumer is less concerned with appearing "normal" and is more driven by internal values. Consistent with this notion, role-relaxed baby boomers score lower on the importance of being well respected than the score on this value in the sample for 1986. In other words, the importance of being well respected seems to be dropping in the 1990s.[23]

Research on the Value of Materialism. Perhaps the value with the greatest impact on consumer behavior is materialism. We have already discussed materialism as an individual difference variable in chapter 6. A number of researchers have attempted to identify whether the emphasis on the cultural value of materialism has changed in the United States. They approached the question by content analyzing popular literature, such as comic books and popular novels. (Content analysis involves coding the themes of written material into various categories.) One study investigated the frequency with which materialistic themes appeared in several comic books such as *Archie, Uncle Scrooge McDuck,* and *Richie Rich.* An example of a materialistic theme is found in a 1965 edition of *Archie:* "Veronica tells Archie that having everything she wants bores her, and Betty convinces Archie to go out with her instead so that Veronica feels challenged. It works, but Veronica wins, thanks to her new outfits that catch Archie's eye."[24]

After examining the time period from the 1940s to the mid-1980s, the author of the study reported finding little evidence of changes in materialistic themes over the 40-year period. Interestingly, he argued that the comic books may have a positive socializing influence on children. The values portrayed in the comic books were generally positive ones. The stories indicated that wealth can be either good or bad. When the role models acted poorly, bad fortune occurred to them. The wealthy characters in the stories were encouraged not to flaunt their riches, and the deserving poor were portrayed as honest, intelligent, and clean—people who lacked only the opportunity or circumstance to be wealthy.

Considering sources other than comic books, however, one does find evidence of changes in materialism as a value. One study, for example, investigated the frequency with which brand names were mentioned in popular novels.[25] It found a more than fivefold increase in the usage of brand names between 1946 and 1975. Some critics charge that the manner in which companies name products is making the "sacred profane." For example, "True" cigarettes and "First Romance" novels can be viewed as taking sacred words and symbols and making them profane by connecting them with products. Indeed, the charges seem to have some merit. The word *truth* could be considered tainted by an association with a cigarette brand—especially because tobacco companies have avoided telling consumers the truth about the harmful effects of smoking.

When one looks at the themes in advertisements, one gains another perspective on materialism in American society. Some authors have distinguished two types of materialism—instrumental and terminal. **Instrumental materialism** involves obtaining a material good in order to perform some activity. It is viewed as benign because the good is an instrument for the accomplishment of something else. In contrast, **terminal materialism** involves the possession of a good as an end in itself. Terminal materialism is viewed as potentially destructive because it leads to such unbecoming traits as envy, possessiveness, selfishness, and greed.[26]

One study investigated 2,000 print advertisements having to do with the interior or the exterior of houses. The ads, spanning the years 1901 through 1979, were content analyzed to determine the frequency with which material goods were cast in terms of their appeal or theme. The results revealed that utilitarian themes, in which the product's benefits were described in terms of practicality and efficiency, decreased in frequency over the time span. In contrast, themes involving luxury appeals increased dramatically, indicating an increase in materialistic themes. However, although appeals to luxury have increased substantially over time, the underlying themes of such ads have more frequently been of an instrumental nature. As the authors explained:

> It is also evident that this materialistic emphasis has been more involved with instrumental themes of using the advertised items than with terminally materialistic themes of having the product for its own sake. If we have become a culture of consumption, it does not yet appear that this consumption is an end rather than a means to other ends.[27]

Do men or do women exhibit greater amounts of materialism? A recent study investigated the materialism and sharing behavior of men and women in Germany and Canada. Across both nationalities women were found to be more sharing, generous, nurturant, and caring than men. One explanation suggested by the authors was that material goods mean different things to men than to women. For men material goods help establish power and competitive relations, whereas for women material goods are a part of social relations.[28]

We usually think of the United States as a clearly materialistic society, but how does it compare in this respect to other industrialized nations? One study compared the degree of materialism in the United States and the Netherlands—countries whose prosperity is about equal.[29] Questionnaires were completed by middle-class households in both countries. The results indicated that levels of materialism were highly similar in each nation across the various scales. The only difference was that the sample in the Netherlands revealed slightly higher levels of "possessiveness" toward material goods than American consumers.

In another study researchers compared materialistic values among consumers in Europe, the United States, and Turkey.[30] These results revealed that Turkish consumers were simultaneously more materialistic and more generous than American and European consumers. In explaining the results, the authors suggested that factors unique to the Turkish culture may account for the surprising findings: Turkey has an ancient history of prosperity, a cultural legacy that may have accustomed the Turks to the idea that they can afford to be generous.

Cross-cultural comparisons of materialistic values suggest that one must avoid simple statements about *why* people are materialistic. Clearly, a variety of factors influence materialistic values—including the overall prosperity and industrialization of a nation, as well as its particular cultural history. The research on materialism as a value in the United States has yielded mixed findings. Some studies find little evidence of an increase in materialism, whereas others find ample evidence. As the housing advertisement study suggested, the answer may lie in the type of materialism studied. Americans do seem to have a mistrust of owning things for their own sake. An emphasis on terminal materialism is inconsistent with American values that emphasize practicality and efficiency. Nonetheless, there is overwhelming evidence that the United States is a materialistic society. As one author noted, "The findings indicate the pervasiveness of a consumer culture in the mid-twentieth century and suggest that the baby-boom generation, reared in material abundance, may be unabashedly materialistic."[31]

CULTURAL RITUALS

Cultural rituals are socially standardized sequences of actions that are periodically repeated, provide meaning, and involve the use of cultural symbols. Rituals can be public or private. They vary from large-scale civic rituals, such as the Super Bowl, to private rituals involving prayer. Ritual behaviors are "scripted" so that they are formal and prescribed by convention, and in many cases they involve the consumption and use of products.

These characteristics of rituals are embodied in its formal definition: The term *ritual* refers to an expressive, symbolic activity constructed of culturally sanctioned behaviors that occur in a fixed, episodic sequence and tend to be repeated over time. Ritual behavior is dramatically scripted and acted out and is performed with formality, seriousness, and inner intensity.[32]

Rituals should be distinguished from habits. Habits are also repetitive, engaged in over time, and can have inner intensity. For example, most of us have a sequence of actions we follow to go from home to work or school. Such sequences of actions, however, are considered habits rather than rituals. Rituals differ from habits on three criteria. First, rituals are prescribed by society rather than by the individual. Second, people are more consciously aware of what takes place in a ritual than they are of what is going on in a habit. Third, rituals have greater symbolic meaning than habits and have more affect attached to them.[33]

Table 13.1 presents a typology of ritual experience. As evident in the table, rituals exist at various levels of abstraction. At their most abstract—as in religious, magic, and aesthetic rituals—they have cosmological value. At their most concrete—as in the grooming and mating rituals of animals—rituals are biologically determined. The types of rituals shown in the table also point out the functional value of rituals. For example, the cultural rituals of graduation and marriage act as rites of passage that symbolically denote a change in a person's status. Similarly, rituals can serve to pass on knowledge and create bonds within groups. Thus, holiday celebrations, the exchange of birthday gifts, and office luncheons are enacted in order to fulfill specific goals within groups.[34]

Rituals commonly have four elements: artifacts, scripts, performance roles, and an audience. Consider, for example, the various aspects of a college basketball game. One can identify in this ritual the artifacts (basketballs, pompons, beer, etc.), the script

A Typology of Ritual Experience

Primary Behavior Source	Ritual Type	Examples
Cosmology	Religious	Baptism, meditation, mass
	Magic	"Healing," gambling
	Aesthetic	Performing arts
Cultural values	Rites of passage	Graduation, marriage
	Cultural	Festivals, Valentine's Day, Groundhog Day, Super Bowl
Group learning	Civic	Memorial Day parade, elections, trials
	Small group	Pancake Day, fraternity initiation, business negotiations, office luncheons
	Family	Mealtime, bedtime, birthday and holiday celebrations
Individual aims and emotions	Personal	Grooming, household rituals
Biology	Animal	Greeting, mating

Source: Dennis Rook, "The Ritual Dimension of Consumer Behavior," *Journal of Consumer Research* 12 (December 1985): 251–64. Reprinted with permission.

TABLE 13.1

(the rules of the game), performance roles (players, referees, coaches), and the audience. Of course, rituals vary in formality and in the extent to which each of the four elements is present.

At the cultural level, researchers have identified four types of rituals.[35] **Exchange rituals** involve the exchange of gifts, information, goods, or money. **Possession rituals** involve acts in which a person engages to lay claim to, display, and protect possessions. For example, housewarming parties and overzealous car waxing can be viewed as possession rituals. **Grooming rituals** act to ensure that the special perishable properties of clothing, hairstyles, and looks are present. In some cases the grooming ritual is not performed on the consumer but on a product. An example is the constant grooming of lawns by many homeowners. A fourth type of ritual is the **divestment ritual,** which may be performed to erase the meaning associated with the previous owner of the good. For example, after buying an older house, consumers will frequently engage in cleaning and redecorating behaviors in order to lay claim to the possession. Similarly, a divestment ritual may occur when a person disposes of a personalized item, such as a special coat, car, or house. When one of the authors sold a prized Camaro and asked the new owner for a ride to work, for example, the new owner asked if he wouldn't like to drive it one last time. She provided him with an additional opportunity for a divestment ritual.

The list of consumption-related rituals is long. They include rites of passage (e.g., weddings, baby showers, and funerals), religious ceremonies, holiday festivities (e.g., Christmas, Thanksgiving), family activities (e.g., television viewing at prescribed times, summer vacation, and Sunday dinner), and large-scale public rituals, (e.g., singing the national anthem, watching parades and sports events).[36] The ritual of Christmas has an unwritten "tree rule": Married couples with children should put up trees. Unmarried persons with no living children should not put up trees. Some of these rituals have both a religious element and an added, commercial element. For example, Easter has both religious and secular significance.

For manufacturers and retailers, success often lies in recognizing the importance of culturally prescribed consumer rituals and tying the company's products to these rituals. By identifying ritualistic patterns of behavior, marketers can design and promote products that might serve as artifacts in the activities. For example, the beauty ritual involves a long series of steps for many women. Some adroit marketers (such as Clinique) have attempted to lengthen the ritual by adding new steps and products, such as using an astringent to close facial pores after washing. DonnaKaran, Clinique and others have assembled similar multistep skin-care systems for men, thus far with only modest success. (Perhaps men are offended by the original use for perfume: counteracting the stench of burning flesh during sacrificial ceremonies).[37] The idea is to change grooming habits into rituals prescribed by the firm by promising to provide the important consumer benefit of more-attractive skin.

A final point of interest to retailers and service providers is the notion of rituals as catalysts for consumers to construct "small worlds"—that is, to develop and maintain social relationships. Although the rituals may differ ("male bonding" occurs at sports events, whereas women might socialize at an arts performance), the end result is similar. If facilities and events facilitate the development of small worlds of interconnected consumers, perhaps including a sense of belonging, the value provided may be enhanced. For example, some participants have noted that they attend certain events more for social purposes than for the value of the actual performance or event.[38]

CULTURAL SYMBOLS

In addition to values and rituals, cultures have symbols. **Symbols** are entities that represent ideas and concepts.[39] Chapter 3 discussed semiotics, a field that investigates the meaning of symbols. As noted there, symbols are important because they communicate complex ideas rapidly with a minimum of effort. For example, if a company wants to communicate the concept of patriotism, a useful symbol is the American flag. By adroitly using symbols, companies and advertisers can tie cultural values to their products or services, enhancing their product's attractiveness to consumers.

It can be argued that people "consume" symbols.[40] That is, products may be evaluated, purchased, and consumed based in part on their symbolic value. For a product to have symbolic value, it must have a shared reality among consumers, meaning that large numbers of consumers must have a common conception of the product's symbolic meaning. For example, in order for an automobile to have "prestige" value, others in the relevant social group must view it in the same manner as the buyer.[41]

Companies frequently symbolize the characteristics of their products via the names chosen for them: One expert insists that names must express the "soul" of the product, as well as strike an emotional chord with consumers.[42] For example, auto manufacturers have been fond of naming their products after cats, suggesting swiftness, agility, and aggressiveness. Examples include the Jaguar, Cougar, Lynx, Wildcat, Bobcat, and Puma.

Numerous symbols exist in American culture. The symbol of money—and occasionally power or greed—is the dollar sign ($). One symbol to denote Christian spiritual meanings is the cross. A smoking pipe might be used to symbolize contemplation. Similarly, wearing glasses can indicate intelligence and possibly physical weakness—á la Clark Kent, Superman's alter ego. Planting a tree suggests permanence, and so forth.

Colors also have symbolic value. In the United States, black can have a variety of symbolic meanings, depending on the context. When worn at funerals, it indicates mourning. In contrast, black bras, garter belts, and panties suggest high levels of sex appeal. Blue indicates coolness—for example, "Ice Blue Aqua-Velva." White means purity, as in wedding dresses and milk products. Pink is feminine, and for babies blue is masculine.

Clothing also has important symbolic meaning for consumers. Table 13.2 identifies a variety of functions that clothing may have for consumers, as well as the potential symbolic value of such clothing. One of the functions of clothing is to act as an emblem of group membership. The popularity of T-shirts and hats that possess a logo

Clothing: Its Functional Uses and Symbolic Meanings

Function of Apparel	Use of Apparel	Symbolic Meaning	Example of Apparel
Camouflage	Hide the body	Sexually conservative	Robes
	Cover blemishes or injuries		Cosmetics, patches
Display	Reveal body parts	Sexually explicit	Tight or skimpy clothing
Utilitarian	Protect the body	"Down-to-earth," practical	Some jeans, raincoats
Aesthetic	Beautify or enhance the body	Love of beauty	Jewelry
Souvenir	Reminder of the past	Love of family or experience	Charm bracelet
Emblematic	Group membership	Show membership in a group	Fraternity jacket
	Connotative	Reveal social class or wealth	Expensive jewelry

Source: Adapted in part from a table in Rebecca Holman, "Apparel as Communication," in *Symbolic Consumer Behavior*, Proceedings of the Conference on Consumer Aesthetics and Symbolic Consumption, ed. Elizabeth Hirschman and Morris Holbrook, (Ann Arbor, MI: Association for Consumer Research, May 1980), 8.

TABLE 13.2

illustrates the symbolic nature of clothing. Clothing with designer logos faded after great popularity in the 1980s, but these logos are now back in big, oversized versions.[43]

Although all cultures use symbols, they may be more important in some cultures than in others. For example, Japan has been called the empire of signs. Indeed, this statement is true both literally and figuratively. Japan's urban landscape is cluttered with signs, some flashing incessantly and others meticulously lettered. Figuratively, the Japanese culture engages in a large number of symbolic activities. The practice of exchanging business cards (*meishi*) has a symbolic function. The great care taken in wrapping and packaging plays a role in the spiritual and cultural life of the country.

The Japanese are also fond of using foreign words in promotional materials that may have several symbolic meanings. The foreign words may connote something new or modern, they may indicate a Western influence, and they may symbolize prestige. One researcher attempted to count the number of English loanwords in a Japanese dictionary but gave up after recording 7,000 instances. Fully 80 percent of loanwords in Japanese are taken from English. Examples of such loanwords include *botsu* (boots), *tobako* (cigarette), and *kitchin* (kitchen).

Two researchers spent a summer in Japan investigating the use of English loanwords by Japanese companies.[44] They observed that Japanese beverage companies frequently include English prose in their advertising. For example, one ad for Kirin beer was written in English: "The legendary KIRIN is a symbol of good luck. Open up KIRIN today, and you'll see what it is all about." Japanese promotional messages frequently use similes and metaphors that sound very strange to Americans. One beverage, called Pokka White Sour, featured a promotional message in English: "Pokka White Sour is refreshing and white like Alpine snow. Its sour taste of yogurt will extend on your tongue softly and be a sweetheart." This usage is merely odd. Contrast it with the far less hospitable Pocari Sweat soft-drink brand name.

We frequently assume that symbols are universal, when they in fact are not. For example, a picture of a snake may represent sex, evil, medicine, energy, or other ideas. In the United States, a cross is typically a religious symbol. In Taiwan, crossing your fingers at right angles represents the number 10.

POPULAR CULTURE

What are the two largest exports by U.S. companies in the 1990s? Aircraft and related equipment were ranked number one, and popular culture was ranked number two. Just one component of the popular culture scene (popular culture software, which includes movies, music, television programming, and home video) provided a surplus of $8 billion to the U.S. balance of trade. In fact, recordings, films, and books together produce almost as much value as civil aircraft, the only area in which the United States is still considered the world's best.[45]

So what is popular culture? Many definitions have been proposed. For the purposes of understanding its impact on consumer behavior, the following definition is most appropriate: "**Popular culture** is the culture of mass appeal." As such, popular culture has the following characteristics:[46]

1. It taps into the experiences and values of a significant portion of the population.
2. It does not require any special knowledge to understand it.
3. It is produced in such a way that large numbers of people have easy access to it.
4. It most frequently influences behavior that does not involve work or sleep.

To understand popular culture, one must distinguish it from "high" culture. **High culture** is exclusive in style, content, and appeal. It frequently harks back to the "old masters" of art, theater, music, and literature. To the advocates of high culture, popular culture frequently appears loud, brassy, and even immoral. The lifestyle of hip-hop music stars is frequently used as an illustration.

As many scholars have noted, however, the distinction between "high" and "popular" culture can be hazy. For example, when Walt Disney produced *Fantasia*, he borrowed from high culture the music of great classical composers, such as Beethoven. A huge success, *Fantasia* has become part of popular culture even though it employs elements of high culture. Indeed, Shakespeare's works originated as popular culture by appealing to mass audiences who sought entertainment in the working-class theaters of his day. Similarly, Paul McCartney and Eric Clapton, once considered rather mindless Brit-pop musicians, are today part of the music world's cultural "establishment."

Examples of Popular Culture

Because popular culture involves anything that has mass appeal and is used in nonwork activities, the range of subject matter encompassed by the term is extremely large.

Advertising. Advertising becomes popular culture when its images, themes, and icons become embraced by the mass public. Examples of figures from advertising that have achieved popular culture status include Ronald McDonald, Tony the Tiger, the Energizer Bunny, and the Pillsbury Doughboy.

Television. As a medium, television acts to create popular culture. Indeed, one scholar has argued that television "has become preeminently *the* popular culture and a primary purveyor of values and ideas."[47] Researchers have found that heavy television viewing affects consumers' views of the world. For example, heavy television viewers have been found to overestimate both the amount of violence in the United States and the degree of affluence in the United States.[48] As a result, a rating system has been devised for television shows to help parents monitor the amount of violence their children are seeing.

Music. Music can also shape popular culture. The phenomenon of rap music illustrates the enormous impact of music on the consumer behavior of a generation. The beginnings of rap music can be traced back to 1968 where it was invented in the Bronx section of New York City. The first rap label was established in 1979. Then, in 1981 Blondie's hit song "Rapture" rose to number one on the charts. In 1985 MTV began a rap program. The first rap-based movie was produced in 1990. By 1993 rap moved into mainstream popular culture when Coca-Cola employed rap music in its advertising with performers dressed in the baggy, hip-hop fashions associated with the music phenomenon.[49]

Fashion. The concept of fashion can be defined either narrowly or broadly. According to the narrow interpretation, fashion is identified with clothing, costumes, and bodily adornment. For example, the practice of body piercing for the purpose of adornment exemplifies fashion in popular culture.

The broader definition of fashion extends the concept to include any use of products to express one's self-image or role position. **Fashion,** then, is a set of behaviors temporarily adopted by a people because the behaviors are perceived to be socially appropriate for the time and situation.[50] From this perspective fashion involves the adoption of symbols to provide an identity. The symbols may include clothing, jewelry, automobiles, housing, artwork, and any other socially visible object that communicates meaning within the popular culture.

Even the books that people read (or whether they read books at all) can act as symbols that communicate information to others. A consumer researcher analyzed the consumption ideology found in a best-selling author's detective stories—Robert B. Parker, who writes the *Spenser for Hire* series. Noting that detective stories have displaced the cowboy novel in popular culture, the researcher stated that such novels express certain American values. In these novels the detective acts as a type of mythical hero who possesses special powers and who overcomes weaknesses often involving alcohol and problems with women. An important theme in the Spenser series is knowing how and what to consume. As the researcher of the study, Cathy Goodwin, noted, "Knowing how and what to consume, but sometimes consciously choosing to be inappropriate, is evidence of superiority, strength or originality."[51]

Fashion is inherently dynamic as it constantly changes over time. One cannot overemphasize the importance of the symbolic value of fashion. Indeed, symbolic value may overwhelm any "utilitarian" value. One merely has to look at the pain endured by women who wear corsets and high-heeled shoes to understand the relative weight people give to symbolic versus utilitarian value of the consumer behavior. Of course, men have their own fashions and, like women, endure physical discomfort to look good—witness hair transplants. Indeed, men dressed about as fashionably as women until the "so-called masculine renunciation of lavish dress in the mid-eighteenth century."[52]

Fashion trends have a number of characteristics:[53]

1. *Type of trend.* Two basic types of fashion trends have been identified. In the **cyclical fashion trend,** members of a society adopt styles that are progressively more extreme in one direction or another. Examples include skirt lengths and tie widths. In the **classic fashion trend,** particular looks become "classic," such as the blue pin-striped suit.

2. *Speed of trend.* The trend may be very fast or slow. Some trends are simple fads and come and go quickly. An example of such a fad would be dyeing one's hair with Kool-Aid. A long-lasting trend is shaving of facial hair by most men and of underarm hair by most women in the United States.

3. *Fashion turning points.* Within cyclical fashion trends, a turning point eventually occurs because a technological or cultural barrier has been reached. For example, in the late eighteenth century, the hoopskirt became progressively wider until women could no longer move through doorways. Similarly, in the early 1970s and again in the 1990s, miniskirts headed upward until a cultural barrier was reached in the form of preserving some modesty. Perhaps the same thing will happen with body piercing, as convenient locations of the body are increasingly "occupied."

4. *The degree of individual-level adherence to the trend.* Although fashion trends can be discerned in the overall society, at the individual level each person appears to behave in an almost random manner regarding the trend. Indeed, some people will take delight in dressing or behaving in exactly the opposite manner prescribed by the trend. In turn, these countertrends may become the basis for new fads.

How Popular Culture Develops

As noted earlier, there are numerous trends and countertrends within the overall cultural matrix of a society. These arise from the interplay of changes in the material environment, the institutional–social environment, and cultural values. The shorter-term trends that bubble up from the cultural matrix come and in most cases, go. Fashion trends were once set by designers, but now many trends start with teenagers. Specialized market research firms find "cool kids" and pay them hundreds of dollars to interview their friends on videotape. This sort of research led to Reebock's introduction of shoes in pastel colors and Burlington Industries' introduction of jeans in darker shades of blue.[54] Given the name *popular culture,* these mass trends, while they last, may influence tens of millions of people in their everyday life.

As popular culture trends arise from the cultural matrix, media and opinion leaders must begin to communicate the symbols that carry the meanings of the trend. The media include television, radio, print, movies, the theater, and so on. Important mass-opinion leaders include performers, songwriters, journalists, advertisers, sports celebrities, and various editors, although other important people can act as opinion leaders as well. For example, in 1961 John F. Kennedy broke custom by walking down Pennsylvania Avenue for his inauguration without a hat. The sight of the youthful, bare-headed president resulted in a shift in fashion that devastated the men's hat industry.

In sum, the diffusion of popular culture occurs through a process that mimics the spread of innovations (discussed in chapter 12). The spread of popular culture can be fast or slow. It diffuses through a process that closely approximates the multi-step diffusion model. It has a life cycle that can be short (a fad) or very long (e.g., the Beatles continue to be popular to this day). But its impact cannot be underestimated. Marketers who want to link their products to the fads and fashions that push the hot buttons of masses of people should develop an advanced understanding of popular culture.

MANAGERIAL IMPLICATIONS

The consumer-behavior concepts that emerge from investigations of culture and popular culture can be applied to each of the PERMS managerial application areas. The following sections summarize some of the possibilities.

Positioning and Differentiation

Brands can be positioned and differentiated based upon important cultural values. Only one brand, of course, can hold the position as largest of the competing brands. Although Coca-Cola is the world's largest soft-drink company, 7-Up successfully made an appeal to the more iconoclastic, against-the-grain aspect of our cultural makeup by positioning itself as the "uncola." This both strengthened the position of 7-Up in consumer minds and appealed to our cultural propensity to engage in a little risky behavior.

Environmental Analysis

Culture and popular culture are of course both creatures of the external environment. Environmental scanning is therefore critical to understanding changes and how those changes should be incorporated into company offerings.

As will be discussed in chapter 15, a major result of political changes in Eastern Europe in the early 1990s was the introduction of consumerism and consumer values into this large region of the world. A number of companies were able to take advantage of this rapid change to introduce their products and services. Perhaps the next area of the globe where dramatic changes may be in the offing is Africa. A company wishing to take advantage of such changes in the future will need to have a keen understanding of the culture and popular culture of this vast area.

Research

Marketing research can help managers gain an understanding of how cultural values change in a society. For example, changes in values—such as increased desires for pleasure, excitement, and fun—could influence how products are named, what their colors are, and how they are designed. In advertising such values would influence the underlying tone of the message and the choice of models. We can see this happening through changes in advertising for established products such as Coca-Cola, whose themes have included "The Pause That Refreshes," "Things Go Better with Coke," "Have a Coke and a Smile," "I'd Like to Give the World a Coke," "It's the Real Thing," "Coke Is It," and "Always Coca-Cola."

Marketing Mix

When developing the marketing mix, companies should analyze core values of every culture involved, as well as the culture to which the product is being marketed. This strategy works both for U.S. firms marketing in foreign countries and for foreign firms marketing in the United States. For example, Anheuser-Busch used Native Americans in an ad to sell Budweiser in Britain. It became Budweiser's most popular campaign ever there, with viewers requesting photos of the primary actor. Brand awareness rose to an all-time high, and sales increased 20 percent. For Britons, the Native American expressed "genuine American values," explained Louis Blackwell, editor of the U.K. advertising publication *Creative Review*. However, other Native Americans in the United States got wind of the ad and asked that it be withdrawn.[55] In Britain the ad managed to represent U.S. values well. For Native Americans the ad called attention to the fact that their population has an alcoholism rate about five times that of the general U.S. population. On both sides of the Atlantic, the ad involved core values, but with different results.

Segmentation

One of the tasks needed to successfully use segmentation is to identify segments of consumers who respond well to a certain product and positioning strategy. Often, these segments are assumed to break out along demographic lines (e.g., young females), but other bases may be important here as well.

For example, among young females there are differences based on popular culture and the lifestyles of popular culture icons. The punk singer Bif Naked, who is pierced in multiple locations, certainly attracts a segment of the population and may be an appealing cultural icon. On the other hand, an expanding segment of the population of young people finds Latin music attractive; Enrique Iglesias, for example, would be a more appealing cultural icon for this segment of the population. Using popular culture icons is of course always somewhat risky because fads can change quickly.

Notes

1. Melanie Wallendorf and M. Reilly, "Distinguishing Culture of Origin from Culture of Residence," in *Advances in Consumer Research*, ed. Richard Bagozzi and Alice Tybout (Ann Arbor, MI: Association for Consumer Research, 1983), 10:699–701.
2. David Tse, Kam-hon Lee, Ilan Vertinsky, and Donald Wehrung, "Does Culture Matter? A Cross-Cultural Study of Executives' Choice, Decisiveness, and Risk Adjustment in International Marketing," *Journal of Marketing* 52 (October 1988): 81–95.
3. This comment was made by the sociologist Chuck Edgley, who made numerous other helpful comments for this chapter.
4. Sunkyu Jun, A. Dwayne Ball, and James W. Gentry, "Modes of Consumer Acculturation," in *Advances in Consumer Research*, ed. Leigh McAlister and Michael L. Rothschild (Provo, UT: Association for Consumer Research, 1993), 20:76–82. Also see James W. Gentry, Sunkyu Jun, and Patriya Tansuhaj, "Consumer Acculturation Processes and Cultural Conflict: How Generalizable Is a North American Model for Marketing Globally?" *Journal of Business Research* 32 (February 1995): 129–39.
5. Henry Fairchild, *Dictionary of Sociology* (Totawa, NJ: Littlefield, Adams, 1970).
6. Peter H. Bloch, "Seeking the Ideal Form: Product Design and Consumer Response," *Journal of Marketing* 59 (July 1995): 16–29.

7. George J. McCall and J. L. Simmons, *Social Psychology: A Sociological Approach* (New York: Free Press, 1982).

8. Joseph Campbell, *Myths, Dreams, and Religion* (New York: E. P. Dutton, 1970).

9. Fara Wagner, "Basketball Thrills Koreans, as NBA Dribbles into Asia," *Wall Street Journal*, May 17, 1996, p. B9.

10. Kelly Shermach, "Gun Advocates Decry Study on Firearms Sales to Women," *Marketing News*, January 16, 1995, p. 14.

11. John P. Robinson and Geoffrey Godbey, "Has Fitness Peaked?" *American Demographics*, September 1993, pp. 36–42.

12. Randall Lane, "A Boxing Boom," *Forbes*, December 18, 1995, p. 207; Gianna Jacobson, "Booming Baby Market," *Success*, October 1995, p. 30.

13. Much of the discussion of the cultural meaning of goods is based on Grant McCracken, "Culture and Consumption: A Theoretical Account of the Structure and Movement of the Cultural Meaning of Consumer Goods," *Journal of Consumer Research* 13 (June 1986): 71–84.

14. Ibid., 78.

15. For an interesting discussion of the definition of values, see L. J. Shrum, John McCarty, and Tamara Loeffler, "Individual Differences in Value Stability: Are We Really Tapping True Values?" in *Advances in Consumer Research*, ed. Marvin Goldberg and Gerald Gorn (Provo, UT: Association for Consumer Research, 1990), 17:609–15.

16. Theodore Wallin, "The International Executives' Baggage: Cultural Values of the American Frontier," *MSU Business Topics* 24 (spring 1976): 49–58.

17. Cora DuBois, "The Dominant Value Profile in American Culture," *American Anthropologist* 57 (December 1955): 1232–39. Also see Janet T. Spence, "Achievement American Style," *American Psychologist*, December 1985, pp. 1285–95.

18. Frank H. Alpert and Michael A. Kamins, "An Empirical Investigation of Consumer Memory, Attitude, and Perceptions toward Pioneer and Follower Brands," *Journal of Marketing* 50 (October 1995): 34–45.

19. D. E. Vinson, J. Scott, and L. Lamont, "The Role of Personal Values in Marketing and Consumer Behavior," *Journal of Marketing* 41 (April 1977): 44–50.

20. Thomas J. Reynolds and David B. Whitlack, "Applying Laddering Data to Communications Strategy and Advertising Practice," *Journal of Advertising Research* 35 (July–August 1995): 9–17; Charles E. Gengler and Thomas J. Reynolds, "Consumer Understanding and Advertising Strategy: Analysis and Strategic Translation of Laddering Data," *Journal of Advertising Research* 35 (July–August 1995); Gerald Zaltman and Robin Higie Coulter, "Seeing the Voice of the Consumer: Metaphor-Based Advertising Research," *Journal of Advertising Research* 35 (July–August 1995): 35–51.

21. Lynn Kahle, Basil Poulos, and Ajay Sukhdial, "Changes in Social Values in the United States during the Past Decade," *Journal of Advertising Research* 28 (February–March 1988): 35–41.

22. Pamela Homer and Lynn Kahle, "A Structural Equation Test of the Value–Attitude–Behavior Hierarchy," *Journal of Personality and Social Psychology* 54 (April 1988): 638–46.

23. Lynn Kahle, "Role-Relaxed Consumers: A Trend of the Nineties," *Journal of Advertising Research* 35 (March–April 1995): 66–71.

24. Russell Belk, "Material Values in the Comics: A Content Analysis of Comic Books Featuring Themes of Wealth," *Journal of Consumer Research* 14 (June 1987): 26–42.

25. Monroe Friedman, "The Changing Language of a Consumer Society: Brand Name Usage in Popular American Novels in the Postwar Era," *Journal of Consumer Research* 11 (March 1985): 927–38.

26. Russell Belk and Richard Pollay, "Materialism and Magazine Advertising during the Twentieth Century," in *Advances in Consumer Research*, ed. Elizabeth Hirschman and Morris Holbrook (Provo, UT: Association for Consumer Research, 1985), 12:394–98.

27. Ibid., 397.

28. Floyd W. Rudmin, "German and Canadian Data on Motivations for Ownership: Was Pythagoras Right?" in *Advances in Consumer Research*, ed. Marvin Goldberg and Gerald Gorn (Provo, UT: Association for Consumer Research, 1990), 17:176–81.

29. Scott Dawson and Gary Bamossy, "Isolating the Effect of Non-Economic Factors on the Development of a Consumer Culture: A Comparison of Materialism in the Netherlands and the United States," in *Advances in Consumer Research*, ed. Marvin Goldberg and Gerald

Gorn (Provo, UT: Association for Consumer Research, 1990), 17:182–85. Other research has suggested that the level of materialism in Europe has not changed much in recent years. See Caolan Mannion and Teresa Brannick, "Materialism and Its Measurement," *Ibar* 16 (1995): 1–16.

30. Guliz Ger and Russell Belk, "Measuring and Comparing Materialism Cross-Culturally," in *Advances in Consumer Research*, ed. Marvin Goldberg and Gerald Gorn (Provo, UT: Association for Consumer Research, 1990), 17:186–92.

31. Susan Spiggle, "Measuring Social Values: A Content Analysis of Sunday Comics and Underground Comix," *Journal of Consumer Research* 13 (June 1986): 100.

32. This definition is based in large part on Dennis Rook, "The Ritual Dimension of Consumer Behavior," *Journal of Consumer Research* 12 (December 1985): 251–64. We have added the idea that rituals are culturally mandated in order to help distinguish the idea of a ritual from that of a habit.

33. These ideas were developed by Mary A. Stanfield Tetreault and Robert E. Kleine III, "Ritual, Ritualized Behavior, and Habit: Refinements and Extensions of the Consumption Ritual Construct," in *Advances in Consumer Research*, ed. Marvin Goldberg and Gerald Gorn (Provo, UT: Association for Consumer Research, 1990), 17:31–38.

34. Rook, "Ritual Dimension."

35. McCracken, "Culture and Consumption."

36. Ray Brown, *Rituals and Ceremonies in Popular Culture* (Bowling Green, OH: Popular Press, 1980). For a discussion of funerals and other aspects of death, see James W. Gentry and Cathy Goodwin, "Social Support for Decision Making during Grief Due to Death," in *Marketing and Consumer Research in the Public Interest*, ed. Ronald P. Hill (Thousand Oaks, CA: Sage, 1996), 55–68; and Terrance G. Gabel, Phylis Mansfield, and Kevin Westbrook, "The Disposal of Consumers: An Exploratory Analysis of Death-Related Consumption," in *Advances in Consumer Research*, ed. Kim P. Corfman and John G. Lynch Jr. (Provo, UT: Association for Consumer Research, 1996), 23:361–67.

37. Holy Finn, "Scent of a Man," *Financial Times Weekend Supplement*, May 29–30, 1999, p. 11.

38. Brenda Gainer, "Ritual and Relationships: Interpersonal Influences on Shared Consumption," *Journal of Business Research* 32 (March 1995): 253–60.

39. Charles Morris, *Signs, Language, and Behavior* (New York: George Braziller, 1946).

40. Elizabeth Hirschman, "Comprehending Symbolic Consumption: Three Theoretical Issues," in *Symbolic Consumption Behavior*, Proceedings of the Conference on Consumer Aesthetics and Symbolic Consumption, ed. Elizabeth Hirschman and Morris Holbrook (Ann Arbor, MI: Association for Consumer Research, May 1980), 4–6, 15. Also see Morris Holbrook, *Consumer Research: Introspective Essays on the Study of Consumption* (Thousand Oaks, CA: Sage, 1995).

41. Objects can, however, possess symbolic value independent of its value as viewed by others. For example, a person is unlikely to swap wedding rings even when the alternative offered is of better quality. See Marsha L. Richins, "Valuing Things: The Public and Private Meanings of Possessions," *Journal of Consumer Research* 21 (December 1994): 504–21.

42. Cacilie Rohwedder, "Name-Finders Save New Products from Fiascos in Global Market," *Wall Street Journal*, April 11, 1996, p. B5.

43. Teri Agins, "Signs of the Times: Logos on Clothing are Back and They're Bigger Than Ever," *Wall Street Journal*, February 22, 1996, pp. B1, B9.

44. This section was based on an article by John Sherry and Eduardo Camargo, "May Your Life Be Marvelous: English Language Labelling and the Semiotics of Japanese Promotion," *Journal of Consumer Research* 14 (September 1987): 174–88.

45. Hamish McRae, *The World in 2020: Power, Culture, and Prosperity* (Boston, MA: Harvard Business School Press, 1995).

46. This definition, as well as the characteristics of popular culture, was taken from Michael J. Bell, "The Study of Popular Culture," in *Concise Histories of American Popular Culture*, ed. M. Thomas Inge (Westport, CT: Greenwood Press, 1982), 443.

47. Robert S. Alley, "Television," in *Handbook of American Popular Culture*, ed. M. Thomas Inge (Westport, CT: Greenwood Press, 1982), 1368.

48. Thomas C. O'Guinn and L. J. Shrum, "The Role of Television in the Construction of Consumer Reality," *Journal of Consumer Research* 23 (March 1997): 278–94.

49. For a discussion of rap music and its impact on children's advertising, see M. Elizabeth Blair and Mark N. Hatala, "The Use of Rap Music in Children's Advertising," in *Advances in*

Consumer Research, ed. John F. Sherry and Brian Sternthal (Provo, UT: Association for Consumer Research, 1992), 19:719–24.

50. George B. Sproles, *Fashion: Consumer Behavior toward Dress* (Minneapolis, MN: Burgess, 1979).

51. Cathy Goodwin, "Good Guys Don't Wear Polyester: Consumption Ideology in a Detective Series," *Advances in Consumer Research,* ed. John F. Sherry and Brian Sternthal (Provo, UT: Association for Consumer Research, 1992), 19:739–45.

52. Craig J. Thompson and Diana L. Haytko, "Speaking of Fashion: Consumer's Uses of Fashion Discourses and the Appropriation of Countervailing Cultural Meanings," *Journal of Consumer Research* 24 (June 1997): 15–42.

53. These characteristics were originally developed by Christopher M. Miller, Shelby H. McIntyre, and Murali K. Mantrala, "Toward Formalizing Fashion Theory," *Journal of Marketing Research* 30 (May 1993): 142–47.

54. Roger Ricklefs, "Marketers Seek Out Today's Coolest Kids to Plug into Tomorrow's Mall Trends," *Wall Street Journal,* July 11, 1996, pp. B1, B2.

55. Tara Parker-Pope, "British Budweiser Ads Rankle American Indians," *Wall Street Journal,* July 16, 1996, p. B1.

CHAPTER 14

Subcultures and Demographics

After reading this chapter, you should be able to discuss each of the following concepts, together with their managerial implications:

1. The term *subculture* and how subcultures differ from demographic variables.
2. Six different types of subcultures in the United States.
3. Baby boomers.
4. The changing age composition of the United States between 1995 and 2005.
5. Three ways in which the elderly process information differently than younger adults.
6. Four factors that make the African-American subculture an important target market.
7. Factors that explain the rapid growth of the Hispanic subculture in the United States.
8. Reasons for regional shifts in population.
9. Social class.
10. Examples of how social classes differ in shopping patterns and in leisure activities.

WHAT IS A SUBCULTURE?

The United States and Canada are composed largely of immigrants from throughout the world and their descendants. Although U.S. and Canadian "cultures" do exist, the so-called melting pot has not created an entirely homogeneous people out of the hodge-podge of settlers. North America is "a mixture of subcultures reflecting the national heritage, language, religious, racial, and geographic diversity of a vast continent populated primarily by waves of immigrants from many diverse cultures and subcultures."[1]

Within the overall culture of North America, subgroups retain some of the values, beliefs, and symbols of their culture of origin. These groups form subcultures that can become important target markets for marketers. For example, the need of Jews to have kosher food makes them an attractive target for marketers willing to adequately control the preparation of food products. Meanwhile, mainstream marketers, such as ConAgra, have begun to market kosher foods because consumers are attracted to the wholesome image of the food products. Indeed, 60 percent of the sales of Hebrew National's frankfurters go to non-Jewish customers.[2]

In addition to originating from immigration, subcultures can also develop from naturally occurring subdivisions within a society. All societies contain such subgroups, which may be based on age, social class, and regional differences. In each case some factor causes differences in values and lifestyles sufficient to create a subculture. For example, a combination of retirement, common physical problems, and similar housing needs has resulted in the development of the elderly subculture.

A **subculture** may be defined as a subdivision of national culture, based on some unifying characteristic, such as social status or nationality, whose members share similar patterns of behavior that are distinct from those of the national culture.[3] Numerous demographic characteristics have been used to identify subcultures, including the following:

Nationality (e.g., Hispanic, Italian, Polish)

Race (e.g., African American, Native American, Asian American)

Region (e.g., New England, Southwest)

Age (e.g., elderly, teenager)

Religion (e.g., Catholic, Jewish)

Gender

Social class (e.g., upper class, lower class)

Subcultures versus Demographics

The concepts of subcultures and demographics are closely related. **Demographic variables** describe the characteristics of populations. Examples of demographic variables include the following:

Nationality	Marital status
Age	Income
Religion	Region
Gender	Ethnicity
Occupation	Education

Of course, many of these demographic variables also describe subcultures. Within the demographic category of religion, for example, one can identify a number of distinct subcultural groups in the United States, including Jews, Christians, and Moslems.

When one speaks of cultures or subcultures, however, the focus is on the group's values, customs, symbols, and actions. Demographic features merely describe the characteristics of a population of people. The reason a marketer might speak of an African-American subculture is that this demographic characteristic conveniently describes a group of people who may have similar behavior patterns.

Changes in age and ethnic distribution, as well as attitudes toward gays and lesbians, have had a major impact on marketing strategy. For example, with the changing nature of the social classes, retailers have either had to go upscale or go to the lower end. Companies such as Sears, which traditionally focused on the middle class, lost market share to specialty stores on the upper end and discount department stores on the lower end. During the 1980s and early 1990s, the sales of specialty stores such as

The Limited and The Gap grew by over 20 percent per year. Sears and J.C. Penney have had to make adjustments to meet this competition.

Also note that large groups of people may form subcultures based on a shared interest in a particular type of product. For example, professional musicians and artists form distinct subcultures that many companies attempt to reach with a unique marketing mix. In the 1960s a psychedelic subculture formed around a shared interest in hallucinogens.

This chapter will discuss certain key subcultural groups that are more "mainstream" than the subculture of users of hallucinogens. It begins with the important topic of age subcultures.

AGE SUBCULTURES

As consumers move through their life cycle, predictable changes in values, lifestyles, and consumption patterns occur. A 5-year-old has a completely different set of needs than a 20-year-old, who in turn has different needs than a 65-year-old. Because various age "cohorts" of consumers have similar values, needs, and behavioral patterns, they form subcultures that may constitute important market segments. Furthermore, changes in the number of people in age categories due to variations in birthrates create new marketing opportunities.

An analysis of age trends is also important to marketers because highly accurate projections of the future age composition of the population can be made more easily than for other demographic factors, such as income or occupation. These projections allow marketers to recognize potential marketing opportunities years in advance, which greatly simplifies the planning process.

Perhaps as profound as the changing ethnic population of the United States is its changing age composition and income distribution. During the 1980s the number of children under 17 years of age living below the poverty line increased from less than 15 percent to over 20 percent (20.8 percent in 1995). However, poverty among people over 65 decreased to 10.5 percent in 1995—a lower poverty rate than among either children or the working-age population (11.4 percent).

One factor that strongly influences the age distribution of the population is immigration. Immigrants, whether legal or illegal, tend to be younger. Immigrant women also tend to have high birthrates. Because of the youth of the immigrants and their higher fertility rates, immigration is the single most important factor retarding the aging trend of the U.S. population.

Four age groups of critical importance to marketers are discussed in this section—the baby-boom generation, Generation X, Generation Y, and the elderly.

The Baby Boomers

Although some debate may exist as to whether the **baby-boom generation** actually forms a subculture, sufficient lifestyle similarities exist among the huge group of Americans born between 1946 and 1964 that the group has a large impact on marketers and the economy as a whole. The United States is currently experiencing fundamental changes in the age characteristics of its population. The major reasons for the shifts in the average age of Americans over the next 40 years lie in the dramatic changes in birthrates over the last half century. During the Great Depression of the 1930s, a **baby bust** occurred. The number of children born to the average woman during her lifetime (i.e., the **fertility rate**) dropped to the replacement level of 2.1 births. Total births dropped 25 percent.[4]

The Depression "birth dearth" was followed by the post–World War II baby boom. The fertility rate shot past 3.8, and the total number of births increased by one-third over

Depression levels. The baby boom lasted through 1964. It was followed, however, by another baby bust. Caused by changes in the technology of birth prevention (e.g., the birth-control pill) and the emergence of the working woman, this baby bust sent fertility rates plunging to as low as 1.8 in 1976—a rate far below replacement level.[5] Lasting from 1965 to 1980, the latest baby bust group is now called Generation X by marketers.

This series of changes in the birthrate created a huge bulge of 77 million people (over half again as large as the previous generation). As time passes and the boomers grow older, the bulge moves through the population like a melon being digested by a boa constrictor.[6] For example, in 1980 there were less than 25 million Americans in their 40s; however, by the year 2000, the number had almost doubled. As the years pass, the bulge moves, growing older and changing the nature of the marketplace. In 1970 the majority of the baby boomers were between 6 and 24 years of age. Marketers of soft drinks and fast foods were ecstatic over the hordes of teenyboppers clamoring for their products. By 1995, however, the earliest baby boomers reached 50, while others are in their 30s and 40s. These consumers tend to be affluent, with a new set of product needs and wants. For example, demand for home furnishings is increasing as baby boomers purchase expensive furniture, draperies, and carpets (one indication of this is that there are now about 100 magazines on home design).

Table 14.1 gives an overview of the projected U.S. population between 1995 and 2005. As can be seen, two age groups will shrink considerably during this period. Those 25 to 34 years old will decrease by 11.7 percent, and the number of children under 5 years old will decrease by 4.2 percent. A huge increase will occur among those between 45 and 64 years old. These are the baby boomers. The second-greatest increase will occur among those 75 years and older.

Implications for Marketing Strategy. One of the prime marketing requirements for consumer-goods companies is the tracking of the baby-boom generation. Indeed, a marketing law might be phrased as "Those who live by the baby boom shall die by the baby boom." As their tastes and preferences change with the passing years, the for-

Projections of the U.S. Population, 1995–2005

Age Group	Population (1,000) 1995	2005	Percentage Distribution 1995	2005	Percentage change 1985–1995	1995–2005
Under 5	20,181	19,333	7.7	6.7	+13.1%	−4.2%
5–17	48,853	53,790	18.4	18.7	+9.1	10.1
18–24	25,465	28,238	10.1	9.8	−11.9	10.9
25–34	41,670	36,792	16.6	12.8	−.1	−11.7
35–44	42,150	43,075	15.7	14.9	33.0	2.2
45–54	30,224	41,219	10.8	14.3	34.6	36.4
55–64	21,241	28,870	8.2	10.0	−4.0	35.9
65–74	18,963	18,623	7.2	6.5	10.9	−1.8
75+	14,685	18,347	5.4	6.4	27.1	25.1
Total	263,432	288,287				

Source: U.S. Department of Commerce, *Statistical Abstract of the United States, 1995* (Washington, DC: U.S. Government Printing Office, 1995).

TABLE 14.1

tunes of manufacturers are dramatically affected. For example, with their traditional target market of 5- to 17-year-olds declining by more than one-half million during the 1980s, McDonald's was threatened with both a possible decline in revenues and the loss of their primary workforce—teenagers. To navigate the changing age demographics, the company hired retired people to work behind the counters.

Other companies had to make adjustments as well. In 1981 Levi Strauss was the world's largest clothing manufacturer when jeans production peaked at 560 million pairs. However, by the mid-1980s profits began to drop dramatically and were down 20 percent by 1988. One of the company's strategic responses was to move into roomier khaki and chino pants, which fit the middle-aged spread of the baby boomers better than jeans. Levi's now sells about $1 billion per year of Dockers slacks. Sales were also helped by the fact that younger males who might prefer jeans still need at least one pair of dressier pants, and Dockers fit the bill. Such upscale designers as Geoffrey Beene and Tommy Hilfinger have used elastic waistbands to cope with the expanding middles of baby boomers.[7] Likewise, although dental care improvements have decreased the number of cavities needing to be filled (in 1984 *Forbes* magazine forecast the end of the dental profession), boomers' concern with continuing to look good led to a 20 percent increase in the number of dentists and a near-doubling of dentists' average income between 1987 and 1996.[8]

Not all is positive for the baby-boom generation, however. Because of their large numbers, the baby boomers have had major problems finding jobs. Many are chronically underemployed. One result is the dependence of some boomers on their parents for financial support even in their 40s.[9] These boomers have been called RYAs (returning young adults who move back in with relatives) and ILYAs (incompletely launched young adults who are not financially independent).

Generation X

Born between 1965 and 1980, the number of **Generation Xers** (the "baby busters") is small, but the group possesses $125 billion of discretionary income. Given a variety of names, such as "afterboomers" and "flyers" (i.e., fun-loving youth en route to success), the group is noted for valuing religion, formal rituals (e.g., proms), and materialism, as well as more negative attitudes toward work and getting ahead than the boomers.[10] Because of the group's small size, employers must compete for them in the job market. For example, the U.S. Army began its Army College Fund, allowing enlistees to save up to $25,200 during their term of service for college. One research group calls Generation Xers in the United States and northern Europe the "new realists," who have resigned themselves to the possibility that they will never achieve the affluence of their parents' generation.[11]

Members of Generation X have until recently been ignored by marketers. As one executive explained: "[A]s baby boomers enter middle age, marketers are being forced to confront Generation X. These people will fuel the growth for product categories from fast food to liquor to apparel to soft-drinks." In the television arena, Fox Broadcasting (e.g., *The Simpsons*) and MTV have specifically targeted Xers. Advertising managers are particularly concerned with how to reach this market. A slew of Generation X magazines has been launched, but they are remarkably similar, focusing on music, celebrities, and lifestyle. Among those that fell shortly after launch are *Real, Forehead, The Nose,* and *Hypno.*[12] Heinz launched a $50 million advertising program in 1999 to lure teenagers back to ketchup, using references to acne, angst, alienation, and irony as an appeal. One example is the dollop of ketchup that will never come out of the bottle because, the advertisement says, it "has issues."[13]

Because of their spending power, Generation Xers are being taken seriously by marketers. In addition, the group is moving into the time span when its members begin to purchase cars, houses, and other big-ticket items. The vice president–general manager of Nissan USA noted that Generation X now accounts for 25 to 30 percent of its automobile sales. He added, "As they age and move up in income, they'll grow in importance. We want to make a good first impression."[14]

Generation Xers are also part of a new infatuation called "global teens." For years international marketers have noticed that people in different countries with similar educational and income backgrounds seem to act in much the same way. The Xers may have become the first generation to share even closer commonalities: Many watch the same television shows, drink Coke and eat Big Macs, see the same movies, "surf" the Internet, and wear the "global teen uniform"— baggy Levi's or Diesel jeans, T-shirt, and Nikes or Doc Martens. This tying together via a worldwide media net may mean that teenagers everywhere are leading "parallel lives," which means that cross-national marketing opportunities are much greater.[15]

Generation Y

The next cohort to appear on the horizon are the 72 million children of the baby boomers, who are now reaching adulthood. They represent 28 percent of the current population, rivaling the baby boomers' 30 percent.

Like the Generation Xers, these so-called Generation Yers are more heterogeneous in racial and socioeconomic terms than boomers. For example, the original boomers were 75 percent non-Hispanic white, whereas the Yers are 67 percent non-Hispanic white. They are the first to have significant numbers (about 1 in 35) to be of mixed race, making the traditional racial categories likely to become obsolete. Although the first half of the boomers were born in the era of segregation, this is not true of any of the Generation Yers. The boomers learned that "Father Knows Best," but for the Yers, "Dad isn't home": In 1970 12 percent of children lived in a one-parent household, but in 1993 27 percent did.[16] One group of Yers is particularly in demand. There are only 7.4 million 12- to 15-year-old girls, the prime baby-sitter pool—and 35 million families with newborns to 11-year-olds who need sitters.[17]

The Yers—also called the millennium generation (M-Gens)—hark back to the political activism of their baby-boomer parents. As in 1968, French students in 1998 took to the streets to protest crowded and poorly equipped schools. Unlike the situation between baby boomers and their parents in the 1960s and 1970, both the boomers and the M-Gens are environmentalists. Manufacturers are appealing to M-Gens by noting that they don't use rabbits to test cosmetics, a theme that appeals as well to former 1960s activists.[18]

The Elderly

A fourth major age trend in the United States is the "graying of America." The aging of the population will be one of the most dominant demographic factors for the foreseeable future. Barring global war or other disasters, the population of those under 30 will never again be as large as it was in 1983. By the year 2020, those over 65 will outnumber teenagers two to one.

A number of factors (birthrates, mortality rates, and immigration rates) influence the projected population and its characteristics in the years ahead. Unfortunately, each is difficult to predict accurately. Birthrates are influenced by the technology available to prevent births as well as by cultural values and lifestyle patterns. **Mortality rates** have been falling since the 1970s. Life expectancy increased by three years during the 1970s and another two to three years in the 1980s. Men born in 1990 will live on average 72 years, and women, 79 years. Because of the striking difference in the life expectancy of men and women, an aging population means more women. Elderly women will increasingly form an important segment for marketers to target. Of those over 85 years old, women outnumber men by almost two-and-a-half to one.

The Mature Consumer. Just who is the **mature consumer**? No specific age is associated with becoming "mature" or reaching one's "golden years." However, a series of events occur between the ages of 55 and 65 that set the aging consumer apart from younger people. During this time period, retirement has either occurred or is anticipated. In all likelihood income is reduced and becomes relatively fixed after retirement, making inflation a threat. Health concerns become more important at about this age, and close friends begin to die.

Mature consumers are well off financially. Although only 23 percent of American consumers are 55 or older, they control 75 percent of the nation's wealth and about half of its discretionary income.[19] Mature consumers also have a great deal of free time. In 1900 60 percent of all men over 65 were still working. In 1940 the figure was 40 percent. In the 1990s only 17 percent of men over 65 are working.[20] This early retirement trend resulted in large part because of the stronger financial position of mature consumers in the 1980s.

Mature consumers—here defined as age 55 or older—differ from younger people in two major aspects. First, in certain ways they process information differently. In particular, their visual, hearing, and taste senses decrease in acuity. One study found that information-processing differences limit the extent to which the elderly are able to use nutritional information about cereals. As compared with younger consumers, the elderly were less able to search intensely for nutritional information on packages and select an appropriate cereal.[21] From a public-policy perspective, the results suggest that, although nutritional information is more readily available to consumers on packages, the elderly may not be able to make appropriate use of it. The changes in information-processing abilities indicate that marketers should be concerned with how much time the elderly are given to make a decision. Providing additional time for information processing—for instance, making an advertisement longer or having a salesperson proceed more slowly—may assist older consumers.

A second way in which mature consumers differ from younger consumers is that their motor skills decline. As people age their ability to walk, write, talk clearly, and drive a car can gradually deteriorate. In many cities companies are now providing a variety of services to the elderly to help them overcome these age-related handicaps. Examples of such services include in-home food delivery, yard and house cleaning, fix-up services, and nursing care. Table 14.2 identifies other ways in which the consumption habits of the elderly differ from that of younger consumers.

One major finding concerning the elderly is that they are cautious consumers. They do not tend to risk being wrong for the sake of acting quickly.[22] In addition, the higher the perceived risk, the less likely the elderly are to try a product.[23]

Another phenomenon that occurs as people grow older is an increase in the amount of time spent watching television. Although all Americans spend more time watching television than any other activity except sleep and work, the elderly especially use the television both for entertainment and for obtaining information. The importance of the television increases in part because elderly people tend to have fewer social contacts.[24]

In addition, the elderly may also be somewhat more vulnerable to scams and fraud, perhaps due to their differences in information processing and motor skills.

On the other hand, marketers find that attitude, more than age, defines the mature marketplace. The elderly generally feel younger than they actually are.[25] One implication for managers is that promotional materials should focus on portraying the elderly at the age they feel, rather than at their chronological age. Furthermore, as the

Consumption Habits of Mature Consumers Compared to Younger Consumers

1. Shopping Behaviors
   a. Shop more frequently.
   b. Spend less per shopping trip.
   c. Shop less often at night.
   d. Use coupons.
   e. Pay with cash—not credit cards.
   f. Shop less at discount stores.
2. Media Habits
   a. Watch 60% more TV, particularly in the daytime.
   b. Read more newspapers.
   c. Listen to less radio, particularly FM.
3. What They Want from Retailers
   a. Courteous treatment.
   b. Personal assistance.
   c. Delivery service.
   d. Rest facilities (e.g., benches).

Sources: Adapted from K. L. Bernhardt and T. C. Kinnear, *Advances in Consumer Research* (Ann Arbor, MI: Association for Consumer Research, 1976), 3:449–52; and Zarrel Lambert, "An Investigation of Older Consumers' Unmet Needs and Wants at the Retail Level," *Journal of Retailing* 55 (winter 1979): 43.

TABLE 14.2

U.S. government's de facto definition of "retirement age" (full Social Security benefit eligibility) creeps up from 65 to 67, we may find that our own working definitions of "the elderly" will change.

ETHNIC SUBCULTURES

Another demographic variable frequently used to describe subcultures is ethnicity. Although used in a variety of ways, the term **ethnicity** generally refers to a group bound together by ties of cultural homogeneity. Such a group is linked by similar values, customs, dress, religion, and language. Ethnicity is frequently closely linked to nationality or region of origin. One may speak of Mexican Americans and Chinese Americans as ethnic groups because each shares a common national or geographic ancestry as well as a similar culture. Table 14.3 provides population projections for several ethnic groups between 1995 and 2020. In this section we will discuss the African-American, Hispanic, and Asian-American subcultures and their importance as potential target markets.

The African-American Subculture

A number of factors shape the African-American subculture, which represents 12 percent of the U.S. population. One major contributor is income deprivation. In the 1990s 37 percent of African-American households had incomes of under $15,000. In contrast, 30 percent of Hispanic and 14 percent of white households had incomes this low.[26] Other factors influencing the subculture are (1) educational disparities, (2) a

U.S. Population Projections for White, Black, Asian, and Hispanic Groups, 1995–2020

	White	Black	Asian	Hispanic*
% Distribution				
1995	82.9%	12.5%	3.7%	10.2%
2000	81.9	12.8	4.4	11.3
2010	80	13.4	5.7	13.5
2020	78.2	13.9	6.9	15.7
% Change				
1995–2000	3.6	7.1	24.3	16.3
2000–2010	6.2	13.4	41.8	30.0
2010–2020	6.0	12.9	31.8	26.4

*Persons of Hispanic origin may be of any race.

Source: U.S. Department of Commerce, *Statistical Abstract of the United States, 1995* (Washington, DC: U.S. Government Printing Office, 1995).

TABLE 14.3

young, highly mobile family structure headed by a high proportion of females, and (3) a concentration of its population in central cities.

Despite these disadvantages, the black subculture is growing in importance as a market segment. As shown in Table 14.4, it has impressive buying power, it is increasing in size faster than the general population, and it is rising in socioeconomic status.

The African-American subculture is also marked by the importance of religious and social organizations. African Americans disproportionately belong to fundamentalist Protestant groups and to the Democratic political party. There is also a recognized speech pattern, known as AAVE—African American Vernacular English—which is used to some extent by 80 percent of the African-American population. This dialect

Factors Making African Americans an Important Market Segment

1. *Spending power.* Over $213 billion in annual expenditures.
2. *Average annual household income.* $22,393.
3. *Increasing size.* During the 1990s, estimated increase in size by 12.2% to represent 12.8% of the U.S. population.
4. *Youth.* Median age is 28 years as compared to 34 for whites.
5. *Geographic concentration.* 65% of African Americans live in the top 15 U.S. markets.
6. *Unique tastes and preferences.* Spend far more than whites on boys' clothing, rental goods, radios, and cognac. Adults are more than twice as likely as whites to own a pager.

Sources: U.S. Department of Commerce, *Statistical Abstract of the United States, 1993, 1995* (Washington DC: U.S. Government Printing Office, 1993, 1995), Eugene Morris, "The Difference in Black and White," *American Demographics,* January 1993, pp. 44–49; Lisa L. Brownlee, "Motorola Gets Signal on Blacks' Pager Use," *Wall Street Journal,* June 24, 1994, p. 86; U.S. Bureau of the Census press release, September 26, 1996.

TABLE 14.4

form appears frequently in television programs, but its use in written or spoken advertising is quite limited.[27]

We should note that the African-American subculture is not homogeneous. For example, different groups of African-American consumers have divergent views of rap music. While the sound is popular with lower-class blacks and youths, older individuals in the middle class frequently respond negatively to it. National advertisers, who employ rap music to reach black audiences, may in fact be offending the very people they are attempting to reach, according to the authors of one study. The researchers noted that perhaps national advertisers should follow the lead of an Atlanta radio station that plays "songs you grew up on, and no rap."[28]

A critical issue marketers face in the promotion of products to black consumers involves liquor and cigarette advertising. Blacks spend relatively more of their income on liquor and cigarettes than whites, and advertising that specifically targets the group frequently draws fire from public-interest groups. For example, in 1991 Heileman attempted to launch PowerMaster, a new brand with a high-alcohol content that was targeted to urban blacks. After a public outcry, the company backed off the brand. The next year the company was again criticized when it sought to bring out Crazy Horse malt liquor—another high-alcohol brand. In 1993 Heileman began a repositioning effort for its Colt 45 malt liquor with an ad in which a young black college graduate gives advice to a younger friend. One official with the Institute on Black Chemical Abuse said: "[I]t's in poor taste. It's inaccurate to portray someone like the gentleman, with this sense of mission, yet acting as a proponent of malt liquor right there on the street."[29]

The Hispanic Subculture

Hispanics are the second-fastest-growing major minority group in the United States (Asian Americans are currently the fastest-growing subcultural group). Hispanics will become the largest minority in the United States by the year 2010 (see Table 14.3). It has been estimated that Mexican admissions alone represent 23 percent of all legal immigration into the United States between 1971 and 1990.[30] A combination of high fertility rates, high immigration rates, the proximity of Puerto Rico (from which Hispanics can legally enter the United States), and continued illegal immigration has led to a rapidly expanding population.

The **Hispanic subculture** is based on a number of factors that bind the group together. A common language unites most Hispanics: The primary language of 82 percent of U.S. Hispanic households is Spanish.[31] A common religion, Catholicism, also imparts a sense of commonality to Hispanics (over 85 percent of Hispanics are Catholic). Hispanics also tend to live in metropolitan areas. Sixty-three percent of Hispanics live in urban areas (compared with 75 percent of the African-American population).[32] Because Hispanics share a similar language and religion and are geographically concentrated, they may make an outstanding target market.

The Hispanic subculture is also marked by a constant influx of new members through legal and illegal immigration. A circular pattern exists: Many Hispanics enter the United States, stay for a length of time, and then leave. It has been estimated that 30 percent of Mexican immigrants eventually return to Mexico, which may be why American products sell so well in our southern neighbor nation.[33]

Hispanics reveal a highly conservative value structure. They are more likely than Anglos to express traditional American values concerning the importance of hard work; they are optimistic regarding their future standard of living; they are materialistic and seek the "good life."[34] Hispanics tend to be more family oriented than Anglos, to live more for the present, and to be somewhat less competitive. Table 14.5 presents a number of important facts about the Hispanic market.

Some Key Characteristics of the Hispanic Subculture

1. Mexican Americans make up two-thirds of U.S. Hispanic households.
2. The average annual household income is $28,330.
3. 14% of Hispanic households have incomes of over $50,000.
4. Hispanics are heavy users of both long-distance and local phone service.
5. On average, Hispanics spend more on in-home food preparation than non-Hispanics. Large meals are at the center of Hispanic home entertainment.
6. Over 80% of Hispanics watch Spanish-language TV and listen to Spanish-language radio—a percentage that has been rising in recent years.

Sources: Patricia Braus, "What Does Hispanic Mean?" *American Demographics,* June 1993, pp. 46–49; U.S. Department of Commerce, *Statistical Abstract of the United States, 1995* (Washington DC: U.S. Government Printing Office, 1995); U.S. Bureau of the Census press release, September 26, 1996; and Roberto R. Ramirez, "The Hispanic Population in the United States," U.S. Bureau of the Census *Current Population Reports,* March 1999.

TABLE 14.5

Hispanic Segmentation. An important aspect of the study of Hispanics is recognizing that they are not one homogeneous group. It is therefore inappropriate to speak of a *single* Hispanic market segment.[35] At least four distinct groups, or segments, exist— Mexican Americans (65.2 percent of U.S. Hispanics), Cubans (4.3 percent), Puerto Ricans (9.6 percent), and Central and South Americans (14.3 percent). Among the four Hispanic groups, there are differences in the way Spanish is spoken, in food preferences (e.g., Mexicans eat refried beans, Cubans eat black beans, and Puerto Ricans eat red beans), and in political attitudes.

Each of the Hispanic groups is also geographically concentrated. Los Angeles, where 2.1 million Hispanics live, is considered to be the prime target area for reaching Mexican Americans. Similarly, Miami contains the largest concentration of Cubans (Miami is 62 percent Hispanic),[36] and New York City has the largest number of Puerto Ricans.

One other point of differentiation is the degree of acculturation. Hispanics range from new arrivals to 10th-generation (or more) descendents of immigrants. In addition to length of stay, fluency in English and general contact with the majority culture also influence the degree of preference for U.S. products. Some products such as clothing are largely free of any language barrier and are easily adopted. Others (e.g., long-distance phone-call procedure, obtaining and using credit cards) require more learning and adjustment. One study found that Mexican Americans consumed more white bread, highly sugared cereals, and other unhealthy foods than either Anglos or Mexicans. It has been suggested that this was due to a time-lag effect: Mexican immigrants had assimilated an outdated version of the Anglo-American lifestyle that didn't reflect contemporary health concerns.[37]

Problems in Marketing to Hispanics. A number of problems exist in trying to market to the Hispanic subculture. As already noted, marketing to Puerto Ricans is not the same as marketing to Cuban Americans or to Mexican Americans. Moreover, cultural differences may exist within each segment. One advertising executive declared that, if the United States and Mexico went to war, Hispanics in California would likely fight for Mexico while those in Texas would fight for the United States.[38]

A second problem in marketing to Hispanics is the differences in the type of Spanish spoken. The word for "earring," *pantella,* can mean "television screen" or even "lampshade" to some Hispanics. In some areas of the United States, *bodega* means a small, Hispanic-owned grocery, but in south Texas *bodegas* are warehouses.[39]

The Asian-American Subculture

What is the fastest-growing ethnic subculture in the United States? The answer is not African Americans or Hispanics, but Asian Americans. In the 1980s over 40 percent of all immigrants to the United States came from Asia. Some estimate that, by the year 2050, the number of Asian Americans will nearly equal the number of Hispanics in the United States, who by then will be the largest minority. Asian Americans are already becoming a potent economic and intellectual force. The percentage of Asian Americans who graduate from college is nearly twice that of white Americans. In addition, family incomes of Asian Americans are significantly higher (by $4,848) than Anglo-Americans, $17,754 higher than Hispanics, and $18,221 higher than African Americans.[40]

To a greater degree than the differences that separate Hispanics, Asian Americans differ widely in language and culture of origin. Chinese, Vietnamese, Japanese, and Korean are the most common Asian languages spoken in the United States and are mutually incomprehensible. Tastes also differ. At the 1996 Olympics in Atlanta, a Chinese athlete complained that appropriate food wasn't available. Told that there was plenty of kimchi (fermented, spicy cabbage), he replied that kimchi was food for Koreans.

Comparing Anglo, African-American, and Hispanic Consumption

One study surveyed Anglo, African-American, and Hispanic consumers in order to compare the groups on a variety of consumption characteristics.[41] The results were inconsistent with a number of stereotypes concerning the groups. First, no evidence was found for differences in brand loyalty among the groups (Hispanics are often assumed to be very brand loyal). For brand loyalty, only an age effect occurred (respondents over 55 reported being more brand loyal). Second, both African Americans and Hispanics viewed trading stamps more positively than did Anglo consumers. No differences were found among the groups on coupon proneness, impulse buying, shopping for generic products, or the tendency to shop for specials. Both African Americans and Hispanics showed a greater tendency to shop for bargains. Overall, however, the results did not reveal large differences among the groups on any of the variables.

In sum, marketers must avoid assuming that stereotypes of ethnic subcultures are accurate. Marketing strategy should be based on sound marketing research and environmental analysis.

Portraying Minorities in Advertisements

One issue of concern has been the degree to which ethnic groups appear in advertising and commercials. Given their proportion in the U.S. population, African Americans are slightly underrepresented in magazine advertisements, but Hispanics are even more underrepresented, whereas Asian Americans are slightly overrepresented. In addition, Hispanics and Asian Americans are more likely to be depicted in a major role in advertisements than are African Americans. On the other hand, the Screen Actors Guild reported that in 1995 nonwhites got 21 percent of jobs in television advertisements, which actually exceeds their proportion of the population.[42]

On a final note, it is important to realize that notions of race and ethnicity are becoming increasingly fluid. For example, one of the common assumptions about Chinese society is that it developed in isolation from the West. But in 1987 an archaeologist found 3,000-year-old corpses with European features and blond hair in western

China, wearing textiles of a Celtic tartan style.[43] Again, caution is needed when using ethnicity or nationality as a marketing segmentation variable.

REGIONAL SUBCULTURES

Another major subcultural variable of interest to marketers concerns how populations locate themselves in the regions of the United States. Measuring and predicting the demographic patterns of **regional subcultures** is important to marketers for two reasons. First, different regions have distinct lifestyles resulting from variations in climate, culture, and the ethnic mix of people. Consequently, different product preferences exist. For example, there are regional preferences for foods and beverages. Some coffee manufacturers blend their coffee differently for the various regions—heavier in the East, lighter in the West, and with chicory in Louisiana.

A second reason for studying regional subcultures is that their growth rates and size may vary dramatically. For many types of goods, it is important to shorten the distribution channel as much as possible. New production facilities, therefore, should be built in areas experiencing the greatest population growth. In addition, companies looking for new growth opportunities should possibly focus on regions expected to experience population increases.

Dramatic changes are occurring in the populations of the regions of the United States. In the past the Northeast and North Central regions were the most heavily populated. However, by the late 1980s, three of the five most populated states (California, New York, Texas, Pennsylvania, and Florida) were in the lower half of the United States. In 1990 California and Texas became the two largest states in terms of population. As a result of shifting demographics, corporations are changing their marketing emphasis—and in many cases their corporate headquarters—to better focus on emerging markets.[44]

Table 14.6 shows regional population winners and losers in the 1980s and mid-1990s. Although California, Florida, and Alaska had large percentage increases during the 1980s, they were replaced by Idaho, Colorado, and Utah in the early to mid-1990s. The likely explanation for the change is that the economic recession of the early 1990s hit the first three states particularly hard, and as a result, their population growth slowed dramatically.

Regional population shifts occur for several reasons. One factor that affects these shifts is the search for jobs. During the severe recession of 1980–82, for example, many workers moved from the North Central states to the West and Southwest in search of employment. People also move for lifestyle reasons. Florida has grown rapidly because of the huge influx of retirees seeking the sun in their retirement years. Consequently, Florida is the nation's "oldest" state, with 18.4 percent of the population 65 or over.[45]

A third reason for regional population shifts is a difference in birthrates. These differences take longer to manifest themselves, but over a 10- to 20-year period, the variations become meaningful. In general, the West is younger than the Northeast and North Central states. The median age in the Northeast is over 30 years, whereas in the West it falls dramatically. For example, Alaska's median age is 28.3. Utah is the "youngest" state, with a median age of 25.5 years. In Utah's case a confluence of demographic factors accounts for the state's youthfulness. The Mormon population and influence in Utah is large. A central focus of the religion is the importance of the family and of childbearing, which, in turn, keeps median age relatively low.

The combination of a net inflow of migration and a youthful population portend future above-average growth in the Western states. The youthful population there will tend to have higher birthrates than the older populations found in the Northeast and North Central states.

Percentage Shifts in Population by State

1990–1997		1980–1990	
Fastest Percentage Growth			
Nevada	39.5%	Nevada	50.1%
Arizona	24.3	Alaska	36.9
Idaho	20.2	Arizona	34.9
Utah	19.5	Florida	32.7
Colorado	18.2	California	25.7
Slowest Percentage Growth			
Rhode Island	−1.6%	West Virginia	−8%
New York	−0.8	Iowa	−4.7
Connecticut	−0.5	North Dakota	−2.1
North Dakota	−0.3	Pennsylvania	0.1
Maine	1.2	Louisiana	0.3

Source: U.S. Department of Commerce, *Statistical Abstract of the United States, 1995, 1998* (Washington DC: U.S. Government Printing Office, 1995, 1998).

TABLE 14.6

Geodemographics

An area of study that is having major impact on marketing research is that of geodemographics. **Geodemographics** takes as its unit of analysis the neighborhood (i.e., census blocks) and obtains demographic information on consumers within neighborhoods. Census blocks found to contain people with similar demographic characteristics are then clustered together to form potential target markets for companies. This process of identifying groups of neighborhoods with households that are demographically similar is called **cluster analysis.** One basic concept of geodemographics is that individuals within a neighborhood have similar demographic characteristics, buying patterns, and values. A second important concept is that neighborhoods may be placed into similar categories, even when they are widely separated.[46] Geodemographic analysis can be an important managerial tool. In particular, geodemographics is a vital component of direct marketing. By directly contacting consumers with similar geodemographic profiles through direct mail or telephone calls, companies can precisely target a market segment. The result is a much more efficient use of a company's resources. A number of national firms offer geodemographic analysis, such as ACORN, ClusterPlus, PRIZM, and Micro-Vision.

Geodemographic analysis is a marketing research technique that is used in segmenting the marketplace, repositioning brands, and designing the marketing mix.

Neighborhoods identified as being in the same cluster then become market segments. L.L. Bean was one of the early users of geodemographic analysis to segment the marketplace. Because the company mails expensive catalogs to potential customers, it had to find a cost-effective way of identifying "L.L. Bean types." A company called PRIZM was hired to develop a geodemographic profile of the market segment that L.L. Bean should target. Catalogs were then sent to zip codes possessing a high percentage of "L.L. Bean–type" neighborhoods. The company slowly built a database that not only identified where their clients lived but also what magazines they read, the television shows they watched, and even the products they owned.[47]

Geodemographic analysis can assist managers in designing the marketing mix by providing a detailed profile of where customers live, what they buy, and what their demographic characteristics are. In particular, the location of stores and the selection of merchandise for stores can be guided by geodemographics. Recently, market researchers have used geodemographic analysis to identify good locations for new golf courses. By determining where golf courses are currently located and by identifying a demographic profile of golfers and where they live, researchers can pinpoint areas of the United States that have a surplus of golfers in relation to the number of courses available. Figure 14.1 presents a map that depicts the concentrations of golfers in the Michigan area, with darkly shaded areas representing high concentrations of golfers. The map was drawn in order to assist managers in deciding whether to build a new golf resort, called Sugar Loaf. Based on the map, do you think the resort would be successful?

Should Companies Segment by Geography?

The question of whether companies should segment by geographical areas is similar to the question of whether global companies should standardize their products across all markets or adapt their offerings to local conditions. There is little doubt that a national marketing effort is less expensive than a regionally based strategy. As one consultant succinctly put it, "Breadth of choice equals complexity; complexity equals increasing costs."[48] For example, when Campbell's divided the country into 22 regions, it had to promote 88 employees to brand sales managers, retrain its sales force, and make major changes in production—all costly moves. In addition, an effort to target a specific region frequently brings retaliation from local companies. When Campbell's introduced Spicy Ranchero Beans into the Southwest, the area's dominant marketer of beans, Ranch Style Beans, retaliated with heavy advertising and sales promotions.

Despite the problems related to developing regional marketing strategies, many companies have begun using regional segmentation. For example, the 30 teams of the NFL present a dilemma for store chains selling league merchandise. Although a few teams such as the Dallas Cowboys have a national following, in many cases regional teams draw the largest interest. A national chain such as Footlocker, therefore, must consider the appropriate mix of "national" versus "regional" teams to feature in their stores.[49]

SOCIAL-CLASS SUBCULTURES

Social classes may be defined as the relatively permanent strata in a society that differ in status, wealth, education, possessions, and values. All societies possess a hierarchical structure that stratifies residents into "classes" of people. Both actual and perceptual factors distinguish the groups. In concrete terms classes differ in occupations, lifestyles, values, friendships, manner of speaking, and possessions. In perceptual terms individuals perceive that different classes have diverging amounts of prestige, power, and privilege. Finally, members of a class tend to socialize with each other rather than with members of other classes. As one theorist observed, social classes are multidimensional.

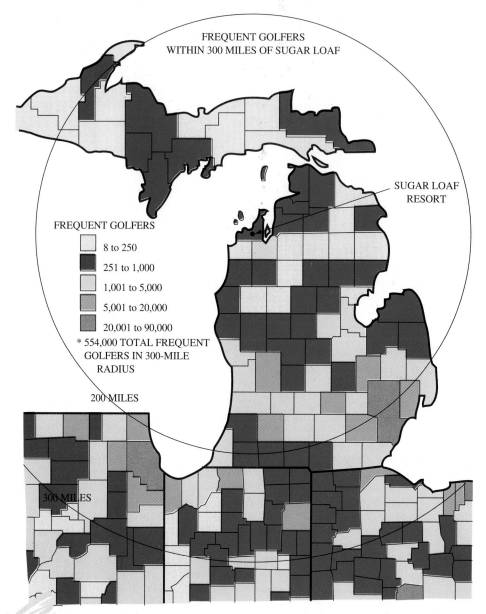

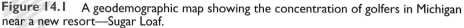

Figure 14.1   A geodemographic map showing the concentration of golfers in Michigan near a new resort—Sugar Loaf.

Three primary factors differentiate the social classes: economic status (e.g., occupation, wealth, house type and location), educational credentials, and behavioral standards (community participation, aspirations, and recreational habits).[50]

In the egalitarian culture of the United States, discussions of social class may make people uncomfortable. When answering an interviewer's question about social class, one woman said, "It's the dirtiest thing I've ever heard of."[51] Despite its unpleasant connotations, the study of social class has important managerial implications for marketers.

In comparison to how the term is used by sociologists, marketing managers interpret the concept of social class more narrowly. Marketers are concerned with how the buying patterns of social classes differ, rather than with the political, institutional, and cultural reasons for their existence. For marketers the social classes are seen as subcultures with distinct lifestyles, buying patterns, and motivations.[52] Thus, they view the social classes as potential market segments possessing divergent needs, wants, and desires for products and services.

What Are the Social Classes?

Table 14.7 provides a **social-class hierarchy** scheme and summarizes some of the characteristics of the social classes. The descriptions given in the table have proved quite

---

The Social-Class Hierarchy

A. Upper Americans

Upper-upper (0.3%). The world of inherited wealth and old family names. Working is a matter of choice, and members often serve on the boards of directors of major corporations. Serves as a reference for lower classes. Not a major market segment because of its small size.

Lower-upper (1.2%). The newer social elite, drawn from current professionals, corporate leadership. May be extremely wealthy, but the money is relatively new. Is an achieving group and will spend money to show its wealth. Will guard its social-class position because of insecurity. Is a major market for specialized luxury goods, such as Mercedes automobiles.

Upper-middle (12.5%). The rest of college-graduate managers, intellectual elite, and professionals. Lifestyle centers on private clubs, causes, and the arts. Collegiate credentials expected. Housing is extremely important to this group—particularly where the house is located. The quality and appearance of products are also important.

B. Middle Americans

Middle class (32%). White-collar workers and their blue-collar friends. Live on "the better side of town," try to "do the proper things." Have white-collar friends and acquaintances. Respectability is a key idea for this group. Home ownership, high moral standards, and focus on the family are important ideals. They tend to have high school educations or some college but do not reach high levels in their organizations.

Working class (38%). Blue-collar workers; lead "working-class lifestyle" whatever their income, school background, and job. Jobs tend to be monotonous, although affluence is possible if they have a union job. Tend to stay close to their parents and relatives and live in older parts of town. Do have money for consumer products and, with the middle class, represent the market for mass consumer goods.

C. Lower Americans

Upper-lower (9%). Working, not on welfare. Living standard is just above the poverty level. Behavior judged "crude," "trashy." Tend to be unskilled workers.

Lower-lower (7%). On welfare, visibly poverty stricken, usually out of work (or have the "dirtiest jobs"). Some are bums, common criminals. Has become separated from the upper-lower group because it exists mainly on government transfer payments. With the upper-lower class, accounts for only 6–7% of disposable income.

Source: Data adapted from Richard P. Coleman, "The Continuing Significance of Social Class in Marketing," *Journal of Consumer Research* 10 (December 1983): 265–80.

TABLE 14.7

accurate for at least the last 50 years in the United States. Recent trends, however, are creating some subtle changes. One trend is a new group of people who could be placed in the lower-upper class. These are professionals who marry and form two-career families. Because of their high incomes and their need to juggle two careers, these families have become a separate target market. For example, when one spouse must move because of job relocation, the other spouse may need help finding employment comparable to the current position, and businesses have sprung up to cater to this need.[53]

Differences between social classes are evident in their communication patterns. One study found that people can identify an individual's social class simply by hearing him or her read something.[54] Social classes differ in their speech cadence, voice modulation, and fluency of speech. The choice of words also varies among the social classes.[55] Lower classes describe the world in more concrete terms than do the middle and upper classes. If asked where he or she obtained bubble gum, a lower-class child would likely state a person's name. An upper-class child would simply say "from the grocery store."

Although most marketers agree that social class is an important concept, published examples of its use in marketing are sparse because there are a number of problems in using social class as a segmentation variable. One problem in measuring social class is that the measures assume that an individual's social class is an average of his or her position on several dimensions of status. The consistency with which an individual reveals a particular social class across a number of dimensions is called **status crystallization.** Some have argued that those who have low crystallization are more prone to express liberal ideas and advocate changes in the social order.[56] An example of low crystallization might be a Hispanic attorney whose parents were laborers.

Social Class and Buying Behavior

Because of the problems of the social-class concept, one must use caution in interpreting the findings of studies investigating its impact on buying behavior. One finding of importance to marketers is that the reasons for shopping differ among the social classes. The upper classes tend to shop not only out of necessity but also for pleasure.[57] Higher-class women tend to favor stores with a high-fashion image, such as the Neiman Marcus chain, whereas lower-class women favor mass merchandisers and stores with price appeal. The shopping patterns of the upper class reveal the importance of maintaining a certain social image. Products that reflect differences in class, like furniture, are viewed as "socially risky." Upper-class consumers tend to purchase such products from specialty shops and department stores geared to providing personal service in an upscale atmosphere. For low-risk products, such as toasters, the upper-class shopper is perfectly willing to buy a brand-name product from a discounter. The relationship between income and willingness to buy store-brand rather than national-brand merchandise may be curvilinear: Low-income and higher-income shoppers are less likely to buy store brands than those in between.[58]

The social classes also differ in the amount and type of information search behavior done prior to and during shopping. Middle- and upper-class consumers tend to engage in more information search prior to making a purchase. For example, before buying appliances they may read newspapers, brochures, and test reports. In contrast, lower-class consumers are more apt to rely on in-store displays and salespeople.[59] In general, lower-class consumers have less product information. They are less informed about product prices and are no more likely to buy products "on sale" than are upper-class consumers. Upper-class consumers are also less likely to use price as an indicator of quality. They tend to judge the quality of products on their merits rather than on their price.

Psychological Differences Among the Classes

Many of the differences noted in the consumption behaviors of the social classes can be explained by differences in the way each view the world. The middle classes tend to focus on the future. They are generally self-confident, are willing to take risks, believe that they can control their fate, and see their horizons as broad. In contrast, the lower classes focus on the present and past. They are concerned with security and with their family and themselves.

Psychological differences in the social classes were demonstrated in a study that investigated how groups of consumers differed in their perception of the symbolism of products.[60] Lower-class individuals tended to believe that owners of big houses and nice cars obtained them because of "good luck." In contrast, consumers with higher social status attributed the ability to purchase status symbols to the self-motivation of the owner. Such results indicate a more fatalistic view of life among the lower classes. These psychological and lifestyle differences are summed up by the following quotation:

> For twenty years researchers have found that "working-class life styles have been almost impervious to change in their basic characteristics—i.e., the limited horizons, the centrality of family and clan. The chauvinistic devotion to nation and neighborhood have been little altered by the automobile, telephone, or television. The modernity—and change—that these people seek is in possessions, not in human relationships or 'new ideas.' "[61]

Social Class and Lifestyles

As a macroenvironmental force, social class strongly influences consumers' lifestyles. Four generalizations can be made concerning the impact of social class on consumer lifestyles: (1) social class influences lifestyle, (2) social class is predictive of resources owned, (3) goods may be purchased as status symbols, and (4) consumption of status symbols is a skill.

Social Class Influences Consumer Lifestyles. Perhaps the most important contribution of social class to the understanding of consumer behavior is that it strongly influences lifestyle. Max Weber was perhaps the earliest researcher to link social class and lifestyle, although he viewed lifestyle as more closely linked to status than to class. Some consumer researchers have even argued that lifestyle is the "essence of social class."[62] The style of consumption (i.e., lifestyle) may be viewed as an expression of a particular social class. How consumers live is directly influenced by their education, household income, occupation, and type of house. Level of education tends to influence a person's activities, interests, opinions, values, and beliefs. Household income influences the capacity to purchase consumer goods and to express other interests. Occupation influences the type of people with whom a person associates as well as the types of products and services that are purchased to play the occupational role. As noted in chapter 12, the products and services that a person must have in order to engage effectively in a particular role are called a *role-related product cluster.*[63] A stereotypical view of the role-related product cluster of a successful young attorney or stockbroker might include an Armani suit, luxury car, and vacation home.

Social Class Is Predictive of Resources Owned. Four resource dimensions have been identified as influenced by social class—financial, social, cultural, and time. First, those in higher social classes tend to have greater financial resources because of their occupations or inherited wealth. Second, as one moves higher in social-class level, opportunities for social participation increase, and associations are made with those of higher social standing. The level of social participation generally rises as social status increases. Social skill and social standing appear to be closely linked.[64] Third, those in higher social classes tend to be familiar with cultural matters. In addition, higher-education credentials provide "cultural capital" for individuals. Finally, those in higher social classes tend to have a broader time horizon than those in lower social classes. The higher social classes require people both to have longer time horizons and to delay gratification while building personal skills through education. Those in higher social classes frequently have less "free time" but have more flexibility in choosing the activities on which to spend their time.

Goods May Be Purchased as Status Symbols. Products and services may be purchased as a means of showing membership in a particular social class. Goods and services may represent social-class standing because of restrictions that make it difficult for individuals not in the social class to own them. These restrictions tend to arise because individuals in lower social classes lack the resources to purchase or effectively use these status symbols. For example, in the United States, owning a Mercedes-Benz has come to represent membership in the lower-upper class for many individuals. Similarly, a high level of educational resources is required to read and enjoy certain magazines, such as the *New Yorker,* that are indicative of upper-middle-class standing.

It has long been recognized that, in order to depict social status, people must display appropriate material items. This is because we frequently encounter individuals who are strangers, and the only way to ascertain the person's status is through visual cues. There is a problem, however, in portraying social class through material goods. If the ownership of a material symbol is diffused across levels of the class hierarchy, it becomes a **fraudulent symbol.**[65] That is, if members of different social classes display the same symbol of status, it will not accurately depict the meaning desired. For a material item to adequately symbolize social-class standing, accuracy is required in both the encoding and decoding stages.[66]

Ownership of the material item must be homogeneous within a single social class in order for accurate encoding to occur. Thus, people within the class should consistently possess the good. In addition, there must be wide agreement that possession of the item symbolizes a particular social-class standing. When a shared status meaning is attached to a material good by society at large, accuracy in decoding occurs. Examples of material symbols that individuals decode in a consistent manner are clothing, health care, automobiles, and housing.[67] Another material symbol that is accurately encoded and decoded is the possession of hired household help. The presence of chauffeurs, cooks, and gardeners is indicative of an individual in the upper classes.

Consumption of Status Symbols Is a Skill. The adroit purchase of goods and services can be used to solidify or help advance an individual's social-class standing. Individuals who fail to represent their social class via the "correct" visible symbols risk scorn and the disrespectful title of "nouveau riche." Learning to make the correct purchases is a type of skill. The problems associated with moving rapidly from one class to another have been grist for Hollywood movie makers. In *King Ralph,* for example, John Goodman is a Las Vegas lounge singer one day and king of England the next. In *Coming to America,* Eddie Murphy goes the other way, from a prince in Africa to working at a fast-food restaurant in the United States.

An argument can be made that a great deal of status anxiety currently exists in the United States. The number of consumption guides, fashion experts, interior decorators, and real estate professionals suggests great concern about appropriate consumption. People would not hire these surrogate consumers if the accurate display of symbolic material goods were unimportant. The need to purchase the "correct" goods and services to support or help advance status has created an entire class of surrogate consumers.

OTHER SUBCULTURES

Because space limitations restrict a full discussion of all the various subcultures available for target marketing, only a few are outlined here. One geographically based subculture is represented by the increase in population of rural areas. From 1990 to 1995, three-quarters of the rural counties in the United States grew in population, reversing the pattern of the 1980s. This movement is spearheaded by those looking for retirement living or for recreational uses. The rise in telecommuting and long-distance driving may be allowing more workers to move into rural areas as well.[68] Another subculture is made up of the some 49 million U.S. citizens who are disabled in some way, a segment of the population that offers additional marketing opportunities.

An Internet Community?

The growth of the Internet may be spawning a new subculture—that of Web users.[69] In demographic terms this community is largely male and well educated. Web users may increasingly be using "Internet friends" as sources of information and product recommendations, eclipsing the influence of family members, coworkers, and friends.

MANAGERIAL IMPLICATIONS

The ideas generated from our discussion of subcultures have applications to each of the PERMS concepts. These applications are described in the following sections.

Positioning and Differentiation

One method of positioning a product is to differentiate it vis-à-vis competitors by making special appeals to subgroups or subcultures. As an example, the appeal of the popular music industry has continued and has even increased due to ever-finer positioning of music to narrower targets. "Rock" music is now subdivided into "light," "punk," "industrial," and other forms.

At the same time, musical "products" once targeted to small subcultural markets are now finding opportunities to "mainstream" themselves. For example, in recent years both country and "Latin" music have expanded well beyond their subcultural roots.

Environmental Analysis

Marketing managers should conduct environmental analysis in order to track changes in the size of a market for any product or service. Segments of appropriate size and buying power can then be identified and specific products developed and promoted for the target groups.

In addition to carefully analyzing age trends, marketers should conduct broader-scale demographic analyses. Environmental analyses should be conducted to identify changes in the ethnic composition of the population, which may reveal new consumer segments to be targeted.

Research

Market research can identify the unmet needs of various subcultures. However, attention also needs to be paid to the possibility that "representative samples" may in fact not be representative. As discussed in this chapter, there are a number of divisive elements within the Hispanic and Asian-American subcultures (for example, country of origin) that can prevent a sample from representing the subculture as a whole.

At the extreme, a third-generation Hispanic attorney from Houston who graduated from Harvard Law School and drives a BMW may have less in common with new immigrants from Central America than she does with other big-city attorneys. Although this case is not typical, marketing mistakes are possible if attention is not paid to the forces that divide, as well as unite, a particular subculture.

Marketing Mix

Differences between age cohorts, ethnic groups, and regions and social classes have implications for differences in promotional, product, and pricing strategy. Multiple examples (e.g., Levi's, Sears) demonstrate the need to respond to changes in age cohorts. The makers of Pokémon face the issue of how to retain interest in new cohorts of preteens; the conventional wisdom is that, like the Teenage Mutant Ninja Turtles and Mighty Morphin Power Rangers, this fad will soon end, and preteens will move on to a new fantasy world. Nintendo has built a $6 billion empire whose survival depends on the outcome. The makers are counting on a synergy between collectible elements (like Beanie Babies, Cabbage Patch Dolls, and baseball cards), a complete mythology (like Power Rangers), and a raft of Web sites (starting with www.pokemon .com), shows, and games to keep interest flowing for years to come. One can even buy sheet music to teach the Pokémon theme to budding pianists and guitar players.

Segmentation

An example of a manufacturer using ethnic subculture appeals as a segmentation device is Mattel. The company now offers the Barbie doll (now, at over 40, herself the age of a baby boomer) as representative of a variety of ethnic and national subgroups. There is, for example, a Puerto Rican Barbie, and Spanish, Swedish, and Northwest Coast Native American Barbies were part of the "Millennium 2000 line." In additional to segmenting on ethnic lines, Mattel also offers a wheelchair Barbie and a "Hacker Barbie" designed to counteract the notion that girls are "numerophobic."

Notes

1. Robert E. Pitts, "Guest Editorial: The Hispanic Subculture: Subcultural Complexity and Marketing Opportunity," *Psychology and Marketing* 3, no. 4 (1986): 243–46.
2. Suein L. Hwang, "Kosher-Food Firms Dive into the Mainstream," *Wall Street Journal*, April 1, 1993, pp. B1, B6.
3. D. O. Arnold, *The Sociology of Subcultures* (Berkeley, CA: Glendasary Press, 1970).
4. R. T. Reynolds, B. Robey, and C. Russell, "Demographics of the 1980s," *American Demographics*, January 1980, pp. 11–19.
5. "Americans Change," *Business Week*, February 20, 1978, pp. 64–80.
6. Campbell Gibson, "The Four Baby Booms," *American Demographics*, November 1993, pp. 37–40. Also see "The Boomer Initiative," <www.babyboomers.com>.
7. Teri Agins, "The Status of Denim: Designer Jeans Make a Comeback," *Wall Street Journal*, July 2, 1996, pp. B1, B3: Teri Agins, "Like Boomers' Middles, Elastic Waistbands S-p-r-e-a-d," *Wall Street Journal*, September 19, 1996, pp. B1, B10.
8. David Plotz, "Defining Decay Down: Why Dentists Still Exist," *Slate* magazine, <www.slate.com> (August 18, 1999).
9. Christina Buff, "Passing the Bucks: Aging Boomers Cut the Cord but Can't Let Go of the Wallet," *Wall Street Journal*, July 8, 1996, pp. A1, A5.
10. Ronald Alsop, "Busters May Replace Boomers as the Darlings of Advertisers," *Wall Street Journal*, November 12, 1987, p. 35: Chris Manolis, Aron Levin, and Robert Dahlstrom, "A Generation X Scale: Conceptualization, Measurement, and Nomological Validity," *Marketing Theory and Applications*, ed. Edward Blair and Wagner A. Kamakura (Chicago, IL: American Marketing Association, 1996), 7:435–36.
11. Diane Summers, "A View of the X-Files," *Financial Times*, January 20, 1996, p. 11.
12. Jennifer DeCoursey, "Growing Pains Plague Generation X Magazines," *Advertising Age*, November 5, 1995, p. S24.

13. Richard Tomkins, "Shaking Out the Last Dollop of Growth," *Financial Times,* June 12–13, 1999, p. 7.

14. Raymond Serafin and Cleveland Horton, "X Marks the Spot for Car Marketing," *Advertising Age,* August 9, 1993, p. 8.

15. Cyndee Miller, "Teens Seen as the First Truly Global Customers," *Marketing News,* March 27, 1995, p. 9. See chapter 19 for a discussion of the possible problems of assuming that markets are the same across the world.

16. Susan Mitchell, "The Next Baby Boom," *American Demographics,* October 1995, pp. 22–31.

17. Emily Nelson, "Why Teenage Sitters Have So Much Power," *Wall Street Journal,* September 26, 1996, pp. B1, B7.

18. Gerald Celente, "Sons and Daughters of Woodstock Say 'Hell, No,' " *Financial Times Weekend Supplement,* January 2–3, 1999, p. 3.

19. Rick Christie, "Marketers Err by Treating Elderly as Uniform Group," *Wall Street Journal,* October 31, 1988, pp. B1, B3.

20. Fabian Linden and Paul Ryscavage, "How We Live," Conference Board and the U.S. Bureau of the Census, 1986; U.S. Department of Commerce, *Statistical Abstract of the United States, 1995* (Washington DC: U.S. Government Printing Office, 1995), 399.

21. Catherine A. Cole and Siva K. Balasubramanian, "Age Differences in Consumers' Search for Information: Public Policy Implications," *Journal of Consumer Research* 20 (June 1993): 157–69.

22. Jack Botwinick, *Aging and Behavior: A Comprehensive Integration of Research Findings,* 2nd ed. (New York: Springer, 1978).

23. L. G. Schiffman, "Perceived Risk in New Product Trial by Elderly Consumers," *Journal of Marketing Research* 9 (February 1972): 106–8.

24. Rose L. Johnson, "Age and Social Activity as Correlates of Television Orientation: A Replication and Extension," *Advances in Consumer Research,* ed. Leigh McAlister and Michael L. Rothschild (Provo, UT: Association for Consumer Research, 1993), 20:257–61.

25. Gabrielle Sandor, "Attitude (Not Age) Defines the Mature Market," *American Demographics,* January 1994, pp. 18–21: Benny Barak and Leon Schiffman, "Cognitive Age: A Nonchronological Age Variable," in *Advances in Consumer Research,* ed. Kent B. Monroe (Ann Arbor, MI: Association for Consumer Research, 1981), 8:602–6; and Robert E. Wilkes, "A Structural Modeling Approach to the Measurement and Meaning of Cognitive Age," *Journal of Consumer Research* 19 (September 1992): 292–301.

26. U.S. Department of Commerce, *Statistical Abstract of the United States, 1995,* 476.

27. Jennifer Edson Escalas, "African American Vernacular English in Advertising: A Sociolinguistic Study, "in *Advances in Consumer Research,* ed. Chris T. Allen and Deborah Roedder John (Provo, UT: Association for Consumer Research, 1994), 21:304–9.

28. Lydia A. McKinley-Floyd, J. R. Smith, and Hudson Nwakanma, "The Impact of Social Class on African American Consumer Behavior: An Interdisciplinary Perspective," in *Marketing Theory and Applications,* ed. C. Whan Park and Daniel C. Smith (Chicago, IL: American Marketing Association, 1994), 5:384–89.

29. Laura Bird, "Critics Shoot at New Colt 45 Campaign," *Wall Street Journal,* February 17, 1993, p. B1.

30. Lisa Peñaloza, "*Atravesando Fronteras/*Border Crossing: A Critical Ethnographic Exploration of the Consumer Acculturation of Mexican Immigrants," *Journal of Consumer Research* 21 (June 1994): 32–54.

31. Lisa A. Yorgey, "Cultured Creative," *Target Marketing,* November 1995, pp. 22–28.

32. Daniel McQuillen, "Cities of Gold," *Incentive,* February 1996, pp. 38–40. Other estimates place the number of Hispanics living in urban areas at up to 88 percent. See Peñaloza, "*Atravesando Fronteras.*"

33. B. G. Yovovich, "Cultural Pride Galvanizes Heritages," *Advertising Age,* February 15, 1982, pp. M9, M44.

34. B. A. Brusco, "Hispanic Marketing: New Application of Old Methodologies," *Theme,* May–June 1981, pp. 8–9.

35. Joel Saegert, Francis Piron, and Rosemary Jimenez, "Do Hispanics Constitute a Market Segment?" in *Advances in Consumer Research,* ed. John Sherry and Brian Sternthal (Provo, UT: Association for Consumer Research, 1992), 19:28–33.

36. Marilyn Lavin, "Acculturating the Hispanic Consumer: The Grocery Shopping Experience," *Marketing Theory and Applications,* ed. David W. Stewart and Naufel J. Vilcassim (Chicago, IL: American Marketing Association, 1995), 6:359–64.

37. Melanie Wallendorf and Michael R. Reilly, "Ethnic Migration, Assimilation, and Consumption," *Journal of Consumer Research* 10 (December 1983): 292–302. Cited in Peñaloza, "*Atravesando Fronteras.*"

38. John Sugg, "Miami's Latino Market Spans Two Continents," *Advertising Age*, February 15, 1982, pp. M9, M44.

39. Additional problems occur when companies are "politically incorrect" in a foreign language. Microsoft accidentally released a Spanish-language thesaurus suggesting that Indians can be equated with man-eating savages and offering "bastard" as a synonym for those of mixed race. Don Clark, "Hey, #@*% Amigo, Can You Translate the Word 'Gaffe'?" *Wall Street Journal*, July 8, 1996, p. B6.

40. U.S. Bureau of the Census, "Income and Poverty Status of Americans Improve, Health Insurance Coverage Stable, Census Bureau Reports," press release, September 26, 1996.

41. Robert E. Wilkes and Humberto Valencia, "Shopping-Related Characteristics of Mexican Americans and Blacks," *Psychology and Marketing* 3 (1986): 247–59. Also see Francis J. Mulhern and Jerome B Williams, "A Comparative Analysis of Shopping Behavior in Hispanic and Non-Hispanic Shopping Areas," *Journal of Retailing* 70 (fall 1994): 231–52.

42. Charles R. Taylor, Ju Yung Lee, and Barbara B. Stern, "Portrayals of African, Hispanics, and Asian Americans in Magazine Advertising," in *Marketing and Consumer Research in the Public Interest*, ed. Ronald P. Hill (Thousand Oaks, CA: Sage, 1996), 133–50; Leon E. Wynter, "Business and Race," *Wall Street Journal*, November 6, 1996, p. B1.

43. Gale Eisenstodt, "Myths and Mummies," *Financial Times Weekend Supplement*, August 28–29, 1998, p. 1.

44. Joe Schwartz, "Fourth to Florida," *American Demographics*, October 1987, p. 14.

45. U.S. Department of Commerce, *Statistical Abstract of the United States, 1995*, 33.

46. David J. Curry, The New Marketing Research Systems: How to Use Strategic Database Information for Better Marketing Decisions (New York: Wiley, 1993).

47. Ibid.

48. Alix M. Freedman, "National Firms Find That Selling Local Tastes Is Costly, Complex," *Wall Street Journal*, February 9, 1987, p. 17.

49. Andrew Gaffney and Andy Bernstein, "Jim Connelly," *Sporting Goods Business*, February 1996, pp. 62–65.

50. Richard Coleman, "The Continuing Significance of Social Class in Marketing," *Journal of Consumer Research* 10 (December 1983): 265–80.

51. R. H. Tawney, *Equality* (London: Union Books, 1981).

52. James Carmen, *The Application of Social Class in Market Segmentation* (Berkeley, CA: Institute of Business and Economic Research, 1965).

53. Bill Leonard and Roger D. Sommer, "Relocating the Two-Income Family," *HR Magazine*, August 1995, pp. 55–58.

54. Dean Ellis, "Speech and Social Status in America," *Social Forces* 45 (March 1967): 431–37.

55. Leonard Schatzman and A. Strauss, "Social Class and Modes of Communication," *American Journal of Sociology* 60 (January 1955): 329–38.

56. Gerhard Lenski, "Status Crystallization: A Non-Vertical Dimension of Social Status," *American Sociological Review* 21 (August 1956): 458–64.

57. Stuart Rich and Subhash Jain, "Social Class and Life Cycle as Predictors of Shopping Behavior," *Journal of Marketing Research* 5 (February 1968): 43–44.

58. Alan Dick, Arun Jain, and Paul Richardson, "Correlates of Store Brand Proneness: Some Empirical Observations," *Journal of Product and Brand Management* 4, no. 4 (1995): 15–22.

59. V. Kanti Prasad, "Socioeconomic Product Risk and Patronage Preferences of Retail Shoppers," *Journal of Marketing* 39 (July 1975): 42–47.

60. Russell Belk, Robert Mayer, and Kenneth Bahn, "The Eye of the Beholder: Individual Differences in Perceptions of Consumption Symbolism," in *Advances in Consumer Research*, ed. Andrew Mitchell (Ann Arbor, MI: Association for Consumer Research, 1981), 9:523–29.

61. Cited in Coleman, "Continuing Significance of Social Class."

62. J. H. Myers and Jonathan Guttman, "Life Style: The Essence of Social Class," in *Lifestyle and Psychographics*, ed. William Wells (Chicago, IL: American Marketing Association, 1974), 235–56.

63. Another group of authors has called this the "standard package" for both different occupational groups and for different cultural groups, for example, Asian Americans. See Cecelia Wittmayer, Steve Schulz, and Robert Mittelstaedt, "A Cross-Cultural Look at the

'Supposed to Have It' Phenomenon: The Existence of a Standard Package Based on Occupation," in *Advances in Consumer Research,* ed. Chris T. Allen and Deborah Roedder John (Provo, UT: Association for Consumer Research, 1994), 21:427–34.

64. Much of this section is based on ideas suggested by James Fisher, "Social Class and Consumer Behavior: The Relevance of Class and Status," in *Advances in Consumer Research,* ed. Melanie Wallendorf and Paul Anderson (Provo, UT: Association for Consumer Research, 1987), 14:492–96.

65. Erving Goffman, "Symbols of Class Status," *British Journal of Sociology* 2 (December 1951): 294–304.

66. Russell Belk, "Developmental Recognition of Consumption Symbolism," *Journal of Consumer Research* 9 (June 1982): 887–97.

67. Scott Dawson and Jill Cavell, "Status Recognition in the 1980s: Invidious Distinction Revisited," in *Advances in Consumer Research,* ed. Melanie Wallendorf and Paul Anderson (Provo, UT: Association for Consumer Research, 1987), 487–91.

68. Scott Kilman and Robert L. Rose, "Population of Rural America is Swelling," *Wall Street Journal,* June 21, 1996, pp. B1, B4.

69. Neil A. Granitz and James C. Ward, "Virtual Community: A Sociocognitive Analysis," in *Advances in Consumer Research,* ed. Kim P. Corfman and John G. Lynch Jr. (Provo, UT: Association for Consumer Research, 1996), 23:161–66.

The International Consumer

After reading this chapter, you should be able to describe each of the following concepts, together with their managerial relevance:

1. The cross-cultural significance of symbols.
2. How cultural values differ around the world.
3. Cross-cultural problem areas.
4. Back translation.
5. Differences in time perception.
6. Nonverbal behavior.
7. Ethnocentricity and animosity.
8. Cross-cultural differences in symbols, friendship, and etiquette.
9. Standardized global marketing strategy.
10. Pattern advertising.

The importance of understanding culture is well illustrated when marketers are unsuccessful at selling their products abroad. By recognizing the differences between their own culture and that of the targeted society, marketing managers can avoid multimillion-dollar mistakes. At the same time, managers should be aware that diverse cultures often share certain interests. For example, enthusiasm for basketball is exploding. In addition, many basic needs are similar across countries and cultures.

Consumer-behavior concepts apply across diverse cultures. The importance of food in France illustrates the role of *cultural rituals* in consumer behavior. Selling cheese to the French would probably be an exercise in futility because the French are very particular when it comes to this item. French *hypermarches* may carry 130 brands of cheese, bottled in oils, rolled in ashes, covered with mold, filled with seasoning, surrounded by rinds or waxes, and even in decay. In France cheese consumption, like food consumption in general, is considered so important that the French government brought top chefs into primary schools in the 1990s to educate young French palates concerning food preparation and consumption rituals. In France cheese is served on a plate, eaten with a knife and fork, and usually accompanied by bread and wine.[1]

CROSS-CULTURAL USE OF SYMBOLS

Differences in cultures are readily seen in the use of symbols. For example, one class of American products that frequently succeeds abroad is motion pictures. American-made movies have strong appeal to many overseas audiences. Because of the high profit potential, a movie may be distributed overseas within six months of its release in the United States. Despite their general popularity, however, it can be difficult to predict which American-made films will be popular overseas. For example, Al Pacino is a well-known actor here, but he is a bigger star abroad. U.S. posters for the movie *Scent of a Woman* featured Pacino less prominently than did the posters used overseas.[2] The difference between the actor's popularity here and in other countries illustrates how symbols may have different meanings to people of different cultures.

As discussed in chapter 13, issues of language usage can tie us into cross-cultural knots. Why, for example, do the Japanese appear to care so little about incorrect use of English terms in naming products? One consultant for Interbrand, a branding consulting firm, says that, in foreign domestic markets, "English is used as a kind of aspirational language. . . . There's not a lot of research done into what the names actually mean because they're not intended for an English-speaking audience." Hence, one gets nonsense names for cars in Japan such as Subaru's Picnic-Car Astonish, Nissan's Pantry Boy Supreme, and Mazda's Bongo Brawny. In addition, any attempt to invent names that will survive across borders is perilous. Toyota's MR2 was a disaster in France, where it was pronounced *merde,* denoting excrement; Ford's Pinto translated into "small penis" in Portuguese, diminishing its appeal to male drivers; and Mitsubishi's Pajero, a macho SUV, translated into "masturbator" in Latin American Spanish slang.[3]

The symbolic meaning of various holidays also differs across cultures. For example, in Japan Christmas has little to do with celebrating the birth of Jesus. Instead, Christmas Eve (more important than the day after) is to young people a night for romance; hotels are booked up to a year in advance. For everyone, it is a good day to eat fried chicken and strawberry shortcake. On Christmas Eve KFC's Japan unit sells about five times that of an average day.[4]

The symbolic meaning of nonverbal communication can also create problems in the international arena. A story is told of an American consultant who rented a car in South Africa and noticed that people were looking at him, then rapidly opening and closing their hands. He assumed this meant something like "hello" and began doing the same thing. He later found that they were telling him, "your car lights are on." And he was signaling back, "and so are yours."

Knowledge of the implicit meaning of symbols is particularly important when a company begins to market its products or services internationally. The next section discusses this important issue.

INTERNATIONAL MARKETING AND CONSUMER BEHAVIOR

For an international marketing campaign to succeed, managers must have an excellent understanding of culture in the target markets. Cross-cultural analysis involves the study of the values, attitudes, language, and customs of other societies.

Table 15.1 identifies seven categories of differences in foreign cultures that affect international business. Of these, perhaps the most important are differences in languages and values. Differences in language can severely impede the communication process. Value differences have a more subtle, but equally important, impact on marketing. For example, values related to the acceptability of body hair on women severely limit the ability of companies to market razors successfully in some countries. The Austrian marketing director for Gillette once remarked, "We don't have to advertise women's razors here. I can personally give razors to all four Austrian women who want them."[5] The fact that Gillette is now advertising the Sensor for women in neighboring Germany shows that cultural values can change over time.

The East Asian Consumer

Over the past couple of decades, the United States' trade ties with Europe have decreased in importance. Foreign trade has increasingly focused on developing countries, as well as on countries around the Pacific Rim. The Pacific Rim includes North America, South America, Australia, Indonesia, East Asia, and Siberia. This region is the home of 50 percent of the world's population and holds 6 of the world's 10 "supercities" (none of the 10 are in Europe).[6]

East Asia in particular should become increasingly important to the United States. Composed of Japan, Korea, China, and Southeast Asia, the region has over one-fourth of the world's population and is the dominant exporter of automobiles, electronics, and computer chips. The culture, however, has marked dissimilarities to that found in the United States. East Asian countries follow the Confucian ethic, a philosophy that does not subscribe to a supreme being and that emphasizes the virtues of work, frugality, and education.

Within East Asia Japan is a major trading partner and economic competitor of the United States. One of the main cultural differences between the countries is how the two societies view the individual. In the United States, the individual is seen as more important than the state, whereas in Japan the group, family, and state are relatively more important.

International Business Cultural Factors

1. *Language.* Spoken, written, mass media, linguistic pluralism.
2. *Values.* As related to time, achievement, work, wealth, change, risk taking, science.
3. *Politics.* Nationalism, sovereignty, power, imperialism, ideologies.
4. *Technology and material culture.* Transportation, energy system, communications, urbanization, science.
5. *Social organization.* Social mobility, status systems, authority structures, kinship.
6. *Education.* Literacy, human resource planning, higher education.
7. *Religion.* Philosophical systems, sacred objects, rituals.

Source: Adapted from Vern Terpstra and Kenneth David, *The Cultural Environment of International Business* (Cincinnati, OH: Southwestern Publishing, 1991).

TABLE 15.1

The differences in the cultures can also be seen in how companies view employees and customers. Japanese companies tend to assume that their customers are correct and honest in all cases. The attitude of American companies may tend to go in the other direction. Similarly, Japanese firms motivate their employees with job security and longevity, although this general statement can be taken too far: part-time workers and women typically do not have job security, and many workers are forced to retire between the age of 55 and 60 and need to continue working elsewhere.[7]

Although cultural values are rather difficult to change, the Japanese are beginning to adopt some values that are more Western in orientation. For example, after years of working longer hours than their counterparts in other rich countries, the Japanese are now learning to value their leisure time. The government asked businesses to reduce the usual five-and-a-half-day workweek and gave government employees a five-day workweek in 1992.[8] Millions of Japanese are engaging in foreign travel, and exposure to shopping in other countries has increased their demand for consumer goods from other countries.

One of the consumption patterns that the Japanese share with Americans—but which has been taken to even greater heights in Japan—is the use of automated vending machines. In Japan these machines are grouped into "stores." A larger variety of goods are sold via machines, and they appear both in residential and commercial-use areas. Although the Japanese may buy an entire meal from vending machines, they don't like to eat in public; thus, the machines must be close enough to either home or work so that food can be eaten in privacy.

Taiwan, South Korea, Singapore, and Hong Kong are also top markets for U.S. products. Many U.S. companies are even more intrigued by the 1.2 billion consumers in the People's Republic of China. China has the world's fastest-growing economy, and consumer preferences are changing, as shown by the composition of the "three bigs," the most longed for consumer items. The "three bigs"—once a watch, bicycle, and a sewing-machine, and in the 1980s a color television, a washing machine, and a tape recorder—in the 1990s were a VCR, air conditioner, and stereo.[9] Wal-Mart operates six stores in China under joint-venture agreements.

Another of the most rapidly expanding markets in the world is Vietnam, where PepsiCo's KFC unit was the first of many U.S. fast-food brands to open stores. North Korea is also opening its doors. The cases of Vietnam and North Korea are illustrative of a growing tendency on the part of Western businesspeople to think of developing countries not only as sites for low-cost production but as groups of real customers who have, or will shortly have, the incomes to purchase significant amounts of Western products.[10]

Researchers have investigated differences in decision making among people in the United States and East Asia. One such study examined differences in the exchange process among executives from China, Japan, Korea, and the United States.[11] In this study the executives engaged in a simulated negotiation exercise in which they had to reach an agreement on the price of three products. In all cases the negotiations occurred within the same culture: Americans negotiated with Americans, Japanese with Japanese, and so on. The study revealed a number of interesting results. First, Japanese and Korean buyers were both found to have greater status than the sellers, and in each case the buyers received greater profits than did the sellers. Second, for Americans the key to successful negotiations was the use of problem-solving strategies, which involved cooperation and information exchange. Third, competitive strategies yielded higher economic rewards for the Chinese. Fourth, the Korean's negotiation style incorporated aspects of the American negotiation model and the Japanese model. The authors concluded that if a universal principle could be found, it was that interpersonal attractiveness strongly influences negotiation outcomes for all four cultural groups. The more interpersonally attractive the partners were to each other, the better the outcomes.

The Latin American Consumer

With the ratification of the North American Free Trade Agreement (NAFTA), we can expect that trade with Mexico—already the United States' third-largest trading partner—will leap upward. Nor will trade-expanding agreements stop there. The United States has agreed to negotiate free-trade agreements with all other Latin American countries, beginning with Chile.

American-made products are viewed positively in Latin America. In Mexico about 90 percent of the movie videos rented are made in Hollywood and are usually adapted with subtitles rather than Spanish dubbing.[12] On one weekend in Buenos Aires, Argentina, no one could view Oliver Stone's film *Nixon* because the only copy in the city had been borrowed by then president Carlos Menem.

Other U.S. exports are also highly prized. The number of U.S. franchises with outlets in Mexico quadrupled in the early 1990s to more than a hundred. *Cristina,* an imported Cuban-American TV talk show, patterns itself after *Oprah* and other American talk shows that dwell on psychological and sexual issues.[13]

Not to be outdone, Grupo Televisa, Latin America's biggest media concern, has exported its racy telenovelas to Turkey, China, India, Russia, and elsewhere. The company is also becoming a force in English-language programming for the U.S. market.[14] In addition, Telmex, Mexico's leading telecommunications company, has opened an Internet portal with Microsoft for all of Latin America. [15]

As trade increases with Latin America, however, cultural differences will create difficulties. For example, a nonverbal activity that can lead to discomfort for North Americans is the *abrazo,* or embrace, a common mode of greeting in Latin America. It may take some practice for *norteamericanos* to learn how to turn their heads a bit so they don't bump noses!

Language is a unifying force among the people of Latin America, but that unity isn't monolithic. We realize that the British, Americans, and Australians speak the same language, but with variations—what are "bangers and mash," anyway?—and the same variability is found in Spanish. For example, café (a place for snacks) can be variously called "un cabaré" in Colombia, "un cafetín" in Mexico, "un milonguero" in Argentina, "un boiti" in Central America, and "una tapesa" in Spain. A variant dialect of Spanish has for years been spoken in Los Angeles, and along the U.S.–Mexican border there is a Spanish–English mix called "Spanglish"[16] or "Tex-Mex." This "border Spanish," spoken in places like McAllen, Texas, is not viewed with favor by those living in the Mexican interior.

As discussed in previous chapters, cosmetic surgery is a consumption phenomenon related to the self-concept. Perhaps this phenomenon has reached its height in Argentina, where an estimated 1 in 30 have undergone plastic surgery. One humorist sums up Argentina's philosophy as, "I have been operated on, therefore I am." Former President Carlos Menem has apparently gone under the knife himself. Appearing one day with a swollen face, the official explanation was that he had been stung by wasps. The more-accepted version laid the blame on collagen injections in the presidential cheeks, while others said it was a reaction to a hair transplant. Whatever the real story, it prompted the birth of a satirical magazine called *The Wasp,* as well as a slogan for a hotel that had been refurbished: "We, too, have been bitten by a wasp."[17]

The Eastern European Consumer

The East Europe landmass stretches from the eastern border of Germany to the Pacific Ocean and is composed of people as diverse as the European Czechs to the

Mongoloid people of far-eastern Siberia. With a population of some 425 million (compared to 357 million in all of Western Europe), this area has enormous potential for marketers.

Incomes in Eastern Europe are much lower than in Western Europe, but productivity is increasing after the early 1990s period of political turmoil and economic readjustments. The retail setting is austere: Typically, stores have had few toilets, no air-conditioning, little in the way of carpeting, and only the most rudimentary displays. In Kazakhstan, understanding of the post-Communist system was so weak that a soap opera was put together to demonstrate how market systems work.[18] On the other hand, demand for Western products is high: One Swedish furniture retailer had to drop catalog sales in Hungary and stop advertising in Hungary and Poland because both generated demand it couldn't satisfy. This combination of high demand and low purchasing power has created new shopping patterns, such as patrons accumulating silverware and tableware one spoon or cup at a time.[19]

Not all Eastern European countries are poor, however. Czechs were the sixth-wealthiest people in the world before World War II. This background contributes to its rapid adaptation to market structures and Western tastes.[20] In the Czech Republic, U.S. products were found to have a good reputation for quality, although generally falling behind that of Germany and Japan. Also, Czech customers are influenced by advertising and price discounting, meaning that U.S. suppliers may be able to use advertising and discounting to compete favorably with Japanese and German products. However, Czech customers at this point prefer German, Japanese, and even Czech products.[21]

The disintegration of the Soviet Union and its satellites threw open a huge market hungry for consumer goods, especially for imported goods banned under communism. *Playboy* has licensed overseas editions in Poland, Hungary, and the Czech Republic. It airs selected pay-per-view television offerings in Bulgaria and sells home videos in Slovenia and Croatia.[22] Not only are the people of Eastern Europe anxious for consumer goods, Western items are status symbols as well. For example, the Twix bar is a favorite for Russian teenage boys hoping to impress their girlfriends with American confections.[23]

Marketing to the Eastern European consumer does require an understanding of the different cultures of the people and of their unfamiliarity with Western-style business practices. When European and American products first began to arrive, East Europeans felt that advertising tricked consumers. When Procter & Gamble introduced its shampoo and conditioner "Wash and Go," customers had not heard of hair conditioner, nor did they want it. Polish bars began serving a drink derisively called "Wash and Go—a shot of vodka with a water chaser."[24] They greeted free samples with suspicion, reasoning that the product must be of low quality if the company was giving it away.[25]

Gradually, however, these consumers have acquired more experience and are more comfortable with marketing activities. One research study found that 89 percent of a 500-person focus group assembled by Leo Burnett's Prague office believed ads provide useful information, and nearly 60 percent said they use the information in deciding what to buy. According to Marek Janicki, managing director of ITI–McCann–Erickson in Warsaw: "In the past, producers were king. Now the customer is king. People are happy someone is trying to get their attention."[26]

Still, advertising sometimes fails to get the message across. Hungarian consumers thought the Eveready Energizer bunny was a promotion for a toy bunny, not a battery.[27] Similarly, an ad selling bath soap for babies showed a young mother holding a baby and wearing a ring on her left hand. Scandalized Hungarians, who wear wedding rings on their right hand, were aghast that she would tell everybody in Hungary that she was unmarried.

The Western European Consumer

By comparison with other areas of the globe, Western Europe can appear to be a very attractive area for U.S. businesses seeking to expand abroad. First, Western Europe is large (there are 364 million people in the European Union) and relatively wealthy. Second, Western Europe seems culturally accessible. Even McDonald's is doing well in the land of haute cuisine, with some 500 French locations.[28]

Despite its size and wealth, Western Europe contains remarkable cultural diversity. Cultural differences exist both between the United States and Western Europe and between the nations and cultures within Western Europe. An important difference between U.S. and German citizens, for example, is their attitude toward debt and credit cards. Although people in the United States use debt relatively freely, the German word for debt—*schulden*—also means guilt. This may be why Germans make only 1 percent of their purchases with credit cards, compared with 18 percent in the United States.[29]

Although the European Union (EU) has a common agricultural policy, a coordinated monetary system, and open borders, there are cultural differences between countries within the union. Also, a small part of Western Europe does not belong to the EU. Countries within Western Europe have different preferences, even on such mundane matters as the appropriate size of paper napkins.[30] Unilever's food division sells a different tomato soup in Rotterdam than in Brussels, uses another recipe in France, and still another in Germany. Unilever found that Germans want detergents that are environmentally safe and will pay a premium for it. Spaniards, however, want a cheaper product that will get shirts white and soft. Greeks want smaller detergent packages to hold down the cost of each store visit.[31] In short, the "Euroconsumer" does not yet exist.

Comparing the United States, Mexico, the Czech Republic, France, and Japan: Key Dimensions

	United States	Mexico	Czech Republic	France	Japan
Attitudes toward uncertainty	Risk acceptant	Risk averse	Risk averse	Risk averse	Risk averse
Individualistic vs. group oriented	Individualistic	Group oriented	Group oriented	Individualistic	Group oriented
Nurturing vs. macho	Macho	Macho	Nurturing	Nurturing	Very macho
Attitudes toward authority*	Low	High	High	High	High

*The degree to which survey respondents felt that authority figures, such as their bosses, were to be deferred to. U.S. respondents were less inclined to defer to their supervisors than were people from the other countries listed.

Source: Adapted from Geert Hofstede, *Culture's Consequences* (Beverly Hills, CA: Sage Publications, 1980).

TABLE 15.2

Table 15.2 identifies some of the key dimensions on which cultures in the United States, Mexico, the Czech Republic, France, and Japan—foreign markets that have been examined—can be compared.

The African Consumer

Approximately 760 million people inhabit over 50 different African countries. The region north of the Sahara is heavily influenced by the Middle East, and most of the population is either Christian or Muslim. The people of this region are primarily Caucasoid and constitute about one-quarter of Africa's total population. Sub-Saharan Africa is more in keeping with our vision of Africa as a combination of vast areas of savanna and thick rain forests. Sub-Saharan Africa is the leading exporter of many precious metals and agricultural products, and Nigeria is a key exporter of crude oil. Although Africa is still predominantly rural, the number (and size) of cities is increasing.

Individuals in Africa tend to be collectivist, be relationship-oriented, and to place a high emphasis on the family. However, much of Africa is changing rapidly, and values may be in a state of flux. Many Africans in sub-Saharan Africa are bilingual, speaking both their own language and that of former European colonial administrators (we discuss the question of languages in the next section).

The business climate and culture is strongly influenced by Europe, with Francophone (former French colony) countries preferring French products. Anglophone countries give high marks to British and German goods. American products are highly regarded but seen as most appropriate for the well-to-do: Expansion opportunities for American products are most obvious in the Anglophone countries. With the exception of cars, Japanese products have not been highly regarded until recently. Thus, Africa has a potential for increases in the consumption of Japanese products as well.

Cross-Cultural Problem Areas

When marketers deal with individuals from a different culture, a number of difficult problems may arise. We discuss some of these issues in this section.

Translations. In addition to dealing with the difficulties of everyday speech in foreign countries, marketers must be aware of the problem of accurately translating their product's brand name into new languages. Examples of mistranslations abound.[32] For example, Colgate-Palmolive introduced its Cue toothpaste into France without changing the name. They did not realize that "cue" is a pornographic word in French. A paper manufacturer accidentally had its name translated into Japanese. The name became "He who envelopes himself in ten tons of rice paper." When the American film *City Slickers* went to France, its title became *Life, Love, and Cows*.[33] The Guatemalan subsidiary of Bayer, Germany's giant chemicals group, ran an unfortunate ad in *La Prensa Libre* for Baygon, an insecticide, which used the slogan *La muerte súbita es una especialidad Alemana*, "Sudden death is a German speciality." Despite clear references to Germany's sudden-death victory over the Czech Republic in the 1996 European soccer championships, the ad was pulled after a number of irate phone calls.

The list of translation faux pas is long. One method of avoiding such problems is called **back translation.** The process involves successively translating the message back and forth between languages by different translators. In this way subtle and not-so-subtle differences in meaning can be located.

Although back translation will solve translation issues, there is the question of whether the context is the same, even if the words are translated accurately. Is leasing a car meaningful in a culture where leasing isn't prevalent? Even using a translator fluent in both languages won't necessarily solve this potential problem. For example, a Nigerian who has spent enough time in the West to speak English with great fluency has also to some degree internalized Western values. To that extent he no longer reflects the same values as his compatriots in Nigeria.[34]

One new technology with considerable promise is translation software, which offers the alluring possibility of foreign language translation at your fingertips (via keyboard). Earlier attempts at computerized translation in the 1950s led to such miscues as "the spirit is willing but the flesh is weak" rendered via computer as "the vodka is strong but the meat is rotten." More recently, when former prime minister Margaret Thatcher visited a Fujitsu plant near Mt. Fuji, the company's intelligent computer translated her remarks on being honored to visit such a marvelous factory as "This company, having been visited by me today, is honorable." Nonetheless, Fujitsu is confident enough that it has put its English–Japanese translator on the Internet.[35]

National Languages and Dialects. Frequently, the language question is more nuanced than simply using the national language. In roughly ascending order of the level of confusion, China, India, and Africa present the greatest linguistic challenges to Westerners.

China, a huge country divided by high mountain ranges and peopled by several major ethnic groups, has a number of Chinese dialects that are mutually unintelligible. One of the authors visited a village in Taiwan where neither the national nor the dominant regional language was spoken, but yet a third "Chinese." He could speak only with children, who had learned the national language in school. But China is slowly being tied together by a common language. Children are taught to speak a national language based on the dialect of the capital, Beijing.

Even more languages exist in India than in China. The Indian constitution recognizes 18 official Indian languages. Although in fact there are only four major language families with more than 1 million speakers each (fewer than in Europe), still there is a great diversity.[36] As a practical matter, coverage of India for marketers is less complicated. Each of the 26 states has three official languages: English, Hindi, and the predominant state language. To assure complete coverage, many advertisers place the same ad in an English paper, a Hindi newspaper, and a local-language newspaper.

Language may even affect the location of foreign businesses in India. Hindi is a northern Indian language, and Indians in the south see little reason to speak it instead of English. Their English is therefore generally better than that of northerners, and foreign businesspeople may find that southern India provides a better environment in which to work.

Although English, French, and to a lesser extent Portuguese are spoken in Africa as a legacy of the colonial past, there are over 1,000 mutually unintelligible languages. Some languages (such as Swahili, Hausa, and Mandingo) had become lingua francas (universal languages) in certain areas of Africa before the arrival of Europeans. Nonetheless, the problem of linguistic appropriateness is a major challenge for marketers in Africa.[37]

Some linguistic impediments are political in nature. When the Soviet Union disintegrated, the former states declared linguistic as well as political independence from Moscow. Kyrgyzstan, Kazakhstan, and Turkmenistan not only use their own languages in preference to Russian—they also decided to use the Latin alphabet instead of the Cyrillic alphabet.[38]

Time Perception. In international settings time can cause problems because different cultures view time differently. Time is a commodity in the United States. Americans, for example, speak of "spending" and "wasting" time. As a consequence, Americans hate to be kept waiting. In many other cultures, time is much less important. A foreign executive may keep an American client waiting for 45 minutes or longer and think nothing of it. To some foreign businesspeople, 45 minutes is an insignificant length of time to wait.[39]

A U.S. professor described his experience of teaching classes in Brazil as traumatic at first because students arrived late to class and then hung around after class for no apparent reason. Part way through the semester, he asked the students how many minutes before and after the agreed time would it be before someone was considered early or late. For Brazilian students the average was 54 and 34 minutes, respectively. For students at a comparable California university, the times were 24 and 19 minutes. The Brazilian students were simply more casual in their approach to time.[40]

Some argue that an emphasis on time denotes a culture that maintains a fast-paced lifestyle. A study was performed that investigated the accuracy of bank clocks, the average walking speed of pedestrians on a city street, and how long it took postal clerks to sell a stamp in several cultures. On all three measures, Japan had the most accurate and fastest times. The United States and England were either second or third on each. Indonesia tended to have the most relaxed pace.[41]

Symbols. As already discussed, divergent cultures may have different symbols to communicate meaning. Thus, a symbol in one culture may not have the same meaning in other cultures. For example, the number seven is unlucky in Ghana and Kenya but lucky in India and the Czech Republic. The number four is unlucky in Japan because the words for "four" and "death" are pronounced identically; Mandarin and Cantonese speakers have the same attitude, for the same reason. In Hong Kong the numbers eight, three, and two are considered good because they have the same pronunciation as "good fortune," "alive," and "easy," respectively. The triangle is negative in Hong Kong and positive in Columbia. Purple is associated with death in many Latin American countries. In Mexico yellow flowers are a sign of death, whereas in France they denote infidelity. The expression "wearing a green hat" means that a man's wife is cheating on him in China. Similarly, gifts may represent different feelings in different cultures.

Never surprise your Japanese host with a gift. By accepting it (and refusal is impossible) he incurs an obligation to reciprocate immediately with a gift of exactly equivalent value. If the gift is not from Japan, the price may be unknown, and your host will agonize over what to do.

Friendship. Americans tend to make friends easily, but they also drop them rapidly. In some countries friendship replaces the legal or contractual system.[42] Therefore, friends are made slowly and retained for great lengths of time. As a consequence, the Chinese, Japanese, and others view with skepticism Americans who come on strong; they tend to see such Americans as insincere and superficial.

Etiquette. Matters of etiquette can also create discomfort and misunderstandings. For example, Americans may not understand the Japanese exchange of business cards, or *meishi*, which is a necessary social ritual. With the exchanges Japanese individuals are able to gauge their respective levels of status. There is a precise ritual to exchanging name cards in Japan. They must be given with both hands, rather than one (this is also true for China and Korea). In China the exchange of name cards is both a matter of etiquette and practicality. Many people have the same names, and many characters sound alike in spoken Chinese (4,800 people are identically named Liang Shuzhen in Shenyang City alone). Name cards are used to build personal "phone books" because calling "information" could easily be an exercise in futility.

The exchange of hugs and a kiss on the cheek among males in Eastern Europe strikes many Americans as strange and inappropriate. However, the ritual is a basic part of the manner in which people greet each other in that part of the world. Another matter of etiquette that differs is how food is eaten. For example, many Europeans consider eating food with your fingers (e.g., sandwiches or french fries) quite crude. The Japanese find the Western practice of blowing one's nose on a handkerchief and putting this effluvia in a pocket or purse, rather than disposing of it, disgusting. Instead of getting formal when embarrassed, Thais giggle. Westerners sometimes assume they have missed a joke when they have embarrassed their counterpart.[43]

Nonverbal Behavior. Nonverbal behaviors are those actions, movements, and utterances that people use to communicate in addition to language. These include movements of the hands, arms, head, and legs, as well as body orientation and the space maintained between people. Different cultures have divergent norms concerning such nonverbal behavior. Such differences can be seen in various cultures as forms of *interpersonal spatial relations*. Americans have four zones surrounding them—intimate, personal, social, and public.[44] The intimate zone is from zero to 18 inches away. Public zones are from 12 feet or further away. Business tends to be conducted in the social zone of four to seven feet.

People in other cultures, however, may not space themselves in the same way as Americans. In Middle Eastern and Latin American cultures, people tend to interact at a much closer distance. Consequently, Americans may become uncomfortable as a foreign businessperson closes in on them. The result of such interaction has been described as a sort of waltz, with the American backtracking and the foreign client pursuing. The problem is that the foreigner sees the American as standoffish, whereas the American sees the foreigner as pushy.[45]

Another aspect of nonverbal behavior is the influence of *context*—how one indicates that something is as important as what one says.[46] The United States is a low-context country. Most of the information in a message is contained in explicit code—that is, language. In Japan, a high-context country, the Japanese look for meaning in what is not being said—silences, gestures, and so on. For example, in the United States, the precise wording of agreements is very important, which means that in business transactions contracts are critical. Because attorneys are specialists in writing contracts, legal input is important. In Japan, however, precise wording is less important than the intentions of the parties to an agreement. Divining intention requires an atmosphere of trust, so agreeing to do business takes a bit longer. Once someone has agreed to do something, words written on paper mean proportionately less. So, in Japan "a person's word is his bond," but in the United States, written contracts tend to be relied upon. A disconcerting result for American businesses is that the Japanese often ask for contracts to be renegotiated based on the intention of the parties. That intention is interpreted from the context of the discussion and not from the precise words used.

Ethnocentricity. Ethnocentrism refers to the common tendency for people to view their own group as the center of the universe, to interpret other social units from the perspective of their own group, and to reject persons who are culturally dissimilar. This natural proclivity leads to a tendency for people to blindly accept those people who are culturally similar. Thus, the symbols and values of the person's ethnic or national group become objects of pride, whereas symbols of other groups may become objects of contempt.[47]

When marketing across cultures, business executives must strenuously avoid the tendency to look down on others because they do things differently. They must stifle the urge to try to change the behavior of their hosts because what they do is not as "good" as the American way.

Similarly, attitudes toward consumption activities differ markedly across cultures. When given the statement, "A house should be dusted and polished three times a week," 86 percent of Italians agreed, whereas only 25 percent of Americans did. Eighty-nine percent of Americans felt that "Everyone should use a deodorant," but only 53 percent of Australians agreed.[48]

The tendency to exhibit ethnocentrism can be used as a segmentation variable. In fact, a consumer ethnocentrism scale has been developed. Research conducted on this scale indicates that those who are high in consumer ethnocentrism are more prone to accentuate the positive aspects of domestic products and to discount the virtues of foreign-made items. They reacted more positively to advertisements that used an "American-made" theme. In addition, a product's American origin and construction was rated higher as a purchase consideration by those with higher levels of ethnocentrism.[49] The consumer ethnocentrism scale has been shown to apply cross-nationally to French, Japanese, and German subjects, as well as to those in Korea and Mexico.

Several studies have been conducted to investigate the extent to which "made in America" themes have a positive impact on consumer attitudes and buying intentions. The use of such themes can potentially evoke feelings of patriotism and prove beneficial for companies. The overall results of the research are, however, quite mixed. For example, one study assessed consumer decision making before and after the introduction of the "Made in the USA" television campaign.[50] The $40 million campaign was run by a coalition of 245 U.S. textile and apparel companies. The campaign used nationally known celebrities who touted American-made apparel as superior in quality and style. The researchers found that the respondents had positive attitudes toward domestically produced goods. When actual purchase preference was considered, however, the campaign had little effect when compared to other product attributes, such as style, quality, and fiber content.

Early research on the country-of-origin issue found evidence that U.S. consumers did consider this factor when making a purchase. For example, a 1985 *Wall Street Journal*/ NBC nationwide telephone poll found that 53 percent of the respondents claimed to look at labels for country of origin. Of those who did, 76 percent claimed to generally choose domestically produced apparel.[51] Follow-up research in the United States and Canada, however, revealed that, when 1,458 consumers were asked why they purchased a clothing product, only one person said "country of origin" was the reason. The authors concluded that "the percentage of those who searched for domestically produced goods because they cared about protection of the home industry was much lower than the percentage of those who expressed a concern for buying Canadian or U.S.-made clothing."[52]

It seems that, although a "Made in the U.S.A." campaign will enhance the overall corporate image, better-made products or price are more important. Still, if quality and price are competitive, American-made goods have a strong appeal, which may be growing.

One possible factor that may influence the tendency of consumers to reveal ethnocentric buying behavior is the specific region in which they live. One study polled consumers in North Carolina about their views on textile imports and the "Made in the U.S.A." campaign.[53] In Greenville, North Carolina, a city whose economy is significantly affected by foreign imports, 92 percent of those polled stated that they would pay more in order to limit imports of both cars and clothing. In a more urbanized city (Winston-Salem), less economically threatened by foreign imports, only 32 percent stated that they would pay more to limit clothing imports and only 23 percent stated that they would pay more to limit car imports. The likely explanation for these dramatic differences is that consumer ethnocentrism increases when foreign competition directly affects one's job and economic viability.

Binational products. The issue of consumer ethnocentrism is made more complicated by the current manufacturing trend to make product components in one country and assemble the product in another, or to design a product in one country and manufacture it in another. How are these "binational" products received? Generally speaking, it appears that consumers are influenced by their view of *both* countries. This means that manufacturers need to carefully consider the locations of all of the steps in processing. For example, having a product designed in Japan can mitigate the effects of having it made in a country that has a poor reputation for quality.[54]

Other Ethnocentrism Effects. Ethnocentrism may also be displayed in the tendency for consumers in richer societies to assume that products from poorer countries are less preferable than those that come from developed countries. This effect may even extend to consumers from poorer countries, who may prefer products from richer countries to their native products.[55] On the other hand, this tendency may not mean that consumers in richer countries do not want to buy any products from poorer countries. It appears that consumers display preferences for goods that match their notion of the country of origin. For example, although athletic footwear from China might not be attractive to U.S. consumers, sandals could be a good match.[56]

Animosity. Related to the concept of ethnocentrism is the notion of animosity: Some people may actively prefer not to buy products from a certain country. Chinese consumers have been found to hold an animosity toward buying Japanese products that is independent of a specific product, and older Mexican consumers may possess animosity toward purchasing American products.[57]

ADAPTING OR STANDARDIZING PRODUCTS AND SERVICES

A major issue in international marketing concerns whether to standardize the marketing plan across national boundaries. No simple answer exists to the question of whether the marketing mix can be standardized. In some countries, such as Japan and Russia, distribution systems are quite different from those found in the United States. Likewise, products must often be adapted to the tastes and preferences of different cultures. For example, U.S. companies typically find that the scent of their personal hygiene products must be made stronger to do well in Thailand.

The issue of standardization strikes most strongly in the advertising area. Impulse, a spray deodorant/perfume, followed a global advertising strategy by using a "boy-meets-girl" love story theme across the 31 countries in which it was marketed. To allow for cultural differences, the company permitted each of the local agencies to shoot its own version of the basic storyboard. Each of the commercials used the same copy line: "If a complete stranger suddenly gives you flowers—that's impulse. Men just can't resist acting on Impulse." The romantic fantasy commercials involved a young man acting irrationally when a woman wearing the perfume walks by. Upon smelling the perfume, he searches for a flower seller, grabs a bunch of flowers, and chases after the woman. The successful brand was first developed in 1972 in South Africa, from where it moved to Brazil. Within two years of its debut in West Germany, it had garnered 36 percent of the country's total deodorant market.[58]

Although standardized marketing efforts across countries are cheaper to develop and put into practice, serious problems occur for many products. The goal of a standardized marketing program is to have what Coca-Cola calls "One sight, one sound, one sell."[59] In most cases, however, too many obstacles get in the way of this goal for it to be implemented. Differences in such variables as government regulations, electrical outlets and voltages for electrical products, and customs make standardized marketing impractical in many instances. Government authorities in Britain, for example, did not allow Philip Morris to use advertisements showing the Marlboro cowboy, on the grounds that children worship cowboys and would take up smoking. So one ad showed a map of the United States, above a tobacco health warning, to advertise Marlboro country.[60] In other cases the issue is "what works." Pepsi ads in Israel have featured a young man in army boots doing push-ups. In Israel the military is held in high esteem by almost everyone, and teenagers idolize soldiers in elite combat units more than rock stars or sports celebrities.[61] This campaign, while appropriate for Israel, might stimulate controversy elsewhere.

Even in the product category of athletic shoes, companies must exercise caution in employing a standardized marketing effort. For example, athletic shoe manufacturers Nike and Reebok now have 50 percent of the $4.5 billion market for athletic shoes in Europe, up from 5 percent just a decade ago. In this case European buyers want the shoes because they are American and are identified with such American icons as Michael Jordan. The popularity of the 1992 Olympic basketball dream team in Europe helped increase the popular image of these American brands at the expense of their European rivals, Adidas and Puma. "America's image may be the last remaining export by U.S. firms," according to Michael Atmere, publisher of *Footwear Plus*.

European buyers of Nike and Reebok shoes are interested in an American experience, so the companies do not alter the physical product for these countries. In both print advertising and on television, tag liners in Italy, Germany, the Netherlands, and France all read the same way, in English: "Just do it" for Nike or "Planet Reebok." But subtle changes are necessary. Reebok deleted weight lifting and boxing from commercials in France because of French aversion to violence. Because Europeans don't play sports as much as Americans and don't visit sporting goods stores as often, Reebok also sells its shoes in about 800 traditional shoe shops in France.[62]

A curious case of adaptation has occurred in the case of beer. In 1531 King Ferdinand of Germany liked a South Bohemian beer so much that he adopted it as the beer of his royal court, the "Beer of Kings." The Germans called the beer "Budweiser" after the German name of the town where it was made, Budweis. In 1876 Adolphus Busch of St. Louis, Missouri, created a new beer, trademarked the name Budweiser, and added a new slogan, "The King of Beers." At the turn of the century, the two Buds clashed over rights to the name. In 1911 they agreed on a settlement. Budweiser (Europe) remained a robust beer brewed in small batches, while Budweiser (U.S.) was adapted to blander American preferences.[63]

Examples of the problems of global marketing abound. Whereas forms of clothing in North America and Western Europe are virtually identical, storage isn't. In Europe walk-in or built-in closets barely exist, so closet wardrobes, almost a curiosity here, are big European sellers.[64] Kool-Aid sells well in Venezuela but cannot be sold in Europe. Nestlé, the huge Swiss company, sells coffee in every country in the free world. However, the advertising and the taste of the coffee varies from country to country. In fact, there may be only a very few products, if any, that one can safely standardize.

Indeed, the idea that companies can completely standardize their marketing plans around the world contradicts the marketing concept. The consumer should be at the center of the marketing plan. Because consumers differ around the world, so too should the marketing plans. Not only does it violate the marketing concept; it is difficult to do. A recent study of "Eurobrands" found that, in order to become pan-European, every single brand had to make some change in an element of the marketing mix: 75 percent had to make changes in distribution and pricing, 79 percent in promotion, some in every element.[65]

A number of companies have adopted a compromise strategy. In this strategy a company develops a base product and customizes the accompanying elements of the offering (i.e., price, promotion, and distribution channels) for a region, such as Latin America, Europe, or Asia. An overall promotional theme may be developed to be employed worldwide, but the implementation of this theme (e.g., deciding whether to translate a slogan directly or to paraphrase it) is done locally. Called pattern advertising, this approach is an example of what the Japanese call *dochakuka:* "Think globally, act locally."[66]

Pattern advertising can even apply to packaging and brand marks. When Coca-Cola expanded into the former Soviet Union, there was already a high level of awareness for their famous script logo. However, the word "Enjoy," which is part of the logo, connoted sensuality when translated into Russian, which is not appropriate for a soft drink. The word "Enjoy" was changed to "Drink".[67] The pattern of the brand mark was retained but slightly changed for the specific environment. The Impulse perfume promotional campaign mentioned earlier is also an example of a pattern-advertising campaign.

Tangible Products versus Services

The degree to which standardization is possible also depends on the nature of the product. As Figure 15.1 illustrates, different types of products are more or less likely to be successful in a standardized format. Generally, services (as well as industrial products) are less likely than consumer products to need adaptation to local markets. Management consultants, lawyers, and accounting firms are able to practice in much the same ways in different countries, although specifics (such as laws and accounting practices) may differ. Similarly, industrial products are seldom country specific because there are few cultural differences in how a screw works! On the other hand, food products are more likely to be country specific. The Chinese may like hamburgers as a break in the usual routine, but they have a saying that if they go three days without eating rice, they're still hungry no matter what else they eat.

A Conclusion to the Standardization Debate?

In the final analysis, both the standardization and the customization arguments contain elements of truth. As incomes increase, people do seem to want many of the same products. And the younger the customer, the more this seems to be true. London yuppies may be more like rich young Parisians than their older countrymen. However, cultural differences remain strong, and it will be some time, if ever, before completely standardized products become the norm.

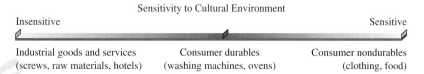

Figure 15.1   Different types of products tend to be more or less sensitive to foreign environment. The more sensitive a product is, the greater the need to adapt the product to the local environment.

THE ROLE OF MARKETING RESEARCH IN INTERNATIONAL MARKETING

In order to identify similarities and differences in taste preferences and in the meaning of symbols across cultures, a company must engage in marketing research. Major problems exist, however, in performing marketing research across cultures. One issue involves how to standardize measures of consumption values. Recently, it was suggested that researchers may be more successful by focusing on perceived attribute importance as a means of standardizing measures across cultures. Thus, a large pool of attributes can be developed that are likely to be important to individuals in diverse cultures. Studies can be done in each culture to identify those attributes most important to individuals in that culture. A pilot study conducted with individuals in Japan, Singapore, Hong Kong, South Korea, and Taiwan supported the general approach.[68]

Other issues in cross-cultural marketing research may involve technical problems. For example, Saudi Arabia officially bans most meetings of four or more people except for family or religious meetings, so a focus group would be difficult to arrange. With no published electoral rolls or phone books, telephone surveys would be difficult. And it is technically illegal to stop strangers on the street or knock on the door of someone's house.[69]

Country versus Segment Targets

When a company does business in several countries, managers can choose two broad segmentation approaches: country segments or market segments. In the first approach, Brazil, for example, may be viewed as a target market segment. Using the second approach, although Brazil is the physical location of a large group of consumers, the important variables for segmentation are commonalities in needs and wants among consumers across nationalities. These consumers reside in different countries and speak different languages, but they have similar needs for a product or service. From this perspective age, income, and psychographics are the essential means of identifying market segments. The relevant marketing question is not where they reside but whether they share similar wants and needs. The targeted consumers may be global teens, middle-class executives, or young families with small children. Each of these segments may share wants and needs across borders.

MANAGERIAL IMPLICATIONS

The consumer-behavior concepts that emerge from an investigation of international consumer-behavior issues can be applied to four of the five PERMS managerial applications areas. Because international differences between nations are themselves part of the environment, we do not separately discuss the environment as an application area here. Applications to the other four areas are summarized in the following sections.

Positioning and Differentiation

Can a product's country of origin be used to differentiate a product from its competitors? This is clearly the case. Because of its positive reputation, a DVD player made in Japan should probably make the country of origin clearly visible, perhaps by using a large label. A player from somewhere else might not fare as well if it focuses attention on country-of-origin information.

A company that has done well in this regard is Philip Morris, which managed to capture a large portion of the market in Turkey for cigarettes (Turkey was once synonymous with tobacco). In their introduction Philip Morris used American tobacco, which has a higher nicotine content than the local variety and therefore creates a more powerful buzz. This appealed to local tastes. It was even able to take advantage of the development of a local myth, which is that their Marlboro brand is mixed with wine to give it a stronger effect. Although untrue, this myth is partly based on Muslim prohibitions against alcohol. Finally, Philip Morris used marketing techniques that were transplanted from the United States. When Marlboro was introduced, the salespeople dressed up like cowboys and rode off in vans painted like Marlboros to visit store owners. And even though Turkey in 1996 passed legislation banning cigarette advertising, Marlboro had already planted itself well enough in consumer minds that it could simply use its familiar red chevron in advertising. In this case a mixture of adaptation to local tastes (raising nicotine levels) was combined with elements of a standard advertising program—the Marlboro cowboy and the red-and-white color scheme.

Research

Cross-cultural analysis should be performed by any company seeking to do business in any other country. Although the need to do so is clear, some of the difficulties in conducting cross-cultural research are also pointed out in the chapter.

Rapid changes in communications—particularly the development of the Internet—may go some way toward making international market research more feasible. With the relatively low cost of sending questionnaires by e-mail, or having respondents register their responses via an Internet site, collecting data may become quite easy. There are two cautionary notes, however. First, the penetration of the Internet varies from country to country. Second (and related), by using the Internet marketers restrict themselves to those with Internet access! This may not be a problem for generating numbers of responses, but consider who has Internet access in restricted markets. At early stages Internet users tend to be male, fairly young, and relatively well educated and well paid. If this is your target market, you may be in luck. Otherwise, your sample may not reflect your target.

Finally, be aware of potential cross-cultural differences that may cause problems with market research. One of the authors recently attempted to have a survey on satisfaction with musical performances administered to a group of students in Poland. The students got together to determine what the questions meant! Styles of music are categorized differently in Poland—so although the students understood English perfectly well (they were taking graduate-level business courses entirely in English), the terms in the survey were meaningless to them.

Marketing Mix

Promotional and product elements that are compatible with different cultures are critical for the marketing mix. As noted previously, there are restrictions on certain types of promotions in certain countries. Other countries may be even more permissive than U.S. standards, making U.S.-style ads seem relatively tame in these markets.

That products should be appropriate for local conditions goes without saying. It is important not to make assumptions about what is appropriate, however, without investigation. An interesting finding of a recent study is that Eastern European men are more fashion conscious than their female counterparts—probably because men in these countries have traditionally been more exposed to outside influences, while women have been expected to lead more cloistered lives. It may therefore be true that male clothing to be offered in Eastern Europe should be relatively more flamboyant and individualistic, whereas female clothing should be duller. This may be particularly true in Romania, where men take their fashion cues from the Italians not far away. [70]

Segmentation

One of the difficulties with segmentation, as discussed in this chapter, is the problem of determining whether national borders are useful segmentation variables. This method in essence violates the marketing principle because it assumes that all members of a nationality share the same needs and wants. We suggest that concentrating on cross-border segments that share commonalities makes more sense.

In fact, it is possible to target segments in different countries that are not the same, at least in a demographic sense. For example, Mercedes targets the upscale segment in the United States but is a major supplier of taxicabs in Germany.

Notes

1. Scott D. Roberts and Kathleen S. Micken, "*Le Fromage* as Life: French Attitudes and Behaviors toward Cheese" (paper presented at the annual conference of the Association for Consumer Research, Minneapolis, MN, October 19–22, 1995).
2. Thomas R. King, "Local Lures: For International Movie Marketers, Posters Are the Center of Attention," *Wall Street Journal Global Entertainment Supplement,* March 26, 1993, p. R13.
3. Richard Tomkins, "Motoring along Memory Lane," *Financial Times Weekend Supplement,* June 26–27, 1999, p. 9.
4. Yumiko Ono, "Love and Chicken Fill Christmas Eve in Very Merry Japan," *Wall Street Journal,* December 17, 1991, pp. A1, A9.
5. Anne B. Fisher, "The Ad Biz Gloms onto Global," *Fortune,* November 12, 1984, p. 80.
6. Donald A. Ball and Wendell H. McCulloch Jr., *International Business: Introduction and Essentials* (Homewood, IL: Irwin, 1996). Also see the Web site of the Megacities Foundation, <http://www.megacities.nl/megaacities/main.htm>.
7. Min Chen, Asian Management Systems: Chinese, Japanese, and Korean Styles of Business (London: Routledge, 1995).
8. "Changes in Japan's Workweek," *Wall Street Journal,* May 4, 1992, p. A17.
9. Valarie Reitman, "Enticed by Visions of Enormous Numbers, More Western Marketers Move into China," *Wall Street Journal,* July 12, 1993, pp. B1, B6.
10. G. Pascal Zachary, "Strategic Shift: Major U.S. Companies Expand Efforts to Sell to Consumers Abroad," *Wall Street Journal,* June 13, 1996, pp. A1, A6; Joseph Kahn, "Cleaning Up: P&G Viewed China as a National Market and Is Conquering It," *Wall Street Journal,* September 15, 1995, pp. A1, A6.
11. John Graham, Dong Kim, Chi-Yuan Lin, and Michael Robinson, "Buyer–Seller Negotiations around the Pacific Rim: Differences in Fundamental Exchange Processes," *Journal of Consumer Research* 15 (June 1988): 48–54. For a discussion of differences between Taiwanese and U.S. negotiators, see Ben S. Liu and Wai-kwan Li, "A Friend Is a Friend Even When Money Is the Issue: Differences between Taiwanese and Americans in Negotiations" (unpublished manuscript, 1996).
12. Matt Moffett, "Mexico: JFK, Si! Madonna, No!" *Wall Street Journal Global Entertainment Supplement,* March 26, 1993, p. R15.
13. Matt Moffett, "Amigos for Now: Mexicans Anticipate Passage of Trade Pact Will Lift Economy," *Wall Street Journal,* April 20, 1993, pp. A1, A13.
14. Craig Torres and Joel Millman, "Televisa Seeks to Get Big Part in Global Play," *Wall Street Journal,* May 30, 1996, p. A14.
15. Luis de la Prida, "Busy Race to Be LatAm Internet King," <www.bizyahoo.com/wi/000323/6071.html> (April 5, 2000).
16. Frances de Talavera Berger, *¡Mierda! The Real Spanish You Were Never Taught in School* (New York: Plume, 1990).
17. David Pilling, "Rich Argentines Live on a Knife Edge," *Financial Times,* June 3, 1996, p. 9.
18. Paul Levy, "Showing Kazakhs the Way the World Turns," *Wall Street Journal,* October 3, 1995, p. A16.
19. Stephen D. Moore, "Sweden's Ikea Forges into Eastern Europe," *Wall Street Journal,* June 29, 1993, p. A6.
20. Frederick Kempe and Cacilie Rohwedder, "Top Executives Name Czech Republic Most Attractive for Future Investments," *Wall Street Journal,* July 9, 1993, p. A6.

21. David B. Klenosky, Suzeanne B. Benet, and Petr Chadraba, "Assessing Czech Consumers' Reactions to Western Marketing Practices: A Conjoint Approach," *Journal of Business Research* 36 (June 1996): 189–98.

22. Susan Carey, "Playboy Looks Overseas as U.S. Climate Grows Hostile," *Wall Street Journal,* September 29, 1993, p. B4.

23. Neela Banerjee, "Russia Snickers after Mars Invades," *Wall Street Journal,* July 13, 1993, p. B1.

24. Dan Michaels and Shailagh Murray, "Advertising: Eastern Europe's Window of Opportunity Is Still Open," *Wall Street Journal Europe,* July 7, 1993.

25. William R. Putsis Jr., "Marketing in Eastern Europe: Lessons from Early Entrants," *Yale Management,* 1993, pp. 14–21.

26. Michaels and Murray, "Advertising: Eastern Europe's Window."

27. Tara Parker-Pope, "Ad Agencies Are Stumbling in East Europe," *Wall Street Journal,* May 10, 1996, pp. B1, B14.

28. Andrew Jack, "McDonald's Makes Fast-Food Inroads on the French Palate," *Financial Times,* February 21, 1996, p. 14.

29. Greg Steinmetz, "Germans Finally Open Their Wallets to Credit Cards but Aren't Hooked Yet," *Wall Street Journal,* April 6, 1996, p. A1.

30. Janet Guyon, "A Joint-Venture Papermaker Casts Net across Europe," *Wall Street Journal,* December 7, 1992, p. B6.

31. E. S. Browning, "In Pursuit of the Elusive Euroconsumer," *Wall Street Journal,* April 23, 1992, p. B1.

32. For an excellent discussion of the problems of translation, see David A. Ricks, *Blunders in International Business* (Cambridge, MA: Blackwell, Grid, 1993).

33. "Did We Say That?" *Playboy,* September 1993, p. 15.

34. Eric J. Arnould and Melanie Wallendorf, "On Identical Methods in Cross-Cultural Research, or the Non-Comparability of Data Obtained with Seemingly-Comparable Measures" (paper presented at the 1993 American Marketing Association Educators' Meeting, Newport Beach, CA, February 20–23, 1993).

35. Emiko Terazono, "Fujitsu Puts First Japanese Translation Package Online," *Financial Times,* April 29, 1996, p. 9.

36. "Language and Dialects," <www.adaniel.tripod.com/Languages1.htm> (April 6, 2000).

37. *Encyclopedia Americana,* international edition, s.v. "African peoples."

38. Martha Brill Olcott, "Central Asia's Catapult to Independence," *Foreign Affairs* 71 (summer 1992): 108–30.

39. Edward T. Hall, *The Hidden Dimension* (New York: Doubleday, 1966).

40. Robert Levine and Ellen Wolff, "Social Time: The Heartbeat of Culture," *Psychology Today,* March 1985, pp. 28–35.

41. Ibid.

42. Hall, *Hidden Dimension.*

43. Karen Swenson, "Roaches and Redheads: Touring a Small Thai Town," *Wall Street Journal,* July 1, 1993, p. A12.

44. Edward T. Hall, *The Silent Language* (New York: Doubleday, 1959).

45. H. W. Smith, "Territorial Spacing on a Beach Revisited: A Cross-National Explanation," *Social Psychology Quarterly* 44 (June 1981): 132–37.

46. Edward T. Hall, *Beyond Culture* (Garden City, NY: Anchor Press, Doubleday, 1976).

47. Terence Shimp and Subhash Sharma, "Consumer Ethnocentrism: Construction and Validation of the CETSCALE," *Journal of Marketing Research* 24 (August 1987): 280–89. Also see Subhash Sharma, Terence Shimp, and Jeongshin Shin, "Consumer Ethnocentrism: A Test of Antecedents and Moderators," *Journal of the Academy of Marketing Science* 23 (winter 1995): 26–37.

48. J. T. Plummer, "Consumer Focus in Cross-National Research," *Journal of Advertising* 6 (spring 1977): 10–11.

49. Shimp and Sharma, "Consumer Ethnocentrism." Also see Joel Herche, "A Note on the Predictive Validity of the CETSCALE," *Journal of the Academy of Marketing Science* 20 (summer, 1992): 261–64.

50. Richard Ettenson, Janet Wagner, and Gary Gaeth, "Evaluating the Effect of Country of Origin and the 'Made in the USA' Campaign: A Conjoint Approach," *Journal of Retailing* 64 (spring 1988): 85–100.

51. H. Gilman, "Clothing Shoppers Talk Domestic but Look First for Style, Savings," *Wall Street Journal,* October 15, 1985, p. 31.

52. Susan Hester and Mary Yuen, "The Influence of Country of Origin on Consumer Attitude and Buying Behavior in the United States and Canada," in *Advances in Consumer Research,* ed. Melanie Wallendorf and Paul Anderson (Provo, UT: Association for Consumer Research, 1987), 14:538–42.

53. Sayeste Daser and Havva Meric, "Does Patriotism Have Any Marketing Value: Exploratory Findings for the 'Crafted with Pride in U.S.A.' Campaign," in *Advances in Consumer Research,* ed. Melanie Wallendorf and Paul Anderson (Provo, UT: Association for Consumer Research, 1987), 14:536–37.

54. Paul Chao, "Partitioning Country of Origin Effects: Consumer Evaluations of a Hybrid Product," *Journal of International Business Studies* 24 (second quarter 1993): 291–306; Richard Ettenson and Gary Gaeth, "Consumer Perceptions of Hybrid (Bi-National) Products," *Journal of Consumer Marketing* 8 (fall 1991): 13–18.

55. David K. Tse and Gerald J. Gorn, "An Experiment on the Salience of Country-of-Origin in the Era of Global Brands," *Journal of International Marketing* 1, no. 2 (1993): 57–76.

56. Myung-Kyoo Choi, John C. Mowen, and Michael S. Minor, "The Effect of Country of Origin on Product Evaluations: A Test of the Matchup Hypothesis" (unpublished manuscript, 1996); Martin S. Roth and Jean B. Romeo, "Matching Product Category and Country Image Perceptions: A Framework for Managing Country-of-Origin Effects," *Journal of International Business Studies* 23 (third quarter, 1992): 477–97.

57. Jill Gabrielle Klein, Richard Ettenson, and Marlene D. Morris, "The Animosity Model of Foreign Product Purchase: An Empirical Test in the People's Republic of China," *Journal of Marketing* 62 (January 1998): 89–100; Wolfgang Hinck and Reto Felix, "!No Quiero Taco Bell! An Empirical Investigation of Mexican Consumer Animosity toward U.S. Products" (paper presented at the Marketing in a Global Economy Conference of the American Marketing Association, Buenos Aires, Argentina, June 28–July 1, 2000).

58. Brian Oliver, "A Little Romance Puts Impulse on Global Path," *Advertising Age,* June 24, 1985, pp. 39–40.

59. Fisher, "Ad Biz."

60. Tara Parker-Pope, "Tough Tobacco-Ad Rules Light Creative Fires," *Wall Street Journal,* October 9, 1996, pp. B1, B6.

61. Amy Dockser Marcus, "Out of Step: The Poor Grow Poorer in Israel as the Army Rejects More Youths," *Wall Street Journal,* August 13, 1993, pp. A1, A6.

62. Joseph Pereira, "Off and Running: Pushing U.S. Style, Nike and Reebok Sell Sneakers in Europe," *Wall Street Journal,* July 22, 1993, pp. A1, A8.

63. Shailagh Murray, "Privatization: Emotion Joins Economics as Factor in Czech Sell-Offs," *Wall Street Journal Europe,* June 21, 1993; Roger Thurow, "The King of Beers and the Beer of Kings Are at Lagerheads," *Wall Street Journal,* April 2, 1992, pp. A1, A8; "Czech Government Closer to Brewery State Auction," *Wall Street Journal,* July 28, 1993, p. A10.

64. Allyson L. Stewart, "U.S. Puts Pier Pressure on Europe's Retailers," *Marketing News,* August 2, 1993, pp. 6–7.

65. Jeryl Whitelock, Carole Roberts, and Jonathan Blakeley, "The Reality of the Eurobrand: An Empirical Analysis," *Journal of International Marketing* 3, no. 3 (1995): 77–95.

66. An excellent discussion of "going local" can be found in Alan S. Parter, *Going Local: How Global Companies Become Market Insiders* (London: Economist Intelligence Unit, 1993).

67. Murray I. Tubliner, "Brand Name Selection Is Critical Challenge for Global Marketers," *Marketing News,* August 2, 1993, pp. 7, 11.

68. David Tse, John Wong, and Chin Tiong Tan, "Towards Some Standardized Cross-Cultural Consumption Values," in *Advances in Consumer Research,* ed. Michael Houston (Provo, UT: Association for Consumer Research, 1988), 15:387–95. Other problems also exist in doing market research across cultures. For a discussion of problems in measurement, see Jagdip Singh, "Measurement Issues in Cross-National Research," *Journal of International Business Studies* 36 (third quarter 1995): 597–620.

69. Tara Parker-Pope, "Nonalcoholic Beer Hits the Spot in Mideast," *Wall Street Journal,* December 6, 1995, pp. B1–B2.

70. Lalita A. Manrai, Dana-Nicoleta Lascu, Ajay K. Manrai, and Harold W. Babb, "Fashion Consciousness and Dress Conformity in Central and Eastern Europe" (paper presented at the Marketing in a Global Economy Conference of the American Marketing Association, Buenos Aires, Argentina, June 28–July 1, 2000).

CHAPTER 16

The Dark Side
of Consumer
Behavior

After reading this chapter, you should be able to discuss each of the following concepts, together with their managerial implications:

1. The categories of deceptive advertising that the Federal Trade Commission has considered in the past.
2. Whether children can tell the difference between commercials and programming.
3. Ways by which companies might make children's advertising more acceptable to parents.
4. Negligent consumer behavior.
5. Product misuse.
6. Possible drivers of compulsive consumption.
7. Corporate social responsibility.
8. Reasons that businesses may actively attempt to portray themselves as socially responsible.
9. The factors that influence consumer reactions to companies that issue product recalls.
10. The various approaches to dealing with corporate rumors.

Consumer behavior has a "dark" side. Companies can prey on consumers through unscrupulous behavior. As we will also see, however, consumers may also engage in negligent behavior. Examples include actions that harm themselves, such as the consumption of drugs such as steroids and cocaine. As one method of decreasing the likelihood that such activities might occur, as well as the harm that results, the government regulates the buying and selling of goods and services.

The **regulatory environment** consists of the laws and regulations that federal, state, and local governments develop in order to exert control over business practices. One goal of such laws and regulations is to protect consumers from the actions of unscrupulous companies. For example, in the United States, the Federal Trade Commission (FTC) prohibits "unfair or deceptive acts or practices" by merchants and attempts to monitor the consumer environment for evidence of such practices.

Regulatory agencies seek to protect consumers against outright scams. In addition, they attempt to control less obvious, but nonetheless illegal activities of companies, such as selling slightly used products as new items. In 1996, for example, Chrysler was charged in California with reselling 116 cars that had been returned to dealers because of major problems. The new owners had not been informed, a violation of California law.[1]

In addition to protecting consumers against unscrupulous companies, regulatory agencies also serve to protect consumers from themselves. Consumers can sometimes engage in negligent behavior that poses risks to themselves and to others. The FDA is charged with enforcing laws that forbid the use of various types of drugs. The use of steroids by consumers represents one such misused product. Some forms of sexual conduct can also pose risks. In fact, advertising campaigns have been initiated to inform consumers of the problems of AIDS.

This chapter presents and analyzes three major public-policy issues: deceptive advertising practices, advertising to children, and telemarketing fraud. This is followed by a discussion of negligent consumer behavior, examples of which are seat-belt use, product misuse, and drinking and driving. The chapter then examines smoking, compulsive drinking, gambling, and other compulsions. Finally, we discuss the importance of corporate social responsibility.

SOME CURRENT PUBLIC-POLICY ISSUES IN THE CONSUMER DOMAIN

A number of public-policy issues are in the consumer domain. Among these are deceptive advertising, advertising aimed at children, and telemarketing fraud.

Deceptive Advertising

Advertisements can be *deceptive* when they are literally false or potentially misleading. Some ads are easy to evaluate. For example, "guaranteed to last 10 years" is a statement that is either true or false. Potentially misleading ads are more difficult to assess because consumer interpretation of the ad is relevant. When ads are interpreted incorrectly, the result is *miscomprehension,* due to the inferences made by consumers.

The possibility of miscomprehension is rather large. One study showed that on average consumers had a miscomprehension rate of 30 percent for television advertisements. A second study by the same authors concerning print advertisements indicated that 21.4 percent of the meanings in magazine advertisements were misunderstood, and in a further 15.5 percent of cases the consumers did not comprehend the message at all.[2] Although the precise rate of miscomprehension and noncomprehension is somewhat controversial, the potential for miscomprehension of advertisements is clearly significant. From a marketing manager's standpoint, the phenomenon of miscomprehension means that a certain proportion of the audience is likely to miscomprehend, or fail to comprehend, the advertising message.

The FTC is charged with regulating deceptive advertising, rather than dealing with the issue of miscomprehension. Table 16.1 shows a number of categories of deceptive safety claims that may be present in advertising considered misleading by the FTC.

Misleading Safety Claims	
Misleading affirmative safety claims	Untrue claims that the product is safe. For example, the manufacturer of Jazz nontobacco cigarettes was enjoined from making claims about the safety of the product and its ability to help people stop smoking.
Deceptive denials of product risks	No assertions that the products are safe are made, but it is asserted that its lack of safety hasn't been scientifically proven. R. J. Reynolds asserted for years that a causal relationship between smoking and heart disease had not been scientifically proven.
Deceptive information omissions	Claims that are partially true but contain significant omissions. For example, liquid diets requiring very low food intake were deceptively called "risk free" because advertisements did not disclose that monitoring by a physician is required to minimize health risks.
Unfair information omissions	A plastic surgery center did not disclose the fact that breast implants interfere with mammography. This is an unfair omission because, while implants may otherwise have an acceptable risk level, this risk is significant.

Source: Based on Ross D. Petty, "Regulating Product Safety: The Informational Role of the U.S. Federal Trade Commission," *Journal of Consumer Policy* 18 (1995): 387–415.

TABLE 16.1

One example of FTC action on deceptive advertising involved Kraft Singles individually wrapped cheese slices. Losing market share to imitation-cheese products, Kraft launched a campaign positioning Singles as containing as much calcium as five ounces of milk. Because about 30 percent of the calcium was lost in processing, however, the actual calcium remaining was that of 3.5 ounces of milk. The FTC determined that this ad was deceptive, and Kraft was ordered to desist from making this claim. One of the controversies in the Kraft case was whether the difference between the calcium in 5 or 3.5 ounces of milk was material. That is, did Kraft want consumers to make their decision based on the fact that Singles had more calcium than its artificial competitors or was the actual amount of increased calcium important? The FTC and consumer researcher David Stewart argued for the latter position, while analyst Jacob Jacoby argued for the former.[3] As you can see, what constitutes deceptive advertising is not always clear-cut.

The FTC has issued a series of advertising guidelines and enforcement policy statements on advertising claims, which range from product-specific (e.g., metallic watchbands and hosiery) to general (e.g., use of the word *free* in advertising, and environmental marketing claims).[4] A recent aspect of the FTC's activity has been the first regulatory cases involving deceptive advertising on the Internet. Many of the early cases involved offers by small companies to repair consumer credit records. [5]

Unfair Advertising. In 1976 the FTC attempted to rule that all advertising aimed at children was unfair. In this case the issue wasn't deception but whether such advertising was unfair because children might not be able to understand the messages. This led to a 14-year battle between Congress and the advertising industry over a legal definition of what was "unfair." During this period the FTC could use the idea of "unfairness" in individual cases but couldn't issue industry-wide rules. As a result, "unfairness" played only a minor role in FTC actions in the 1980s and early 1990s. Agreement on a definition was finally reached in 1994. However, it is unclear whether this will prompt major new rulings from the FTC.[6]

Corrective Advertising. In response to the increased attention given to deceptive advertising tactics in the 1960s and early 1970s, the FTC began to order corrective measures from some of the guilty parties. The incident that sparked the idea of corrective advertising involved Campbell's soup advertisements in which clear marbles were placed in the bottom of a soup bowl, forcing the vegetables to the surface. Consumers believed that the soup contained more vegetable pieces than it actually did. The FTC issued a cease-and-desist order that banned this practice.[7]

Perhaps the most famous of all corrective advertising cases involved Warner-Lambert's claim that Listerine mouthwash could prevent or lessen the severity of colds and sore throats. The company began manufacturing Listerine in 1879 and advertising the product in 1921: Warner-Lambert had been making this claim for over half a century. In 1975 the FTC ordered that the company must attempt to correct misimpressions that their advertisements had created. Between 1978 and 1980, Warner-Lambert spent more than $10 million on corrective advertising. Nearly 95 percent of this money was devoted to television commercials.[8]

Children's Advertising

Both marketing managers and public-policy makers have reacted to criticisms of advertising directed at children. As noted in chapter 12, children are influential in family decision making. They also directly control a significant amount of purchases. Children under 12 have an annual income of $27.5 billion in the United States and influence some $188 billion in U.S. purchases, about $1.87 trillion worldwide. Professor James Neal has coined the term *filiarchy* (like patriarchy or matriarchy) to describe children's growing spending power within the family.[9]

In addition, children prefer nationally labeled brands (which are often more profitable than private-label brands). Whereas 70 percent of adults have become major buyers of private-label store brands, only 7 percent of children would even consider the stuff: They want brand-name gifts and designer clothes. Brands offer children a common commercial language, something that identifies them as part of a group.[10]

Marketing managers and public-policy makers have benefited from consumer-behavior research and theory that examines children's responses to advertising. Some key issues that researchers have investigated include the following:

➤ Can children tell the difference between commercials and programming?

➤ Do children understand the selling intent of commercials?

➤ Do commercials make children want products that are not good for them?

The need for continued concern regarding children's exposure to television is related to the influence television has on children. The influence of television may have slipped in recent years as such techniques as children's membership clubs, catalog-marketing programs, and marketing to children on the Internet have flourished.[11] One other reason the influence of television may have declined is that children may be seeing fewer commercials. In 1990 the Children's Television Act limited the advertising children would see on children's television programs—no more than 10.5 minutes per hour on weekends and no more than 12 minutes per hour during the week. A more recent agreement commits television stations to carry at least three hours of educational children's shows a week.[12] In Europe Sweden has already banned advertising to children under 12 and, with a Swede assuming the presidency of the EU in 2001, a trans-European ban on children's advertising may be possible. Norway has already followed Sweden's example.

Telemarketing Fraud

Recent statistics indicate that telemarketing fraud costs Americans about $40 billion annually.[13] A recent effort to combat telemarketing fraud is known as the Know Fraud program (www.consumer.gov/knowfraud). Among the organizations involved in the Know Fraud educational effort are the American Association of Retired Persons (AARP), Council for Better Business Bureaus Foundation, the FBI and the Department of Justice, the U.S. Post Office, and others. This particular program is funded by about $4 million confiscated from a fraud case in Des Moines, Iowa, which could not be returned to the victims.

The reason for the involvement of the AARP is easy to determine. As discussed in chapter 14, the elderly may be vulnerable to fraud due to changes in the ways they process information, as well as decreases in their motor skills. Televised public information announcements provide advice about avoiding telemarketing scams.

NEGLIGENT CONSUMER BEHAVIOR

Most of us would agree with the following statements: "Seat belts save lives," "Smoking is hazardous to your health," "Drinking and driving don't mix." Yet many consumers, in some manner or another, exhibit what might be termed negligent behavior. **Negligent behavior** is composed of those actions and inactions that may negatively affect the long-term quality of life of individuals and society. This type of behavior can occur in two different contexts. The first form of negligent behavior occurs because the consumption of a product in and of itself presents a hazard of some sort. The consumption of cigarettes and certain drugs are two examples that fall into this category. A second type of negligent behavior occurs when the consumer uses a product in an unsafe manner or fails to use safety features and follow safety instructions. Failure to use seat belts and not following dosage instructions for over-the-counter drugs are examples of this form of negligent behavior.[14]

There are two common approaches to induce people to act in a safer manner. One involves legislation that creates laws forcing consumers to wear seat belts, bans the advertising and sale of cigarettes, and imposes stiffer penalties for drunk driving. A second approach involves the use of marketing techniques to encourage more appropriate consumer actions. Consumer-behavior research and theory provide insight into how marketers and public-policy makers can influence consumers to behave in a safer manner.

Product Misuse

Many of us would never think of using a blow dryer in the shower or a lawn mower to trim the hedges. Nor would we think that using a cellular phone in a car may lead to an accident because our concentration is diverted from the road. Consumers' misuse of products in just such a fashion, however, has prompted marketers and public-policy makers alike to exert special precautions in the design and testing of products. In fact, the majority of product-related injuries result not from a flaw in the product itself but through misuse of an otherwise safe product.[15] As one individual put it, "The most dangerous component is the consumer, and there's no way to recall him."[16] Table 16.2 shows various possible explanations for consumer misuse of "safe" products.

As mentioned earlier, one method of inducing people to act in a safer manner is legislation. In addition to regulating consumer behavior, this might involve setting

Consumer Misuse of "Safe" Products: Some Potential Explanations

1. *Action slip.* A performance error resulting from faulty cognitive processing. This is particularly likely when the consumer is focusing on desired end results rather than the more mundane actions necessary to arrive at the desired state.
2. *Error proneness.* The tendency not to be vigilant, especially during routinely performed activities.
3. *Reinforcement.* The consumer takes a risk but doesn't suffer any consequences. Each successive trial that doesn't result in harm reinforces the proneness to risky behavior.
4. *Hedonic goals.* Consumers focused on fantasy, fun, and feelings are less likely to calculate the risks involved in their behavior.
5. *Ritual/socially sanctioned misuse.* Campus beer bashes, for example.
6. *Individual irrationality.* The actions of obsessive, compulsive, or addictive personalities.
7. *Advertising.* Advertising representations may be partially responsible for unsafe behavior because they encourage extreme forms of product use.

Source: Adapted from Jeffrey Stoltman and Fred Morgan, "Psychological Dimensions of Unsafe Product Usage," in *Marketing Theory and Applications* eds.. Rajan Varadarajan and Bernard Jaworski (Chicago: American Marketing Association, 1993) 4:143–50.

TABLE 16.2

government safety standards for almost every type of industry. If a company's products fail to meet such standards, then the products are subject to recall. However, it has been estimated that "no more than 20 percent of all consumer product related injuries can be addressed by feasible regulation of the production and distribution of consumer products."[17]

We also noted earlier that a second method of preventing product misuse lies in increasing consumer information. However, this second alternative has been called into question. There is a practical limit to the amount of information that can be presented on a label, and inserts and manuals are usually discarded early in the life of products such as power tools. Even experience may not be helpful because novices are often more careful and vigilant than the experienced user.

The argument has been made that a third alternative is needed that relies on product design. From this perspective we need more study of how products are actually used in order to incorporate into a design an increased level of safety: "[T]he actual hazard arises in the kitchen or in the hedgerow, not in the store."[18] For example, the oval-shaped Ford Taurus instrument panel is a departure from previous designs. It was in part the result of customer complaints that previous panels had too many small buttons that were too close together and were too difficult to manage while driving.[19]

Drinking and Driving

Alcohol-related traffic fatalities declined by one-third between 1988 and 1998, to a still-substantial 15,935.[20] In the 1980s increased attention was given to the issue of drinking and driving, in part because of the efforts of the national organization Mothers Against Drunk Driving (MADD). Public-policy makers could make greater use of consumer-behavior research concerning this area. This section describes some of the methods currently used, along with their strengths and weaknesses.

Informing and Educating. Using the approach of informing and educating assumes that individuals act rationally in an effort to further their self-interest. Thus, the public should be presented with objective information about the hazards of drunk driving.[21] When developing such information campaigns, advertisers have frequently used a fear-inducing message appeal. The Department of Transportation and the Ad Council initiated an advertising campaign against drinking and driving.

Social Controls. The majority of liquor advertisements portray the beverage as a drink consumed in the presence of others and as a means of heightening one's acceptability. The strategy of social controls plays on the understanding that individuals are influenced by the actions and attitudes of those around them. The dominant theme employed in this tactic is to have social influencers disapproving of drunk driving. Examples of this strategy include campus meetings of the SADD (Students Against Drunk Driving) organization or commercials showing family or friends taking car keys away from the person who overindulged.

Economic Incentives. Using concepts derived from behavior modification theory, one approach might be to reward individuals for demonstrating the desired behavior. Insurance companies currently use this approach by providing reduced rates to individuals who agree not to drink and drive. Some restaurants give a free meal to a designated nondrinking driver who will drive his or her friends who are drinking home. The limitation of this approach is that some individuals may refrain from drinking and driving only if they perceive the benefits as outweighing the costs.

Economic Disincentives. Rather than rewarding individuals for not drinking and driving, the use of economic disincentives punishes individuals who drink and drive. This punishment could occur directly—through fines, car repair costs, and high insurance premiums—or indirectly, for example, through an excise tax on alcohol that would result in higher liquor prices. However, consumers may continue to drink and drive if they feel the benefits of their behavior still outweigh the costs.

COMPULSIVE BEHAVIOR

Some negligent behaviors are the consumption of products that are hazardous in and of themselves, as discussed in the previous section. Many of these behaviors become compulsive or addictive over time. Other behaviors are not harmful in moderation but become harmful when the behavior becomes compulsive.

Smoking

Until the late 1960s, consumers were exposed to nearly 3,000 cigarette commercials per week, representing 38 different brands. Concern over the health hazards of cigarette smoking had begun in the 1950s. However, it was not until the issuance of the surgeon general's report in 1964 that policy makers began to exert considerable efforts to alter the public's smoking behavior. The Department of Health and Human Services used such tactics as bumper stickers that read "Smoke, Choke, Croak" and endorsements from athletic stars such as Peggy Fleming and Bart Starr proclaiming, "I don't smoke." In general, the approach was to depict smokers as distraught coughers, whereas nonsmokers were portrayed as happy and healthy.[22]

Thirty years later, the campaign was still in full swing. During the mid-1990s the negative publicity concerning smoking and the actions of cigarette manufacturers grew in intensity. In particular, the advertising campaign employing "Joe Camel" was attacked for targeting the youth of America. In 1994 *Advertising Age* and the Roper organization conducted a national poll that found that 68 percent of Americans believe that cigarette ads influence children and teens to smoke. The results further revealed that two-thirds of Americans, including half of all smokers, wanted the U.S. government to increase restrictions on cigarette advertising. Over 50 percent of those polled wanted all cigarette advertising banned.[23]

In 1996 a series of new restrictions on cigarette advertising and sales whose aim was halving tobacco use by children and adolescents was introduced by the federal government. The new guidelines ban vending machines and self-service displays except where those under 18 also aren't allowed, require photo identification for anyone under the age of 27 buying cigarettes, ban billboards near schools and playgrounds, limit billboards and advertisements in magazines with a young readership to black-and-white text only, and restrict the distribution of promotional items (such as clothing).[24]

The increased antismoking activity has not led to a continuing decline in cigarette consumption. Although smoking dropped from the 1960s through 1992, from 1995 to 1997 the percentage of adult smokers remained at 24.7 percent. Smoking has declined among most age groups, but the percentage of smokers aged 18–24 actually increased during that period, from 24.5 percent to 28.7 percent.[25] New cigarette brands appealing to young adults, such as Red Kamels (revived after a 60-year hiatus) and Moonlight Tobacco, have been introduced, and the controversial Joe Camel was brought back as well. A recent study indicates that adolescents are three times more responsive to cigarette ads than adults, leading the study's authors to conclude that "cigarette advertising for market share is primarily a battle of brands for consumption by the young."[26] So the battle over the issue is by no means over. Some researchers argue that poor communications strategies by antismoking groups are in part to blame, but the root causes are the strong social reward for smoking in some circles (such as among teenagers) and certain deeply held cognitive positions. In fact, consumer awareness of the major health effects of smoking is now quite high. Researchers have found that smokers now overestimate, rather than underestimate, the risk of lung cancer from smoking.[27] These results suggest that many smokers simply tune out, or develop counterarguments for, antismoking messages.

Another new group of actors entering the antismoking arena in the late 1990s are makers of products such as nicotine gums and patches. The drug companies attempt to "switch" smokers to their products, which are available as over-the-counter drugs. Because these manufacturers are well versed in consumer advertising, their antismoking message may be successful in ways that public-interest commercials could not be.

Compulsive Drinking

The decline in alcohol-related deaths on the road, mentioned earlier, may be part of an overall decline in alcohol consumption. The National Institute on Alcohol Abuse and Alcoholism reports that in 1991 drinking per capita fell to its lowest mark since 1965, with hard liquor intake declining to near-1949 levels.[28] In 1995 alone consumption of hard liquor dropped 1.6 percent. This created interest among distillers such as Jack Daniels and Bacardi in developing beers under their labels. As further evidence of the downward trend, a decades-old voluntary moratorium on television advertising by makers of hard liquor ended with Seagram's airing of commercials in 1996.[29]

Despite the decrease in sales of hard liquor, there are at least three disturbing trends in alcohol consumption. First, one of the newer drinking fads involves alcoholic soft drinks ("alcopops"), which taste like colas or fruit juices but may contain more alcohol than beer does. Going under such names as Cola Lips, Two Dogs, Mrs. Puckers', Hooper's Hooch, Lemonhead, and Moog in Britain (where they were first introduced), these products have been test-marketed in the United States. Second, in the 1990s "binge" drinking increased dramatically. Forty-two percent of college students have engaged in binge drinking (more than five drinks at a time), and 35 percent of college women now drink to get drunk, over three times the average found in 1977.[30] Third, the "gender gap" in use of alcohol by teenagers is disappearing. On average, boys and girls now start to drink at the same age—15 years old.[31]

Gambling

Gambling is a form of addictive consumption that affects an estimated 8 to 12 million people. Although a compulsive gambler is most likely to make less than $25,000 a year, many are high-income professionals. Like drug users, compulsive gamblers may exhibit a "high" while engaging in the activity, followed by depression when they stop.[32]

We often think of gambling in connection with casinos, which have spread from landlocked locations in Las Vegas and New Jersey to such locales as riverboat gambling. In addition, a majority of states now have state-run lotteries, which make it easy to gamble with nothing more than a visit to the local convenience store.

Gambling exists in many countries. In Japan 17.8 billion yen a year, equal to one-fourth of the national government's budget and more than the Japanese car industry's production revenues, is spent on *pachinko*, a game that appears to be addictive for the Japanese. The game is played on an upright pinball-like machine, where steel balls drop through formations of nails. *Pachinko* is even more convenient to play than the state lotteries in the United States because *pachinko* parlors can be found on virtually any busy street, with over 14,500 parlors and 3.1 million machines in operation. *Forbes* magazine lists one owner of a *pachinko* machine manufacturing company, Kenkichi Nakajima, among the wealthiest individuals in the world.[33]

Other countries with gambling include Taiwan, where a state-run lottery was reinstated in 1993, and Katmandu, Nepal, which may be the gambling capital of South Asia. In China lotteries are run under the name of "social welfare projects" to avoid government prohibitions. Gambling on horse racing is called an "intelligence competition"—participants guess which horse is "smart enough" to finish first or in an "intelligence trifecta," first, second, and third![34]

Compulsive Shopping

As described in chapter 6, compulsive buying is a major societal problem. Compulsive buyers use shopping the way other addicts use alcohol or drugs. Like other addicts, they seek the experience to protect their self-image, but when they end the experience they feel more self-loathing and are subject to the disapproval of others, which in turn produces guilt. They attempt to escape this self-loathing by engaging in the experience again. According to some psychologists, this type of experience isn't pleasurable even while the addict is engaged in the activity.[35] Perhaps surprisingly, certain drugs have been found to relieve compulsive shopping.[36]

It has also been suggested that compulsive shopping may be hereditary. Ten percent of the relatives of compulsive shoppers are compulsive shoppers themselves, whereas only 2 to 3 percent of the entire population suffers from this compulsion.[37]

Other Compulsions

Other forms of compulsive consumption are shown in Table 16.3. One of the more interesting compulsions is overwork. In 1996 a Japanese court ordered Dentsu, the world's largest advertising agency, to pay $1.2 million to the survivors of Ichiro Ishima, who during his last eight months of employment by Dentsu had worked from early in the morning to 2 A.M. for 105 days and beyond 4 A.M. for 49 days. His family said he averaged only two to four hours of sleep a night.[38]

Prior to the 1980s, perspectives on compulsive behavior emphasized sociological and psychological influences. However, recent research on compulsive behavior has

Compulsive Consumption: Some Examples

Substance abuse	Alcoholism
	Stimulants and sedatives
	Cannabis, opioids, cocaine, hallucinogens
Eating disorders	Anorexia
	Bulimia
	Binge eating disorder
Impulse-control disorders	Compulsive gambling
	Compulsive buying
	Compulsive sexuality
	Kleptomania
	Compulsive working
	Compulsive exercising
	Compulsive television watching

Source: Based on Elizabeth C. Hirschman, "The Consciousness of Addiction: Toward a General Theory of Compulsive Consumption," *Journal of Consumer Research* 19 (September 1992): 155–79; and Ronald J. Faber et al., "Two Forms of Compulsive Consumption: Comorbidity of Compulsive Buying and Binge Eating," *Journal of Consumer Research* 22 (December 1995): 296–304.

TABLE 16.3

evolved in two directions. One is based on the possibility that various forms of addiction may have physical roots[39] and may be due to imbalances in neurochemicals. That certain addictive tendencies seemed to be inheritable (for example, evidence that alcoholism "runs" in families) is suggestive of physical causes.

The other new direction of research suggests that several forms of compulsive behavior may be driven by the same forces, that is, they may occur together. A recent study, for example, found that compulsive buyers also tended to suffer from binge eating. In fact, compulsive buyers were more likely to suffer from a range of eating disorders, substance abuse or dependence (alcohol, sedatives, cocaine, etc.), and other disorders such as gambling and kleptomania.[40]

Future research on compulsive consumption will add to our knowledge base. These new directions, as well as sociologically and psychologically oriented studies, may one day enable us to more completely understand the "dark-side" aspects of consumer behavior. These behaviors may actually be more widespread than currently thought when one considers that much research on compulsive behaviors depends on self-reporting. Because these attitudes and behaviors aren't socially desirable, respondents may be unwilling to report on their behavior.[41]

CORPORATE SOCIAL RESPONSIBILITY

Prior to the 1960s, most individuals generally accepted the idea that business's primary objective was to obtain economic profit. This thinking began to change, however, as social values in the United States changed. Today, 95 percent of Americans believe companies have responsibilities to employees and communities beyond making profits.[42]

Many companies exert much energy, time, and money to portray themselves as good corporate citizens who act in a socially responsible manner—companies spend well over $1 billion annually in cause-related marketing alone. **Corporate social responsibility** refers to the idea that business has an obligation to help society with its problems by offering some of its resources. Several arguments support the notion that developing a positive image in terms of social responsibility is important for companies.

Succeeding in the Long Run

One argument for being socially responsible involves a long-term rather than short-term perspective. A business's self-interest could be advanced if the business embraced a long-run view. This position would permit expenditures in support of socially responsible activities and provide future benefits in the form of consumer approval and loyalty. A focus on short-run profits would discourage expenditures devoted to societal problems. For example, in 1996 the nation's largest waste company, WMX Technologies, secretly sponsored an engineering study for an environmental group, the North Valley Coalition of Concerned Citizens. The coalition, which was underfunded, needed sophisticated evidence that would aid them in their efforts to keep the second-largest waste management company, Browning-Ferris, from reopening their Sunshine Canyon Landfill in the Los Angeles area.[43] Although this behavior might keep the dump from reopening in the near term, in the longer term waste companies will probably make the job of securing approval of dump sites more difficult for themselves and the industry as a whole.

Acquiring a Positive Public Image

Companies can create a positive public image by acting in socially responsible ways. For example, one study revealed that customers are less likely to blame the company for accidents when the product has safety standards that exceed, rather than simply meet, those of the government. Also, consumers are less likely to blame the manufacturer when products include safety warnings.[44]

Another way that companies may reveal socially responsible behavior is by making speedy product recalls. A product recall could even be seen as a corporate opportunity, in that the situation allows the company to show its ability to act professionally in a proconsumer fashion.[45] A series of studies by John Mowen examined the impact that product recalls could have on consumer impressions of a company. These studies found that consumers perceived a familiar company as significantly less responsible for a product defect than an unfamiliar company; consumers viewed companies who reacted to product defects prior to intervention by the Consumer Product Safety Commission as less responsible for the defects;[46] and consumer impressions of the company were influenced by the speed with which it initiated a product recall.[47] Table 16.4 gives an overview of the implications of these findings.

Finally, it is important to note that the influence that the perceived corporate responsibility of a company may have on product evaluations is not direct. That is, perceptions of corporate social responsibility affect the overall corporate image. This image then has an effect on product evaluations.[48] But an improved image doesn't directly improve product evaluations.

The Diffusion of Rumors

A positive public image can also be affected by the diffusion of rumors. Rumors periodically plague both large and small companies. They are a kind of group contagion that results from fears and anxieties. For example, national hysteria over the AIDS epidemic has spawned rumors. In at least two instances, rumors were spread that an employee of a restaurant had AIDS and was infecting food. As soon as such a rumor begins to spread, business falls dramatically.

Overview of Product-Recall Implications

- Companies should strive to maintain a highly visible positive corporate image. Such a company is less subject to a negative consumer response when a recall is initiated.
- Companies should establish a recall plan that can be quickly implemented should disaster strike. Consumers have a more favorable impression of companies that react quickly in a product-safety situation.
- When a problem is first discovered, it may be best to overstate the problem to the public. Consumers will subsequently develop more favorable impressions of the company when they hear that the problem is not as severe as first expected. If the company displays the reverse behavior—that is, minimizes the problem, only to later discover that the difficulty is worse than first announced—the result can be negative consumer impressions.
- Companies should endeavor to manufacture the safest products possible. The safer the products, the less likelihood of severe injuries, negative consumer opinions, and product liability awards.
- Companies should not shy away from press coverage of product recalls. Information from independent sources such as the media, especially when the company is described as behaving in a socially responsible manner, can generate favorable consumer impressions.

Source: Adapted from Joshua Wiener and John C. Mowen, "Product Recalls: Avoid Beheading the Messenger of Bad News," *Mobius* 4 (1985): 18–21.

TABLE 16.4

Rumors have caused problems for all types of companies. In 1979 Procter & Gamble (P&G) began to be plagued by the rumor that the firm embraced Satanism. Flyers circulated among fundamentalist Protestant congregations noted that the P&G symbol contained a sorcerer's head and 13 stars—a proported sign of Satan. McDonald's has also been hit by rumors alleging Satanism. Even more disturbing has been the fiction that the company added ground worms to their hamburger meat. In 1995 rumors began to spread that subliminal sexual references were included in Disney movies *Aladdin, The Lion King,* and *The Little Mermaid.*[49] The K (for kosher) sign that appears on bottles of Snapple has been interpreted as meaning that the company is a supporter of the Ku Klux Klan. A rumor has circulated that Liz Claiborne stated on the Oprah Winfrey show that she didn't want African Americans wearing her clothes, a rumor persisting despite Ms. Winfrey's own insistence that she has never interviewed Liz Claiborne.[50] Since the first Tylenol poisoning incident in 1982, the FDA has logged some 500 tampering complaints per year, reaching a peak of over 1,700 complaints in 1986.[51]

Types and Causes of Rumors. Sociologists and psychologists have identified a number of different types of rumors. **Pipe dream** rumors represent wishful thinking on the part of the circulators. They are positive hopes concerning something that might happen, such as the size of the Christmas bonus given by a corporation.

Another type of rumor, the **bogie,** is a fear rumor that spooks the marketplace. These are the type that have plagued McDonald's and Procter & Gamble. A bogie demolished the first king-sized menthol cigarette, Spud, in the 1940s.[52] A rumor spread that a leper worked in the plant where the brand was packaged. In six months the cigarette had disappeared.

Rumors can also be **self-fulfilling.** In this case the rumor is based on a perception of what could happen in the future if something else were to occur. "Bank runs" are examples of self-fulfilling rumors. It is true that if all of the depositors in a bank suddenly withdraw their money, any bank will fail. In bad times this knowledge can spook people and result in the very behavior that is the source of the fear.

In **premeditated** rumors individuals with something to gain set out to spread rumors that may help them financially or otherwise. Such premeditated rumors can spread through the stock market and cause short-term shifts in the value of companies, from which unscrupulous individuals can make a profit. Procter & Gamble believed that its Satan rumors resulted in part from the salespeople of a competing firm distributing flyers describing P&G's supposed Satanic activities. P&G has had a particularly hard time with Amway distributors: It has sued Amway distributors six times for statements linking the company to Satanism.[53]

Finally, rumors can be **spontaneous** when people seek explanations for unusual events. One author suggested that the ground-worm rumors striking McDonald's may have begun when a consumer found "tubular" matter in a hamburger.[54] Such matter could easily be a small blood vessel not ground up well. In order to explain the material, the consumer leapt to the conclusion that the tube must have been a worm.

The right environment is required for rumors to be nourished to the point that they can move through the population. The two factors that seem to be required are uncertainty and anxiety. Rumors generally occur and spread most rapidly when times are bad and people are uncertain about their future. It is not surprising that the rumors that struck McDonald's and P&G were at their worst during the severe recession between 1980 and 1983.

In addition to uncertainty and anxiety, researchers have found that the importance and the ambiguity of a rumor influences its spread. A formula was developed to express the relationship:[55]

$$\text{Rumor} = \text{Ambiguity} \times \text{Importance}$$

Urban legends, a phenomenon related to rumors, are realistic stories about incidents that are reputed to have occurred. They diffuse through the population like rumors and often appear to have a local connection. One legend has a groom mounting a chair at his wedding party, announcing that the marriage was going to be annulled and that the reason was underneath everyone's dinner plate. When the stunned guests flipped their plate, there was the bride in flagrante delicto with the best man. This story has been set in New York City, New Hampshire, Medford, Massachusetts, and Schenectady, New York, and a similar version set in St. Paul, Minnesota, has the groom consorting with the maid of honor. A University of Utah folklorist has found over 400 of these legends. Nearly everyone knows that alligators prowl New York sewers. Many may have heard about the good Samaritan who approaches a woman slumped in her car. She moans that she's been shot in the head and shows grey matter oozing from the wound. She's actually been hit in the head by the tin at the end of a tube of Pillsbury biscuits that exploded in the heat, and the "brains" is biscuit dough.[56]

Managers should also monitor the environment for the spread of rumors. One expert suggested that companies should go through a series of actions if a rumor strikes them:[57]

Step 1. Ride out the rumor.

Step 2. Trace its origins.

Step 3. Treat it locally.

Step 4. Rebut it with facts, but don't deny the rumor before the public hears about it.

Rumors, however, are rarely eradicated completely. Procter & Gamble's Satan rumor resurfaced in the mid-1990s, some 16 years after it began. In fact, rumors can move from company to company. The worms-in-hamburger rumor struck Wendy's prior to jumping to McDonald's.

There is a potential problem with the use of refutational strategies to eliminate the spread of rumors. A study was done to investigate the worm rumor and McDonald's hamburgers.[58] The authors found that, when the rumor was refuted with facts (e.g., red worms cost five dollars per pound and could not possibly be used), the negative impression of McDonald's remained. When a refutational strategy mentions the rumor, the consumer is reminded of the negative information. One way around the problem may be to give the facts without mentioning the rumor. McDonald's did this with a major promotional campaign advertising the fact that the hamburgers are made with 100 percent pure beef. No mention of the rumor was made in the advertising campaign.

In 1999 Coca-Cola was forced to remove its products from shelves in France, Belgium, the Netherlands, and Luxembourg after slight contamination was found in products produced in Dunkirk and Antwerp. The company at first attempted a targeted withdrawal only from the actual affected market—but governments raced ahead and Coca-Cola appeared to be avoiding the issues. This contrasts strongly with the Tylenol scare in 1982, when Johnson & Johnson recalled all product immediately, and an incident in 1995 in which Philip Morris recalled all Marlboro cigarettes from the U.S. market due to contamination of a batch of filters. In the latter case, although the recall cost about $200 million, Marlboro's market share actually rose.[59]

Avoiding Government Regulation

A final reason to act in a socially responsible manner is to avoid government regulation. Given current societal values, if a business does not respond to societal demands on its own, consumer groups may exert pressure on governments to intervene.

All business functions concern themselves to some degree with social responsibility. However, the burden falls mostly to the marketer. Indeed, when a company is perceived as acting unethically or in an irresponsible fashion, marketing is the function most likely to be blamed.[60] Marketers can best avoid this label by following the strategies suggested previously—namely, maintaining a positive initial corporate image and responding quickly when difficulties arise.

MANAGERIAL IMPLICATIONS

The consumer-behavior concepts that emerge from investigating the dark side of consumer behavior apply to each of the PERMS managerial application areas. The following section discuss the implications.

Positioning and Differentiation

The concept of corporate social responsibility has direct implications for the positioning of a company. Efforts to create a "good-citizen" image help to position a company as one that puts customers first.

European companies have tried to position themselves as responsible corporate citizens by adopting the notion of product stewardship. It may be that the opportunity exists to use product stewardship as a point of differentiation with competitors in the United States as well.

Environmental Analysis

It is clearly important to ensure that a company's actions are in compliance with laws and regulations. This is particularly true for start-up firms.

Perhaps equally important, it is critical that the company is seen as socially responsible. Enhanced perceptions of corporate social responsibility lead directly to increased company image and indirectly to enhanced product evaluations.

Finally, environmental scanning is also needed to monitor whether rumors concerning the company are developing. Because the company needs to be in a position to respond promptly if a response is warranted, an "early-warning system" needs to be in place and functioning continuously.

Research

Along with environmental scanning, market research should be used to determine how consumers view the company. In particular, it may be important to monitor the degree to which the public's view of the company's approach to corporate social responsibility is accurate.

Market research may also need to be used to determine whether customers are using a company's product in a novel, unplanned manner that may be unsafe or have other negative consequences.

Marketing Mix

Pricing, promotion, product development, and distribution should be undertaken in a manner that is socially responsible. The company should communicate these actions through its public relations activities.

Pricing can be an issue of contention. One of the dilemmas posed by medical advances is evident most clearly in the case of pharmaceutical companies. When these companies develop a new drug with significant health care benefits, the companies' right to a good return on their investment may conflict with corporate social responsibility. Developing new drugs certainly entitles a company to the fruits of its labor. On the other hand, from this perspective very useful drugs may be available only to the relatively well off, especially early in the product life cycle when the company typically wishes to recoup R&D costs. This problem will almost certainly increase over the next decade as improvements in health care treatments accelerate.

Segmentation

Some segments of the population are more concerned with issues of corporate social responsibility than are other segments. As an example, we suggested in chapter 14 that Generation Y—or the millennium generation—teenagers are politically active and perhaps more interested in social issues than has been the case since the 1960s and 1970s. This may present opportunities for marketing managers to segment the market into groups of the more, and less, socially involved. Because the more socially involved are also of a certain age group, targeted campaigns may be useful.

Notes

1. John Howard, "Chrysler Faced with 'Lemon Law' Sanctions," *McAllen Monitor,* June 1, 1996, p. 7A.
2. Jacob Jacoby and Wayne D. Hoyer, "Viewer Miscomprehension of Televised Communication: Selected Findings," *Journal of Consumer Research* 15 (March 1989): 434–43. Also see Jacoby and Hoyer, "The Miscomprehension of Mass-Media Advertising Claims: A Re-Analysis of Benchmark Data," *Journal of Advertising Research* 30 (June–July 1990): 9–16.
3. Jacob Jacoby and George J. Szybillo, "Consumer Research in FTC vs. Kraft (1991): A Case of Heads We Win, Tails You Lose?" *Journal of Public Policy and Marketing* 14 (spring 1995): 1–14; David M. Stewart, "Deception, Materiality, and Survey Research: Some Lessons from Kraft," *Journal of Public Policy and Marketing* 14 (spring 1995): 15–28; and Seymour Sudman,

"When Experts Disagree: Comments on the Articles by Jacoby and Szybillo and Stewart," *Journal of Public Policy and Marketing* 14 (spring 1995): 29–34.

4. Arent Fox, "FTC Advertising Guidelines," <www. webcom.com/lewrose/guides. html> (June 11, 1998).

5. "Sellers Beware On-Line," *Sales and Marketing Management,* December 1994, p. 16: Arent Fox, "FTC Tackles Fraud on the Information Superhighway, Charges Nine On-Line Scammers," <www.webcom.com/lewrose/article/ftc-net.html> (April 28, 1996).

6. Ivan L. Preston, "Unfairness Developments in FTC Advertising Cases," *Journal of Public Policy and Marketing* 14 (fall 1995): 318–20. Also see 1997 remarks by FTC commissioner Roscoe Starek, <www. ftc.govspeeches/starek/ minnfin.htm>.

7. For an account by an advertising executive involved in the controversy, see Dick Mercer, "Tempest in a Soup Can," *Advertising Age,* October 17, 1994, pp. 25–29.

8. William L. Wilkie, Dennis L. McNeill, and Michael B. Mazis, "Marketing's 'Scarlet Letter': The Theory and Practice of Corrective Advertising," *Journal of Marketing* 48 (spring 1984): 11–31.

9. Richard Tomkins, "Selling to a Captivated Market," *Financial Times,* April 23, 1999, p. 10. Also see Jennifer Gregan-Paxton and Deborah Roedder John, "Are Young Children Adaptive Decision Makers? A Study of Age Differences in Information Search Behavior," *Journal of Consumer Research* 21 (March 1995): 567–80.

10. Kyle Pope, "Better to Receive: How Children Decide on Gifts They Want, and Plot to Get Them," *Wall Street Journal,* December 24, 1993, pp. A1, A5.

11. For an example, view opportunites to shop for Barbie dolls at such Web sites as <www.dollattic .com> (November 8, 1999).

12. Elizabeth Jensen and Albert R. Karr, "White House, TV Industry Compromise on Educational Programs for Children," *Wall Street Journal,* July 30, 1996, p. B14.

13. Cindy Long, "Agencies Join Forces to Combat Billions of Dollars Lost from Telemarketing Fraud," *McAllen Monitor,* November 19, 1999, pp. 1C–12C.

14. Thomas C. Kinnear and Cynthia J. Frey, "Demarketing of Potentially Hazardous Products: General Framework and Case Studies," *Journal of Contemporary Business* 7 (1978): 57–68.

15. Richard Staelin, "The Effects of Consumer Education on Consumer Product Safety Behavior," *Journal of Consumer Research* 5 (June 1978): 30–40. For a philosophical view of why safety devices lead to complacency and similar paradoxes, see Edward Tenner, *Why Things Bite Back: Technology and the Revenge Effect* (New York: Knopf, 1996).

16. Walter Guzzardi, "The Mindless Pursuit of Safety," *Fortune,* April 9, 1979, pp. 54–64.

17. Staelin, "Effects of Consumer Education."

18. Jeffrey J. Stoltman and Fred W. Morgan, "Expanding the Perspective on Consumer Product Safety," in *Marketing and Consumer Research in the Public Interest,* ed. Ronald P. Hill (Thousand Oaks, CA, Sage Publications, 1996).

19. John Pierson, "Ford Labors Over Tiny Buttons and Dials in Quest for a Driver-Friendly Dashboard," *Wall Street Journal,* May 20, 1996, pp. B1, B7.

20. See the Web site of the National Drunk and Drugged Driving (3D) Prevention Coalition, <www.3dmonth.org/idf.htm> (April 7, 2000).

21. Janet R. Hankin, Ira J. Firestone, James J. Sloan and Joel W. Ager, "The Impact of the Alcohol Warning Label on Drinking during Pregnancy," *Journal of Public Policy and Marketing* 12 (spring 1993): 10–18.

22. Kinnear and Frey, "Demarketing of Potentially Hazardous Products."

23. Steven W. Colford and Ira Teinowitz, "Teen Smoking and Ads Linked," *Advertising Age,* February 21, 1994, pp. 1, 36.

24. Richard Tomkins, "Advertising Curb May Lift Tobacco Industry Profits," *Financial Times,* August 26, 1996, p. 4. Also see Tara Parker-Pope, "Tough Tobacco-Ad Rules Light Creative Fires," *Wall Street Journal,* October 9, 1996, pp. B1, B6.

25. Russ Bynum, "CDC: Anti-Smoking Campaigns Haven't Been Effective," *McAllen Monitor,* November 5, 1999, p. 3A.

26. Richard W. Pollay, S. Siddarth, Michael Siegel, Anne Haddix, Robert K. Merritt, Gary A. Giovino, and Michael P. Eriksen, "The Last Straw? Cigarette Advertising and Realized Market Shares among Youths and Adults, 1979–1993," *Journal of Marketing* 60 (April 1996): 1–16. Also see Cornelia Pechmann and Chuan-Fong Shih, "Smoking Scenes in Movies and Antismoking Advertisements before Movies: Effects on Youth," *Journal of Marketing* 63 (July 1999): 1–13.

27. John E. Calfee and Debra Jones Ringold, "The Cigarette Advertising Controversy: Assumptions about Consumers, Regulations, and Scientific Debate," in *Advances in*

Consumer Research, ed. John F. Sherry Jr. and Brian Sternthal (Provo, UT: Association for Consumer Research, 1992), 19:557–62.

28. Tim W. Ferguson, "Calm Down: Risk Is Not All Around," *Wall Street Journal,* December 14, 1993, p. A17; Judith Valente, "Scotch Makers Tell Youth It's Hip to Be Old-Fashioned," *Wall Street Journal,* December 29, 1993, pp. B1, B5.

29. Yumiko Ono, "Some Liquor Makers Are Happy if You Switch to Beer—As Long as It's Theirs," *Wall Street Journal,* May 23, 1996, pp. B1, B5; Sally Goll Beatty, "Seagram Flouts Ban on TV Ads Pitching Liquor," *Wall Street Journal,* June 11, 1996, pp. B1, B6.

30. J. Craig Andrews and Richard G. Netemeyer, "Alcohol Warning Label Effects: Socialization, Addiction, and Public Policy Issues," in *Marketing and Consumer Research in the Public Interest,* ed. Ronald P. Hill (Thousand Oaks, CA: Sage Publications, 1996).

31. "Women and Drugs," *Wall Street Journal,* June 6, 1996, p. A14.

32. Bob Smith, "Compulsive Gamblers: In Over Their Heads," *HR Focus,* February 1992, p. 3.

33. "Lots of Lovely Silver Balls," *Financial Times,* May 22, 1996, p. 13; "The World's Richest Individuals," <www.forbes.com/tools/toolbox/billnew/richmain.99.asp?value2-1133> (April 7, 2000).

34. "Gambling on the Rise in China," *China News Daily,* June 27, 1996.

35. Gerhard Scherhorn, "The Addictive Trait in Buying Behavior," *Journal of Consumer Policy* 13 (1990): 33–51; Elizabeth C. Hirschman, "The Consciousness of Addiction: Toward a General Theory of Compulsive Consumption," *Journal of Consumer Research* 19 (September 1992): 155–79; Elizabeth C. Hirschman, "Cocaine as Innovation: A Social-Symbolic Account," in *Advances in Consumer Research,* ed. John F. Sherry Jr. and Brian Sternthal (Provo, UT: Association for Consumer Research, 1992), 19:129–39.

36. For more information on potential pharmacological treatments for compulsive shopping, see the second author's Web site on compulsive shopping, <www.baclass.panam.edu /courses/minor/compulsive.htm>.

37. "Compulsive Shopping Could Be Hereditary," *Marketing News,* September 14, 1998, p. 31.

38. Emiko Terazono, "Suicide of Employee Who Worked Excessive Hours Costs Japanese Company $1.2 Million," *Financial Times,* March 30–31, 1996, p. 3.

39. Elizabeth C. Hirschman, "Professional, Personal, and Popular Culture Perspectives on Addiction," in *Marketing and Consumer Research in the Public Interest,* ed. Ronald P. Hill (Thousand Oaks, CA: Sage Publications, 1996), 33–53; James A. Roberts, "The Antecedents and Incidence of Compulsive Buying in the Baby Bust Generation" (paper presented at the 1996 Texas Marketing Faculty Consortium, Waco, TX, April 12, 1996).

40. Ronald J. Faber, Gary A. Christenson, Martina de Zwann, and James Mitchell, "Two Forms of Compulsive Consumption: Comorbidity of Compulsive Buying and Binge Eating," *Journal of Consumer Research* 22 (December 1995): 296–304.

41. David Glen Mick, "Are Studies of Dark Side Variables Confounded by Socially Desirable Responding? The Case of Materialism," *Journal of Consumer Research* 23 (September 1996): 106–19.

42. Nancy Dunne, "Portrait of an American Dilemma," *Financial Times,* June 17, 1996, p. 1.

43. Jeff Bailey, "The Dump's Foe Is Indignant and Has Money for a Fight," *Wall Street Journal,* June 7, 1996, pp. A1, A4.

44. Mitch Griffin, Barry J. Babin, and William R. Darden, "Consumer Assessments of Responsibility for Product-Related Injuries: The Impact of Regulations, Warnings, and Promotional Policies," in *Advances in Consumer Research,* ed. John F. Sherry Jr. and Brian Sternthal (Provo, UT: Association for Consumer Research, 1992), 19:870–78.

45. G. Fisk and R. Chandran, "How to Trace and Recall Products," *Harvard Business Review,* November–December, 1975, pp. 90–96.

46. John C. Mowen, "Further Information on Consumer Perceptions of Product Recalls," in *Advances in Consumer Research,* ed. Jerry Olson (Ann Arbor, MI: Association for Consumer Research, 1980), 7:519–23.

47. John C. Mowen, David Jolly, and G. S. Nickell, "Factors Influencing Consumer Responses to Product Recalls: A Regression Analysis Approach," in *Advances in Consumer Research,* ed. Kent Monroe (Ann Arbor, MI: Association for Consumer Research, 1981), 8:405–7.

48. Tom J. Brown and Peter A. Dacin, "The Company and the Product: Corporate Associations and Consumer Product Responses," *Journal of Marketing* 61 (January 1997): 66–84.

49. Lisa Bannon, "Bazaar Gossip: How a Rumor Spread about Subliminal Sex in Disney's 'Aladdin,' " *Wall Street Journal,* October 24, 1995, pp. A1, A6.

50. Dorothy Rabinowitz, "Race and Rumor," *Wall Street Journal,* April 29, 1996, p. A20.

51. John Stockmeyer, "Brands in Crisis: Consumer Help for Deserving Victims," in *Advances in Consumer Research,* ed. Kim P. Corfman and John G. Lynch Jr. (Provo, UT: Association for Consumer Research, 1996), 23:429–35.
52. Robert Levy, "Tilting at the Rumor Mill," *Dun's Review,* July 1981, pp. 52–54.
53. Zachary Schiller, "P&G Is Still Having a Devil of a Time," *Business Week,* September 11, 1995, p. 46.
54. James Esposito and Ralph Rosnow, "Corporate Rumors: How They Start and How to Stop Them," *Management Review,* April 1983, pp. 44–49.
55. G. W. Allport and L. Postman, *The Psychology of Rumor* (New York: Holt, Rinehart & Winston, 1947).
56. Neal Gabler, "The Lure of Urban Myths," *Playboy,* August 1996, pp. 70–153.
57. Levy, "Tilting at the Rumor Mill." Problems with aggressive approaches to crisis management are discussed in Stockmeyer, "Brands in Crisis."
58. Alice Tybout, Bobby Calder, and Brian Sternthal, "Using Information Processing Theory to Design Marketing Strategies," *Journal of Marketing Research* 18 (February 1981): 73–79.
59. Richard Tomkins, "A Spillage of Goodwill," *Financial Times,* June 17, 1999, p. 19.
60. Patrick Murphy and Gene Laczniak, "Marketing Ethics: A Review with Implications for Managers, Educators, and Researchers," in *Review of Marketing,* ed. Ben M. Enis and Kenneth J. Roering (Chicago, IL: American Marketing Association, 1981), 251–66.

Index